P9-AFZ-684

METHODS IN CELL PHYSIOLOGY

VOLUME I

Methods in Cell Physiology

Edited by

DAVID M. PRESCOTT

BIOLOGY DIVISION, OAK RIDGE NATIONAL LABORATORY

OAK RIDGE, TENNESSEE

VOLUME I

1964

ACADEMIC PRESS New York San Francisco London

A Subsidiary of Harcourt Brace Jovanovich, Publishers

ACADEMIC PRESS INC.
111 Fifth Avenue, New York, New York 10003

United Kingdom Edition published by
ACADEMIC PRESS, INC. (LONDON) LTD.
24/28 Oval Road, London NW1

Library of Congress Catalog Card Number: 64-14220

PRINTED IN THE UNITED STATES OF AMERICA

LIST OF CONTRIBUTORS

Numbers in parentheses refer to the page on which the author's contribution begins.

Helen H. Baldwin, McArdle Memorial Laboratory for Cancer Research, University of Wisconsin, Madison, Wisconsin (9)

M. A. Bender, Biology Division, Oak Ridge National Laboratory, Oak Ridge, Tennessee (381)

W. F. Benton, Division of Molecular Biology, Vanderbilt University, Nashville, Tennessee (55)

I. L. Cameron, Biology Division, Oak Ridge National Laboratory, Oak Ridge, Tennessee (127)

J. Gordon Carlson, Department of Zoology and Entomology, The University of Tennessee, Knoxville, Tennessee (229)

Lucien G. Caro, The Rockefeller Institute, New York, New York (327)

R. F. Carrier, Biology Division, Oak Ridge National Laboratory, Oak Ridge, Tennessee (85)

Cicily Chapman-Andresen, Department of Physiology, Carlsberg Laboratory, Copenhagen, Denmark (277)

John W. Daniel, McArdle Memorial Laboratory for Cancer Research, University of Wisconsin, Madison, Wisconsin (9)

Julie Micou Eastwood, Department of Zoology, University of California, Berkeley, California (403)

J.-E. Edström, Department of Histology, University of Gothenburg, Gothenburg, Sweden (417)

Mary Esther Gaulden, Biology Division, Oak Ridge National Laboratory, Oak Ridge, Tennessee (229)

Lester Goldstein, Department of Biology, University of Pennsylvania, Philadelphia, Pennsylvania (97 and 403)

Edmund Guttes, Department of Biology, Loyola University, Chicago, Illinois (43)

Sophie Guttes, Department of Biology, Loyola University, Chicago, Illinois (43)

T. W. James, Zoology Department, University of California, Los Angeles, California (141)

Konrad Keck, Department of Biology, Johns Hopkins University, Baltimore, Maryland (189)

Adolf Kuhl, Pflanzenphysiologisches Institut der Universität, Göttingen, Germany (159)

Harold Lorenzen, Pflanzenphysiologisches Institut der Universität, Göttingen, Germany (159)

O. L. Miller, Biology Division, Oak Ridge National Laboratory, Oak Ridge, Tennessee (371)

R. J. Neff, Division of Molecular Biology, Vanderbilt University, Nashville, Tennessee (55)

G. M. Padilla, Gerontology Branch, National Heart Institute, National Institutes of Health, Bethesda and Baltimore City Hospitals, Baltimore, Maryland (141)

Robert P. Perry, Department of Molecular Biology, Institute for Cancer Research, Philadelphia, Pennsylvania (305)

D. M. Prescott, Biology Division, Oak Ridge National Laboratory, Oak

Ridge, Tennessee (85, 365, 371, and 381)

S. A. Ray, Division of Molecular Biology, Vanderbilt University, Nashville, Tennessee (55)

Jesse E. Sisken, Department of Experimental Pathology, City of Hope Medical Center, Duarte, California (387)

G. E. Stone, Biology Division, Oak Ridge National Laboratory, Oak Ridge, Tennessee (127 and 371)

Vance Tartar, Department of Zoology, University of Washington, Seattle, Washington (109)

R. C. von Borstel, Biology Division, Oak Ridge National Laboratory, Oak Ridge, Tennessee (1)

M. Wilborn, Division of Molecular Biology, Vanderbilt University, Nashville, Tennessee (55)

Sheldon Wolff, Biology Division, Oak Ridge National Laboratory, Oak Ridge, Tennessee (215)

PREFACE

Much of the information on experimental techniques in modern cell biology is scattered in a fragmentary fashion throughout the research literature. In addition, the general practice of condensing Materials and Methods sections of journal articles to the most abbreviated form has led to descriptions that are frequently inadequate guides to techniques. This volume is intended to bring together into one compilation, complete and detailed treatments of a number of widely useful techniques which have not been published in full form elsewhere in the literature.

In the absence of firsthand personal instruction, researchers are often reluctant to take up new techniques. This hesitancy probably stems mostly from the fact that descriptions in the literature do not contain sufficient detail concerning methodology; or there may be insufficient information to estimate the difficulties or practicality of the technique or to judge whether the method can really provide a suitable solution to the problem under consideration. The presentations in this volume are intended to meet this situation. They are comprehensive to the extent that they may serve not only as a practical introduction to experimental procedures but they also provide some evaluation of the limitations, potentialities, and current applications of the methods. Only those theoretical considerations needed for proper use of the method are included.

The book may have particular usefulness for those working with intact cells, and the first chapters deal with culturing and experimental manipulation of a variety of cell types. There are numerous descriptions of techniques designed for working with single cells and of procedures for studying cellular activities in relation to the cell life cycle. The chapters on autoradiography include detailed treatment of qualitative and quantitative aspects of the method as well as simple procedures for using liquid and dry emulsions.

Finally, special emphasis has been placed on inclusion of much reference material in order to guide readers to the earlier and the current, pertinent literature.

David M. Prescott

November, 1963

CONTENTS

Chapter 1

Survey of Cytochemistry

R. C. VON BORSTEL

Biology Division, Oak Ridge National Laboratory,[1]
Oak Ridge, Tennessee

I. Survey

Chemically defined dyes became available in the nineteenth century. Their first use with cells and tissues was to help in identification of the cellular elements in terms of microanatomical structure. Specific staining was seen in biological terms and not in chemical terms, even though basic and acidic charges on dyes were early recognized as important factors in stainability [see Conn (1948) for a thorough historical treatment of the staining of tissues]. As a field apart from the morphology of cells and tissues, the chemistry of cells and tissues began early in the nineteenth century when glycogen was identified *in situ*. Raspail, who is regarded as the father of histochemistry (Lison, 1936; Pearse, 1960), was its spokesman and the person who used many chemical techniques for identifying compounds in tissues by their chemical nature.

A case can be made that the modern era of description of cells and tissues in chemical terms began when Feulgen and Rossenbeck (1924) used the Schiff reagent to identify deoxyribonucleic acid (DNA) in chromosomes [see Kasten (1960) for a complete account of cytochemical application of the Schiff-type dyes]. Lison must be regarded as the father of the modern era of cytochemistry and histochemistry, as evidenced by his thoughtful and comprehensive book (1936), which defined with precision the limits of this science. Brachet (cf. 1944), in his extensive analyses of develop-

[1] Operated by Union Carbide Corporation for the United States Atomic Energy Commission.

ment, was the first to demonstrate broadly the applicability of this new science to biological problems.

In the early 1930's there began several comprehensive attempts to describe the chemical molecules in the micromorphological province. Caspersson launched a new enterprise when he developed microphotometric methods for studying the ultraviolet absorption spectra of cell parts *in situ* (cf. Caspersson, 1947, 1950). His approach attained a high degree of fulfillment during his collaboration with Schultz on cytogenetic experiments, since Schultz was able to focus the method on specific problems by his genetic manipulations of biological material (Caspersson and Schultz, 1939; 1940). These methods and those used by Brachet were instrumental in fixing attention to the possible role of nucleic acids in directing protein synthesis (Schultz, 1941; Caspersson *et al.*, 1941; Brachet, 1941). This discovery of Caspersson, Schultz, and Brachet stands as one of the great contributions to cell biology from the field of cytochemistry.

The techniques of cytochemistry used by Brachet and Caspersson were fused by Pollister and Ris (1947) and their colleagues who used specific stainability together with microspectrophotometric methods in the visible region of the spectrum to define as quantitatively as possible the chemical nature of cells and their parts [see Shugar (1962) for an authoritative review of quantitative staining methods, and Caspersson *et al.* (1960) for recent advances in instrumentation]. Visible light microspectrophotometry became extremely useful in the confirmation and extension of the discovery that the content of DNA per haploid chromosome complement is constant for any given species (Vendrely and Vendrely, 1956). That DNA synthesis occurred during interphase (Swift, 1950; Walker and Yates, 1952) was also demonstrated by microspectrophotometric means.

Caspersson and Brachet also added another facet to cytochemical analysis by their use of proteolytic enzymes and nucleases for specific removal of biochemical entities. This, particularly in the hands of Kaufmann and his collaborators who worked with enzymes of proven high purity, became the most powerful tool for dissection of cells already dead [see Kaufmann *et al.* (1960) and Macgregor and Callan (1962) for complete historical and critical discussions of the use of enzymes for chromosome analysis]. Degradative enzymes are not the only type of enzymes that can be used. DNA polymerase or RNA polymerase can be incubated with labeled triphosphate nucleotides using fixed cells as primer. The newly synthesized DNA and RNA can be detected autoradiographically. The demonstration of the priming activity of cells after fixation is a kind of revivification and can be regarded as a step toward making cytochemistry into a synthetic science.

Enzyme kinetic methodology as an analytical tool in cytochemistry has seldom been used. However, Gall (1963) used enzyme kinetics in a straightforward manner for specifically analyzing the structure of a cell component when he counted the number of deoxyribonuclease-induced breaks of loops of lampbrush chromosomes as a function of time. Gall's data provide evidence that in areas of the chromosome where DNA is accessible to the action of deoxyribonuclease, a single molecule of DNA is the structural continuum. The experiment implies that the DNA of lampbrush chromosome loops are equivalent to the Watson-Crick helix and are not made up of multiple strands of DNA.

Other than enzymatic digestion, three main approaches have been used in determining the location of proteins in cells: the first is simply that of specific stainability, usually through specific chemical reactions with amino acids. For instance, the Sakaguchi reaction is useful as a specific stain for arginine-containing proteins (Baker, 1944; Serra, 1946; Thomas, 1946); fast green at a pH above 8 as a specific stain for histone was developed by Alfert and Geschwind (1953). Other reactions also have been used, and it is known that the amino acids rather than the proteins themselves are usually the agents conferring specificity (cf. Lison, 1960; Glick, 1949; Pearse, 1960; Cowden, 1960). The second approach is the use of immune sera bound to fluorescent dyes as a cytochemical reagent (Coons, 1958; Beutner, 1961), and this has been a powerful tool for studying cellular origins of antigens and serum globulins. The third approach is the use of substrates, which after being acted upon by enzymes localized in cells, cause a precipitate to be formed by the reaction product at the enzyme site. The application of this hydrolytic type of reaction on cells was first done independently by Gomori (1939) and Takamatsu (1939).

There is another area of cytochemical analyses that is really outside the domain of microscopic localization of chemical elements in cells. This is ultramicroanalytical methodology, which was pioneered for enzyme analyses by Linderstrøm-Lang and his colleagues (Linderstrøm-Lang, 1939, 1952; Glick, 1961). This constitutes a scaling down of macrotechniques to the microlevel. The great contribution of Linderstrøm-Lang and Gomori was their conclusive demonstration by entirely different means that enzymatic activities of the cell are specifically localized. Previously the cell had been considered as a bag of enzymes. The clear realization of intracellular partitioning of enzymatic activities gradually grew through the research of Linderstrøm-Lang and his collaborators. Gomori's work was really a climax to an accomplished fact, but it in turn opened a door to a plethora of possible enzyme localization procedures (cf. Burstone, 1962).

The analytical method per se in cytology is to macerate cells and tissues and to separate out for chemical analysis the cellular components that can be compared *in vitro* to the same components *in situ*. The older observations include the first isolations of single nuclei by Ransom (1867) and nuclei in large quantity by Ackermann (1904), and of numerous other cell components by Plosz (1873). Chemical analyses were begun on the nucleus by Miescher (1872), on yolk platelets by McClendon (1909), on chloroplasts by Ewart (1896), and on mitochondria by Warburg (1913) (see also Needham, 1931, and Pearse, 1960, for accounts of early works of other investigators). More recently, the renaissance of cell-particulate isolation began with the separation of mitochondria from liver cells by Bensley and Hoerr (1934), who also noted that free nuclei were present in the homogenates. Claude (1940) is generally accorded the credit for the first isolation of microsomal particulates which he at first believed to be mitochondria; it seems certain that his original isolations were in fact mixtures of particles (see Bensley, 1942). It is now known that Claude's microsomes are pieces of endoplasmic reticulum (Palade and Siekevitz, 1956). Nuclei have been isolated singly for many years (e.g., Duryee, 1937; see Chambers, 1940). Mass isolation of nuclei stemmed directly from the research of Bensley and Hoerr. Isolation procedures for large quantities of pure nuclei were first developed by Behrens (1938). Nucleoli were first isolated in large quantity by Vincent (1952), and the mitotic apparatus was separated from other cellular constituents by Mazia and Dan (1952).

From these studies and from the work of the entire group of biochemists who worked on soluble compounds of biological interest grew the non-genetic aspects of molecular biology. Now the central problem is the functional roles of isolated cell components, particularly with respect to gene action. When the interactions of DNA and RNA in protein synthesis could be studied without limiting membranes, and controlled by substrate addition, molecular biology was no longer a strictly analytical science, and reconstruction by synthesis became possible. At the same time, genetic science was scaled down to the microlevel. Benzer (cf. 1957), with genetic fine structure analysis, took genetic methodology virtually to the level of the nucleotides. All of these studies, grouped around the DNA model of Watson and Crick (1953), have made possible firm experimental approaches to the theoretical aspects of cell biology.

Tracer techniques with autoradiographic emulsion or film straddle the border between cell physiology and cytochemistry. The isotopically labeled compounds are put in the metabolic pool of the live cell, and the compounds or their metabolic products are recorded later by autoradiographic means on fixed and stained preparations. Of course, controls must be run in which a variety of cytochemical tests are employed, usually those of specific solubility of compounds or digestion by specific enzymes, so here cell physiology and cytochemistry merge into one. Autoradiography was used for a number of years at the tissue level [see Hamilton (1942) for a review of the early literature] before it was used at the intracellular level to measure the diffusion coefficient of sodium (Duryee and Abelson, 1947; Abelson and Duryee, 1949). Cytological autoradiography became generally useful shortly thereafter largely through the efforts of Howard and Pelc (see 1952 for a useful summary of their early work with isotopic labeling). Howard and Pelc divided the interphase of the cell cycle into three parts, G_1, S, and G_2, for before, during, and after DNA synthesis. Their work provided a clear demonstration that DNA synthesis occurs in interphase and was done independently from the similar demonstration done microspectrophotometrically by Swift (1950) and Walker and Yates (1952). The partition of the formerly completely enigmatic interphase into stages related to DNA synthesis has been beneficial to cell biology since that time.

Another important experiment involving the use of autoradiography was the transplantation of nuclei containing labeled RNA to unlabeled cells (Goldstein and Plaut, 1955). This experiment clearly showed that the site of RNA synthesis is in the nucleus. An autoradiographic experiment related to this one, which implicates the nucleolus also, was done by Perry *et al.* (1961) who showed that RNA synthesis was dramatically lowered if the nucleolus were irradiated with ultraviolet radiation from a microbeam.

Autoradiographic analysis came into full fruition as a tool of high resolving power when the tritiation of compounds was accomplished for cytological use by Taylor *et al.* (1957). Their work stands as another of the great contributions to cell biology from the field of cytochemistry. In their publication, the semiconservative nature of chromosome distribution after DNA replication was revealed.

Stain technology and cytochemistry are in general passing through the same evolution for electron microscopy as they did for light microscopy. Contrasts in tissues prepared for the electron microscope are enhanced by heavy metals attached to the tissue components (electron staining). Development of specific stains for electron microscopy is just beginning. There is some evidence that the uranyl salts which are used as a positive stain have some specificity for nucleic acid residues (Zobel and Beer, 1961). Other positive stains that increase contrasts in tissues are indium (Watson and Aldridge, 1961) and lead hydroxide (Watson, 1958). Phosphotungstic acid (Brenner and Horne, 1959) is an example of a negative stain that increases the density of the surrounding medium and is an excellent stain for demonstrating surface detail clearly. Silver reduction as a counterpart for the Feulgen reaction has been used (see Kasten, 1960). Identification of specific proteins by ferritin-conjugated antisera has been accomplished (cf. Baxandall *et al.*, 1962), as has enzyme localization by methods approximating those of enzyme localization for light microscopy (Sheldon *et al.*, 1955; Novikoff, 1959; see also Burstone, 1962, and Harris, 1962).

Electron microscopy can resolve structural detail at a size scale of 8 Å (cf. Fernandez-Moran, 1962). When adequate fixation methods were found and thin sectioning methods devised, electron microscopy revised entirely the concepts of cell structure, particularly with respect to the cytoplasmic elements and enclosing membranes (see Harris, 1962). For general use in biochemistry, electron microscopy has been particularly helpful in the identification of small particles from cells during steps of chemical isolation. In this way, the ribosome was identified as a separate cellular component (cf. Palade and Siekevitz, 1956).

Autoradiography coupled with electron microscopy has been successfully used by a number of investigators (see Caro, Chapter 16 of this volume). With tritium, the limit of resolution appears to be about 0.1μ, unfortunately about 100 times larger than the present resolving power of the electron microscope itself.

II. Summary and Conclusions

There have been several major discoveries in biology through the agency of cytochemistry. These include (1) the emphasis on the possible role of nucleic acid in direction of protein synthesis by Caspersson, Schultz, and Brachet, (2) the general nature of the constancy of DNA in the haploid chromosome complement of a species following the original biochemical discovery of DNA constancy by Boivin, Vendrely and Vendrely, (3) the discovery by Linderstrøm-Lang and Gomori that enzymes are associated with specific structural components of cells; (4) the demonstration that DNA synthesis occurs during interphase by Howard and Pelc, Swift, and Walker and Yates, and (5) the demonstration of the semiconservative nature of chromosome distribution after DNA replication by Taylor, Woods, and Hughes.

The field of cytochemistry often anticipates, and at other times follows closely behind, the advances in biochemistry and molecular biology. In biochemistry, cells are used as a source of biological compounds which are often refined by the investigators to a high degree of purity. In cytochemistry, the cell can be regarded as a "dirty enzyme preparation" or a "crude protein and nucleic acid preparation." Cells from a variety of sources can be used easily with cytochemical methods for a comparative study of a particular reaction or molecule where purity is not essential. Cytochemical methodology can be used wherever precipitable reactions are involved and wherever locations within cells are of paramount importance. It is to be hoped that eventually it may be possible to study cytochemically the synthesis of cell parts from molecules, and cells from cell parts.

References

Abelson, P. H., and Duryee, W. R. (1949). *Biol. Bull.* **96,** 205.

Ackermann, D. (1904). *Z. Physiol. Chem.* **43,** 299.

Alfert, M., and Geschwind, I. I. (1953). *Proc. Natl. Acad. Sci. U. S.* **39,** 991.

Baker, J. R. (1944). *Quart. J. Microsp. Sci.* **85,** 1.

Baxandall, J., Perlmann, P., and Afzelius, B. A. (1962). *J. Cell Biol.* **14,** 144.

Behrens, M. (1938). *In* "Handbuch der biologischen Arbeitsmethoden" (E. Abderhalden, ed.), Vol. V, Part 10, II, pp. 1363–1392. Urban and Schwarzenberg, Berlin.

Bensley, R. R. (1942). *Science* **96,** 389.

Bensley, R. R., and Hoerr, N. H. (1934). *Anat. Record* **60,** 449.

Benzer, S. (1957). *In* "A Symposium on the Chemical Basis of Heredity" (W. D. McElroy and B. Glass, eds.), pp. 70–93. Johns Hopkins Press, Baltimore, Maryland.

Beutner, E. H. (1961). *Bacteriol. Rev.* **25,** 49.

Boivin, A., Vendrely, R., and Vendrely, C. (1948). *Compt. Rend.* **226,** 1061.

Brachet, J. (1941). *Arch. Biol. (Liege)* **53,** 207.

Brachet, J. (1944). "Embryologie Chimique." Masson, Paris.

Brenner, S., and Horne, R. W. (1959). *Biochem. Biophys. Acta* **34,** 103.

Burstone, M. S. (1962). "Enzyme Histochemistry." Academic Press, New York.

Caspersson, T. O. (1947). *Symp. Soc. Exptl. Biol.* **1,** 127.

Caspersson, T. O. (1950). "Cell Growth and Cell Function." Norton, New York.

Caspersson, T., Landström-Hyden, H., and Aquilonius, L. (1941). *Chromosoma* **2,** 111.

Caspersson, T., Lomakka, G., and Caspersson, O. (1960). *Biochem. Pharmacol.* **4,** 113.

Caspersson, T., and Schultz, J. (1939). *Nature* **143,** 602.

Caspersson, T., and Schultz, J. (1940). *Proc. Natl. Acad. Sci. U. S.* **26,** 507.

Chambers, R. (1940). *In* "The Cell and Protoplasm" (F. R. Moulton, ed.), pp. 20–30. American Association for the Advancement of Science, Washington, D. C.

Claude, A. (1940). *Science* **91,** 77.

Conn, H. J. (1948). "The History of Staining." Biotech Publications, Geneva, New York.

Coons, A. H. (1958). *In* "General Cytochemical Methods" (J. F. Danielli, ed.), pp. 399–422. Academic Press, New York.

Cowden, R. R. (1960). *Intern. Rev. Cytol.* **9,** 369.

Duryee, W. R. (1937). *Arch. Exptl. Zellforsch.* **19,** 171.

Duryee, W. R., and Abelson, P. H. (1947). *Biol. Bull.* **93,** 225.

Ewart, A. J. (1896). *J. Linnean Soc. London (Botany)* **31,** 364.

Fernández-Morán, H. (1962). *In* "The Interpretation of Ultrastructure" (R. J. C. Harris, ed.), pp. 411–427. Academic Press, New York.

Feulgen, R., and Rossenbeck, H. (1924). *Z. Physiol. Chem.* **135,** 203.

Gall, J. G. (1963). *Nature* **198,** 36.

Glick, D. (1949). "Techniques of Histo- and Cytochemistry." Wiley (Interscience), New York.

Glick, D. (1961). "Quantitative Chemical Techniques of Histo- and Cytochemistry," Vol. I. Wiley (Interscience), New York.

Goldstein, L., and Plaut, W. (1955). *Proc. Natl. Acad. Sci. U. S.* **41,** 874.

Gomori, G. (1939). *Proc. Soc. Exptl. Biol. Med.* **43,** 23.
Hamilton, J. G. (1942). *Radiology* **39,** 541.
Harris, R. J. C. (ed.) (1962). "The Interpretation of Ultrastructure." Academic Press, New York.
Howard, A., and Pelc, S. R. (1952). *Heredity* **6,** Suppl., 261.
Kasten, F. H. (1960). *Intern. Rev. Cytol.* **10,** 1.
Kaufmann, B. P., Gay, H., and McDonald, M. R. (1960). *Intern. Rev. Cytol.* **9,** 77.
Linderstrøm-Lang, K. U. (1939). *Harvey Lectures* **34,** 214.
Linderstrøm-Lang, K. U. (1952). "Lane Medical Lectures," Vol. 6. Stanford Univ. Press, Stanford, California.
Lison, L. (1936). "Histochemie Animale." Gauthier-Villars, Paris.
Lison, L. (1960). "Histochemie et Cytochemie Animales," Vols. I and II. Gauthier-Villars, Paris.
McClendon, J. F. (1909). *Am. J. Physiol.* **25,** 195.
Macgregor, H. C., and Callan, H. G. (1962). *Quart. J. Microscop. Sci.* **103,** 173.
Mazia, D. and Dan, K. (1952). *Proc. Natl. Acad. Sci. U. S.* **38,** 826.
Miescher, F. (1872) [cf. Greenstein, J. (1943). *Sci. Monthly* **57,** 523].
Needham, J. G. (1931). "Chemical Embryology," Vols. I, II, and III. Cambridge Univ. Press, London and New York.
Novikoff, A. B. (1959). *In* "Analytical Cytology" (R. C. Mellors, ed.), pp. 69–168. McGraw-Hill, New York.
Palade, G. G., and Siekevitz, P. (1956). *J. Biophys. Biochem. Cytol.* **2,** 171.
Pearse, A. G. Everson (1960). "Histochemistry," Churchill, London.
Perry, R. P., Hell, A., and Errera, M. (1961). *Biochem. Biophys. Acta* **49,** 47.
Plosz, P. (1873). *Arch. Ges. Physiol. Pflüger's* **7,** 371.
Pollister, A. W., and Ris, H. (1947). *Cold Spring Harbor Symp. Quant. Biol.* **12,** 147.
Ransom, W. H. (1867). *Trans. Roy. Soc. London* **158,** 431.
Schultz, J. (1941). *Cold Spring Harbor Symp. Quant. Biol.* **9,** 55.
Serra, J. A. (1946). *Stain Technol.* **21,** 5.
Sheldon, H., Zetterquist, H., and Brandes, D. (1955). *Exptl. Cell Res.* **9,** 592.
Shugar, D. (1962). *Prog. Biophys. Biophys. Chem.* **12,** 153.
Swift, H. H. (1950). *Physiol. Zool.* **23,** 169.
Takamatsu, H. (1939). *Trans. Soc. Pathol. Japan* **29,** 429.
Taylor, J. H., Woods, P. S., and Hughes, W. L. (1957). *Proc. Natl. Acad. Sci. U. S.* **43,** 122.
Thomas, L. E. (1946). *J. Cellular Comp. Physiol.* **28,** 145.
Vendrely, R., and Vendrely, C. (1956). *Intern. Rev. Cytol.* **5,** 171.
Vincent, W. S. (1952). *Proc. Natl. Acad. Sci. U. S.* **38,** 139.
Walker, P. M. B., and Yates, H. B. (1952). *Proc. Roy. Soc. London, B* **140,** 274.
Warburg, O. (1913). *Arch. Ges. Physiol. Pflüger's* **154,** 599.
Watson, J. D., and Crick, F. H. C. (1953). *Nature* **171,** 737.
Watson, M. L. (1958). *J. Biophys. Biochem. Cytol.* **4,** 727.
Watson, M. L., and Aldridge, W. G. (1961). *J. Biophys. Biochem. Cytol.* **11,** 257.
Zobel, C. R., and Beer, M. (1961). *J. Biophys. Biochem. Cytol.* **10,** 335.

Chapter 2

Methods of Culture for Plasmodial Myxomycetes

JOHN W. DANIEL and HELEN H. BALDWIN

McArdle Memorial Laboratory for Cancer Research,
University of Wisconsin, Madison, Wisconsin

I. Introduction

The plasmodial myxomycetes are an unusually interesting, but relatively little known, group of organisms. In these multinucleate organisms a veinlike system of channels which supports a cyclic, reciprocating flow of cytoplasm replaces conventional cellular organization. Syncytial organization, synchronous mitotic division, and several discrete phases in their life cycle typify many of the myxomycetes. Until recently investigators of the myxomycetes have focused their attention on two primary subjects: morphology and taxonomy, and protoplasmic flow and motility. Reviews by Martin (1960) and Alexopoulos (1960, 1963) summarize the large number of contributions on the morphology and taxonomy of the plasmodial myxomycetes and emphasize the many interesting problems which remain to be solved. Only recently have the last of the major links in the life cycle of the much studied member, *Physarum polycephalum*, been sketched in (Ross, 1957, 1961; Dee, 1960, 1962). A number of valuable studies have described the physiology of cytoplasmic flow and motility (Kamiya, 1960; Ohta, 1954) and a contractile protein associated with these phenomena (Loewy, 1952; Ts'o *et al.*, 1956, 1957).

The plasmodial form and synchronous mitotic division of these organisms make them appealing models for many studies of cell biochemistry and physiology. This use has been seriously hindered, however, by the difficulty of establishing pure cultures and the absence of suitable culture techniques. The recent development of axenic culture of *P. polycephalum* on soluble media (Daniel and Rusch, 1956, 1961) has made possible biochemical analysis of many aspects of its life cycle. Further applications of this technique will certainly extend knowledge of the less familiar members of the group and increase our understanding of basic life processes.

The following chapter briefly summarizes methods of culture of plasmodial myxomycetes and especially the isolation and axenic culture of *P. polycephalum*. Although this review does not consider the cultivation of the cellular slime molds, pure culture of *Dictyostelium* (Bradley and Sussman, 1952), *Labyrinthula* (Vishniac, 1955; Watson and Ordal, 1957), and *Polysphondylium pallidum* (Hohl and Raper, 1963) on defined or semidefined media has been reported.

II. Culture of Impure Myxomycetes

Cultivation of plasmodial myxomycetes in the laboratory began more than one hundred years ago. Plasmodia collected in the field or derived from germinated spores were grown in moist chambers on their natural substrate, e.g., rotting wood, or on tan bark (deBary, 1864; Baranetzki, 1876). Although biologists continue to use this method of culture for certain purposes (Brandza, 1926b; Nauss, 1943), early curiosity regarding the nutrition of the myxomycetes led to a search for preferred nutrients.

Lister (1888) fed *Badhamia utricularis* several species of fungi and observed that it engulfed and digested particles as an ameba does. Fungi proved to be satisfactory substrates for many myxomycetes (Macbride, 1900; Howard, 1931b). Howard and Curry (1932a,b) compared the feeding preferences of thirty-three myxomycetes for the mycelia and sporophores of a variety of fungi; they described the nutritional relationship as both saprophytic and parasitic. Crude cultures such as these were frequently overgrown by contaminating molds, bacteria, and protozoa. Miller (1898) attempted to improve growth conditions for *Physarum cinereum* and three species of *Stemonitis* by using sterile media, killing mold mycelia by heating the culture to 37°C, and attempting to eliminate protozoa by drying. He refers to the growth conditions as aseptic; however, "bacteria were found in all the cultures."

Pinoy's observations (1902, 1903, 1907) led him to believe that bacteria were essential to the growth and spore germination of the plasmodial myxomycetes. To control better the nutrition of myxomycetes he heated spores at 50°C for 1 hour to destroy contaminating bacteria; he then germinated the spores on agar streaked with pure suspensions of *Bacillus fluorescens*. Since plasmodia grow well in such "pure," two-membered cultures, the technique has been frequently used, with either yeast or bacteria as the feeder organism (Cohen, 1939, 1941; Sobels, 1948, 1950; Hok, 1954). Following Pinoy (1907), many thought the myxomycetes to be obligate parasites or symbionts. Actually, the relationship between the myxomycete and bacteria or yeasts is more often a mutualistic association or "ecological balance" (Raper, 1937; Cohen, 1941).

The growth of impure cultures on a substrate of oatmeal or oatmeal agar has been common. Howard (1931b) successfully grew several myxomycetes in crude culture on oatmeal agar. The moist chamber procedure developed by Camp (1936) has also been frequently followed. Camp supported the plasmodium on a bridge of filter paper, bent so its edges dipped into the water below. Pulverized rolled oats (or Pablum) were dropped on the filter paper to feed the organism.

While it appeared to many investigators that particles were essential to the nutrition of the myxomycetes, others tested growth on a great variety of soluble nutrient media (Cayley, 1929; Howard, 1931b; Parker, 1946; Alexopoulos, 1959). Because bacteria were present as a supplementary or alternate food source, their efforts did not establish whether soluble nutrients were used. Only when pure culture methods were developed was it shown that a myxomycete could grow on soluble substrates.

III. Isolation and Pure Culture

A. Isolation Methods

Three general methods, singly or in combination, have been used to isolate myxomycetes from contaminating organisms. These are the migration method, the enrichment method, and the antibiotic method. The techniques of the migration method have been described fully by Cohen (1939) and by Raper (1937, 1951). A plasmodium is permitted to migrate over a sterile, nonnutrient agar plate. A plasmodial branch that has not intersected its own path during migration is excised and transferred to a second agar plate. This process is repeated until the contaminants have been left behind the moving plasmodium. The method is quite successful with organisms which are highly motile (Cohen, 1939; Sobels, 1950), but if the plasmodium migrates slowly, the motility and rapid proliferation of contaminating bacteria interfere. Cohen (1939) has also described the enrichment method for isolation. After one migration over agar to remove gross contaminants the plasmodium is transferred to a sterile, nonnutrient agar plate streaked across its diameter with a heavy suspension of yeast, preferably *Saccharomyces ellipsoideus* or *S. cerevisiae*. The plasmodium, inoculated at one end of the streak, moves along it, feeding as it goes and leaving contaminants behind. After two successive transfers a "pure" two-membered culture is established. Removal of the yeast is easily achieved by one or two migrations. The enrichment method helps preserve plasmodial vigor.

Antibiotic decontamination has been used by Locquin (1949, reported by Hok, 1954), Sobels (1950), Sobels and Cohen (1953), and Hok (1954). Sobels and Cohen (1953) found that penicillin G (200 units/ml) and dihydrostreptomycin sulfate (1 mg/ml) added to the agar eliminated bacteria from five out of twelve cultures. The remainder were not decontaminated even on successive transfers. After one migration to remove gross contaminants, Hok (1954) transferred his plasmodia to agar slants containing 20 units/ml of streptomycin and penicillin, or placed the plasmodium on the surface of an agar plate flooded with the antibiotic solution for 5 hours. Low concentrations of bacitracin, tyrothricin, and subtilin were also nontoxic (Hok, 1954). The increased speed of isolation that can result from antibiotic treatment was reported by Watson and Ordal (1957) for a cellular myxomycete. They successfully isolated the cellular marine myxomycete *Labyrinthula* by ten repeated transfers on sterile seawater agar fortified with human blood or beef serum. By adding 200 units/ml penicillin and 300 μg/ml streptomycin to the medium, culture purity was achieved in only two transfers.

Parker (1946) attempted isolation by germinating spores on sterile agar and laboriously selecting under the microscope the gametes that were free of bacteria. These were transferred individually to sterile plates. The attempt was unsuccessful, as she did not obtain fusion of the gametes and development of a plasmodium. Although painstaking, the method should be successful, especially if applied to the zygotes rather than gametes. Isolation might also be obtained by plating zygote suspensions. Similarly, suspensions of spherules obtained by grinding laboratory sclerotia (see Section VI) could be plated in agar media and colonies selected.

B. Criteria of Purity

In 1928 Skupienski (cited in Parker, 1946) claimed to have achieved pure cultures of *Didymium difforme* plasmodia by sowing old sporangia. The weak plasmodia that formed survived for several months on agar. As evidence of the culture purity he mentions only that the water of condensation was clear and the surface of the agar was shiny. Howard (1931a) states that "uncontaminated plasmodia [of *P. polycephalum*] were transferred to plugs of sterile *Polyporus frondosus*" on which they grew rapidly. However, no criteria of purity were given. Cohen (1939), Parker (1946), and others have discounted both Skupienski's and Howard's report.

Cohen (1939) achieved pure culture of *Badhamia foliicola, Didymium squamulosum, Fuligo septica, Stemonitis axifera, Badhamia utricularis,* and *Physarum polycephalum.* As criteria of growth in pure culture, he states that (1) no microorganisms should grow in nutrient media, including at least one medium comparable in composition to that on which the plasmodium grew, and (2) cultures should grow indefinitely without permanent loss of vigor. Sobels (1948, 1950) maintained pure cultures of *Licea flexuosa* from 1942 to 1946. No microbial growth was observed on a variety of nutrient broths. She also developed pure cultures of *B. utricularis*, using a bacteriological analysis of the plasmodial path on agar as a test for purity. Hok (1954) inoculated nutrient broth with bits of plasmodia or agar from the plasmodia track. If no growth appeared in the preliminary test, more diverse media were used to verify successful isolation.

Adequate tests of purity should eliminate with certainty all classes of microorganisms and should include in the testing conditions a wide range of temperature, pH, aeration conditions, and types of media. Tests should be made on viable and nonviable samples in an effort to detect intracellular or symbiotic organisms. Cytological examination by visible and electron microscopy should be included.

C. Substrates for Isolated Myxomycetes

The most common substrates have been particulate, sterile food placed on nonnutrient, buffered agar. Killed or autolyzed yeast (Cohen, 1939; Sobels, 1948, 1950; Hok, 1954), killed bacteria (Sobels, 1950; Hok, 1954), or rolled oats (Daniel and Rusch, 1956, 1961) have been used. Figure 1a

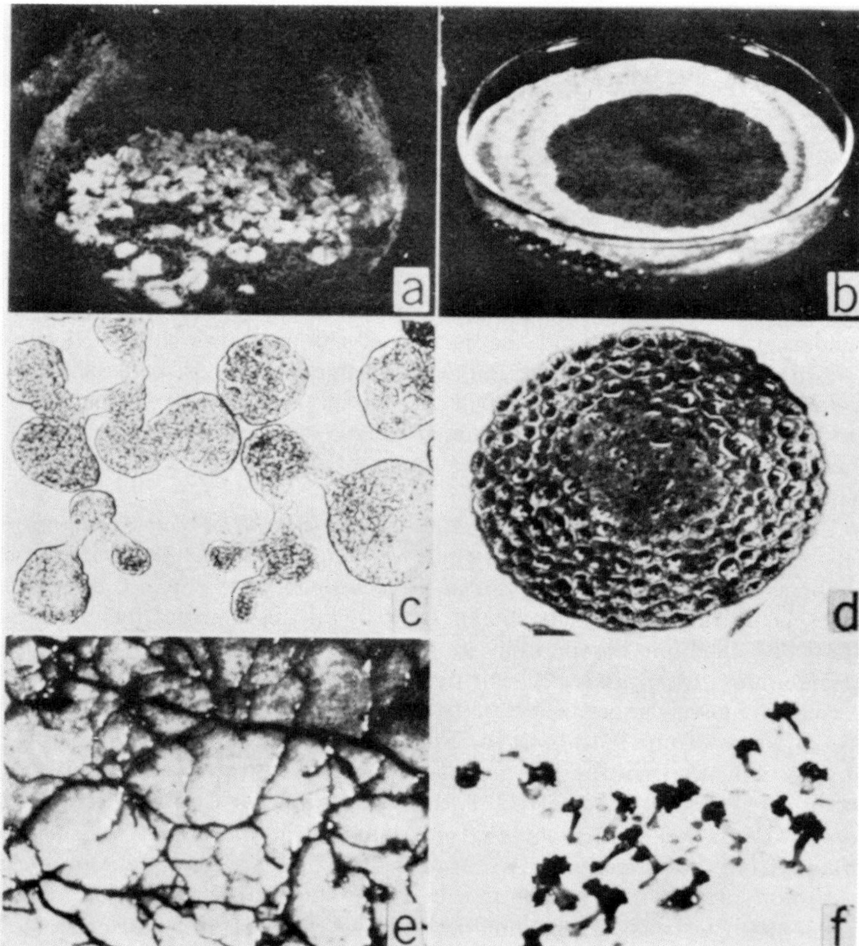

FIG. 1. (a) *Physarum polycephalum* (Schw) in pure culture on oat flakes. × 0.45. (b) A plasmodium supported on filter paper and growing on the semidefined, citrate-hematin medium. × 0.45. (c) Microplasmodia grown in submersed culture on the semidefined, citrate-hematin medium. × 98. (d) Cluster of spherules derived from a microplasmodium grown in submersed culture, fixed in 2% formaldehyde—5% acetic acid—45% ethanol and stained with iron-alum-hematoxylin. × 264. (e) A plasmodium after 5 days' incubation on the sporulation medium, prior to illumination (supported on filter paper). × 3.80. (f) Mature sporangia formed after illumination of a plasmodium as in (e). × 4.01.

shows *P. polycephalum* growing on sterile, rolled oats. Hok (1954) tested a wide variety of nutrient, solid media including oatmeal agar, ground brown rice, Pablum, and soybean meal, supplemented with autolyzed yeast; growth was always suboptimal. He found that a suspension of nitrogen mustard-killed yeast streaked on agar was the only nutrient giving growth equal to that in two-membered cultures with living yeast. Yeast killed by heat or other means was inferior.

Sobels (1950) grew *Licea flexuosa* and *B. utricularis* for periods up to 5 weeks on a soluble medium of buffered agar supplemented with 10% alcoholic yeast extract and peptones or sugar. Subcultures were not made. While growth was limited and cultures could not be maintained permanently, her work was the first evidence that myxomycetes might not require particulate nutrients.

Kerr (1961) reported growing myxamebae of *Didymium nigripes* from spores on a liquid medium containing formalin-killed *Aerobacter aerogenes*.

IV. Axenic Culture of *Physarum polycephalum* on Soluble Media

The strain of *P. polycephalum* whose growth is described in the following sections was isolated by the migration method of Cohen (1939), and its purity was established by bacteriological and microscopical means (Daniel and Rusch, 1961). Additional evidence of successful isolation came from electron microscopy (Sachs, 1958; Slautterbach and Bradke, 1961).

A. Media

1. Semidefined Soluble Media

Since the technique for growth of *P. polycephalum* on a semidefined, soluble medium was published in detail earlier (Daniel and Rusch, 1961), only a brief review of that method will be given.

The medium, whose composition is given in Table I, is made up of 1.0% tryptone, 0.15% yeast extract, 1.0% glucose, chick embryo extract, and a balanced salt solution containing Ca^{++}, Mg^{++}, Fe^{++}, Mn^{++}, Zn^{++}, PO_4^{3-}, SO_4^{--}, and Cl^- ions. It is buffered with $CaCO_3$ at pH 5.0. All ingredients except the chick embryo extract and $CaCO_3$ are mixed from stock solutions and are stored at 5°C with a few drops of toluene until autoclaving. The $CaCO_3$ is autoclaved separately as a 10% suspension and added to the cooled medium. The lyophilized chick embryo extract (Difco)

TABLE I

SEMIDEFINED GROWTH MEDIUM

Component	Concentration (gm/100 ml medium)	Component	Concentration (gm/100 ml medium)
Tryptone (Difco)	1.0	Citric acid · H_2O	0.048
Yeast extract (Difco)	0.15	HCl, conc.	0.006 ml
Glucose, anhydrous	1.0	Distilled water	to 100 ml
KH_2PO_4	0.20	$CaCO_3$	0.30
$CaCl_2 \cdot 2H_2O$	0.06	Chick embryo extract[a]	1.5 ml
$MgSO_4 \cdot 7H_2O$	0.06	[Hematin (Sigma Chem. Co., 2 × crystallized)	0.05[b]]
$FeCl_2 \cdot 4H_2O$	0.006	[Citric acid · H_2O	0.306[b]]
$MnCl_2 \cdot 4H_2O$	0.0084		
$ZnSO_4 \cdot 7H_2O$	0.0034		

[a] Difco ampoule containing 2 ml of a lyophilized 50% extract reconstituted with 8.3 ml distilled H_2O.

[b] The bracketed components may be substituted for HCl, $CaCO_3$, and chick embryo extract to prepare the citrate-hematin medium. The total gm/100 ml of citrate · H_2O = 0.3538 gm in the citrate-hematin medium.

is reconstituted with 8.3 ml sterile water per ampoule and added to the medium after addition of $CaCO_3$. Using care to keep the $CaCO_3$ in suspension, 20 ml of this medium is added to 500 ml Erlenmeyer flasks or 10 ml to 25 × 150 mm culture tubes for agitated submerged culture. For surface culture 12–15 ml is added below the filter paper in 100 × 15 mm Petri dishes.

Several acceptable modifications in the medium can be made. Tryptone can be replaced by enzymatic (Difco) or acid (General Biochemicals Inc.) casein hydrolyzates, peptone (Difco), or protone (Difco) (Daniel and Rusch, 1961). The chick embryo extract may be replaced by 5 μg/ml hematin or hemoproteins (Kelley *et al.*, 1960; Daniel *et al.*, 1962). The hematin solution, which is added just prior to inoculation, is prepared by dissolving hemin (Sigma Chemical Co., twice crystallized) in 1% NaOH, final concentration, 0.05%. The solution is autoclaved for 20 minutes at 15 psi and can be stored at 5°C (Daniel *et al.*, 1962). When particulates are to be avoided, 0.03 *M* citrate buffer, added to the salt solutions and adjusted to pH 4.6, may be substituted without significant change in growth rate. The citrate-containing medium, complete except for hematin, is autoclaved for 20 minutes at 15 psi and the sterile hematin solution added afterwards.

Chick embryo extract-$CaCO_3$ and hematin-citrate media have been used routinely from 1955 to the present, subculturing the organism from shaken cultures every 3 or 4 days with no evidence of decline in growth rate. Characteristic growth curves with both media appear in Fig. 2.

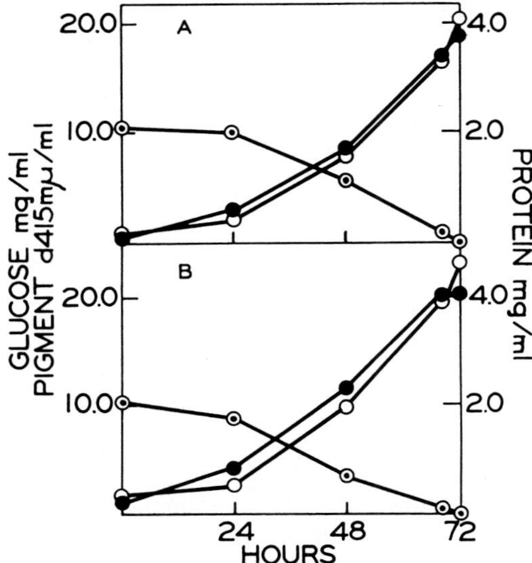

FIG. 2. Glucose utilization and growth of *Physarum polycephalum* on the semidefined media. Growth measured by protein content (Lowry *et al.*, 1951) and pigment density. Glucose measured by glucose oxidase (Glucostat®) method (Teller, 1956). (A) Hematin-citrate medium. (B) Chick embryo extract-$CaCO_3$ medium. ● protein in microplasmodia; ○ pigment in microplasmodia; ⊙ glucose in medium.

Specimens of *P. polycephalum* obtained from other sources than the original isolate have been grown satisfactorily on the semidefined media, but no survey of other myxomycetes has been made.

Relatively few compounds have been found to replace glucose as energy sources for growth of this strain of *P. polycephalum*. Table II summarizes the compounds utilized and the growth obtained with them. Glucose, fructose, disaccharides, and soluble starch are well utilized. Figure 2 shows typical glucose utilization. Potato starch, D-galactose, L-arabinose, xylose, sorbose, glycerol, gluconate, and glucuronate support little or no growth and elicit no adaptive response. Pyruvate, L-lactate, oxalacetate, L-malate, succinate, methanol, acetoin, tartrate, glycolate, fumarate, citrate, and α-ketoglutarate are also inactive. Acetate (0.5%) is quite toxic either in the presence or absence of glucose. Ethanol (0.5%) supports a slow rate of growth, and diauxic growth occurs on ethanol and a limiting amount of glucose.

TABLE II

CARBON SOURCES FOR GROWTH OF *Physarum polycephalum* ON SEMIDEFINED MEDIUM

Compound	Concentration (gm/100 ml)	Control growth (Per cent)
Glucose (control)	1.0	100
Fructose	1.0	50
	0.5	44
Maltose	1.0	94
Soluble starch (reagent grade)	1.0	97
Potato starch	1.0	41
Ethanol	0.5	47
	1.0	91[a]
No glucose	—	49
	—	36

[a] Growth at 157 hours; all other values at 72 hours.

2. SYNTHETIC MEDIA

The completely synthetic medium developed for growth of *P. polycephalum* is the first established for a plasmodial myxomycete and has facilitated detailed nutritional and biochemical studies. Three synthetic media are presented here, in the order of increasing simplicity. These have been designated A (excess vitamins and amino acids), AV-40 (minimum vitamins), and OV-40 (minimum amino acids and minimum vitamins). The organic and inorganic constituents of each of these is given in Table III.

For the A medium a four times concentrated basal solution (4× Basal) is prepared. This is composed of all of the inorganic constituents, glucose, and vitamins listed in Table III, but four times the weight of each compound per liter is used. The citric acid is dissolved first, then the $FeCl_2$. The glucose is dissolved separately in water and added to the $FeCl_2$-citrate solution. Each salt except $CaCl_2$ is added separately in the order listed and completely dissolved before the next is added. The vitamins are added and dissolved similarly. To prevent precipitation of $CaSO_4$, the volume is brought to approximately 900 ml before the final constituent, $CaCl_2$, is added. After the $CaCl_2$ is in solution, the volume is brought to 975 ml and the pH adjusted to 4.60 with approximately 23 ml of 30% KOH. The 4× Basal is completed by adjusting the volume to 1000 ml.

The 4× Basal for AV-40 and OV-40 is prepared similarly except that no vitamins are included. Both of these basal media are stable for 2–3 months at 5°C as determined by chemical assay and bioassay. Only thi-

TABLE III

COMPOSITION OF SYNTHETIC MEDIA A, AV-40, AND OV-40

Component	Concentration (mg/liter)	Component	Concentration (mg/liter)	Component	Concentration (mg/liter)
1[a,b]		2[a]		3[d]	
Citric acid·H_2O	2850	Inositol	11.9	DL-Methionine[e]	252
Glucose	10250	Choline hydrochloride	8.57	Glycine	454
NH_4Cl	2020	Biotin[c]	0.158[g]	L-Arginine hydrochloride	605
KH_2PO_4	656	Thiamine hydrochloride	42.4[g]	L-Cysteine hydrochloride·H_2O	502
$K_2HPO_4 \cdot 3H_2O$	875	Pyridoxal hydrochloride	60.9	L-Histidine hydrochloride·H_2O	268
$FeCl_2 \cdot 4H_2O$	46.5	Pyridoxine hydrochloride	8.72	L-Leucine	524
$MnCl_2 \cdot 4H_2O$	65	Niacin	4.22	L-Lysine hydrochloride	630
$ZnSO_4 \cdot 7H_2O$	33.6	Calcium pantothenate	4.5	DL-Isoleucine	348
Na_2SO	300	p-Aminobenzoic acid	0.816	DL-Phenylalanine	434
$CuCl_2 \cdot 2H_2O$	2.56	Fiolic acid	0.407	DL-Tryptophan	177
$CoCl_2 \cdot 6H_2O$	0.36	Vitamin B_{12}	0.0049	DL-Serine	470
$MgSO_4 \cdot 7H_2O_4$	232	Rboflavin	4.36	DL-Threonine	376
$CaCl_2 \cdot 2H_2O$	933			DL-Valine	432
				(DL-Alanine)[f]	2437

Volumes of Stock Solutions Used to Prepare Media

Medium	4X Basal with vitamins (ml)	4X Basal no vitamins (ml)	Thiamine (ml)	Biotin (ml)	Amino acids (ml)	H_2O (ml)
A	252	—	—	—	260	581
AV-40	—	252	20	20	260	541
OV-40	—	252	20	20	120	680

[a] Columns 1 and 2 comprise the constituents for the 4× Basal for medium A.
[b] Column 1 comprises the constituents of the 4× Basal for media AV-40 and OV-40.
[c] Only the underlined vitamins (Column 2) are used in the AV-40 and OV-40 media.
[d] Column 3 is the amino acid composition of the A and AV-40 media.
[e] Only the underlined amino acids (Column 3) appear in the OV-40 medium.
[f] DL-Alanine appears only in the OV-40 medium.
[g] For AV-40 and OV-40 media; ×100 for A medium.

amine and biotin are included in the AV-40 and OV-40 media. Thiamine HCl, 21.2 mg/100 ml, and biotin, 0.79 mg/100 ml, are prepared as separate, fifty times concentrated solutions and are stored frozen.

The amino acid stock solution for the A and AV-40 media is prepared in the manner following: fifty times the weight of each of the amino acids listed in Table III, column 3 is dissolved separately in 100 ml distilled water. Equal volumes of each amino acid solution are mixed for the stock solution. The amino acid solution for the OV-40 medium contains only the four underlined amino acids. The weights per 100 ml of stock amino acid solution for the OV-40 medium are: 3.024 gm L-arginine HCl, 2.268 gm glycine, 0.642 gm L-methionine, 8.114 gm DL-alanine. Each is prepared separately and equal volumes are mixed for the amino acid stock solutions. All amino acid solutions are stable for about 2 weeks at 5°C with a few drops of toluene.

Table III also lists the volumes of the stock solutions that are mixed to prepare 1000 ml of each final medium. The volume in excess of 1000 ml represents the extra 9% of water provided for evaporation on autoclaving. The media are stable for 1 week at 5°C if a few drops of toluene are added.

After 23.5 ml of medium without hematin is pipetted into 500-ml Erlenmeyer flasks, the flasks are capped with stainless steel culture tube closures (Bellco Glass) and autoclaved for 20 minutes at 15 psi. The volume after cooling is approximately 20 ml; 0.2 ml of sterile hematin solution (Section IV,A,1) is then added. Alternatively, 11 ml of medium can be pipetted into 25 × 150 mm test tubes, autoclaved, and supplemented with 0.1 ml of sterile 0.05% hematin solution. Suitable volume adjustments must be made for media which are autoclaved in bulk as less water is lost on autoclaving. Sterile hematin solution is also added separately to bulk media.

If the media described above are sterilized by Seitz or Millipore filtration rather than by autoclaving there is an increase of not more than 20% in maximum protein level attained for the standard growth cycle. Figure 3 shows growth curves of flask cultures on all synthetic media using a reciprocating shaker. Glucose utilization during growth on the A medium is shown in Fig. 4.

3. Minimal Organic Requirements

To determine which of the organic elements in medium A were required for growth of *P. polycephalum*, the vitamins and amino acids were deleted singly and the remaining components were combined in a new, simplified medium. Of the vitamins in the A medium only thiamine and biotin were necessary. Growth on the AV-40 medium (Fig. 3) shows the effect of

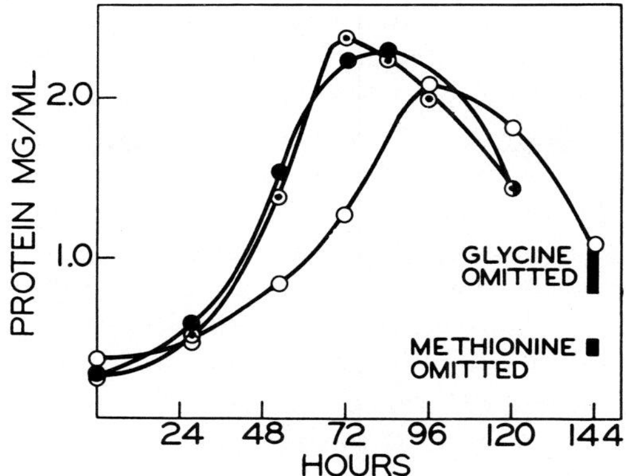

FIG. 3. Growth of *Physarum polycephalum* on synthetic media. Growth measured by protein content of microplasmodia (Lowry *et al.*, 1951). Twenty-milliliter cultures in 500-ml flasks incubated at 22°C on reciprocating shakers. ● A medium; ⊙ AV-40 medium; ○ OV-40 medium.

Glycine omitted, growth on AV-40 medium without glycine.

Methionine omitted, growth on AV-40 medium without methionine.

deleting all but these two vitamins as well as the lack of growth if either is omitted from the medium. The biotin and thiamine present in the initial inoculum permit growth for three generations but are exhausted by the fourth. Adding back thiamine or biotin at one tenth the original concentration allows growth at a rate indistinguishable from the control.

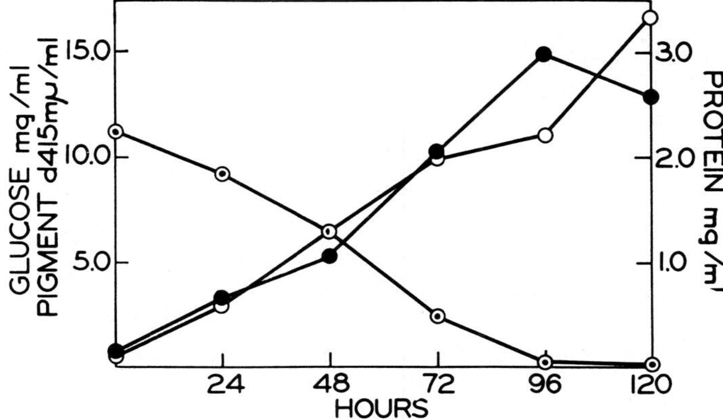

FIG. 4. Glucose utilization and growth of *Physarum polycephalum* on A medium. Growth measured by protein content of microplasmodia (Lowry *et al.*, 1951) and pigment density. Glucose measured by glucose oxidase (Glucostat®) method (Teller, 1956). ● protein in microplasmodia; ○ pigment in microplasmodia; ⊙ glucose in medium.

Approximately 8 mμg/ml of thiamine and 0.16 mμg/ml of biotin allow 50% growth on the AV-40 medium under standard conditions.

Hematin is required for growth on the semidefined and all of the synthetic media. The optimum concentration for growth on the AV-40 medium is 5 μg/ml. δ-Aminolevulinic acid, a number of porphyrin derivatives, and protoporphyrin IX are inactive as substitutes for hematin. Native or heat-denatured hemoproteins are approximately tenfold more active than free hematin on the basis of heme content (Daniel *et al.*, 1962).

The amino acid requirements were established by single, progressive deletions from the AV-40 medium. Three categories of amino acids developed: (1) those not essential for growth, (2) those absolutely required or strongly stimulatory, and (3) those necessary only in the OV-40 (minimal) medium. The nonessential amino acids are leucine, isoleucine, valine, tyrosine, alanine, proline, aspartic acid, glutamic acid, and lysine. The second group of amino acids consists of methionine and glycine. The effect of their deletion from the AV-40 medium is shown in Fig. 3. The glycine requirement is not absolute. Cultures may be maintained indefinitely in its absence but at approximately one fourth of the rate in its presence. Arginine is stimulatory on the OV-40 medium but not the AV-40. Alanine supplies the necessary amino nitrogen in the OV-40 medium but may be deleted from the A or AV-40 media with no effect. Glutamate and glutamine, but not aspartate, can also serve as amino nitrogen sources; NH_4Cl does not serve as a source of amino nitrogen.

B. Culture Techniques and Conditions

Physarum polycephalum and other plasmodial myxomycetes have traditionally been grown in surface culture. Because of the syncytial and ambulatory nature of the large plasmodia and the lack of pure culture methods, this mode of growth appeared obligatory. For studies of synchrony and sporulation, surface culture of large plasmodia is still required; however, Daniel and Rusch (1961) have successfully grown *P. polycephalum* in submersed culture. To obtain qualitatively and quantitatively constant cultures, to maintain purity, and to initiate replicate surface cultures, the submersed method of growth is preferable. Other plasmodial myxomycetes should respond similarly to submersed culture.

1. Surface Culture

A large, single plasmodium may be grown in surface culture (Fig. 1b) using any of the described media and the following technique. A 9-cm disc of filter paper is supported on a monolayer of 3.0–4.0 mm glass beads either in 100 × 15-mm Petri dishes or in 500-ml Erlenmeyer flasks. Millipore membrane (type HAWP, 0.45 μ pore size) may be substituted for filter paper. The Petri dish or flask, filter paper, and glass beads are autoclaved together. The culture is then inoculated with a plasmodial fragment cut from another surface culture and the growth medium added. The medium volume of approximately 12 ml must wet the filter paper without flooding its surface. The liquid should be added at the edge and under the filter paper; care must be taken to prevent formation of air pockets under the filter paper. Alternatively, the inoculum may be a 50% (v/v) suspension of microplasmodia from shaken cultures. One-tenth ml or larger samples are pipetted directly onto the dry filter paper; after several hours the microplasmodia fuse into a single plasmodium and growth medium is added (Section IV,B,3). These methods have been described more fully elsewhere (Nygaard *et al.*, 1960; Daniel and Rusch, 1961; Guttes *et al.*, 1961).

The doubling time for surface cultures on filter paper is 12–16 hours, until depletion of the medium. It is also possible to grow *P. polycephalum* on an agar medium prepared by adding 1–2% agar to any of the media, autoclaving, and then adding hematin just before pouring.

2. Submersed Culture

To initiate agitated submersed culture, a plasmodial fragment from surface culture is placed on the bottom of a slanted 500-ml Erlenmeyer flask containing 20 ml of growth medium. The plasmodium is allowed to migrate to the liquid surface, the floating plasmodium is then incubated upright for 48 hours in the dark at 22°C. Care must be taken to avoid submersion and resultant degeneration. After 48 hours agitation is begun. The organism fragments into multinuclear microplasmodia of varying sizes and shapes (Fig. 1c). Some cytolysis appears to occur during the initial agitation but not on continued culture. Within three transfers a standard growth cycle is established.

a. Inoculation and incubation. For the semidefined, soluble medium a 1.0 ml (approximately 3.5 mg protein) inoculum from a 72-hour culture is used for 20-ml shake cultures. Flask cultures grown on A and AV-40 media are inoculated with 2.5 ml of a 96-hour A or AV-40 culture containing approximately 2.4 mg protein/ml. After 96 hours of growth in the dark at 22°C on a reciprocal shaker (Section IV,B,2,b), the cultures again have a protein density of 2.4 mg/ml. Tube cultures grown on A or AV-40 media are inoculated with 0.8 ml of 120-hour A or AV-40 cultures containing approximately 2.0 protein/ml. Growing more slowly than the flask cultures, they regain the plasmodial density of the inoculum in 120 hours. Flask cultures grown on OV-40 medium are inoculated with 5.0 ml of a

120-hour OV-40 culture (2.0 mg protein/ml) and attain a similar density after 120 hours.

Both the age and amount of inoculum affect the resulting growth rate. For A and AV-40 media the doubling time is constant when the inoculum is taken at peak culture growth and when the initial protein density is between 0.1 and 0.3 mg/ml. Use of inocula from cultures more than 4 hours older than the age of maximum yield results in longer doubling time for the next cycle.

b. Aeration. Since *P. polycephalum* appears to grow only under aerobic conditions (Daniel *et al.*, 1962), the type and amount of agitation used is important to obtain optimum growth. For 20-ml volumes in a 500-ml flask a reciprocating shaker operating at 170 reciprocations/minute with a stroke length of $1\frac{5}{8}$ inches is satisfactory. The Eberbach Variable Speed shaker or New Brunswick shakers R-8 and R-8D are suitable. Inadequate aeration and splashing make volumes larger than 50 ml impractical on reciprocating shakers. The effect of aeration on reciprocating shakers has been shown by Daniel and Rusch (1961). An Eberbach Rotary shaker operating at 180 rpm with a 1-inch radius of gyration provides aeration and fragmentation for 50–100-ml cultures in a 500-ml Erlenmeyer flask.

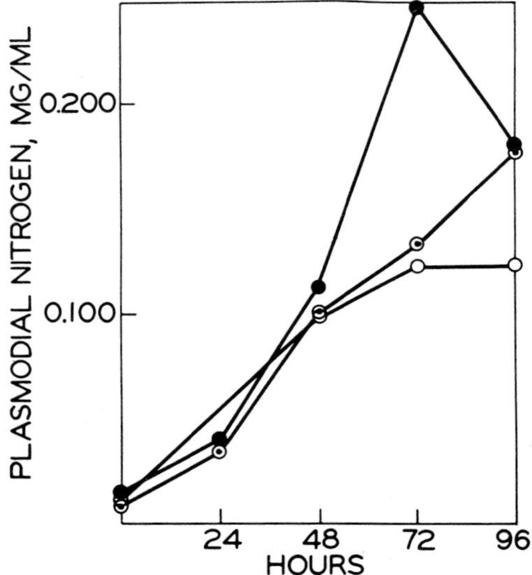

FIG. 5. The effect of aeration on growth of *Physarum polycephalum*. Grown on chick-embryo extract–$CaCO_3$ form of semidefined medium. Growth measured by nitrogen content of microplasmodia (Johnson, 1941). Twenty-milliliter cultures incubated in 500-ml flasks on an Eberbach rotary shaker with 1-inch radius of gyration. ● 180 rpm; ⊙ 160 rpm; ○ 130 rpm.

Under these conditions the growth rate is comparable to that shown in Figs. 2 and 3. Figure 5 shows the effect of varying the speed of rotation on culture growth. Use of smaller volumes with rotary agitation often causes clumping and fusion of microplasmodia, resulting in slower and highly variable growth rates. Five to 10-ml volumes may also be incubated conveniently and economically in 25×150-mm culture tubes held upright in racks placed on a rotary shaker (New Brunswick, model VS) operating at 240 rpm with a 1-inch radius of gyration. A reciprocating shaker may also be adapted to incubate culture tubes at a 55° angle from the vertical.

c. Effects of pH and temperature. Table IV shows the effect of pH on

TABLE IV

EFFECT OF pH ON GROWTH OF *Physarum polycephalum* ON SEMIDEFINED AND A MEDIA

Semidefined[a]			A		
Initial pH	Final pH	Growth at 72 hours (mg N/ml[b])	Initial pH	Final pH	Growth at 96 hours (mg N/ml[b])
4.6	4.4	0.277	4.7	3.7	0.193
5.0	4.6	0.222	4.9	3.8	0.177
5.3	4.7	0.203[c]	5.2	3.9	0.161

[a] Citrate-hematin form.

[b] Milligrams of plasmodial nitrogen per milliliter culture.

[c] Yellow pigment in medium.

growth in citrate-buffered, semidefined and A media. In all cases the pH drops during the growth cycle. Between 4.1 and 4.6 growth is maximal, but it declines slightly at pH 5.2. At a pH higher than 5.2, growth inhibition increases. If $CaCO_3$ is used as a buffer in the synthetic media at pH 5 or higher, growth is poor and serial transfers cannot be maintained. With the semidefined medium, $CaCO_3$ and citrate serve equally well.

Optimum growth temperature on the semidefined, A, and AV-40 media lies between 22° and 28°C. At 31°C growth on the semidefined medium cannot be maintained for more than one transfer. On the OV-40 medium growth at 28°C is at a rate almost comparable to that of AV-40 at 22°C, suggesting that amino acid uptake or metabolism may be a rate-limiting and highly temperature-sensitive reaction. The effect of temperature on growth rate with the semidefined medium is shown in Table V. Temperatures should always be measured within the culture flask, as the shaker motors tend to heat the cultures above the incubator temperature.

TABLE V

THE EFFECT OF TEMPERATURE ON DUPLICATION TIME OF *Physarum polycephalum*[a]

Temperature (°C)	Strain	Initial protein density (mg/ml)	Duplication time[b] (hours)
21.5	M2[c]	0.08–0.15	18.8
	M3[d]	0.08–0.17	18.8
24.0	M2	0.14–0.19	15.3
	M3	0.16–0.20	15.7
27.5	M2	0.12–0.17	14.3
	M3	0.13–0.18	13.1

[a] On semidefined (citrate-hematin) medium. Reciprocal shaker at 150 reciprocations/minutes, 1$\frac{5}{8}$ inch stroke.

[b] Average of determinations within noted concentration range.

[c] Maintained in submersed, axenic culture for approximately 4 years.

[d] Maintained in submersed, axenic culture for 8 months. Strains tested simultaneously.

Since uniform incubation temperature is of critical importance in studies of synchrony using surface cultures, the use of a small incubator with good circulation rather than an incubator room is suggested.

d. Effect of light on growing plasmodia. Axenic cultures of *P. polycephalum* grown on soluble media are inhibited by exposure to light, as has been frequently observed in the past (Baranetzki, 1876; Gray, 1938; Sobels and Van der Brugge, 1950). Because of this, cultures should be grown in darkness and shielded from artificial lighting used in the incubator room. In our laboratory this is achieved by permitting only infrequent, low-level illumination of wave lengths longer than 500 mμ during growth. A number of comparisons between cultures grown in complete darkness, except when inoculated, and those exposed briefly and intermittently to 40-watt "cool white" G. E. fluorescent lamps at a distance of 3–4 feet showed erratic amounts of growth inhibition in all light-exposed cultures. Although variable in extent under these conditions, inhibition can be as great as 50% after several cycles. On the semidefined medium bleaching of pigment and growth inhibition occur as a result of exposure to light. Under controlled illumination the extent of inhibition of growth and pigment can be measured. Pigment formation is suppressed disproportionately to growth as measured by protein. Intermittent illumination causes inhibition of growth and pigment formation which are reversed when dark incubation is resumed. Continuous growth in light does not induce adaptation. (However, for adaptation under natural conditions, see Brandza, 1926a.)

3. Interconversion of Macro- and Microplasmodia

The fragmentation of a synchronously dividing, multinucleate plasmodium to a population of individually synchronous but collectively asynchronous microplasmodia has been described (Section IV,B,2). Fragmentation continues throughout the growth period in agitated cultures; the microplasmodia often have a dumbbell-like shape which suggests the mode of subdivision (Fig. 1c).

TABLE VI

Composition of Sporulation Medium

Compound	Concentration (mg/liter)
HCl	40
$FeCl_2 \cdot 4H_2O$	59
$MnCl_2 \cdot 4H_2O$	82
$ZnSO_4 \cdot 7H_2O$	33
Citric acid $\cdot H_2O$	1200
$CaCl_2 \cdot 2H_2O$	590
$MgSO_4 \cdot 7H_2O$	590
$CuCl_2 \cdot 2H_2O$	23
KH_2PO_4	390
$CaCO_3$	1100
Niacin	98
Niacinamide	98

Microplasmodia suspended in salts medium (Table VI), growth medium, or distilled water, fuse fully within 3 hours on filter paper. Daniel and Rusch (1962a) and Guttes (this volume, Chapter 3) describe in detail the conditions for fusion of microplasmodia using salts medium; this is especially useful for sporulation purposes. To initiate synchronous growth in surface cultures, a 0.3-ml sample of a 50% suspension of microplasmodia in distilled water or semidefined growth medium can be used. Microplasmodia grown in agitated culture in the semidefined medium with citrate and hematin are harvested after 65 hours of growth by centrifuging at 500*g* for 3 minutes. The packed microplasmodia are resuspended with an equal volume of semidefined medium or water. If water is used they must be suspended very carefully to prevent excessive damage and loss of pigment; this is particularly true if the microplasmodia have been grown on a synthetic medium. Samples of 0.3 ml are transferred to the center of filter paper arranged as described in Section IV,B,1. Fusion begins within 2 hours; after this the appropriate medium can be adde

When microplasmodia are suspended in water or a salts medium, fusion may be detected within 2 hours by formation of fan-shaped branches at the periphery of the plasmodium. On continued incubation the entire plasmodium assumes an arborescent, migratory form. Addition of growth medium suppresses migration and promotes growth of a circular, compact, and relatively homogeneous plasmodium (Fig. 1b). Microplasmodia suspended in the semidefined medium fuse well but do not show the arborescent, migratory form until the medium is exhausted of nutrients. Cultures to be used for synchrony must not be allowed to migrate after fusion.

C. Analytical Techniques

1. Protein

Two types of protein determinations have been used successfully for *P polycephalum*. The older micro-kjeldahl method of Johnson (1941) was carried out on trichloroacetic acid (TCA) precipitates of the plasmodia. The centrifuged plasmodia are suspended in a small volume of water to which an equal volume of 8% TCA in acetone (8.0 ml of 100% w/v TCA diluted to 100 ml with acetone) is added. The samples stand 15 minutes or more and are then centrifuged. The yellow supernatant liquid is saved for pigment analysis and the precipitate is dissolved in 0.3 *N* NaOH prior to analysis by the Johnson procedure. Acetone may be omitted if pigment recovery is not required.

Before analysis by the Lowry protein method (Lowry *et al.*, 1951), the protein-containing precipitate obtained either by the foregoing TCA precipitation method or as a 0.5 *N* perchloric acid precipitate (Fig. 6) is dissolved in twenty volumes of 0.4 *N* NaOH.

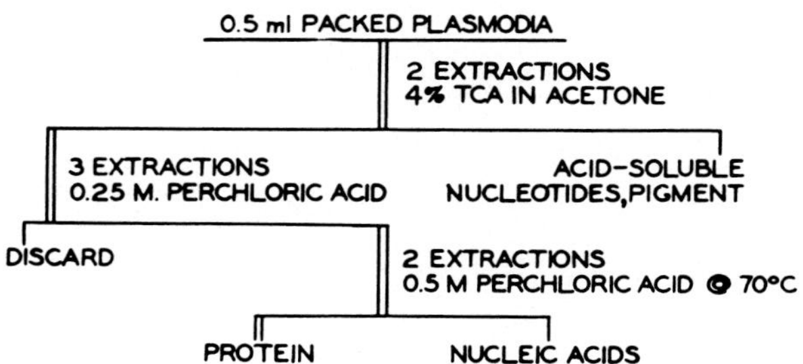

FIG. 6. Extraction scheme for plasmodia of *Physarum polycephalum*.

2. Nucleic Acids

Deoxyribonucleic acid (DNA) and ribonucleic acid (RNA) determinations have been carried out on hot 0.5 *N* perchloric acid (PCA) extracts using Keck's (1956) method for DNA and Ceriotti's (1955) procedure for RNA. Between 0.2 and 0.8 ml of packed plasmodia are suspended in distilled water. An equal volume of 8% TCA in acetone is added and the samples refrigerated for at least ½ hour. This supernatant and two subsequent washes with 4% TCA in acetone contain the pigment and the acid-soluble nucleotides. Acetone is removed from the precipitate by two washes with cold 0.25 *N* PCA. The precipitate is extracted twice with five volumes of 0.50 *N* PCA in a 70°C hot water bath. The combined supernatants are then analyzed for DNA and RNA. The precipitate can be analyzed for protein if desired. Figure 6 shows the extraction procedure.

Nygaard *et al.* (1960) used the orcinol method for determination of RNA from *P. polycephalum*. They also described procedures for hydrolysis of RNA and DNA and chromatographic analysis of acid-soluble nucleotides.

3. Pigment Determination

The amount of pigment dissolved in 4% TCA-acetone is determined by absorption at 415 mμ with a 1-cm cell in a Beckman DU spectrophotometer. The pigment has a broad peak of maximum absorption at approximately 385 mμ in alkaline solutions and at approximately 415 mμ in acid solutions. Although the chemical nature of the pigment has not yet been established, it apparently consists of several components, and there is good evidence (Kuraishi *et al.*, 1961) that it is not a pteridine as Wolf (1959) has suggested.

All of the analytical procedures described are applicable to microplasmodia and the large plasmodia obtained from surface cultures.

V. Sporulation (Fruiting) of *Physarum polycephalum* in Pure Culture

A. Sporulation as a Morphogenic Process

Specific nutritional conditions, differing from those required for growth, regulate the ability of the mold to sporulate. Under these conditions (Section V,B) plasmodia of *P. polycephalum* form sporangia when exposed to light. Briefly, the following changes occur: several hours after illumination the plasmodium segregates into many small spheres, each of which elevates to form a fruiting body or sporangium consisting of a supporting stipe and a head containing the sporogenous material. Meiosis then occurs, followed by cytoplasmic segregation to form uninucleate, gametic spores. The morphology of sporulation has been described by Howard (1931b) and in detail by Guttes *et al.* (1961) for axenic cultures maintained under the conditions described by Daniel and Rusch (1958, 1962a,b).

As observed from the procedures required for sporulation of *P. polycephalum* in axenic culture, three obligatory stages are involved. The first, immediately following the growth phase, is a period of minimum exogenous nutrition in the presence of niacin, during which the mold develops the ability to respond to light and thus enters the second phase. During this light-sensitive stage, visible light initiates the photochemical events which determine the third phase, the morphological expression of sporulation.

Guttes *et al.* (1961) used the word "sporulation" in a restricted sense to include only the events in the third phase. Since both the biochemical processes which follow the conclusion of net growth and the light reaction are required to induce the events included by Guttes *et al.* (1961), we will include all three phases described above in the term sporulation.

From a general and more basic point of view, morphogenesis can be described as the result of coupled cell processes (cell differentiation) controlling transition from one metabolic steady state to another in response to changes in environment. These changes result in genotypic expression establishing new metabolic pathways, allowing utilization of products of the new environment and reutilization of cell components. The organism finally stabilizes in a new state, characterized by altered energetics and cell structure.

It is useful from this point of view to consider growth as the idealized reference state. From an environment of minimal complexity which supplies stoichiometrically balanced substrates, an organism duplicates the minimum components necessary for its perpetuation at a maximal rate. Any stable departure therefrom, occasioned by change in environment (including mutation), could be considered differentiation. A coupled series of such changes would constitute morphogenesis. A basically unstable system would lead to cell death. One index of morphogenesis would be the newly established growth rate as compared with the reference state. The resultant lower net rate of growth would serve as a measurement of the organism's ability to adjust to a new rate-limiting reaction imposed by the new environment. New cell structures, subparticulate or more complex, would be the end products and the manifestation of morphogenesis. Haldane (1954) has noted an approximate correlation between the number of mutations (blocked reactions) and the viability of an organism under conditions promoting growth of the parent. The capacity of a cell to select and reject alternative pathways, that is, to evoke selectively or suppress its genotype, may correspond to such a morphogenic model. In a broad sense morphogenesis may be considered as ordered or accumulated differentiation conferring enhanced potential for survival.

The limiting physical and nutritional conditions of the environment which induce transition from the growth to the sporulation state reduce the flux of available free energy in the organism. Energy consumption per cell unit for net synthesis and osmotic work declines. This essential conservation of vital organization and cell material is apparently accomplished by a coordinated shift in cell structure and energy metabolism. Mitchell (1962) has recently emphasized the significance of the association between aerobic phosphorylation pathways and cell-interfacial structure for control of metabolite transport.

If a series of reactions leading to a new state is limited by a high energy-requiring step, an intermediate, metastable state may be established from which the cell may proceed in several directions depending on the stimulus, e.g., growth, sporulation, vegetative dormancy, or metabolite accumulation. Introduction of a source of free energy such as light, oxidizable substrate, or high energy phosphate compounds would produce an unstable state resolved as a new steady state of higher potential energy. The system reacting with the energy source would, by definition, be a controlling one. Chance (1959) has defined a controlling substance as a catalyst (enzyme or coenzyme) which can exist in two different states and which functions in a cycle linking two processes together. For induction of sporulation in *P. polycephalum*, and because under growth conditions light inhibits without inducing sporulation, the metabolic function of the pigment and its subsequent alteration by light would appear to be the controlling system.

The following sections describing the culture conditions required for induction of sporulation illustrate this concept of morphogenesis and serve to define a system for biochemical analysis.

B. Method of Obtaining Sporulation

The following method was developed to obtain sporulation of *P. polycephalum* under axenic conditions (Daniel and Rusch, 1958, 1962a). Microplasmodia, grown on the semidefined medium, are harvested near the peak of their growth cycle. At this time the culture is characterized by maximal growth of the organism as measured by protein and pigment content, exhaustion of the nutrient medium (Figs. 2 and 4), and maximal sporulation potential. A packed volume of 0.5 to 1.5 ml (1.0–3.0 mg nitrogen) is suspended in 1.0 ml of a balanced salts solution supplemented with niacin and niacinamide (Table VI). The inorganic elements of the sporulation medium are similar to the growth medium; however, the only organic components are the citrate buffer and 98 mg/liter of both niacin and niacinamide. The suspension of microplasmodia is pipetted onto a 9-cm disc of filter paper resting on a monolayer of glass beads in a 500-ml Erlenmeyer flask. The flask is then incubated in the dark at 22°C for 5 to 6 hours to permit fusion. After fusion is complete approximately 12 ml of sporulation medium is added. Dark incubation is continued for 96 hours at 22°C, during which time the plasmodium is transformed into a veinlike network (Fig. 1e). The flasks are then placed for 2 hours on a screen 2.5 cm above two 40-watt fluorescent lamps. Additional air circulation during the 2-hour illumination period is necessary to keep the temperature within the flasks below 24°C. After illumination the flasks are returned to the incubator for sporangial development. Within 8 hours the first macroscopic signs of sporulation are evident; sporulation is complete after 12 to 16 hours (Fig. 1f). Spores formed in this manner from normal strains of *P. polycephalum* germinate to form swarm cells (gametes) and zygotes which initiate a new plasmodium.

C. Factors Affecting Sporulation

The conditions inducing sporulation in myxomycetes have been much studied and little understood. In 1936 Seifriz and Russell attempted to analyze the conditions responsible for sporulation of *P. polycephalum* in unisolated culture. They considered, and discounted as of relatively little importance, the nine following factors: dryness, depletion of nutrients, character of nutrition and substrate, temperature, light, toxins, pH, gamma radiation, and injury. They concluded that the organism has an intrinsic growth rhythm or cycle and that disturbances of this mysterious cyclic pattern can prevent but not induce sporulation. While our findings do not bear out most of their points, there may be a correlation in the discovery of the brief period of sporulation potential after logarithmic growth is complete. As yet we do not know what biochemical state this represents or what biochemical composition characterizes the period when microplasmodia exhibit optimum sporulation potential. This metastable state can be followed by biological death, growth, sporulation, or vegetative dormancy (spherule formation), depending on the environmental conditions.

Discovery of the niacin requirement for sporulation and the effect of other organic compounds helps to clarify the contradictory reports of the role of feeding and starvation on sporulation (Seifriz and Russell, 1936; Camp, 1937; Gray, 1938; Schure, 1949). While no growth-supporting compound is necessary for sporulation, sporulation in *P. polycephalum* cannot occur unless niacin or one of a small group of biosynthetically related compounds is present during the dark incubation period preceding illumination (Daniel and Rusch, 1962b). Glucose, among the elements of the synthetic growth medium, prevents sporulation. It is completely inhibitory at a concentration of less than 2 μmoles/ml. Pyruvate, lactate, oxalacetate, malate, and fumarate also inhibit sporulation but tryptone and yeast extract do not. It becomes apparent that a "starved" plasmodium could not sporulate unless changes inducible by niacin had been accomplished, and that a "fed" organism might sporulate if glucose and some of its metabolites were absent from the medium.

While further investigation into the role of niacin in sporulation is essential, the following points have been established about the post-growth dark incubation period with niacin and have been published elsewhere (Daniel and Rusch, 1962b):

(1) Niacin, or any of the active compounds, must be present during a 4-day incubation period. Nicotinamide-adenine dinucleotide (NAD), $NADH_2$, triphosphopyridine nucleotide (NADP), or $NADPH_2$ replace niacin but do not shorten the required incubation time. Preincubation in the dark does not shorten the required contact time with niacin.

(2) Reduced pyridine nucleotides play an important part in development of light sensitivity. Folic acid, *p*-aminobenzoic acid (*p*ABA), and *p*-aminobenzenesulfonamide (*p*ABS) prevent sporulation if added at any time during the 4 days of dark incubation and are especially effective during illumination or during the 24 hours immediately preceding it. It seems likely that folic acid, *p*ABS, and *p*ABA are reacting with reduced pyridine nucleotides through the *meta* position of the *p*ABA moiety. This reaction occurs *in vitro* (Guardiola *et al.*, 1958). In our system addition of $NADH_2$ or $NADPH_2$, but not NAD or NADP, overcomes the *p*ABA inhibition.

(3) Recent studies (Daniel and Rusch, 1962c) have shown an aerobic, coupled, photooxidation-reduction reaction between pigment and pyridine nucleotides which results in an accumulation of reduced pyridine nucleotides. These reduced nucleotides are utilized in sporulating plasmodia previously incubated with niacin, but not in those lacking exogenous niacin.

(4) At high concentrations in relation to niacin, D-gluconic acid and D-glucoheptulose replace niacin. A common mode of action seems likely, and yet it does not appear that these compounds function as precursors of niacin via shikimic acid.

Just how niacin functions in the development of light sensitivity is not known. At present it appears that niacin or a distal metabolite of niacin may induce anabolic pathways whose products are essential for sporulation. Perhaps reduced pyridine nucleotides are among these. Niacin may act in the control role described by Chance (1959). Niacin may also act to inhibit the function of a niacin-containing compound and in this way control the dark period metabolism.

Under the conditions of minimal nutrition during dark incubation the quantity of plasmodium as measured by protein and nucleic acid declines (Fig. 7). Although no net growth occurs, mitosis continues (Guttes *et al.*,

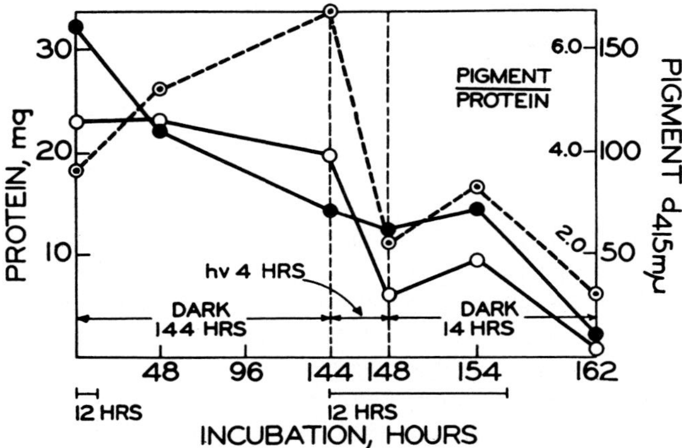

FIG. 7. Protein, pigment, and pigment to protein ratio during sporulation of *Physarum polycephalum*. Protein and pigment determined as total plasmodial content per plate. Dark incubation at 22°C. Illumination at 24°C, 2.5 cm above two 40-watt fluorescent lamps. ● protein; ○ pigment; ⊙ pigment/protein.

1961), suggesting that energy-yielding, endogenous oxidations of protein and/or nucleic acids are still coupled to support net duplications of certain cell structures. This also implies an unusually efficient coupling of anabolism to catabolism. Of particular significance for the sporulation mechanism may be the occurrence of mitosis before illumination in contrast to meiosis following this event.

As early as 1876 Baranetzki had implicated light in the sporulation process. Gray (1938) considered the effect of light on sporulation of ten species of myxomycetes, including members of each order of Myxogastres. Although he was unable to achieve sporulation of all of these, he showed that illumination was essential for sporulation of *P. polycephalum* and certain other yellow-pigmented myxomycetes and that it was not necessary for some unpigmented forms. Under his conditions there was a definite correlation between light intensity and frequency of sporulation, and he demonstrated that "shorter wavelengths [of light] are necessary for fruiting; long wavelengths and infrared do not permit [it]." Gray (1953) employed three isolated bands of a mercury arc light as an illumination source and showed that the percentage of sporulation was greater and the hours required to induce sporulation were shorter with an illumination of 4360 Å than one of 5460 Å or 5770–5790 Å. By use of filters and special flasks we found that light was an absolute requirement and that the active wavelengths lie between 350 and 500 mμ (the absorption peak of the yellow pigment in an acid medium is approximately 415 mμ), confirming Gray's findings (Daniel and Rusch, 1962a).

Gray (1938) reported that cyclic illumination lengthened, rather than shortened, sporulation time. (He used two cycles; either 8-hour illumination, 16-hour dark; or 0.5-minute illumination, 2.5-minute dark). Daniel and Rusch (1962a) showed that the illumination period must be of finite length but need not exceed 2 hours. Longer illumination, up to 8 hours, was not inhibitory.

Schure (1949) developed an empirically successful method of obtaining sporulation with *Physarum didermoides,* an organism which behaves similarly to *P. polycephalum* both in its negative phototropism while growing and in its requirement for light in order to sporulate. Sobels and Van der Brugge (1950) adapted Schure's technique successfully to pure culture of *B. utricularis* and to two-membered cultures of *P. polycephalum.* Although they showed light dependence, sporulation was too infrequent to be considered well controlled.

Gray (1939) showed that pH and temperature have an interdependent effect on sporulation. With increasing temperature the maximum pH permitting 100% sporulation decreased from 6 to 3. Under the controlled conditions described here both temperature and pH affect sporulation (Daniel and Rusch, 1962a). Although sporulation occurs through a pH range from 4 to 6, a higher pH is inhibitory. Plasmodia incubated at 6°C for 12 hours after illumination and returned to 22°C showed a delay of 12 hours before sporulation occurred normally.

Two main advantages result from the controlled conditions for sporulation described here: (1) reproducible sporulation of plasmodia grown under uniform conditions; (2) means for a systematic study of nutritional factors leading to a definition of the underlying biochemical determinants. Although apparent requirements may vary among methods, in a state of pure culture and defined nutrition they should reflect genuine metabolic requirements and serve as a means of analyzing the morphogenic mechanism. It seems possible that the light requirement, essential under the conditions described, may after further study be replaceable by altered environmental conditions or by addition of actual metabolites produced through the photochemical reaction. Similarly, the niacin requirement may reflect a regulation of metabolism achieved in a different manner by plasmodia derived under different nutritional conditions. This is suggested by the ability of gluconic acid to replace the niacin requirement.

VI. Sclerotia and Spherule Formation

If a myxomycete plasmodium is cooled (Hilton, 1908; Jump, 1954) or slowly dried to a water content of 10 to 15% (Hodapp, 1942; Gray, 1939; Jump, 1954) or exposed to certain other adverse conditions such as low pH, high osmotic pressure, or the presence of heavy metal ions (Jump, 1954), the plasmodial material assumes a dormant form known as a sclerotium. While the sclerotia of the various myxomycetes differ somewhat in gross appearance, all are composed of enwalled subunits named spherules by Brandza (1928), which are mono- or polynucleate (Brandza, 1928; Jump, 1954). The process of sclerotization has been described by Jump (1954), whose photomicrographs of sclerotization in *P. polycephalum* over a 36-hour period of drying show formation of spherule membranes starting within 2–4 hours and completed by 24 hours. During the next 12 hours, the plastic sclerotium becomes brittle. Reconstitution of the plasmodium from a plastic sclerotium induced by cooling rather than dehydration is a rapid process in which the spherules merge with adjacent ones, protoplasmic streaming is reinitiated, and the entire plasmodium is reformed within 4–6 hours (Jump, 1954). When rehydration is necessary the process is similar but slower.

Reports of the longevity of sclerotia vary. Gehenio (1944) found 75% of *P. polycephalum* sclerotia viable after 1 year but only 10% viable after 2 years of storage. Hodapp (1942) reports that 60% of sclerotia of the same organism had lost viability when 8 to 13 months old. However, Nollen (1957) reported greater longevity and hardiness of *P. polycephalum* sclerotia. Although many workers controlled conditions for sclerotia formation carefully, few have adequately controlled the subsequent storage period (Luyet and Gehenio, 1944).

Hodapp (1942) observed aggregation of the plasmodia before sclerotization and felt that this was a necessary precursor to formation of a viable sclerotium. However, Jump (1954) noted that no aggregation takes place before cold-induced sclerotization; the sclerotium assumes the same form as the precursor plasmodium and is only microscopically distinguishable from it. He also observed that single spherules are formed at the trailing edge of a moving plasmodium and states "since a single spherule is capable of developing into a plasmodium, and since, in culture at least, individual spherules frequently form apart from the main mass, the organization is a casual one and the spherule should be regarded as the functional unit." The work of Hemphill (1962) has supported this belief.

Hemphill developed a method for producing spherules and packets of spherules (microsclerotia) from plasmodia grown in submersed, pure culture (Fig. 1d). Microplasmodia are cultured in the usual way on the semidefined medium with citrate and hematin. The cultures are harvested by centrifugation at 1000*g* after 72 hours of growth, and the washed microplasmodia are suspended in salts medium without niacin (Table IV). Half of the microplasmodial suspension is transferred to each of two 500-ml flasks and 20 ml of salts medium is added. The "starvation" flasks are agitated in the usual manner for 48 hours in the dark. The microsclerotia are then harvested by centrifugation, washed, and resuspended in salts medium. From the initial growth culture eight samples of 0.2 to 0.3 ml each are obtained. Each sample is pipetted onto a narrow strip of filter paper placed on a disc of filter paper arranged in a Petri dish as described in Section IV,B,1. The closed Petri dish preparations are allowed to dry in the dark at 22°C. After 2 days the spherules have dried on the supporting paper strips and may be stored at 5°C in sterile tubes.

Spherules prepared in this way are cytologically equivalent to the subunits of sclerotia prepared by more conventional methods and show equivalent longevity as tested by viability after storage at 60°C (17 days), at −7°C (at least 85 days), and in absolute ethanol (95 days) (Hemphill, 1962). It is too early to know the longevity of her preparations, but spherules described by Guttes *et al.* (1961) and Daniel and Rusch (1961), which developed spontaneously in aged growth cultures and were stored in sterile sealed tubes at 5°C, are still viable after 3 years. Spherule preparation, therefore, is a desirable and convenient means of preserving material and provides a method of testing for strain alteration and adaptation.

To reconstitute plasmodia from spherules or microsclerotia, the filter paper carrying the spherules is placed in a 25 × 150 mm tube and 10 ml of nutrient medium is added. Within 4–5 days of dark incubation at 22°C on a rotary tube shaker a microplasmodial suspension is obtained. The culture has a growth cycle comparable to cultures maintained in the vegetative state after two to three transfers to growth medium.

Physarum polycephalum grown under sterile conditions described in this paper may also be induced to form sclerotia under desiccating conditions (Stewart and Stewart, 1961).

VII. Changes Observed after Prolonged Growth in Pure Culture

A. Growth Rate

Over a period of several years different isolates from our original *P. polycephalum* sclerotium and other isolated strains have been observed for changes in growth rate on the semidefined medium. The observations may be summarized as follows. (1) Newly isolated cultures from a single sclerotium adapt from oat culture to the semidefined medium rapidly. Within a few weeks a 3- or 4-day transfer cycle is established and thereafter the cultures have a stable growth rate. (2) Other isolated strains show the same adaptive behavior but establish their own characteristic growth rates. (3) Cultures transferred serially on oats slowly decline in ability to grow on this substrate. The decline may stop, giving a stable, slowly growing strain, or it may continue, making it difficult or impossible to maintain the strain on oats. Poorly growing oat cultures accumulate slime and migrate much more slowly on oats or agar than do vigorous strains. The presence of contaminating organisms could not be demonstrated in such cultures although contaminants may inhibit the growth of unisolated, oat-grown plasmodia. (4) Isolates from the same sclerotium have developed differences in pigment production, sugar utilization, spherule formation, and sporulation ability after several years of transfer.

B. Sporulation

After growth on the semidefined medium for approximately 3 years, a *P. polycephalum* isolate began to sporulate with decreasing frequency until no sporulation could be obtained either under conditions described by Daniel and Rusch (1962a) or from oat-grown cultures. During the development of this asporogenous strain, normal sporangial development persisted, but the spores had abnormal cytology, irregular size, and were unable to germinate. Cultures which were declining in ability to sporulate required a longer period of dark preceding illumination and a longer period of illumination. There was no change in the niacin requirement. The decline was more rapid for cultures maintained on the citrate than on the carbonate-buffered, semidefined medium.

A new isolate (M3) was derived from the same sclerotium and compared with the asporogenous one (M2). These studies by Dunn (1960) showed that in contrast to the new isolate (M3), the asporogenous strain utilized oats slowly and incompletely, fused slowly, and at the end of the growth cycle formed spherules slowly and incompletely. The asporogenous strain grew slightly less well on the semidefined medium. To obtain isolates of both strains spherules were plated and late developing colonies (presumably those containing one or few nuclei) were selected. After one or two growth cycles spherules were prepared and the plating repeated. The isolates showed the characteristics of the parent strain, but a few isolates having some properties of the opposite strain were found in both cases (Table VII). When equal amounts of the two strains were fused and tested

TABLE VII

NUMBER AND CHARACTERISTICS OF ISOLATES DERIVED FROM M2 AND M3 STRAINS

Parent strain	Number of isolates		
	M2	M3	Mixed
M2	11	0	2
M3	0	8	2
M2 + M3 composite	14	1[a]	3
	Characteristics of isolates after cloning		
	M2	M3	Mixed
	Poor growth on oats; good growth on semidefined medium; no sporulation	Good growth on semidefined medium and oats; plasmodia sporulate and spores germinate on either medium	Good growth on semidefined media but given isolate variable with respect to growth on oat culture and sporulation

[a] Growth and sporulation typical but spores did not germinate.

for sporulation, none was obtained. Isolates of the composite strain were almost completely of the M2 type with only a few M3 types persisting. Any bias caused by poorer spherule formation or growth rate of M2 would have favored the opposite response. In the same internal environment and maintained under the pure culture conditions of minimal nutrition for sporulation, M3 nuclei are apparently altered or suppressed by factors present in the M2 strain which exhibit a strong competitive advantage. Spores of the M3 strain germinate and give rise to competent zygotes, as demonstrated by their ability to establish new plasmodia. Supernatants from cultures of the M2 strain did not affect the ability of M3 to sporulate.

These as yet incomplete results indicate the development or selection of an asporogenous strain during prolonged growth on the semidefined medium. No strain used in this laboratory has indefinitely maintained its ability to sporulate. The mechanism of this effect is of considerable interest, especially in regard to the effect that prolonged culture at a rapid growth rate may have on the persistence of actual or potential pathways ultimately required for sporulation.

References

Alexopoulos, C. J. (1959). *Am. J. Botany* **46,** 140.

Alexopoulos, C. J. (1960). *Mycologia* **52,** 1.

Alexopoulos, C. J. (1963). *Botan. Rev.* **29,** 1.

Baranetzki, J. (1876). *Mem. Soc. Natl. Sci. Nat. Cherbourg* **19,** 321.

Bradley, S. G., and Sussman, M. (1952). *Arch. Biochem. Biophys.* **39,** 462.

Brandza, M. (1926a). *Compt. Rend.* **182,** 488.

Brandza, M. (1926b). *Compt Rend.* **182,** 987.

Brandza, M. (1928). *Botaniste* **20,** 117.

Camp, W. G. (1936). *Bull. Torrey Botan. Club* **63,** 205.

Camp, W. G. (1937). *Am. J. Botany* **24,** 300.

Cayley, D. M. (1929). *Trans. Brit. Mycol. Soc.* **14,** 227.

Ceriotti, G. (1955). *J. Biol. Chem.* **214,** 59.

Chance, B. (1959). *In* "Regulation of Cell Metabolism" (G. E. W. Wolstenholme and M. O'Connor, eds.), p. 367. Little, Brown, Boston, Massachusetts.

Cohen, A. L. (1939). *Botan. Gaz.* **101,** 243.

Cohen, A. L. (1941). *Botan. Gaz.* **103,** 205.

Daniel, J. W., and Rusch, H. P. (1956). *Federation Proc.* **15,** 513.

Daniel, J. W., and Rusch, H. P. (1958). *Federation Proc.* **17,** 434.

Daniel, J. W., and Rusch, H. P. (1961). *J. Gen. Microbiol.* **25,** 47.

Daniel, J. W., and Rusch, H. P. (1962a). *J. Bacteriol.* **83,** 234.

Daniel, J. W., and Rusch, H. P. (1962b). *J. Bacteriol.* **83,** 1244.

Daniel, J. W., and Rusch, H. P. (1962c). *Abstr. 2nd Meeting Am. Soc. Cell Biol., San Francisco,* p. 38.

Daniel, J. W., Kelley, J., and Rusch, H. P. (1962). *J. Bacteriol.* **84,** 1104.

deBary, A. (1864). "Die Mycetozoen." Engelmann, Leipzig.

Dee, J. (1960). *Nature* **185,** 780.

Dee, J. (1962). *Genetics Res. Cambridge* **3,** 11.

Dunn, K. (1960). Unpublished studies.

Gehenio, P. M. (1944). *Biodynamica* **4,** 359.

Gray, W. D. (1938). *Am. J. Botany* **25,** 511.

Gray, W. D. (1939). *Am. J. Botany* **26,** 709.

Gray, W. D. (1953). *Mycologia* **45,** 817.

Guardiola, A. L., Paretsky, D., and McEwen, W. (1958). *J. Am. Chem. Soc.* **80,** 418.

Guttes, E., Guttes, S., and Rusch, H. P. (1961). *Develop. Biol.* **3,** 588.

Haldane, J. B. S. (1954). "The Biochemistry of Genetics," p. 30. Allen and Unwin, London.

Hemphill, M. D. (1962). Master's Thesis. University of Wisconsin, Madison, Wisconsin.

Hilton, A. E. (1908). *J. Quekett Microscop. Club* **10,** 263.

Hodapp, E. L. (1942). *Biodynamica* **4,** 33.

Hohl, H. R., and Raper, K. B. (1963). *J. Bacteriol.* **85,** 199.

Hok, K. A. (1954). *Am. J. Botany* **41,** 792.

Howard, F. L. (1931a). *Am. J. Botany* **18,** 116.
Howard, F. L. (1931b). *Am. J. Botany* **18,** 624.
Howard, F. L., and Curry, M. E. (1932a). *J. Arnold Arboretum (Harvard Univ.)* **13,** 270.
Howard, F. L., and Curry, M. E. (1932b). *J. Arnold Arboretum (Harvard Univ.)* **13,** 438.
Johnson, M. J. (1941). *J. Biol. Chem.* **137,** 575.
Jump, J. A. (1954). *Am. J. Botany* **41,** 561.
Kamiya, N. (1960). *Ann. Rev. Plant Physiol.* **11,** 323.
Keck, K. (1956). *Arch. Biochem. Biophys.* **63,** 446.
Kelley, J., Daniel, J. W., and Rusch, H. P. (1960). *Federation Proc.* **19,** 243.
Kerr, N. S. (1961). *Bacteriol. Proc. (Soc. Am. Bacteriologists)* p. 86.
Kuraishi, S., Garver, J. C., and Strong, F. M. (1961). *Plant Physiol.* **36,** xlvi.
Lister, A. (1888). *Ann. Botany (London)* **2,** 1.
Locquin, M. (1949). *Bull. Mens. Soc. Linneenne Lyon* **18,** 4.
Loewy. A. G. (1952). *J. Cellular Comp. Physiol.* **40,** 127.
Lowry, O. H., Rosebrough, N. J., Farr, A. L., and Randall, R. J. (1951). *J. Biol. Chem.* **193,** 265.
Luyet, B. J., and Gehenio, P. M. (1944). *Biodynamica* **4,** 369.
Macbride, T. H. (1900). *Rhodora* **2,** 75.
Martin, G. W. (1960). *Mycologia* **52,** 119.
Miller, C. O. (1898). *Quart. J. Microscop. Sci.* **41,** 43.
Mitchell, P. (1962). *J. Gen. Microbiol.* **29,** 25.
Nauss, R. N. (1943). *Bull. Torrey Botan. Club* **70,** 153.
Nollen, P. M. (1957). Master's Thesis, University of Wisconsin, Madison, Wisconsin.
Nygaard, O. F., Guttes, S., and Rusch, H. P. (1960). *Biochim. Biophys. Acta* **38,** 298.
Ohta, J. (1954). *J. Biochem. (Tokyo)* **41,** 489.
Parker, H. (1946). *J. Elisha Mitchell Sci. Soc.* **62,** 231.
Pinoy, E. (1902). *Bull. Soc. Mycol. France* **18,** 288.
Pinoy, E. (1903). *Compt. Rend.* **137,** 580.
Pinoy, E. (1907). *Ann. Inst. Pasteur* **21,** 686.
Raper, K. B. (1937). *J. Agricult. Res.* **55,** 289.
Raper, K. B. (1951). *Quart. Rev. Biol.* **26,** 169.
Ross, I. K. (1957). *Am. J. Botany* **44,** 843.
Ross, I. K. (1961). *Am. J. Botany* **48,** 244.
Sachs, I. (1958). Unpublished studies.
Schure, P. S. J. (1949) *Antonie van Leeuwenhoek. J. Microbiol. Serol.* **15,** 143.
Seifriz, W., and Russell, M. A. (1936). *New Phytologist* **35,** 472.
Skupienski, F. X. (1928). *Acta Soc. Botan. Poloniae* **5,** 225.
Slautterbach, D. B., and Bradke, D. (1961). Unpublished studies.
Sobels, J. C. (1948). *Ann. Inst. Pasteur* **75,** 147.
Sobels, J. C. (1950). *Antonie van Leeuwenhoek. J. Microbiol. Serol.* **16,** 123.
Sobels, J. C., and Cohen, A. L. (1953). *Ann. N. Y. Acad. Sci.* **56,** 944.
Sobels, J. C., and Van der Brugge, H. F. J. (1950). *Koninkl. Ned. Akad. Wetenschap. Proc. Ser. C* **53,** 1610.
Stewart, P. A., and Stewart, B. T. (1961). *Exptl. Cell Res.* **23,** 471.
Teller, J. D. (1956). *Abstracts 130th Meeting Am. Chem. Soc.* p. 69c.
Ts'o, P. O. P., Eggman, L., and Vinograd, J. (1956). *J. Gen. Physiol.* **39,** 801.
Ts'o, P. O. P., Eggman, L., and Vinograd, J. (1957). *Biochim. Biophys. Acta* **25,** 532.
Vishniac, H. S. (1955). *J. Gen. Microbiol.* **12,** 455.
Watson, S. W., and Ordal, E. J. (1957). *J. Bacteriol.* **73,** 589.
Wolf, F. T. (1959). *In* "Photoperiodism" (R. B. Withrow, ed.), Vol. 55, p. 321. Am. Assoc. Advance. Sci., Washington, D. C.

Chapter 3

Mitotic Synchrony in the Plasmodia of Physarum polycephalum *and Mitotic Synchronization by Coalescence of Microplasmodia*[1]

EDMUND GUTTES and SOPHIE GUTTES

Department of Biology, Loyola University, Chicago, Illinois

I. Introduction

A better understanding of the mechanisms controlling the alternation between cell growth and mitosis depends on the availability of cellular material representative of defined stages of the cell cycle in quantities large enough to allow the application of biochemical procedures. Since single cells are too small for this purpose, methods have been designed to

[1] This work was supported in part by grants from the National Cancer Institute (No. C-3584) and the Alexander and Margaret Stewart Fund to Professor Dr. H. P. Rusch, McArdle Memorial Laboratory, University of Wisconsin, Madison, Wisconsin; and by NIH Grant GM-8495 to the authors.

synchronize large numbers of cells. This is achieved either by interfering with the cellular metabolism (Zeuthen, 1958) or by selecting cells in a specific stage of the mitotic cycle from an asynchronous culture (Maruyama and Yanagita, 1956). Other investigators have solved this problem by using material which exhibits natural mitotic synchrony. This is the case, for example, in sea urchin eggs (Mazia, 1959), in lily anthers (Erickson, 1947; Stern, 1956), and in organisms where several nuclei share the same cytoplasmic environment, such as plant endosperm (Jungers, 1931), insect eggs during early cleavage (Sonnenblick, 1950), giant amebae (Kudo, 1947), and myxomycetes (Lister, 1893; Howard, 1932). Among these, the myxomycetes are particularly attractive because they combine mitotic synchrony with giant size. Lack of suitable methods for growing them in an axenic culture has precluded their full use in the past. Such methods are now available for the myxomycete *Physarum polycephalum* (Daniel and Rusch, 1961). When grown on one of the media described by Daniel and Baldwin (this volume, Chapter 2), the nuclei of the plasmodia of *P. polycephalum* divide in synchrony approximately every 12–14 hours until the plasmodia reach a diameter of 5–6 cm and contain approximately 10^8 nuclei. Thus, with regard to the nuclear behavior such a plasmodium resembles one giant cell.

In the course of our studies it became desirable to have the same stage of the cell cycle available in several plasmodia simultaneously and at a predetermined time. This was achieved by a simple and reliable method which essentially consists in allowing large numbers of plasmodial fragments ("microplasmodia") growing in submersed agitated culture (Daniel and Rusch, 1961; Daniel and Baldwin, this volume, Chapter 2) to coalesce on filter paper (Guttes *et al.*, 1959, 1960; Nygaard *et al.*, 1960). These microplasmodia are smaller than 1 mm (Fig. 1) but still multinucleate. Agitated cultures contain microplasmodia of all stages of the cell cycle at random, although within each one of them the nuclei divide in synchrony. During coalescence (Fig. 2), the microplasmodia lose their identity and their respective constituents are mixed. The resulting surface plasmodium (Fig. 3) behaves like a single cell. Immediately after coalescence, this "cell" is at a stage of the mitotic cycle which is simply the arithmetic average of all stages present in the microplasmodial suspension before coalescence (Guttes *et al.*, 1959). A period follows during which nuclear division does not occur. This period is terminated by the first synchronous postfusion mitosis in which all nuclei participate. After that, the nuclei continue to divide in synchrony until the medium is exhausted.

It is not entirely unexpected that nuclei representing different stages of the mitotic cycle become mitotically synchronized when they are allowed, by experimental coalescence, to share the same cytoplasmic environment. Tahmisian (1959), for instance, observed that the nuclei of grasshopper neuroblasts, which were fused by roto-compression, divided in synchrony. Daniels (1951) found the same phenomenon when he fused pieces of multinucleate giant amebae with one another. The following

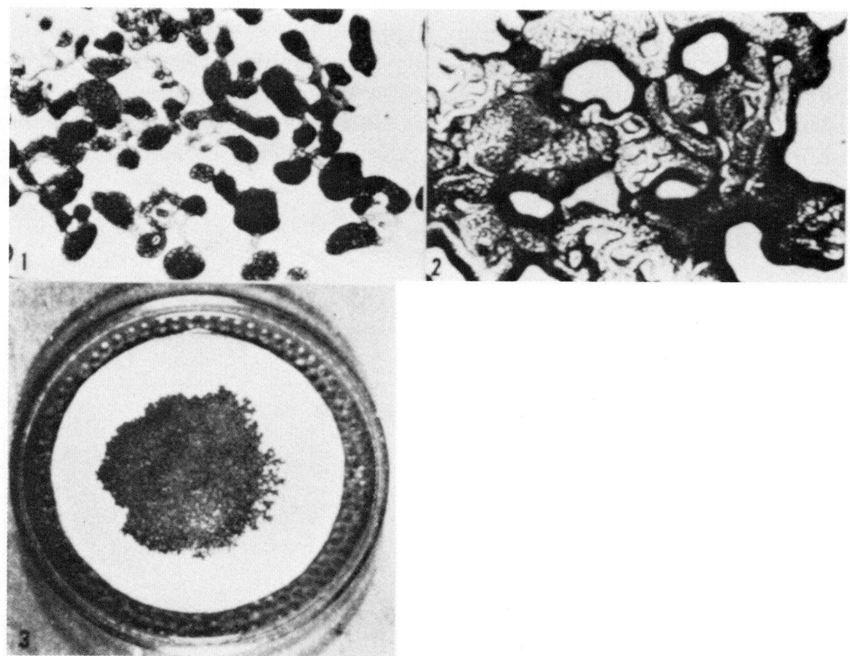

FIG. 1. Microplasmodia on agar. × 33.
FIG. 2. Microplasmodia of Fig. 1, 15 minutes later; coalescence has begun.
FIG. 3. Surface plasmodium growing on filter paper supported by glass beads in a Petri dish.

procedure for the mitotic synchronization of microplasmodia is based on the same principle. However, since the plasmodia of *P. polycephalum* coalesce spontaneously, they can be fused in large quantities without need for complicated manipulation of individual pieces (Guttes *et al.*, 1961). For details concerning the isolation of *P. polycephalum* and methods for preparing and culturing microplasmodia, the reader should consult the contribution by Daniel and Baldwin in this volume (Chapter 2).

II. Life History of *Physarum polycephalum*

Physarum polycephalum (Fig. 4) is a myxomycete. This group of organisms lives as motile, coenocytic plasmodia on deteriorating organic material. The plasmodium of *P. polycephalum* has a bright yellow color, which is caused by numerous yellow pigment granules. Under our conditions, on semidefined liquid yeast-tryptone medium (Daniel and Rusch, 1961), the plasmodium forms a flat disc which is composed of a dense meshwork of thin strands (Guttes *et al.*, 1961). As long as the environment is humid and nutrients are available, the organism grows indefinitely by

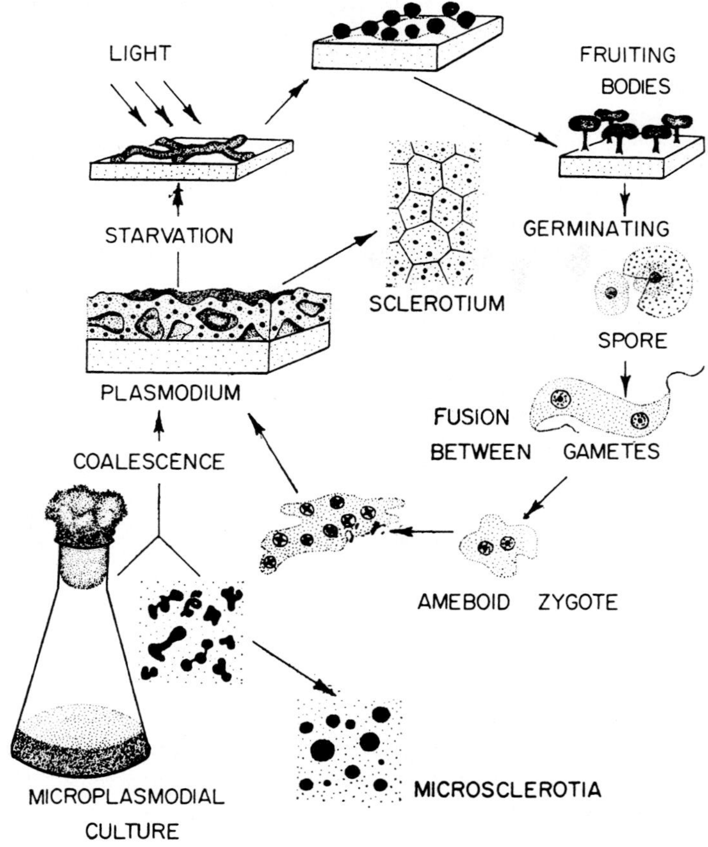

FIG. 4. Life cycle of *Physarum polycephalum*.

synchronous nuclear division, and cytoplasmic fission never occurs. When the plasmodium is being starved, its mobility increases. Most of the thin strands fuse with one another, and a coarse network of plasmodial strands is formed which is usually oriented toward an advancing front. If such a plasmodium is exposed to light after several days of starvation (Gray, 1945; Rusch, 1959), it forms fruiting bodies containing mostly uninucleate spores. After germination and fusion of gametes, ameboid zygotes are formed (Howard, 1931). These zygotes are miniature plasmodia, and they develop into larger ones by successive synchronous nuclear divisions which are not accompanied by cytoplasmic fission.

When a plasmodium is subjected to slow desiccation, it forms internal walls and is eventually converted into a brittle layer of mostly multinucleate "spherules" (Jump, 1954) called a sclerotium (DeBary, 1860). The sclerotium is relatively resistant to changes in temperature, light, and dryness and can survive in a dormant state for years. The sclerotia are revitalized when exposed to humidity.

III. The Experimental Material

The details which are given below apply to cultures maintained on citrate-buffered, semidefined yeast-tryptone medium fortified with hemin (see Daniel and Paldwin, this volume, Chapter 2). They are grown as suspensions of a 40-ml volume in agitated 500-ml Erlenmeyer flasks. Inocula of 2 ml are transferred twice a week.

For preparing large surface plasmodia, suspensions of microplasmodia are concentrated by centrifugation and allowed to coalesce on filter paper. Prompt and even coalescence is the main prerequisite for obtaining optimal mitotic synchrony within, as well as between, plasmodia. For this purpose two factors are of prime importance: the type of agitation and the age of the microplasmodial culture. We have found that when the microplasmodia are grown in 500-ml flasks as indicated above, an alternating agitation of 100 strokes per minute with an amplitude of 4 cm is optimal for subsequent coalescence. When the cultures are agitated less vigorously, the slime formed by the microplasmodia tends to adhere to their surface and later inhibits coalescence. On the other hand, too intensive agitation causes damage to the microplasmodia, resulting in a retardation of coalescence. The age of the cultures is important for similar reasons. Vigorously growing young cultures should be used because aging cultures produce excessive slime. Since the slime increases the viscosity of the medium, the sedimentation velocity of the microplasmodia serves as a criterion for the amount of slime present. Microplasmodia which are to be used for the preparation of surface plasmodia should sediment within a fraction of a minute when the culture flasks are removed from the shaker.

A. Preparation of Surface Plasmodia

1. Solutions, Glassware, and Equipment

a. Solutions

Erlenmeyer flasks (500 ml), each containing 200 ml of growth medium (for composition see Daniel and Baldwin, this volume, Chapter 2).

Erlenmeyer flasks (125 ml), each containing 50 ml distilled water.

Screw-capped vials, each containing 2.0 ml of 0.05% hemin (for preparation see Daniel and Baldwin, this volume, Chapter 2).

The flasks should be stoppered with nonabsorbent plugging cotton.

All solutions are autoclaved for 20 minutes under 15 pounds pressure (121°C).

b. Glassware

Petri dishes (15 cm in diameter) containing a single layer of glass beads (4 mm in diameter) covered with circular Whatman No. 40 filter paper (12.5 cm in diameter).

Graduated centrifuge tubes (40 ml), inverted in a 400-ml glass beaker which is tightly closed with aluminum foil.

A Petri dish (9 cm in diameter) containing pieces of aluminum foil (approximately 4 × 4 cm).

Volumetric pipettes (50 ml) with tips broken off and fire polished.

Volumetric pipettes (1.0 ml) with wide orifice.

All-glass syringes (2.0 ml) with 22-gauge needles. Syringes and needles may be assembled before autoclaving in a test tube stoppered with a cotton plug.

All glassware is autoclaved for 45 minutes under 15 pounds of pressure (121°C).

c. Equipment

Metal rack for supporting the centrifuge tubes in a slanted position.

Forceps to handle the pieces of aluminum foil.

International Clinical Centrifuge.

Bunsen burner.

2. Procedure

Throughout the following procedure the necessary precautions for work under aseptic conditions should be observed.

The microplasmodial suspensions are transferred with the 50-ml pipettes from the culture flasks to the 40-ml centrifuge tubes standing on the slanted rack. Each tube is then covered with a piece of aluminum foil. After centrifugation for 2 minutes at approximately 50 *g*, the supernatant is decanted and the tubes are returned to the slanted rack. The surface of the microplasmodial sediment in each tube is rinsed once with 1.0 ml of distilled water to remove excess slime. Each sediment is then resuspended with a volume of distilled water approximately twice that of the packed sediment. All suspensions are finally pooled in one centrifuge tube.

Of the pooled suspension, 1.0-ml aliquots are evenly spread with 1.0-ml pipettes in circular areas of approximately 3 cm in diameter on the filter paper in the Petri dishes. Since the microplasmodia readily settle down, the suspension must be stirred gently each time before removing an aliquot from the centrifuge tube.

Since growth medium is inhibitory to coalescence, it is important to allow sufficient time for the microplasmodia to establish contact with one another and to coalesce prior to its addition. This usually requires approximately $1\frac{1}{2}$ hours. The precise length of this period depends upon the efficiency with which the filter paper withdraws the liquid separating the microplasmodia from one another in suspension. As a rule, coalescence may be considered as completed when the peripheral and the central areas of the microplasmodial aggregate begin to curl up slightly and assume a velvetlike appearance.

At this time, the growth medium, fortified with hemin, is applied to the Petri dishes from the side, with the necessary precautions to avoid contamination. The volume of the added medium should be sufficient to fill the space between the glass beads and the filter paper without leaving large air bubbles. Occasional small air bubbles are removed by lifting the filter paper momentarily with flamed forceps.

All of the plasmodia prepared from a vigorously growing culture will enter the first synchronous postfusion mitosis approximately 6–7 hours after they were placed on the filter paper. The precise time depends on the condition of the culture used. However, for plasmodia obtained from the same microplasmodial suspension, the beginning of the first postfusion mitosis should not vary by more than ±5 minutes.

B. Pilot Plasmodia

It is often desirable to know several hours in advance, with a precision of ±10 minutes, at which time a group of plasmodia will enter mitosis. In that case, two groups of plasmodia are prepared in such a way that the onset of mitosis in the plasmodia of the first group (pilot plasmodia) precedes that in the second group (experimental plasmodia) by a period of predetermined length. This is achieved by preparing a few pilot plasmodia from a group of pooled microplasmodial aliquots from culture flasks which are immediately returned to the shaker. A few hours later the experimental plasmodia are prepared from the remaining microplasmodia. The pilot plasmodia will precede the experimental plasmodia in the onset of mitosis by a period which is equal to the interval between removing the two groups of aliquots from the cultures. This is due to the fact that the growth characteristics of the microplasmodial cultures, which determine the onset of the first postfusion mitosis, do not change appreciably during the few hours between removing the first and the second group of aliquots (Daniel and Rusch, 1961; Guttes *et al.*, 1961).

C. Microscopic Technique

For studying the morphology of a plasmodium, small explants are fixed for 24 hours in Champy's liquid (Gurr, 1953) and incubated for 3 days in the dark with 3% potassium dichromate. They are embedded in paraffin (melting point 60°–63°C) for 30 minutes, and thin sections (3μ) are stained according to Altmann's procedure (Gurr, 1953).

The morphology of the nuclei is best examined in smear preparations obtained from pieces of the plasmodial periphery which are then fixed at room temperature for 2 hours in 0.2% osmic acid and stained with a solution of azocarmine B (Gurr, 1953).

For specific staining of the chromosomal deoxyribonucleic acid (DNA), the application of Barger and DeLamater's (1948) modification of the Feulgen reaction to smear preparations which are fixed in ethanol chilled with dry ice is recommended. Hydrolysis is optimal with heating for 3 minutes at 60°C in 1 N HCl.

For fast determination of the mitotic stage of a given plasmodium, a small explant (less than 1 mm in diameter) is removed with a sharp blade from the plasmodial periphery and fixed in ethanol as a smear preparation on a thin 18-mm square cover slip (No. 1). After a few seconds, the unstained preparation can be examined in ethanol under high magnification with phase contrast. This method is particularly useful when plasmodia are to be harvested at a specific stage of mitosis.

D. The Mitotic Cycle

The drawings in Fig. 5 illustrate the appearance of the nuclei in ethanol-fixed, unstained smear preparations under phase contrast at various stages of the mitotic cycle.

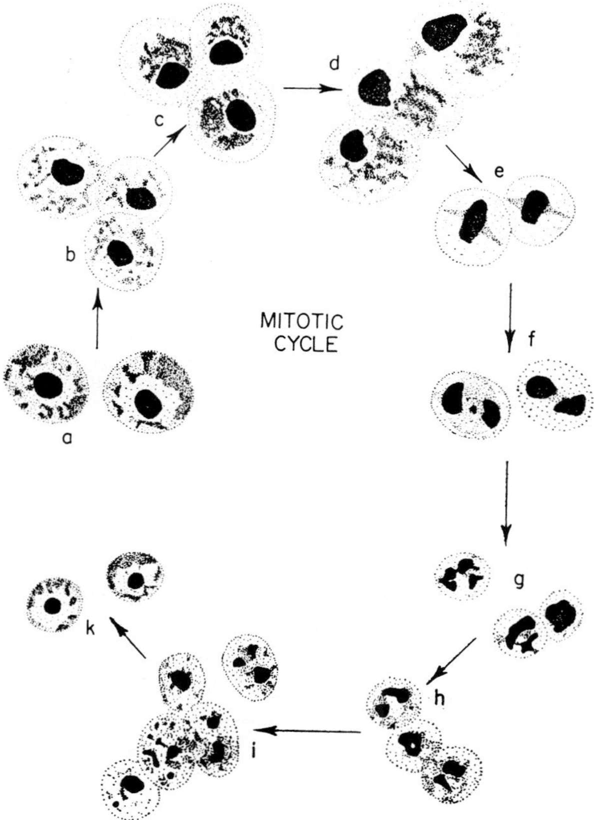

FIG. 5. Mitotic cycle. Schematic drawings from microphotographs (Guttes *et al.*, 1961). a, late interphase; b, approximately 1 hour prior to prophase; c, beginning prophase; d, prophase, nucleolus is beginning to disappear; e, metaphase; f, anaphase; g, daughter nuclei, 20 minutes after metaphase; h, daughter nuclei, 35 minutes after metaphase; i, daughter nuclei, 60 minutes after metaphase; k, daughter nuclei, 90 minutes after metaphase.

During interphase, each nucleus has one central nucleolus, and the chromosomes are arranged near the nuclear periphery. Approximately 1 hour before prophase, the chromosomes begin to spread more evenly throughout the nucleus. The nucleolus increases in size and begins to assume a slightly eccentric position. At the beginning of prophase, the chromosomes form a dense globular mass with the enlarged nucleolus at the periphery of the nucleus. Toward the end of prophase, the nucleolus becomes crescent-shaped, decreases in volume, and disappears. At metaphase, the chromosomes are separated by an intranuclear spindle. In anaphase, the spindle elongates and the connection between the daughter plates breaks. The telophase nuclei first appear as optically dense bodies of a diameter of little more than 1μ. Within the next 10 minutes they increase considerably in size, and prenucleolar bodies begin to be segregated from the chromosomes and to fuse with one another. Eventually, one central nucleolus is formed, and the chromosomes again assume a more peripheral position.

IV. Discussion

The degree of mitotic synchrony during the first, second, and third postfusion mitosis is such that there is no need to establish a synchronization index. During the first and second postfusion mitosis, more than 99% of the nuclei enter prophase within less than 5 minutes. The onset of the third postfusion mitosis may vary within one plasmodium by ± 10 minutes. However, since the preceding intermitotic period lasts for approximately 12 hours, this variation is negligible for studies concerning processes which occur during interphase.

The degree of mitotic synchrony between plasmodia also changes as the plasmodia grow. At the first postfusion mitosis, the nuclei of all plasmodia prepared from different aliquots of the same microplasmodial suspension enter prophase within less than 5 minutes. At the second mitosis, $\frac{2}{3}$ of the plasmodia enter prophase with the same precision, and the others may vary by not more than ± 10 minutes. At the third mitosis, the beginning of prophase may vary for different plasmodia from the same microplasmodial suspension by ± 30 minutes.

With regard to the precision of mitotic synchrony, experiments oriented around the first postfusion mitosis would appear to be technically most convenient. However, this mitosis has some features which render it less desirable in experiments for which it is necessary that not only mitosis proper, but also biosynthetic processes of the intermitotic period, be synchronized. The behavior of some nuclei during the first postfusion mitosis suggests that the latter might not fully be the case. For instance, prior to the first postfusion mitosis, some nuclei are able to incorporate DNA precursors in pulse experiments using radioactive tracers (Guttes and Guttes, 1963), whereas, during the following intermitotic periods, all nuclei can incorporate DNA precursors only for a few hours after mitosis.

Another indication that the first postfusion mitosis is premature for some of the participating nuclei is the occasional occurrence, during prophase, of nuclei which resemble postmitotic nuclei (Guttes and Guttes, 1963). Their chromosomes are spread as in typical prophase nuclei. However, they are smaller than the others, and they contain several nucleoli, a condition typical for postmitotic nuclei.

Some ($< 0.5\%$) of the nuclei participating in the first postfusion prophase are exceedingly large. Their origin is as yet unknown. It is possible that they derive from nuclei which, at the time of coalescence, have reached a late premitotic stage and, being unable to enter mitosis after the change of the cytoplasmic environment during coalescence, continue to increase in size. There is also the possibility that they originate from nuclei which, at the time of coalescence, have already entered mitosis and, being unable to complete mitosis after coalescence, became polyploid.

The applicability of *P. polycephalum* to problems of cell growth and mitosis has been illustrated in recent years. Nygaard *et al.* (1960) were able to investigate with biochemical procedures the synthesis of DNA during the intermitotic period in single plasmodia by removing different sectors from the same plasmodium at regular intervals, leaving one sector as control. In a similar fashion, Sachsenmaier and Rusch (1961) investigated the effect of 5-fluorodeoxyuridine upon RNA and DNA synthesis and upon the onset of mitosis. In another line of work, we have recently studied the responsiveness of nuclei at various stages of the mitotic cycle to a DNA-synthesizing environment when implanted by coalescence into DNA-synthesizing host plasmodia (Guttes and Guttes, 1962).

V. Summary

Large quantities of microplasmodia of the myxomycete *Physarum polycephalum* growing in submersed agitated culture are mitotically synchronized by coalescence. In the resulting surface plasmodia, the nuclei divide simultaneously and at a predictable time.

References

Barger, J. D., and De Lamater, E. D. (1948). *Science* **108,** 121.

Daniel, J. W., and Rusch, H. P. (1961). *J. Gen. Microbiol.* **25,** 47.

Daniels, E. W. (1951). *J. Exptl. Zool.* **117,** 189.

DeBary, A. (1860). *Z. Wiss. Zool.* **10,** 88.

Erickson, R. O. (1947). *Nature* **159,** 275.

Gray, W. D. (1945). *Am. J. Botany* **32,** 157.

Gurr, E. (1953). "A Practical Manual of Medical and Biological Staining Techniques." Wiley (Interscience), New York.

Guttes, E., and Guttes, S. (1962). *Federation Proc.* **21,** 381.

Guttes, E., and Guttes, S. (1963). *Experientia (Basel)* **19,** 13.

Guttes, E., Guttes, S., and Rusch, H. P. (1959). *Federation Proc.* **18,** 479.

Guttes, E., Guttes, S., and Rusch, H. P. (1961). *Develop. Biol.* **3,** 588.

Guttes, S., Guttes, E., and Rusch, H. P. (1960). "*Physarum polycephalum*—an Ideal Organism for Cell Research." Motion picture. John Ott Pictures, Inc., Lake Bluff, Illinois.

Howard, F. L. (1931). *Am. J. Botany* **18,** 116.

Howard, F. L. (1932). *Ann. Botany* (*London*) **46,** 461.

Jump, J. A. (1954). *Am. J. Botany* **41,** 561.

Jungers, V. (1931). *Cellule* **40,** 291.

Kudo, R. R. (1947). *J. Morphol.* **80,** 93.

Lister, A. (1893). *J. Linnean Soc. London Botany* **29,** 529.

Maruyama, Y., and Yanagita, T. (1956). *J. Bacteriol.* **71,** 542.

Mazia, D. (1959). *In* "Sulfur in Proteins" (R. Benesch *et al.*, eds.), pp. 367–389. Academic Press, New York.

Nygaard, O. F., Guttes S., and Rusch, H. P. (1960). *Biochim. Biophys. Acta* **38,** 298.

Rusch, H. P. (1959). *In* "Biological Organization and Function—Cellular and Sub-Cellular" (C. H. Waddington, ed.), p. 263. Pergamon Press, New York.

Sachsenmaier, W., and Rusch, H. P. (1961). *First Ann. Meeting Am. Soc. Cell Biol., Chicago,* 1961, Abstract, p. 186.

Sonnenblick, B. P. (1950). *In* "Biology of *Drosophila*" (M. Demerec, ed.), pp. 62–163. Wiley, New York.

Stern, H. (1956). *Science* **124,** 1292.

Tahmisian, T. N. (1959). *In* "Mitogenesis" (H. S. Ducoff and C. F. Ehret, eds.), p. 26 Univ. of Chicago Press, Chicago, Illinois.

Zeuthen, E. (1958). *Advan. Biol. Med. Phys.* **6,** 37.

Chapter 4

Induction of Synchronous Encystment (Differentiation) in Acanthamoeba *sp.*

R. J. NEFF[1], S. A. RAY, W. F. BENTON, and M. WILBORN

Division of Molecular Biology, Vanderbilt University, Nashville, Tennessee

---

[1]Work reported in this article was supported by grants from the Public Health Service (E-1908 and RG-6731), National Institutes of Health, and by an equipment grant from the Natural Sciences Research Committee, Vanderbilt University. The support is gratefully acknowledged.

I. Introduction

The formation of a cyst wall by amebae, known as encystment, is one example of protozoan differentiation (Trager, 1963). It shares with other differentiating systems the characteristic that macromolecules are synthesized which are not present in the undifferentiated state. In *Acanthamoeba* sp. the end product of differentiation is the cyst wall. It is composed largely, if not entirely, of polysaccharide (Neff and Benton, 1962). At least one third of the wall is cellulose (Tomlinson and Jones, 1962). The wall components are not present in the ameba but are synthesized from endogenous sources during encystment.

This paper describes simple methods of inducing synchronous encystment in axenic cultures (see Section III). Limitations of the methods are also presented (see Section IV). The stages and end products of encystment are the same in induced or naturally occurring encystment. The important difference is that induced cultures yield masses of cells that are largely in phase in all stages of the encystment process whereas naturally encysting cultures are largely out of phase (see Section II). The advantage of a synchronized mass differentiation is the ability to follow in time and with macro physical and chemical methods the changes that occur prior to and during the actual differentiation. In the present system either large aliquots or single cells may be taken for study at progressive stages.

The ultimate value of the *Acanthamoeba* system may be that it will serve as a simple model for understanding more complex embryonic systems. As yet no guiding principle or mechanism common to all differentiations has emerged. Should there be one it should be identifiable in this system. The simplicity of the *Acanthamoeba* system argues strongly for an intensive study of it in the near future.

II. The Encystment Process: A Description

The primary stimulus inducing encystment in *Acanthamoeba* is removal of food. Cells exposed to starvation conditions eventually encyst. In natural encystation, this is accomplished by a gradual depletion of food bacteria in mono- or polyxenic cultures, or by a gradual depletion of some nutrient in the liquid medium of axenic cultures. In experimentally induced encystment, food is removed very rapidly and from all cells simultaneously by washing them free of growth medium. It is this rapid food removal that is largely responsible for the synchronous encystment which follows.

A. Natural and Induced Encystment

Encystment of *Acanthamoeba* sp. on agar plates, with or without bacteria, has been previously described (Neff, 1957). It is asynchronous and may continue for several days or even weeks.

In axenic cultures grown in shallow liquid medium, cells multiply until they reach a maximum concentration of 1–1.5 $\times$ 10^6 cells per milliliter. They remain at this level for 5–10 days. At the end of this period, an asynchronous encystment begins. Over a period of a month or longer, all cells either encyst or break up. In these shallow cultures breakage is extensive so that only 50–60% of the cells present at the plateau number become mature cysts. Large amounts of cellular debris are present.

Aerated mass cultures in the same medium reach a population density of 3–4 $\times$ 10^6 cells per milliliter (Klein, 1959). They remain at this plateau number for 2 or 3 days and then begin to encyst. Encystment is largely complete 24 hours after it begins. Only 60–70% of the cells become mature cysts. Cellular debris is extensive.

In the experimental system to be described in Section III, cells from aerated mass cultures are harvested, washed, resuspended, and aerated in encystment medium. These cells begin to encyst 5–6 hours after washing. Eighty to 90% of the cells have begun to encyst by the ninth or tenth hour. All cells form mature cyst walls by the twentieth hour. Usually, over 90% of the original cells are recovered as mature cysts. Cells which do not encyst disintegrate; breakage occurs after encystment has started. No cell division is observed after induction, i.e., washing in encystment medium. Encystment curves are shown in Figs. 3, 4, 5, and 6.

B. Morphological Stages in Encystment

Microscopic examination of cultures induced to encyst under optimal conditions permits recognition of three morphological stages in encystment. They are: *pre-encystment*, *cyst initiation*, and *cyst wall synthesis;* these stages are shown in Fig. 1.

1. Pre-encystment

The pre-encystment stage has not been identified in naturally encysting cultures because the cells during pre-encystment are morphologically indistinguishable from amebae in growing cultures. Pre-encystment cells

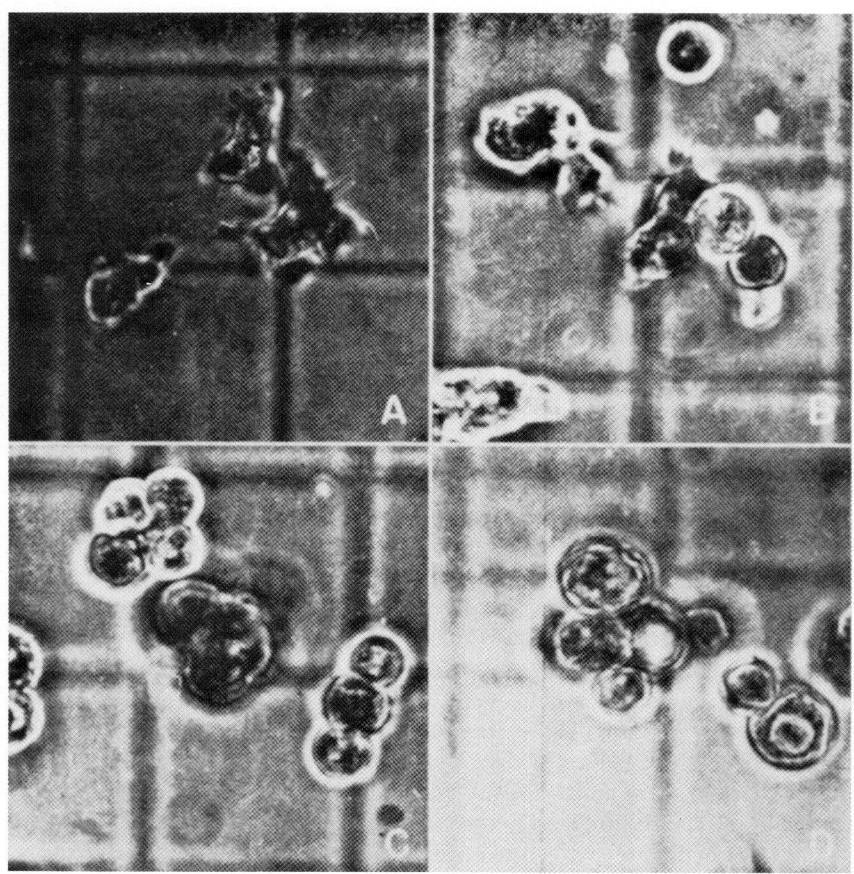

FIG. 1. Stages in synchronous encystment. Photomicrographs were made on samples for counting from a synchronous encystment experiment at four successive intervals after induction. Experimental conditions were: EM, optimal bicarbonate buffer (Section III,A,1,b); cell concentration, 2×10^6 cells per milliliter; temperature, 30°C; aeration, 4 cfh (cubic feet per hour) per liter of EM. In this experiment, 70% cyst initiation was completed in 3.6 hours.

Cells were photographed as they appeared in the counting chamber. The chamber used was 0.1 mm deep, had no undersurface concavity, and was used with a Number 1 cover slip. The out-of-focus squares which appear in the photographs are 50 μ on a side.

All photomicrographs were made with Tiyoda phase contrast optics (B.M.) using a 40 × objective, and a 10 × ocular. (A) Fifteen minutes after induction. Cells are all pre-encystment amebae, which attach to the floor of the counting chamber; they extend both limax and filar pseudopodia. (B) Eight and one-half hours after induction. Cyst initiation has occurred in 30–40% of the cells. The photomicrograph shows late pre-encystment amebae and young cysts. (C) Twelve hours after induction. Cyst initiation has reached over 90%; this counting sample contains only clumps of young cysts. (D) Nineteen hours after induction. Ninety per cent of the cells are mature cysts, with completed double walls.

are ameboid; they retain their ability to attach to glass and to form the limax and filar pseudopods characteristic of the species. Early pre-encystment cells cannot be distinguished morphologically from those on the threshold of encystment.

However, the pre-encystment stage is marked by rapid and important *physiological* changes in the cells. During pre-encystment, progressive changes occur in volume, in mass, in the concentrations of protein, ribonucleic acid, lipid and carbohydrate, and in the activities of several enzymes. These changes will be described in future communications by members of our group. This data suggests that the pre-encystment period is comparable to the "inductive period" in embryonic differentiating systems. Early pre-encystment cells are seen in Fig. 1A.

2. Cyst Initiation

The first morphological change evident in a suspension of encysting amebae is a sudden rounding up of amebae, beginning approximately 5–6 hours after induction. Cells that have just rounded up are called young cysts. They are no longer capable of attaching to glass or of forming pseudopods. The surfaces of these rounded cells are smooth. When rounding begins, the cell surface appears to be "sticky"; the rounded cells tend to clump or to attach to ameboid cells. Small particles in the encystment medium may also stick to their surfaces. This "stickiness" may signal the beginning secretion of cyst-wall material, although it should be emphasized that *no wall can be resolved* at the young cyst surface with bright-field, dark-field, phase-contrast, or interference microscopes. A mixture of late pre-encystment cells and young cysts is shown in Fig. 1B. Clumps of young cysts are seen in Fig. 1C.

The time required for all cells in a mass culture to enter the cyst initiation stage may extend over several hours. However, studies on encystment in isolated single cells demonstrate that the transition from the ameba to the young cyst occurs very rapidly. It is complete in less than 1 hour, and probably requires only a few minutes. Once a pre-encystment ameba has rounded up, no further morphological changes can be detected for several hours.

3. Cyst Wall Synthesis

Although it is probable that the synthesis of cell wall material begins at the time the cell rounds up, several hours elapse before the cyst wall is sufficiently thick to be resolved. In a single cell preparation a cyst wall 0.5–1.0 μ in thickness can be seen as soon as 6–7 hours after the onset of cyst initiation. Two layers are visible at this time. An encysting cell possessing a double cyst wall is scored as an *old cyst* regardless of wall thickness.

Clumps of mature cysts (20 hours after induction) are seen in Fig. 1D.

The cyst wall continues to thicken during the next few hours. The thickening is gradual. Mature cyst walls reach a final thickness ranging from 1.5 to 2.0 μ. Synthesis appears to be completed in about 12 hours after the onset of cyst initiation, but no exact criterion for defining the end of synthesis has been found. It should be emphasized that cyst initiation and cyst wall synthesis probably represent one continuous process divided into two stages for convenience. We believe that rounding up represents the first morphological sign of wall synthesis, and that the synthesis of cell wall material continues gradually from cyst initiation until it is completed. The two stages, however, provide useful classes in the analysis of encystment curves of mass cultures.

To summarize, for a single cell induced to encyst under optimal conditions, the approximate lengths of the three stages are the following: pre-encystment, 7 hours; cyst initiation, 15 minutes; cyst wall synthesis, 10 hours. In the mass synchronized systems, the same periods are about 7, 3.5, and 12 hours, respectively. The mass system is discussed in Section III,C. Finally, although there are three distinct morphological stages, it seems likely there are only two distinct functional stages: pre-encystment and cyst wall synthesis. The short stage of cyst initiation is probably the first sign of cyst wall synthesis.

III. Induction of Synchronous Encystment: The Method

Encystment is induced by removing cells from their nutrient medium, washing them, and transferring them to an encystment medium devoid of nutrients. This step is called "induction." All operations are carried out aseptically. The transferred cells are sampled at intervals, and the samples are counted differentially. From this data, encystment curves are plotted. This section will be divided into four parts. The first will describe suitable encystment and growth media; the second, apparatus used in our laboratory; the third will describe the cell handling, sampling, and counting procedures; and the fourth section will describe the treatment of data.

A. Encystment and Growth Media

1. Preparation of Encystment Medium (EM)

Two different encystment media have been designed. The first maintains a constant pH (between 8.6 and 9.0) at low cell concentrations. The second EM gives a progressive increase in pH (from 7.0 to 8.8) during encystment. Both are described below.

a. An EM Maintaining Constant pH during Encystment. An EM giving good synchrony in all stages of encystment has the following composition:

KCl	0.1 *M*
Amine buffer	0.02 *M*
$MgSO_4$	0.008 *M*
$CaCl_2$	0.0004 *M*
$NaHCO_3$	0.001 *M*

The pH is adjusted to 8.9 or 9.0 before autoclaving. After cooling it is used without further adjustment. Potassium chloride may be replaced in part or *in toto* by NaCl. The amine buffer, tris(2-amino-2-hydroxymethyl-1,3-propanediol) has been used in most of the studies reported in this paper. It is satisfactory for experiments in which the cell concentration is 10^5 cells per milliliter or less. Any one of three amine buffers (diethanol amine; 2-amino-2-methyl-1,3-propanediol; or 2-amino-2-ethyl-1,3-propanediol) is superior to tris at 0.02 *M* for cell concentrations up to 5×10^5 cells per milliliter because of their greater buffering capacity near the optimal pH for cyst initiation.

Although the same EM is used with higher cell concentrations, up to 2×10^6 cells per milliliter, the pH of the EM must be adjusted periodically back to 8.9 during encystment (see Section IV,F).

b. An EM Giving a Progressive pH Increase during Encystment. An EM giving an excellent synchrony is the following:

KCl	0.1 *M*
$NaHCO_3$	0.04 *M*
$MgSO_4$	0.008 *M*
$CaCl_2$	0.0004 *M*
2-Amino-2-methyl-1,3-propanediol	0.00032 *M*

All ingredients are dissolved in water and the medium is autoclaved. On autoclaving a precipitate of carbonates forms. After cooling, the EM is gassed with CO_2 until the suspended precipitate dissolves. This reduces the pH to 6.4–6.5. The EM is then gassed for 5 minutes with a 95% O_2-5% CO_2 mixture at 4–5 cubic feet per hour (cfh). This treatment restores O_2 and retains the low pH. If the pH remains below 7.0 at the end of this treatment, it is brought to 7.0 by bubbling air. The EM is now ready for use and is aerated at 4 cfh per liter of medium after the cells have been introduced.

The pH of this EM increases progressively during pre-encystment from the pH range for the maximal rate of growth (7.0) to that for the most rapid rate of cyst initiation (8.6–9.0). The progressive rise in pH is due to evaporation of CO_2 during aeration. The amine buffer serves to put a ceiling or lid on the pH rise. Its concentration is so arranged that the pH of EM approaches, but does not exceed, the pK of the buffer. Two other amine buffers, diethanol amine and 2-amino-2-ethyl-1,3-propanediol, can be used at the same molar concentration. The rate of aeration is critical in this system. At 4 cfh (for which the EM was designed) the pH rises rapidly to 8.5 or 8.6 during the first 5–6 hours of pre-encystment and then approaches the pH of the lid buffer asymptotically. The above system is *extremely* reliable with cell concentrations up to 2×10^6 cells per milliliter. The upper limit of cell concentration has not been determined. Limits of this method are discussed in Section IV,F.

In both of these EM's (constant pH and increasing pH) the breakage is 10% or less. This is determined by total counts made at the time of placing cells in EM and on termination of the experiment—18 or more hours in EM. It is possible there is much less breakage than indicated. As seen in Fig. 1C and D, the cysts attach to each other and counting is difficult with the larger clumps. There is very little debris in the optimal EM's after encystment. It is certainly small compared to the cellular debris found in natural encystment or in EM where the divalent cations are low or absent. We believe we have little or no breakage in our optimal EM's.

2. Optimal Growth Medium (GM)

Encystment synchrony is best if the cells used are taken from a GM in which the generation time is as short as possible. The following GM supports the most rapid growth yet attained for soil ameba in aerated mass cultures. In it, the generation time for *Acanthamoeba* sp. is 11–12 hours at 30°C. The composition is as follows:

Proteose peptone (Difco)	0.75%
Yeast extract (Difco)	0.75%
Glucose	1.5%
$MgSO_4$	0.001 M
$CaCl_2$	0.00005 M
KH_2PO_4	0.002 M
Ferric citrate	0.0001 M
B_1 hydrochloride	1.0 mg per liter
Biotin	0.2 mg per liter
B_{12}	1.0 μg per liter

The medium is prepared by making up two stock solutions, sterilizing them separately, and mixing just before inoculation.

All ingredients, except glucose, are dissolved in water; this solution is not made to volume at this time, since glucose is added after autoclaving. The pH of the GM without glucose is adjusted to pH 7.0, and the solution is centrifuged or filtered to remove debris. A concentrated solution of glucose is prepared and autoclaved separately. The correct volume of the concentrated glucose solution (to give the correct final volume of GM and the correct final concentration of glucose) is added to the incomplete, sterile GM just before inoculation.

Two-liter aspirator bottles are used for mass aerated cultures. The assembly is like the one shown in Fig. 2, except that there is no sampling port. Cells are grown at 29–32°C and aerated at 3 cfh.

B. Encystment-Sampling Apparatus

The apparatus used routinely in our experiments consists of a 2-liter Pyrex aspirator bottle which is fitted to: (1) an aeration train, and (2) a sampling port. The assembled apparatus is shown in Fig. 2.

Clean aspirator bottles are oven dried and then coated inside with a thin layer of Dow Corning High Vacuum Silicone Grease applied with a large dry bottle brush. The silicone grease prevents cells from adhering to the walls: it is inert. The bottle is closed by a vented stopper prepared by inserting a short length of glass tubing into a one-hole stopper. To the glass tubing protruding from the outside of the stopper is attached a vent consisting of a short length (about 5 mm) of rubber tubing. The stopper is wired securely in place in the mouth of the bottle after cells have been inoculated into the EM. The vent is covered by crimping a small piece of aluminum foil around its end. This permits escape of air from the culture but prevents contamination during storage. Under standard conditions, each bottle contains 1 liter of EM; however, volumes ranging from 0.4 to 1.4 liters have been used without detectable change in synchrony.

The aeration train consists of an air filter and a humidifying water trap connecting the aeration bottle to a pump or to the building air line. The air filter is made by sealing a length of U-shaped 8 or 9 mm Pyrex tubing into the end of a 25 × 200 mm Pyrex test tube. It is packed *loosely* with many pieces of nonabsorbent cotton. The filter effectively excludes bacterial and fungal spores if properly prepared. The water trap is placed in the train to prevent water loss from the culture during aeration. A trap constructed from a 500-ml Erlenmeyer flask is shown on the right in Fig. 2.

The sampling port permits the aseptic removal of samples of any size

FIG. 2. Encystment-sampling apparatus. The construction and use of this apparatus are described in the text. The bottle, as shown, is ready for aeration. The aluminum foil has been removed from the vent stopper to show the stopper wired in place. Normally, the wire is over the aluminum foil when the bottle is used.

from the encysting culture and minimizes opportunities for contamination. The sampling port is listed in current catalogs as a "test tube filling attachment." The port is inserted in one hole of a two-hole stopper of the correct size to fit the mouth of the sampling vial or flask. Into the second hole is inserted a glass tube with a 90° bend, to which is attached a rubber mouth tube used to start siphoning the sample from the bottle. A Y tube connects the outlet of the air filter, the sampling port, and the rubber air inlet to the bottom of the aspirator bottle. The Y tube is made from 8 mm Pyrex tubing.

All rubber tubing connections are made with $\frac{1}{4}$-inch rubber tubing. Two types of tubing have proved satisfactory: either amber gum of the type that will withstand repeated autoclaving, or the heat-resistant rubber tubing supplied by A. H. Thomas Co., Philadelphia, Pa. The rubber stoppers should also be made of heat-resistant rubber.

The air filter, sampling assembly, and air inlet tube are held in place by wiring the Y tube to the neck of the bottle. EM is added to the bottle before autoclaving. The vent stopper is placed in the mouth of the bottle and covered loosely with aluminum foil. The air inlet tube is clamped shut above the level of the EM. This prevents the EM from boiling over during autoclaving and wetting the cotton in the air filter. The entire assembly can then be sterilized as a unit by autoclaving for 30 minutes at 121°C.

C. Procedures for Cell Handling, Sampling, and Counting

1. Induction

Growing or stationary phase cells in GM are transferred to sterile, 40-ml, heavy-walled graduated centrifuge tubes. The centrifuge tubes may be either of the screw-cap type or wide-mouth type covered with aluminum foil. The cells are collected by centrifugation. A 2-minute centrifugation at 600–1000*g* packs the cells sufficiently for the supernatant medium or wash fluid to be decanted aseptically without loss of cells.

Enough cells are collected to provide the concentration of cells desired in the experiment when they are resuspended in a standard volume of EM in the encysting-sampling apparatus. A useful rule of thumb is that 1 ml of packed cells grown under standard conditions contains about 2.5×10^8 cells.

The harvested cells are washed centrifugally 2 or 3 times in sterile EM. After each centrifugation, the sedimented cells are resuspended in fresh sterile EM by mixing gently with a sterile, wide-tipped 10-ml serological pipette. The washed cells are finally suspended in a small volume of EM and aliquots transferred to encystment-sampling bottles so that the final concentration is approximately that desired. Large-tipped pipettes are used for all transfers and mixings to minimize cell breakage.

The inoculated bottles are placed in a water bath adjusted to a chosen temperature, and the aeration train attached to the air line. The air flow is adjusted to 4 cfh per liter of EM. Air flow from the air line is monitored with any of several commercially available flow meters which read between 0.5 and 10 cfh. All clamps are removed except that on the rubber tubing leading from the Y tube to the sampling port; it remains closed except when samples are taken. This inoculation completes induction. Zero time is defined as the time of inoculation of washed cells into EM.

2. Sampling

Aliquots of the encysting suspension are removed at intervals for counting and analysis. The following procedure is used: The air line is disconnected. The clamp is transferred from the rubber tubing connecting the Y tube and the sampling port to the tubing connecting the air filter and the Y tube. The sampling vial is attached to the stopper of the sampling port. The sample is siphoned into the sampling vessel. The siphoning is started by a brief application of mouth suction to the bent tube in the second hole of the sampling port stopper. To stop sampling after a suitable sample volume has been siphoned out, the clamp is removed from the tubing connecting the air filter and Y tube and returned to its original position. The air filter is again attached to the air line.

Some cells may attach to the walls and floor of the coated bottle in time, even with vigorous aeration and mixing. They can be easily removed by inverting the bottle several times before sample withdrawal. Inverting is done *only* after the air line has been disconnected and after the air inlet tubing and the vented stopper have been clamped shut. Encystment media drains cleanly from the silicone-coated surface and removes attached cells without rupturing them. Two or three inversions usually remove all cells from the sides and bottom of the bottle. Repetition of this inversion procedure before each sampling is strongly recommended.

3. Counting

Samples are withdrawn and counted to determine total cell concentration of the encysting population at the beginning and termination of each experiment. Methods of counting total cell populations have been described previously (Neff, 1963).

The degree of encystment achieved in an experiment is determined by performing differential counts on the population at hourly intervals after induction. In the differential counts, three cell types are scored in each sample. They are: *pre-encystment amebae*, *young cysts*, and *old cysts*. These classes are defined by the criteria given in Section II,b. The total count at each interval is the sum of the three classes.

Since the characteristic distinguishing between pre-encystment amebae and young cysts is the ability of the amebae to attach and extend pseudopods, the environmental conditions during counting must permit the amebae to form pseudopods. The conditions that must be met are: a clean glass surface, an adequate oxygen supply, and no cover slip compression. All conditions can be met by diluting the counting sample to a level of 5×10^5 cells per milliliter or less, and performing the count in a blood counting chamber which is 0.1 mm deep. The chamber is filled with the sample, and the cells allowed to stand undisturbed for 3–5 minutes to permit ameba to attach and extend their pseudopods. Then the differential count is performed. All classes are scored simultaneously using a Clay-Adams, Five Key, Laboratory Counter.

The counts are performed with the high-dry objectives. The high-dry objectives of most microscopes can be used with a counting chamber 0.1 mm in depth, if a Number 1 cover slip is substituted for the thick one customarily supplied. Phase-contrast optics are used to facilitate recognition of the three classes. Phase can be used most effectively if the counting chamber is one *without* a concavity on its under surface. The total number of cells counted at each sampling interval depends upon the statistical confidence levels to be satisfied. If a total of 1000 cells per sample is counted, then one person can perform hourly counts on four bottles with ease.

D. Treatment of Data

At each sampling interval the results are tabulated and the percentage of cells in each of the three classes is calculated. From this data an encystment curve is constructed by plotting the percentage of each class present at each sampling interval against the time elapsed since induction. Since the percentage of pre-encystment amebae and the percentage of cysts in the population are reciprocally related, the plot of the pre-encystment amebae may be omitted and the course of the encystment can be clearly visualized by following the changes in relative numbers of total cysts and old cysts. The curve for old cysts lags behind that for total cysts by several hours but is nearly indentical to it in its characteristics.

From an encystment curve, the three stages of encystment may be determined for a mass culture of encysting cells. The encystment stages in a mass culture may be defined as follows:

1. Pre-encystment: that period between induction and the time when the total cysts constitute 10% of the total cells present. In the optimal system, this is 6–7 hours.

2. Cyst initiation: that period extending from the time when the total cysts reach 10% of the total population until they constitute 80% of the total. In the optimal system this is 3–4 hours long.

3. Cyst wall synthesis: that period beginning with 10% cysts and continuing until 80% of the total cells are old cysts. In the optimal system, this requires 10–12 hours after 10% cyst initiation.

It will be noted that the slope of the curve defining the percentage of total cysts in the culture is immediately diagnostic of the degree of synchrony achieved in the experiment. Under optimal conditions, this slope is very great; the percentage of total cysts (mostly young cysts at this time) in the population may go from 10% to 80% in 3–3.5 hours in an experiment lasting 20 hours, indicating a high degree of synchrony in the encystment process (see Figs. 3, 4, 5, and 6).

IV. Optimal Conditions for Synchronous Encystment

Encystment will occur under a wide variety of experimental conditions. For high degrees of synchrony in encystment, however, the experimental conditions are more circumscribed. Recently, we have explored several variables which affect the degree of synchrony achieved. They are: competence of cells, cell concentration, ionic composition of EM, rate of aeration during encystment, temperature, and pH of EM. A discussion of these factors will be presented in this section. An understanding of them will permit conditions to be varied somewhat for special experimental purposes, so long as the conditions are kept within the limits discussed below.

A. Competence of Cells

1. Growth Medium and Encystment Synchrony

Acanthamoeba may be successfully grown on any of several growth media (Adam, 1959; Band, 1959; Neff, 1957; Neff and Neff, 1963; Neff *et al.*, 1958). However, cells grown on different media differ in their response to induction of encystment. In general, a GM which supports most rapid growth (as measured by a short generation time) also promotes most rapid and synchronous encystment. Furthermore, in media which do not support maximal growth rates, the cell breakage is greater during encystment. Consequently, we recommend that cells for encystment experiments be grown in the optimal GM given in Section III,A,2, and under the conditions specified.

2. Effect of Culture Age on Synchronous Encystment

Test cells were harvested from a single mass culture growing under optimal conditions. The first cells were withdrawn when the population density was 2.6×10^5 cells per milliliter; these cells were in the logarithmic phase of growth. A second sample of cells was collected from the same culture when the cell density reached a level of 2.8×10^6 cells per milliliter; they were in the stationary or plateau phase of growth. Both samples were induced to encyst under identical conditions and resuspended in EM at a concentration of 4×10^5 cells per milliliter. The encystment was allowed to proceed under optimal conditions, and encystment curves plotted. The encystment curves for both logarithmic phase and stationary phase cells are shown in Fig. 3.

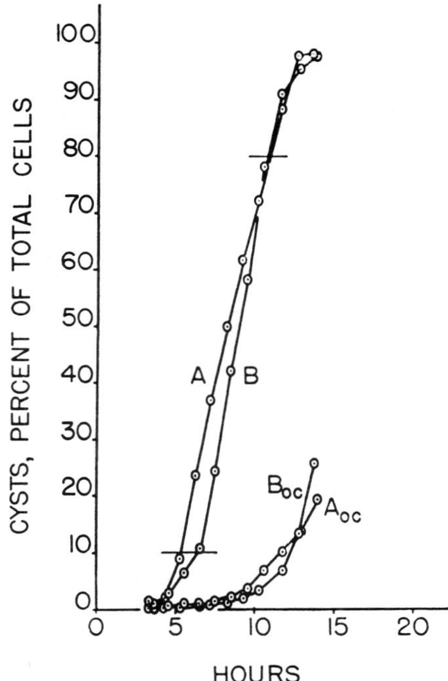

FIG. 3. The effect of culture age on encystment synchrony. Experimental conditions: EM, buffered at constant pH 8.8 with 0.02 *M* tris (Section III,A,1,a); cell concentration in EM, 4.0×10^5 cells per milliliter; aeration, 3 cfh per liter of EM; temperature, 30°C.

Curves A and A_{OC} represent the increases in total cysts and mature cysts, respectively, in the encysting population. The cells were taken from a culture harvested in the logarithmic phase of growth (2.6×10^5 cells per milliliter). Curves B and B_{OC} show the increases in total cysts and mature cysts, respectively, in an encysting population. Cells were derived from the same culture as those of A but when the culture had entered the stationary phase of growth (2.8×10^6 cells per milliliter).

In the figure, horizontal lines are drawn at 10 and 80% levels. The time required for 70% cyst initiation for the log phase cells was 5.5 hours; for the stationary phase cells, 3.5 hours.

It will be noted that the stationary phase cells required 90 minutes longer than the log phase cells to enter the cyst initiation phase (cysts = 10% of total). However, once they had done so, encystment proceeded rapidly and with great synchrony so that both populations reached the 80% cyst level at 10.5 hours after induction. Therefore, the stationary phase cells required 3.5 hours to go from 10 to 80% cysts, while the log phase cells needed 5.5 hours. Similar results have been obtained in other experiments.

To summarize: synchrony of encystment is greatest for cells which have been grown in media supporting rapid growth and which are harvested in the maximum stationary phase of growth.

B. Cell Concentration

Good encystment synchrony is obtained under some of the conditions described in Section III up to 2×10^6 cells per milliliter. Without exception the greatest synchrony has been observed when the cell concentration is 10^5 cells per milliliter or less. This is attributed to the difficulty of maintaining the optimal pH for cyst initiation at high cell concentrations with

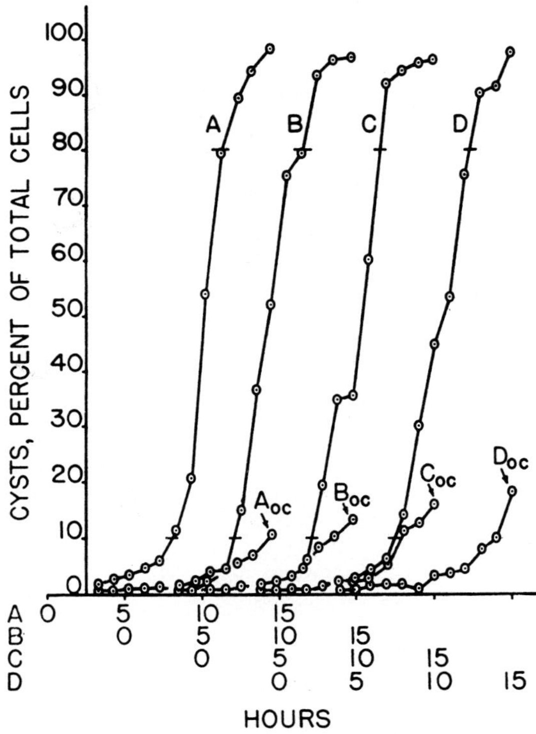

FIG. 4. The effect of cell concentration on encystment synchrony. Experimental conditions: EM, buffered at pH 8.8 with 0.02 *M* tris (Section III,A,1,a); temperature, 30°C; aeration, 6 cfh per liter of EM. Encystment was studied at four cell concentrations, viz., 1.2×10^5, 4.6×10^5, 8.3×10^5, and 1.5×10^6 cells per milliliter. Cyst initiation at each concentration is shown in curves A, B, C, and D, respectively. A_{OC}, B_{OC}, etc., show the increases in numbers of old cysts. The time required for 70% cyst initiation in curve A was 3.3 hours; in B, 4.5 hours; in C, 4.3 hours; and in D, 5.0 hours. It was necessary to re-adjust the pH to 8.9 every 2 hours in the three highest concentrations.

tris (see Section IV,F). The effect of cell concentration on synchrony is illustrated in Fig. 4. It should be noted that pH was periodically adjusted in all but the lowest cell concentrations.

There apparently is no minimal cell concentration; single cells encyst nicely in either of the EM's described. Single cells, isolated in droplets of EM, have been followed throughout encystment in an oil compression chamber of the type first described by de Fonbrune (1939). If there is no excessive cover slip compression, and if the oxygen supply is adequate, the time scale for encystment is similar to that observed in mass cultures. Encystment is in no way dependent upon the presence of other cells.

At the highest cell concentration studied, 4.4×10^6 cells per milliliter, only 8% cyst initiation was observed after 17 hours, even though experimental conditions were optimal for suspensions of lower concentration. The factors responsible for the failure of encystment in this case have not been unequivocally identified; they are probably related to inadequate aeration and poor control of pH at this high cell concentration.

C. Ionic Composition of EM

Ions are of importance in encystment for both nonspecific and specific reasons. First, they provide an adequate tonicity; second, two cations, Mg^{++} and Ca^{++}, are required for encystment.

1. TONICITY

The isotonic salt concentration for *Acanthamoeba* (ameboid stages) is in the range of 0.1 to 0.15 *M* KCl. This fact has been established by two independent methods. First, that salt concentration in which contractile vacuole formation just ceased was determined. By this criterion, the isotonic concentration of KCl, of NaCl, or of mixtures of these two salts, is very close to 0.1 *M*. Second, studies of the packed cell volume of cells in salt solutions of different tonicities under anaerobic conditions were conducted. Under anaerobiosis, the contractile vacuole does not function and the cells shrink in hypertonic solutions and swell in hypotonic ones. Results indicated that the isotonic concentration lies in the range of 0.1 to 0.13 *M* KCl. Within this range, the packed cell volume remains close to that of aerobic cells.

Synchronous encystment has been studied at KCl concentrations from 0.05 to 0.2 *M*. The results of this study are shown in Table I. The results at these four concentrations of KCl are nearly identical. Minor variations observed are at the lowest and highest concentrations studied. In 0.05 *M* KCl the pre-encystment time is lengthened. At 0.20 *M* the cyst initiation time is lengthened. Concentrations of KCl greater than 0.20 *M* have not

TABLE I

EFFECT OF EM CONCENTRATION ON ENCYSTMENT[a]

KCl conc. (molarity)	Time for 10% cyst initiation (hours)	Time for 70% cyst initiation (10–80%) (hours)	Cell breakage during 17 hours of encystment (% of original cells)
0.05	9.5	4.7	12
0.10	8.5	5.0	16
0.15	8.5	4.5	17
0.20	8.7	5.8	15

[a] Conditions: cell concentration, 4.5×10^5 cells per milliliter; initial pH, 8.3; final pH, 8.5. Other salts of the EM: $NaHCO_3$, 0.01 *M*; $MgSO_4$, 0.001 *M*; $CaCl_2$, 0.00005 *M*; KH_2PO_4, 0.002 *M*. Temperature, 30°C.

been studied. Concentrations lower than 0.05 *M* were not tested because cell breakage is very great at tonicities lower than 0.02 *M*, even in the presence of divalent cations. In designing optimal EM's, the total ionic concentration has been held within a range equivalent to 0.1–0.15 *M* KCl. Potassium chloride has been used routinely as the major salt; however, it may be replaced by NaCl, in part or totally, with no detectable change in the encystment pattern.

2. REQUIREMENT FOR DIVALENT CATIONS

The ionic requirements for encystment in a closely related soil ameba, *Hartmanella rhysodes*, have been described by Band (1963). In agreement with his results we have also found that both magnesium and calcium ions are required for encystment in *Acanthamoeba*. Cyst wall formation can be prevented for 1–2 days in an aerated suspension of cells in EM from which divalent cations have been excluded. However, as soon as cells begin to break, some of the remaining cells begin to encyst; it is proposed that the release of divalent cations from broken cells permits encystment in the remaining cells. It is possible that divalent cations are absolute requirements for completion of encystment, but this remains to be proved. The inhibition of encystment by increased concentrations of phosphate buffer (Section IV,F) can also be attributed to the removal of Mg^{++} and Ca^{++} from the EM by complex formation at the higher pH's.

Either Mg^{++} or Ca^{++} alone will support a limited encystment. They are most effective when both are present and when the concentration of Mg^{++} exceeds that of Ca^{++}. We do not know the optimal ratio of $Mg^{++}:Ca^{++}$ but find little difference in any phase of synchronous encystment when the molar ratio $Mg^{++}:Ca^{++}$ falls between 20:1 and 10:1. The ratio of $Mg^{++}:Ca^{++}$ in GM is also in this range.

The effects of total Mg^{++} and Ca^{++} concentrations on synchronous encystment have been studied in a limited range. In one experiment a series of EM's were prepared in which the ratio of $Mg^{++}:Ca^{++}$ was kept at 20:1, but in which the concentration of Mg^{++} was varied from 10^{-3} to 8.3×10^{-3} *M* with proportional changes in the Ca^{++} concentrations. Encystment was tested at two cell concentrations—5×10^5 and 1×10^6 cells per milliliter. Effects were the same at both concentrations; at Mg^{++} concentrations of 4×10^{-3} and 8.3×10^{-3}, the cyst initiation period was slightly shortened. Furthermore, at these two concentrations of Mg^{++}, the time required for thickening of the cyst wall was about half that required at lower Mg^{++} concentrations. It would be desirable to extend these to higher divalent cation concentrations.

Other polyvalent cations have been studied but appear to be either dispensable or inhibitory. They are: Fe^{++}, Mn^{++}, Zn^{++}, Cu^{++}, and Co^{++}. We have found no special anion requirement. Synchrony is high when chloride is the only anion present.

D. Aeration

Both growth and encystment of *Acanthamoeba* have an absolute requirement for oxygen. Aerated cultures which have been switched to continuous gassing with nitrogen will not encyst. Neither will shallow stationary cultures encyst if the air is replaced with nitrogen and the culture sealed off from air.

Optimal rates of aeration for synchronous encystment have been established for cell concentrations between 10^5 and 2×10^6 cells per milliliter. Rates of aeration below 1.5–2.0 cfh per liter of medium result in lengthening of all stages of encystment. Little difference in the encystment pattern is observed between 3 and 10 cfh per liter of EM. Breakage is increased at air flows above 6 cfh. At high cell concentrations, oxygen may become limiting. At cell concentrations of 4 and 5×10^6 cells per milliliter aerated at 3 cfh little encystment is observed even after cells have been in EM for 20 hours. Greater air flow or the use of pure oxygen may permit the use of these high cell concentrations. Neither has been tested. For optimal synchrony in encystment, aeration rates of 4 cfh per liter of EM have been used with cell concentrations of 10^5 to 2×10^6 cells per milliliter.

E. Temperature

All phases of synchronous encystment are most rapid in the 30 to 32°C range. All phases of encystment are lengthened either above or below this temperature range. The upper temperature that permits encystment is 40°C. Here the pre-encystment and cyst initiation times are at least double those at 32°C. Encystment has not been followed to completion at 40°C—if indeed it goes to completion. Encystment does not occur at 42°C; at this temperature over half the cells are dead 8 hours after induction.

In Table II, results from 4 temperature experiments are recorded. Of a

TABLE II

EFFECT OF TEMPERATURE ON PRE-ENCYSTMENT AND CYST INITIATION TIMES[a]

Temperature (°C)	Pre-encystment (hours)	Cyst initiation (hours)	Ratio
15	20	20?	1.0?
20	11	9.5	1.16
	18	17.0	1.06
25	9.0	7.0	1.28
30	7.2	4.6	1.56
	8.0	4.5	1.74
	7.7	5.5	1.50
32	7.0	5.5	1.27
	7.7	5.8	1.33
	8.5	5.0	1.70
34	8.2	9.3	0.88
36	8.5	12.9	0.66
	9.2	7.3	1.24
38	9.6	11.4	0.84

[a] Conditions: cell concentration, 3.5–5 $\times 10^5$ cells per milliliter; initial pH, 8.3; final pH, 8.5–8.8. Salts of EM: KCl, 0.1 M; $NaHCO_3$, 0.01 M; $MgSO_4$, 0.001 M; $CaCl_2$, 0.00005 M; KH_2PO_4, 0.002 M. Concentration of cells at harvest, 2.5 $\times 10^5$ to 3 $\times 10^6$ cells per milliliter.

number of temperature experiments, these were selected because the conditions of the experiment were similar though not optimal. Each experiment has at least one control curve run at 30° or 32°C. This data on temperature is sufficient to establish clearly that the most rapid encystment occurs in the 30° to 32°C range. Further, the increase in ratios at 30° and 32°C suggests that cyst initiation is more temperature sensitive than preencystment.

F. Hydrogen Ion Concentration

1. Problems of pH Control

There are two major problems of pH control in the synchronous encystment system. First, the pH of an encysting culture changes toward neutrality with time. This effect is illustrated by the following experiment. Two bottles of EM buffered with 2×10^{-3} M phosphate were prepared. The initial pH of the first was adjusted to pH 8.5; the pH of the second was adjusted to pH 5.0. Both bottles were inoculated with 4.5×10^5 cells per milliliter and aerated at a rate of 2 cfh. In the first bottle the pH dropped from the initial value of 8.5 to 7.3 in 3 hours. In the second the pH changed from pH 5.0 to 6.6 in the same time period. Similar shifts toward neutrality have been observed in other experiments in which the cell concentration was varied; the time required for the shift was inversely proportional to the cell concentration, suggesting that the pH change is due to cellular activity. It is probable that the encysting cells release alkali at acid pH's and produce acid above neutrality.

The second major problem to be considered in determining pH control in the encysting system is that the pH optimum for the pre-encystment stage and the pH optimum for the initiation and completion of cell wall synthesis are clearly different. The pH optimum for pre-encystment is not sharp or exactly defined; it appears to be close to neutrality. The pH optimum for cyst initiation has not been determined with precision. However, it is high and in the range of pH 8.6 to 9.0. The upper limit of pH permitting cyst initiation is clearly defined and must be avoided. At pH 9.2 or above, the cells die within a few hours.

An experiment demonstrating the difference in pH optima for the two stages in encystment is summarized in Table III. It will be noted that at

TABLE III

EFFECT OF pH ON PRE-ENCYSTMENT AND CYST INITIATION[a]

pH		Pre-encystment	Cyst initiation
Initial	Final	Time from placing in EM to formation of 10% young cysts (hours)	Time for young cysts to increase from 10 to 80% (hours)
7.0	7.0	5.5	7.0
9.1	8.8	7.5	3.5

[a] Conditions: optimal EM with 0.02 M tris; cell concentration, 1.7×10^5 cells per milliliter; length of experiment, 18 hours after placing cells in EM.

pH 9.1 the cyst initiation period is shortened and the pre-encystment period increased in comparison with the times required for these stages at pH 7.0. This effect has been observed consistently at other cell concentrations and with different buffers. The pH optimum for the completion of the cyst wall synthesis has not been studied specifically; it seems to be the same as that for cyst initiation, viz., 8.6 to 9.0.

These problems of pH control have been attacked in three different ways. First, we have tested EM buffered at a constant pH; second, we have developed a buffer in which the pH increases from neutrality to about 9.0 during the first hours of encystment; and third, we have conducted preliminary experiments in which the pH is maintained near neutrality during the pre-encystment period and then shifted rapidly to the alkaline level. Each approach will be discussed.

2. Encystment at Constant pH

The first experiments to be reported were performed in EM in which the pH was controlled at a constant level throughout the encystment; experiments have been performed at neutrality and at pH 8.8–9.0. It is simple to maintain pH at neutrality throughout encystment, even without buffer. However, at neutrality the cyst initiation period is long and synchrony poor. Since cyst initiation is most rapid at alkaline pH's, most of our experiments have been conducted with EM buffered to pH 8.8–9.0. The problem at this pH is to neutralize acid as rapidly as it is formed. Any buffer to be useful must have a pK close to pH 9.0 and must be nontoxic to cells at concentrations sufficiently high for good buffering capacity.

Although the growth medium is buffered with phosphate, this buffer is not useful in the encystment system because its pK's are either too low (pK_2 = 7.1) or too high (pK_3 = 12.3). At a concentration of phosphate which gives good buffering at pH 8.8 (0.05–0.1 M) cyst initiation is largely inhibited. This is probably due to removal of required Mg^{++} and Ca^{++} from EM by formation of insoluble precipitates. Ammonium ions have a more reasonable pK (9.25) but cannot be used since the undissociated form, NH_3, is volatile in the optimal pH range for cyst initiation. Upon aeration, NH_3 is lost and the pH of EM buffered with ammonium ions drops rapidly, presumably due to the uptake of CO_2 from the air.

The amine buffer tris has been used most extensively in our encystment studies. Its pK is 8.08. At a concentration of 0.02 M it is excellent for buffering EM in experiments where the cell concentration does not exceed 10^5 cells per milliliter. Unfortunately, it does not maintain the pH at the desired level at higher cell concentrations. For example, in several experiments in which 10^5 cells per milliliter were suspended in EM containing 0.02 M tris adjusted to pH 9.2 at the beginning of the experiment, the pH dropped only to 8.8 during 20 hours of aeration; cyst initiation required 3–3.5 hours. However, when an identical experiment was performed at a cell concentration of 2×10^6 cells per milliliter, the pH dropped from 9.2 to 8.5 by the end of the first hour and to 7.8 by the end of the fourth hour. It remained at this level until the experiment was terminated at 18 hours. The time for cyst initiation increased to 8–12 hours. This greatly increased cyst initiation period was due largely, if not entirely, to the large change in pH. This was demonstrated by repeating the experiment at 2×10^6 cells per milliliter, and readjusting the pH to 8.9 at hourly intervals by addition of dilute alkali. When the pH was controlled in this manner, the time of cyst initiation was decreased to 4–5 hours (see Fig. 4).

Tris is not toxic to cells, even at low cell concentrations. Unfortunately, at buffer concentrations greater than 0.02 *M* there is an increase in the pre-encystment period, although there is no detectable effect on cyst initiation. Thus, the major limitation of tris at high cell concentrations is that its p*K* (and therefore its optimal buffering range) is too low to maintain the optimal pH for cyst initiation at buffer concentrations where there is no delaying effect on pre-encystment. The chief virtue of tris, as with all amine buffers, is that it is a cation in its dissociated form and does not form insoluble salts with divalent cations.

Recently, we have used three other amine buffers which have p*K* values closer to the pH optimum for cyst initiation. They are: diethanol amine (Eastman), 2-amino-2-methyl-1,3-propanediol (Eastman), and 2-amino-2-ethyl-1,3-propanediol (California Biochemicals Corp.). The p*K*'s of these compounds are 8.88, 8.79, and 8.80, respectively (Bates, 1961). Even though all three can be obtained in practical grade only, none is toxic to cells at concentrations of 0.02 *M*. At this concentration, all are satisfactory buffers for cell concentrations up to 5×10^5 cells per milliliter. This represents a fivefold improvement over tris-buffered EM. At a cell concentration of 5×10^5 cell per milliliter, the pH of the encysting culture drops from an initial value of 9.0 to 8.6 during 15 hours of encystment; under these conditions, the cyst initiation time is 3.5–5.0 hours. Higher concentrations of these three amine buffers have not yet been studied systematically.

With all of the four amine buffers tested, it is not uncommon to find a "lag" of an hour or more (see Fig. 4) during the otherwise most rapid phase of cyst initiation. The reason for this phenomenon is not known. Lags occur most often in EM with buffer concentrations above 0.02 *M*, or if the pH of the EM exceeds 9.2 before cells are inoculated. (These lags are rarely encountered in the buffer systems using bicarbonate; see Section IV,F,3.)

To summarize: the EM currently in use, if a constant pH of 8.8–9.0

is required throughout encystment, is one which is 0.02 M in 2-amino-2-methyl-1,3-propanediol (Section III,A,1,a). This EM can be used for experiments in which the cell concentration does not exceed 5×10^5 cells per milliliter, without pH adjustment during the encystment process. If higher cell concentrations are needed (up to 2×10^6 cells per milliliter), the pH must be periodically adjusted to 9.0 during the experiment, as for tris.

3. EM WITH A PROGRESSIVE INCREASE IN pH

A real improvement in synchrony has resulted from our introduction of a buffered EM in which the pH changes predictably during encystment. This scheme attempts to satisfy the pH requirements for both pre-encystment and cyst initiation stages. The method we have developed utilizes a bicarbonate as a built-in supply of hydroxyl ions which can be externally controlled. This bicarbonate-EM has been described (Section III,A,1,b). It is excellent for cell concentration to 2×10^6 per milliliter.

In solution, the sodium bicarbonate added to the EM is in equilibrium with carbonic acid and dissolved CO_2. During aeration of the encysting culture inoculated into EM, the dissolved CO_2 may be volatilized. Each molecule of CO_2 lost from the medium in this manner releases one hydroxyl ion into the buffered EM. If the aeration rate is sufficiently rapid so that CO_2 is volatilized and removed from the system more rapidly than it is replaced by trapping CO_2 from the incoming air, or CO_2 resulting from cellular metabolism, then appreciable amounts of hydroxyl ions will be released and the pH of the culture will rise until a new equilibrium is established. The pH at which this equilibrium occurs will be a function of the bicarbonate concentration in the EM, the cell concentration, and the rate of aeration.

Under the experimental conditions recommended in Section III,A,1,b, the rate of alkali production depends almost exclusively upon the rate of aeration until the culture reaches a pH of approximately 8.5. At this pH the trapping of CO_2 from the incoming air supply and metabolic sources becomes more important and may affect the equilibrium position, particularly at high cell concentrations. Consequently, in this pH range, the pH of the entire culture may be controlled by relatively small adjustments of the rate of aeration, until the desired pH is established.

With low cell concentrations (1 to 2×10^5 cells per milliliter) CO_2 trapping from all sources is greatly exceeded by CO_2 volatilization; the pH rises rapidly and soon exceeds the optimal pH range for cyst initiation before equilibrium is reached. For this reason, we have added a lid buffer at such a concentration that the pH cannot exceed the pK of the buffer, e.g., 8.8 for 2-amino-2-methyl-1,3-propanediol. The concentration of the lid buffer is calculated from the Henderson-Hasselbach equation, assuming that all of the CO_2 available from the bicarbonate may be volatilized. Figure 5 demonstrates the effect of the rate of aeration on the rate of pH increase and on the rate of cyst initiation. In this experiment, no lid buffer was used, since it was not required by the concentration of cells used in this experiment. We believe that the smooth cyst initiation curves resulting from the use of the bicarbonate system is due to the gradual increase in

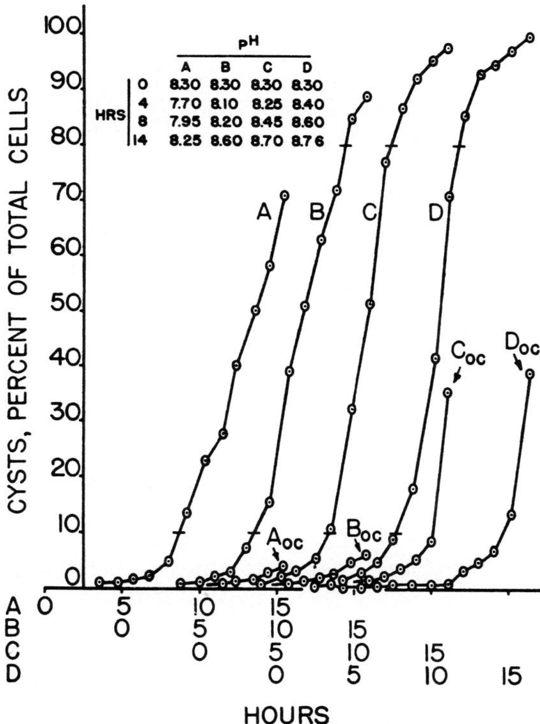

FIG. 5. The effect of the rate of aeration on encystment synchrony and on pH in EM buffered with bicarbonate. Experimental conditions: EM composition, KCl, 0.1 *M*; $NaHCO_3$, 0.01 *M*; $MgSO_4$, 0.001 *M*; $CaCl_2$, 0.00005 *M*; and KH_2PO_4, 0.002 *M*. The pH was 8.3 before inoculation. The temperature was 30°C, and the cell concentration, 4.5×10^5 cells per milliliter. Four identical cell suspensions were induced and aerated at rates of 1, 2, 4, and 8 cfh per liter of EM. Cyst initiation for these four populations is shown in curves A, B, C, and D, respectively. A_{OC}, B_{OC}, etc., represent the corresponding curves for old cysts.

The time required for 70% cyst initiation in these four cultures was: A, 7.5 hours (estimated); B, 6.0 hours; C, 3.7 hours; and D, 4.5 hours.

The pH of each culture was measured at 0, 4, 8, and 14 hours; results are summarized in the inset.

pH from neutrality to the optimal pH for cyst initiation. No lags are observed in the encystment curves.

In the bicarbonate-buffered EM experiments, the major increase in pH occurs early in the pre-encystment period. If, as we believe, the pH optimum of the pre-encystment stage is close to neutrality, then the synchrony of encystment might be improved by a system in which the pH remains near neutrality during pre-encystment, and is increased abruptly to the pH optimum for cyst initiation just before cyst initiation begins. A simple and direct attack is to add a suitable amount of alkali to EM buffered at pH 7 toward the end of pre-encystment. Incorporation of a suitable concentration of a lid buffer into the neutral EM would prevent overshooting the optimal pH for cyst initiation.

A preliminary experiment of this design has just been completed. The results are presented in curve A of Fig. 6. The lid buffer in this experiment was 0.02 *M* 2-amino-2-methyl-1,3-propanediol. The pH was maintained at neutrality during the first 5 hours following induction. At the fifth hour, 1 *N* NaOH was slowly added to the encysting culture until the pH reached 8.8. Curve B is a control experiment performed on an aliquot of the same cells using the optimal bicarbonate system. The synchrony obtained in both experiments is excellent. The encystment curves are similar. Testing of this system at higher cell concentrations continues.

V. Evaluation of the Method

Questions and data closely related to the usefulness and development of synchronous encystment are considered briefly.

A. How Good Is the Synchronous Encystment?

Two aspects of this question which will be considered are (1) the degree of perfection of the method, and (2) its usefulness in unraveling the mechanisms of ameba differentiation.

It is obvious that the synchrony of encystment is not perfect. A perfect synchrony in this system would be identified by all cells beginning cyst initiation at the same time. This perfection has not been realized in this mass system and probably never will be. However, a closer approach to the perfect system seems possible. To avoid such terms as good, bad, or half-bad, we have arbitrarily defined goodness in terms of the time required for cyst initiation. In these terms, our best encystment to date is 70% cyst initiation in 3 hours.

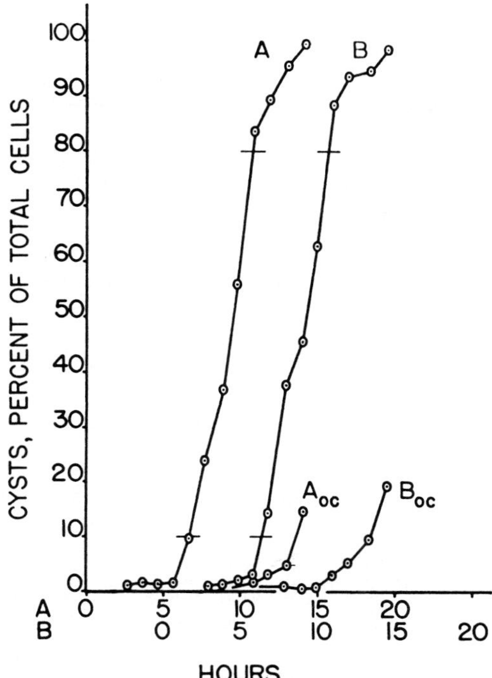

FIG. 6. The effect of the rate of change of pH on encystment synchrony. In curve A, the EM composition was: KCl, 0.1 *M*; 2-amino-2-methyl-1,3-propanediol, 0.02 *M*; $MgSO_4$, 0.008 *M*; and $CaCl_2$, 0.0004 *M*. The initial pH was 7.0; it remained at this level until the end of the fifth hour after induction, when it was raised rapidly to 9.0 by the addition of 10 ml of 1.0 *N* NaOH (per 1 liter of EM) during 15 minutes. The pH dropped to 8.82 by the fifteenth hour. Curve A represents the increase of total cysts, and A_{OC} the increase of old cysts in the population. The time required for 70% cyst initiation was 3.7 hours.

In curve B, the cyst initiation for an induced population in which the pH rises gradually during pre-encystment is shown. The EM was the bicarbonate buffered EM described in Section III,A,1,b. The initial pH was 7.5. Three hours after induction, the pH was 8.7; at 7 hours, it was 9.0; at the end of 15 hours, 9.1. Curve B shows the increase in total cysts during the experiment, and B_{OC} the increase in mature cysts. The time required for 70% cyst initiation was 4.1 hours.

Both experiments were conducted at 30°C and at a cell concentration of 2.5×10^5 cells per milliliter. The cells used were aliquots from the same culture. The aeration rate was 4 cfh per liter of EM.

We believe a better criterion of the goodness of the synchronous encystment system is its potential usefulness in solving the mechanisms of amebae differentiation. Although not perfect, we propose that the synchrony which has been obtained will permit the complete specification of the sequence of physical-chemical events in this differentiation. This is due to two facts. First, under controlled conditions, the duration of the various stages in the mass encystment are very reproducible. The duration of pre-encystment and cyst initiation can be accurately defined and thus serve as distinct points of reference in the encystment process. Secondly, we can relate the stages in the imperfect mass synchrony to stages in the encystment of a single cell. Thus new data obtained by macro physical and chemical methods on changes in cell constituents during mass encystment can be absolutely correlated with the stages of single cell encystment. Finally, with the system, one should be able to decide what mechanisms are responsible for differentiation. For example, it is now possible to test the hypothesis that differentiation is the result of enzyme induction or derepression.

B. Agreement with Other Data

There is no other data on synchronous encystment in amebae available. However, the recent papers of Band (1963) and Collinge and Balamuth (1961) on conditions for encystment in a related soil ameba, *Hartmanella rhysodes*, have been published and contain a great deal of useful information. In general, our data on basic conditions agree with theirs. However, Band has found a higher total osmotic requirement for encystment than we have for the synchronous encystment in *Acanthamoeba*. The reason for this descrepancy is not apparent. One possible explanation is species difference. We have not yet tested our system with their ameba or with any of several other soil amebae now in axenic culture. A second possible explanation is difference in procedure. For example, Band's induced encystment was followed in shallow cultures on rotary shakers. How this might change the encystment picture is not predictable.

C. Is Encystment a Differentiation?

Throughout this presentation, it has been assumed that encystment is a differentiation. This view is in harmony with the theme of a recent and elegant review of protozoan differentiation by Trager (1963). From this article, there is little doubt that encystment is easily identified as an example of protozoan differentiation. It is a cytodifferentiation in the best sense, since it involves a change in cell type. Trager deals with some of the semantics of the term differentiation but does not attempt to establish identity of common stages in protozoan and embryonic systems.

The ultimate value of the synchronous encystment method will reside largely in the light it helps to shed on embryonic differentiation. In this regard a useful question to pursue is: Can differentiation in amebae be identified with embryonic differentiation? From the work presented it is now possible to see general similarities between the two systems. In both we can identify an inductive period. In amebae this stage has been called pre-encystment. In both, the actual period of differentiation is characterized by synthesis of new macromolecules not present in the undifferentiated state. To cite only one example, in the process of initiation and continued wall synthesis in ameba encystment, one finds close parallels with the process of initiation and continued secretion of the cartilaginous matrix by differentiating chondrocytes.

In other aspects, the ameba system may not be like the embryonic system. One aspect is this: cyst initiation does not require specific exogenous macromolecules for induction. Inducers such as proteins, as demonstrated by Yamada (1962), or nucleic acids, as indicated by Niu *et al.*, (1962), do not seem to be required. It would seem that inducers in amebae, if there are such, are of endogenous origin and result from internal changes after food removal. Certainly isolated cells encyst efficiently.

We conclude that both amebae and embryonic systems have at least two events in common: (1) an inductive or predifferentiative period followed by, (2) a period of differentiation where specific new macromolecules are synthesized. In biology we recognize and anticipate unity in basic mechanisms. If all differentiative systems do have common mechanisms at the genic and/or molecular levels, we would expect first identification of them in the simpler systems.

References

Adam, K. M. G. (1959). *J. Gen. Microbiol.* **21,** 519.

Band, R. N. (1959). *J. Gen. Microbiol.* **21,** 80.

Band, R. N. (1963). *J. Protozool.* **10,** 101.

Bates, R. G. (1961) *Am. N. Y. Acad. Sci.*, **92,** 341.

Collinge, J. C., and Balamuth, W. (1961). *J. Protozool.* **8,** Suppl., 15.

de Fonbrune, P. (1949). "Technique de Micromanipulation." Masson, Paris.

Klein, R. L. (1959). *J. Cellular Comp. Physiol.* **53,** 241.

Neff, R. J. (1957). *J. Protozool.* **4, 176.**

Neff, R. J. (1963). *In* "Synchrony in Cell Division and Growth" (E. Zeuthen, ed.), Chapter 21. Wiley, New York.

Neff, R. J., and Benton, W. F. (1962). *J. Protozool.* **9,** Suppl., 11.

Neff, R. J., and Neff, R. H. (1963). *In* "Synchrony in Cell Division and Growth" (E. Zeuthen, ed.), Chapter 8. Wiley, New York.

Neff, R. J., Neff, R. H., and Taylor, R. F. (1958). *Physiol. Zool.* **31,** 73.

Niu, M. C., Cordova, C. C., Niu, L. C., and Radbill, C. L. (1962). *Proc. Natl. Acad. Sci. U. S.* **48,** 1964.

Tomlinson, G., and Jones, E. (1962). *Biochim. Biophys. Acta* **63,** 194.

Trager, W. (1963). *J. Protozool.* **10,** 1.

Yamada, T. (1962). *J. Cellular Comp. Physiol.* **60,** Suppl. 1, 49.

Chapter 5

Experimental Procedures and Cultural Methods for Euplotes eurystomus *and* Amoeba proteus

D. M. PRESCOTT AND R. F. CARRIER

Biology Division, Oak Ridge National Laboratory,[1]
Oak Ridge, Tennessee

I. Introduction

Although numerous species of protozoa can be maintained in culture, only a relative few can be propagated in pure culture under aseptic and defined conditions. Of the latter group, *Tetrahymena pyriformis* is the most widely used since it grows rapidly, all of its nutrient requirements are known, and it can be induced to undergo synchronous cell division in

[1] Operated by the Union Carbide Corporation for the United States Atomic Energy Commission.

mass culture (Scherbaum and Zeuthen, 1954). Single cell techniques for *Tetrahymena* are described by Stone and Cameron in this volume (Chapter 8). The flagellate, *Astasia longa*, is a second example of an organism that grows well in pure culture, but, in general, it is too small for single cell techniques. *Astasia* should prove to be valuable experimental material, however, because of the methods that have been developed for its maintenance in mass culture with a high degree of continuous synchrony of cell division (Padilla and James, this volume, Chapter 9).

Unfortunately, most species of protozoa, including those that are most useful for micrurgy and other single cell techniques, must still be maintained in a mixed culture in which combinations of bacteria, yeasts, algae, molds, or other protozoa serve as food. This shortcoming reduces the experimental possibilities with such large organisms as *Amoeba proteus*, *Chaos chaos*, *Stentor*, and *Euplotes* in certain kinds of work, particularly in some biochemical studies. Their large size, general ruggedness, and diversity in organizational patterns, however, are so advantageous that the deficiencies in culture technique become relatively less important. The mixed culturing of such organisms contains an element of art, and in this chapter reliable techniques for growing *A. proteus* and *Euplotes eurystomus* will be described with as much definition as is currently possible. The discussions will include, in addition, some information on special experimental techniques.

II. *Euplotes eurystomus*

A. *Euplotes* Culture

Euplotes eurystomus has a short and reproducible generation time and grows to a heavy concentration of organisms in lettuce infusion medium containing *Aerobacter aerogenes* and *Tetrahymena* as food organisms. Probably the bacteria could be replaced by the relatively complex synthetic medium described by Doll and Lilly (1959) for *Euplotes patella*. The dried lettuce powder is prepared from fresh lettuce, as described by Sonneborn (1950), made up in a 1.5% solution (w/v) with glass distilled water, and sterilized by autoclaving. Two or three days before use, the solution is inoculated with *A. aerogenes* and kept at about 25°C. To initiate a *Euplotes* culture, bacterized lettuce infusion is diluted with nine parts of distilled water to one part of infusion solution and added to a Petri dish (60 mm diameter) to a depth of about 5 mm. Keeping cultures in Petri dishes allows convenient observation with a dissecting microscope. A few thousand tetrahymenae and one euplotes to several hundred are added. The euplotes will continue to proliferate until all tetrahymenae have been ingested (usually several days, but this depends on the number of euplotes in the initial inoculum). Such stock cultures can be allowed to starve for a few days, or proliferation can be maintained by adding more tetrahymenae and a small amount of sterile lettuce infusion (about one part of infusion to nine parts of culture fluid). Cultures of this type last one to several months when kept at 16°–18°C and require only a few minutes of care every few days. Culture life can be extended and proliferation more easily maintained by regular reduction of the number of euplotes using a braking pipette.

To make fresh cultures from an already well-established stock, it is only necessary to transfer healthy euplotes and tetrahymenae to sterile lettuce infusion. Tetrahymenae are added as the supply is exhausted, but bacterized medium need then be added only every few months.

B. The Cell Cycle

In young cultures grown at 24°–25°C the generation time is 10–12 hours, but this increases when the density of euplotes becomes high. The cell cycle of *Euplotes* is particularly interesting because of the wavelike manner in which deoxyribonucleic acid (DNA) synthesis proceeds through the macronucleus (Gall, 1959; Prescott and Kimball, 1961). The waves of DNA synthesis are reflected in the cytologically distinct replication bands, and these markers can be used to advantage for studying aspects of the initiation and control of DNA synthesis (Kimball and Prescott, 1962). DNA synthesis in the macronucleus begins a few hours after cytokinesis, lasts for about 8 hours, and is followed shortly by the next cytokinesis. The DNA synthesis period of the micronucleus is short, occurs at the time of cytokinesis, and does not overlap with the DNA synthesis period of the macronucleus (Prescott *et al.*, 1962).

The initiation and progress of DNA synthesis in the macronuclei in mass cultures can be synchronized by starvation of the organisms for about 5 days at 24°–25°C, followed by refeeding with tetrahymenae and a small amount of sterile lettuce infusion. The status of DNA synthesis can be checked by observing the replication bands in a few sample cells fixed and stained with acetocarmine and flattened under a coverslip. Eighteen to twenty hours after refeeding, the DNA replication bands appear at the tips of the macronucleus with a high degree of synchrony. The end of the first DNA synthesis period in the culture is followed by a moderately synchronous cell division, but the synchrony of both DNA synthesis and cell division disappears rapidly over the few subsequent cycles.

C. Isotope Labeling

Gall's (1959) excellent work of demonstrating by thymidine-H^3 labeling that the reorganization bands are reflections of waves of DNA synthesis led to further work involving radioisotope labeling of ribonucleic acid (RNA) and protein, as well as short-pulse labeling with thymidine-H^3 (Prescott and Kimball, 1961; Kimball and Prescott, 1962). In these latter experiments the entrance of free, radioisotopically labeled nucleosides or amino acids into *Euplotes* from the medium was found to be slow and highly variable in rate. Rapid and intense labeling was achieved by feeding *Euplotes* with *Tetrahymena* that had been prelabeled with the particular radioactive precursor for one or more hours. *Tetrahymena* apparently contains pools of amino acids and nucleosides (and their derivatives) that are available to *Euplotes* synthesis systems almost immediately after ingestion. For example, the DNA in the replication band has been found to be labeled within 2 minutes after ingestion of a tetrahymena that had been preincubated with thymidine-H^3. This system of introducing labeled precursors has not given consistent results but probably would be reliable if the euplotes to be labeled are not permitted to ingest any tetrahymenae for some hours prior to being fed on radioactive tetrahymenae. This short period without food will probably have little or no effect on the rate of macronuclear replication because of the nutrients stored in food vacuoles, and an initial rapid ingestion of labeled Tetrahymenae will occur at the end of the brief period of semistarvation.

D. Micrurgy

Only a limited amount of study has been done with micrurgical experiments on *Euplotes*. Yow (1961) has recently carried out some work on regeneration of parts in *Euplotes* after micrurgical alterations and has combined this experiment with observations on the replication bands and behavior of the micronucleus. References to the few earlier works on micrurgy of *Euplotes* are given by Yow.

E. Isolation of the Macronucleus

The organization and pattern of replication in the *Euplotes* macronucleus described above makes it uniquely suitable for experiments in nuclear cytochemistry and physiology (see, for example, Gall, 1959; Kimball and Prescott, 1962). Experiments requiring autoradiographic detection of radioactivity in the macronucleus can be considerably simplified if the macronucleus is isolated from the cytoplasm before autoradiography. This is true for two reasons: (1) the pellicle and cytoplasm lying between the macronucleus and the photosensitive emulsion in whole cells will absorb radioactivity (this is particularly serious in tritium labeling) and (2) in experiments involving labeling of proteins and RNA, it is difficult and often impossible to distinguish macronuclear labeling from labeling of the overlying and surrounding cytoplasm.

The macronucleus of *Euplotes* can be cleanly isolated from all cytoplasm at the time of fixation by the following procedure. All steps are performed under a dissecting microscope with a braking pipette of the type described by Stone and Cameron in this volume. Living cells are transferred with a minimum of culture medium to glacial acetic acid in a small dish or watch glass. The euplotes become very fragile in the acetic acid and are next broken by pipetting in and out of a braking pipette that has a bore diameter at the tip a little less than the width of a single euplotes. The nucleus will usually float free and can be transferred to a slide with the pipette and allowed to air-dry. The nucleus is 100–150μ long and is most easily seen with a dissecting microscope if the mirror is arranged to give oblique lighting.

Nuclei dried from the acetic acid solution appear ragged, torn, and generally distorted. While this may be of no consequence for some types of experiments, much better preservation of normal nuclear cytology can be obtained by drying from 95% alcohol. To do this, a "subbed" microscope slide (see Caro, this volume, Chapter 16, for subbing method) is placed in the bottom of a Petri dish containing 70% alcohol to a depth of about 5 mm. The isolated nuclei in the acetic acid solution are gently pipetted into the alcohol over the slide. The acetic acid and nuclei are denser than the alcohol and will drop onto the slide. The acetic acid spreads out and flows off the edges of the slide, but the nuclei will remain affixed to the slide. The dish should not be disturbed for several minutes, to allow the nuclei to attach firmly. The slide is then rinsed in 95% alcohol and air-dried. The nucleus in Fig. 1 was isolated by this procedure from a cell which had been incubated in thymidine-H^3 for 15 minutes.

III. *Amoeba proteus*

A. *Amoeba proteus* Culture

Although the following descriptions are primarily for culturing *A. proteus*, the method has been used successfully for maintaining cultures of *Chaos chaos* and *A. discoides*. The method has not changed in principle

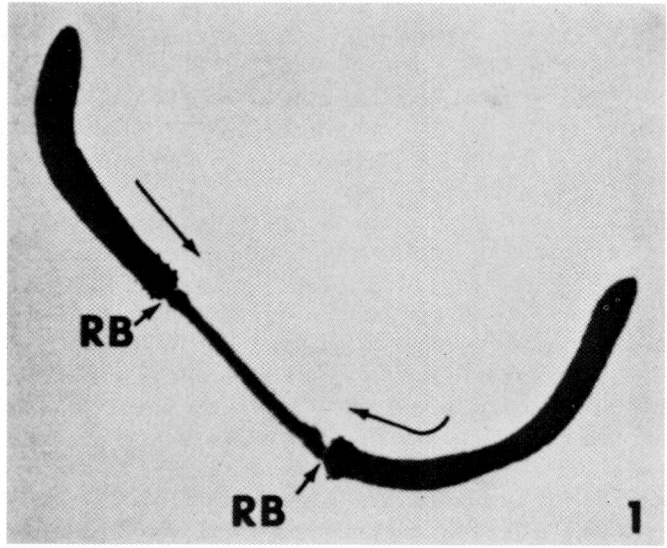

FIG. 1. An autoradiograph of a macronucleus isolated from a euplotes which had been incubated in thymidine-H^3 for 15 minutes. The two waves of DNA synthesis are moving in the directions indicated by the arrows, and the replication bands (RB) are located at the points indicated.

from that described previously (Prescott and James, 1955; Prescott, 1956); however, a little more is now known about the physiology and nutritional requirements of amebae, and this information allows more specific description of some phases of the art of ameba culturing.

The principal source of nutrient for the ameba is tetrahymenae. Attempts to grow *A. proteus* on tetrahymenae in the absence of all other organisms have failed, even when the culture is supplemented with liver extract or other complex sources of nutrients. Therefore, it is still necessary to have bacteria present in the ameba cultures; some progress in defining the types of bacteria required has been reported by Nardone (1959).

The amebae were formerly cultured on a nonnutrient agar surface, but growth is just as rapid on a glass surface and the agar has therefore been eliminated. The inorganic medium has been modified and now is made up with 10 mg $CaCl_2$, 6 mg KCl, 2 mg $MgSO_4 \cdot 7\ H_2O$, 10 mg NaCl, and 4 mg $CaHPO_4$ in 1 liter of distilled water. A culture is initiated by adding inorganic medium to a clean Petri dish to a depth of about 5 mm. One ameba to several hundred are added. The bacteria carried over with the amebae from the previous culture help to establish the conditions required for ameba growth. A few thousand washed tetrahymenae are added. This is the point of greatest uncertainty about the culture method. The tendency is to add too many tetrahymenae, and for unknown reasons an overabundance of tetrahymenae inhibits ameba growth and may even kill the culture. Underfeeding is not serious since the cultures remain healthy, the only effect being a slower ameba growth rate. The cultures are kept at 15°–20°C.

The tetrahymenae are grown aseptically at 20°–25°C in aliquots of about 100 ml proteose peptone (1%) in 250 ml Erlenmeyer flasks. The cultures should be used 2–4 days after inoculation. The tetrahymenae from cultures older than 4 days tend to cytolyze during washing. Washing is accomplished by centrifuging the tetrahymena culture at a few hundred times gravity in a conical bottom tube and resuspending the cells in the inorganic ameba medium. The centrifuging is repeated to remove final traces of proteose peptone, which is toxic for *A. proteus*. The tetrahymenae are kept concentrated about tenfold by using a smaller volume of inorganic medium for the final resuspension. In washing, the tetrahymenae should be centrifuged with enough force to form a loose pellet at the bottom of the tube. Too much force will cause some cytolysis, and the materials released from broken tetrahymenae usually have adverse effects on the ameba cultures. Washed tetrahymenae can be stored for several days at 15°–20°C. In addition to the production of gram amounts of amebae for biochemical studies, the culture method is reliable for producing clones. We have used this method for following cell lineage in ameba for as many as 60 generations.

B. The Cell Cycle

Because the conditions in mixed cultures cannot be controlled with much precision, the generation time varies from one culture to another. In the best cultures, however, the cell cycle lasts about 24 hours at 24°C. This generation time can also be obtained with single cells if medium from a healthy, growing culture is used to set up the single cell culture. The DNA synthesis period occurs during the first half of interphase; DNA synthesis begins almost immediately after the end of cytokinesis and is completed before 14 hours. More precise or detailed information is not yet available. Measurements of mass, protein, and volume increase of cells and volume increase of the nucleus over the cycle are described in an earlier paper (Prescott, 1955). The dividing forms of amebae are easily recognized (see Chalkley, 1935), and groups of several hundred daughter cells can be obtained by selecting dividing cells with a braking pipette.

C. Micrurgy of *Amoeba*

The two main micrurgical techniques with *Amoeba* are nuclear transplantation (see Goldstein, this volume, Chapter 21) and cutting into nucleated and enucleated fragments. The latter technique is extremely simple and can be done by hand or with a micromanipulator with a glass needle under a dissecting microscope. The operation is most easily done in a Petri dish containing inorganic medium and a layer of 1% nonnutrient agar. The amebae are transferred and allowed to attach to the agar and to elongate into the usual streaming form. When they are transected, the nucleus is usually found in the rear portion. Enucleated cells detach from the agar, tend to become spherical, and show only sporadic and sluggish motility. They are easily distinguished from nucleated fragments since the latter reattach to the agar and resume normal ameboid streaming. Nucleated fragments will grow and proliferate, and enucleated fragments cytolyze after 1–3 weeks. In experiments on enucleate amebae, particularly using radioisotopic tracers, it should be remembered that ameba cytoplasm contains several thousand rickettsial-like particles which apparently continue to synthesize both DNA and RNA, and probably protein, for some time after enucleation (Rabinovitch and Plaut, 1962a,b). All *A. proteus* and *A. discoides* strains tested so far contain these particles, and no method for eliminating them has been devised.

D. Compression of Living Amebae

A special chamber has been designed for flattening amebae to a thickness of 20μ to permit measurements on cell and nuclear volumes and to permit ultraviolet microbeaming of the nucleus and cytoplasm separately (Jagger and Prescott, unpublished observations). Amebae are placed in a groove 20μ deep by 1 or 2 mm wide and cut in an ordinary microscope slide (A. D. Jones Optical Works, Cambridge, Massachusetts). The groove is covered with a cover glass (quartz, for ultraviolet microbeaming), but enough inorganic medium is kept on the slide to prevent immediate compression of the amebae. Any ameba that may have moved out of the groove at this point can be repositioned by gently sliding the cover glass. The excess inorganic medium is gradually withdrawn at the edge of the cover glass and the amebae are gradually compressed. Two living amebae compressed to 20μ are shown in Fig. 2.

E. Preventing Cytokinesis

In connection with studies on single cell growth, a reliable technique was devised for inhibiting cytokinesis with a protein solution, thereby

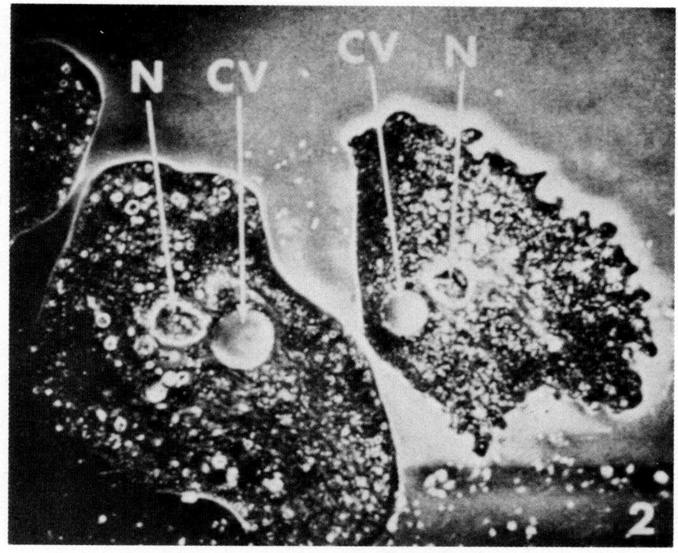

FIG. 2. Two living *Amceba proteus* flattened to 20μ in a special chamber. The nucleus (N) and contractile vacuole (CV) are clearly visible.

producing binucleated cells (Prescott, 1959). The cytokinetic inhibition is an interesting phenomenon in itself but has never been studied in detail. Dividing amebae that have not yet begun to form a cytokinetic furrow are immersed in a 1% solution of egg albumin for about 1 hour. This relatively long exposure is necessary because treated cells remain capable of division for about 20 minutes after untreated controls have completed cytokinesis. Control amebae require about 30 minutes to complete division. Mitosis is unaffected by the treatment and two nuclei are produced. The protein solution induces pinocytosis in interphase amebae, but dividing amebae do not show this reaction. At the next mitosis, four nuclei are produced and these are distributed in the 2, 3, or 4 daughter cells produced. After several cell cycles, all of the progeny are usually uninucleate. If the cytokinesis inhibition is repeated at several successive divisions, an *A. proteus* with 4, 8, or 16 nuclei can be produced. Guttes and Guttes (1960) have described a mechanical method for preventing cytokinesis in *A. proteus*.

F. Isotope Labeling

The proteins and nucleic acids of amebae become labeled slowly when isotopically labeled precursors are added to the inorganic medium. The labeling process can be accelerated by two methods: inducing pinocytosis or feeding prelabeled food organisms. Intense pinocytosis can be induced with a 0.5% (w/v) egg albumin solution (for a full discussion of pinocytosis by ameba, see Chapman-Andresen, this volume, Chapter 14). By the pinocytotic method, the uptake of isotopically labeled material can be sharply increased (Chapman-Andresen and Holter, 1955), but the rate of incorporation is only moderately increased (see, for example, Chapman-Andresen and Prescott, 1956), possibly because of competition from materials derived from food vacuoles. If a food organism, such as *Tetrahymena*, is prelabeled with the particular precursor, the rate of incorporation can be increased many fold. For example, amebae take up only enough $P^{32}O_4$ from the medium to give a few disintegrations per minute per ameba. If tetrahymenae grown in the presence of $P^{32}O_4$ are fed to amebae, the number of disintegrations per minute per ameba can be increased up to 10,000. The same technique has been used successfully for introducing H^3-amino acids, thymidine-H^3, cytidine, uridine, and adenosine into ameba protein and nucleic acids. *Tetrahymena* is particularly suitable because it can be labeled very heavily (see Stone and Cameron, this volume, Chapter 8) and does not mutate most precursors in such a way that the subsequent labeling of *Amoeba* becomes nonspecific or unknown.

G. Fixation of *Amoeba*

Preparations of *A. proteus* usually need to be considerably flattened, particularly to make the nucleus clearly visible. In tritium autoradiography, very flat preparations are required to allow registry of radioactivity from the nucleus. This is usually done by placing one or a few amebae on a clean slide in a very small amount of inorganic medium and flattening them with a cover glass. A small drop of fixative (usually 70% alcohol or acetic acid:alcohol) is placed on the underside of a clean cover glass and the glass dropped onto the amebae. The slide is immediately frozen in liquid nitrogen (15 seconds immersion), the cover glass flipped off, and the slide rinsed in 95% alcohol and air-dried. If liquid nitrogen is unavailable, slides can be frozen with dry ice, but acetic acid should be used as the fixative (Rabinovitch and Plaut, 1962a) because the alcohol-containing fixatives are not frozen by the dry ice method. The amebae almost always remain on the slide, but occasionally do not. Losses can be minimized by using 70% alcohol as the fixative and flattening the amebae on "subbed" slides.

If an ameba is caused to cytolyze by tearing with glass needles, the nucleus will float free. Such nuclei can be air-dried, fixed, and then autoradiographed without interference from the cytoplasm. The DNA synthesis period was determined on such nuclei, but the procedure is not recommended in the case of RNA and protein labeling since these macromolecules rapidly leak out of isolated ameba nuclei.

References

Chalkley, H. W. (1935). *Protoplasma* **24,** 607.

Chapman-Andresen, C., and Holter, H. (1955). *Exptl. Cell Res. Suppl.* **3,** 52.

Chapman-Andresen, C., and Prescott, D. M. (1956). *Compt. Rend. Lab. Carlsberg Ser. Chim.* **30,** 57.

Doll, N. E., and Lilly, D. M. (1959). *J. Protozool.* **6,** Suppl., 10.

Gall, J. G. (1959). *J. Biophys. Biochem. Cytol.* **5,** 295.

Guttes, E., and Guttes, S. (1960). *Nature* **187,** 520.

Kimball, R. F., and Prescott, D. M. (1962). *J. Protozool.* **9,** 88.

Nardone, R. M. (1959). *J. Protozool.* **6,** Suppl., 9.

Prescott, D. M. (1955). *Exptl. Cell Res.* **9,** 328.

Prescott, D. M. (1956). *Compt. Rend. Lab. Carlsberg Ser. Chim.* **30,** 1.

Prescott, D. M. (1959). *Ann. N. Y. Acad. Sci.* **78,** 655.

Prescott, D. M., and James, T. W. (1955). *Exptl. Cell Res.* **8,** 256.

Prescott, D. M., and Kimball, R. F. (1961). *Proc. Natl. Acad. Sci. U. S.* **47,** 686.

Prescott, D. M., Kimball, R. F., and Carrier, R. F. (1962). *J. Cell Biol.* **13,** 175.

Rabinovitch, M., and Plaut, W. (1962a). *J. Cell Biol.* **15,** 525.

Rabinovitch, M., and Plaut, W. (1962b). *J. Cell Biol.* **15,** 535.

Scherbaum, O. M., and Zeuthen, E. (1954). *Exptl. Cell Res.* **6,** 221.

Sonneborn, T. (1950). *J. Exptl. Zool.* **113,** 87.

Yow, F. W. (1961). *J. Protozool.* **8,** Suppl., 18.

Chapter 6

Nuclear Transplantation in Ameba

LESTER GOLDSTEIN

Department of Biology, University of Pennsylvania,
Philadelphia, Pennsylvania

I. Introduction

The value of nuclear transplantation in ameba has been demonstrated on a number of occasions (see, e.g., Comandon and de Fonbrune, 1939; Lorch and Danielli, 1953; and Goldstein and Plaut, 1955). The technique, however, has been used surprisingly little in the past. This infrequent employment is surprising because the technique apparently is the only one that provides for the introduction into a new cytoplasmic environment of a physiologically active (i.e., interphase) nucleus under circumstances that permit worthwhile cytological investigation. For a discussion of specific experimental rewards of such an operation see Goldstein (1963).

Transplantation of interphase nuclei by other techniques has been carried out with embryonic amphibian cells (King and Briggs, 1953) and *Acetabularia* (Hämmerling, 1953) but with different objectives than those of comparable operations on amebae. The method of nuclear transplantation in amebae is unique and has, among others, the particular advantage of not involving the transfer of any significant amount of cytoplasm as a result of the operation. This permits studies of the behavior of macromolecules in amebae that would be more difficult with embryonic amphibian cells or *Acetabularia* because of the cytoplasmic "contamination" that seems unavoidable in the latter cases. As far as this writer is aware, the type of operation to be described here has been successfully carried out only with large, free-living amebae such as *Amœba proteus.*

II. Equipment

The equipment, as well as the entire nuclear transplantation procedure, has been described before (de Fonbrune, 1949), and few changes have been made since then. De Fonbrune should be consulted for more detailed consideration of all aspects of the methodology.

A. The Micromanipulator

A variety of manipulators may be employed for these operations, but it is the writer's opinion that the commercially available instrument of choice remains the de Fonbrune micromanipulator. (Manipulators employing advance mechanisms of the screw-type seem to be completely unfitted for nuclear transplantations in amebae.) A combination of two features makes the de Fonbrune instrument particularly well suited for ameba nuclear transplantations: (a) a nonmechanical connection between the hand-operated control lever and the microtools, and (b) the facility for mounting on the same manipulator head two microtools, one of which can be moved independently of the other.

The nonmechanical connection between the control lever and the microtools (a pneumatic device in the de Fonbrune instrument) has two important virtues. First, it eliminates the transmission of disturbing vibrations from the operator's hand to the microtools. Second, it permits the positioning of the control lever in such a way that the operator's hand moves in the same direction as the microtool image seen in a compound microscope. (The microtools, of course, would then actually be moving in the opposite direction.) A beginner will immediately appreciate that this feature enables one to learn the operative technique in a much shorter time than otherwise would be possible.

The facility for mounting two independently moving microtools on the same operating head has three important virtues. Because, as we shall see, the nuclear transplantation operation requires a microhook to hold amebae *stationary* and a microprobe for *pushing* a nucleus from one cell to another, it is an obvious advantage to have two independently moving microtools; otherwise two manipulator heads would be required, the equipment expense would be greater, and the arrangement of the apparatus would be awkward. The second virtue is that the construction of the microhook is appreciably simpler than would be necessary if it were mounted on a manipulator head other than the one carrying the microprobe. Finally, because both tools are mounted close together on one manipulator head, positioning of the tools in the operating chamber is simpler; if mounted on separate manipulators, they need to be positioned separately—resulting in greater inconvenience to the operator.

The de Fonbrune micromanipulator manufactured in the United States (by A. S. Aloe Co., St. Louis, Missouri) has the serious drawback of poor construction. (It is also manufactured in France but the former is the only version available in this country through normal commercial channels.) Because of what appears to be a restraint in international trade, it is suggested that prospective American buyers investigate the possibility of purchasing the instrument in Europe.

Modifications of the Micromanipulator

During micromanipulator operation, subtle vertical microprobe movements frequently need to be made but may be difficult to execute; at other times involuntary vertical displacements of microtools may occur to the operator's disadvantage. Some adjustments of the instrument can be made to overcome these difficulties, at least to some extent.

Because there is no provision on the de Fonbrune micromanipulator for modifying the ratio of hand-to-tool control of vertical motions as there is for horizontal movements, it is advisable to increase the volume of the air space in the vertical control pneumatic system and thereby enable the operator to achieve finer movements than otherwise would be possible. Since there is more air to compress, this modification results in less movement of the relevant aneuroid diaphragm in response to an equivalent movement of the hand control stick. An increase in the volume of any of the 3 pneumatic systems can be achieved by placing a closed flask (of about 100 ml capacity, G in Fig. 1) in the pneumatic tube between control stick and microtool.

A major imperfection of the version of the de Fonbrune instrument distributed in this country is that a gratuitous vertical motion of the microprobe (see below) often results when the operator is attempting a horizontal motion along the right-left axis (as viewed in Fig. 1). Needless to say, this leads to difficulties in controlling the precise direction of microtool motions. As far as can be determined, this defect appears to be due largely to poor construction of the front aneuroid diaphragm—the one upon which the microtool holder is mounted. (Prospective purchasers of this manipulator are advised to select, if possible, an instrument that shows a minimum of this imperfection.) The trouble sometimes can be reduced by making adjustments in the shape and length of the rods connecting the three aneuroid diaphragms with the integrating yoke and perhaps by adjusting the angle of micromanipulator head. The modification to achieve finer vertical control described above also makes it easier for the operator to make rapid accommodations to compensate for the gratuitous motion.

A modification of another kind that may be necessary for more effective operations is the attachment of a heavy base to the bottom of the manipulator head (see Fig. 1), thus making the instrument more stable. If

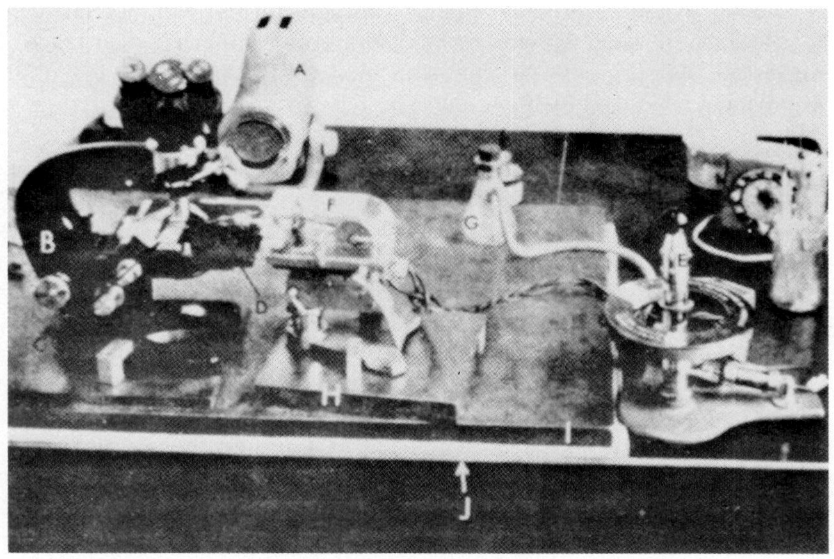

FIG. 1. Photograph of the complete apparatus for nuclear transplantation operations. (A) Microscope lamp; (B) microscope; (C) operating chamber; (D) microtools; (E) control stick for pneumatic movements; (F) micromanipulator head; (G) air-containing flask attached to pneumatic tube of vertical fine control; (H) base attached to bottom of micromanipulator head; (I) heavy steel plate; (J) foam rubber pad.

vibrations in the laboratory are disturbing, it also may be worthwhile to place the entire apparatus, particularly the microscope and the manipulator head, on a heavy steel plate resting on a ca. 2.5 cm thickness of foam rubber, as shown in Fig. 1.

B. The Operating Chamber

The operating chamber (available from A. S. Aloe Co.) is a slightly modified version of the original "huile chambre" design by de Fonbrune (see Fig. 2). The oil chamber has been modified by us only to the extent

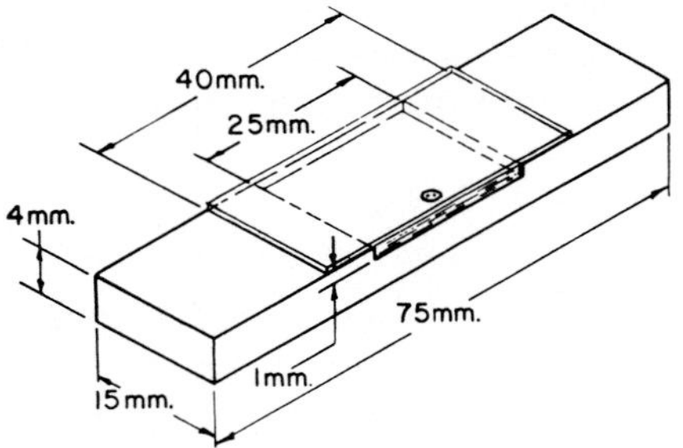

FIG. 2. Diagram of assembled operating chamber. An aqueous drop containing two amebae is depicted in the oil layer.

that it is cut in two longitudinally to allow easier handling (and, incidentally, to save expense, since this doubles the number of chambers at only a slightly extra cost).

In use the chamber is filled with mineral oil (liquid petrolatum) and covered with a 15 × 40 mm cover glass from which hangs a drop of culture medium containing amebae. One thus has a hanging drop surrounded by oil, which eliminates evaporation from the drop of medium and dampens extraneous vibrations of the operating tools. The microtools are inserted into the chamber directly through the oil via the open side of the 1 mm depression. They enter the chamber at a slight angle to the horizontal (Fig. 3); thus it is advantageous to place the drop containing the cells near the edge of the chamber. This is one reason that the "half" chamber is quite suitable for the operations.

FIG. 3. Diagrammatic side view of microtools entering operating chamber.

C. The Microtools

Two glass microtools, a microhook and a microprobe, are required for ameba nuclear transplantations and are so minute that they can be made only on some sort of microforge. (The de Fonbrune microforge is probably the only commercially available model that is reasonably satisfactory, although it is possible to construct an effective one at a more reasonable cost.) The manufacture of a variety of microtools has been described by de Fonbrune (1949); only the essential features of the two microtools that interest us will be discussed here. Experience has shown that the most crucial and difficult aspect of the entire nuclear transplantation procedure is usually the manufacture of suitable microtools, and the novice in nuclear transplantation experiments is thus urged to work hard at perfecting this part of the methodology.

1. The Microhook

A diagram of two views of the microhook is given in Fig. 4. Only the hook at the tip need be made on the microforge; the other angles should be made on a microburner. (A modified hypodermic needle, about 20

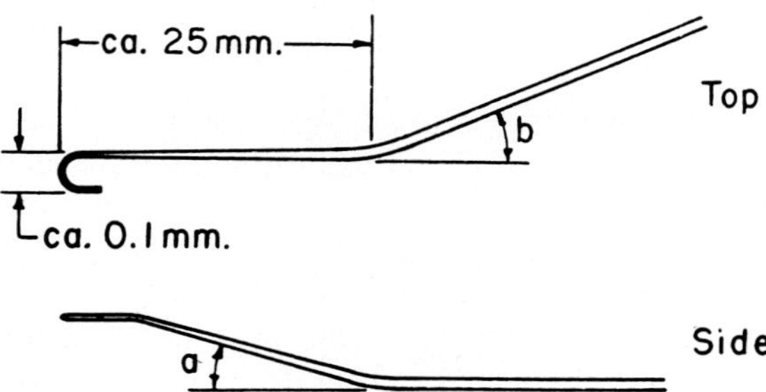

FIG. 4. Diagram of top and side views of microhook. Angle *a* is approximately 10° and angle *b* is approximately 10°–15°.

gauge, attached to a fuel gas line will do as a microburner.) The diameter of the rod making the hook proper should be about 20–40μ.

The hook should be flat in the horizontal plane so that it makes good contact with the cover glass from which the amebae hang. This will prevent the amebae from slipping between hook and cover glass during the operation. Angle *a* on the shaft simplifies the introduction of the microhook into the operating drop; angle *b* enables the microhook to be almost parallel to the microprobe during the operation.

2. The Microprobe

A diagram of two views of the microprobe is given in Fig. 5. The tip of the microprobe, which is made on the microforge, should be about

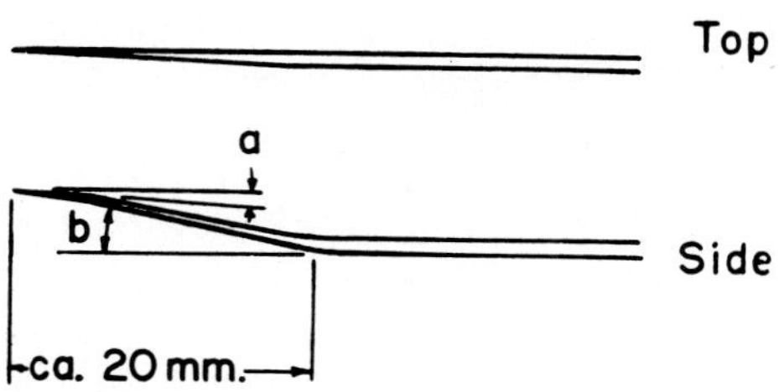

Fig. 5. Diagram of top and side views of microprobe. Angle *a* is approximately 5° and angle *b* is approximately 10°.

2–5μ in diameter. Only the last 2–4 mm need be pulled out on the microforge, with the taper being determined by experience.

III. Operating Procedure

The operating procedure will be presented here in fair detail but it will be obvious to the beginner that reasonable skill can only be achieved through practice. The investigator would be wise not to undertake serious experiments until better than 50% of his attempts consistently result in successful operations. The best test of a successful operation is to transplant a nucleus into an enucleate cell and have the cell feed, grow, and divide. One should note, however, that the first cell division after an operation is often delayed beyond the time that normal cells would be expected to divide.

A. Assembly of Operating Chamber with Cells

Since most nuclear transplantations are effected between two cells that are probably invisibly different from one another (e.g., radioactive vs. nonradioactive), it is necessary to distinguish by some means which cell is which when they are observed under the operating microscope. This distinction can be made simply by feeding one ameba until just before the operation while keeping the other without food for approximately 1 day; they then can be distinguished readily by the presence or absence of food vacuoles.

Should more than two cells be involved in a particular operational sequence, it is possible to distinguish (but with some difficulty) one ameba from another by shape and position in the chamber, as well as by the presence or absence of food vacuoles.

The steps in the assembly of the operating chamber are as follows:

(1) The depression of the oil chamber is filled with mineral oil. (We have a subjective impression that the operations are easier to perform when the oil is cooled to 5°–10°C.)

(2) Under a dissecting microscope, amebae are placed in a small drop of medium near the middle and edge of a long side of a cover glass about 15 × 40 mm. Three amebae—a donor, a recipient, and a third ameba—are placed in the same drop. (The presence of the third ameba will be explained below.) The individual amebae are handled with relative ease with a braking pipette (Holter, 1943). Excess medium should be withdrawn from the drop until its volume is approximately 10 times that of the 3 amebae.

(3) The cover glass is inverted and placed over the oil-containing depression of the operating chamber, which is then placed on microscope stage as shown in Fig. 1. Note that the microscope stand is at right angles to the normal eyepiece position. This arrangement facilitates the entrance into the chamber of the microtools after the cells are positioned in the center of the microscope field.

B. Introduction of the Microtools into the Chamber

The microtools, which earlier should have been oriented with respect to one another as shown in Fig. 6, are carefully introduced into the chamber's open side by movement of the manipulator coarse controls. After they have entered the chamber, the microtools are positioned in the center of the microscope field where the amebae already have been placed by movement of the microscope stage. The operator previously should have arranged that the microprobe could be moved with the fine pneumatic controls at least 20μ above and below the microhook and at least 100μ beyond all lateral limits of the microhook; this should be checked again after the tools are in the chamber. These observations and all further operations under the compound microscope are best carried out at a magnification of 100–150 ×.

C. Positioning of the Cells in the Chamber

Before the amebae are manipulated further, the "third ameba" (mentioned above) is sacrificed by being impaled on the microprobe and drawn

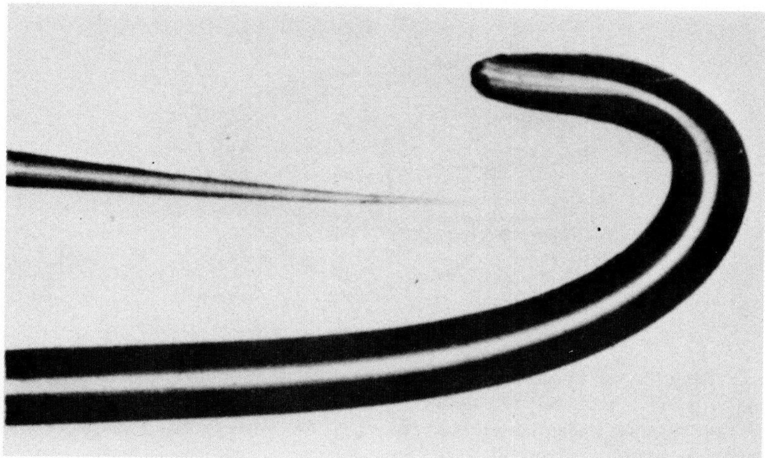

FIG. 6. Photomicrograph of the two microtools in proper orientation with respect to one another.

to the water-oil interface. Contact with the interface, along with harsh action of the microprobe, causes the cell to burst, after which the liberated contents are stirred through the drop of medium. This procedure greatly reduces, for unknown reasons, the chances of the remaining amebae bursting during subsequent manipulations.

To proceed further, the two remaining amebae must be immobilized to some extent. This is best accomplished by drawing them out of the drop with the microhook to a more remote region of the chamber. (In practice, the amebae are held in the microhook and the stage is moved perpendicularly to the axis of the tools.) Drawn with the amebae is a small amount of aqueous medium; it is then relatively simple to trap the cells in a loop made by the hook and the oil-water interface (Fig. 7).

It is of course necessary—either early or late—to position the amebae correctly with respect to one another: the donor of the nucleus should be on the left (in the microscope field) and the recipient should be abutting it on the right. This positioning is done by gentle movements of the microtools and/or movement of the microtools in combination with microscope stage movements.

D. Enucleation

Should the recipient of a grafted nucleus need to be, for experimental purposes, an enucleate cell, the host cell nucleus will have to be removed

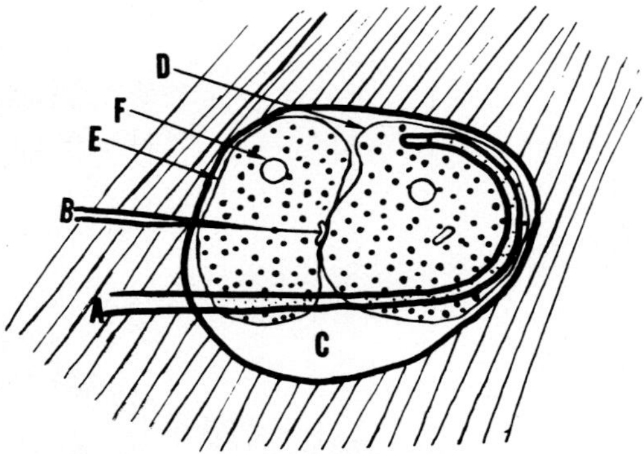

FIG. 7. Diagram of operating arrangement. (A) Microhook; (B) microprobe; (C) aqueous drop; (D) host cell; (E) donor (of nucleus) cell; (F) contractile vacuole. The nucleus that is being transplanted is at the tip of the microprobe. The drop containing the amebae is surrounded by oil.

before the introduction of the donor nucleus. For this, one draws the would-be recipient ameba into a small drop of medium by itself; it is then immobilized with the hook and the microprobe is introduced into the cell on the side away from the hook and slightly to the lower part of ameba. Finally, the nucleus is pushed with the probe directly to the right and out of the cell. (It will take some training to recognize the nucleus, which is frequently near the contractile vacuole.) Upon completion of this operation the probe is withdrawn and all punctured cell surfaces seal themselves almost immediately. One can then bring the would-be donor ameba into the drop and proceed with further manipulations.

E. Nuclear Transplantation

The manipulations leading to the transplantation of a nucleus from one cell to another are similar to those of the enucleation operation just described, except that they are likely to be considerably more difficult to perform. The probe is inserted into the donor as described above and the donor nucleus is pushed (and *not* punctured, although such a condition is tolerable for a nucleus that is sacrificed for enucleation purposes) through the donor cell membrane, through the host cell membrane, and into the cytoplasm of the recipient (Fig. 7). *The passage of the nucleus must occur without exposing it to the surrounding medium, since such exposure irreversibly injures the nucleus.* Because the two cells are not completely immobilized and may move independently of one another, this step tends to be the most difficult one of the entire procedure. Difficulty sometimes arises because one or both cell membranes do not readily puncture as the nucleus is being pushed; this may be overcome after a number of attempts or it may be necessary to start anew on a fresh pair of cells. Once the nucleus has entered the recipient cell the probe is withdrawn, leaving the transplanted nucleus in the host cell cytoplasm and permitting the punctured cell surfaces to seal themselves.

F. Removal of Postoperative Cells from the Chamber

After the operation is complete, removal of the cells from the operating chamber should be effected as soon as possible. Since one must discriminate between two cells when the chamber is disassembled, one of the amebae is drawn back to the "large" drop of medium with the microhook and the other is left in the "small" operating drop. The drops, but not the cells, can be distinguished under a dissecting microscope.

Following the above separation, the cover glass, upon which the aqueous drops unfailingly remain, is removed and examined under a dissecting microscope; the cells are removed one by one with a braking pipette and placed in appropriate incubating vessels. (It is desirable to add some ameba medium to the drops to facilitate removal of the cells.) If food organisms are present in the incubating vessels, cell recovery can usually be recognized in nucleate amebae—by feeding and movement behavior—within an hour or less of the transplantation operation.

IV. Conclusion

Nuclear transplantation in amebae is not a technique that can be learned simply by following detailed instructions. Neither, however, is it a technique that requires unique talents. With diligent application and careful attention to instructions (very little of the guidance offered here is gratuitous), a patient worker should be reasonably proficient after approximately 2 weeks of practice.

When trained, the degree of proficiency may vary to some extent; I have known an investigator to be able to perform an operation approximately every 4 minutes, but the average is likely to be on the order of 8–10 minutes. It is possible to work as a team, with one member assembling the chamber and recovering the animals after the operation and the other member performing the operation proper. Under the latter conditions it routinely is possible for the average practitioner to execute an operation every 3–4 minutes—if everything is going well. Even so, under the best of circumstances the nervous tension is sufficiently great that we have never performed more than approximately 90 successful operations in one day. For an individual working alone 50 successful operations per day would be a good yield indeed.

References

Comandon, J., and de Fonbrune, P. (1939). *Compt. Rend. Soc. Biol.* **130,** 740.
de Fonbrune, P. (1949). "Technique de Micromanipulation." Masson, Paris.
Goldstein, L. (1963). "Protoplasmatologia." Springer-Verlag, Vienna. *In Press.*
Goldstein, L., and Plaut, W. (1955). *Proc. Natl. Acad. Sci. U. S.* **41,** 874.
Hämmerling, J. (1953). *Intern. Rev. Cytol.* **2,** 475.
Holter, H. (1943). *Compt. Rend. Trav. Lab. Carlsberg, Ser. Chim.* **24,** 399.
King, T. J., and Briggs, R. (1953). *J. Exptl. Zool.* **123,** 61.
Lorch, I. J., and Danielli. J. F. (1953). *Quart. J. Microscop. Sci.* **94,** 461.

Chapter 7

Experimental Techniques with Ciliates

VANCE TARTAR[1]

Department of Zoology, University of Washington, Seattle, Washington

I. Introduction

The methods described in this chapter relate to three experimental designs. (1) The initial, starting organization of cells can be altered and their subsequent response compared with the normal. When the protozoa are not large enough to permit direct manipulation, a machine is provided for producing these alterations. (2) Two cells distinguished by some difference can be fused by grafting, and the resulting interaction can reveal a great deal about normal phases of the cell such as cell differentiation, the effects of external treatments like radiation damage, and the nature of racial or species differences. (3) In the most common design

[1] Support by PHS grant C-3637 from the National Cancer Institute, U. S. Public Health Service, is gratefully acknowledged.

the cell environment is altered, changing the cell indirectly. One interesting possibility of this type is suggested.

II. Experimental Possibilities with *Stentor*

A. Cell Grafting

The genus *Stentor* includes some species so large in cell size and of such a consistency as to permit the most complex microsurgical operations which have ever been performed on unicellular life. Stentors therefore rank high among the few types of cells in which grafting, enucleation, and nuclear transfers are possible, the others being *Acetabularia* (Hämmerling, 1953), amebas (see Comandon and de Fonbrune, 1939; Danielli, 1959; Daniels, 1959; Brachet, 1957), *Actinosphaerium* (see Okada, 1930), and various eggs (see Wilson, 1934; Briggs and King, 1955).

Largest of the stentors is *S. coeruleus*. When contracted into a sphere, it has a diameter of approximately 350μ; naturally, it is the preferred species for micrurgy. These ciliates are obtainable in culture from several biological supply houses. Illustrated details of grafting and other operations on stentors, with a summary of results so far obtained, have been presented elsewhere (Tartar, 1961a), as well as a history of the development of grafting in protozoa (Tartar, 1961b). The present account will therefore merely indicate the nature of certain techniques by which preparations of potential significance for cell physiology may be obtained.

The basic operation whereby two stentors are fused into one protoplasmic continuum is shown in Fig. 1. Since fusion is accomplished by

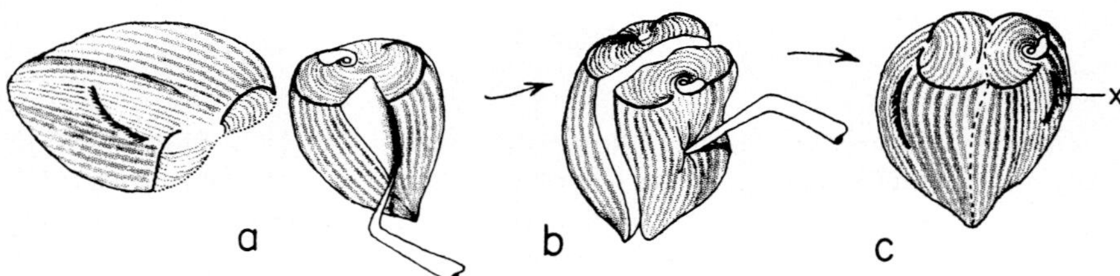

FIG. 1. Parabiotic grafting of two *Stentor coeruleus*. a, Cell to the left has been split longitudinally, opened, and placed flat against the slide to prevent quick healing. Second cell then split likewise with a glass needle. b, First cell is turned over, and, with exposed endoplasms apposed, the two cells are thrust together until they join. c, Resulting fusion pair. In this case a stentor with mouthparts excised and bearing an oral regeneration primordium was grafted to a smaller morphostatic cell. Activation state of the regenerator then induces formation of a comparable reorganization anlage (x) in the partner, and the bistomial biotype is produced.

the endoplasm, the cells are first cut open in quick succession and then pressed together before the openings close in healing. As soon as the endoplasms are exposed, a delicate membrane forms, probably by the orientation of polar molecules at the new surfaces, and prevents swelling and cytolysis. The two cut areas, which always tend to contract to a minimum in healing, expand when pressed together and the membranes break against each other so that fusion between the endoplasms is effected. Once this fusion is accomplished at any site, it spreads to complete the union. Before the union becomes firm, the cells can still be moved by the needle into any desired orientation with respect to each other. All of this should be done with a needle from which the fine tip has been broken, for in the pressing together, this slightly blunt instrument will push rather than impale the cells.

Throughout this basic operation, the stentors are quieted by placing them in a large drop of viscous methyl cellulose and working against the slide-methocel interface. This method of quieting ciliates was introduced by Marsland (1943) and applied to stentor grafting by Weisz (1951). Preparation of a methyl cellulose solution was also described by Wichterman (1953, p. 411). Uhlig (1960) noted that the shedding of pigment which sometimes accompanies abrupt contact with the quieting agent could be reduced to a minimum by first allowing the experimental animals to swim in the methyl cellulose before working against the slide-methocel interface. The ciliates were introduced into the methyl-cellulose by a micropipette with a small drop of culture fluid surrounding them.

What is made possible by this grafting? First, one can produce cells or protoplasmic continuums much larger than normal. As many as 100 stentors have been grafted together (Tartar, 1954b). These fusion masses show that normal maximum size is not due to immediately critical restrictions from surface-volume relationships, for they live quite well for a week or two. Yet eventually, large internal vesicles usually develop, as well as other interesting consequences described in the reference cited.

Second, persisting biotypes are produced by parabiotic grafting: doublet and triplet stentors with single "tails" and two and three sets of mouth parts, respectively, which may grow and reproduce as such for a long time (up to 2 months) but eventually revert to the normal single form.

Third, and most important, intrinsic differences between cells are revealed and investigated by grafting. *Intraclonal* grafts have demonstrated that the stentor cell passes through striking phase differences. A regenerating animal is somehow "activated" so that it can induce the formation of a comparable oral primordium in a nonregenerating fusion partner (Fig. 1) (Weisz, 1956; Tartar, 1958). Conversely, a morphostatic specimen, i.e., one that is not in regeneration, reorganization or division, is not only continually inhibiting its own redifferentiation but can occasion the resorption of even a well-formed oral primordium in a regenerating stentor to which it is grafted (Tartar, 1958). These cell states somehow involve the whole or some pervasive aspect of the cell, because the direction in which the interaction progresses depends on the relative size of the two graft components. If one of the partners is beginning division it may be possible to induce the other to do likewise (Weisz, 1956), and this is potentially a new approach to the study of cell division. However, further work is required to clarify the issues (Tartar, 1961a).

Interracial grafts reveal similarities and differences between stentors from different localities. Many combinations are harmonious, yet others are strikingly incompatible (Tartar, 1963b). "Shattering reactions" such as those described in the reincorporation of fragments of *Arcella* by Reynolds (1924) characterized one combination, and in others various potentially instructive abnormalities in cell differentiation were manifested long before the eventual demise of the chimeras. Thus, even on the unicellular level we find an anticipation of those specificities which so sharply limit the interindividual grafting of tissues in man.

Interspecific grafts also yield persisting unions, as if the basis of adhesion were common to the genus. But incompatibility in the performance of the combined cells is now very evident. To cite one expression of this disharmony, an admixture of *S. coeruleus* cytoplasm causes ejection of the symbiotic *Chlorella* characteristic of *S. polymorphus*, and reciprocally, a bit of *S. polymorphus* leads to depigmentation or loss of the blue-green stentorin in *S. coeruleus*. Eventual death of the chimera is almost always the rule, yet it is possible that a subtle "tincturing" of one species by a very small addition of self-reproducing material from another could lead to instructive blockages and abnormalities in the host (Tartar, 1961a).

B. Enucleation, Renucleation, and Nuclear Transfers

For a detailed account of these techniques the reader is again referred to the recent summary of the biology of *Stentor* (Tartar, 1961a). We may ignore the many micronuclei present, except in conjugation, for we are fortunate in having direct experimental evidence that the macronucleus alone is effective in the vegetative life of stentors (Schwartz, 1935). Since emacronucleated stentors live 3–7 days, there is ample time to measure such a capacity as respiration (Whiteley, 1960) and even to test by renucleation the point of irreversible denaturation of the cytoplasm (Tartar, 1961a). At this critical point, some cell systems might conceivably be reconstituted while others are not, thus producing models on the cell level in which separate functions are dissociable for analysis (Mazia, 1952).

When compacted just before fission, the macronucleus is easily removed with a needle (Fig. 2), though one has to be wary of stray nodes which may not have participated in this condensation. Division proceeds, so

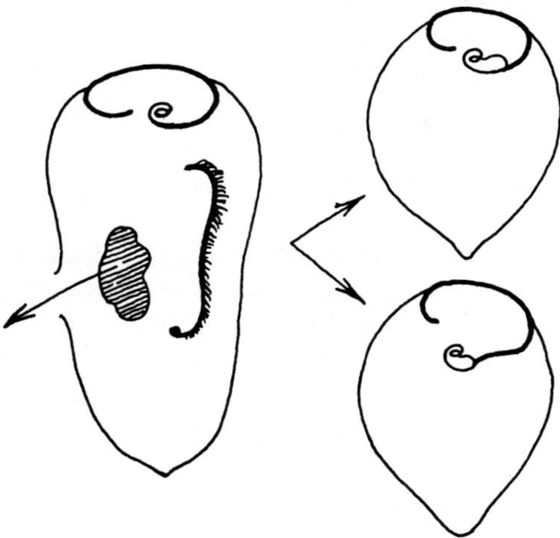

FIG. 2. Dividing stentor with compacted macronucleus excised. Division continues nevertheless, yielding two amacronucleate cells.

that one usually not only has two enucleate specimens, but also information relevant to the problem of furrow formation in dividing cells. Even when fully extended, all the nodes of the nucleus can be teased out of the cell after they have been exposed by a cut which runs along the macronuclear chain (Fig. 3a).

These operations are carried out with a glass needle on starved animals not filled with confusing food vacuoles. Dark-field illumination is provided by placing the drop of methyl cellulose on a square of black cloth fastened to a slide with melted paraffin and operating, as always, with reflected light. When exposed by the incision, the nuclear beads stand out even more clearly than in the intact stentor. Finally, since the beaded macronucleus maintains a quite constant location within the cell just beneath the ectoplasm and is deployed as illustrated, it should be possible by one transection to rapidly produce a large number of enucleate fragments almost as easily as with uninucleate amebas and to retain the companion pieces as controls (Fig. 3a).

Nuclei can be introduced into the stentor cell most readily by taking advantage of the fact that adhesion and fusion are accomplished by the endoplasm. The donor cell is cut open and one or more of its nuclear beads are teased out but left enclosed within a thin capsule of endoplasm. The surrounding envelope protects the beads from injurious direct exposure to the medium and is also the means of transplantation. The host cell of the same or another species, previously enucleated or not, is then brought nearby within the same drop of methocel and sliced open to expose its endoplasm. The nucleus to be implanted is picked up with the tip of the needle, and the envelope of surrounding cytoplasm is broken against the host's endoplasm. Renucleations and nuclear transfers are accomplished in this manner. The transplanted nuclei persist and perhaps even multiply, but effective interaction occurs only between species which are presumably closely akin.

As in similar experiments with *Acetabularia* (Hämmerling, 1953) and eggs (Briggs and King, 1955), a minor amount of cytoplasm is transferred with the nucleus in the above procedure. Alternatively, a presumably naked nuclear node can be implanted into a stentor as a pat of butter is put in a bun: by slicing open the receiving cell, placing the nucleus deep in the split, and quickly closing the cell to trap the nucleus inside (Tartar, 1953). The operation must be completed with great rapidity, or else the nucleus will be injured by exposure to the medium.

C. Altering the Nucleocytoplasmic Ratio

The dimorphic nuclear complement of ciliates suggests that the unique macronucleus, like the unusual nuclei of dipterous salivary gland cells or of germinal vesicles, should have something special to teach us. It is clear that the ciliate macronucleus is highly polyploid and that nuclear size follows cell size and not the reverse, as in most cells. Therefore, in a form such as *Stentor* the quantity of nucleus in relation to the volume of cytoplasm can be altered to extremes in either direction not heretofore possible without introducing the qualitative difference of chromosomal deletions.

Enucleations as just described can be stopped short of removing the last node (Fig. 3), yielding preparations of approximately normal cytoplasmic volume having only about one fourteenth the normal amount of nucleus. As Schwartz (1935) first indicated, such stentors are slow in regenerating and their digestive processes are impaired. Consequently, there is a quantitative aspect to nucleocytoplasmic relations or interactions, and this feature, quite apart from specificities of DNA, can be investigated experimentally in a form like *Stentor* (Tartar, 1963a). The proportions can be shifted still further in favor of the cytoplasm by grafting one or more enucleated cells to the mononodal stentor (Fig. 3d), though in practice it is the mononodal animal which is engrafted last in order

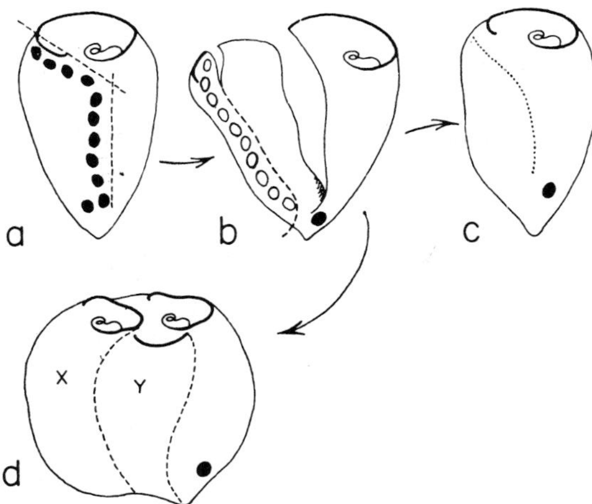

FIG. 3. Reducing the proportion of nucleus to cytoplasm. a, Two cuts through the stentor along the chain macronucleus make it accessible. (This or a similar diagonal *transection* would produce nucleate and enucleate parts.) b, Cell is opened to prevent quick healing and a strip bearing most of the nuclear beads is excised, leaving a single one behind. c, Healed cell with single macronuclear node in an approximately normal volume of cytoplasm. d, Mononodal stentor fused to graft of two stentors from which all the macronucleus has been removed (X, Y), decreasing still further the proportion of nucleus.

that its nucleus can be watched to insure its not being ejected during the disturbances of grafting. The disproportion is eventually corrected by compensatory growth of the nucleus, but this occurs only a day or two later in the course of regeneration or reorganizational replacement of the mouthparts. Thus there is sufficient time to test the capacities of these hyponucleates and provide a valuable supplement to parallel tests on enucleated cells.

Stentors with macronuclear material greatly in excess of the normal proportion can be produced by excising a strip of the cytoplasm containing the macronuclear chain (Fig. 4a). All or most of the nucleus is then isolated into a small amount of cytoplasm (Fig. 4b). Such fragments, however, are not always viable for reasons that remain obscure. A better method is to graft several of these fragments (Fig. 4c) to form a cell of approximately normal cytoplasmic volume containing several nuclear complements. From visible indications such specimens are in no way abnormal, which is in itself interesting. Again, the disproportion is corrected, but even more gradually than in the case of too little nucleus, so that an entire week may be spent in the hypernucleate condition.

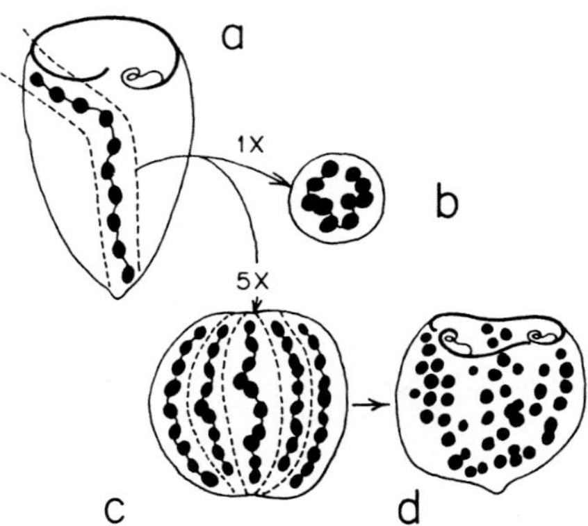

FIG. 4. Increasing the proportion of nucleus to cytoplasm. a, Cuts paralleling the macronuclear chain (or as in Fig. 3b) confine all the nucleus within a small fragment (b). c, Grafting five such nucleate strips produces a doublet (d) of approximately normal cell volume with greatly increased nuclear mass.

D. Synchronous Mass Regeneration

To have large numbers of cells simultaneously performing some cell process is naturally useful in the experimental analysis of that process. Similar animals are then available in abundance for operations, statistical treatment of the effects of external agents, or biochemical analysis. Already we can at least coordinate stentors with respect to cell redifferentiation by causing the shedding of feeding organelles in all animals of a sample, however large. In effect this imposes a simultaneous stimulus to oral regeneration, following which the similarity of the clonal cells can be relied upon to produce approximately synchronous oral primordium formations and development.

For details of this method the reader is referred to published accounts (Tartar, 1957, 1961a). In brief, we take advantage of the discovery that stentors respond to dilute solutions of urea, sucrose, and many other compounds, first by a neat and selective sloughing of the band of membranelles which encircles the anterior end and extends into the gullet. Prolonged exposure leads to gradual dissolution of all cortical structures and eventual death of the cell. The point then is to stop the process at the right time, when the shedding of membranelles is sufficient to elicit regeneration of the entire ingestive structures and yet recovery is complete.

To a known volume of a stentor culture, an equal volume of 4% urea or 20% sucrose is added. After gentle mixing, a sample is removed to observe under low magnification until the proper timing has been determined. When all specimens have shed their membranellar bands, the major preparation is decanted and washed several times with the culture fluid because in lower concentrations the shedding agents also act as inhibiters of regeneration, a point of considerable interest in itself. Now all the animals have to regenerate and will do so simultaneously. The weaker the agent, the longer the time required; therefore, time and concentration can be varied until the cleanest effect is produced, viz. complete shedding of the band without any dissolution of the lateral striping.

Such coordination of regeneration recalls synchronization of cell division by repeated heat shocks in *Tetrahymena* and other smaller ciliates. That this relationship may be more than analogous, and the two methods prove supplemental, is suggested by recent studies (Williams and Scherbaum, 1959; Frankel, 1962) indicating that suspension of division may be due to blockage of development of the early division primordium, which is in most respects very similar to the regeneration anlage.

E. Culturing Stentors

Again we refer to a review of this topic which is already available (Tartar, 1961a). A few remarks will suffice here. Stentors are carnivorous, feeding on smaller protozoa such as *Paramecium bursaria*, *Halteria*, and colorless flagellates with which they are to be supplied. A few stentors are best started in a small volume of water (15 ml) with food organisms and an added rice grain preheated to prevent germination. The gradual decay of the rice grain prevents sudden changes in pH, etc. When well started, the culture can be nutrified every week or two by modest additions of skimmed milk—a complete food, ready-mixed. For biochemically cleaner cultures, food organisms are grown separately and, at the stationary phase following the log phase of growth, added to the stentor cultures.

III. Techniques with *Paramecium*

Although much less amenable to microsurgery than *Stentor*, *Paramecium* is outstanding as the unicellular form in which Mendelian inheritance was first demonstrated (Sonneborn, 1937) and of which the most complete genetic analysis has been worked out, including the discovery of important phenomena in physiological genetics such as the cytoplasmic determination of nuclear differentiation in respect to mating types, nucleocytoplasmic relations in expression of the killer trait, and shift in manifest serotype by external agents (Sonneborn, 1947; Beale, 1954). Moreover, it has been shown that paramecia have an unusual rigidity of cell construction, resulting in a so-far unique manner of regeneration (Tartar, 1954a). Methods for producing new experimental situations therefore should be of considerable promise because of this background, and they are also potentially applicable to other ciliates, e.g., *Frontonia*.

A. Preparing Cells with Two Macronuclei

The procedure is at once apparent from inspection of Fig. 5. A paramecium in a late stage of division is confined to a small drop, preferably

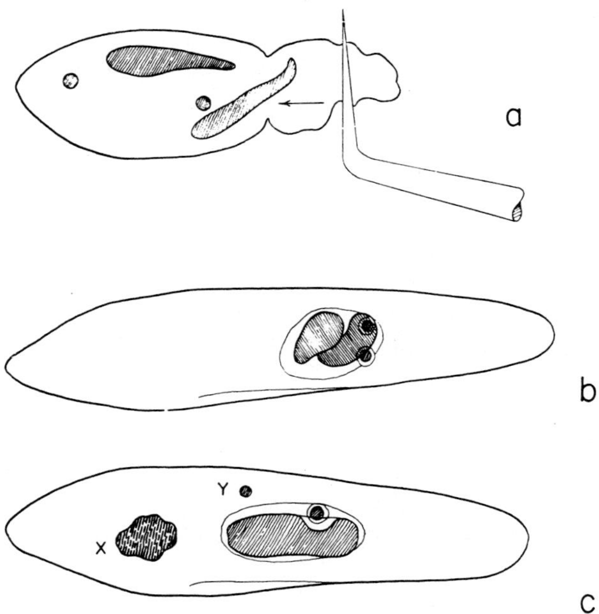

FIG. 5. Preparing a line of *Paramecium caudatum* with double nuclear complement. a, In a dividing cell the nuclear content of one product is forced through the fission constriction into the other. b, Sample of cell line with macronuclei and micronuclei twice the normal number. c, Eventually one of the macronuclei (x) is selectively resorbed in the cytoplasm, and the excess micronucleus (y) may also become "lost."

with some quieting agent. Using a glass needle, pressure is applied to one of the forming daughter cells to drive its macronucleus through the narrowing neck of the division furrow into the other cell. The isthmus prevents dissolution of the remaining cell under tension, as the completion of constriction precludes rejection of the translocated cell contents. The specimen is then rescued by using the needle to coalesce the tiny drop with a large drop of culture medium previously placed adjacent to it. A paramecium with two macronuclei is the result. Its micronuclear complement may also have been doubled or otherwise altered, as can be determined by staining one of the subsequent division products.

These cells grow and multiply as such, producing lines with two macronuclei. Eventually, however, nucleocytoplasmic proportions are corrected, not by segregation of the nuclei as in postconjugational division or by both macronuclei becoming smaller, but by the disintegration and resorption of one (Tartar, 1940). Extra micronuclei are likewise selectively resorbed (Fig. 5c).

B. Preparing Amicronucleate Clones

In ciliates, with their dimorphic nuclei, removal of the macronucleus soon leads to cell death, but deletion of the micronucleus or micronuclei affords a test of the possible distribution of functions between the two types of nuclei in the performance of the emicronucleated cells. Possible aging effects in the amitotic macronucleus can be determined when autogamous replacement of the macronucleus from the micronucleus is thus precluded. Conjugating amicronucleates with normal cells of opposite mating type should be one way of producing haploid animals, if the former receives but one pronucleus whose division products yield both micronuclei and new macronuclei (see Sonneborn, 1938; Schwartz, 1939, 1946).

Using *P. caudatum* as an example, selective removal of the single micronucleus is possible because the products of the dividing micronucleus move to the extremities of the cell (Fig. 6). Then excision of one end with a fine glass needle removes one of the new micronuclei and division continues to completion, yielding one emicronucleate daughter cell and one normal control. Were we dealing with *P. aurelia,* the probability is that both of the two new micronuclei would be removed, because they migrate together in the same manner. Success of the operation is determined by staining one of the early fission products of the operated side. For the emicronucleate cell does grow and divide, but only at about half the rate of the control, producing an amicronucleate line, the nature of whose deficiencies have, however, not yet been analyzed (Tartar, 1940). A similar retardation of growth and division was reported by Schwartz (1947) in *P. bursaria* emicronucleated by *delayed* effects of excising the end of the cell, but eventually the deficiency was somehow compensated and the normal generation time recovered. This could explain the occurrence in nature of vigorous amicronucleate races of various ciliates. In Schwartz's (1958) animals the micronucleus, remarkably, might even be regenerated from the macronucleus, and this eventually should be watched for. By com-

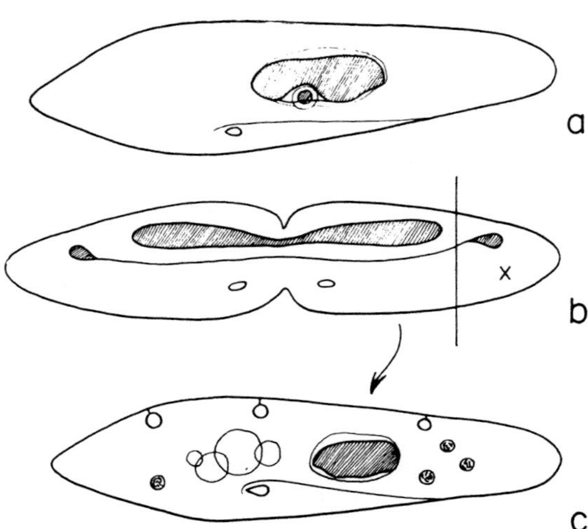

Fig. 6. Preparing an amicronucleate line of *Paramecium caudatum*. a, Predivision cell with micronucleus resting within a crypt in the macronucleus and therefore inaccessible. b, During fission the micronucleus emerges and its division products migrate to the far ends of the cell. Removing one cell tip (x) at this time excises one of the new micronuclei. c, Cut cell yields a line of cells with food and contractile vacuoles but no micronucleus.

bining this and the preceding operation, cell lines with various nuclear complements could be prepared.

In *Euplotes*, direct emicronucleation may be performed on nondividing cells (Taylor and Farber, 1924), and the rotary cutter presently to be described should do the same more easily.

C. The Rotary Razor-blade Cutter

The study of regeneration or redifferentiation in unicellular forms is often limited by the difficulty of obtaining abundant viable fragments. Referring only to the ciliates, many are too small for easy manual cutting (*Tetrahymena*), some tend to cytolyze with extrusion of a highly fluid endoplasm (*Paramecium*), and in others, the rigid pellicle resists neat transection (*Euplotes*). For preparing ablated cells in forms such as these, the rotary razor-blade cutter orginally designed for cutting paramecia is ideal (Tartar, 1954a). Operating on a statistical principle and without the necessity of anesthetizing the material, this device produces thousands of fragments from which viable pieces, cut as desired, may be selected.

As shown in Fig. 7 the instrument applies the bow-and-spindle principle of a fire-by-friction device for rotating the blades. The illustration should

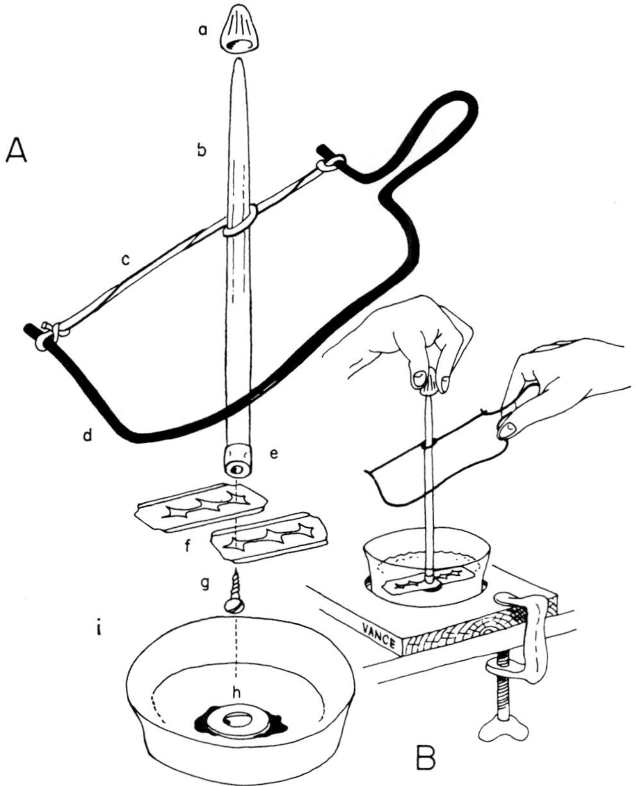

FIG. 7. The rotary razor-blade cutter. A, somewhat disassembled instrument. a, Socket; b, paintbrush handle with ferrule (e) minus bristles; c, leather thong; d, coping saw handle; f, two double-edged blades held in stem by round-headed screw (g) which fits loosely into socket made by cementing washer (h) to bottom center of fruit dish (i). B, cutter in operation, dish filled with protozoan sample and held within hole cut in board clamped to the table.

be largely self-explanatory, with only a few remarks regarding details necessary. Starting from the top, a porcelain joint binder for electric wiring is used as the socket. A paintbrush with bristles removed is used as a spindle because the ferrule prevents splitting where the round-headed screw is inserted to hold the blades. The round head makes a bearing of minimum friction which fits in a washer fastened to a fruit dish with glass-sealing cement. A coping saw handle is used for the bow and its string is a leather thong or shoelace. The spindle may be whittled into hexagonal cross section to prevent slipping on the thong.

In operation a quantity of concentrated culture of the organisms to be cut sufficient to cover the razor blades, is poured into the dish. A few sharp thrusts of the bow are sufficient for cutting. Since the blades rotate first one way and then the other, a whirlpool is produced in which the cells follow the blades; the blades come back against the cells and cut them by chance. The contents of the fruit dish are then poured into shallow dishes and allowed to stand for half an hour, during which time the nonviable fragments will have disintegrated. One can then pick out and isolate the fragments desired, for by their shape one can tell from which part of the cell they came. On this statistical basis several highly improbable pieces, such as anterior cell tips bearing the macronucleus, can be obtained.

Using this device, it was possible in one day to produce more fragments than in all previous studies of regeneration in *Paramecium*. They showed that if the mouthparts are excluded, as in anterior-end pieces, the same are not regenerated unlike the situation in many other ciliates, e.g., *Stentor*. Regeneration of the truncated ends of the cell is accomplished by a building-out (Tartar, 1954a), not by the remodeling of the fragment ("morphallaxis") which we find in *Stentor* and its allies. Therefore, *Paramecium* is the only known case among animals (*Acetabularia* would be a comparable case in plants) in which feeding or growth subsequent to ablation is essential for regeneration. Both points testify to the fixity of construction of the paramecium cell. Such may also be the case in the ciliate *Frontonia*, which likewise has a thick ectoplasm reinforced with trichocysts.

That the instrument described is applicable to cutting the tiny *Tetrahymena* was shown by Albach and Corliss (1959).

D. Culturing

Growing paramecia (also obtainable from biological supply houses) is now a well-established practice and one need only refer to the accounts of Sonneborn (1950), Needham *et al.* (1959), and Wichterman (1953) for ample instructions. Here I would like only to report some interesting consequences of an abnormal type of culture, very similar to results reported by Fauré-Fremiet (1945). *Paramecium multimicronucleatum* were grown in hay infusion in large Erlenmeyer flasks with loose caps in the usual way, but when well started the culture was overnutrified by adding skimmed milk. A highly putrid condition resulted. Many cells developed inverted ends, like those described as a morphological mutant in *P. aurelia* by Dawson (1926); but the posterior as well as the anterior end might be turned in, though less frequently (Fig. 8). This is as if cell growth were thrown out of balance, the ectoplasm increasing faster than the endoplasm to produce buckling. By pressure under a cover slip, the

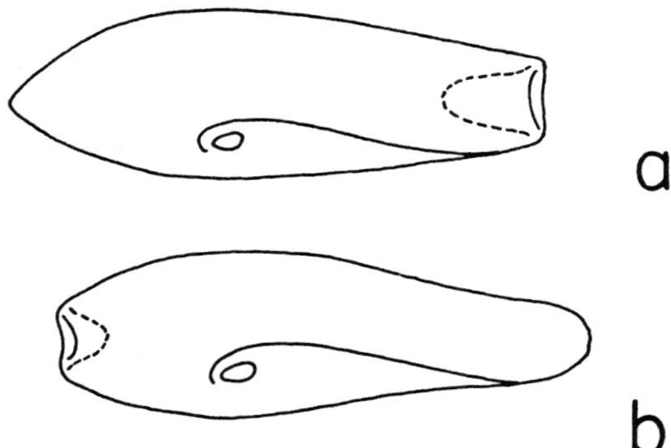

FIG. 8. *Paramecium* grown in hay infusion overnutrified with milk, showing inverted anterior (a) and posterior (b) cell ends.

end of a truncated cell could be everted and give rise to a normal line in normal culture medium. This demonstrated that the complete cell end is indeed present, as well as that the abnormality is probably of nutritional rather than genetic origin.

The other result was abortive fission by which fully formed daughter cells failed to achieve final separation and formed chains of two or more cells (Fig. 9), similar to those produced in dilute formalin by Fauré-Fremiet

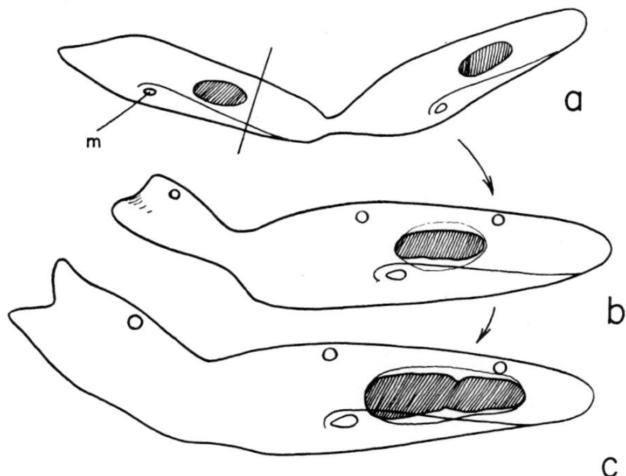

FIG. 9. Abnormal *Paramecium* from strong hay-milk culture. a, Chain of two cells from failure of daughter cells to separate. b, Cut as shown in (a), anterior cell carries anterior portion of posterior partner. c, Growth occurs throughout and the macronucleus consequently also increases in size but mouthparts (m) are not regenerated in the trailing partner.

(1945). When the posterior member of such a tandem pair was hand-cut so that its anterior half, devoid of ingestive structures, was carried along and fed by the complete anterior partner, no mouthparts were regenerated in the posterior portion (Fig. 9c). This indicates that oral regeneration in *Paramecium* requires either pre-existing mouthparts or oral sites. Such specimens often become monsters, as if the guide lines for normal growth had been set askew.

References

Albach, R. A., and Corliss, J. O. (1959). *Trans. Am. Microscop. Soc.* **78,** 276.

Beale, G. H. (1954). "The Genetics of *Paramecium aurelia.*" Cambridge Univ. Press, London and New York.

Brachet, J. (1957). "Biochemical Cytology." Academic Press, New York.

Briggs, R., and King, T. J. (1955). *In* "Biological Specificity and Growth" (E. G. Butler, ed.), pp. 207–228. Princeton Univ. Press, Princeton, New Jersey.

Comandon, J., and de Fonbrune, P. (1939). *Compt. Rend. Soc. Biol.* **130,** 740.

Danielli, J. F. (1959). *Ann. N. Y. Acad. Sci.* **78,** 675.

Daniels, E. W. (1959). *Ann. N. Y. Acad. Sci.* **78,** 662.

Dawson, J. A. (1926). *J. Exptl. Zool.* **44,** 133.

Fauré-Fremiet, E. (1945). *Bull. Biol. France et Belg.* **79,** 106.

Frankel, J. (1962). *Compt. Rend. Trav. Lab. Carlsberg* **33,** 1.

Hämmerling, J. (1953). *Intern. Rev. Cytol.* **2,** 475.

Marsland, D. A. (1943). *Science* **98,** 414.

Mazia, D. (1952). *In* "Modern Trends in Physiology and Biochemistry" (E. S. G. Barron, ed.), pp. 77–122. Academic Press, New York.

Needham, J. G., Galtsoff, P. S., Lutz, F. E., and Welch, P. S. (1959). "Culture Methods for Invertebrate Animals." Dover, New York.

Okada, Y. K. (1930). *Arch. Protistenk.* **69,** 39.

Reynolds, B. D. (1924). *Biol. Bull.* **46,** 106.

Schwartz, V. (1935). *Arch. Protistenk.* **85,** 100.

Schwartz, V. (1939). *Naturwissenschaften* **27,** 724.

Schwartz, V. (1946). *Biol. Zentr.* **65,** 89.

Schwartz, V. (1947). *Z. Naturforsch.* **2b,** 369.

Schwartz, V. (1958). *Biol. Zentr.* **77,** 347.

Sonneborn, T. M. (1937). *Proc. Natl. Acad. Sci. U. S.* **23,** 378.

Sonneborn, T. M. (1938). *Genetics* **23,** 169.

Sonneborn, T. M. (1947). *Advan. Genet.* **1,** 263.

Sonneborn, T. M. (1950). *J. Exptl. Zool.* **113,** 87.

Tartar, V. (1940). *Anat. Record* **78,** Suppl., 109.

Tartar, V. (1953). *J. Exptl. Zool.* **124,** 63.

Tartar, V. (1954a). *J. Protozool.* **1,** 11.

Tartar, V. (1954b). *J. Exptl. Zool.* **127,** 511.

Tartar, V. (1957). *Exptl. Cell Res.* **13,** 317.

Tartar, V. (1958). *J. Exptl. Zool.* **139,** 479.

Tartar, V. (1961a). "The Biology of Stentor." Pergamon Press, New York.

Tartar, V. (1961b). *Biologist* **44,** 7.

Tartar, V. (1963a). *J. Protozool.* In press.

Tartar, V. (1963b). *Proc. Interm. Conf. Protozool., 1st, Prague* 1961. In press.

Taylor, C. V., and Farber, W. P. (1924). *Univ. Calif. (Berkeley) Publ. Zool.* **26,** 131.
Uhlig, G. (1960). *Arch. Protistenk.* **105,** 1.
Weisz, P. B. (1951). *Biol. Bull.* **100,** 116.
Weisz, P. B. (1956). *J. Exptl. Zool.* **131,** 137.
Whiteley, A. H. (1960). *Compt. Rend. Trav. Lab. Carlsberg* **32,** 49.
Wichterman, R. (1953). "The Biology of Paramecium." McGraw-Hill (Blakiston), New York.
Williams, N. E., and Scherbaum, O. H. (1959). *J. Embryol. Exptl. Morphol.* **7,** 241.
Wilson, E. B. (1934). "The Cell in Development and Heredity." Macmillan, New York.

Chapter 8

Methods for Using Tetrahymena *in Studies of the Normal Cell Cycle*

G. E. STONE[1] and I. L. CAMERON

Biology Division, Oak Ridge National Laboratory,[2]
Oak Ridge, Tennessee

I. Introduction

Many difficulties in studies of the cell growth-duplication cycle revolve around the problem of obtaining and manipulating cells of known position in the cell life cycle. One approach to this problem has been to synchronize large populations of cells by various treatments (see review by Prescott, 1961). However, synchronization treatments often introduce parameters that may be undesirable for the study of the normal growth-duplication cycle. Consequently, there is a need for techniques involving a minimum of disturbance to the cells.

The purpose of this chapter is to describe some simple and expedient

[1] NIH Postdoctoral Fellow under Grant No. CPD-332-C1.

[2] Operated by Union Carbide Corporation for the United States Atomic Energy Commission.

techniques for obtaining and manipulating protozoan cells in definable positions of the growth-duplication cycle. Although these techniques have been applied primarily to *Tetrahymena pyriformis*, strain HSM, they are also largely applicable to other protozoans. Examples of how these techniques have been used and possible suggestions for future problems are discussed.

II. Special Equipment

A. Braking Pipette

The braking pipette, because of its slow, even rate of air flow, is probably the most important single piece of equipment in the techniques to be described. Like most other studies on the growth-duplication cycle, the following techniques depend upon the readily observable event of cell division as a beginning and end point of the cycle. The braking type of pipette allows the selection and isolation of cells in similar stages of division from relatively large populations in logarithmic growth.

Although Holter (1943) and Claff (1947) described braking pipettes more intricate in design than the type used by Prescott and his group (Fig. 1), the latter type is quite satisfactory for the techniques to be described here. Its primary advantages are that it is easy to make, sterilize, and clean.

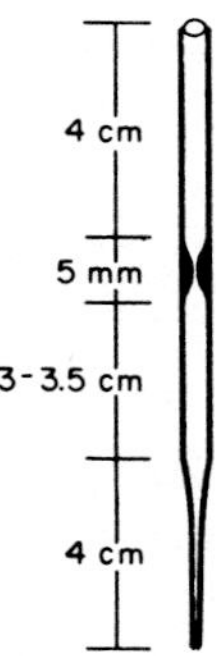

FIG. 1. Braking pipette used for selecting cells.

The following is a description for making such pipettes. Approximately 12-cm sections of Pyrex glass tubing, 4 mm outside diameter and 2 mm inside diameter, are washed free of dirt. Although the over-all dimensions of the pipette can vary, the following may be used as a guide. The braking area of the pipette should be about 5 mm long with an aperture diameter of about 5–15 μ. This aperture is produced by collapsing the tubing over a very hot, fine point flame while applying slight pressure toward the flame from either side. Next, one end of the pipette is drawn out about 4 cm with an outside diameter of 1–1.5 mm. If required, this portion of the pipette can be calibrated to deliver a standard volume. The chamber between the braking area and the drawn-out portion should be 3–3.5 cm long. The finished pipette has a total length of 12 or 13 cm. The bore size at the tip is governed by the size of the cells being selected. The tip should be drawn with a sharp taper over a microflame to avoid undesirable flexibility. When required, new tips may be produced repeatedly by fusing the old tip to another piece of glass and then pulling out a new tip.

For best results, the fluid uptake in the pipette due to capillary forces should be so slow that it is almost imperceptible. When suction is applied to the pipette by mouth through rubber tubing, the fluid should rise slowly and evenly and should cease immediately upon release of the suction. If the fluid rises by capillary action or rises too fast when suction is applied, the bore of either the tip or braking area is too large. Most frequently at fault will be the bore of the braking area. The bore can be reduced by reheating and drawing the tube out slightly. The proper rate of uptake is best determined by trial and error.

After a period of using the pipette, obstructions in the tip or braking region may occur. For example, a small amount of fluid usually remains in the tip and upon drying may form a residue that interferes with the fluid flow rate of the pipette. The tip area should therefore be kept clean. Water sometimes condenses in the braking area and blocks the even flow of air. This fluid often can be forced out by air pressure but the brake usually becomes occluded again unless the pipette is dried out over a flame.

B. Capillary Culture Pipettes

Capillary culture pipettes, as described by Prescott (1957), are used to incubate experimental and control groups of cells. The capillary culture pipettes avoid problems of evaporation and other difficulties that may be encountered when using depression slides and hanging-drop culture methods. With the pipette technique, large numbers of cells can be cultured in relatively little medium, and constant temperature conditions are easily maintained. The cells can be observed and counted, permitting accurate determinations of culture growth rate and of individual cell generation times.

The same glass tubing used to make the braking pipette can be used

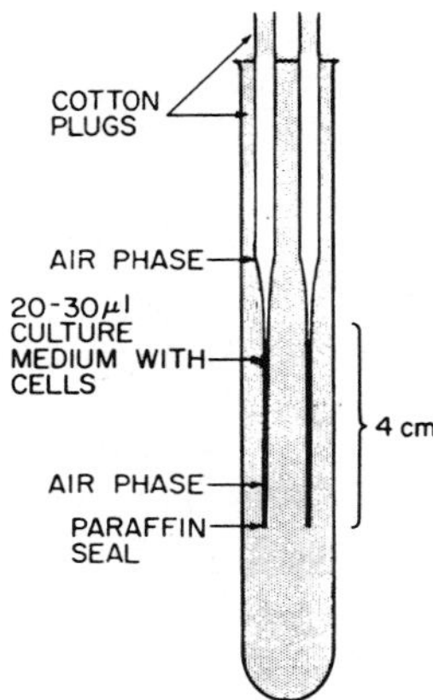

FIG. 2. Capillary culture pipette inserted into cotton-stoppered test tube in a constant temperature bath.

to make the capillary culture tubes (Fig. 2). The approximate dimensions of the capillary portion of the pipette are $\frac{1}{4}$–$\frac{1}{2}$ mm inside diameter and 4–6 cm in length. Capillary tubes, which are to be used for counting cells, are prepared by heating the glass tubing to a very flexible state and drawing out slowly. This results in thick walls for the capillary portion, and the cells will then stand out as bright spots in oblique, transmitted light (dark field effect). The capillary portion should not be drawn too thin since very flexible tubes break too easily and are generally difficult to work with. However, the tubes should be long enough so that they can be inserted into a cotton-stoppered test tube in a constant-temperature water bath as shown in Fig. 2. Pefore sterilizing, a cotton plug is inserted in the top of the pipette.

III. Manipulation of Cells

A. Maintenance of Stocks

Sterile stock cultures are routinely maintained in 10 ml of synthetic medium (Elliott *et al.*, 1954) plus 400 mg per liter of proteose peptone and 1 mg per liter of cholesterol. The pH is adjusted to 7.2–7.4 with NaOH. Stock cultures kept at 15°C require subculturing only about every 2 weeks. Cells that are to be used in an experiment, however, are taken from cultures that have been maintained in logarithmic growth for several days by daily subculture into fresh medium. Although it would be desirable in many instances to maintain stocks in a synthetic medium without the 0.04% proteose peptone, without this supplement the multiplication rate is slow and the individual generation times are quite variable (Prescott, 1959). Adding the small amount of proteose peptone to the synthetic medium results in a constant, reproducible generation time and still allows a relatively favorable circumstance for introducing experimental compounds.

B. Obtaining and Culturing Synchronously Dividing Populations

Cultures from which dividing cells are to be selected are prepared in the following manner. Ten ml of fresh medium is inoculated with about 0.03 ml of a 24-hour culture and incubated overnight. The resulting population is generally dilute enough so that dividing cells can be selected with a braking pipette. The population should be dense enough, however, to assure a sufficient number of dividing cells. A culture that is too dense should *not* be diluted with fresh medium to obtain the proper concentration since this may result in an abnormally long generation time for the subsequent cell cycle (Prescott, 1957). To be sure of obtaining the proper concentration of cells, several cultures can be started, varying the size of inoculation.

For selection of dividers, the culture is poured into a small, sterile Petri dish (6 cm in diameter). Within a minute or two, cells in division will begin to settle to the bottom. To reduce the danger of breaking the tip of the pipette, it is helpful to use a Petri dish with a bottom layer of nonnutrient agar. Dividing cells, including those in very early stages of cytokinesis, are easily recognized under a dissecting microscope, at a total magnification of about × 50. Since the fission process lasts about 20 to 25 minutes (from the first visible formation of the furrow to separation of the duaghter cells), it is preferable to select cells in the early cytokinetic stages so that by the time they have been selected and transferred to capillary culture pipettes they are still in the process of division, and the exact separation time can be determined. One to 2 hours of practice is sufficient to develop reasonable proficiency, e.g., selection in 3–5 minutes of 10–25 cells in similar stages of division. The more care taken to select cells in the same stage, the better the synchrony in the subsequent cycle. After selection, the dividing cells are blown into the culture pipette after inserting the tip of the braking pipette into the capillary tip of the culture pipette. This transfer is more easily carried out under the dissecting microscope. Once the cells are transferred, the medium containing the cells is drawn up further into the capillary by slight suction of the rubber tubing, which is attached to the cotton-stoppered end of the culture pipette.

When the medium is well up in the capillary, the tip is sealed by dipping into and drawing in a small amount of melted paraffin. The paraffin is kept in a salt cellar over an alcohol lamp with a short piece of glass tubing partially immersed in the melted paraffin. When the glass tubing is picked up, some melted paraffin is retained in the tubing, and the tip of the culture pipette is then inserted into this tubing, thus avoiding the possibility of directly heating the cells.

The actual separation time for dividing cells can be determined by direct observation. The beginning of the cycle for a synchronous group is taken as the time when one half of the cells have separated. For example, a 10- to 15-minute period usually separates the division of the first and the last cells in a sample of 15 carefully selected, dividing cells. Figure 3

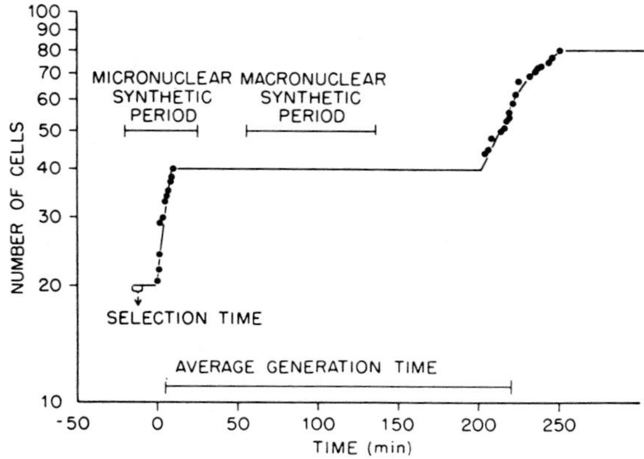

FIG. 3. Degree of synchrony of 20 cells selected in early stages of division. Times required to collect dividing cells, subsequent separation, and micronuclear and macronuclear synthetic periods of these cells are indicated.

shows the degree of synchrony and the position of micronuclear and macronuclear synthetic periods that can be expected under the conditions just described. At the next division, the time elapsing between the separation of the first and last daughter cells is about 40 minutes, representing about 18% of the generation time.

Generation times of *T. pyriformis* (McDonald, 1958) and *Paramecium* (Kimball and Barka, 1959) sister cells from a single division show a positive correlation when compared to nonsister cells. This information allows a more critical estimate of the position in the cell cycle of a killed experimental cell. One daughter cell is retained as control for estimating the generation time of the experimental cell if the experimental is to be killed at some time during the interdivision interval. The time at which the experimental cell is killed is expressed as a percentage of the cell cycle. Kimball and Barka (1959) estimated the position of the experimental cell from the correlation coefficient of sister cells and the average generation time of all the control cells for a particular experiment rather than using the absolute generation time of the sister cell. The reader is referred to their paper for details of the method.

C. Experimental Manipulations

Several experimental manipulations are available for obtaining information about the events occurring during the cell cycle; in addition, the effect of modifying the environment at some specific point of the interdivision interval can be determined.

A "pulse" exposure of the organism to a radioisotope or other treatment is frequently useful, and two methods for giving such pulse treatments at known times in the cell's growth-duplication cycle are described below.

Individual cells or small groups of synchronous cells can be introduced into experimental solutions from the culture pipette. With the aid of a diamond pencil the tip of the culture pipette is broken off between the paraffin seal and the fluid meniscus, and the cells are gently forced into a slide depression containing the experimental solution. At the end of exposure to the experimental solutions, the cells can be picked up with the braking pipette and washed by transfer into fresh medium in slide depressions. By calibrating the braking pipette and delivering a known amount of medium into a known volume of wash solution, the dilution factor can be calculated. It is possible to wash 20–30 cells through three changes of medium in a 3- to 4-minute period with a dilution factor of 10,000–20,000. If the experiment calls for continued incubation of the cells after treatment, they can be reintroduced into the culture pipette.

Tetrahymena often lyse when transferred from a medium such as proteose peptone to a synthetic medium. It has been found that adding 0.1–0.5% (v/v)Tween 80 to the synthetic medium eliminates lysis.

Another method for washing experimental cells involves the use of a Reduced Capillary Tip, Hopkins Vaccine Centrifuge tube (Kimble No. 45225). A mass culture of *Tetrahymena* can be exposed to an isotopically labeled precursor or other material and subsequently washed several times by alternate centrifugation and resuspension in fresh medium. The freshly washed cells can then be poured into a Petri dish, and dividing cells, for example, can be collected using a dissecting scope and a braking pipette as described in Section III,B. By varying the time after washing, one may obtain dividers that were pulse-labeled or treated at different parts of the previous interphase. Washing in fresh medium may cause a small increase in generation time, although this effect can be minimized by filtering the cells out of part of the original mass culture and using this "conditioned," cell-free medium for the washing procedures. Any increase in generation time can be detected by recording the time of the next cytokinesis.

When 10 ml graduated, reduced capillary tip tubes are used, the cells can be concentrated in 0.05 ml of medium; resuspending the cells in 10 ml of fresh or "conditioned" medium gives a dilution factor of 200, i.e., one washing removes at least 99.5% of the experimental medium. Care must be taken not to injure the cells by too much force of centrifugation. An International Equipment Company centrifuge (Model SBV) spun at about 600 rpm for 3–4 minutes will concentrate the cells without injury. The supernatant is removed by aspiration, and cells are resuspended in 10 ml of fresh medium by gentle mixing with a culture pipette attached to a mouth tube.

D. Preparation of Cells for Autoradiography and Cytology

1. Fixation and Extraction

Well-flattened cells are essential for spectrophotometric and autoradiographic measurements. To accomplish flattening a small drop of medium containing the cell(s) is placed on a slide, and as much fluid as possible is drawn from the drop with a braking pipette without picking up the cell(s). If a few of the cells are accidentally picked up, these can be redeposited and dried separately by repeating the original procedure. As many as 50 cells can be dried in 30 seconds. To facilitate subsequent observations, it is helpful to circle with a diamond pencil the position of the cells on the under surface of the slide. Cell breakage during drying may occur under certain conditions but this can be prevented by using slides subbed with gelatin. The subbing medium is a 0.5% solution of gelatin plus 0.05% chrome-alum (see Caro, Chapter 16, this volume). Subbing is accomplished by dipping clean slides into this solution and then allowing them to drain and air-dry in a vertical position.

Air-dried cells can be fixed with a 3:1 fixative (3 parts 95% ethyl alcohol to 1 part glacial acetic acid) at room temperature for 10–30 minutes, followed by several quick changes of 95% alcohol. Cells may be air-dried from the alcohol and stored indefinitely at room temperature.

Enzymatic or chemical extraction procedures may be carried out on the slides prior to staining, autoradiography or Geiger-Müller tube counting. Some of the extraction procedures we have used successfully are outlined here. All of them are preceded by acid-alcohol (1:3) fixation.

Enzymatic removal of deoxyribonucleic acid (DNA) is achieved in most materials by digesting in a 0.01% solution of DNase (Sigma, 1 × crystallized), 0.003 *M* $MgSO_4$, pH 6.5, 37°C for 2 hours. Ribonucleic acid (RNA) is removed with a 0.02% RNase solution (Sigma, 5 × recrystallized) at pH 6.8, 24°C for 2 hours. Both RNase and DNase treatments may be run consecutively on the same slide. To remove acid-soluble products from the cells a 5-minute treatment at 0°C in 5% trichloroacetic acid followed by four washings in 70% alcohol over a 3-hour period is usually sufficient. Most of the nucleic acids can be extracted from the cells by a 10-minute treatment in 5% trichloroacetic acid at 90°C followed by an alcohol wash for 10–30 minutes to remove the acid.

2. Autoradiography

Tetrahymena can be labeled heavily with tritiated precursors of RNA, protein (Prescott, 1962), and DNA (McDonald, 1962) in a matter of 5–15 minutes. An exposure time of 1–2 weeks is required to obtain autoradiographic images (Figs. 4–7). The simplified autoradiographic technique described by Prescott (this volume, Chapter 19) gives excellent results on *Tetrahymena*.

Grain count analysis can be done on the autoradiographs, but interpretations of such data must take into account the various points raised by Perry (this volume, Chapter 15) in his detailed discussion of quantitative aspects of autoradiography. *Tetrahymena* flattened by the drying method are still quite thick in relation to the path length of tritium β-particles; therefore, the number of grains is a measure of the concentration of the isotope in a volume that is determined by the area counted and the average range of the β-particles. These considerations become more critical when counting silver grains produced by radiation originating within the nucleus because of the layer of cytoplasm interposed between the nucleus and the emulsion.

Better autoradiographic resolution between nucleus and cytoplasm is frequently obtainable with sectioned material. Rudzinska (1955) has described a technique for paraffin embedding of mass populations centrifuged into a pellet. The pellet can be handled as a piece of tissue. The success of this technique depends on a large population and is not readily adapted to small numbers of cells.

Kimball and Perdue (1955) have described a procedure for sectioning small numbers of *Paramecium*. They have recently refined this technique (personal communication, 1963) as follows: A small amount of melted agar is placed in the end of a piece of glass tubing previously sealed at one end over a flame. The radioactive cells are pipetted on top of the agar and fixative is added. After the cells have settled on the agar, the excess fixative

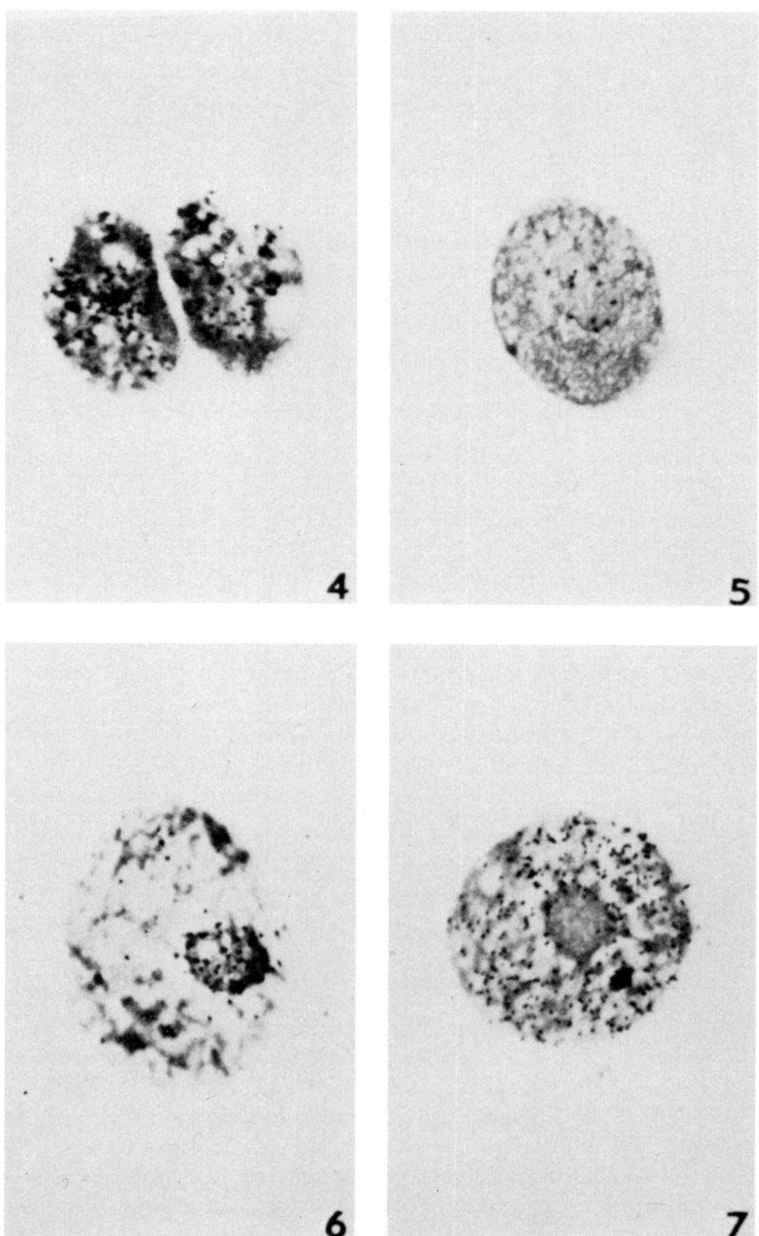

FIG. 4. Autoradiograph of *Tetrahymena* incubated in tritiated thymidine for 15 minutes. Silver grains are localized over the nuclei. Stained with toluidine blue.

FIG. 5. Autoradiograph of a *Tetrahymena* exposed to tritiated cytidine for 1.5 minutes. Labeling is concentrated over the nucleus. Stained with Giemsa.

is drawn off and more melted agar, mixed with a counterstain, is added to cover the cells. After the additional agar has solidified, the entire block is forced out by inserting a pipette down the side of the agar block and forcing water under the block. The piece of agar containing the cells is treated as a piece of tissue for dehydration and clearing. The position of the cells is easily recognized at the site where the agar containing the counterstain meets the agar lacking counterstain. The agar block is then embedded in paraffin and sections prepared with a rotary microtome and floated onto water. Cooling the microtome blade and water bath is necessary for the last procedure. The advantage of this technique is that the few cells are localized in a small, recognizable area and extensive sectioning is not necessary to be assured of obtaining cell sections.

Figures 4–7 are micrographs of *Tetrahymena* autoradiographs stained according to some of the procedures outlined below. These micrographs are intended to illustrate the results one can expect to obtain after labeling with tritiated thymidine and uridine. The specific experimental conditions are given in the figure legends.

3. STAINING

It is the purpose of this section to review only a few special procedures for *Tetrahymena* that have been found to be practical for routine use. Most of the staining is done through the emulsion after development of the autoradiograph. Toluidine blue, 0.25% (w/v), pH 6.3, has been found to be a practical and utilitarian method for staining virtually all types of cells through the emulsion. In the case of *Tetrahymena*, staining takes 1–2 minutes, and after excess stain is washed off with 95% alcohol the preparation is air-dried. To counterstain, the cells can be placed in eosin for 2 minutes prior to staining in toluidine blue.

Another staining procedure that has been found to work well for autoradiographs is the use of 0.3% aqueous methyl green for 20 minutes, followed immediately by 3 minutes in 0.5% pyronine and washing in 3 parts tertiary butyl alcohol to 1 part ethyl alcohol (Kurnick, 1955). Gude *et al.* (1955) describe a procedure for using Giemsa stain for autoradiographs. Slides are placed in buffered distilled water (pH 6.8) for 1 hour and then dried. When dry, they are stained 1–2 hours by a modification

FIG. 6. Autoradiograph of *Tetrahymena* after a 12-minute exposure to tritiated cytidine. Some silver grains appear over the cytoplasm. Stained with toluidine blue.

FIG. 7. Autoradiograph of a *Tetrahymena* exposed to tritiated cytidine for 12 minutes and then incubated in a nonlabeled medium for 88 minutes. The silver grains over the nucleus are greatly reduced but the cytoplasm is now heavily labeled. Stained with Giemsa.

of Wollbach's Giemsa mixture. Figures 5 and 7 illustrate the use of this stain on autoradiographed *Tetrahymena*.

Feulgen stain is useful when one is attempting to resolve silver grains over the nucleus. Because of the necessity of hydrolysis at high temperature, this staining is carried out before coating with emulsion. Procedures for microspectrophotometric measurement of Feulgen-positive material in *Tetrahymena* have been described by McDonald (1958).

4. Microchamber for Studying Living Cells

Whole-cell volume and macronuclear measurements can be made on individuals or groups of living *Tetrahymena* by using a simple microchamber described by Cameron and Prescott (1961). The chamber can be made with simple laboratory equipment. Three or more parallel glass wool fibers are placed about 1 mm apart on a clean microscope slide and are held in place by two pieces of cellulose tape placed near the edges of the slide (see Fig. 8). The fibers in many lots of glass wool are uniformly

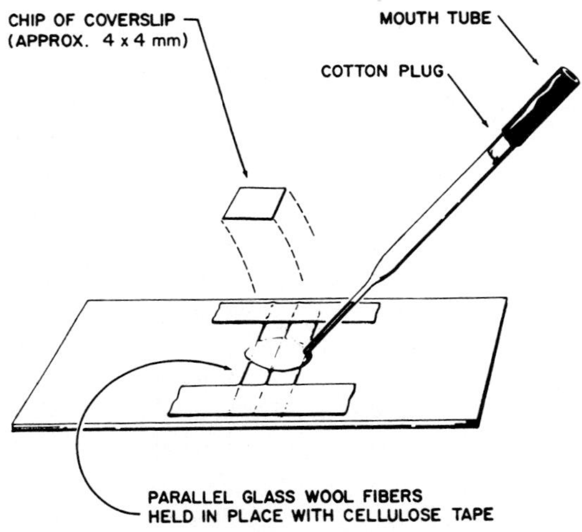

FIG. 8. Drawing of the culture chamber used to keep individual *Tetrahymena* flattened to 8 μ during growth and division. The edge of the cover slip can be sealed with immersion oil to prevent evaporation of the medium.

8 μ in diameter and therefore assure a constant thickness of the preparations.

A drop of medium containing one or several cells is placed on the slide in the area of the glass fibers, then a small chip of cover slip is lowered onto the drop. Excess medium is removed from around the cover slip with a filter paper blotter until the cover slip lies firmly on the glass fibers;

this procedure yields a preparation that is 8 μ thick. Flattening to this thickness reduces the motility of the cells considerably. This permits observation of contractile vacuole activity, ciliary movement, interference microscope measurements, etc. The chamber can be sealed around the edges with mineral or immersion oil to prevent evaporation of the medium. A chamber prepared in this manner is useful for the study of volume changes or other observations for extended periods of time, especially when combined with photography. As a convenient 8 μ reference standard, a section of the glass fiber can be included in the photographs (see Fig. 9).

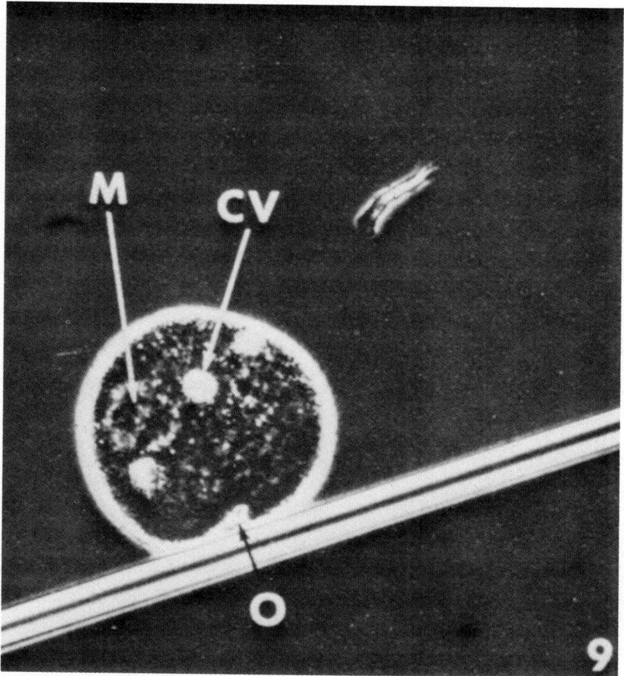

FIG. 9. A microchamber preparation of a living *T. pyriformis* HSM flattened to 8 μ. The photomicrograph was taken with a phase microscope using a flash exposure of 1/3000 second. Exposure times as long as 1/20 second have, however, been used successfully. Macronucleus (M), oral area (O), and contractile vacuole (CV).

The photographs can be enlarged and cell size measured with the aid of a planimeter [see Cameron and Prescott (1961) for details of nuclear and volume computations].

References

Cameron, I. L., and Prescott, D. M. (1961). *Exptl. Cell Res.* **23,** 354.
Claff, C. L. (1947). *Science* **105,** 103.
Elliott, A. M., Brownell, L. E., and Gross, J. A. (1954). *J. Protozool.* **1,** 193.
Gude, W. D., Upton, A. C., and Odell, T. T., Jr. (1955). *Stain Technol.* **30,** 161.
Holter, H. (1943). *Compt. Rend. Trav. Lab. Carlsberg (Ser. Chim.)* **24,** 399.
Kimball, R. F., and Perdue, S. W. (1955). *Exptl. Cell Res.* **27,** 405.
Kimball, R. F., and Barka, T. (1959). *Exptl. Cell Res.* **17,** 173.
Kurnick, N. B. (1955). *Stain Technol.* **30,** 213.
McDonald, B. B. (1958). *Biol. Bull.* **114,** 71.
McDonald, B. B. (1962). *J. Cell Biol.* **13,** 193.
Prescott, D. M. (1957). *Exptl. Cell Res.* **12,** 126.
Prescott, D. M. (1959). *Exptl. Cell Res.* **16,** 279.
Prescott, D. M. (1961). *Intern. Rev. Cytol.* **2,** 255–282.
Prescott, D. M. (1962). *J. Histochem. Cytochem.* **10,** 145.
Rudzinska, M. A. (1955). *J. Protozool.* **2,** 188.

Chapter 9

Continuous Synchronous Cultures of Protozoa[1]

G. M. PADILLA[2] AND T. W. JAMES

Gerontology Branch, National Heart Institute, National Institutes of Health, PHS, U. S. Department of Health, Education and Welfare, Bethesda, and the Baltimore City Hospitals, Baltimore, Maryland and Zoology Department, University of California, Los Angeles, California

---

I. Introduction

One natural outgrowth of the development of synchronous cultures of various cell types has been the establishment of a system which can be maintained for an indefinite number of generations without loss of cell division synchrony. We have called such systems "continuous synchronous cultures." This may be considered a misnomer since the term "continuous culture" is usually applied to a system in which a continuous inflow of

[1] This research has been supported in part by National Science Foundation Grant G-19297.

[2] Present address: Biology Division, Oak Ridge National Laboratory, Oak Ridge, Tennessee.

sterile medium and a concomitant washout of cells results in a steady state population in the growth vessel. The chemostat (Novick and Szilard, 1950), bactogen (Monod, 1950), and turbidostat (Myers and Clark, 1944) are typical examples of this type of continuous culture, although they differ widely from each other. In the present situation, a "continuous synchronous culture" is a system which is regularly permitted to expand from one population level to another in a stepwise fashion by a synchronous burst of cell division. The culture is then rapidly diluted to the population density level existing before the synchronous burst took place. Such systems can be shown to have certain properties common to a chemostat, irrespective of the method used to induce cell division synchrony. However, since dilution is intermittent rather than continuous, the system is continuous only in the long term sense of its operation.

Development of such culturing methods also serves to provide a partial answer to a criticism which is often leveled against synchronized systems. The criticism hinges on the concept of "balanced growth" which stipulates that growth of a cell can be considered "balanced" only if all the major constituents of a cell double during each cell cycle (Barner and Cohen, 1956). In many synchronized cultures this does not occur, particularly if they are dependent on batch culture techniques.

Through the various phases of the growth cycle in batch cultures, cells continuously adapt to an ever changing environment as the cell population increases. Such adaptations may be reflected in the biochemical profile of cellular constituents, so that cells in the early logarithmic phase of growth differ sharply from those in the deceleratory phase (Buetow and Levedahl, 1962). If synchrony-inducing forces are applied to such batch cultures, it is not surprising to find cells exceeding the prescribed limits of balanced growth, and in fact, fluctuations in the median values may be amplified and intensified through synchrony. Through the adoption of continuous culture techniques, the cells are offered a more stable environment which, in part, results in repetitive synchronous bursts whose characteristics are easily duplicated with a substantial degree of precision each time the cycle is repeated. In fact, if the continuous system is well controlled, the data from one cycle can be superimposed on that of another cycle with confidence.

A. Selection for Synchronized Cells

The use of stepwise dilution procedures in a continuous synchronized culture provides an added dividend that is not immediately evident but that is analogous to a chemostat's tendency to select for short generation time organisms. In a chemostat the washout rate determines the mean generation time of the cells. It has been shown experimentally (Novick and Szilard, 1950) as well as on mathematical and statistical grounds (Moser, 1958), that there is a selection for the shortest mean generation time in the culture. For example, short generation time mutants are selected (Novick and Szilard, 1951). In a continuous synchronized culture with stepwise dilution, the synchronized generation time is determined by the length of the cyclical program which brings the cells into simultaneous division. If halving the volume by dilution is carried out once each cycle (preferably as soon as the burst of division is completed), the number of cells at any fixed time in the cycle will be the same from cycle to cycle, but the proportion of cells that obey the cycle to those that do not will increase progressively. In other words, those cells which do not divide will be diluted or washed out of the culture more rapidly than those which do divide, and unless more nondividing cells are generated in the course of time, the culture will consist exclusively of dividing cells.

This is, of course, an oversimplified view of what is actually occurring. In practice, some small percentage of disobedient cells will be produced at a constant rate, but if their rate of production is much lower than the rate of production of obedient cells, i.e., synchronized cells, they will be reduced by repeated dilutions to a small proportion of the total population. This model offers an opportunity to determine the size of the nondividing class of cells and to change experimentally its dimensions through imposition of cyclical regimens of varying severity. The time of dilution is of some importance, but this will depend on the method by which synchrony is obtained. As a rule, some time in the nondividing period of the cell cycle will be favorable in bringing about this type of selection.

B. Balanced Growth

Another serious criticism often leveled against the product of synchronization is that the cells are not "normal" because of the temporary physiological states (transients) introduced by the synchronizing techniques or procedures being employed (Abbo and Pardee, 1960). For example, a temperature cycle may induce synchronous division by distorting the pattern of biochemical activities that are present in a "normal" cell, i.e., one that is grown at a constant temperature (Scherbaum and Zeuthen, 1954; Zeuthen, 1958). There is no complete answer to this criticism, since this is most likely what happens. Yet, the importance of the question can be appraised by a second one: Are "normal" cells essential to understanding the patterns of biochemical events that are important to cell division? Obviously, if cell division can occur in synchronized systems, a knowledge of just what the distortions are may provide an insight into the essential activities for the process of cell division. The discomfort which arises in some minds is undoubtedly associated with the difficulty in understanding the kinetics of physiological transients. Furthermore, the aim of many investigators who have attempted to use synchronized cultures has not been to understand the process of cell division, and the supposition may have been made that other aspects of the cell cycle are synchronized to the same degree to which the division activities are controlled. The introduction of continuous culture techniques into the problem will provide greater reproducibility in the synchronized systems and will help circumvent some of these difficulties (James, 1961a).

II. Light-Induced Synchrony in *Euglena gracilis*

Recently, the green flagellate, *Euglena gracilis*, has been added to those photosynthetic cell types that can be experimentally induced to divide synchronously by means of a repetitive light-dark cycle. We shall limit our discussion of the system to its continuous culture features, since the various other attributes of the system have been well described elsewhere (Cook, 1960, 1961, 1962; Cook and James, 1960). The discussion below summarizes some of these findings.

A. Development of the Light-Dark Cycle

The light-dark cycle which brought about repetitive synchrony in *Euglena* was derived from a series of considerations encompassing not only the growth of this cell as a function of light exposure but also its biochemical profile and kinetic responses following cessation of illumination (Cook, 1960). In particular, the basis for constructing a repetitive 24-hour cycle rested in great measure on the minimum energy (light) requirements for growth and cell division for *Euglena* at 20°C, cultured on the chemically defined Cramer-Myers (1952) medium (Table I). This medium, which is identical to that also used for *Astasia longa,* consists primarily of inorganic salts chelated by citrate, to which vitamins B_1 and B_{12} are added. In addition, as shall be discussed in more detail later, a source of reduced sulfur is required for maintenance of synchrony. With *Euglena,* this need was filled by cysteine and methionine added to final concentrations of 6.4×10^{-4} M and 10^{-5} M, respectively (Cook, 1960). Both vitamins and SH-bearing compounds were aseptically added to pre-autoclaved medium.

TABLE I

GROWTH MEDIUM[a]

Compound	Mg/liter
$(NH_4)_2HPO_4$	1000
KH_2PO_4	1000
$MgSO_4 \cdot 7H_2O$	200
Na citrate $\cdot 2H_2O$	645
$CaCl_2 \cdot 2H_2O$	265
$Fe_2(SO_4)_3 \cdot XH_2O$	3.0
$MnCl_2 \cdot 4H_2O$	1.8
$CoCl_2 \cdot 6H_2O$	1.3
$ZnSO_4 \cdot 7H_2O$	0.4
$Na_2MoO_4 \cdot 2H_2O$	0.2
$CuSO_4 \cdot 5H_2O$	0.02
Vitamin B_1 (thiamine $\cdot$ HCl)	0.02
Vitamin B_{12}	0.01
Distilled water to one liter	
Na acetate	5000
pH (Acetate)	6.8

[a]Modification of basal medium of Cramer and Myers (1952).

Repeated determinations revealed that *Euglena* grows at 20°C under a saturation intensity of incandescent white light of 130 foot-candles with an average generation time of about 20 hours. If during exponential growth the light is suddenly turned off, a proportion of the population continued to divide for about 6.2 hours. These would be, of course, cells that had been continuously exposed to light in the preceding 13.8 hours of their life time, the other cells being unable to divide (Cook, 1960). They thus mobilized, in that period of time, sufficient energy to complete their generation. If now a population of cells were to be exposed to alternating periods of light and darkness, in which the same relationship is maintained, i.e., 13.8 hours of light followed by 6.2 hours of darkness, one would expect that initially only a small proportion of cells would complete division after the first light shut-off. As the cycle is repeated, and if there occurs little or no depletion of "stored" energy, a greater proportion of cells would complete cell division in the dark period. Eventually, the entire population would behave as a unit and synchrony would result. The results shown in Fig. 1 indicate that this is indeed the case. For a 24-hour cycle the light period was set at 16 hours and the dark period at 8 hours. At population densities below 5000 cells per milliliter 90–95% of the cells complete division at each burst; this is shown in the upper portion of the

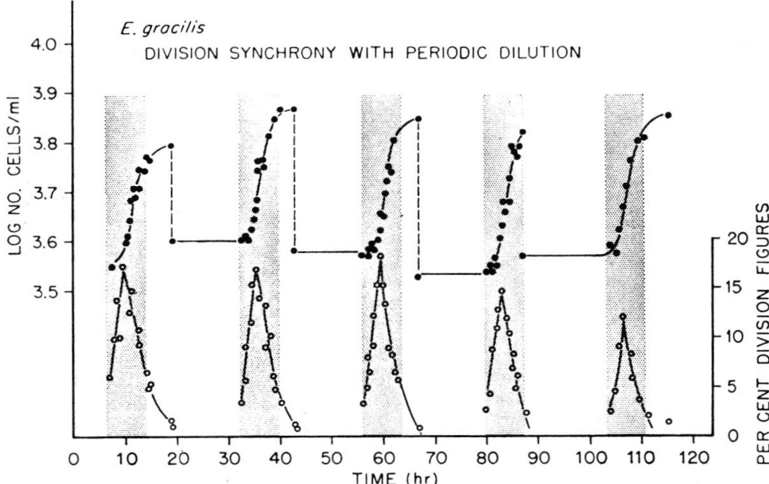

FIG. 1. Light-induced division synchrony in *Euglena gracilis*. The upper curve is a plot of the logarithm (to the base 10) of the population density. The 8-hour dark periods are represented by the shaded areas. The light periods are of 16 hours duration. The broken lines indicate dilution with fresh salt medium at the temperature of the culture (20°C). The lower curve shows the proportion of cells in recognizable fission. (From Cook, 1962; reproduced by permission of the publishers).

graph as the logarithm of the number. The division index, i.e., the fraction of cells in cytokinesis, indicates that the system is highly repetitive, the peak value being achieved regularly in the middle of the dark period.

B. Continuous Culture Techniques

The results shown in Fig. 1 also typify the continuous aspects of synchrony in *Euglena*. Continuity, which is interrupted only by accidental contamination, is achieved in this system with a culture vessel of simple design. The cells are grown in a Spinner Flask (Bellco Glass Co., Vineland, New Jersey), which is a cylindrical vessel equipped with two ports and a magnetically operated stirring bar. Stirring assures adequate gas exchange as well as uniform illumination. The culture is diluted daily in the early portion of the light period, taking care that the inflowing sterile medium is at the same temperature as the parent culture. Samples and excess cells are removed by a siphon suitably equipped with a contamination-preventing mantle at the delivery tip. As shown by the cell counts, performed on an electronic cell counter (Coulter Co., Hialeah, Florida), this method of sampling is adequate.

The primary deficiency in this system is the present inability to synchronize *Euglena* at high population densities. This difficulty, however, is offset by the finding that samples from separate cycles can be pooled and continuous patterns of change indicating balanced growth can be derived from such samples (Cook, 1962). This point again illustrates one of the advantageous features of a continuous synchronous culture.

III. Temperature-Induced Synchrony in *Astasia longa*

A. Growth vs. Temperature

One would expect that since growth is a complex of chemical and physical processes, a cell's response to temperature shifts would assume a variety of forms. In some instances a given function may be inhibited by reduced temperature (e.g., respiration) while an apparent compensatory change will be seen in the opposite direction (e.g., increase in size). Indeed, the parameter under examination may be said to alter the quality of the event being measured. Thus in attempts to derive an over-all formulation of stress vs. response, temperature effects on cell division and growth must be considered in general terms before examination is made at the molecular or even particulate level.

To derive a synchrony-inducing temperature cycle, it becomes necessary to limit one's choice of the range and duration of the temperature periods of the cycle, as well as its periodicity. To this end, the primary measure of a cell's response to temperature is its growth rate. At the same time one should also determine the biochemical profile of the cell at each steady state level of growth, so that with standard calculations based on the kinetics of cellular proliferation (Hutchens *et al.*, 1948) an estimate can be made of a cell's capability or effectiveness as a function of temperature. This may be in terms of substrate utilization as well as rates of synthesis of one or all the major components of protoplasm. To be sure, these determinations need not forecast a successful synchrony but will presage the temperature cycle best suited for its attainment.

In *A. longa* a variety of parameters were examined as function of ambient temperature (James and Padilla, 1959) and the results provided sufficient clues for the subsequent formulation of a synchrony-inducing temperature cycle (Padilla and James, 1960). In essence, it was found that *Astasia* is twice as effective at 25°C than at 15°C in its rate of dry weight production, even though it divides 3.3 times faster at the higher than at the lower temperature (James and Padilla, 1959). This was meant to imply that for a 24-hour temperature cycle, ignoring for the moment the effects of repetitive temperature shifts, the 15°C portion of the cycle must be twice as long as the 25°C portion in order for the cells to produce equivalent amounts of protoplasm in that span of time. In addition, as the 15°C-grown *Astasia* were considerably larger than their 25°C counterparts, the cold cells upon shifting to a higher temperature *could* operate their larger mass of respiratory machinery to greater advantage under temperature cycling than in a constant environment. As it turns out, one of the early temperature programs, set within these conjectural limits, gave a reasonably good synchrony provided two other criteria were met: (a) the temperature transition periods were rapid and (b) the medium was either organic (e.g., 2% proteose peptone) or supplemented with SH-bearing compounds (Padilla and James, 1960). We shall consider the question of the medium later.

The above criteria were met through the development of improved culture vessels, controlling units, and provision for optimum conditions of growth (Padilla, 1960; Blum and Padilla, 1962). The most adequate temperature program to date consists of a 17.5-hour period at 14.5°C and a 6.5-hour period at 28.5°C. With this cycle, highly repetitive synchrony is achieved and is characterized by a close phase relationship of cellular events to the temperature program (Padilla and Cook, 1963). With the development of continuous culture techniques, to be described below, the system approaches the qualifications of a model for a single cell.

B. Development of Continuous Culture Techniques

As with *E. gracilis*, maintenance of continuous cultures in synchrony rests simply with the adoption of techniques for serial dilution. The first problem one faces is the construction of a culture vessel that allows large yields of cells growing at optimum conditions.

1. Culture Apparatus

Figure 2 shows the type of culture vessel found to be most adequate in the continuous synchrony of *A. longa* (Blum and Padilla, 1962). An almost identical unit has been used by Wilson for studies on the oxygen consumption of synchronized cultures of *A. longa* (Wilson, 1962; Wilson and James, 1963). The vessel consists of a cylindrical Pyrex glass jar 10 inches in diameter and 12 inches high, to which is clamped a $\frac{1}{4}$-inch stainless steel plate as a cover. The jar is separated from the cover by rubber and gauze gaskets which prevent contamination and avoid undue strain on the glass surface. In lieu of these materials, gaskets of autoclavable inert plastic foam are now available (Gay-Mar Industries, Buffalo, New York).

Several ports are drilled through the plate cover for the following items:

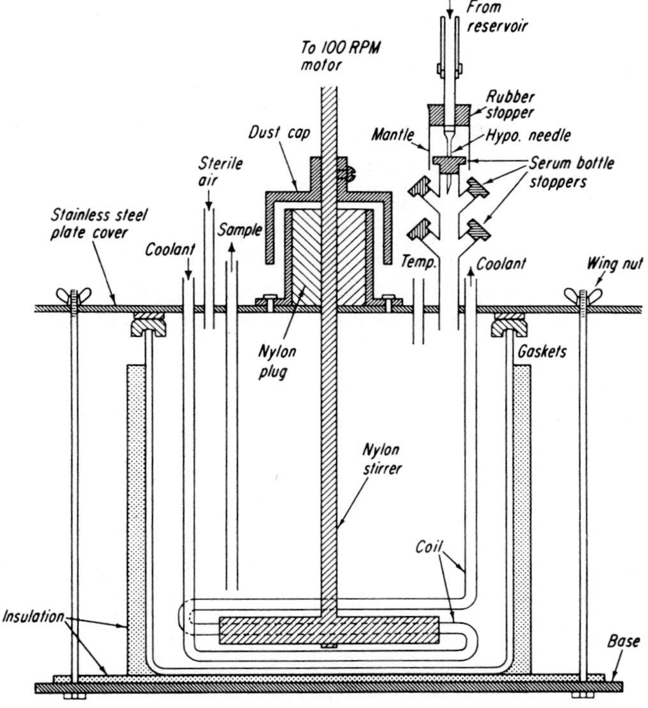

FIG. 2. Schematic representation of the culture apparatus. See text for details.

two $\frac{3}{8}$-inch OD stainless steel tubes of the cooling coil; inlet and outlet ($\frac{1}{4}$-inch OD, stainless steel tubes) for sterile air, flowing at a minimum rate of 3.5 liters per hour and 20 pounds per square inch (a lower rate is permitted if the air is bubbled through the medium); a stainless steel sampling tube ($\frac{1}{4}$-inch OD) connected to an automatic pipetter (Brewer Co., Baltimore, Maryland); an autoclavable thermistor probe (Yellow Springs Co.) for recording the temperature; a stainless steel inoculation tube ($\frac{1}{2}$-inch OD) provided with multiple stoppered inoculation ports; and lastly, a central opening ($\frac{1}{2}$-inch bore) for the stirrer collar. As shown in Fig. 2, the stirrer shaft, consisting of a $\frac{3}{8}$-inch diameter nylon rod (Zytel type, Du Pont and Co., Wilmington, Delaware), passes through a cylindrical nylon plug which is enclosed in a brass housing attached to the plate cover. The two nylon surfaces are self-lubricating and will withstand repeated steam sterilization. An aluminum cap covers the stirrer and its collar. A 3-inch steel or nylon blade completes the stirring mechanism.

Several methods are available for securing air-tight seals to all these ports and the plate cover: welding, cementing with heat-resistant epoxy resins, etc. The most advantageous method involves the use of stainless steel compression-type tube fittings which are available from industrial suppliers in a variety of sizes and forms. If other materials are contemplated in the construction of the culture apparatus, a recent study itemizing those materials found to be inert toward algae (Dyer and Richardson, 1962) may serve as a guide.

The culture vessel is inoculated with a hypodermic syringe. Dilution is also accomplished via a hypodermic needle attached to a tube passing through a rubber stopper (cf. Fig. 2). A glass mantle, consisting of a 25-mm glass tube section, covers the pierced serum bottle stopper and allows for repeated inoculations. An overhead reservoir, consisting of a 20-liter aspirator bottle (Corning Co., Corning, New York) contains sterile medium which is added by gravity flow. An in-line solenoid valve (not shown) permits unattended dilution of the culture. Heat-labile compounds, such as vitamins and SH-compounds, are sterilized by filtration and may be added directly to the culture vessel. If a more permanent setup is desired, the empty culture vessel and reservoir may be pre-sterilized and complete medium added and cold-sterilized by passage through high-capacity ceramic filter candles (Selas Co., Spring House, Pennsylvania) or membrane filters (Pall Corp., Glen Cover, Long Island, New York).

2. Controlling Units

A program clock (Paragon Electric Co., Two Rivers, Wisconsin) equipped with dual sets of trippers independently activates a sequence-delay timer and an 8 pole, double throw latching relay. The sequence timer (Herbach and Rademan, Philadelphia, Pennsylvania) consists of a slow moving clock motor whose shaft turns several adjustable cams. These cams sequentially depress circumferentially mounted microswitches which emit intermittent pulses to an automatic pipetter coupled to a fraction collector (Gilson Medical Electronics, Middleton, Wisconsin). The pipetter samples the culture four times and delivers each 15-ml sample to test tubes in the rotating fraction collector table. The first three samples are discarded since they serve to flush out the connecting lines and only the fourth sample, which is rapidly mixed with 0.2 ml of Bouin's fixative previously placed in each tube, is retained for counting. Cell counts are performed on properly diluted aliquots with an electronic cell counter (Coulter Co., Hialeah, Florida) previously calibrated for this cell type.

The latching relay governs the phases of the temperature cycle by alternatively directing the flow of water through the coils in the culture vessel from either a "hot" or a "cold" water bath. Paired solenoid valves (Automatic Switch Co., Florham Park, New Jersey) control the inflow and outflow of each bath. In addition the temperature level of each bath is also controlled through the switching of the relay: during the cold period a pair of thermoregulators sets the cold bath at the desired cold period temperature (in this case 14.5°C) and permits the hot bath to rise to a temperature higher than that of the warm period. During the warm period a second pair of thermoregulators is put into operation and the cold bath is now set to drop below 14.5°C while the hot bath is kept at 28.5°C (the temperature of the warm period). Thus, by allowing the hot bath to be warmer and the cold bath to be colder than the ultimate temperature levels of the cycle (when their water is not being circulated through the culture), an artificially higher temperature gradient is established at each temperature shift and the extra heat capacity of each bath is employed to reduce the transition periods considerably. We have found that by this device even two 5-liter cultures can be rapidly cooled and heated with conventional size water baths (Forma Scientific, Inc., Marietta, Ohio) of 20- to 30-gallon capacity. Additional refinements can be introduced in each bath so that the temperature constancy is kept well below ±0.1°C.

3. Synchrony Stability and Repetitiveness

A direct result of conducting these studies against a well-defined chemical background has been the finding that very subtle but necessary synchrony stabilizing agents are some reduced sulfur compounds (Padilla and James, 1960; James, 1960). Among several, thioglycollic acid (2-mercaptoacetic acid) is the most effective. This substance appears to perform at least two interrelated functions: (a) it permits *Astasia* to respond to the synchrony-inducing temperature cycle, and (b) it stabilizes the synchronized population so it does not drift out of phase with the temperature program. To be sure, stability in the synchronized system derives from a rigorously applied temperature cycle, as well as maintenance of optimum conditions for growth (such as proper aeration) (Blum and Padilla, 1962). But even with the temperature cycle outlined above, thioglycollic acid is required for the system to operate satisfactorily, as shown in Fig. 3.

The upper portion of Fig. 3 shows six consecutive cycles for cells repeatedly diluted with fresh medium but kept at a constant thioglycollic acid concentration (5×10^{-5} M). The lower portion shows a parallel culture "synchronized" in the absence of this compound and similarly diluted. It is obvious that without thioglycollic acid the bursts of division gradually drift into the cold period with a resultant departure from complete cell doublings at the end of each warm period. Moreover, the slope of the log-linear portion of each burst decreases, possibly indicating a progressive lengthening of the time required for cytokinesis. In essence, without a reduced sulfur source continuous synchrony is lost, and the

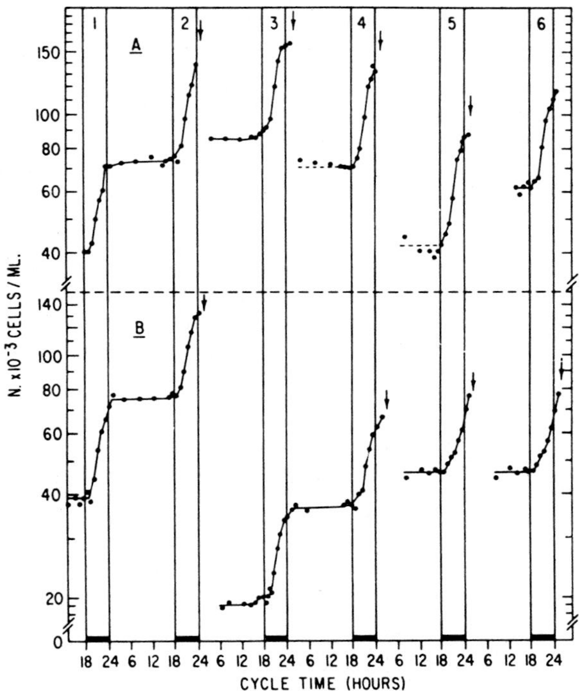

FIG. 3. The effect of thioglycollic acid on the synchrony pattern of *Astasia longa* grown on Cramer-Myers medium. The upper portion of the graph (A) shows the behavior of a culture to which thioglycollic acid was added to a concentration of 5×10^{-5} *M* at the time of dilution shown by each arrow. The lower portion of the graph (B) shows a parallel culture repeatedly diluted without addition of thioglycollic acid. The ordinate gives the population density and the abscissa shows the cycle time. The cold period (14.5°C) was 17.5 hours long and the warm period (28.5°C), indicated by the bar, was of 6.5 hours duration.

quality of repetitiveness decreases in the system. The metabolic function of thioglycollic acid itself is not yet known, but the rapid uptake at a time coincident with the burst of division suggests it is closely linked to the process of cell division (James, 1961b).

The question naturally arises as to whether repetitiveness of cell division is reflected in the biochemical activities of the synchronized cells. In other words, does synchrony occur in cellular processes other than cytokinesis? In partial answer to this question the protein and dry weight contents of *Astasia*, assayed colorimetrically and gravimetrically, were examined in consecutive synchronous cycles. The results of such determinations are shown in Fig. 4. The upper portion of the graph shows the pattern of

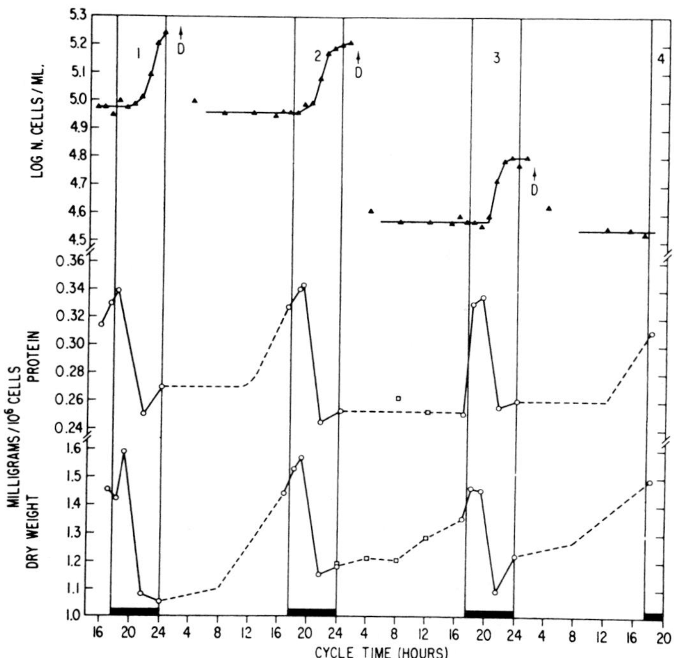

FIG. 4. Total protein levels and dry weights of synchronized *Astasia longa* during four consecutive cycles. The abscissa shows the cycle time, with the 6.5-hour warm period (28.5°C) indicated by the black bar. The upper tracing (▲——▲) represents the synchrony pattern expressed as the logarithm of the population density. The middle and lower curves relate to the total protein content and dry weights expressed in milligrams/10^6 cells. Total proteins were determined by the Lowry method (Lowry *et al.*, 1951). Between the second and third warm periods several samples of cells were stored at 2°C overnight before being assayed. The corrected values of such determinations are indicated by the open squares. All other determinations were performed on fresh samples and represent mean values of triplicate aliquots.

synchrony and the middle and lower tracings indicate the changes in the protein and dry weight contents of the cells.

In spite of some variation in the timing of the onset of cell division, the pattern of protein synthesis appears unaffected. The cells regularly attain maximum protein level of approximately 0.34 mg/10^6 cells in the first 2 hours of the warm period, and a minimum level of 0.25 mg/10^6 cells in the last 2 hours of the warm period. This value is not one half of the maximum level since the interval of cytokinesis and minimum protein production are not coincident throughout the entire population of cells, some protein being synthesized during the burst of division (Blum and

Padilla, 1962). In any event, it is clear that protein synthesis is repetitively synchronized and closely parallels the cytological events.

Changes in the dry weight content, on the other hand, show some fluctuations, but in amplitude rather than periodicity. As with the protein content, the maximum dry weight of the cells is achieved in the first 2 hours of the warm period, but with each ensuing warm period this level decreases slightly. In the fourth warm period, only a portion of which is shown, the maximum level rises again, showing a return to the previous level.

To determine the patterns of synthetic activity occurring in the cold period, suggested by the broken lines, samples of cells were removed, stored in culture medium at 2°C overnight, and assayed for their total protein and a dry weight content. Cells stored at this temperature for 8 hours or longer lost as much as 25% of their protein content. This loss was in part reflected in the decreased dry weight of the cells which was found to be constant for the duration of the cold storage. The corrected values are shown in Fig. 4 only to suggest the over-all patterns of change. It is not clear at this time why cells should lose so much material when stored at low temperatures.

The above results clearly indicate that in the over-all aspects, *A. longa* is finely attuned to its temperature program. As reported elsewhere, such a phase relationship relates also to the time course of nucleic acid synthesis, which, as in the case of proteins, occurs in the latter portions of the cold period and most of the warm period, exclusive of the time of cytokinesis (Blum and Padilla, 1962). It is to be emphasized, however, that these values still relate to an *average* cell and not a single cell. As such, however, they are amenable to statistical considerations. In this sense then, fluctuations do not necessarily reflect deviations of a single cell from its norm, but rather represent the retention of variability usually associated with cell populations (James, 1961a). If the population is approaching the behavior of a single cell, is its synchrony dependent on the continual imposition of the temperature cycle? How will a synchronized population of cells behave when placed at constant temperature? The results shown in Fig. 5 indicate that for some time, at least, the temperature-induced alignment is retained by *A. longa.*

In this particular experiment, the temperature cycle was interrupted at the end of the second warm period and the cells were then kept at the higher temperature (28.5°C). The cell population, upon completing its division, paused slightly and then resumed cytokinesis in a phased manner. This phased pattern persisted for approximately two generations, after which the characteristic log-linear rate of growth was resumed, with a generation time of approximately 11 hours. Although not clear at the

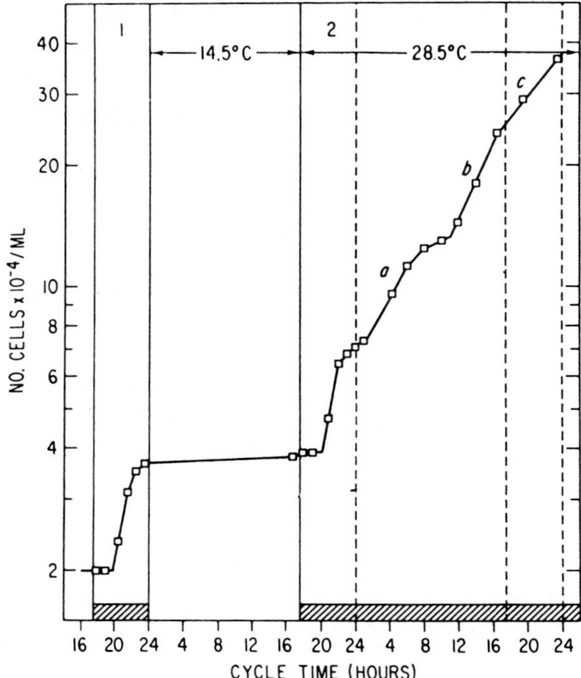

FIG. 5. Oscillatory pattern of growth of synchronized *Astasia* released from the temperature cycle. The curve shows the behavior of cells subsequent to their release from the temperature-inducing cycle to the temperature of the warm period (28.5°C). The dotted vertical lines indicate the times at which the ensuing temperature shifts would have occurred. In the first burst the cells doubled in number in 2.5 hours, in the second burst in 3.0 hours. Following release they showed three distinct log-linear rates of division with slopes equivalent to the following generation times: a = 6.5 hours, b = 6.5 hours, and c = 11 hours.

present time, a variety of feedback mechanisms must be involved in the retention of such an alignment and may be related to some form of control which is lost by the cells after two cell divisions at constant temperature.

IV. Concluding Remarks

The inherent quality of repetitiveness that is seen in the synchrony of *Euglena* and *Astasia*, it is hoped, does not rest with a uniqueness of these organisms, but rather represents the ability of the cell cycle to adapt to an externally applied cycle of stresses. If one considers a cell lineage as a discontinuous series of events grossly subdivided into an interphase and a mitotic phase, synchrony derived by these methods becomes but an alignment of cellular activities. In terms of developmental patterns, synchrony is the segregation of age classes, which in turn reflects temporally distributed cellular events.

It is apparent that at the present time synchrony in *Euglena* and *Astasia* cannot be operationally described in molecular terms. But it is also clear that since under these systems the cells are able to grow and divide, this presents an experimenter with a well-defined model of cellular growth and division for further experimentation (Padilla and Blum, 1961, 1962). That the present approach does not represent a cul de sac is to be determined by future studies, particularly in terms of whatever useful information can be derived from such synchronized systems. It is hoped, moreover, that the present approach will be extended to other cell types by those investigators least fearful of adventure.

References

Abbo, F., and Pardee, A. B. (1960). *Biochim. Biophys. Acta* **39,** 478.

Barner, H. D., and Cohen, S. S. (1956). *J. Bacteriol.* **72,** 115.

Blum, J. J., and Padilla, G. M. (1962). *Exptl. Cell Res.* **28,** 512.

Buetow, D. D., and Levedahl, B. H. (1962). *J. Gen. Microbiol.* **28,** 578.

Cook, J. R. (1960). "Light-Induced Division Synchrony of *Euglena gracilis* and the Effects of Visible Light on Related Cells." Doctoral dissertation, Univ. of California, Los Angeles.

Cook, J. R. (1961). *Plant Cell Physiol.* **2,** 199.

Cook, J. R. (1962). *Biol. Bull.* **121,** 277.

Cook, J. R., and James, T. W. (1960). *Exptl. Cell Res.* **21,** 583.

Cramer, M., and Myers, J. (1952). *Arch. Mikrobiol.* **17,** 384.

Dyer, D. L., and Richardson, D. E. (1962). *Appl. Microbiol.* **10,** 129.

Hutchens, J. O., Podolsky, B., and Morales, M. F. (1948). *J. Cellular Comp. Physiol.* **32,** 117.

James, T. W. (1960). *Ann. N. Y. Acad. Sci.* **90,** 550.

James, T. W. (1961a). *Ann. Rev. Microbiol.* **15,** 27.

James, T. W. (1961b). *Pathol. Biol. Semaine Hop.* **9,** 510.

James, T. W., and Padilla, G. M. (1959). *In* "Proceedings of the First National Biophysics Conference" (H. Quastler, ed.), p. 694. Yale Univ. Press, New Haven, Connecticut.

Lowry, O. H., Rosebrough, N. J., Farr, A. L., and Randall, R. J. (1951). *J. Biol. Chem.* **193,** 265.

Monod, J. (1950). *Ann. Inst. Pasteur* **79,** 390.

Moser, H. (1958). *Carnegie Inst. Wash. Publ. No.* **614.**

Myers, J., and Clark, L. B. (1944). *J. Gen. Physiol.* **28,** 103.

Novick, A., and Szilard, L. (1950). *Proc. Natl. Acad. Sci. U. S.* **36,** 708.

Novick, A., and Szilard, L. (1951). *Cold Spring Harbor Symp. Quant. Biol.* **16,** 337.

Padilla, G. M. (1960). "Studies on the Synchronization of Cell Division in the Colorless Flagellate *Astasia longa*." Doctoral dissertation, Univ. of California, Los Angeles.

Padilla, G. M., and Blum, J. J. (1961). *First Ann. Meeting Am. Soc. Cell Biol., Chicago, Illinois, 1961*, p. 160.

Padilla, G. M., and Blum, J. J. (1962). *Second Ann. Meeting Am. Soc. Cell Biol., San Francisco, California, 1962*, p. 41.

Padilla, G. M., and Cook, J. R. (1963). *In* "Synchrony in Cell Division and Growth" (E. Zeuthen, ed.). Wiley (Interscience), New York. In press.

Padilla, G. M., and James, T. W. (1960). *Exptl. Cell Res.* **20,** 401.

Scherbaum, O., and Zeuthen, E. (1954). *Exptl. Cell Res.* **6,** 221.

Wilson, B. W. (1962). "Controlled Growth and the Regulation of Metabolism of the Flagellates *Astasia* and *Euglena*." Doctoral dissertation, Univ. of California, Los Angeles.

Wilson, B. W., and James, T. W. (1963). *Exptl. Cell Res.* In press.

Zeuthen, E. (1958). *Advan. Biol. Med. Phys.* **6,** 37.

Chapter 10

Handling and Culturing of Chlorella

ADOLF KUHL and HARALD LORENZEN

Pflanzenphysiologisches Institut der Universität Göttingen, Germany

I. Introduction

Since the year 1919, when Warburg—in the course of his early studies on photosynthesis—introduced the unicellular green alga *Chlorella* into physiological research work, an immense number of studies in photosynthesis and in nearly all fields of plant physiology has been done with this organism or closely related types. It was soon proven that among the main advantages of this organism in research work were the relatively simple handling and culture methods under conditions which could be easily controlled. In addition, a much better reproducibility of experimental results could be obtained than with "higher plants." It is therefore understandable that great effort was spent and will continue to be in order to determine the best conditions for culturing and growing these valuable experimental organisms. It cannot be the task of this article to compile all the facts about the culturing of unicellular algae and to discuss them in every respect, but we will try to give an introduction to the handling of these organisms by providing the information necessary for the successful culturing and growing of *Chlorella* and other unicellular green algae.

The reader of this article, however, should keep in mind that its perusal should be accompanied by the study of the basic facts of plant physiology, especially algal physiology. For this purpose we have listed a number of books and review articles helpful for a general study of algal culture and metabolism. Pertinent articles not cited in the text are listed in the references and are marked with an asterisk.

II. The Organisms and Their Growth

A. General Considerations

The organisms comprising the genus *Chlorella* are nonmotile, globular, unicellular green algae with an average diameter of 4 to 10μ (Fig. 1).

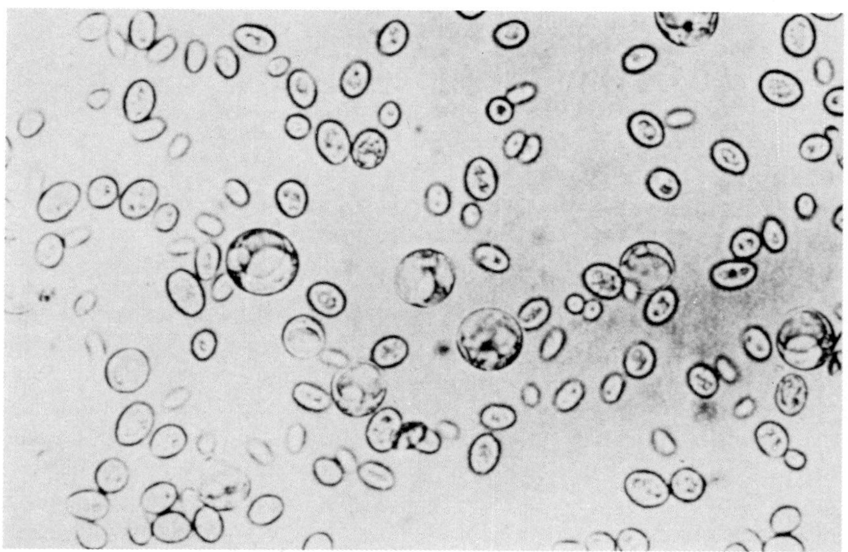

FIG. 1. Microphotograph of a *Chlorella* culture grown at 25°C in continuous fluorescent light (6000 lux) and provided with an air-CO_2 mixture (98:2). The average diameter of the large cells is 20–25μ (All the microphotographs in this article represent *C. pyrenoidosa*, strain 211-8b, of the "Algensammlung des Pflanzenphysiologischen Instituts der Universität Göttingen").

Under favorable environmental conditions the cells grow rapidly and reproduce by asexual division into 2, 4, 8, or 16 autospores. The number of autospores (daughter cells) released by a so-called "mother cell" is controlled either by internal or external conditions. The autospore liberation process itself is not light dependent and can take place in darkness after *Chlorella* has actively increased its cell mass in light. To promote a vigorous and healthy growth of an experimental culture, *Chlorella*, suspended in a liquid medium with a suitable composition of mineral nutrients in adequate concentration, must be supplied with sufficient carbon dioxide as well as with light energy in the visible range of the spectrum. Likewise, the culture must be held at a favorable temperature and be continuously agitated to prevent sedimentation of the algal cells. The agitation ensures, in addition, that all the cells of a culture on the average are equally exposed to light. For normal propagation of *Chlorella* the cultures are illuminated continuously. In such a culture, algae at all stages of the life cycle are present at the same time. If the course of the growth of an algal culture is demonstrated by plotting cell number, cell substance, or packed-cell volume against time, a characteristic S-shaped curve (growth curve) results.

Chlorella are strictly dependent on light for autotrophic growth; therefore, the course of the growth curve is governed by the illumination of the culture. Provided that all external conditions are held constant, the course of growth can be discussed, in a very abbreviated form, as follows: at the start, in a culture inoculated with a small number of active cells, the light energy received by each cell is above the saturation point and does not limit growth. The increase in cell quantity proceeds "exponentially" (exponential phase of growth). Due to the increasing number of algal cells in the suspension, the organisms shade each other so that the light input per cell is approximately constant. From this fact it follows that the increase in cell quantity plotted against time becomes "linear" (linear phase of growth). The third region of the growth curve is characterized by the high density of the suspension. The increase in cell quantity per unit of time now decreases, almost approaching zero. These are only a few remarks about the characteristics of the kinetics of algal growth. They are very incomplete, but in this article we will deal principally with the culturing of *Chlorella* from a more practical point of view. More complete treatments of the theoretical considerations of the relations between the growth of the culture as a whole and the illumination are given by Tamiya *et al.* (1953b) and Myers (1953, 1962a). Often, the growth of an algal culture is expressed as production, which means the rate of increase in cell quantity within a certain time. Another characteristic of the growth of an algal culture may be given by the "generation time." It is defined as the time in which the cell number doubles (James, 1961).

These considerations are necessary because of the fact that the physiological and biochemical characteristics of a *Chlorella* culture are known to vary to a great extent during the different growth phases. It is therefore important to control the conditions, especially with respect to the time of harvesting of *Chlorella* cells for experimental work, in order to obtain reproducible experimental results. Changes of physiological and biochemical characteristics of *Chlorella* are brought about by changes in the environmental conditions too. Changes in the supply of the mineral nutrients especially result in very marked differences in the chemical composition of *Chlorella* (Spoehr and Milner, 1949). The organic matter of a normally grown culture of *C. pyrenoidosa* is composed of 53% C, 7.5% H, 28.5% O, and 10.8% N (Myers, 1960, 1962b). From this the approximate percentage of the main cell compounds can be calculated. On a dry weight basis these are: protein, 50%; carbohydrate, 30%; lipid, 15%; and ash, 5%. The chlorophyll content may vary between 1.5 and 4.0% on the average. Under certain conditions a great part of the ash may consist of phosphate originating from inorganic, condensed phosphates (polyphosphate) which can be accumulated by *Chlorella* to a great extent (Kuhl, 1960, 1962).

Under autotrophic conditions (with only an inorganic carbon source available) *Chlorella* grows photosynthetically. If the organisms are supplied with glucose or another suitable organic compound as the sole carbon source, they will grow as well heterotrophically. In the latter case the organic compound will be partially oxidized to release energy which in turn is necessary to convert the remaining part of the compound into cellular material. The problems of heterotrophic nutrition of algae are discussed in detail by Pringsheim (1959).

For most investigations three species of *Chlorella* are in use. These are *C. vulgaris*, *C. pyrenoidosa*, and *C. ellipsoidea*. In all of these species different strains are known which differ markedly in physiological characteristics. It seems appropriate, therefore, to make some short remarks about the taxonomy of the genus *Chlorella* before we deal with the handling and culturing of these organisms.

B. Taxonomic Remarks

One should be aware of the fact that in a strict sense the name *Chlorella* in many cases only represents a type. It is not easy to distinguish the *Chlorella* species taxonomically on the basis of microscopic examination alone. This is the one important reason we advise the use of a culture whose identity is known beyond any doubt. There are a great many differences in physiological behavior and great variations in metabolism (Myers, 1962b) which are not reflected in clearly marked differences in morphology. Pure cultures are therefore labeled with strain numbers. To prevent misunderstandings and discrepancies in interpreting experimental results, it should be a general rule for anyone working with an algal culture to describe his culture and techniques as exactly as possible. Such a description should state—in addition to culture methods—the genus, strain number, and the origin of the culture. For most investigations it is desirable to use a defined algal strain of one of the well-known culture collections (Appendix).

Recently there were published some very interesting and promising attempts to revise the old and imperfect classification of the genus *Chlorella* on the basis of a comparative study of the occurrence and specific combination of a number of morphological, physiological, and biochemical criteria. Morphological differences alone are not sufficient. Kessler (1962) and Kessler and Soeder (1962) proposed using hydrogenase activity to differentiate between the species *C. pyrenoidosa* (+ hydrogenase activity) and *C. vulgaris* (− hydrogenase activity). This difference partly parallels the ability to produce secondary carotinoids or inability to produce them in the case of nitrogen deficiency (Kessler *et al.*, 1963). Soeder (1962, 1963) compared cell morphology under standardized conditions and completed the description by the statement of biochemical and physiological characteristics. Shihira and Krauss (1963) investigated the physiology of nutrition of a series of known *Chlorella* strains, and their results in general correspond to those of Kessler and Soeder (1962) as far as classification is concerned.

III. The Culture of *Chlorella*

A. Normal Culture Methods

1. Stock Cultures

For most investigations it is desirable to start with a pure culture, which should best be obtained from one of the aforementioned culture collections. Such pure cultures are always derived from a single parent cell and are propagated with the precautions necessary to prevent contamination by other microorganisms. To retain these cultures over a longer period of time, it is advantageous to prepare test tube cultures using media solidified with 1% agar. Contamination of algal stock cultures by bacteria can be easily observed by adding peptone (0.1%) and glucose (1.0%) to the media in a convenient concentration; this will promote bacterial growth much more rapidly than algal growth. Tube cultures are normally kept at room temperature under artificial or natural light but not in direct sunshine. A transfer of these algae onto fresh agar slants every 6–8 weeks is, in most cases, sufficient. For regular inoculation of experimental cultures, however, liquid stock cultures are superior since agar slant cultures are not as uniform because the cell layers on the agar surface are differently supplied with light and nutrients, a situation involving shading and diffusion problems. An inhomogeneous inoculum is therefore obtained by simply washing the cells from the agar surface. From the liquid stock cultures the algae are transferred to the culture vessel under sterile conditions when necessary. A box containing an ultraviolet lamp is very helpful for maintenance of sterile conditions during the inoculation procedure. Microscopic examination of the stock culture, preferably with phase contrast equipment, before the inoculation of vessels should be a matter of course. If a stock culture of a strain under investigation should become contaminated with other microorganisms, it can best be purified by the methods extensively used and demonstrated by Pringsheim (1949, 1951).

In connection with the handling and keeping of stock cultures over a period of years, the problem of constancy with respect to morphological and physiological characteristics is very important. Fortunately, it seems that among most of the frequently used strains of *Chlorella* there is no evidence of a tendency for much spontaneous mutation. On the other hand, there exist a great number of mutant strains of *Chlorella*, the mutation of which were induced by ultraviolet radiation. Most of these have alterations with respect to their carotenoid composition. The characteristics of numerous ultraviolet-induced mutant strains of *Chlorella* are given by Bendix and Allen (1962).

2. Carbon Sources

The results of an elementary analysis reveal that approximately one half of the ash-free dry substances of *Chlorella* is carbon (Myers, 1960). Therefore, the most important problem of algal nutrition in liquid cultures is an adequate carbon supply. This problem is met by aerating the algal suspensions with a mixture of air and carbon dioxide, most often in the ratio 95:5 as suggested by Warburg (1919). In many laboratories air-CO_2 mixtures with a lower CO_2 concentration (1–2% CO_2) are in use. The gas stream bubbling through the suspension must in any case be sufficient to support a satisfactory CO_2 diffusion gradient between the gas and the liquid phases. In an illuminated algal suspension the medium is not in equilibrium with the gas phase with respect to CO_2 because the algae take up CO_2 to an extent that a gradient results between the gas and liquid phase which is proportional to the CO_2 uptake. The effectiveness of providing a sufficient CO_2 level in the media by raising the CO_2 concentration of the gas mixture is limited, according to the results of Steemann Nielsen (1955). The continuous bubbling of the air-CO_2 mixture influences the pH value maintained in the culture, which on the other hand governs the equilibrium of the three different forms: free CO_2, HCO_3^- and $CO_3^=$ (Emerson and Green, 1938). This fact may be of importance, for most *Chlorella* strains take up CO_2 principally in the undissociated form. Using culture vessels of the types which are shown in Fig. 4, approximately 20 liters of gas per hour for each vessel are sufficient. From the elementary analysis of algal dry substance one can easily calculate that for a production of 1 gm of this matter, 1.83 gm of CO_2 are needed. This amount corresponds to nearly 1 liter of CO_2 under laboratory conditions. For smaller scale cultures the gas mixture can be taken directly from high pressure cylinders containing air-CO_2 mixtures. Larger quantities of the gas mixture are more economically prepared by a continuously working gas mixing device in which the two gases are combined by utilizing calibrated glass capillary tubes under constant pressure. In addition to providing the carbon as CO_2, most strains of *Chlorella* are able to grow on glucose or acetate as the sole carbon sources (Pringsheim, 1959). Using glucose as the carbon source, the pigmentation of several strains may be altered since chlorophyll, which is present in autotrophically grown cultures, can decrease to such a degree that the culture appears yellow (Bergmann, 1955; Pringsheim, 1959; Lie, 1963). In working with organic carbon sources, it is important to prevent contamination of the cultures with bacteria or molds because the growth of these organisms is selectively promoted over that of the algae.

3. Nutrient Media

One finds in the literature liquid media in which unicellular algae of the *Chlorella* type grow vigorously, although the compositions of these media vary to a great extent. Fortunately, most *Chlorella* strains tolerate a broad range of salt and hydrogen ion concentrations so that normally the composition of the medium is not so very critical. Often, a culture medium which has been used with good success in a particular laboratory for a specific organism can be utilized without any modifications. The formula shown in Table I (from Kuhl, 1962) represents a nutrient medium that has been in use for years in the Pflanzenphysiologisches Institut der Universität Göttingen for cultures grown under continuous illumination, for synchronized cultures of *Chlorella*, and for many unicellular green

TABLE I

NUTRIENT MEDIUM FOR UNICELLULAR GREEN ALGAE[a]

Compound	Mg/liter	Concentration (moles/liter)
KNO_3	1011.10	1×10^{-2}
$NaH_2PO_4 \cdot 1H_2O$	621.0	4.5×10^{-3}
$Na_2HPO_4 \cdot 2H_2O$	89.0	0.5×10^{-3}
$MgSO_4 \cdot 7H_2O$	246.50	1×10^{-3}
$CaCl_2 \cdot 2H_2O$	14.70	1×10^{-4}
$FeSO_4 \cdot 7H_2O$ Fe-EDTA complex[b]	6.95	2.5×10^{-5}
H_3BO_3	0.061	1×10^{-6}
$MnSO_4 \cdot 1H_2O$	0.169	1×10^{-6}
$ZnSO_4 \cdot 7H_2O$	0.287	1×10^{-6}
$CuSO_4 \cdot 5H_2O$	0.00249	1×10^{-8}
$(NH_4)_6Mo_7O_{24} \cdot 4H_2O$	0.01235	1×10^{-8}
pH about 6		

[a] From Kuhl (1962).

[b] Preparation of the Fe-EDTA complex: 0.69 gm $FeSO_4 \cdot 7H_2O$ and 0.93 gm disodium-salt of EDTA are dissolved in 80 ml of double distilled H_2O by boiling for a short time. After the solution is cooled to room temperature it is made up to 100 ml. It contains in 1 ml the iron concentration stated above.

algae. Its composition has not been the subject of a critical investigation in every respect. Other formulas are to be found in the valuable articles of Krauss (1953) and Myers (1960). Nutrient solutions are commonly prepared by using concentrated "stock solutions" of the individual components. These solutions are then mixed in the proper proportions and diluted to the concentration desired. Time can be saved by combining the trace elements in one "stock solution," which should be slightly acidified to prevent contamination with living organisms. Freshly made culture media may be sterilized after filling the culture vessels or reserve bottles either in flowing steam or by autoclaving at higher pressure. During this procedure, a very slight precipitate may be formed which has proven to be without influence on the growth of *Chlorella*. Usually, glass distilled water is used for preparing nutrient solutions. De-ionized water from an ion exchange column is just as useful. If water with a higher degree of purification is indispensable, quartz distilled water may be necessary. If the algal culture in continuous light is to be grown to a dense suspension, the amount of nitrogen supplied in the media listed in Table I may not be sufficient. Taking into account the fact that most unicellular algae contain about 8% nitrogen on a dry weight basis (Myers, 1960), the nitrogen supplied by the above KNO_3 concentration makes possible a dry weight production of 1.75 gm per liter of solution. If very dense suspensions are required, KNO_3 can be supplied in a concentration two or three times higher than normal or repeatedly given in smaller portions during the course of growth. Since NO_3^- uptake is accompanied by a decrease in hydrogen ion concentration, which in turn markedly influences the availability of certain ions (precipitation of Ca, Mg, and Fe-phosphates), it may be advantageous to replace the NO_3 ion by the NH_4 ion. In this case the pH value will be lowered. No change in pH occurs if the culture is supplied with urea; however, not all strains of *Chlorella* can utilize this source of nitrogen. These questions were discussed in detail by Syrett (1962). The pH value of the freshly prepared media (Table I) is between 6.1 and 6.3, which is due to the buffering action of the two phosphate ions. Lower pH values are preferable since the precipitation of Ca^{++}, Mg^{++}, and Fe-phosphates is restricted. It may be helpful to note that most *Chlorella* strains tolerate phosphate concentrations much higher than normally supplied. This fact is important if it is necessary to maintain the pH value of the nutrient solution fairly constant. Even a tenfold higher phosphate ion concentration will not prevent good growth of most *Chlorella* strains. For a steady and sufficient supply of the trace elements the introduction of chelating agents is very valuable. By using these compounds, the trace element cations easily form reversible complexes, the splitting of which steadily supplies the algae with the amounts required. By far the most commonly used chelating agent today is ethylenediamine tetraacetic acid (EDTA). It is not metabolized by most microorganisms so that even in a nonsterile medium it does not support the growth of contaminants. Instead of supplying it as the disodium salt, which is the common practice, we prefer to produce an Fe-EDTA complex solution by which the availability of iron is greatly increased above the level obtained with normal methods.

It should be noted here that the proposed concentrations and the number of trace elements (in Table I) are not the result of a detailed study. The work of Walker (1953, 1954) pertains to these problems. The addition of these trace elements (Table I) will satisfy the known requirements and be a matter of precaution when other requirements are suspected but unconfirmed. These short statements about the composition of the nutrient media can not cover all the details of algal nutrition. It is to be emphasized that the effects and importance of single components are not discussed here. Answers to these problems are comprehensively provided in the review articles of Krauss (1953, 1958) and Ketchum (1954). The article of Wiessner (1962) concerns the physiological effect of micronutrients. For the functional aspects of mineral nutrition one should refer to Pirson (1955).

4. Light

Laboratory cultures of algae are customarily provided with artificial illumination. For photosynthetic activity and growth these organisms are able to employ that light which they can absorb by their chlorophylls or the accessory pigments. This means in a practical sense that for cell production, only light in the spectral range between 400 and 700 mμ is effective. Unfortunately, all artificial light sources have emission spectra which are not very similar to natural light. Usually, tungsten or fluorescent lamps are used to illuminate algal cultures. The emission of the former continuously increases from the blue to the red parts of the visible spectrum with a relatively high heat development, which is often a disturbing factor. In comparison to incandescent lamps, fluorescent lamps are more efficient, for they convert a larger part of electric energy to light. In this type of lamp, however, the radiation from the persisting mercury lines could be responsible for unfavorable effects on algal growth. This is one reason why the use of fluorescent lamps has often met with some criticism. In a recent investigation Tipnis and Pratt (1962) compared the influence on algal culture of light emitted by fluorescent lamps with that emitted by incandescent lamps. This study revealed very interesting effects in the chemical composition of the algae indicating that incandescent lamps are preferable. In many laboratories, however, different types of fluorescent lamps are successfully used to illuminate algal cultures so that they can be recommended without any reservation.

The light intensities commonly chosen for vigorous growth of *Chlorella* in continuously illuminated cultures are in the range between 6000 and 12,000 lux as measured at the surface of the culture vessel. The growth of cultures is not limited to this range, for even with lower light intensities (500–3000 lux) a healthy growth can be obtained. An examination of growth with respect to light intensity and temperature was reported by Halldal and French (1958).

Xenon high pressure lamps, with their high light output and favorable spectra, have been used with great success by Warburg and Krippahl (1962) to produce large amounts of *Chlorella* in ordinary glass beakers. Using lamps which emit light with differences in the spectral composition, one must always be aware of the fact that the chemical composition of *Chlorella*, especially with respect to protein and carbohydrate, can vary widely if the red or the blue parts of the spectrum prevail (see Kowallik, 1962; Hauschild *et al.*, 1962). A great difficulty in connection with the illumination is the comparison of light intensities, especially when different light sources are being used. This is so because the relative sensitivity of the different types of photocells may lead to false results. Without giving detailed descriptions of measuring devices and methods, the intensities of different light sources cannot be compared without reservation. It is desirable in these cases to describe as exactly as possible the type of lamp and the precise distance between it and the culture vessel.

5. Temperature

The rate of growth of an algal culture is influenced by the temperature applied. Many of the standard species and strains of *Chlorella* grow best at a certain temperature characteristic for each strain (optimum temperature). Although temperature sensitivity may differ from one strain to another, constant temperatures of the nutrient solution in the range from 20° to 30°C will be quite satisfactory for normal culture techniques. The optimum temperature for the most frequently used strains of *Chlorella* lies within this range, 25°C being most often used. Certain strains, however, may have higher optimum temperatures. Sorokin and Myers (1953) isolated a high temperature strain of *Chlorella* with optimum growth at 39°C. The duration of the life cycle of this particular strain is extremely short, as was revealed in experiments with synchronous culture (Section III,C). It is evident, however, that for preserving cultures on agar slants, especially the temperature should ideally be between 16° and 18°C since growth should not be so vigorous as to require frequent transfers to fresh agar slants.

6. Apparatus for Usual Culture Methods

A great variety of culture apparatus is described in the literature. It is common to all of them that they must fulfill the demands for constant conditions: temperature, light, and an air-CO_2 mixture, all of which in addition to an adequate supply of nutrient media are necessary for healthy growth of algal cultures. By far most types of culture apparatus make use of a water bath in which the culture vessels are placed. The volume of such a bath must be of sufficient dimensions so that sudden external temperature changes do not affect the temperature of the culture. As an example, an arrangement designed and in successful use in this institute is demonstrated in Figs. 2 and 3. This type of a light thermostat consists of a well-dimensioned water bath (volume, 120 liters) with Plexiglas® windows (66 × 35 cm) opposite each other. Behind these windows and just in front of a white plastic reflector (for better light utilization), culture vessels of type B or C (Fig. 4) are inserted on each side and connected with the gas supply. The amount of air-CO_2 mixture bubbling through the suspension can be regulated separately for each vessel by a needle valve (maximum of 25 liters per vessel per hour). The gas mixture is delivered

FIG. 2. Light thermostat for the cultivation of *Chlorella* or other unicellular algae. For a detailed description see text. The device for producing the constant air-CO_2 mixture is located behind the culture apparatus.

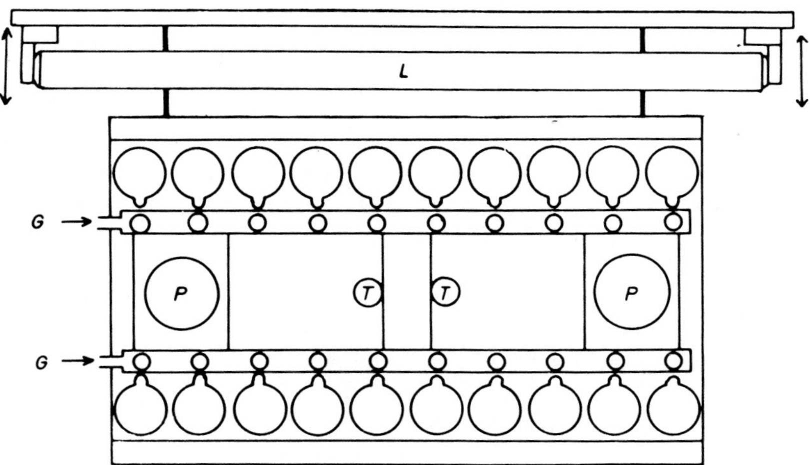

FIG. 3. Schematic representation of the light thermostat (Fig. 2) as viewed from above. G = gas inlets; P = water pumps; T = contact thermometers; L = movable fluorescent lamps mounted on a board.

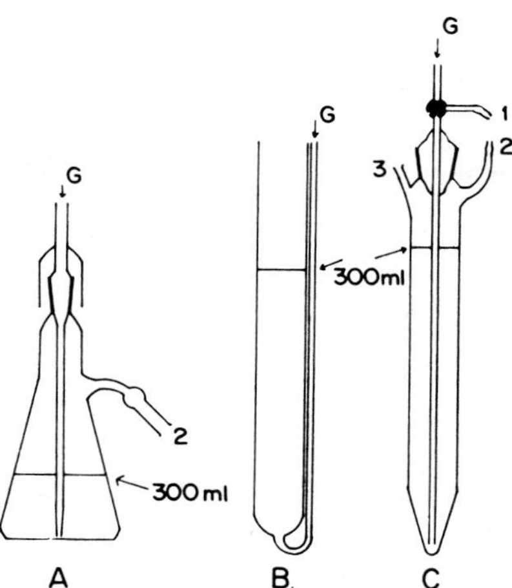

FIG. 4. Culture vessels for laboratory cultures. G = gas inlet. For type C, 1 = sample outlet; 2 = gas outlet; 3 = tube normally closed by a rubber cap. The inner diameter for the vessel of types B and C is about 35 mm.

by a continuously working mixing arrangement. The constant temperature of the water bath is maintained by an immersion heater controlled by a contact thermometer in conjunction with a relay. Normally the bath can be cooled by tap water flowing through a closed cooling system. In other types, designed for use at low temperatures, cooling is accomplished by using a refrigerating machine. To obtain a uniform temperature distribution within the whole bath, especially when illuminated, the bath is equipped with two pumps to circulate the water. The cultures can be darkened on each side of the apparatus separately by sliding a sheet of dark plastic before the Plexiglas® window and by putting a cover over the vessels and the gas inlet tubes to avoid the necessity of darkening the whole room.

Each of the two sides of the thermostat is illuminated by five fluorescent lamps (three of the type, Philips TL 40 W-1/32; and two of the type, TL 40 W-1/55). The fluorescent lamps are mounted on a board that can be moved to change the light intensity within a certain range. An arrangement for switching each lamp on or off separately has proven to be advantageous (Fig. 2). The water bath should be filled with deionized water to retard the growth of undesired microorganisms (including algae) as much as possible. The water must be partially renewed from time to time. For the growth of algae on a smaller scale in filtered light (Schott Glas-Filter), a special light thermostat has been used by Kowallik (1962). If it is not necessary to control strictly the temperature of the cultures, the vessels can be placed around an incandescent lamp and kept at normal room temperature. To reduce the heat radiation from the bulb it can be immersed in a glass jar containing distilled water which is continually cooled by tap water flowing through a copper coil (Pringsheim, 1949).

To grow *Chlorella* over a longer period in an atmosphere of $^{14}CO_2$ (to obtain uniform labeling) a closed system is indispensable. Detailed descriptions are given in the articles of Ellner (1959) and Erb and Maurer (1960).

7. Culture Vessels for Laboratory Cultures

An Erlenmeyer flask closed with a rubber stopper with a gas inlet tube reaching the bottom of the vessel and an outlet tube in a somewhat higher position is often used as a simple and inexpensive culture vessel. These flasks may be placed around an incandescent lamp or can be immersed in a constant water bath and illuminated from either above or below. Higher efficiencies are obtained with glass vessels of different design such as illustrated in Fig. 4. Type A must be either shaken by hand or mechanically to prevent the settling of the algae, while type B or C vessels provide a good mixing of the suspension by aeration. The algae are agitated in order that the light energy input per cell remains fairly constant within a suspension. A special design is the vessel type C, which allows the removal of samples without taking the vessel out of the water bath. Its greatest advantage, however, is the possibility for obtaining samples from the suspension under conditions preventing the contamination of the remaining culture. It works in the following way: turning the three-way stopcock which is normally opened to the gas inlet (G), the sample can be driven out through the inlet now open to the sample outlet (1) with the help of filtered air or nitrogen which is led into the vessel through the normal gas outlet (2), which is normally sealed by a cotton batting. The small tube (3) opposite the gas outlet, which is closed by a rubber cap, can be used to supply the suspension aseptically with injections of substances under investigation. For normal laboratory use culture vessels made of glass are satisfactory. Special investigations may need equipment made of quartz. Despite the fact that plastic material in many instances is very advantageous, it is not commonly used as material for algal culture vessels in the laboratory. For culturing unicellular green algae on a larger scale, especially in outdoor plants, plastic containers are often used. An investigation concerning material used for constructing containers for algal culture was published by Dyer and Richardson (1962).

B. Continuous Culture

In a culture growing in continuous illumination, the increasing cell number is responsible for a decrease in the light intensity received per cell because of mutual shading. This fact, together with changes in the nutrient medium, is the main reason why samples of cells taken from such a culture at different times vary greatly in photosynthetic and biochemical behavior and in chemical composition. These difficulties may be partially overcome by standardized procedures, particularly with respect to the inoculation technique and time of harvesting the samples. Much better results are obtained, however, by the use of samples taken from a culture which is held at a steady state level of growth by the continuous addition of fresh nutrient medium. A culture produced in this way is called a continuous culture, and samples taken from it are very uniform. The first authors to describe an apparatus for the continuous culture of *Chlorella* were Myers and Clark (1944). Their apparatus holds the density of a *Chlorella* population constant by means of an automatic dilution (controlled by a photometric system) of the growing culture with fresh medium from a reservoir. The steady state device offers many advantages; for "both in theory and in practice the continuous culture apparatus yields reproducible experimental material day after day" (Myers, 1960), although, according to the same author, the samples taken from a steady state device do not contain cells which are homogeneous with respect to "age." The frequency distribution of cells at different stages of their life cycle is nevertheless constant. The value of the continuous culture, not only for algae but also for other microorganisms, has been especially demonstrated in the past few years by a great number of relevant articles and detailed descriptions of apparatus. Of great interest in connection with this article is the description of an automatic apparatus for the continuous cultivation of *Chlorella* constructed for special use in the light thermostat shown in Fig. 2 (Senger and Wolf, 1963). We can not deal with all the problems concerning continuous culture here. In this respect the reader is referred to two recent valuable articles of James (1961) and Pfennig and Jannasch (1962). An experimental approach to homogeneous algal cultures arose from the introduction of the methods of synchronization, which are discussed in the following section.

C. Synchronous Culture

1. General Remarks

During the last several years, the well-known methods for the culturing of the green alga *Chlorella* have been extended with techniques of synchronous culture. In the usual type of culture, as well as in continuous cultures, there is always mixed population present which contains cells at all different stages of the algal life cycle. With the aid of the technique of synchronous cultures, it is possible to observe physiological and biochemical activities which are inherently dependent on a particular cell age. Thus, we are able to obtain information concerning the biochemical changes in cell composition and metabolic shifts during the life cycle and to observe the specific effects of trace elements, vitamins, temperature changes, light intensity, light and dark changes, and CO_2 level on the different stages of cell development.

In synchronized cultures the division of cells is restricted to a short time ("bursting division"), while in normal cultures cell divisions occur randomly in time. In connection with these problems, our interest is directed to those methods allowing only complete synchronization, i.e., all or more than 98% of the cells participate in each bursting division and are in phase during the life cycle. In such a culture the degree of synchronization is nearly 1.0. By changing the external conditions we may observe incompletely synchronized cultures. It is necessary to distinguish between two different types of the latter: partially synchronized cultures which are synchronized in two or more groups (Lorenzen, 1957; Pirson and Senger, 1961; Senger, 1961). The most successful methods for the synchronous culture of *Chlorella* and the problems involved are outlined in the following paragraphs.

2. Method of Tamiya and Co-workers

The first method for synchronizing *Chlorella* was developed by Tamiya and his co-workers (1953). They employed a strain of *C. ellipsoidea* and a culture medium with the following composition (Morimura, 1959) per liter: 5.0 gm KNO_3; 2.5 gm $MgSO_4 \cdot 7H_2O$; 1.25 gm KH_2PO_4; 0.0028 gm $FeSO_4 \cdot 7H_2O$; and 1 ml of Arnon's A_5 solution (containing B, Mn, Zn, Cu, and Mo).

At the start, pure algae are taken from an agar slant culture some weeks old (20°–25°C under illumination with daylight fluorescent lamps of 5 kilolux intensity) and transferred into 50 ml of culture solution (25°C, 10 kilolux with daylight fluorescent lamps and with constant aeration with 5% CO_2 in air). This so-called *inoculum* grows over a week, then a 25 ml sample is transferred under sterile conditions into a culture vessel containing 500 ml of solution. This *preculture* is started for the first 5 days with a light intensity of 10 kilolux (250 watt incandescent lamps instead of fluorescent lamps), and following this for 3 days with 0.8 kilolux. The preculture is constantly aerated with CO_2-enriched air and kept at 25°C. At this stage more than 90% of the cells have diameters ranging from 2.5 to 3.5μ. After nearly a 20-fold dilution with fresh culture medium the suspension is centrifuged at 1200*g* for 5 minutes to obtain cells of uniform size. The supernatant cells are centrifuged once more at 1200*g* for 15 minutes, and the Japanese authors now use the packed cells, more than 80% of which are 3.0μ in diameter, as starting material for their *synchronous culture*; such cells are called active dark cells (D_a).

These procedures for obtaining synchronized cells extend over a period of 14 days. The D_a cells are suspended in 500 ml flasks to give an initial cell concentration of about 7×10^6 cells per milliliter. A temperature of 22°C is now used in comparison to a temperature of 16°C, which was employed earlier by the authors. The light intensity of the incandescent lamps remains 10 kilolux. Figure 7A shows the changes in cell number during the one life cycle the authors observe; after nearly 30 hours the division of all cells into 4 daughter cells (autospores) starts and is completed after 10 hours. Therefore, the complete life cycle of *Chlorella* under these external conditions lasts nearly 40 hours, 25% of this time being used for cell division. The cell number at the end of this time is four times larger than the initial number of D_a cells.

3. Method of Sorokin

Sorokin and Myers (1953) introduced the high temperature strain 7-11-05 of *C. pyrenoidosa* for scientific research. Sorokin (1957, 1960) employed synchronous cultures using a continuous culture apparatus (Myers and Clark, 1944) with steady dilution to the desired optical density. Air containing 3.5% CO_2 is bubbled through the algal suspension (39°C and 15 kilolux with fluorescent lamps, pH 6.8). The culture solution contains per liter, in grams: KNO_3, 1.25; KH_2PO_4, 1.25; $MgSO_4 \cdot 7H_2O$, 1.00; $CaCl_2$, 0.0835; H_3BO_3, 0.1142; $FeSO_4 \cdot 7H_2O$, 0.0498; $ZnSO_4 \cdot 7H_2O$, 0.0882; $MnCl_2 \cdot 4H_2O$, 0.0144; MoO_3, 0.0071; $CuSO_4 \cdot 5H_2O$, 0.0157; $Co(NO_3)_2 \cdot 6H_2O$, 0.0049; and EDTA (as a chelating agent), 0.5.

The algae are grown under diurnally intermittent illumination of 9 hours light and 15 hours darkness. After 3 or 4 cycles of this light phase regimen, the suspension at the end of a dark phase contains up to 99% autospores. In all the many papers of Sorokin dealing with synchronous cultures of *Chlorella*, a diagram pertaining to changes in cell number during the growth cycle is not given. He states that "after 9 hours of illumination the walls of the mother cells begin to rupture. During dark periods cells continue to divide" (Sorokin, 1960). Schmidt and King (1961) used the same strain of *Chlorella* (after a preculture at 25°C) at 38.5°C with a light-dark change of 9:9 hours (light intensity: 15 kilolux); in this case the cell divisions start after 11 hours and continue during the following 2 hours. The average yield is 19 daughter cells from each mother cell.

4. Method of Pirson and Lorenzen

The method of Pirson and Lorenzen (1958; Lorenzen, 1956, 1957) is based on light-dark changes in connection with daily dilutions of the suspension to a standard cell number with fresh culture medium. *Chlorella pyrenoidosa* (culture collection of Pflanzenphysiologisches Institut der Universität Göttingen, 211-8b) is washed from the sterile agar slant and transferred into a culture tube (Fig. 4B) containing 300 ml nutrient solution (Table I). In this first phase of growth in the liquid medium the algae are subjected to exactly the same external conditions as during the following periods of synchronous culture. After 2 light-dark changes of 14:10 hours (i.e., 2 periods of 24 hours), the culture has grown to such a density that it is possible to start with a daily dilution to the arbitrary "standard cell number" of 100 ($100 = 1.5 \times 10^6$ cells per milliliter of suspension). At this time the cells have already become completely synchronous; at the beginning of the light phase at least 98% of the cells counted in the first hour of the dark phase have divided. Further manipulations to induce synchronization, such as changes of temperature and light intensity or fractionated centrifugation, are not required. After counting the cells in a counting chamber or hemacytometer, the suspensions are diluted with fresh, sterile culture medium to the "standard cell number." Immediately after this dilution, a new period is started with the application of light. These conditions (30°C, 1.5% CO_2 in air, 10 kilolux) allow a vigorous growth. It is not necessary to maintain the algae under sterile conditions beyond this point. It is only necessary to work under sterile conditions when the cultures are supplied with glucose (Senger, 1962) or other organic nutrients and in all experiments under suboptimal growth conditions (e.g., the use of temperature shocks).

As an example of a completely synchronous culture, Fig. 7C shows that the course of the cell number increases in several succeeding periods of light-dark change (14:10 hours). The differences between the numbers of autospores in each period are very small and do not exceed the error of counting and dilution. There are no cell divisions during illumination, a period when only assimilation and increase in cell volume are taking place. The sum of light provided to each cell is decreasing during the light phase because of growth; this occurs in every culture without continuous dilution. However, it is not an unfavorable influence. By this progressive diminution of light intensity per cell, the organisms will be protected against an inhibitory action of high light intensity. This sensitivity to high light intensities gradually develops as the cells become older (Pirson and Ruppel, 1962). After 14 hours in light (Fig. 5A) the culture must be darkened. At first there are no changes in the cell number, but regularly at the beginning

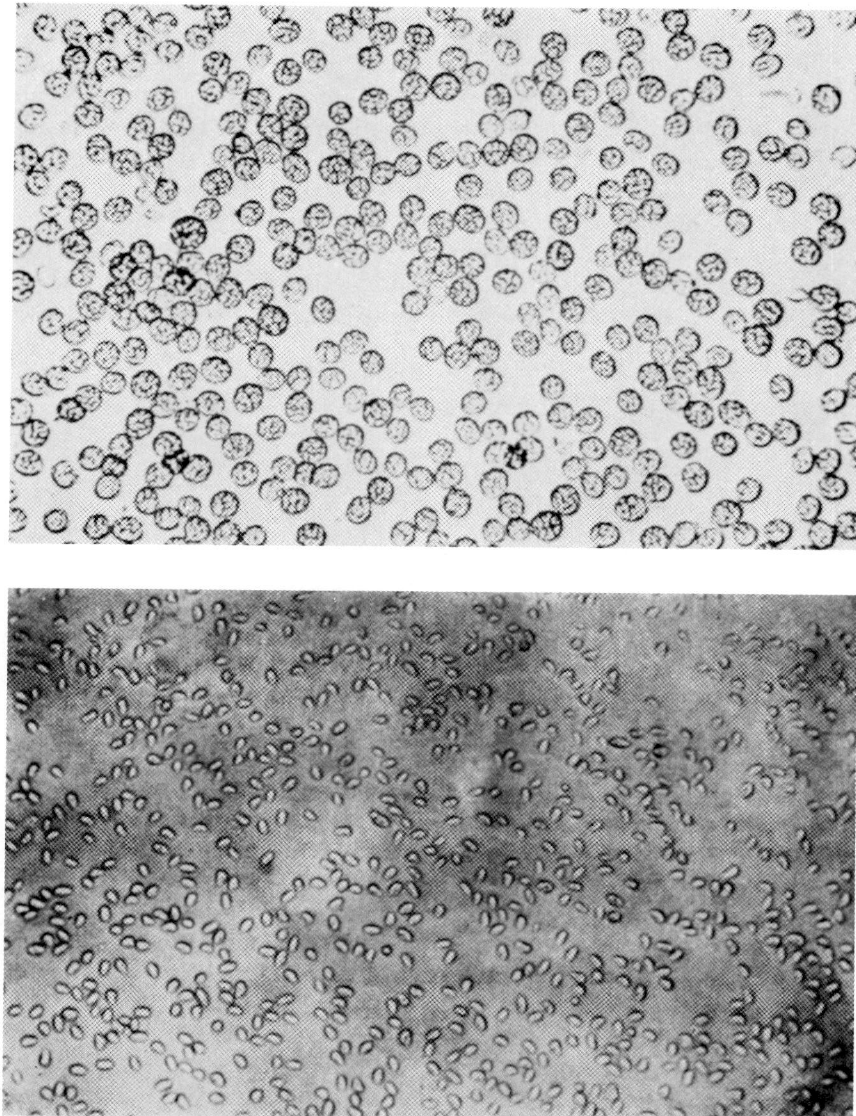

FIG. 5. Microphotograph of a synchronized *Chlorella* culture at different stages. (A) Culture at the end of the light exposure (cells harvested by centrifugation). (B) Culture at the end of the dark time (autospores).

of hour 20 after the start of the period the cells begin to divide. The bursting division reaches a maximum during hour 21. After 23 hours only a few dividing cells remain. Preceding the end of the 24 hour period, the suspension of autospores (Fig. 5B) is diluted to the standard cell number and exposed to light to introduce a new period. During one period (24 hours) the pH increases from 6.2 to approximately 6.5, thus the pH changes caused by dilution are very small. With this method the algae can be constantly maintained as a synchronous culture for several weeks or longer in optimum growth conditions (permanent synchronization). An inhibition of growth (lag phase) following the dilution has never been observed. As shown in Fig. 6 each cell divides, on an average, into 16 daughter cells.

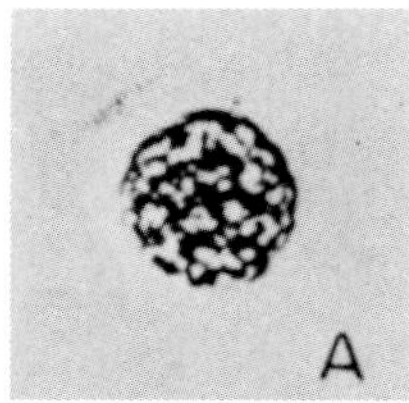

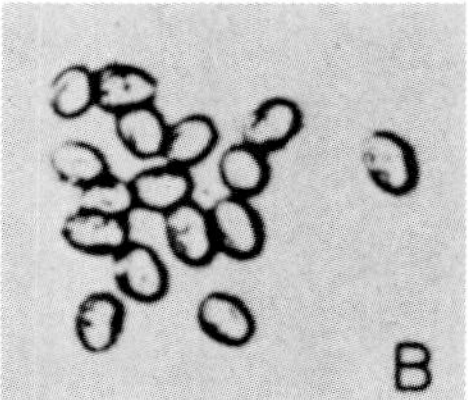

FIG. 6. (A) *Chlorella* cell just before division (diameter, 15μ). (B) 16 daughter cells (autospores) originating from division of cell A (diameter, 3–4μ). Culture conditions for the cells demonstrated in Figs. 5 and 6: light-dark change, 14:10 hours; 30°C; 9000 lux fluorescent light.

To prove that all cells participate in the division activity, the frequency curves of cell sizes can be compared before and after the bursting division. In case of complete synchronization both curves should not overlap (Metzner and Lorenzen, 1960) or only to a small degree (Senger, 1961).

During illumination the dry weight must increase nearly to the same degree as the cell number does in the succeeding division. In a dark phase only a small loss of dry weight by respiration takes place; on the other hand, considerable intracellular metabolic conversions occur (Lorenzen and Ruppel, 1960; Ruppel, 1962). At the end of each period, all essential cell compounds have been multiplied by the same factor as the cell number. The cycles are quite repetitive.

5. CONCLUDING REMARKS

To obtain synchronization in cultures of *Chlorella* (or other microorganisms) a change of at least one external factor is required. Although autotrophic microorganisms can generally be grown in continuous light, the light-dark change seems to be the most suitable procedure to synchronize *Chlorella*. The three methods mentioned use light-dark changes. The Japanese authors use, in addition, fractionated centrifugation. With these methods it is possible to synchronize the algae without employing any type of shock, such as those that are widely used in synchronizing other microorganisms (Zeuthen, 1958; Scherbaum, 1960). It is very important to work with repetitive periods, one immediately following the other. Only under these conditions can we neglect uncontrolled influences arising from the synchronizing procedure. Therefore, from this point of view the method of Tamiya and co-workers must be criticized, as pointed out by Iwamura and Myers (1959). The initial cells used were smaller than those developed in the one synchronous cycle of growth observed. These conditions do not allow the cells to grow with their shortest possible life cycle (see Lorenzen, 1962a), and, therefore, irregularities result in the beginning as well as in the duration of the cell divisions (cf. Tamiya *et al.*, 1962: In this article the control experiments always under the same external conditions are very different with respect to the onset of cell division. In the case of Fig. 6 the divisions are already finished after 32 hours; in the case of Figs. 3, 4, 7, 9, and 11, divisions start after 32 hours or later). It seems that each cell divides exactly into 4 autospores. Tamiya *et al.* (1961) refer to the cultures of Lorenzen and Ruppel (1960) as "not homogeneous with respect to the mode of nuclear and cellular division." It is to be emphasized that with our method we obtain cells that release different numbers of daughter cells. In the experiment (Fig. 7C) with 14 hours light and 10 hours darkness, nearly 80% of the mother cells divide into 16 autospores (Table II). If the synchronization in the cultures of Tamiya *et al.* is really superior it should be possible to demonstrate a much greater sharpness

TABLE II

AVERAGE DISTRIBUTION OF 100 MOTHER CELLS IN CLASSES WITH RESPECT TO THE NUMBER OF DAUGHTER CELLS RELEASED[a]

Number of daughter cells released	Number of mother cells
8	8
16	78
24	2
32	6
Uneven numbers between 8 and 32 not specially noted above	6

[a] Light-dark change 14:10 hours, 30°C, 9000 lux, fluorescent lamps (see Lorenzen 1962b).

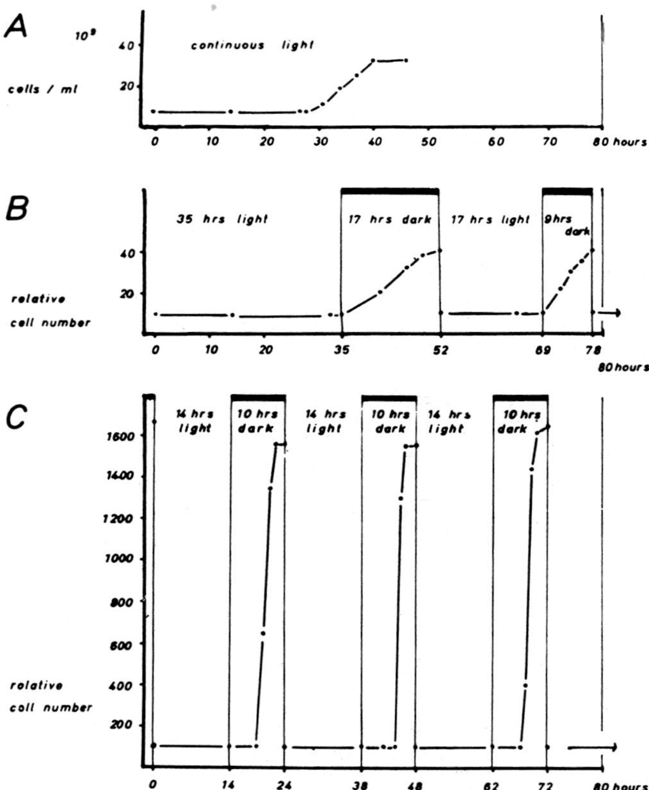

FIG. 7. Cell number versus time. *Chlorella* cultures synchronized with the methods of (A) Tamiya *et al.*, cf. Morimura (1959); (B) Tamiya *et al.* (1961); (C) Lorenzen (1962a,b).

in the bursting division ("Synchronisationsschärfe"). The best method is perhaps a combination of the two methods; Tamiya *et al.* (1961) recently started a culture with periodic dilution. This is the method of the German authors, and Tamiya uses, moreover, a "homogeneous population" gained by fractionated centrifugation following preculture. Tamiya *et al.* call this the "DLD-method" and now attain repetitive cycles (Fig. 7B). The cells are at first retarded by preculturing and then divide during a dark phase after 35 hours in the light. The cells are now adapted and grow under exactly the same external conditions in cycles of 17 hours light to 9 hours darkness (dilution periods of 26 hours!). The duration of cell division (9 hours) is very long, amounting to more than 30% of the whole life cycle. In our method (cf. Fig. 7C) the time of cell divisions is less than 15% of the cycle. In the latter case the cells are more in phase although they do not divide into the same number of daughter cells (cf. Table II).

With respect to the method of Sorokin we know that the cycles of 9 hours of light to 15 hours of darkness were not the shortest period possible for this strain. We obtain a complete synchronization (degree of synchronization $\cong$ 1.0) with this strain by light-dark changes of 7:5 hours (Lorenzen, 1961). Sorokin (1962) himself now uses 7-hour cells for experiments to study the influences of certain factors on cell division.

Certainly the three methods mentioned above are suited to investigate the changing cell activities during cell development. According to our experience and the current literature, we suggest that the following points are important in order to obtain a good permanent synchronization ("Dauersynchronisation") with a repetitious pattern of growth and division:

1. The culture conditions have to be chosen in such a way that the cells complete their life cycle in the shortest possible time and that synchronization be easily achieved.

2. The synchronization must include more than 98% of the cells, and the time of cell division must be as short as possible. The number of daughter cells per mother cell should be uniform ($2n$) and for most purposes as high as possible.

3. At corresponding stages of the life cycle the physiological activities and the chemical composition of the cells should be nearly constant from one period to the succeeding ones (permanent synchronization or "Dauersynchronisation").

D. Mass Culture of Unicellular Algae

It is beyond the scope of this article to deal in detail with the problems concerning the production of a mass of unicellular algae. This special application of algal culture has for years attracted scientists, for algae are known to convert light energy with a very high efficiency into valuable chemical substances. In addition to this the average chemical composition of unicellular green algae is such that these organisms may be used as a source of food. In World War II in Germany, Harder and von Witsch (1942) proposed the mass cultivation of diatoms to produce urgently needed fat, which under certain conditions was synthesized by these organisms to a very high extent. In America, Spoehr and Milner (1947–1948) suggested the use of unicellular algae as a source of food to satisfy the increasing demand of a steadily expanding world population. Following these early discussions, innumerable articles were published covering nearly all fields of algal mass culture. All of them reflect effort spent in the investigations of the conditions necessary for a vigorous propagation of unicellular algae on a large scale. In many countries, especially in Japan, the large scale cultivation of unicellular green algae as a source of food or useful organic compounds has greatly advanced in the last 10 years. The main problems in connection with the mass culture of algae did not stem from biological or physiological reasons. Far more important was the necessity of overcoming frequent technical difficulties in connection with the need to use natural daylight and to supply the cultures with a sufficient concentration of carbon dioxide. Particularly, the construction of pilot plants in Japan revealed the technical potential for production and harvesting of large amounts of algae.

For a study of all the details of algal mass culture the reader of this article is referred to the publication of the Carnegie Institution of Washington, No. 600 (Burlew, 1953), which compiles a great deal of interesting and fundamental articles. Wassink (1954) discussed the problems of various aspects of mass culture. The literature of the following years was reviewed by Tamiya (1957). Krauss (1962) gave an excellent summary from which it can be concluded that in the future the importance of mass culture of algae will further increase. This is especially true with regard to the application of algal mass cultures in photosynthetic gas exchangers. These devices make use of the photosynthetic capacity of the algae to produce oxygen continuously while they remove carbon dioxide from the surrounding environment. In particular, these devices may be of importance if man must live in enclosed space, e.g., during space flight or in a long range submarine. To design and operate a workable unit a great many difficulties have to be overcome. Some of them are discussed in the articles of Rich *et al.* (1959), Krall and Kok (1960), Gaucher *et al.* (1960), and Gafford and Richardson (1960), to which the reader also is referred for an introduction to the many problems of this special application of algal mass culture.

Appendix

Institutions Which Maintain Culture Collections of Algae and Other Microorganisms

Culture Collection of Algae
Department of Botany, Indiana University
Bloomington, Indiana
see Starr (1960)

Collection of Pure Cultures of Bacteria, Yeasts and Molds, and Algae
Hopkins Marine Station of Stanford University
Pacific Grove, California

Collection of Algae and Related Microorganisms
Laboratory of Comparative Biology
Kaiser Foundation Research Institute
S, 14th Cutting and Boulevard
Richmond, California
The collection contains a great number of mutant strains of *C. pyrenoidosa.*
see Bendix and Allen (1962)
Collection of the Institute of Applied Microbiology
University of Tokyo
Bunkyo-ku
Tokyo, Japan
see Watanabe (1960)
Sammlung von Algenkulturen des Pflanzenphysiologischen Instituts der Universität Göttingen.
Nikolausberger Weg 18
34 Göttingen, Germany
Collection of E. G. Pringsheim
Culture Collection of Algae and Protozoa
The Botany School of the University of Cambridge
Downing Street
Cambridge, Great Britain
Algothèque du Laboratoire de Cryptogamie
Muséum National d'Histoire Naturelle
12, Rue de Buffon
Paris, France
Collection of Algal Cultures
Department of Botany of the Hebrew University of Jerusalem
Algal Laboratory
Jerusalem, Israel
Collection of Autotrophic Organisms
Czechoslovak Academy of Sciences
Sbirka kultur autotrofnich organismů ČSAV
Viničná 5
Praha 2, Czechoslovakia
see Baslerová and Dvořáková (1962)
Algal Collection
Biological Research Institute of the Hungarian Academy of Sciences
Tihany, Hungaria

References

*Baslerová, M., and Dvořáková, J. (1962). Algarum, Hepaticarum Muscorumque in culturis collectio. Nakladatelstvi Ceskoslovenske akademie ved Praha.

Bendix, S., and Allen, M. B. (1962). Ultraviolet-induced mutants of *Chlorella pyrenoidosa*. *Arch. Mikrobiol.* **41,** 115–141.

Bergmann, L. (1955). Stoffwechsel und Mineralsalzernährung einzelliger Grünalgen. II. Vergleichende Untersuchungen über den Einfluß mineralischer Faktoren bei heterotropher und mixotropher Ernährung. *Flora* **142,** 493–539.

*Bold, H. C. (1942). The cultivation of algae. *Botan. Rev.* **8,** 69–138.

[1]Included in this list are some review articles and books. These references are marked with an asterisk.

*Brunel, J., Prescott, G. W., and Tiffany, L. H. (eds.) (1950). "The Culturing of Algae." Phycological Society of America, 144 pp. Charles F. Kettering Foundation.

*Burlew, J. S. (ed.) (1953). "Algal Culture: from Laboratory to Pilot Plant," Carnegie Inst. Wash. Publ. 600. Washington, D. C.

*Cook, P. M. (1950). Large-scale culture of *Chlorella*. *In* "The Culturing of Algae," (J. Brunel, G. W. Prescott, and L. H. Tiffany, eds.), Phycological Society of America. Charles F. Kettering Foundation.

Dyer, D. L., and Richardson, D. E. (1962). Materials of construction in algal culture. *Appl. Microbiol.* **10,** 129–131.

Ellner, P. D. (1959). An improved technique for the growth of *Chlorella* in $C^{14}O_2$. *Plant Physiol.* **34,** 638–640.

Emerson, R., and Green, L. (1938). Effect of hydrogen-ion concentration on *Chlorella* photosynthesis. *Plant Physiol.* **13,** 157–168.

Erb, W., and Maurer, W. (1960). Biosynthese von C^{14}-markiertem Eiweiss mit *Chlorella pyrenoidosa*. *Biochem. Z.* **332,** 388–395.

*Fogg, G. E. (1953). "The Metabolism of Algae," Methuen Monograph, *London.* 149 pp. Methuen, London (2nd ed., Wiley, New York, in press).

Gafford, R. D., and Richardson, D. E. (1960). Mass algal culture in space operations. *J. Biochem. Microbiol. Technol. Eng.* **2,** 299–311.

Gaucher, T. A., Benoit, R. J., and Bialecki, A. (1960). Mass propagation of algae for photosynthetic gas exchange. *J. Biochem. Microbiol. Technol. Eng.* **2,** 339–359.

Halldal, P., and French, C. S. (1958). Algal growth in crossed gradients of light intensity and temperature. *Plant Physiol.* **33,** 249–252.

Harder, R., and von Witsch, H. (1942). Bericht über Versuche zur Fettsynthese mittels autotropher Mikroorganismen. *Forschungsdienst* **16,** 270–275.

Hauschild, A. H. W., Nelson, C. D., and Krotkov, G. (1962). The effect of light quality on the products of photosynthesis in *Chlorella vulgaris*. *Can. J. Botan.* **40,** 179–189.

Iwamura, T., and Myers, J. (1959). Changes in content and distribution of the nucleic acid bases in *Chlorella* during their life cycle. *Arch. Biochem. Biophys.* **84,** 267–277.

James, T. W. (1961). Continuous culture of microorganisms. *Ann. Rev. Microbiol.* **15,** 27–46.

Kessler, E. (1962). Hydrogenase und H_2-Stoffwechsel bei Algen. *Vortr. Botan. hrsg. Deut. Botan. Ges.* [N. F.] **1,** 92–101. Fischer, Stuttgart.

Kessler, E., and Soeder, C. J. (1962). Biochemical contributions to the taxonomy of the genus *Chlorella*. *Nature* **194,** 1096–1097.

Kessler, E., Langner, W., Ludewig, J., and Wiechmann, H. (1963). Bildung von Sekundär-Carotinoiden bei Stickstoffmangel und Hydrogenase-Aktivität als taxonomische Merkmale in der Gattung Chlorella. *In* "Studies on Microalgae and Photosynthetic Bacteria." *Plant Cell Physiol.* (*Tokyo*), pp. 7–20 (Special Issue).

Ketchum, B. H. (1954). Mineral nutrition of phytoplankton. *Ann. Rev. Plant. Physiol.* **5,** 55–74.

Kowallik, W. (1962). Über die Wirkung des blauen und roten Spektralbereiches auf die Zusammensetzung und Zellteilung synchronisierter *Chlorellen*. *Planta* **58,** 337–365.

Krall, A. R., and Kok, B. (1960). Algal gas exchangers with reference to space flight. *Develop. Ind. Microbiol.* **1,** 33–44.

Krauss, R. W. (1953). Inorganic nutrition of algae. *In* "Algal Culture: from Laboratory to Pilot Plant" (J. S. Burlew, ed.), Carnegie Inst. Wash. Publ. 600, pp. 85–102. Washington, D. C.

Krauss, R. W. (1958). Physiology of the fresh-water algae. *Ann. Rev. Plant Physiol.* **9,** 207–244.

Krauss, R. W. (1962). Mass culture of algae for food and other organic compounds. *Am. J. Botany* **49**, 425–435.

Kuhl, A. (1960). Die Biologie der kondensierten anorganischen Phosphate. *Ergeb. Biol.* **23**, 144–186.

Kuhl, A. (1962). Zur Physiologie der Speicherung kondensierter anorganischer Phosphate in *Chlorella*. *Vortr. Botan. hrsg. Deut. Botan. Ges.* [N. F.] **1**, 157–166. Fischer, Stuttgart.

*Lewin, R. A. (ed.) (1962). "Physiology and Biochemistry of Algae," 929 pp. Academic Press, New York.

Lie, H. S. (1963). Personal communication.

Lorenzen, H. (1956). Über Wachstum und Stoffwechsel von Grünalgen mit besonderer Berücksichtigung periodischer Erscheinungen. Dissertation, Marburg.

Lorenzen, H. (1957). Synchrone Zellteilungen von *Chlorella* bei verschiedenen Licht-Dunkel-Wechseln. *Flora* **144**, 473–496.

Lorenzen, H. (1961). Neue Erfahrungen mit synchronisierten *Chlorellen*. *Ber. Deut. Botan. Ges.* **73**, 58–59.

Lorenzen, H. (1962a). Studies on permanent synchronization of *Chlorella pyrenoidosa*, with special reference to the effects of temperature. Proc. *Intern. Union Physiol. Sci.*, 22nd *Intern. Congr., Leiden (1962)*, pp. 772–782.

Lorenzen, H. (1962b). "Temperatureinflüsse auf *Chlorella pyrenoidosa* unter besonderer Berücksichtigung der Zellentwicklung." Habilitationsschrift, Göttingen.

Lorenzen, H., and Ruppel, H. G. (1960). Versuche zur Gliederung des Entwicklungsverlaufs der Chlorella-Zelle. *Planta* **54**, 394–403.

Metzner, H., and Lorenzen, H. (1960). Untersuchungen über den Photosynthese-Gaswechsel an vollsynchronen Chlorella-Kulturen. *Ber. Deut. Botan. Ges.* **73**, 410–417.

Morimura, Y. (1959). Synchronous culture of *Chlorella*. I. Kinetic analysis of the life cycle of *Chlorella ellipsoidea* as affected by changes of temperature and light intensity. *Plant Cell Physiol.* **1**, 49–62.

*Moyse, A. (1956). Les bases scientifiques des perspectives nouvelles d'utilisation de la photosynthèse. Les cultures accélérées d'algues. *Ann. Biol.* **32**, 101–128.

Myers, J. (1951). Physiology of the algae. *Ann. Rev. Microbiol.* **5**, 157–180.

Myers, J. (1953). Growth characteristics of algae in relation to the problems of mass culture. *In* "Algal Culture: from Laboratory to Pilot Plant" (J. S. Burlew, ed.), Carnegie Inst. Wash. Publ. 600. pp. 37–54. Washington, D. C.

Myers, J. (1960). Culture of unicellular algae. Manometric techniques for measuring photosynthesis. *In* "Handbuch der Pflanzenphysiologie" (W. Ruhland, ed.), Vol. V/1, pp. 211–233. Springer, Berlin.

Myers, J. (1962a). Variability of metabolism in algae. *Vortr. Botan. hrsg. Deut. Botan. Ges.* [N. F.] **1**, 13–19. Fischer, Stuttgart.

Myers, J. (1962b). Laboratory cultures. *In* "Physiology and Biochemistry of Algae" (R. A. Lewin, ed.), pp. 603–615. Academic Press, New York.

Myers, J., and Clark, L. B. (1944). Culture conditions and the development of the photosynthetic mechanisms. II. An apparatus for the continuous culture of *Chlorella*. *J. Gen. Physiol.* **28**, 103–112.

Pfennig, N., and Jannasch, H. W. (1962). Biologische Grundfragen bei der homokontinuierlichen Kultur von Mikroorganismen. *Ergeb. Biol.* **25**, 93–135.

Pirson, A. (1955). Functional aspects in mineral nutrition of green plants. *Ann. Rev. Plant. Physiol.* **6**, 71–144.

Pirson, A., and Lorenzen, H. (1958). Ein endogener Zeitfaktor bei der Teilung von *Chlorella*. *Z. Botan.* **46**, 53–67.

Pirson, A., and Ruppel, H. G. (1962). Über die Induktion einer Teilungshemmung in synchronen Kulturen von *Chlorella*. *Arch. Mikrobiol.* **42**, 299–309.

Pirson, A., and Senger, H. (1961). Synchronisationstypen bei *Chlorella* im Licht-Dunkel-Wechsel. *Naturwissenschaften* **48**, 81.

*Pringsheim, E. G. (1949). "Pure Cultures of Algae, Their Preparation and Maintenance," 119 pp. Cambridge Univ. Press, London and New York.

Pringsheim, E. G. (1951). Methods for the cultivation of algae. *In* "Manual of Phycology" (G. M. Smith, ed.), pp. 347–357. Chronica Botanica, Waltham, Massachusetts.

Pringsheim, E. G. (1959). Heterotrophie bei Algen und Flagellaten. *In* "Handbuch der Pflanzenphysiologie" (W. Ruhland, ed.), Vol. XI, pp. 303–326. Springer, Berlin.

*Pringsheim, E. G. (1963). Die Ernährung der Algen. *Naturwissenschaften* **50**, 146–150.

Rich, L. G., Ingram, W. M., and Berger, B. B. (1959). A balanced ecological system for space travel. *Proc. Am. Soc. Civ. Engrs. J. Sanit. Eng. Div.* **85**, 87–94.

Ruppel, H. G. (1962). Untersuchungen über die Zusammensetzung von *Chlorella* bei Synchronisation im Licht-Dunkel-Wechsel. *Flora* **152**, 113–138.

Scherbaum, O. H. (1960). Synchronous division of microorganisms. *Ann. Rev. Microbiol.* **14**, 283–310.

Schmidt, R. R., and King, K. W. (1961). Metabolic shifts during synchronous growth of *Chlorella pyrenoidosa*. *Biochim. Biophys. Acta* **47**, 391–392.

Senger, H. (1961). Untersuchungen zur Synchronisierung von *Chlorella*-Kulturen. *Arch. Mikrobiol.* **40**, 47–72.

Senger, H. (1962). Uber die Wirkung von Glucose und Kohlensäure auf das Wachstum synchroner Chlorella-Kulturen. *Vortr. Botan. hrsg. Deut. Botan. Ges.* [N.F.] **1**, 205–216. Fischer, Stuttgart.

Senger, H., and Wolf, H. J. (1964). Eine automatische Verdünnungsanlage und ihre Anwendung zur Erzielung homokontinuierlicher Chlorella-Kulturen. *Planta* (in press).

Shihira, J., and Krauss, R. W. (1963). "*Chlorella*—Physiology and Taxonomy of Forty-one Isolates." Port City Press, Baltimore, Maryland.

*Smith, G. M. (ed.) (1951). "Manual of Phycology," 375 pp. Chronica Botanica, Waltham, Massachusetts.

Soeder, C. J. (1962). Zur Taxonomie der Gattung *Chlorella*. *Ber. Deut. Botan. Ges.* **75**, 268–270.

Soeder, C. J. (1963). Weitere zellmorphologische und physiologische Merkmale von Chlorella-Arten. *In* "Studies on Microalgae and Photosynthetic Bacteria." *Plant Cell Physiol.* (*Tokyo*), pp. 21–34 (Special Issue).

Sorokin, C. (1957). Changes in photosynthetic activity in the course of cell development in *Chlorella*. *Physiol. Plantarum* **10**, 659–666.

Sorokin, C. (1960). Injury and recovery of photosynthesis. The capacity of cells of different developmental stages to regenerate their photosynthetic activity. *Physiol. Plantarum* **13**, 20–35.

Sorokin, C. (1962). Effects of acidity on cell division. *Exptl. Cell Res.* **27**, 583–584.

Sorokin, C., and Myers, J. (1953). A high temperature strain of *Chlorella*. *Science* **117**, 330–331.

Spoehr, H. A., and Milner, H. W. (1947–1948). *Chlorella* as a source of food. *Carnegie Inst. Wash. Yearbook* **47**, 100–103.

Spoehr, H. A., and Milner, H. W. (1949). The chemical composition of *Chlorella*; effect of environmental conditions. *Plant Physiol.* **24**, 120–149.

Syrett, P. J. (1962). Nitrogen assimilation. *In* "Physiology and Biochemistry of Algae" (R. A. Lewin, ed.), pp. 171–188. Academic Press, New York.

Starr, R. C. (1960). The culture collection of algae at Indiana University. *Am. J. Botan.* **47,** 67–86.

Steemann Nielsen, E. (1955). Carbon dioxide as carbon source and narcotic in photosynthesis and growth of *Chlorella pyrenoidosa. Physiol. Plantarum* **8,** 317–335.

Tamiya, H. (1957). Mass culture of algae. *Ann. Rev. Plant Physiol.* **8,** 309–334.

Tamiya, H., Iwamura, T., Shibata, K., Hase, E., and Nihei, T. (1953a). Correlation between photosynthesis and light-independent metabolism in the growth of *Chlorella. Biochim. Biophys. Acta* **12,** 23–40.

Tamiya, H., Hase, E., Shibata, K., Mituya, A., Iwamura, T., Nihei, T., and Sasa, T. (1953b). Kinetics of growth of *Chlorella,* with special reference to its dependence on quantity of available light and on temperature. *In* "Algal Culture: from Laboratory to Pilot Plant" (J. S. Burlew, ed.), pp. 204–232. Carnegie Inst. Wash. Publ. 600.

Tamiya, H., Morimura, Y., and Kunieda, R. (1961). Mode of nuclear division in synchronous cultures of *Chlorella*: comparison of various methods of synchronization. *Plant Cell Physiol* **2,** 383–403.

Tamiya, H., Morimura, Y., and Yokota, M. (1962). Effects of various antimetabolites upon the life cycle of *Chlorella. Arch. Mikrobiol.* **42,** 4–16.

Tipnis, H. P., and Pratt, R. (1960). Protein and liquid content of *Chlorella vulgaris* in relation to light. *Nature* **188,** 1031–1032.

Walker, J. B. (1953). Inorganic micronutrient requirements of *Chlorella.* I. Requirements of calcium (or strontium), copper, and molybdenum. *Arch. Biochem. Biophys.* **46,** 1–11.

Walker, J. B. (1954). II. Quantitative requirements for iron, manganese, and zinc. *Arch. Biochem. Biophys.* **53,** 1–8.

Warburg, 0. (1919). Über die Geschwindigkeit der photochemischen Kohlensäurezersetzung in lebenden Zellen. *Biochem. Z.* **100,** 230–270.

Warburg, O., and Krippahl, G. (1962). Züchtung von *Chlorella* mit der Xenonhochdrucklampe. *Z. Naturforsch.* **17b,** 631.

Wassink, E. C. (1954). Problems in the mass cultivation of photo-autotrophic microorganisms. *In* "Autotrophic Microorganisms" (B. A. Fry and J. L. Peel, eds.), pp. 247–270. Cambridge Univ. Press, London and New York.

Watanabe, A. (1960). List of algal strains in collection at the Institute of Applied Microbiology, University of Tokyo. *J. Gen. Appl. Microbiol.* **6,** 283–292.

Wiessner, W. (1962). Inorganic micronutrients. *In* "Physiology and Biochemistry of Algae" (R. A. Lewin, ed.), pp. 267–286. Academic Press, New York.

*von Witsch, H. (1958). Die Algenkultur. *In* "Handbuch der Pflanzenphysiologie" (W. Ruhland, ed.), Vol. IV, pp. 90–99. Springer, Berlin.

Zeuthen, E. (1958). Artificial and induced periodicity in living cell. *Advan. Biol. Med. Phys.* **6,** 37–73.

Chapter 11

Culturing and Experimental Manipulation of Acetabularia

KONRAD KECK

Department of Biology, Johns Hopkins University, Baltimore, Maryland

I. Introduction to the Organism

More than 30 years ago the unicellular and mononucleate nature of the marine alga *Acetabularia* was recognized by Hämmerling (1931). The giant dimensions of this algal cell make it an ideal object for the study of nucleo-cytoplasmic interactions. Microsurgical operations, such as nuclear transplantation or cytoplasmic grafting, can easily be performed with inexpensive equipment. In fact, such operations are quite suitable for class room experiments. And yet, investigations on this organism have so far been limited to very few laboratories. One of the reasons for this may have been the fact that the culture methods for *Acetabularia* have never been summarized in practical form. Although the procedures per se are rather simple, it would take the new investigator virtually several years to gather the necessary experience on his own, due to the inherently slow growth of *Acetabularia*, which has a generation time of approximately 6 months.

The present article has been written with the intention to fill this gap and to serve as a guide to routine culturing and experimental handling of *Acetabularia*. For details concerning the taxonomy, anatomy, and the sexual reproduction of this organism, the reader is referred to the original literature. Problems of nucleocytoplasmic interactions in general are discussed in review articles by Mazia (1952), Prescott (1960), and Brachet (1961).

In the recent literature the designation *Acetabularia* has been widely used as a collective term to encompass members of the subfamily Acetabularieae. Not all genera in this subfamily carry the name *Acetabularia*, e.g., *Acicularia*. The Acetabularieae belong to the family Dasycladaceae, which in turn are a division of the order Siphonocladiales.

The natural habitat of *Acetabularia* is the littoral zone of tropical and subtropical waters, where these algae are found, as a rule, in a depth of a few feet, although some species have been recovered by dredging from a depth of 100 to 150 feet. In its natural environment *Acetabularia* is calcified and quite brittle, a feature that is not observed in culture plants.

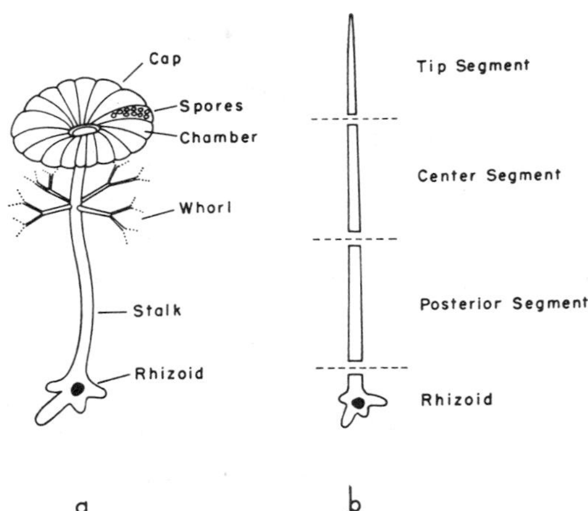

FIG. 1. (a) Schematic illustration of the morphology of a mature cell of *Acetabularia mediterranea*. (b) Diagram of the dissection of a full-grown cell without cap into defined segments.

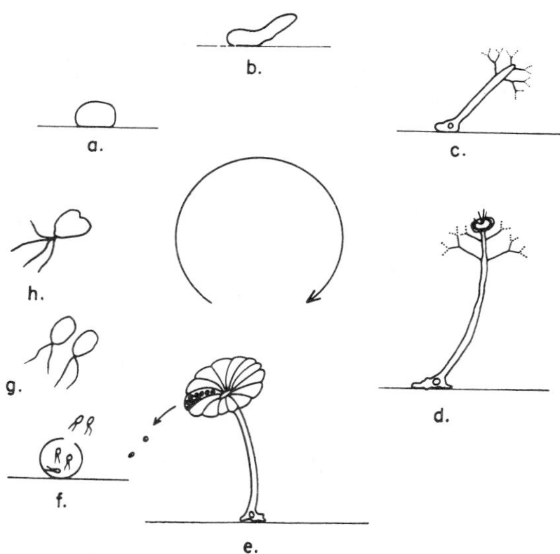

FIG. 2. Life cycle of *Acetabularia*. (a) Zygote, attached to substratum; (b) beginning differentiation of a stalk; (c) young plant with two whorls; (d) cell with a small cap; (e) mature cell with a spore-bearing cap; (f) spore, releasing gametes; (g) pair of bi-flagellate gametes; (h) fusing gametes.

The main phase of the life cycle of *Acetabularia* is mononucleate (Hämmerling, 1931) and diploid (Schulze, 1939). Meiosis precedes the formation of gametes, and the diploid condition is restored after the fusion of two gametes. The resultant zygote soon attaches to a substratum and loses its flagellae (Fig. 2a). After a short period of nonpolar growth, the differentiation of an apex initiates the outgrowth of a stalk (Fig. 2b). As the stalk grows in length, whorls of fine, branched processes develop periodically below the tip (Fig. 2c). The oldest whorls toward the basal end of the stalk disintegrate as new ones are added at the tip. After the cells have reached a certain size, a cap anlage differentiates at the tip (Fig. 2d). In some species the stalk terminates with the cap; in others, e.g., *Acetabularia crenulata*, several caps are formed on top of one another. Generally, only the most apical cap is fertile; the others degenerate sooner or later. During this period of growth the zygote nucleus has remained in the basal rhizoid (Fig. 1a), increasing up to 20,000-fold in volume (Hämmerling *et al.*, 1959). At maturation of an alga this so-called primary nucleus, which is assumed to be diploid despite its large size (Schulze, 1939), gives rise through many mitotic divisions to several thousand secondary nuclei. Massive cytoplasmic streaming now sets in, transporting the secondary nuclei and the stalk cytoplasm into the full-grown cap. Inside the cap-chambers a cytoplasmic region is demarcated around each nucleus; the cytoplasmic aggregates are enclosed by cell walls and comprise the spores (cysts) of *Acetabularia* (Fig. 2e). A spore maturation period follows during which mitotic activity is resumed until several hundred nuclei result per spore. Then the spores enter a resting period which may last from 1 week to several months. Meiosis precedes the production of gametes. Mature spores open at a preformed site, each releasing up to 2000 biflagellate gametes (Figs. 2f, 2g). *Acetabularia* is isogametic; however, both + and − gametes are produced in an individual cap. On the other hand, each spore is dioecious in the sense that only + or − gametes are released by any one spore (Hämmerling, 1931, 1934a, 1944a).

II. Culture Techniques

A. General Procedures

The culture techniques described in this section are based in principle on procedures which have been worked out by Hämmerling and his coworkers for growing *Acetabularia* in cultures free from autotrophic contaminant organisms (Hämmerling, 1944a; Beth, 1953). Modifications of these original procedures are introduced whenever it has proven possible to simplify and standardize the culture conditions without impairing optimum growth. The steps described below are designed to facilitate routine culturing of various species of *Acetabularia*. For certain experiments, however, controlled deviations from the standard techniques will be required. In instances in which enough data are available, such special culture conditions will be referred to in the relevant experimental part of this article.

Absolute sterility is not required in handling the cultures; however, any contamination with autotrophic organisms, "green infections," will ultimately result in a loss of the culture due to overgrowing and crowding out of *Acetabularia*, which unfortunately grows slower than most infecting algae. Certain sterility precautions therefore have to be taken to avoid an infection with algae from fresh sea water, soil, and other sources. Once infected, a culture can only be rescued through its sexual reproduction cycle. The gametes can be purified on the basis of their positive phototactic behavior. This process of decontamination is described later on. Normally, bacterial growth is negligible. If essential in certain experiments, bacterial sterility can be achieved at any stage of the growth cycle by treating the cells with antibiotics as outlined below.

Best growth is obtained in Erd-Schreiber medium (Föyn, 1934), a chemically undefined medium which is prepared from natural sea water by additions of $NaNO_3$, Na_2HPO_4, and small amounts of soil extract. The additives are stored in the form of sterile solutions and the culture medium is prepared by mixing proper volumes of the stock solutions with sterile sea water.

Sea water which can be obtained from the Marine Biological Laboratory in Woods Hole, Massachusetts, was found suitable for the culture medium. The sea water is shipped in 5 gallon carboys and can be stored in this form for many months, preferably in a cool basement. Prior to use, the sea water is filtered through pyrex glass wool and sterilized by boiling for 3 minutes under normal atmospheric pressure. Complete sterilization of sea water by autoclaving leads to the formation of a precipitate and is therefore not recommended. Brief boiling, however, is sufficient to assure the elimination from the culture of autotrophic organisms. After cooling of the sea water to room temperature, it can be used directly for the preparation of Erd-Schreiber medium or stored at room temperature for many weeks. Sterile sea water alone is frequently needed for the maintenance of stock cultures, storage of spore-bearing caps, and other purposes, and should be kept on hand at all times.

Only dark, humus-rich soil should be taken for the preparation of the soil extract. Leaf compost serves remarkably well and is now exclusively used in our laboratory. Dry soil is freed from larger foreign objects and 100 gm suspended in 1000 ml of sea water. The extraction is accomplished by autoclaving for 20 minutes at 120°C. The steaming hot suspension is then quickly poured over pyrex glass wool and immediately filtered through a folded filter (Schleicher & Schuell, No. 588, or equivalent). The filtrate is sterilized by reautoclaving for 10 minutes and can be stored in the refrigerator for 2–3 months. A small brownish precipitate may form on storage and, although in itself not harmful, can be excluded from the culture medium by carefully decanting the required aliquots of the soil extract. One word of caution: Extreme care should be exerted in the handling of samples of soil in the laboratory or culture rooms, since soil is a very potent source of algae, notably diatoms, and negligent handling of soil can cause contamination of *Acetabularia* cultures.

The exact composition of Erd-Schreiber medium as well as the preparation of the individual stock solutions are summarized in Table I.

Although a definite need exists for a synthetic medium for *Acetabularia*, not much success has been achieved thus far in finding such a chemically defined medium which equals Erd-Schreiber medium in its capacity to sustain growth. Recently, Rila Marine mix[1] with additions of $NaNO_3$ and Na_2HPO_4 was tested in the author's laboratory and found quite suitable.

[1] Utility Chemical Company, Paterson, New Jersey.

TABLE I

COMPOSITION OF ERD-SCHREIBER MEDIUM

Stock Solutions

1. Soil extract: 100 gm of dry soil are suspended in 1000 ml of sea water, autoclaved for 20 minutes, filtered and sterilized by reautoclaving. Store in refrigerator.
2. Salt concentrate: Dissolve 4.0 gm of Na_2HPO_4 and 20.0 gm of $NaNO_3$ in 1000 ml of distilled water and sterilize by autoclaving.
3. Distilled water: Sterilize by autoclaving.
4. Sea water: Filtered sea water is boiled for 3 to 5 minutes.

Erd-Schreiber Medium

Combine sterilely	5000 ml sea water
	200 ml distilled water
	70 ml soil extract
	30 ml salt concentrate

Preliminary tests indicated that the growth rates of *Acetabularia mediterranea* and of *Acicularia schenckii* were only slightly lower in this synthetic medium than in Erd-Schreiber medium. Fertile caps were obtained with both species. The Rila Marine mix was made up according to the Company's formula and boiled for 5 minutes. The solution could also be autoclaved without the formation of a significant amount of precipitate, another advantage over natural sea water. To each liter of the cooled, sterile Rila Marine mix solution were added 2 ml of the sterile salt concentrate which is listed in Table I.

Should the presence of bacteria become a problem, either because of contamination of the culture with a rapidly growing strain, or perhaps, because a particular experimental approach requires absolute sterility, a brief treatment of *Acetabularia* cells with combined solutions of penicillin and streptomycin will suffice to produce the required sterility of the culture with respect to bacteria. To each 100 ml of culture medium are added 0.05 ml of a solution containing 100,000 units of penicillin G and 100 mg of streptomycin sulfate per milliliter. The algae are left in this medium for 48 hours and are subsequently transferred to fresh synthetic medium of which all components have been autoclaved.

Pyrex crystallizing dishes, 90 × 50 mm, covered with 100 mm Petri dish lids, are very suitable culture containers. The covered dishes are sterilized by autoclaving (15 minutes at 120°C) or heating in an electric oven (3 hours at 150°C) and stored in dust-proof cabinets. Prior to use, the dishes are filled one-half full with culture medium (about 150 ml), and, after receiving the desired number of cells, they are placed on the shelves of an illumination rack. Any rack design will suffice, as long as some practical considerations such as even illumination, ready accessibility of all shelves, and compactness are incorporated in the design. Fluorescence lamps are recommended as a light source since they offer the advantage of diffuse illumination and minimum heat production. Best growth of the algae is obtained with a light intensity of approximately 2500 lux and a 12-hour light-dark cycle of illumination (Beth, 1953).

The temperature optimum for *Acetabularia* varies considerably from species to species. The tropical species, for instance *A. crenulata* develops best at a temperature of about 27°C, while the mediterranean types, as *A. mediterranea* and *Acetabularia wettsteinii*, need lower temperatures, around 21°C. As a compromise for simultaneously culturing representatives from both groups, the temperature should be maintained between 23° and 25°C.

B. Stock Cultures

During the final stages of maturation of *Acetabularia* cells, the cytoplasm of the stalk streams into the cap and, together with cap cytoplasm, is used up in the differentiation of the spores. Spore-bearing caps can be recognized with the unaided eye on the basis of their dark green color. The stalks of mature plants appear pale green due to the loss of cytoplasm. In some species, as for instance *A. wettsteinii* and *A. schenckii*, spores are also formed in the anterior part of the stalk, probably due to incomplete migration of the secondary nuclei into the cap, or due to the absence of a cap (Hämmerling, 1939).

The spores of some species (*A. mediterranea* and *A. crenulata*) can be stored in the dark at room temperature for several years, and, whenever desired, gametogenesis can be induced by reillumination. Indeed, in certain species a massive release of gametes cannot be induced without a preceding dark period of at least 1 to 2 weeks. The spores of other species (*A. schenckii*, *A. wettsteinii*, *Acetabularia calyculus*) do not withstand long storage in the dark. Gametogenesis takes place shortly after the spores have been formed and a dark period is not required. The methods of propagation for these two types of algae are somewhat different and for practical reasons are discussed separately.

Spore-bearing caps of the first group of algae disintegrate structurally during long storage and thereby release most of the spores; some spores, however, will still be loosely retained in the chambers of cap fragments. Approximately 50 caps or their spore equivalent are washed by repeated resedimentation in sea water, collected in one culture dish, and exposed to reillumination. The first massive release of the positively phototactic gametes may take place anytime between a few days and 2 weeks after light induction and is readily recognized by the appearance of a large green spot on the side wall of the culture dish which is facing the light source. The gametes can be concentrated in a narrow horizontal zone by slightly tilting the culture dish away from the light and thus forcing them to follow the liquid level. The gametes are drawn up into a Pasteur pipette and transferred to another dish with fresh medium. A sporadic release of gametes may recur on the following day or in periods of a few days thereafter. The transferred gametes will again collect along the lighted side of the dish where mating occurs. The zygotes, which are no longer positively phototactic, will turn away from the light and eventually settle and attach themselves to the bottom of the dish, preferentially on the dark side. In the low power dissecting microscope the zygotes remain invisible for 1 to 2 weeks.

Once the zygotes have increased in size and the outgrowth of a stalk is barely discernible (Fig. 2b), they should be brushed loose from the bottom of the dish by means of a fine camel hair brush in order to prevent a firm attachment of the cells at a later stage, which would preclude future transfers without damage to the algae. Gentle brushing should be continued twice a week until the cells have reached a length of 0.5–1.0 mm. At this time they should be suspended in sea water and stored in the dark as stock cultures.

The culturing of algae from the second group, i.e., with spores that do not endure long storage in the dark, necessitates slight changes in the scheme outlined above. Since it is always desirable to obtain large numbers of gametes at one time, particularly for the purification procedure to be described below, spore-bearing caps are collected over a few weeks and kept in sea water in the dark in order to prevent early and irregular gametogenesis. The spore chambers are opened manually here by cutting the caps into several pieces. This step is necessary because in freshly harvested caps of culture plants the chambers remain intact for many weeks and tend to trap gametes inside. The short dark period often helps to synchronize the production and release of gametes, which is induced by reillumination. Some species, however, tend to release the gametes gradually over a period of many days despite a preceding dark treatment. In such a case a green spot never forms and the gametes can therefore not be transferred to fresh medium. Consequently, the zygotes will germinate in the same dish among cap fragments and empty spores. After brushing loose the young cells, their separation from cap fragments and spores is easily achieved by normal gravity sedimentation in graduate cylinders, in that the cells sediment much slower than the other components.

According to Hämmerling (1934a), gametogenesis can be artificially induced or accelerated by exposing the spores to an osmotic shock. Spores which have been freed from cap fragments are suspended in a few milliliters of distilled water. After 1 minute an excess of sea water is added to restore the normal tonicity of the medium. The success of this shock treatment varies greatly from species to species but is generally greater with spores that have been stored in the dark prior to treatment with distilled water.

Irrespective of the resistance of their spores to prolonged storage, algae of both these groups can be kept in the form of standby stock cultures over many years, if young cells are kept under light starvation (Hämmerling, 1944a). Cells of approximately 1 mm length are kept in sterile sea water in the dark with intermittent illumination for 3 days every 3 months. The short periods of light are sufficient to keep such cells alive for over 5 years, but do not permit any significant growth. The above suggested illumination rhythm may be changed slightly in either direction to compensate for differences between species or in the illumination intensity. A pale appearance of the stock culture would warrant an increase in the light dose, whereas noticeable growth can be counteracted by reducing the light period.

It is recommended to keep available stock cultures even in the case of species with storage-resistant spores. The unpredictable lag period between the reillumination of the spores and gametogenesis, as well as the period of time required by the zygotes to grow into cells comparable in size to those in stock cultures, may cause a considerable delay (4–5 weeks) in raising a new culture.

The positive phototaxis of the gametes together with their high mobility

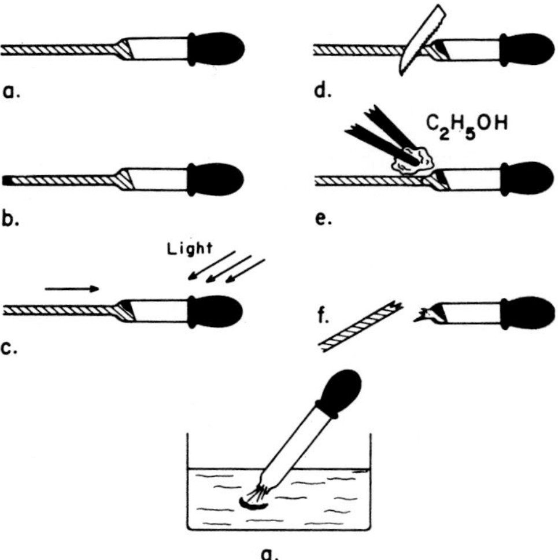

FIG. 3. Process of purifying a culture by making use of the phototactic behavior of the gametes. For details of the procedure see Section II, B.

is the basis for a simple and efficient purification procedure to eliminate contaminant organisms. This technique is particularly valuable if cultures are to be established from samples of *Acetabularia* which have been freshly collected from the ocean. The process is schematically illustrated in Fig. 3. A Pasteur pipette with a narrow tip that is at least 150 mm long, serves as a microchamber. The pipette is filled with sea water slightly beyond the tapered portion (Fig. 3a). A small amount of liquid is then expelled and this amount replaced with a dense suspension of gametes by drawing up some material of the green spot (Fig. 3b). The pipette is placed horizontally on a shelf with the rubber bulb pointing in the direction of the light source (Fig. 3c). In approximately 10 minutes the gametes will collect at the inner meniscus of the sea water. After swabbing the site of the intended break (Fig. 3d) with ethanol (Fig. 3e), the tip of the pipette is broken off and discarded, thus removing the contamination which was drawn in with the gametes (Fig. 3f). The purified gametes are then expelled into fresh medium (Fig. 3g).

C. Working Cultures

The final growth and differentiation of the algae takes place in the working cultures in which the cells are raised to the desired stage. The plants are rather sensitive to crowding and will respond to this with spindly or abnormal growth (Hämmerling, 1944b). Therefore a subculture must be inserted between the stock culture and the actual working culture in order to decrease in steps the number of cells per dish along with increasing cell size.

A few drops of the green sediment from a stock culture bottle are pipetted into 50 × 90 mm culture dishes, each containing about 150 ml of Erd-Schreiber medium. After the cells have settled, a brief check under a low power dissecting microscope will indicate whether enough cells have been transferred. About 300–400 cells per dish should be considered the maximum number. In some species the rhizoids of the cells tend to stick to the bottom of the dish during their growth in subculture. Should this occur, the cells can be detached by occasional brushing. After the cells in subculture have reached a length of 2–4 mm (after about 2 weeks), the working culture is started by transferring these cells to new dishes, counting 50–60 cells into each dish. All the cells that are needed for a given experiment must be counted within 1 or 2 days to assure uniformity in the stage of development. Only individual, healthy cells should be selected; cells which are joined by the rhizoids into tufts cannot be separated later and are to be discarded, together with unusually small or misshaped cells.

Cells of the working culture are transferred to fresh culture medium every 2 to 3 weeks. If at any time green or brown patches begin to spread over the inside of a dish, an infection with other algae is to be suspected and the affected culture should be discarded in order to prevent spreading of the contaminant organism within the remaining working cultures.

III. Microsurgery

A. Equipment

The unusually large size of an *Acetabularia* cell makes it feasible to carry out a variety of microsurgical operations, as enucleation, nuclear transplantation, and multinuclear grafting, without the need for complicated and expensive equipment. Most operations are done either with the unaided eye or under a low power (10 × to 30 ×) dissecting microscope. DeWecker iridectomy scissors with short, pointed blades are recommended for cutting the cell into various segments. During the grafting operations, the components are held and manipulated with fine forceps (Watchmaker's Forceps). Both types of instruments should be of highest quality stainless steel to withstand corrosion by sea water. Throughout the microsurgical operations the instruments are frequently dipped in boiling water to insure sterility. For this purpose a small electric water bath should be at hand. Culture dishes are generally unsuitable for microsurgery because of their high side walls, which limit access by instruments. Tall Petri dishes (20 × 90 mm) combine good accessibility with a sufficiently high level of liquid to prevent the collapsing of cut cells in the interphase with air.

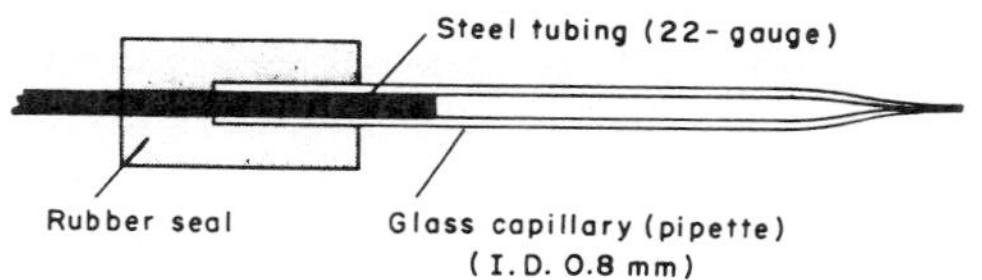

FIG. 4. Detailed drawing illustrating the attachment of a glass micropipette to the steel tubing of the injection system.

A rather inexpensive but highly efficient injection system was recently developed for the injection of controlled amounts of solutions or suspensions of subcellular particles into the vacuole space of *Acetabularia* (Keck and Choules, 1963). The all-hydraulic system consists of a Hamilton[2] microliter syringe #705 (50 μliters) operated by a micrometer drive.

[2] Hamilton Company, Whittier, California.

Attached to the tip of the syringe and sealed in place with epoxy resin are 3 feet of 22-gauge stainless steel tubing (needle stock). The tip of the glass micropipette is hand-drawn from pyrex precision capillary tubing, 1.00 mm outer diameter and 0.80 mm inner diameter.[3] The pipette fits tightly over the steel tubing and is held in place, as well as sealed, by a piece of soft rubber (Fig. 4). This mount permits the quick exchange of pipettes. Distilled water serves as the hydraulic fluid and the material to be injected is separated from it by a silicon oil seal. The pipettes are guided with a Singer Microdissector.[4]

B. Basic Manipulations

Almost all microsurgery with *Acetabularia* is based upon two operational steps, viz., cutting of the cell into defined sections, and the grafting together of two or more parts. Sections from different species can be combined in a graft.

Upon cutting through the stalk, the cell vacuole is opened momentarily, causing a sudden release of the turgor pressure. As a consequence, a significant portion of the cell sap is lost together with some cytoplasm. The cytoplasm at the open end of the stalk joins along the edges of the cut almost immediately, thereby forming a new vacuole. Losses of cytoplasm during cutting of the cell can be minimized by keeping the plants in the dark 1 or 2 days prior to the operation and thus reducing the turgor of the cells.

A cytoplasmic surface exposed by a cut will retain its tendency for fusion when brought in contact with similarly exposed cytoplasm of another cell section. In practice, the components are joined by inserting the cut end of the narrower stalk into the opening of a slightly wider stalk. The cytoplasm of both parts fuses into a uniform tube which includes the combined vacuole spaces. In such a telescopic joint the cell walls of the graft partners should overlap, as a rule, for at least three stalk diameters. The question as to whether tight or loose fits are to be preferred depends very much upon the nature of the graft and will be dealt with in the next section. The joining of two stalk ends can be greatly facilitated by making the plane of the cut slightly oblique to the long axis of the cell. A word of caution concerning the manipulation of cell parts during microsurgery: A cut cell has lost all its normal rigidity and therefore must be handled

[3] Drummond Scientific Company, Philadelphia, Pennsylvania.

[4] Singer Instrument Company, Reading, England.

with extreme care. Any excessive kink or bend may disrupt the continuity of the cytoplasm and cause its fragmentation into two or more parts within the cell wall of the stalk. Furthermore, while intact cells can be lifted from the medium without any damage, cells which have been freshly cut or grafted should under no circumstances be taken out of the dish or raised into the liquid-air interphase. During the grafting operation the partners should be gently pushed in place; parts may also be guided by holding them in the gap above closed tips of forceps. Any hard pinching with forceps will cause a local fragmentation of the cytoplasm.

Approximately 12 hours after grafting, a certain number of grafts will show discontinuity of the cytoplasm at the joint; these plants can be discarded since a fusion will not occur at this time. From the remaining apparently successful grafts a small percentage will be lost later. In such cases the cytoplasm of both partners becomes separated shortly after the operation and, many hours later, the two cytoplasmic surfaces come in contact a second time due to rising turgor pressure. At this late stage, however, the two surfaces will not fuse any longer and eventually a new cell wall is formed between them. Although microscopically not readily recognizable, such pseudo-grafts will later on separate spontaneously.

It seems appropriate to include here a few considerations concerning routine grafting on a larger scale. Irrespective of the total number of grafts desired, not more than 10 to 15 grafts should be prepared in any one operating dish. Cut cells release certain toxic substances into the medium which, when present in excessive amounts, bring about spotty appearance of even the unoperated cells in the dish. This effect, caused by aggregation of chloroplasts, is usually reversible but nevertheless indicates some damage to the cells. The accumulation in the medium of cytoplasmic proteins, released in small amounts from the operated cells, will furthermore introduce the danger of excessive bacterial growth.

Careful selection of cells for proper stalk diameter, and their arrangement within the operating dish, will substantially facilitate the grafting procedure. Certain graft components from different species cannot always be distinguished from each other and identification errors are prevented by keeping cells separated in groups in the operating dish. One cell from each group is then brought into the center of the dish, the desired transplantation operation performed, and the graft gently pushed to a distant place within the dish and thus out of the working area.

Grafts are allowed to recover in dim light. Unnecessary moving or jarring of the dishes should be avoided for at least 12 hours after the operation. Although the grafts may be examined microscopically after this time, they should not be transferred to regular culture dishes for another day or two.

C. Individual Operations

1. Cell Segments

Acetabularia is an example of a highly differentiated unicellular organism. In addition to their readily recognizable morphological differentiation, various portions of the cell differ in their regenerative capacities (Hämmerling, 1932, 1934b, 1953) as well as in their biochemical activities (Hämmerling *et al.*, 1959; Keck and Clauss, 1958; Clauss and Keck, 1959; Richter, 1958; Clauss, 1958). These parameters, although not detectable in the intact cell, nonetheless become apparent after the isolation of such cell segments. An apical-basal gradient of morphogenetic capacities (Hämmerling, 1934b), which is not necessarily accompanied by similar gradients of synthetic activities (Keck and Clauss, 1958), has been revealed in dissection experiments. Of all anucleate cell parts, the tip segments are endowed with the highest morphogenetic power; posterior segments, at the other extreme, are hardly capable of morphological differentiation. However, a posterior segment of the stalk that includes the rhizoid and therefore the nucleus, is capable of full regeneration and will give rise to a mature plant.

Any desired portion of the cell can be isolated by dissection (Fig. 5c) and will remain alive for many weeks if not months (Hämmerling, 1932, 1934b). From a practical viewpoint, however, the capacities of the various regions of the cell are adequately represented by the comparative analysis of tip, center, and posterior segments, the latter with and without the rhizoid (Fig. 1b). For many experiments, especially for those involving biochemical techniques, a great number of cell segments of a definite length must be cut. For economical reasons it is desirable to utilize each cell for more than one particular segment. It is even possible to cut each alga into tip, center, and posterior segments, provided a sufficient number of cells of very similar length is available. In cases where the supply of algae is limited, the center segment can be omitted, thus restricting the investigations only to tip and posterior segments of definite length. With a small center part of varying length being discarded, a greater variability in length of the selected algae is permissible, which in turn will provide an increase in the yield of usable cells in a given working culture.

Various segments differ with respect to the percentage of the parts recovering from the operation. Tip segments with whorls frequently suffer a fragmentation of the cytoplasm into many small, dense lumps, an injury which invariably leads to complete disintegration. Posterior segments which include the rhizoid, on the other hand, almost always survive the

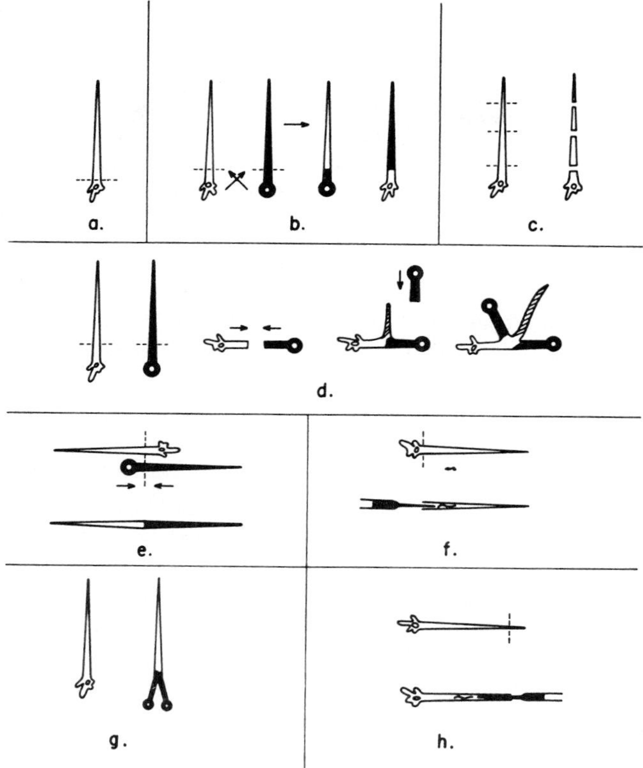

FIG. 5. Classification of microsurgical operations with *Acetabularia*. (a) Rhizoid amputation (enucleation); (b) reciprocal rhizoid transplantation; (c) dissection into defined segments; (d) preparation of bi- and trinucleate cells; (e) anucleate cytoplasmic grafting; (f) injection into anucleate cells; (g) double grafting of rhizoids to an anucleate stalk; (h) injection into nucleate cells.

operation. The percentage of surviving center fragments is intermediate between those of the terminal segments. These differences in the yield must be taken into account when an equal number of various cell segments is to be prepared for an experiment. As a rule, 30%–50% of the cut tip segments will be lost, together with about 15% of center segments or posterior segments without the rhizoid.

The cutting operation is best carried out in tall Petri dishes without the use of the dissecting microscope. The desired length of the segments to be cut is measured with a piece of graph paper which is placed underneath the operating dish. Since most of the cells are moderately curved, a correction of the measured length will be necessary. With experience the required increment in length can be estimated with adequate accuracy. A dark period of 1–2 days prior to the dissection will minimize losses of cytoplasm during the operation.

The classic enucleation of *Acetabularia* (Hämmerling, 1932) is, in essence, an amputation of the rhizoid from the stalk (Fig. 5a). In more precise terms, however, a small but not necessarily insignificant amount of cytoplasm is removed in the rhizoid together with the nucleus. Some cytoplasm is, of course, also lost into the medium during the dissection. The latter loss can be prevented most effectively by ligation of the stalk a few days prior to the rhizoid amputation. In order to compare, for instance, the metabolic activities of anucleate cells with those of intact, nucleate cells on a realistic basis, the rhizoid amputated stalks should equal in length the stalk plus rhizoid, rather than the stalk only, of the intact cells.

2. Nuclear Transplantation

Nuclear transplantation or, correctly, rhizoid transplantation (Fig. 5b) can be carried out between cells of the same or of different species. Transplantations of the first kind, i.e., intraspecific transplantations, permit for example the grafting of a nucleus from a full-grown cell to the stalk of a younger cell and vice versa (Hämmerling, 1939). Another example is the back-transfer of a nucleus to a cell or cell segment which has been anucleate for a certain period of time (Hämmerling, 1932). In the case of interspecific nuclear transplantation, the nucleus of one species is combined with the cytoplasm from another species (Hämmerling, 1935, 1940, 1943). Control activities of the nucleus can be recognized in such grafts by following the appearance of species-specific traits (Keck, 1960, 1961). However, in theoretical considerations concerning this and similar experiments, one has to keep in mind that in addition to the nucleus the rhizoid also contains a small amount of cytoplasm which could be responsible for some of the effects commonly attributed to the transplanted nucleus.

Isolated rhizoids rapidly regenerate a new tip. This tendency is also apparent after the transplantation of a rhizoid to the basal end of a stalk in that some of the grafts will form an extra tip at the site of the joint, eventually giving rise to a cell with two stalks. A rather loose fit of the inserted rhizoid will enhance the tendency for lateral outgrowth of a new tip. This usually undesirable effect can be greatly suppressed by preparing tightly fitting joints and also by inserting the rhizoid into the stalk instead of fitting it over the stalk. Quite a problem arises if the rhizoid donor species has inherently thicker cells than the species supplying the stalks. Should matching be impossible despite rigorous selection of cells with proper diameter from cultures of comparable age, younger cells can be used as rhizoid donors.

3. Bi- and Multinucleate Cells

There are two basically different ways of obtaining binucleate cells of *Acetabularia*. In the first procedure two rhizoids are grafted together. A new stalk tip will regenerate at the site of the joint and grow out to give rise to a binucleate cell of normal size (Hämmerling, 1943; Beth, 1943; Maschlanka, 1943). In the second procedure, two rhizoids are simultaneously transplanted to a full-grown stalk with or without a cap.

Binucleate grafts of the first kind, i.e., with stalk regeneration, can be prepared from rhizoids of the same or of different species (Fig. 5d). Most of the cellular material of a regenerated binucleate cell has thus been synthesized under the control of both nuclei. In the case of interspecific combinations, a hybrid cytoplasm is produced. These conditions are comparable to those found in heterokaryons of certain fungi. A small amount of species-pure cytoplasm is, however, present in each of the rhizoids before the onset of stalk regeneration. In order to minimize the amounts of parental cytoplasm, the rhizoids are cut to a total length not exceeding 3–5 mm. A rather loose fit between the telescopically joined rhizoids is of advantage here, since it will facilitate the early regeneration of a new tip. Tightly fitted rhizoids regenerate only after great delay, either at the joint or, in some instances, from one or both of the rhizoids by converting rhizoidal branches into new tips.

Trinucleate cells are obtained from binucleates by amputating the young stalk after it has reached a length of at least 15 mm, and grafting a third rhizoid in its place (Fig. 5d). The same process can be repeated to obtain tetranucleate grafts. In this way any combination of genomes, intra- or interspecific, can be obtained microsurgically. Problems of gene dosage and gene interactions have been studied in such cells with respect to morphological (Hämmerling, 1946; Werz, 1955) and biochemical traits (Werz, 1957; Keck, 1961).

In binucleate grafts of the second type, two rhizoids are transplanted simultaneously to a full-grown stalk (Fig. 5g). Cellular materials which are synthesized after implantation of the nuclei represent but a small percentage of the total preexisting cytoplasmic substance. Therefore, such grafts are very suitable for a study of short term nuclear control activities and their gene dosage relationship. Unfortunately, there are geometric limitations on the choice of the components in that the combined diameters of both rhizoids cannot exceed by much the stalk diameter. In practice, however, the elasticity of the cell walls will permit the insertion of slightly larger rhizoids, especially if they are provided with obliquely cut surfaces. Nevertheless, rhizoids from young plants will have to be used for intraspecific grafts, and reciprocal grafts cannot be prepared between two species which differ drastically in their stalk diameter.

The survival of all nuclei in a multinucleate cell can easily be tested at the end of the growth period. The individual rhizoids are cut off, transferred to small labeled culture dishes, and allowed to regenerate. The presence of a functional nucleus in a given rhizoid is proved by successful regeneration.

4. Nuclear Implantation

From the theoretical viewpoint the implantation of an isolated cell nucleus into an anucleate stalk would be preferable to rhizoid transplantation. The feasibility of such an operation was mentioned by Hämmerling (1955), but the experimental conditions were not described. According to a more recent paper by Richter (1959a), viable, isolated nuclei can be obtained by squeezing out the contents of a rhizoid in ice-cold 0.25 *M* sucrose solution. The isolated nucleus is then quickly picked up and injected into a freshly cut stalk by means of a micropipette. No extensive data concerning the yield of successful implantations or the adaptability of this operation to a large scale are available at the present time.

5. Anucleate Cytoplasmic Grafts

Interactions between the cytoplasm of different species in the complete absence of any cell nucleus can be studied in anucleate graft combinations. These are prepared by joining two rhizoid-amputated stalks at their basal ends (Fig. 5e). The yield of successful grafts is, however, quite low: approximately 20% in combinations of *A. mediterranea* and *A. schenckii*. The inverse polarity of the partners with respect to one another may partly contribute to the low yield. Nevertheless an intermixing of the cytoplasm of both stalks seems to occur, as is indicated by the exchange of species-specific enzymes (Keck and Choules, 1963).

6. Injection

The large vacuole space of an *Acetabularia* cell is very suitable for the injection of solutions of chemical compounds as well as of suspensions of subcellular particles from *Acetabularia*. The cell is cut open and the vacuole exposed either at the apical end by removing a small portion of the tip, or at the basal end by amputation of the rhizoid. In this way nucleate (Fig. 5h) or anucleate cells (Fig. 5f), respectively, can be injected. A micropipette is inserted through the stalk opening and slowly guided into the cell until the pipette extends halfway into the stalk. Great care should be taken during this step to avoid injuring the wall-lining cytoplasm and thus causing its collapse. Immediately after withdrawing the pipette, the open end of the cell is ligated with fine nylon thread in order to prevent leakage of the injected material.

Fairly large amounts of material can be injected into an *Acetabularia* cell. Thus, enough of a solution can be introduced to replace almost all of the cell sap, provided the tonicity is adjusted to that of sea water. Solid particles, as for instance subcellular components, should best be suspended in sea water for the injection. Inside the cell the particles will soon adhere to and be taken up by the host cytoplasm. The injection technique is of great value whenever the cells are to be treated with solutions of large molecules, as for instance enzymes, which would normally permeate very slowly, if at all, through the thick cell walls. Injections of small quantities of liquid offer the additional advantage of permitting the introduction into the cell of known amounts of material.

IV. Biochemical Analysis

A. General Procedures

The biochemical analysis of *Acetabularia* meets certain limitations which are imposed by the unique anatomy of the cell. The interior space of the cell is occupied by a giant cell vacuole, while the cytoplasm is topographically confined to an extremely thin layer which lines the inside of the cell wall. Therefore, even the most concentrated cell homogenate, prepared by grinding cells without the addition of any liquid, results in great dilution of the cytoplasmic constituents by vacuolar fluid. On a dry weight basis, the cytoplasm also contributes but a small portion when compared with cell wall material.

The unfavorable balance between the amounts of cytoplasm on one hand, and of cell wall material and cell sap on the other hand, together with the slow growth of *Acetabularia* and its sensitivity to crowding in culture, calls for biochemical techniques which compromise between economy of culture material and simplicity and accuracy of analysis.

Significant differences exist in the chemical composition as well as in the metabolic activities of individual cells of comparable age and size (length), even if they are selected from the same working culture. These differences average out when at least 25, better 50, cells or segments are combined in one assay sample. For many analytical techniques such a number of cells also comprises the minimum amount of cellular material required if the reactions are to be carried out on the milliliter scale. Some variations in the data can be expected when experiments are repeated with cells from another working culture of the same age. Consideration should also be given to the time of collection of the cells from the culture, since the pool size of some metabolic intermediates fluctuates sharply in relation to the daily illumination cycle. Differences will be most pronounced between the beginning and the end of the light period. In order to compare the cellular content with respect to such intermediates on a long range basis, it is imperative to harvest all cell samples at the same point in the illumination cycle.

Cell homogenates can be prepared in several ways depending upon the concentration needed. In low concentrations, up to 10 full-grown cells per milliliter of buffer, a relatively wide-spaced homogenizer with a teflon pestle works best. The cell walls break into large fragments and can easily be removed by low speed centrifugation or even by normal gravity sedimentation. A drastic grinding procedure is appropriate for preparations of higher concentrations, including the aforementioned homogenization of cells without the addition of liquid, a preparation which is often used for electrophoretic analysis. An all-glass Potter-Elvehjem type tissue grinder serves well in breaking up densely packed cells. The cell wall fragments are then separated from the slurrylike homogenate by pressing the suspension through a fine mesh cheese cloth.

For certain injection experiments undiluted preparations of cytoplasm are required. It is hardly possible to withdraw the cytoplasm directly from donor cells due to the already discussed anatomical features of *Acetabularia*. However, in using the cell stalk as a "centrifuge tube," practically all of the wall-lining cytoplasm can be centrifuged into the tip where it accumulates as a compact, dark green mass. A specially designed Lucite adapter (Fig. 6) permits centrifugation of 10 to 15 cells at a time. The algae are first enucleated by rhizoid amputation and subsequently

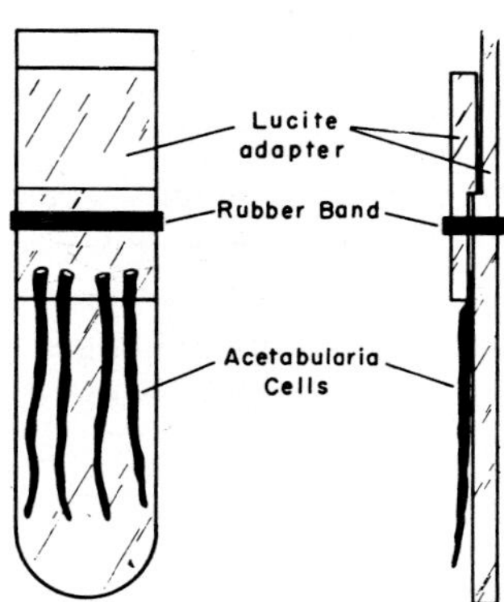

FIG. 6. Front and side view of a Lucite adapter for the centrifugation of *Acetabularia* cells.

attached to the adapter, as shown in the illustration. The adapter is inserted into a plastic centrifuge tube filled with sea water and the cells spun for 15 minutes at 5000*g* with the tips pointing in the direction of the centrifugal force (Swinging Bucket Head). After centrifugation, the dark portions of the tips are cut off under sea water and the cytoplasm withdrawn from the tips with a micropipette.

Electrophoretic analysis of proteins in starch gel has recently proven a powerful tool for the separation of multiple molecular forms of enzymes (isozymes). Applying this technique to *Acetabularia*, it became possible to recognize species-specific enzyme proteins in this alga (Keck, 1960). The histochemical demonstration in starch gel of acid phosphatase is sensitive enough to permit the analysis of individual cells. Although only microliter volumes are needed for the insertion in starch gel, a relatively high concentration of protein is required. Suitable preparations are obtained from single cells by placing an alga on a small Lucite block, making a small cut at the apical or basal end of the stalk, and squeezing out its contents. The small drop produced, which contains cytoplasm and cell sap, is then absorbed to a piece of filter paper for the insertion in starch gel.

B. Biochemical Review

A brief discussion of biochemical approaches to problems of nucleocytoplasmic interactions in *Acetabularia* is included here for a dual purpose, viz., to serve as a source of references for various techniques and to present a sketchy review of the present state of knowledge on the subject.

The morphogenetic activities of anucleate cells of *Acetabularia* are accompanied by the synthesis of relatively large amounts of protein. Increases in the amount of total protein, defined as trichloroacetic acid insoluble Kjeldahl nitrogen remaining after the extraction of liquids and nucleic acids, were first demonstrated by Vanderhaeghe (1954) and Brachet *et al.* (1955). The incorporation of C^{14}-labeled precursors into proteins of nucleate and anucleate cells were studied by Brachet and Chantrenne (1951, 1952, 1956) and Chantrenne *et al.* (1953). "Soluble" proteins, which were obtained from cell homogenates after the sedimentation of subcellular particles, can be assayed colorimetrically according to the Lowry procedure (Keck and Clauss, 1958). Clauss (1958) has studied the synthesis of chloroplast protein and of "soluble" protein after the enucleation of the cells.

The activity of several enzymes was found to increase significantly after enucleation, indicating that highly specific proteins are also synthesized in the absence of a cell nucleus. Individual enzymes differ characteristically in their response to enucleation. The synthesis of phosphorylase, for instance, continues for 3 weeks and its activity increases 600% over this period of time (Clauss, 1959). Acid phosphatase synthesis, on the other hand, is strongly affected after 1 week (Keck and Clauss, 1958). Aldolase (Baltus, 1959) and invertase (Keck and Clauss, 1958) lie between these extremes. Acid phosphatase exists in species-specific molecular forms which seem to be partially interconvertible (Keck, 1960, 1961).

The question of whether ribonucleic acid (RNA) is synthesized in anucleate cells of *Acetabularia* has become a controversial subject. Although anucleate cell parts incorporate C^{14}-orotic acid into RNA at a slower rate than the corresponding nucleate controls, they do so consistently over a period of 70 days (Brachet and Szafarz, 1953). Net RNA synthesis has also been reported to take place in the absence of the cell nucleus, as was determined by the isotope dilution technique with C^{14}-labeled adenine (Brachet *et al.*, 1955; Vanderhaeghe and Szafarz, 1955). These experiments were later repeated with both labeled adenine and guanine. This time, however, the previously found net synthesis of RNA in anucleate cells could not be confirmed (Naora *et al.*, 1959). Similarly, no significant increase in the RNA content after enucleation was detectable when the more conventional Ogur-Rosen procedure was applied (Richter, 1959b). Later it was reported that cells which were enucleated after a prolonged dark period would synthesize appreciable amounts of RNA, which could be determined by the Schmidt-Thannhauser procedure (Schweiger and Bremer, 1961). Naora *et al.* (1960) recovered 81% of the cytoplasmic RNA from a "chloroplast" fraction and reported that synthesis of "Chloroplastic" RNA continued after enucleation, probably at the expense of other cytoplasmic fractions.

Other metabolic systems have been investigated with the aim of explaining the cessation of protein synthesis in anucleate algae. Reducing and nonreducing carbohydrates begin to accumulate from the time protein synthesis declines (Clauss and Keck, 1959). The pool of free amino acids is not affected within 20 days after enucleation (Giardina, 1954; Bremer *et al.*, 1962). Both these results seem to rule out the lack of precursors as the responsible factor for cessation of protein synthesis. Similarly, chemically utilizable energy does not seem to be limiting. Thus respiration and photosynthesis (Chantrenne-Van Halteren and Brachet, 1952; Brachet *et al.*, 1955), including the synthesis of photosynthetic pigments in normal proportions (Richter, 1958), are not affected by enucleation for many weeks and can therefore provide energy-rich polyphosphates (Stich, 1953, 1955; Thilo *et al.*, 1956) for anabolic processes.

V. Potentialities and Limitations

It is a unique feature of *Acetabularia* that a great variety of cellular systems can be assembled or reconstructed microsurgically. Nuclei and cytoplasms, the components of such systems, can be taken from cells of different ages and from different species; they can even be recovered from previous graft combinations. The flow of genetic information from any one nucleus into the cytoplasm can be experimentally interrupted and re-established at various stages of development of a cell or graft.

The amazingly high synthetic capacities of the anucleate cytoplasm of *Acetabularia*, as well as the possibility to remove, replace, or substitute genomes at will, make *Acetabularia* a very suitable object for a study of the nature and properties of the cytoplasmic pool of genetic information and its relationship to the cell nucleus. The buildup of the cytoplasmic informational pool is subject to experimental interference by varying either the physiological conditions of the cell or the number and species-character of the nuclei present in the system prior to enucleation. In a similar manner, the depletion of this pool is amenable to investigation, in particular with reference to its stability in the presence or absence of protein synthesis.

There still exists a need for fractionation procedures which permit the isolation and purification of well-defined subcellular particles. As an example, the role of chloroplasts, or chloroplastic RNA, in the synthesis of protein could then be investigated with respect to its dependence on the cell nucleus. Furthermore, the controversy concerning the synthesis of RNA in anucleate systems could possibly be resolved by a detailed analysis of individual subcellular fractions. Also, the injection of cytoplasmic fractions into a recipient anucleate cell, perhaps from a different species, may well prove to be a suitable test for cellular material carrying genetic information.

Although in *Acetabularia* the *de novo* appearance of a given protein at a particular stage of development has not yet been described, it is quite conceivable that cellular differentiation of this organism is based on time-specific differential gene activity and thus on nuclear differentiation on the gene level. In the case that stage-specific proteins are indeed found in future investigations, the nuclear implantation technique would permit the testing for functional differences in nuclei from cells of various age.

One of the major limitations in approaching any of the above outlined problems is caused, as already pointed out in Section IV, A, by the exceedingly slow growth of *Acetabularia* and by the difficulties one experiences in obtaining large quantities of cytoplasmic constituents. Therefore, the isolation and purification of, for instance, particular proteins, should not be attempted unless the investigator is in control of a vast number of culture rooms.

Thus far, genetic studies with *Acetabularia* are virtually nonexistent. Some crosses between different species have been attempted but without success. Again, the long generation time of *Acetabularia* may have discouraged investigations in this direction.

References

Baltus, E. (1959). *Biochim. Biophys. Acta* **33,** 337.

Beth, K. (1943). *Inductive Abstammungs Vererbungslehre* **81,** 271.

Beth, K. (1953). *Z. Naturforsch.* **8b,** 334.

Brachet, J. (1961). *In* "The Cell" (J. Brachet and A. E. Mirsky, eds.), Vol. II, pp. 771–841. Academic Press, New York.

Brachet, J., and Chantrenne, H. (1951). *Nature* **168,** 950.

Brachet, J., and Chantrenne, H. (1952). *Arch. Intern. Physiol.* **60,** 547.

Brachet, J., and Chantrenne, H. (1956). *Cold Spring Harbor Symp. Quant. Biol.* **21,** 329.

Brachet, J., and Szafarz, D. (1953). *Biochim. Biophys. Acta* **12,** 588.

Brachet, J., Chantrenne, H., and Vanderhaeghe, F. (1955). *Biochim. Biophys. Acta* **18,** 544.

Bremer, H. J., Schweiger, H. G., and Schweiger, E. (1962). *Biochim. Biophys. Acta* **56,** 380.

Chantrenne-Van Halteren, M. B., and Brachet, J. (1952). *Arch. Intern. Physiol.* **60,** 187.

Chantrenne, H., Brachet, J., and Brygier, J. (1953). *Arch. Intern. Physiol.* **61,** 419.

Clauss, H. (1958). *Planta* **52,** 334.

Clauss, H. (1959). *Planta* **52,** 534.

Clauss, H., and Keck, K. (1959). *Planta* **52,** 543.

Föyn, B. (1934). *Arch. Protistenk.* **83,** 2.

Giardina, G. (1954). *Experientia* **10,** 215.

Hämmerling, J. (1931). *Biol. Zentr.* **51,** 633.

Hämmerling, J. (1932). *Biol. Zentr.* **52,** 42.

Hämmerling, J. (1934a). *Arch. Protistenk.* **83,** 57.

Hämmerling, J. (1934b). *Arch. Entwicklungsmech. Organ.* **131,** 1.

Hämmerling, J. (1935). *Arch. Entwicklungsmech. Organ.* **132,** 424.

Hämmerling, J. (1939). *Biol. Zentr.* **59,** 158.

Hämmerling, J. (1940). *Notiz. Ist Biol. Rovingno* **2,** 18.

Hämmerling, J. (1943). *Inductive Abstammungs Vererbungslehre* **81,** 114.

Hämmerling, J. (1944a). *Arch. Protistenk.* **97,** 7.

Hämmerling, J. (1944b). *Biol. Zentr.* **64,** 266.

Hämmerling, J. (1946). *Z. Naturforsch.* **1,** 337.

Hämmerling, J. (1953). *Intern. Rev. Cytol.* **2,** 475.

Hämmerling, J. (1955). *Biol. Zentr.* **74,** 545.

Hämmerling, J., Clauss, H., Keck, K., Richter, G., and Werz, G. (1959). *Exptl. Cell Res. Suppl.* **6,** 210.

Keck, K. (1960). *Biochem. Biophys. Res. Commun.* **3,** 56.

Keck, K. (1961). *Ann. N. Y. Acad. Sci.* **94,** 741.

Keck, K., and Choules, E. A. (1963). *J. Cell Biol.* **18,** 459.

Keck, K., and Clauss, H. (1958). *Botan. Gaz.* **120,** 43.
Maschlanka, H. (1943). *Naturwiss.* **31,** 549.
Mazia, D. (1952). *In* "Modern Trends in Physiology and Biochemistry" (E. S. G. Barron, ed.), pp. 77–122. Academic Press, New York.
Naora, H., Richter, G., and Naora, H. (1959). *Exptl. Cell Res.* **16,** 434.
Naora, H., Naora, H., and Brachet, J. (1960). *J. Gen. Physiol.* **43,** 1083.
Prescott, D. M. (1960). *Ann. Rev. Physiol.* **22,** 17.
Richter, G. (1958). *Planta* **52,** 259.
Richter, G. (1959a). *Planta* **52,** 554.
Richter, G. (1959b). *Biochim. Biophys. Acta* **34,** 407.
Schulze, K. L. (1939). *Arch. Protistenk.* **92,** 179.
Schweiger, H. G., and Bremer, H. J. (1961). *Biochim. Biophys. Acta* **51,** 50.
Stich, H. (1953). *Z. Naturforsch.* **8b,** 36.
Stich, H. (1955). *Z. Naturforsch.* **10b,** 281.
Thilo, E., Grunze, H., Hämmerling, J., and Werz, G. (1956). *Z. Naturforsch.* **11b,** 266.
Vanderhaeghe, F. (1954). *Biochim. Biophys. Acta* **15,** 281.
Vanderhaeghe, F., and Szarfarz, D. (1955). *Arch. Intern. Physiol.* **63,** 267.
Werz, G. (1955). *Planta* **46,** 113.
Werz, G. (1957). *Experientia* **13,** 79.

Chapter 12

Handling of Root Tips

SHELDON WOLFF

Biology Division, Oak Ridge National Laboratory,[1]
Oak Ridge, Tennessee

I. Introduction

Cells from growing roots of plants have long been used in cytological studies and, with the advent of new techniques, are now being used extensively in studies on cellular physiology. Among the reasons for using such cells, other than their intrinsic value as representatives of the plant kingdom, are that it is very easy to obtain a large number of them and they are nongreen, i.e., there are no chloroplasts in the roots, and, consequently, results are not confounded by the production of oxygen from photosynthesis.

It may also be pointed out that actively growing roots are easily handled and may be treated simply with various chemicals and metabolic inhibitors. Unlike many other plant cells, those in the meristematic region of the root tip have very small vacuoles and are relatively undifferentiated, i.e.,

[1] Operated by the Union Carbide Corporation for the United States Atomic Energy Commission.

are isodiametric and do not have secondary cell walls. In some cases, if the roots are treated before seed germination has proceeded very far, a uniform population of cells in regard to the stage of the cell cycle will be treated. For example, all the meristematic cells will be in the pre-deoxyribonucleic acid (pre-DNA) synthetic period.

In the past these cells were used to a great extent in studies of somatic chromosomes. Root tips were, in fact, the classical material for chromosome cytology. The reasons for this were that plants can be obtained having a small number of chromosomes that in many cases are morphologically distinct from one another and very large. The availability of chemical inhibitors and markers containing radioactive isotopes that can be incorporated into these chromosomes has led to studies that help elucidate the chemical structure of chromosomes and the nature of the processes involved during normal cell division.

II. Germination of Seeds and Growing of Roots

In this chapter the discussion will center mainly upon roots grown from *Vicia faba* (the horse bean), *Allium cepa* (the onion), and *Hordeum vulgare* (barley). The techniques discussed are fairly uniform, however, and with suitable modifications any of these techniques can be used for other roots.

To grow onion roots from bulbs, all that is necessary is that the base of the bulb be scraped clean to expose the fresh root primordia and then immersed or suspended in water. The water should be changed every day and within a short while roots will grow from the base of the bulb. Roots can be obtained from onion seeds if seeds are simply scattered on moist filter paper in Petri dishes. It is, however, necessary with these seeds, as with many others, to wash them to destroy any fungus that might overgrow on the filter paper. This can be done by rinsing the seeds in a 2% solution of any commercial hypochlorite bleach, which is already a 5% hypochlorite solution. Similarly, the seeds may be shaken with arsenical compounds such as Arasan or even washed with yellow laundry soap. Some seeds may have seed coats exceedingly impermeable to water, and to facilitate germination it is necessary to scarify them. With large seeds this may be done by scraping the individual seeds with a file. For smaller seeds, however, it may be easier just to rub large groups of them between two pieces of sandpaper. Occasionally, some seeds will be found that require cold temperatures for germination. These may be germinated by placing them between layers of moist filter paper in Petri dishes and allowing them to remain in the refrigerator for a period of time depending on the seed used. When the seeds are subsequently taken out of the cold they will germinate.

Barley seeds may be germinated on moist filter paper in Petri dishes. It is often not even necessary to disinfect barley seeds.

There are other seeds, however, that need different treatment. For instance, the germination of *V. faba* seeds does not give uniformly good results if only placed in Petri dishes. These seeds can be germinated by either soaking them for 24 hours and then removing the seed coat and subsequently suspending the seeds in vials so that their embryos are immersed in water, or the seeds can also be germinated in moist sand or moist vermiculite. These methods, however, do not give as uniform results as the method devised by Gray and Scholes (1951). They soaked the seeds for 24 hours, peeled them, and then germinated them with a modification of the old-time "rag doll germination." The seeds were placed in bundles made up of moistened sterile cotton batting or cotton wool and sterile filter paper. The whole unit was then bound with stiff boards of cardboard, plywood, or aluminum. The order of the bundle was the board, cotton batting, filter paper, the seeds, filter paper, cotton batting, and a board. If this method is used the unit can be bound with rubber bands and placed upright in a dark cabinet for the seeds to germinate. Each day the filter paper is replaced with fresh moistened filter paper, and if it is found that bacteria or fungi are growing on the beans, they may be dipped briefly in a 2% Chlorox solution to inhibit this growth. When the roots are 2–3 cm long, the beans can then be transferred to vials of distilled water or may be pierced with wooden skewers and suspended with their roots in culture dishes of water. Best results are often obtained if spring water is used. Growth is better if the water is aerated constantly during this period.

If a large number of roots is desired at this stage, the primary root tip may be cut off to stimulate the production of lateral roots, which will appear within a few days.

Occasionally, it is important to control as much as possible the environment in which the cells grow. A technique was devised by Brown and Possingham (1957) to culture *Pisum* (pea) roots. Their method was modified by Cohn and Merz (1959) to allow the culture of *Vicia* and onion roots. Merz's modification of their medium is presented in Table I. Lateral roots of either *Vicia* or *Allium* are excised when they are about 2–4 cm long, and 0.5–1.0 cm of the root tips are placed in sterile Petri dishes that contain either filter paper, fine graded pure silica sand, or Pyrex glass wool. The roots in the dishes are moistened with sterile medium. Enough medium is used to wet the glass wool, sand, or filter paper thoroughly, and the dishes are incubated at 20°–25°C and kept moist, but not covered,

TABLE I

COHN AND MERZ'S MEDIUM FOR PLANT ROOT TIP CULTURE

Compound	Stock solution (gm/liter)	Milliliters of stock solution per liter of final solution
Glucose	20	867.4
$Ca(NO_3)_2 \cdot 4H_2O$	0.236	100
$MgSO_4 \cdot 7H_2O$	0.036	1
KNO_3	0.081	10
NaCl or KCl	0.065	10
KH_2PO_4	0.012	10
$Fe(SO_4)_3$	0.002	0.1
Trace elements	(mg/liter)	
H_3BO_3	0.06	0.1
$CuSO_4 \cdot 5H_2O$	0.04	0.1
$MnSO_4 \cdot 4H_2O$	0.04	0.1
$ZnSO_4 \cdot 7H_2O$	0.04	0.1
$NaMoO_4 \cdot 2H_2O$	0.02	0.1
$FeCl_3 \cdot 6H_2O$	2.00	1

with the medium during growth. Two days after excision the roots are transferred to fresh medium in fresh dishes and are subsequently transferred every 4 or 5 days.

III. Fixation of Root Tips

Many methods to fix root tips before staining have been used. Different fixation procedures are followed depending on the components of the root one wishes to preserve and whether squashes or sections will be made of the material. Comprehensive treatments for plant microtechnique have been written by Johansen (1940) and by Sass (1951). A compilation of the techniques used when chromosomes are to be studied can be found in Darlington and La Cour (1960).

One of the most commonly used fixatives for root tips is Carnoy or Farmer fluid which consists either of three parts 100% ethyl alcohol to one part glacial acetic acid or six parts 100% ethyl alcohol to three parts chloroform to one part glacial acetic acid. These fixatives penetrate the tissues very rapidly and cause immediate dehydration. They have been found to be particularly useful to prepare squashes for chromosome studies. They have, however, the disadvantage of being exceedingly powerful solvents that extract basic substances and other compoments, such as lipids, in which one might be interested. Most materials, such as onion root tips, can be smeared adequately when fixed for only a few hours; whereas other materials, such as barley root tips, are often not soft enough to squash unless stored in the 6:3:1 fixative in the refrigerator for about a week.

Since plant cells contain a middle lamella of calcium pectate that cements the cells together, it is often necessary to soften the material to make squashes. Several methods for softening have been devised. Warmke (1935) very simply placed the Carnoy-fixed material into a solution consisting of one part 95% ethyl alcohol to one part concentrated HCl for about 1 minute. After this treatment the root tips were returned to the fixative for a short time and then squashed on the microslides.

If a temporary preparation is wanted, it is possible simply to heat the unfixed root tips in nine parts of acetocarmine to one part concentrated HCl. This fixes, stains, and softens the material so that it may be squashed immediately. This method is adequate for making cursory examinations of the chromosomes and detecting the amount of mitosis occurring. For lengthy, careful examination of the cells, however, it is generally better to fix and stain the material by the standard techniques.

Other methods have been devised for softening the middle lamella to enable the roots to be squashed. A good example is the use of pectinase to dissolve the middle lamella as devised by Setterfield *et al.* (1954) or the use of a cytase found in the stomach of snails (Fabergé, 1945). The pectinase is made up in a 5% solution, rapidly filtered, and then adjusted to pH 4 with normal HCl. This enzyme solution can be stored in the freezer for future use.

Some plant chromosomes, such as those in the root tips of *V. faba*, do not respond well to 3:1 fixation. A superior method for fixation and softening of these root tips was devised by C. E. Ford (unpublished observations, 1953). The method consists of fixing the root tips in a modification of Fleming's chromic acid-osmic acid fixatives. La Cour's 2BD may be used, but Ford has found it is better to omit the acetic acid from the formula. The roots are fixed in a cold solution of six parts distilled water, five parts 2% chromic acid, and three parts 2% osmic acid. The material is exhausted in a vacuum for a minute to aid in penetration of the fixative, then taken out and left at 0°C overnight. Next the roots are washed in several changes of distilled water for about 10–15 minutes until the wash water no longer changes color.

Since osmic acid stains the cells black, it is necessary to bleach material that has been fixed with this substance. Ford has combined the bleach with a softening agent that is designed to remove the middle lamella. He combined hydrogen peroxide bleach with a saturated aqueous solution of ammonium oxylate which ostensibly removes the calcium from the calcium pectate. If primary roots are used, they may be treated for 15 minutes in a mixture containing three parts of saturated ammonium oxylate aqueous solution to one part of a 40-volume hydrogen peroxide solution. One hundred volumes hydrogen peroxide is a 30% solution. Therefore, the final concentration of hydrogen peroxide in the mixture as used is about 3%. When lateral roots of *V. faba* are treated, they are bleached and macerated for only 10 minutes in a 1:1 solution of 10-volume hydrogen peroxide and saturated aqueous solution of ammonium oxylate. After treatment with these substances, the roots are usually rinsed in distilled water and then hydrolyzed in hydrochloric acid for Feulgen staining.

Ford's fixative also gives excellent results with onion root tips. However, with onion root tips it is necessary to omit the ammonium oxylate treatment because it makes the tissue too soft. The Feulgen hydrolysis alone is adequate to soften the roots for smearing.

IV. Staining of Cells

In order to stain the nuclei and chromosomes of the cells, it is only necessary to treat the root tips either before or after smearing with aceto-carmine or aceto-orcein (Darlington and La Cour, 1960). It is usually better, however, to stain the nuclei according to the Feulgen method, which is specific for DNA. In addition, as mentioned above, the Feulgen hydrolysis tends to soften the material so that the cells may be separated from one another. The usual Feulgen hydrolysis is performed at 60°C with 1 *N* HCl. After alcoholic fixation, the material is hydrolyzed for about 6–8 minutes; longer hydrolysis will result in decreased stainability. After aqueous fixation, however, such as that used by Ford, a 12–15 minute hydrolysis period is needed for maximum stainability. After hydrolysis the roots are placed in Feulgen stain (see Darlington and La Cour, 1960) until the tips have become darkly stained, usually 30 minutes. Squashes are then made in 45% acetic acid.

With barley root tips it has been found (Wolff and Luippold, 1956) that the roots are inadequately softened following an overnight 3:1 fixation and Feulgen hydrolysis. The root tips may then, however, be treated with 5% pectinase solution for 30 minutes to 1 hour, at which time they are soft enough to spread.

To preserve the basic protein components of the nucleoli and chromosomes, it is necessary to fix the roots in neutral formalin because acid fixatives extract the basic proteins such as histones. After a fixation time in neutral formalin of about 30 minutes to an hour, the roots may be stained with Feulgen reagent. To preserve completely all the basic proteins, it is sometimes desirable to substitute one normal trichloroacetic acid for the HCl as the hydrolysis fluid and in the make-up of the Feulgen stain itself (Bloch and Godman, 1955). The material can also be fixed by freeze substitution. This too will preserve the protein (Woods and Pollister, 1955). The ribonucleic acid (RNA) of the cell can be stained with pyronin and the basic protein with alkaline-fast green (Alfert and Geschwind, 1953). Protein, in general, may be stained with acid-fast green. In order to make microphotometric studies on basic proteins in plant nuclei, McLeish (1959) has resorted to the Sakaguchi reaction, which is specific for arginine, a basic amino acid that is present in relatively large amounts in histone. Slides containing the material to be stained are coated with celloidin according to the method presented in Baker (1947), air dried, and passed through an alcohol series to water. They are then treated with the Sakaguchi reaction mixture, which is prepared by adding 1 ml of 1% 2,4-dichloroalphanaphthol in 70% ethanol to 47 ml of 1% NaOH. The mixture is shaken vigorously and 2 ml of NaOCl (Hopkin and Williams reagent) containing 10–14% (w/w) available chlorine diluted ten times with distilled water is blown in rapidly from a fine pipette. The mixture is then shaken and used immediately. The slides are immersed in the mixture for 6 minutes at 20°C, drained, rinsed in a large volume of 1% NaOH for 10 minutes, and then mounted in alkaline glycerol at pH 11.3. The slides are then ready for photometric measurements.

McLeish (1959) has also found it possible to make both Feulgen and Sakaguchi comparisons on the same preparation by following a modification of the procedure of Bloch and Godman (1955). After fixing the material in 4% formaldehyde, he stained it by the Feulgen reaction and checked the absorption photometrically. The positions of the nuclei checked were carefully mapped and the preparations then destained by treatment in 5% trichloroacetic acid at 90°C for 30–40 seconds and washed in several changes of distilled water. Celloidin was then put on the preparations and they were stained by the Sakaguchi reaction. The same nuclei could then be relocated and measured again photometrically.

V. Making Slides Permanent

The easiest method by far for making slides permanent is to remove the cover slip (used for making the squash preparation) by the quick freeze method first published by Conger and Fairchild (1953). The slides are placed on a block of dry ice until the material is solidly frozen. The cover slip can then be popped off the material with a razor placed under one end of the cover glass. The slide should remain on the dry ice while this is being performed. The temperature differential between the bottom of the slide and the cover glass is such that all the material will stick to the slide, which may then be passed directly into 95% alcohol and then to 100% alcohol for 1 minute each. Next, a drop of Euparal or Diaphane is added and the cover glass replaced. Modifications of this technique, in which the low temperatures are provided not by a block of solid CO_2 but by expanding compressed gaseous CO_2 from a cylinder or immersing the slides in liquid nitrogen, have been devised.

VI. Autoradiographic Methods

Roots of plants can grow in plain water. This is particularly true for young seedlings in which the cotyledon or endosperm will produce most of the needed nutrients. In addition, the roots are the main absorbing organs of the plant, and, consequently, it is very easy to treat them with radioactive precursors for the various plant constituents. To study the incorporation of tritiated thymidine into DNA or of labeled amino acids into the proteins of the plant, it is only necessary to suspend the seedlings with their roots in solutions of the labeled precursors for short periods of time. After treatment with some precursors such as thymidine, it is usual to place the roots in high concentrations of nonradioactive precursor to dilute the pool of radioactive substance and thus control the time of incorporation of label. The roots can then be fixed and treated as described above. The choice of fixative will depend on whether the substance to be studied is soluble in the fixative. For example, to study incorporation of labeled amino acids into basic proteins, it is necessary to use neutral formalin.

After the cover slips have been removed from the squashed material, the slides are passed through an alcohol series to water. After several changes of water an autoradiographic emulsion is applied to them. This can be done either by applying stripping film or by dipping the slides into liquid emulsion (see chapters on autoradiography in this volume). After the slides have dried, they are then treated according to standard autoradiographic procedures (see Boyd, 1955). They are placed in light-tight boxes, preferably with an inert gas and a desiccant, and stored in the refrigerator to be exposed. The above procedures prevent the fading of the latent image formed when an ionizing particle from the disintegration of the radioactive compound penetrates and exposes the emulsion. After the proper length of time for exposure to occur, the slides are developed in the darkroom under a red safe-light.

Since the emulsions are very thin (this is particularly so when slides are dipped into liquid emulsion), they should not be overdeveloped. Overdevelopment results in an enlargement of the grains produced in the emulsion and a consequent loss of resolution. For stripping films treated at 68°C, a 4-minute development time is adequate, whereas with slides dipped in liquid emulsion, only a 2- to 3-minute development time is needed. After development the slides are fixed with acid fixer. A fixation time twice as long as necessary for the emulsion to clear is adequate. Longer fixation times could remove grains. After the slides are fixed, they are washed in water to remove the fixative and then passed through an alcohol series and mounted in either Euparal or Diaphane.

VII. Isolation of Nuclei

In some cases the study of the physiology of a particular organelle within the cell may be obscured because similar compounds may be produced or found in other parts of the cell. This is true when nuclear proteins are studied either by staining reactions or by autoradiographic techniques. Cells can be sectioned and the nucleus cut so that no cytoplasm is above the nucleus in any given cell. When such nuclei are studied, the results are not obscured by cytoplasmic constituents (Sisken, 1959).

To perform quantitative experiments on nuclear proteins, however, it is much better to free the nuclei from cytoplasmic contamination and thus to study whole, isolated nuclei. McLeish (1959) found that many of the nuclei could be expressed if he crushed unfixed roots between two glass slides. After fixation these nuclei could be stained by the Sakaguchi reaction for arginine.

A method has been devised whereby it is possible to obtain a large quantity of clean nuclei from either fixed or unfixed root tips (Mattingly, 1963). The roots are homogenized in a tissue homogenizer with 10% sucrose to which 0.01% calcium chloride has been added. Vigorous homogenization with a swift vertical and slightly rotatory movement of the homogenizer completely disrupts both cell walls and cytoplasm and releases the nuclei. The degree of homogenization may be checked by taking up small amounts of the homogenate in a pipette and placing a drop on a slide with acetocarmine for direct microscopic observation of the numbers of free nuclei. When homogenization has been carried to the desired point where no macroscopic fragments remain and many free nuclei are found under the microscope, the brei is filtered through eight layers of cheesecloth in a Buchner funnel. When fixed roots are used, the residue is liberally washed with distilled water and the filtrate is centrifuged at 2000 *g* for 10 minutes. The supernatant is discarded and the pellet resuspended in distilled water, after which the nuclei are again centrifuged, the supernatant again discarded, and a drop of residue placed on a clean slide. A cover slip is placed on the drop and the preparation flattened with pressure. The cover slip is removed by the dry ice method and the slide is then ready to be stained, mounted, or covered with autoradiographic emulsion, depending upon the experiment. Wolff and Mattingly (unpublished observations, 1963) also found that nuclei can be obtained very readily from fixed root tips by exposing them to ultrasonic vibrations from a Branson Sonifier.

Mattingly (1963) has also found that after grinding fresh unfixed root tips in chilled sucrose-calcium chloride mixtures the homogenate may be centrifuged in chilled 10% sucrose, the supernatant discarded, and the residue, which contains nuclei, resuspended in chilled 10% sucrose. If this is now layered over a sucrose gradient in a test tube containing layers, in descending order from the top, of 10, 20, and 40% sucrose, then after a short period of centrifugation the material that had been layered over the top of the gradient will be distributed into two layers. The top layer will consist chiefly of nuclei that are free of cytoplasm. These may then be drawn into a fine pipette and placed on a microslide for subsequent treatment.

It is possible to study the chemical components of whole cells by grinding roots in a mortar and pestle with sea sand and separating the different components with straightforward chemical methods. Although this method is adequate for a coarse analysis, it does not allow discrimination between the components in the various organelles of the cell.

VIII. Special Uses

Root tips have been valuable for studying the physiology of living cells, especially the physiology of nuclear phenomena.

It was with growing root tips of *V. faba* that Howard and Pelc (1953) were first able to measure accurately the cell cycle with the use of radioactive precursors for DNA. They were able to divide the interphase portion of the cell cycle into three independent fractions: *G1* (gap one) or prechromosomal duplication interphase, *S* or the period of DNA synthesis, and *G2* or the interphase gap between *S* and visible prophase. They also determined the fraction of the cell cycle spent in *S* from the fraction of nuclei labeled with short-burst treatments. They could then measure the length of time that the cells spent in *G2* by the length of time from treatment with label until labeled mitotic cells appeared. Similarly, they were able to characterize the length of time for all the periods in the cell cycle. Modifications of these methods are now standard ways to measure the cell cycle in all living cells.

In experiments on *Vicia* and *Bellevalia* root tips, Taylor *et al.* (1957) were able to demonstrate that the segregation of labeled chromosomal material is semiconservative, that is, at the first division after labeling of the DNA both chromatids are labeled, but at subsequent replications in the absence of radioactive precursors, the label is found to stay in an individual chromatid and not to be dispersed among all the chromatids produced.

Combined autoradiographic and cytochemical studies on the synthesis of DNA, RNA, and protein in the various components of the cell have been carried on in many laboratories (Woods, 1959; Woodard *et al.*, 1961; Mattingly, 1963; Sisken, 1959; Taylor *et al.*, 1957).

Root tips have also been particularly valuable in studies on the mitotic process. For instance, Evans *et al.* (1957) and Neary *et al.* (1959) have been able to study radiation-induced delays in mitosis by accumulating metaphases in root tip meristematic cells by treatments with colchicine. The dynamics of accumulation of metaphases has enabled them to measure the mitotic delay that occurs in cells that have been irradiated or treated with radiomimetic compounds.

The small number of very large chromosomes that are found in many plants have made root tips the ideal tissue in which to study the effects of various agents on chromosomes. For many years studies have been carried out on the effects of ionizing radiations on the chromosomes of plants (see reviews by Wolff, 1961; Evans, 1962) and also on the effects of radiomimetic compounds on chromosomes (see reviews by D'Amato, 1958; Kihlman, 1961). The latter group of compounds tends to break chromosomes in specific locations usually associated with heterochromatin. It looks promising, therefore, that chromosomal studies with such compounds on root tips will lead to an understanding of the nature of heterochromatin.

By using small, thin timothy roots, Brumfield (1955) has been able to study cell growth and differentiation in living cells. He has suspended the very small timothy roots in a moist chamber and projected an image of the roots through a microscope onto photographic paper. By taking successive photographs he can measure the change in individual cells as they divide, elongate, and differentiate. With such techniques he has been able to study the effects of ultraviolet radiation and metabolic inhibitors on these processes.

IX. Conclusion

Because seeds are easy to germinate and roots are easy to grow and handle, they have been favorable materials for studying various cellular physiological functions. Some of the simple methods for growing, fixing, and handling root tips have been presented. It is hoped that these methods will be an adequate introduction to the means of handling and treating roots to encourage those who have been dissuaded from their use in physiological studies.

References

Alfert, M., and Geschwind, I. I. (1953). *Proc. Natl. Acad. Sci. U. S.* **39,** 991.

Baker, J. R. (1947). *Quart. J. Microscop. Sci.* **88,** 115.

Bloch, D. P., and Godman, G. C. (1955). *J. Biophys. Biochem. Cytol.* **1,** 17.

Boyd, G. A. (1955). "Autoradiography in Biology and Medicine." Academic Press, New York.

Brown, R., and Possingham, J. V. (1957). *Proc. Roy. Soc. London Ser. B* **147,** 145.

Brumfield, R. T. (1955). *Am. J. Botany* **42,** 958.

Cohn, N. S., and Merz, T. (1959). *Nature* **183,** 412.

Conger, A. D., and Fairchild, L. M. (1953). *Stain Technol.* **28,** 281.

D'Amato, F. (1958). *Scientia (Milan)* **52,** 1.

Darlington, C. D., and La Cour, L. F. (1960). "The Handling of Chromosomes," 3rd ed., Allen and Unwin, London.

Evans, H. J. (1962). *Intern. Rev. Cytol.* **13,** 221.

Evans, H. J., Neary, G. J., and Tonkinson, S. M. (1957). *J. Genet.* **55,** 487.

Fabergé, A. C. (1945). *Stain Technol.* **20,** 1.

Gray, L. H., and Scholes, M. E. (1951). *Brit. J. Radiol.* **24,** 348.

Howard, A., and Pelc, S. R. (1953). *Heredity* **6,** *Suppl.,* 261.

Johansen, D. A. (1940). "Plant Microtechnique." McGraw-Hill, New York.

Kihlman, B. (1961). *Advan. Genet.* **10,** 1.

McLeish, J. (1959). *Chromosoma* **10,** 686.

Mattingly, A. M., Sr. (1963). *Exptl. Cell Res.* **29,** 314.

Neary, G. J., Evans, H. J., and Tonkinson, S. M. (1959). *J. Genet.* **56,** 363.

Sass, J. E. (1951). "Botanical Microtechnique." Iowa State Univ. Press, Ames, Iowa.

Setterfield, G., Schreiber, R., and Woodard, J. (1954). *Stain Technol.* **29,** 113.

Sisken, J. E. (1959). *Exptl. Cell Res.* **16,** 602.

Taylor, J. H., Woods, P. S., and Hughes, W. L. (1957). *Proc. Natl. Acad. Sci. U. S.* **43,** 122.

Warmke, H. E. (1935). *Stain Technol.* **10,** 101.

Wolff, S. (1961). *In* "Mechanisms in Radiobiology" (A. G. Forssberg and M. Errera, eds.), Vol. 1, p. 419. Academic Press, New York.

Wolff, S., and Luippold, H. E. (1956). *Stain Technol.* **31,** 201.

Woodard, J., Rasch, E., and Swift, H. (1961). *J. Biophys. Biochem. Cytol.* **9,** 445.

Woods, P. S. (1959). *Brookhaven Symposia Biol.* **12,** 153.

Woods, P. S., and Pollister, A. W. (1955). *Stain Technol.* **30,** 123.

Chapter 13

Grasshopper Neuroblast Techniques

J. GORDON CARLSON AND MARY ESTHER GAULDEN

Department of Zoology and Entomology,
The University of Tennessee,[1] *Knoxville, Tennessee*
and
Biology Division, Oakridge National Laboratory,[2]
Oak Ridge, Tennessee

---

[1] Supported in part by the United States Atomic Energy Commission under Contract No. AT-(40-1)-2575.

[2] Operated by Union Carbide Corporation for the United States Atomic Energy Commission.

I. Introduction

As a material for cytological study, the grasshopper occupies the place among invertebrates that the amphibian does among vertebrates. It has germ and somatic cells that are relatively large and contain correspondingly large chromosomes. A variety of techniques has been developed over the past two decades in our laboratories to utilize to good advantage the large neuroblasts present in an early embryonic stage of the grasshopper.

Neuroblasts have a number of advantages in addition to size (Carlson, 1961). All the features of the cell that can be identified in the fixed and stained cell, with the exception of central bodies, can also be distinguished in the living cell, and a minimum of 14 distinct stages in the mitotic cycle can be identified. At the stage of embryonic development when the neuroblasts are largest and most active mitotically, they may be within a micron of the surface of the embryo, where they can be observed with oil immersion objectives and reached by radiations of low penetrating capacity, such as ultraviolet, beta, and alpha radiations. Each neuroblast maintains a relatively fixed location with respect to its neighbor neuroblasts through repeated unequal cell divisions, and so can be reidentified with confidence during long-term observations over many cell generations in culture preparations or in sectioned material at the end of a known mitotic history in culture. Because they divide unequally, and only the larger daughter cell retains the morphological and physiological characteristics of the neuroblast, the number of neuroblasts per segment and per given series of segments remains constant during active division. A constant cell population is particularly advantageous in studies that involve counting cells in different mitotic stages at repeated intervals of time. Unlike avian and mammalian cultures, in which a certain proportion of the cell population does not divide, all neuroblasts undergo mitosis—some, however, at a faster rate than others. The neuroblast culture also differs from avian and mammalian cultures in that the piece of embryo in the hanging drop maintains its histological integrity during the whole period of study.

Concurrently with the development of cytological techniques, it has been necessary to evolve methods of handling grasshoppers and their eggs, so that a continuous supply of young embryos is available throughout the year. These methods have been, however, merely by-products of our cytological investigations, and so have mostly been arrived at haphazardly to meet the needs of the moment. What information we have accumulated about selecting a species, maintaining individuals in cages, and collecting and storing eggs is included in this chapter and is sufficient for obtaining large numbers of embryos. There are many gaps in our knowledge that a few well-devised and well-executed experiments could fill.

II. Selection of Species

Chortophaga viridifasciata (De Geer) is the species we have used almost exclusively in our studies because it has distinct advantages over most others. It is widely distributed in eastern North America, ranging from Ontario on the north to Texas and Georgia on the south and as far west as Saskatchewan, Minnesota, and Colorado. A subspecies of this genus, *C. viridifasciata australior* Rehn and Hebard, is found in Florida; in the present paper, however, when we refer to *Chortophaga*, we mean *C. viridifasciata*.

Other species of grasshoppers in this country have a diapause, an interruption of development at an early embryonic stage. Such species winter-over in the egg stage, hatch in the spring, and develop to the adult stage in the summer. Their eggs are laid during the summer and fall months but, because of the diapause, are prevented from completing their embryonic development and hatching until diapause has been broken by exposure to the low temperatures of winter. Such species are limited to one generation a year and adults can be collected only in the late summer and fall.

The eggs of *Chortophaga* are laid in spring or early summer and hatch in the late summer or fall. The nymphs pass the winter in protected places, emerge to feed whenever it is warm, and reach the adult stage in the spring. In the north *Chortophaga*, like other species, has only one generation a year. In the milder climate of Missouri, for example, there are two main broods of adults a year, one in April and one in September. In even warmer climates, Tennessee and Alabama, for example, three main broods occur; adults are abundant in the field in early spring, in July, and again in

October. Because *Chortophaga* reared in cages do not produce eggs of the quantity and often of the quality of those collected in the field as large nymphs or adults, we depend on collections from the field for most of our egg-laying adults. It is distinctly advantageous, therefore, to be able to collect them more than once a year.

If there were a species of grasshopper in which diapause occurred at a stage of development earlier than the stage at which we use them for cytological study, namely, 14 days of development at 26°C, the egg storage problem would be greatly simplified. Most of the species other than *Chortophaga* that we have examined, however, undergo diapause at stages later than this; therefore, development of their eggs, like those of *Chortophaga*, must be retarded by storage at low temperature. On the other hand, in research that calls for the use of embryos at a stage of development later than diapause, a species with a diapause has a definite advantage over one that does not, for development stops automatically after a short time and does not begin again until the eggs have been held at low temperature for a certain period of time. Such eggs can, therefore, be stored for long periods of time without undergoing development (Carothers, 1923; Bodine, 1929; Parker, 1930). Only *Truxalis* appears from preliminary investigation to have a diapause close to the optimum stage for neuroblast study, but this needs confirmation.

Of the species that we have examined, *Chloealtis conspersa* (Harris), *Chorthippus curtipennis* (Harris), *Circotettix verruculatus* (Wm. Kirby), *Dissosteira carolina* (Linnaeus), *Trimerotropis maritima* (Harris), and *Truxalis brevicornis* (Linnaeus) appear to have neuroblasts the equal of *C. viridifasciata* for cytological work. *Melanoplus differentialis* (Thomas) and *M. femur-rubrum* (De Geer) have somewhat smaller and in other ways less satisfactory neuroblasts for the cytological research we have been doing.

Chortophaga is a small to medium-sized grasshopper (Fig. 1). The males are considerably smaller and are stronger fliers than the females. Both have brown and green color phases, which are responses to temperature and humidity and not genetically controlled (Whiting, 1915). Under cooler and more humid conditions green individuals predominate; during hotter and drier periods a greater proportion are brown. This applies to the females more than to the males, among whom green individuals are quite scarce. Green individuals sometimes contain purple areas, and the brown shades grade into gray. The wings are yellow with a brown distal band. At the end of its flight the male makes a buzzing or rattling sound when he approaches the ground. Also, in late spring and early summer *C. viridifasciata* is the only species of grasshopper likely to be found in any abundance.

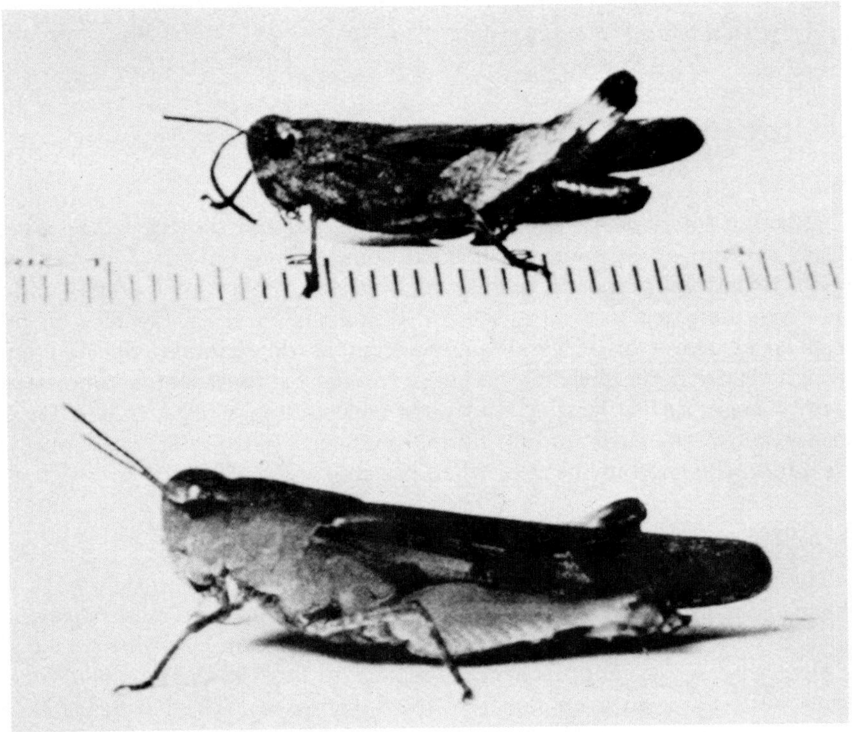

FIG. 1. *Chortophaga viridifasciata* (De Geer). Male above, female below. Smaller divisions of scale are millimeters.

III. Collecting

Chortophaga viridifasciata occurs most abundantly in fields and pastures with bare areas and grass of short to medium height. Adult females and nymphs frequent areas where the grass is densest, but in hot, sunny weather both males and females are frequently found on bare ground, especially after they have been flushed from the grass. Since their activity varies directly with the temperature, collecting is easiest when the day has warmed enough that they can easily be flushed out of the grass, but before it is so hot that they take flight too quickly to be caught with a net. Nymphs can usually be caught by hand more easily than by net. Wintering-over occurs in the nymphal stage, and so nymphs can be collected on any warm day during the winter months, particularly in sheltered places with a southern exposure.

IV. Rearing

Although *Chortophaga* can be reared in cages from the egg to the adult stage, the life cycle under such conditions is long—about 3 months (6 weeks to hatching and an additional 6 weeks to the adult stage) under the best conditions and more often 5–6 months—and the females do not produce as many or as good quality eggs as do animals collected and brought in from the field in the late nymphal or adult instar. The latter usually begin to lay earlier, the pods contain more eggs, and a larger proportion of the eggs contain normal embryos. We prefer, therefore, to use adults collected in the field when possible.

A. Cages

The cage we use is similar to the type described by Carothers (1923). Our main modification is the addition of a platform of fine-mesh hardware cloth level with, but not covering, the tops of two staining dishes; one dish is filled with moist sand, in which the females deposit their eggs, and the other with water to keep the food from drying up. The hardware cloth platform facilitates egg-laying and feeding by keeping the grasshopper at the same level as the sand and food (Fig. 2). It also permits small bits of unused food and droppings to fall to the bottom of the cage. Lucite may be used instead of glass for the front of the cage. It has the advantages of being lighter in weight and not breaking easily; on the other hand, it soon becomes badly scratched from rubbing against the cage top as it is raised and lowered. If the cages are to be sterilized or washed frequently, they should be constructed of a moisture resistant wood such as cedar or cypress. In cages measuring 9 inches high × 7.5 inches wide × 6 inches deep, we place about 12 males and 6–8 females.

B. Food

Both nymphs and adults will eat a great variety of foods. Among those we have used with success are Kentucky blue grass, lettuce leaves, crab grass, Italian rye grass, carrot tops, wheat seedlings, and alfalfa pellets prepared commercially as rabbit food. Unless the leaves of fresh foods are placed with one end in water, they will dry out and will have to be replaced

FIG. 2. Grasshopper cage. Shown are raised hardware cloth platform and dishes containing wet sand for egg-laying and water to keep leaves fresh.

once or twice a day, depending on the temperature and humidity. Alfalfa pellets are spread on moist filter paper laid over wet absorbent cotton or sand in a Petri dish. They will remain moist and edible for 24–48 hours. It is our experience, however, that *Chortophaga* does not feed as readily on pellets as, for example, *Melanoplus* does, and the eggs from *Chortophaga* females that have been fed for a long time on pellets are not in as good condition as the eggs from those fed on grass or lettuce. Carothers (1923) found that certain foods, for example, growing oats, although adequate for growth and development of grasshoppers, resulted in the failure of females to develop eggs and in the production of abnormal germ cells in males. We have found it helpful in using grasses to wet them thoroughly under a faucet before placing them in the cage. This keeps them moist and fresh longer. Grasshoppers often ingest drops of water from the grass, but we have no evidence regarding the value of this to their well-being.

C. Temperature

Maximum rate of egg production is obtained by keeping the grasshoppers at high temperature. For this purpose we use an infrared lamp of the kind that can be purchased at almost any drug store. It is placed as close to the cage as possible without driving the grasshoppers to seek shelter behind the wood sides of the cage. A high rate of egg production, however, shortens the adult lives of the grasshoppers and their period of laying. If it is preferred to have a smaller number of eggs spread over a longer period, use of the lamp can be limited to 2 or 3 days a week.

If the grasshoppers are kept in a humid environment, the use of an infrared lamp greatly lessens their death from infection with a fungus (species unidentified). If heat is provided with an ordinary incandescent light bulb or by placing the cages in an incubator, this fungus may infect a large proportion of the animals. Within a week or two after collection of grasshoppers in the field the fungus makes its appearance on their surfaces as a whitish, threadlike material. Mycelia are found throughout the internal organs of infected individuals.

V. Eggs

A. Laying

The females insert their ovipositors in the sand to the full length of the abdomen and deposit the eggs, together with certain secretions, as they gradually withdraw the abdomen. The secreted material holds the eggs together in a pod that is covered by an outer layer of adhering sand (Fig. 3). Each female lays a pod of eggs about once in 4–6 days.

B. Storage

Egg pods are harvested by removing the dishes of sand from the cages, usually at intervals of a week or less, emptying out the sand, and fingering through it carefully for the pods. These must be handled gently, because at early stages of development the egg envelope is delicate and easily punctured by sharp sand particles. The pods are stored in Petri dishes

FIG. 3. Petri dish containing two intact grasshopper egg pods on wet sand. On the filter paper are two eggs and the divided egg pod from which they were removed.

containing a $\frac{1}{8}$–$\frac{1}{4}$-inch layer of wet sand (Fig. 3), which holds the moisture well and does not support bacterial or fungal growths. They may be left at room temperature or, if it is desired to accelerate development as much as possible, they may be incubated at a temperature as high as 38°C. At this temperature, development is about twice as fast as at 26°C. Thirty-eight degrees is close to the maximum safe temperature, for at 42°C chromosome irregularities are induced.

Because a supply of adult grasshoppers from the field is not obtainable throughout the year, it is necessary to retard development of the eggs soon after laying so that embryos of optimum age (14 days at 26°C) will be available in the intervening periods. *Chortophaga* eggs will not survive prolonged exposure to temperatures near 0°C. For many years we stored them at 17°C. At this temperature they require 6 weeks to reach the stage of development they attain in 2 weeks at 26°C and suffer few deleterious effects. It means, however, that there is a gap of several weeks in the winter between the time the eggs of the fall brood of adults is exhausted and the time that the spring brood of adults will be producing eggs. For about the last 3 years we have attempted to store them at 14°C, at which they can be held below the 2-week stage for over 6 months. We find, however, that after about 4 months the embryos begin to show bad effects of the long storage. Some embryos of a pod show less development than others. After returning these eggs to higher temperatures, that is, 26°–38°C, the mitotic cycle is appreciably longer and the living cells in culture do not exhibit the series of clear and easily identified mitotic stages that cells from eggs stored at 17°C do. We are now storing eggs at 16°C.

The eggs must be kept moist at all times because prolonged drying of the egg pods may cause death of the embryo and at the time of hatching prevent the escape of the hatching grasshoppers from the pod. Hatching and emergence of the nymphs begin with the egg laid last and proceed along the pod to the other end, the hatching period for all eggs in a pod normally requiring 1–2 hours.

VI. Development

A. Embryo

Early embryonic development in Orthoptera has been described by Wheeler (1893), Nelsen (1931), and Slifer (1932). The stage most suitable for studies of neuroblasts is shown in Fig. 4, which is a prerevolution stage

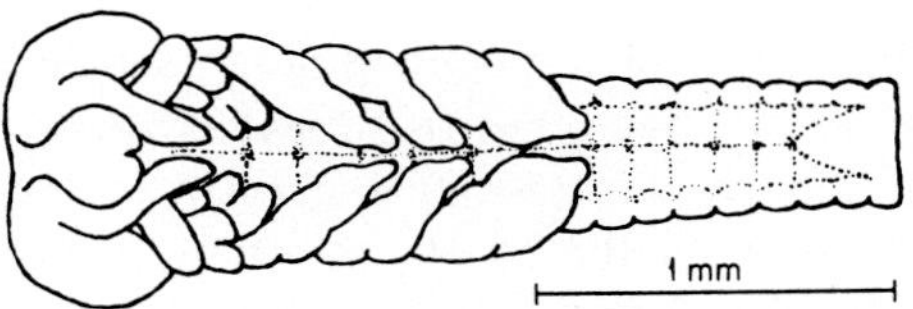

FIG. 4. *Chortophaga viridifasciata* embryo at an age equivalent to 14 days at 26°C (from Carlson, 1961).

equivalent to 14 days development at 26°C. Several features distinguish it from earlier and later stages. The thoracic appendages of the two sides meet in the middle but have not begun to grow posteriorly at the distal ends. The sides of the embryo have not begun to grow upward and enclose the yolk dorsally, and the eyes are unpigmented. The abdomen has broadened from its earlier slender form but is still distinctly longer than wide. The neuroblasts of the first maxillary through the first abdominal segment are well developed and form the ventral covering in the nerve cord region of the embryo. In younger embryos the neuroblasts are smaller and are often covered to varying degrees by the dermatoblasts, while in older embryos the neuroblasts are gradually covered ventrally by a layer of hypodermal cells. The 14-day stage is, therefore, ideal for *in vitro* studies of hanging-drop preparations of the embryo, for most of the neuroblasts then lie very close to the cover glass.

B. Nymph

Eggs that are not used during the embryonic stage may be allowed to hatch, and the nymphs can be reared to the adult stage. A few minutes after hatching the first instar nymphs undergo the first molt, casting off tiny white exuviae. Not later than a day after hatching, these nymphs should be removed from the Petri dish and placed in a cage with free air circulation. They begin to feed on the second day after hatching and must have a readily accessible supply of tender grass or other green plant food. Unlike older nymphs and adults, these 2-day-old nymphs will not move about in search of food, but often remain in one place on the side of a cage, until they shrivel up and die. They can be made to jump by blowing on them or tapping the side of the cage, and if they happen to land on food they will immediately begin to feed. The high mortality of newly hatched nymphs in a cage is due to starvation resulting from failure to move about in search of food. Though we have no valid supporting data, it has seemed to us that the survival of nymphs, especially younger ones, is greatest in cages containing a certain amount of dried-up grass that has settled to the bottom of the cage. The nymphs remain concealed in this loosely piled dry grass much of the time, except when they are on top of it eating newly added grass, or on the screens forming the sides of the cage exposing themselves to the warm rays of sun or lamp. Under hot, dry conditions fresh food should be placed in the cage 3 to 4 times a day when the nymphs are young, unless the lower ends of the stalks are in a vessel containing water.

Chortophaga molts 7 times; there are, therefore, 7 nymphal instars and 1 adult instar. The time required for development from hatching to adult partly depends on the temperature at which the nymphs are kept. Other factors are involved, however; nymphs living in the field and subjected to warm days and cool nights seem to develop faster than those maintained in the laboratory at a higher average temperature. The most effective means we have found of accelerating development in the laboratory is to shine an infrared lamp on the back of the cage (Section IV, C).

VII. Culture Techniques

A. Materials

1. Culture Media

The grasshopper neuroblast is very sensitive to relatively slight differences in osmotic pressure of the culture medium; therefore, it is desirable in the more exacting experiments to use different concentrations of solutions for dissecting and for making hanging-drop preparations of the embryo. The medium in which the embryos are removed from the egg chorion, separated from the yolk, and dissected should be exactly isotonic. On the other hand, the medium that is to be used in the hanging drop should be slightly hypotonic, so that the change in tonicity caused by evaporation of water from the hanging drop, until the moist chamber is saturated, will bring the hanging-drop solution to isotonic level. The former solution is hereafter referred to as the dissecting medium, the latter as the hanging-drop medium. Solutions that are combined and diluted in making these media are referred to as stock solutions.

The osmotic pressure is usually the same for all eggs in one pod but often differs from one pod to another. Our usual procedure is to estimate the correct tonicity and then to check hanging-drop preparations of embryos made up in this medium. Criteria for determining whether a solution has the right osmotic pressure are given in Section VII, F, 1. Adjustments of osmotic pressure are made by varying the amount of water in the dissecting and hanging-drop media, normally within the limits given in the media formulations (Section VII, A, 1, a, b). Dissecting and hanging-drop media should, of course, be varied together. The most commonly required quantities of water are, respectively, 3.2 and 4.2 ml for Carlson's medium (Section VII, A, 1, a) and 3.5 and 4.5 ml for Shaw's medium (Section VII, A, 1, b).

To minimize errors arising from different amounts of water taken up by chemicals from the air, we keep all chemicals in a desiccator over Drierite with color indicator. The amounts given for chemicals in Carlson's and Shaw's media are those for completely dried crystals. The water used in all of these solutions is double-distilled in Pyrex.

a. *Carlson's Medium.* Carlson's medium (Carlson, 1946; Carlson *et al.*, 1947; Carlson, 1961) is a modified Ringer-Tyrode solution containing grasshopper egg yolk. It is made as follows:

Stock Solution *A:*

6.8 gm NaCl; 0.2 gm KCl; 0.2 gm $CaCl_2 \cdot 2H_2O$; 0.1 gm $MgCl_2 \cdot 6H_2O$; and 0.2 gm NaH_2PO_4. Add water to 100 ml.

Stock Solution *B:*
0.125 gm $NaHCO_3$; add water to 100 ml.

Stock Solution *C:*
7.7 gm glucose · H_2O; add water to 100 ml.

Dissecting medium:
A, B, C, 1.0 ml of each; water, 3.2–4.2 ml.

Hanging-drop medium:
A, B, C, 1.0 ml of each; water, 6.1–8.1 ml.

The grasshopper egg yolk is added to the hanging-drop at the time the preparation is made (Gaulden and Kokomoor, 1955) (Section VII, D, 4).

b. *Shaw's Medium.* In an attempt to develop a medium which more closely approximates that surrounding the cell *in vivo*, Shaw (1955, 1956a) analyzed the contents of the 14-day-old grasshopper egg. On the basis of this analysis, he formulated a medium in which the ratios of sodium to potassium and of chlorides to organic anions more closely resemble those ratios found in the egg than does Carlson's medium. Shaw's medium greatly prolongs the period of optimal mitotic activity in the embryo cultures and, with few exceptions, has been used for neuroblast studies since 1956. Stock solutions of this medium are made in five parts as follows:

Stock Solution *A:*
7.35 gm glutamic acid and 3.75 gm glycine. Adjust to pH 7.3 with conc. KOH and add water to 100 ml.

Stock Solution *B:*
7.35 gm glutamic acid and 3.75 gm glycine. Adjust to pH 7.3 with conc. NaOH and add water to 100 ml.

Stock Solution *C:*
0.15 gm $CaCl_2 \cdot 2H_2O$ and 0.05 gm $MgCl_2 \cdot 6H_2O$; add water to 100 ml.

Stock Solution *D:*
0.8 gm NaH_2PO_4 and 0.5 gm $NaHCO_3$; add water to 100 ml.

Stock Solution *E:*
7.7 gm glucose · H_2O; add water to 100 ml.

Dissecting medium:
A, 0.75 ml; *B,* 1.25 ml; *C, D, E,* 1.0 ml of each; water, 3.3–3.6 ml.

Hanging-drop medium:
A, 0.75 ml; *B,* 1.25 ml; *C, D, E,* 1.0 ml of each; water, 4.4–5.0 ml.

A small amount of grasshopper egg yolk is added to the hanging-drop at the time the preparation is made (Gaulden and Kokomoor, 1955).

c. *Storage.* Stock solutions may be sterilized (Section VII, C) and stored in flasks in a refrigerator. A better method, however, is to freeze and store them (unsterilized) in a deep-freeze unit. The three stock solutions of Carlson's medium or the five of Shaw's medium may be combined in their final proportions, and when dissecting and hanging-drop media are wanted the frozen solution is thawed, the necessary amount of fluid removed from the bottle, and the remainder refrozen.

When making up either dissecting or hanging-drop medium, it is important to have the stock solutions and water at room temperature (24–26°C in our laboratory), for temperature has a pronounced differential effect on the volumes of these fluids.

2. Glassware

a. *Storage Containers.* If an autoclave is used for sterilization, stock solutions are stored in Pyrex flasks. After sterilization the cotton stoppers are replaced by corks dipped in melted paraffin.

If ultraviolet radiation is used to sterilize culture media (Carlson *et al.*, 1947) it is necessary to use fused quartz (Vitreosil) flasks, which will transmit the radiation. We use flat-bottomed, Florence style flasks of approximately 125 ml capacity, obtainable from Thermal American Fused Quartz (18–20 Salem St., Dover, New Jersey). These flasks do not usually have perfectly rounded necks, but we have found that corks coated with paraffin will form a good seal. The paraffin has an added advantage in that it coats and fills cracks in the cork and prevents the growth of mold.

Milk dilution bottles of 100 ml capacity with screw caps are convenient for storing stock solutions in a deep-freeze unit.

b. *Syracuse Watch Glasses.* Dissection of the embryos is carried out in 67 mm diameter Syracuse watch glasses.

c. *Petri Dishes.* For ease of handling and for preventing contamination of the medium by air-borne organisms, the Syracuse watch glasses are usually sterilized inside 100 mm diameter Petri dishes. Petri dishes are also used to hold sterile filter paper, one piece to a dish.

d. *Slides.* Embryo cultures are made on 3 × 1 inch depression slides 1.38–1.60 mm thick. The one or two concavities are 16–17 mm in diameter, 0.6–0.8 mm deep, and 0.0531–0.0594 ml in volume.

e. *Cover Glasses.* We use No. 1 cover glasses, 22 mm square, and 0.12–0.14 mm thick. Thickness is measured with a micrometer caliper and those thicker than this are rejected for hanging-drop preparations, if high-dry objectives are to be used. For experiments in which the hanging drop is to be treated with low-penetrating radiations, special types of covers are necessary (Section X, A, 2, 3, 4).

f. *Graduated Pipettes.* For measuring the components of the dissecting and hanging-drop media, graduated pipettes of 1, 5, and 10 ml capacity are used.

3. Instruments

a. *Shielded Stereoscopic Microscope.* Dissection of the embryo and preparation of the hanging-drop culture are performed under a dissecting microscope equipped with 9× oculars and 2× objectives. A glass plate (window glass), 7.5 × 9 inches, is placed on the stage of the microscope and clipped in place (Fig. 5). Such a plate enables the operator to slide

FIG. 5. Dissecting microscope equipped with rectangular glass plate to enlarge the stage, and plastic dust shield to decrease chance of contamination during manipulation of embryo in culture media. Aluminum cover of ultraviolet sterilization box shows openings for instruments, slides, and cover glasses. Cover with dust shield lifts off box (from Carlson *et al.*, 1947).

the two dishes containing dissecting and hanging-drop media in and out of the field of the microscope as desired. The working area of the microscope is covered with a piece of thin plastic or unexposed processed X-ray film, which serves as a dust cover (Fig. 5). The light for the microscope is passed through a glass heat filter.

b. *Knives.* Two small knives for dissecting the embryo are required (Fig. 6). We use Hagedorn No. 1852, straight, 2-inch stainless steel surgical

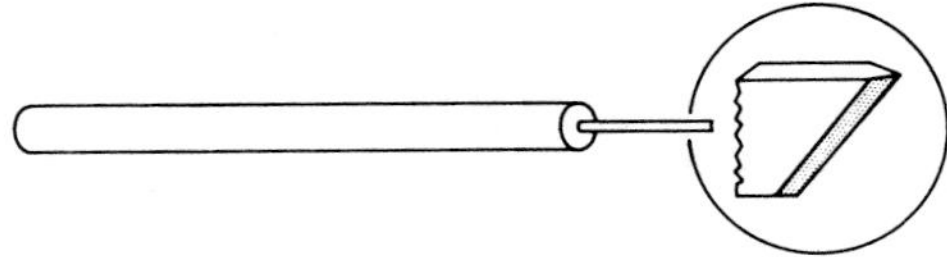

FIG. 6. Dissecting knife with enlarged view of tip to show blade (drawing courtesy of William M. Leach).

needles. The blades of these are reshaped, roughly with an emery wheel and then with a fine hone under a dissecting microscope. Each knife should have a straight, sharp edge ending in a sharp point. The cutting edge should make a 30° angle with the back of the knife. Knives are fastened in dissecting needle holders for use.

c. *Transfer Pipettes.* Tissue is transferred with a pipette made of $\frac{5}{16}$ inch inner diameter glass or quartz tubing. One end is pulled out to about a 0.75 mm inner diameter and fire polished. The pipette is bent about 1 cm from the tip to approximately a 45° angle for ease of handling in the Syracuse watch glass under the dust cover of the dissecting microscope. The total length, including the bulb, is about 12 cm. The rubber bulb of the pipette may be wrapped with cotton approximately $\frac{1}{4}$ inch thick and covered with paper held in place by Scotch tape. This protective covering of the bulb helps prevent the heat of the fingers from expanding the air in the pipette and expelling the embryo during transfer.

d. *Forceps.* For handling the eggs we use curve-tipped forceps, the tips of which have been filed to a dull, rounded shape. This is necessary because eggs are easily punctured.

4. SEALING SUBSTANCES

Cover glasses holding the hanging drop are sealed over the depression slide with heavy mineral oil or Shillaber's heavy immersion oil. Under certain special conditions petrolatum is useful (Sections VIII, B; XIII). All are inert, giving off no vapors that are harmful to cultures. Our usual procedure is to place three small drops of oil equally spaced around the depression of the slide at the time the slide is inverted over the ultraviolet sterilization box (Fig. 5) (Section VII, C, 3).

B. Cleaning Precautions

Weak solutions of commercial detergents in enamel or stainless steel containers are used in cleaning all glassware, which is then rinsed several times, soaked overnight, and rinsed again in Pyrex-distilled water, dried, and sterilized. Cover glasses, new or used, are cleaned and rinsed in the same way but are dried from a 70% alcohol solution. Slides and covers are dried with a lint-free material, such as a linen handkerchief, and stored in covered containers.

If quartz covers are used for ultraviolet irradiation of hanging-drop preparations, they are transferred from rinse water through several changes of absolute alcohol, then into xylene, then into several changes of absolute alcohol, and back to water overnight. These steps complete removal of all immersion and mineral oil which might otherwise absorb ultraviolet radiation.

Embryo-transfer pipettes should be washed frequently in nitric acid or in bichromate-sulfuric acid mixture to remove bits of tissue that adhere to the inner surface and tip of the pipette. If quartz pipettes are used, adhering tissue will absorb the ultraviolet radiation to which they are exposed for sterilization. After the acid washing, the pipettes are rinsed several times and soaked overnight in Pyrex-distilled water.

C. Sterilization

1. Dry Heat

Graduated pipettes, flasks, and Petri dishes containing Syracuse watch glasses or filter paper are sterilized with dry heat. The flasks are plugged with cotton. Petri dishes are stacked in copper boxes or wrapped individually in a double layer of tissue paper. Graduated pipettes are packed in copper containers or wrapped individually in heavy paper. If the Petri dishes are sterilized for the proper amount of time and temperature (2–3 hours at 160–180°C), the tissue paper will not char but will remain strong so that the dishes stacked on a shelf or in a cabinet will remain sterile for days. We question the advisability of using cans for holding the Petri dishes because cultures made from dishes stored in cans may show a slightly abnormal mitotic rate, possibly as a result of some vapor from the cans deposited on the dishes. Individually wrapped dishes are advantageous, because after a can has been opened a number of times over several days the unused dishes may be contaminated.

2. Autoclave

The stock solutions of Carlson's medium can be autoclaved. Since some water is lost from the solutions during autoclaving, it is necessary to replace this before the next autoclaving (Section VII, A, 2, a). The correct temperature and time (120°C for 20–30 minutes) must be carefully observed, otherwise heat-induced reactions among the constituents of the various stock solutions will result. Sterilization must be further limited to the stock solutions because heat reaction between glucose and inorganic salts occurs when the final mixture is autoclaved.

3. Ultraviolet Radiation

We now use ultraviolet radiation almost exclusively (Carlson *et al.*, 1947) for sterilizing culture medium, solutions, slides, cover glasses, knives, forceps, and embryo-transfer pipettes (Fig. 5). Unexposed, processed X-ray film, thin plastic, or heavy Lucite may be used as a cover to shield the eyes from the ultraviolet radiation. Lucite is easier to clean and is rigid enough so that materials can be placed on top of it for storage within easy reach of the microscope. Cover glasses and slides are sterilized by inverting them over openings in the aluminum cover. Smaller openings hold forceps, dissecting knives, and the embryo-transfer pipette. Exposure during the intervals between normal use is sufficient for sterilization.

The same or a separate box may be used for sterilizing medium. We have found the most convenient size to be 19 × 7 × 6 inches deep, lined with aluminum to reflect the ultraviolet radiation in all directions, and covered with a sheet of aluminum or plastic (Fig. 7). It contains a 15 w germicidal lamp at one side near the bottom. The distance between the center of the lamp and the center of each flask is approximately 10 cm. The lamp cord to the box is plugged into a timer that automatically cuts off the lamp at the end of a selected time. Fresh medium is placed in dry heat-sterilized quartz flasks and capped with paraffined corks. Fresh medium is irradiated for 10 minutes. Medium which has been stored is exposed for 3 or 4 minutes before and after opening the container.

Glutamic acid and glycine are nonaromatic amino acids and absorb very little 2537 Å ultraviolet radiation, the predominant wavelength emitted by the germicidal lamp. Solutions containing them can, therefore, be effectively sterilized with such a lamp. Exposure of stock solutions *A* and *B* of Shaw's medium to as much as an hour of radiation does not result in deleterious effects to the medium. Neither the inorganic salts nor glucose in Carlson's or Shaw's medium absorb any significant amount of

FIG. 7. Aluminum lined box for sterilizing culture medium components contained in quartz flasks.

2537 Å ultraviolet, and so are not altered chemically. Excessive exposures, such as half a day or longer, must be avoided, for oxygen within the flask may be transformed into ozone, a toxic substance.

No labels or writing with wax pencil should be placed on the quartz flasks because such materials will absorb the ultraviolet radiation before it reaches the medium. The grease in fingerprints will also absorb ultraviolet radiation; therefore the flasks should be handled by the necks only.

4. MILLIFORE FILTER APPARATUS

Occasionally we have had contamination with yeast in solutions *A* and *B* of Shaw's medium and in the dissecting and hanging-drop solutions of this medium, especially when the solutions are stored in a refrigerator for a long period of time. One way to eliminate this difficulty is to filter these solutions through a millipore apparatus equipped with disc type HA (0.45 μ pore size), which removes all yeast. It also removes carbonate particles that interfere with ultraviolet sterilization.

5. 70% Alcohol

The surface of the egg is sterilized with a 70% alcohol solution.

The procedures outlined above have given us adequate antisepsis for our techniques, for such cultures usually remain uncontaminated for several weeks.

D. Preparation of Hanging-Drop Cultures

1. Checking Embryonic Development

Because all the eggs of a pod develop at the same rate, it is necessary only to check one embryo to find out the stage of development of the remaining embryos. The embryo is removed from the yolk and chorion according to the method described in Section VII, D, 3, but for checking age of development a nonsterile 0.7% solution of NaCl is used instead of the culture medium. The 14-day embryo used for most cytological studies is shown in Fig. 4.

2. Preparation of Eggs

The desired number of eggs (at least 2) is taken from a pod, and adhering sand is carefully removed with forceps or fingers so as not to puncture the chorion. The eggs are dropped into 70% alcohol solution, left for 1 minute, and then transferred with sterile forceps to sterile filter paper in a Petri dish. When the surfaces of the eggs are dry and opaque, the eggs are transferred with sterile forceps to dissecting or hanging-drop medium in a Syracuse watch glass enclosed in a Petri dish. Wetting the end of the forceps first in culture medium facilitates the transfer.

3. Removal and Dissection of Embryo

The dish of hanging-drop medium is placed at the back of the microscope stage and one sterilized egg is immersed in it. This egg will furnish yolk for the hanging-drop preparation and for coating the dish and instruments so that the dissected embryo will not stick to them. The flat side of one of the knives is placed gently on top of the egg to hold it in place. The tip of the other knife is used to puncture the more pointed, caudal cap (Carothers, 1923) to relieve internal pressure during cutting (Fig. 8). The blades of the two knives are now placed side by side with tips pointing in opposite directions close to the puncture and are drawn apart to slice off the caudal tip of the egg, cutting against the bottom of the Syracuse watch glass. The portion cut off is pushed aside and the tips of the two knives are used to restore the circular form to the cut end. The intact end

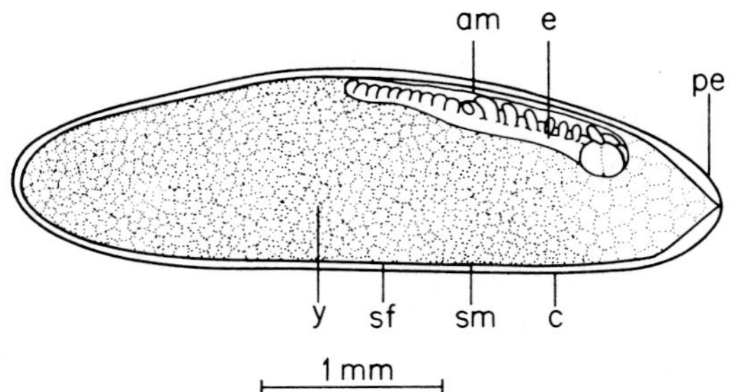

FIG. 8. Cutaway view of embryo in egg. am, Amniotic membrane; c, chorion; e, embryo; pe, caudal end of egg; sf, serosal fluid; sm, serosa; y, yolk (from Gaulden and Kokomoor, 1955).

of the egg is held firmly against the bottom of the dish with one knife, while the side of the blade of the other is drawn toward the cut end with only enough downward pressure to squeeze out the yolk and embryonic material. The embryo and outer envelope (chorion and serosa) are discarded. The anterior fourth of the yolk is cut off and pushed aside to be added later to the hanging drop. The remaining yolk is gently swirled around in a small area that will receive the embryo to be made into a hanging-drop preparation. The dish is then pushed gently to the back of the stage of the microscope.

The dish of dissecting medium is now placed under the field of the microscope and a sterilized egg is placed in it. Yolk and embryo are removed from the egg envelope as described in the preceding paragraph, except that the anterior end of the egg is cut off. The yolk is separated from the embryo, which is then oriented with the appendages upward. The tips of the two needles are brought past each other, with the amniotic membrane covering the appendages between them. This operation rips the membrane down the center, so that it falls away from the embryo. Extreme caution must be taken in this operation to see that the tips of the needles do not damage the ventral surface of the embryo.

The three thoracic appendages are removed as follows. The embryo is steadied with one knife and the cutting edge of the other is placed against the juncture of the appendages and thorax of one side (Fig. 9). The blade is pressed against the dish and rocked, if necessary, to cut off the appendages. This operation is repeated for the other side. The head of the embryo is now severed just anteriorly to the first maxillary segment and discarded. The remaining two pairs of cranial appendages are now readily accessible and are removed. Most of the abdomen is cut off at the junction of the second and third abdominal segments.

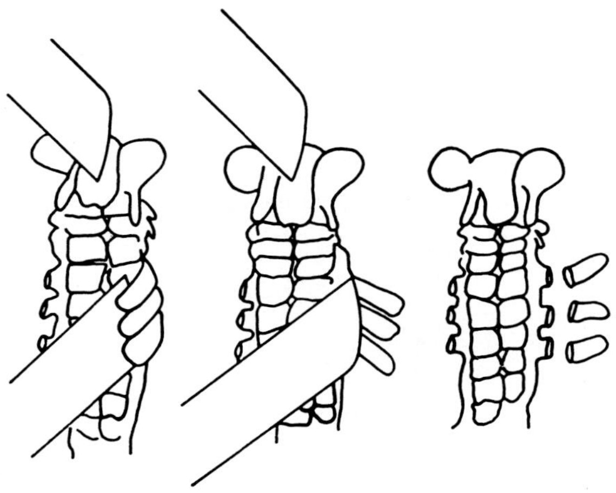

FIG. 9. Method of removal of embryonic appendages with knives (drawing courtesy of Richard A. McGrath).

4. MAKING THE HANGING DROP

All operations to this point have been done with the embryo on its dorsal surface. It is now turned with its ventral surface down and with its long axis parallel to the front edge of the dissecting microscope stage, the abdominal segments to the right. Yolk is drawn into and expelled from the tip of the transfer pipette to coat the surface, and approximately 1.5–2 cm of the end of the pipette is filled with medium. The embryo is drawn up into the end of the pipette, preferably so that the embryo lies within 1–2 mm of the tip. If the embryo is in this position with all pressure released from the pipette bulb, the chance of sucking the embryo up too far or expelling it from the pipette before desired is practically eliminated. The embryo is gently expelled, with as little medium as possible, in the middle of the previously prepared yolk of the hanging-drop medium. The medium remaining in the pipette is discarded and the pipette rinsed several times with hanging-drop medium.

The dish containing dissecting medium is pushed to the back of the stage and the dish containing the dissected embryo brought forward into the field of the microscope. If the embryo transfer and movement of the dish have been done carefully and gently, the embryo will have the same orientation it did in the dissecting medium. The fluid immediately around the embryo is gently stirred with the end of the pipette to disperse any dissecting medium transferred with the embryo. The central area (6–8 mm in diameter) of a sterile cover glass is coated with yolk, which is then replaced with a thin film of hanging-drop medium. The embryo is drawn into the pipette and gently expelled into the fluid on the cover glass as the tip of the pipette is slowly drawn across it. Enough medium should be over the tissue to permit positioning it, but not so much that it can float above the cover glass. The tip of the pipette is now placed next to the embryo and all excess medium withdrawn. This operation pulls the ventral surface of the embryo close to the cover glass—the ventral surface will not adhere but will remain closely appressed. More medium is now added to the embryo in an amount approximately equivalent to 5 to 10 μl. One-quarter of the yolk from the dish of hanging-drop medium is placed around the embryo and any excess fluid removed from the hanging drop. The cover glass is inverted and placed over a depression of a slide. The whole procedure of mounting the embryonic tissue must be performed as soon as it is placed in the dish of hanging-drop medium, so that the cells will not take up much water from the hypotonic medium and evaporation of water from the hanging drop will be kept to a minimum before it is sealed over the depression. All operations from the placing of the egg in the dissecting medium to sealing the cover glass on the depression slide can be performed within 1 minute. Complete osmotic adjustment of the cells requires about 7 minutes.

As soon as the oil has made a complete seal, any excess is removed with the edge of a piece of cleansing tissue or filter paper. It is necessary to take care that one does not warm the cover glass by breathing on it or keeping the fingers close to it. If it is warmed, water will evaporate from the drop and condense on the bottom of the depression. This will change the tonicity of the medium surrounding the embryo and can be counteracted by holding the bottom of the slide firmly against the back of the hand for 10–15 seconds.

E. Study of Hanging-Drop Preparations

1. Microscope Equipment

An ordinary light microscope equipped with 12.5× compensating oculars and 8 mm, 3 or 4 mm dry, and 2 mm oil immersion apochromatic objectives is needed. It is usually necessary to remove the top of the condenser so that the image of the lamp's field diaphragm can be focused in the plane of focus of the microscope. If the lower part of the microscope is not enclosed in an incubator, it is necessary to cover the stage of the microscope with a piece of pliable plastic or unexposed processed X-ray film to shield the slide against the heat of the observer's breath and the warmth irradiated from his body. It is also desirable to use the microscope in a room that is at fairly constant temperature and free of strong air currents.

Because of the thickness of hanging-drop preparations, which are many cell layers thick, phase contrast microscopy does not offer any real advantages over ordinary light microscopy. Phase contrast optics can, however, be used to advantage when the cells are separated and only one layer thick (Section VIII, A, B).

2. Microscope Incubator

If observations are to be made at temperatures higher than those of the room, it is necessary to enclose the microscope in a box that can be heated. Figure 10 shows the setup which we have found to be both convenient and efficient. It is equipped with a small blower (Aminco 4-690 A) which passes air over two 40 w bulbs in a compartment at the left end of the box, through a perforated partition into the main part containing the microscope, and then back to the blower through an insulated pipe leading from the right end of the box. The heat is controlled by a mercury thermo-

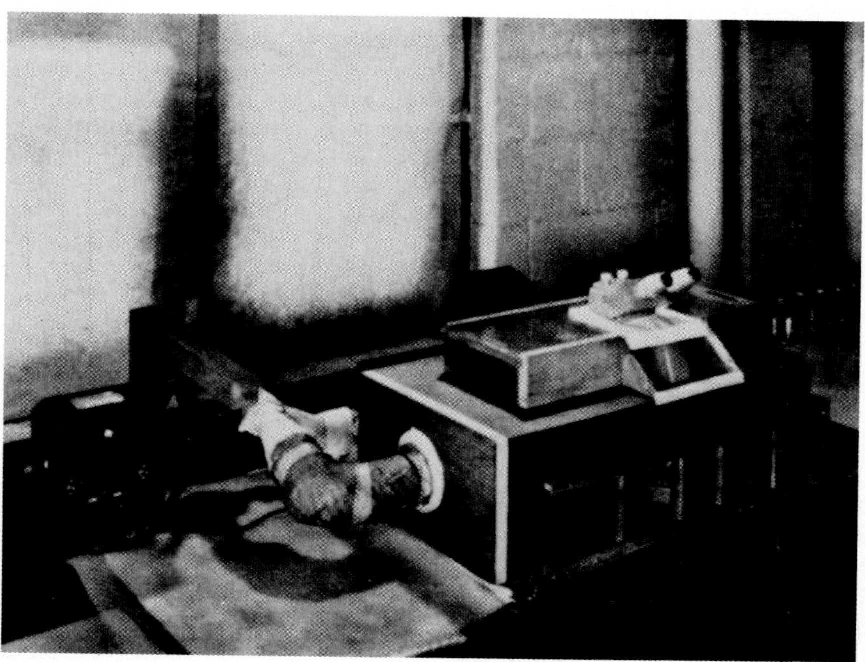

Fig. 10. Microscope incubator with circulating air and thermostatic control. Air ducts from box are connected to blower at rear.

regulator and relay. The thermoregulator should be as near the microscope stage as possible. The temperature of such an incubator should fluctuate no more than ±0.5°C. When a culture slide is put in the incubator, it is placed first on the solid portion of the microscope stage for about 20 seconds so that it is warmed more rapidly than the cover glass. Otherwise water will evaporate from the hanging drop and condense on the bottom of the slide depression.

If several culture preparations are used in one experiment, the slides when not being observed must be kept at the same temperature as when on the microscope stage, and there must be no temperature differential between the top and the bottom of the slide. We have found that a small copper box affords an optimal arrangement. This was constructed in our machine shop and consists of $\frac{1}{4}$ inch copper on all sides, top, and bottom, with three layers of copper racks so placed that only the ends of the slides rest on copper. Its outside dimensions are 7.5 cm high, 12.5 cm wide, and 9.5 cm deep.

The back of the microscope box has a plastic- or glass-covered opening through which the light from the microscope lamp is directed to the mirror of the microscope. The light is filtered through a Pyrex cell containing a solution of copper sulfate (5%) or Zettnow's solution (8.75 gm $CuSO_4$, 0.9 gm $K_2Cr_2O_7$, 0.25 ml H_2SO_4, 150 ml H_2O) to remove heat and prevent a rise in temperature of cells illuminated for observation. The two solutions are equally efficient in filtering out heat, but the latter has the advantage of transmitting a narrower spectrum of visible light. Best illumination is obtained with a ribbon filament bulb arranged to provide Kohler Illumination.

3. Reidentifying Selected Cells

Figure 11 shows the arrangement of neuroblasts at the ventral surface of the dissected embryo as seen with the low power of the compound microscope. They lie roughly in rows at right angles to the midventral line, and so can be designated by number for identification. For example, the cell in solid black is identified as 5R32, because it lies in the fifth segment, on the right side of the body, in the third row, and is the second cell in that row. The segments are easily identified because number 6, the first abdominal segment, has a small appendage, the pleuropodium, which is not removed during dissection. The third thoracic segment is designated the fifth segment and the first maxillary segment is designated the first. Because division of a neuroblast results in a neuroblast and a small ganglion cell, and because the daughter neuroblast occupies the same relative position as the mother cell, the positions of the neuroblasts with respect to one another do not change appreciably during repeated divisions.

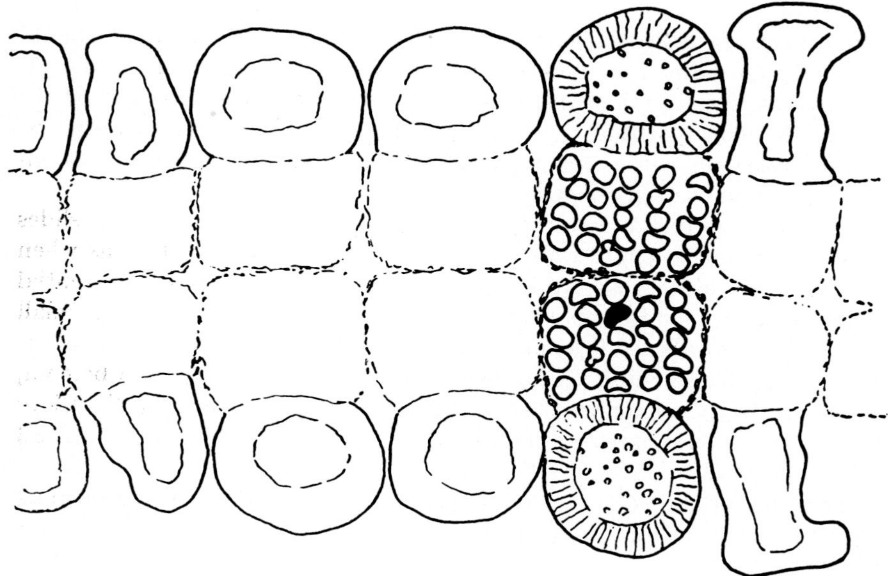

FIG. 11. Useful segments of grasshopper embryo and arrangement of neuroblasts on one of these, the 3rd thoracic segment. From left to right are half of 1st maxillary segment; 2nd maxillary segment; 1st, 2nd, and 3rd thoracic segments; and 1st abdominal segment. The neuroblast in solid black would be designated 5R32 (from Carlson, 1961).

This makes it possible to select a cell and return to it repeatedly over hours or days with assurance that the observations are being made on the same cell.

This identification scheme may also be used to study fixed, sectioned, and stained cells that were first examined when living (Section IX, B, 4, a).

F. Precautions

1. Osmotic Pressure of Medium

The single most important factor in culturing grasshopper neuroblasts in hanging drops is the osmotic pressure of the medium relative to the neuroblasts. A rough estimate of the tonicity of the dissecting medium can be made when the embryo is first separated from the yolk. If the tonicity of the medium is correct, the amniotic membrane as viewed from the side will barely contact the appendages on the ventral surface.

If the medium is hypotonic to the embryo, this membrane will be pushed away from the appendages by passage of water through it into the amniotic cavity. If the medium is hypertonic to the embryo, the membrane will hug the appendages so closely that it will not be visible in side view.

More accurate criteria of correct osmotic pressure of the medium are the appearance and behavior of neuroblasts in hanging-drop preparations. If the solution is strongly hypertonic, nearly all nuclei appear to contain late prophase chromosomes, the chromosomes clump at metaphase, sister chromatids adhere at anaphase, and the mitotic rate is slowed. If it is slightly hypertonic, the metaphase chromosomes appear unusually sharp in outline, clear vacuolelike bodies arise in the protoplasm among the outer ends of the metaphase chromosomes, the nucleoli are invisible, and mitosis is accelerated. If the solution is strongly hypotonic, an excessive number of cells appear to be in the interphase stage, nucleoli are unusually sharp and clear in outline, prometaphase and metaphase chromosomes are barely visible, and mitotic progress is slowed. If the solution is slightly hypotonic, there is a decrease in the number of early and middle prophase stages and mitotic progress is retarded until the cells have adjusted to the lower osmotic pressure.

Even if the solution used has the correct osmotic pressure, certain factors that are often difficult to control may make it hypertonic through evaporation of water. The lapse of too long a time between placing the hanging drop on the cover glass and sealing it over a depression slide can allow excessive evaporation to take place. Differential temperature changes of the cover glass and slide resulting from too much handling, drafts over the slide, changes in the temperature of the air to which the slide is exposed, warm breath, or heat radiated from the body of the observer can cause the cover glass to warm faster than the thick slide, with resulting evaporation from the hanging drop and condensation on the bottom of the depression. It is a wise precaution to see that conditions are such that the slide is always as warm as the cover glass. If condensation does appear in the bottom of the depression, it should be evaporated at once by placing the slide on the warm skin of the arm. A small hanging drop will lose proportionately more water from evaporation than a larger one.

If a person inexperienced in the neuroblast technique wishes to determine whether he is using the proper concentration of solution, he can make counts of the neuroblasts in midmitosis (prometaphase + metaphase + anaphase) at short intervals starting immediately after preparing the hanging drop (Section X, B, 1). If several slides, when averaged, show a rise in the second and third counts, the solution is probably hypertonic; if they show a fall, it is probably hypotonic.

2. Abnormal Embryos

There are several conditions that should immediately warn the observer that an optimal preparation is not being used. If the midmitotic stages and occasionally the prophase stages contain in their cytoplasm refractile round bodies, the division rate of these cells will probably be slower than normal.

If an embryo seems to be flaccid, it should be discarded. Flaccid embryos usually appear more whitish than normal and are not suitable for cytological studies.

If an embryo in culture preparation contains a large number of very small oil droplets that resemble yolk, the neuroblasts do not usually divide at a normal rate. Such cultures should be discarded.

If it is found that some embryos in a given egg pod vary in age by as much as 2 days, none of the embryos should be used for culture preparations. We have found that the neuroblasts in embryos from such egg pods often divide more slowly than normal.

Embryos from eggs laid by old females or by females that have been reared in the laboratory usually show considerable variation in development rate and are not, therefore, optimal material for mitotic studies. Tipton and St. Amand (1954) examined the respiration rate of embryos from old females (termed by them "winter eggs," i.e., eggs laid in January and February by females collected in the field during September and October, either as nymphs or as adults). They found a lower respiration rate in such embryos than in embryos from recently collected females. There would appear, therefore, to be an inherent physiological basis for the slower mitotic rate of neuroblasts in embryos from old females. These observations pertain to eggs that are stored at 17°C until they reach a stage of development equivalent to that reached in 14 days at 26°C.

3. Oxygen and Carbon Dioxide Tension

The neuroblast requires oxygen for mitotic activity, but it seems to tolerate oxygen tension below that of air. Increased oxygen tension has little or no effect. Increased CO_2 tension, however, has pronounced effects.

The buffering qualities of Shaw's culture media and the volume of the depression slides described above are adequate at 26°C for maintaining the neuroblast in division at approximately normal rate for about 5 days. At 38°C, however, division proceeds at normal rate for only 10–12 hours and at lower rates for days. The gradual slowing down of division, which ends in permanent cessation of mitosis 3–4 weeks after preparation of the hanging-drop cultures, may possibly be due, in part, to abnormal partial pressure of CO_2. That this is not wholly responsible for decline of the cultures is demonstrated by lack of revival with periodic changes of culture medium.

G. pH

With the exception of some studies involving chemicals which act best at different pH's, we have prepared our culture media at pH 6.5–7.3. Neuroblasts seem to tolerate wide variations in pH without noticeable immediate effects on cell structures or on mitotic rate, but we have not made a thorough study of the effects of pH.

VIII. Separated Cell Techniques

A. Mechanical Separation

Embryos are prepared in the usual way for the hanging-drop technique and placed in a small amount of Shaw's culture medium on a cover glass. This is inverted over a plain glass slide that has on it a ring of mineral oil slightly smaller in diameter than the smallest dimension of the cover glass. The weight of the cover glass causes the tissue to spread out in a thin layer and some of the neuroblasts are separated mechanically from adjacent cells. The degree of flattening can be controlled by the amount of mineral oil used. With just the right amount, neuroblasts in a single layer can be obtained. This technique and its use are described by Kawamura and Carlson (1962).

B. Chemical Techniques

A method for obtaining large quantities of suspended cells for physiological studies has been described by St. Amand and Tipton (1954) and has been modified for cytological work by Roberts (1955) and Gaulden and Perry (1958). The following procedure will yield a large number of single neuroblast cells and numerous tissue fragments. Fifteen to 20 embryos, 13.5–14 days old (at 26°C), are separated from yolk and membranes in Carlson's dissecting medium, which contains 3.2 ml of water and from which the calcium chloride has been omitted (no adjustment in the sodium chloride content is required). Embryos are transferred with a medicine dropper to 4 ml of this medium, to which has been added 3 mg each of trypsin and hyaluronidase, and are incubated in a covered dish at 35°C for 35 minutes. Very little medium will be transferred if all the embryos are drawn into the pipette and allowed to settle to the tip. They are passed through two 3-minute rinses of Shaw's dissecting medium containing 3.3 ml of water but minus calcium chloride, and placed in Shaw's 3.3 complete medium for 3 minutes. Embryos are transferred to a tapered tube (we use 2 ml centrifuge tubes) containing approximately 0.25 ml of Shaw's 6.0 medium. For separating the cells a pipette of 0.85 mm inside diameter is used, the tip of which has been fire polished. The end has an abrupt taper so that only the tip constricts the embryos. The pipette bulb is equipped with a cotton and paper cover (Section VII, A, 3, c) to prevent expansion of the contained air by heating of the bulb by the fingers. Some medium is drawn up into the pipette and then the embryos are drawn into and expelled very slowly from the pipette about 10–15 times. It is essential that no air bubbles be mixed with the embryos. This is an exceedingly crucial step in the procedure because the neuroblasts can be easily damaged at this time. A small square or circle is outlined on the cover glass by extruding petrolatum from a 26-gauge hypodermic needle; as thin a film of brei as possible is placed within this area, so that the single cells will not, when on the bottom of the drop, be out of range of the objective of the microscope. The cover glass is sealed over a depression slide with heavy mineral oil. Fat-bottomed depressions should be used if the cultures are to be observed by phase contrast microscopy or with reflecting objectives. Shaw's medium with 6.0 ml of water provides enough water to saturate the moist chamber without becoming hypertonic.

Cultures prepared in this way have a large number of single neuroblasts and many small and large fragments of embryonic tissue. Some fragments consist of sheets of neuroblasts one cell thick. Single neuroblasts floating in the culture will complete division only if they are in prophase-anaphase at the time of separation, and we have not seen these cells go into a second division. They do not attach to the cover glass even when cultures are left inverted overnight. A few hours after separation all isolated cells appear to be in a stage similar to normal interphase. Neuroblasts in tissue fragments of several to many cells, however, do divide normally and have been observed to continue division for several weeks (Gaulden and Perry, 1958). That the cells in these fragments are in good condition is also evidenced by the fact that differentiation, i.e., formation of pigment and development of nerve fibers, begins approximately 3 days after preparation (Gaulden and Perry, 1958). Cultures prepared as described above will not tolerate temperatures much above 26°C. The reason for this has not yet been determined.

In the separation procedure all instruments and glass with which the embryos come in contact are coated with yolk. This is an essential step to prevent cells and tissue fragments from adhering to the glass and instruments.

The cells in the tissue fragments divide normally and the daughter cells are no different from those *in situ* with the exception of cells on the edges of the fragments. These will often form processes similar to those observed in chick fibroblast cultures.

If only a few isolated cells are required, a much simpler procedure can be used. An embryo is dissected in Carlson's 3.2 medium minus calcium, placed in the enzyme solution, and mounted on a cover glass with the dorsal surface against the cover in a drop of the enzyme solution and sealed over a depression slide. At 38°C the neuroblasts are extruded from the embryo within a few minutes, and many of the cells form attenuating processes at the surface and edges of the embryo.

Recent unpublished observations by Richard A. McGrath indicate that under certain conditions large fibroblastlike cells migrate out from the embryonic moiety and divide, forming thin sheets of cells against the cover glass. We are not certain of the conditions conducive to this, but preliminary tests suggest that it may result when, during the removal of the appendages of the embryo, much of the tissue lateral of the neuroblast area is also removed.

IX. Fixed Cell Techniques

A. Squashes

1. Thick Squashes

For examination of chromosomes as well as a number of other cytological features of the neuroblast, the squash preparation, made in a modification of Zirkle's (1937) mounting medium, is a useful technique. A large number of squashes can be prepared relatively quickly, and since the cover glass does not have to be removed for permanent mounting, no cells are lost during preparation of the slide.

a. *Acetocarmine.* The embryo is fixed for 1 minute in 3 parts absolute alcohol and 1 part glacial acetic acid. This brief period gives excellent fixation but does not harden the embryo. It is then placed in a solution of acetocarmine for approximately 20–30 minutes, care being taken to submerge the embryo. If fresh acetocarmine is used, it is advisable to open the staining dish about 30 minutes prior to staining the embryo so that some of the acetic acid can evaporate; otherwise the embryo will become so soft that it will break up when transferred to the slide. The stained embryo is placed in the center of a slide and the excess staining fluid withdrawn by a pipette. One drop of a mixture of 3 parts acetocarmine, 3 parts distilled water, and 2 parts white Karo syrup is placed on the embryo. A cover glass with one drop of the mixture in its center is lowered slowly onto the slide so that the two drops coalesce and spread to the edges of the cover glass without inclusion of air bubbles. The cells are separated and spread by letting the eraser end of a pencil strike the cover glass vertically from a height of about 2 inches. To prevent any sideward movement, which will break the cells, the pencil moves inside a 3 inch segment of glass tubing clamped to a ring stand.

b. *Feulgen.* Embryos are fixed in 3 parts absolute alcohol to 1 part glacial acetic acid for 20 minutes, run through the alcohol series to water, hydrolyzed in 1 *N* HCl at 58°C for 6 minutes, rinsed in distilled water, and then transferred to Feulgen solution for 10 minutes at room temperature. Excess solution is removed by two washes of SO_2 water followed by one rinse in distilled water. After 1 minute in 45% acetic acid, an embryo is placed in the center of a slide, excess acetic acid is removed with a pipette, and one drop of a mixture of 1 part formalin, 1 part white Karo syrup, and 3 parts water is added. One drop of this mixture is placed on a cover glass and the squash prepared as described for the acetocarmine stain (Section IX, A, 1, a). It should be noted that the embryos easily adhere to glass after hydrolysis unless surrounded by fluid, and so require careful handling.

Evaporation of water at the edge of the cover glass in both the acetocarmine and Feulgen squashes results in a semipermanent seal by the Karo residue, which will, however, absorb water and become soft if stored under conditions of high humidity. This can be prevented by drying the slides and then ringing the cover glass with balsam or other cement. The Karo mounting medium has a refractive index close to that of balsam and Euparol. It is fluid enough to allow flattening of the cells, and its water base permits mounting of cells in it directly from the acetocarmine stain or from the 45% acetic acid wash. The acetic acid and the formalin both prevent the growth of microorganisms and preserve the cells. If no air bubbles are included in the squashes, and if the preparations are kept at a fairly constant temperature, the chromosomes will retain their original clarity and intensity of stain for several years.

2. Thin Squashes

A squash technique involving the crushing of neuroblasts with heavy pressure, rather than simply separating them, has been developed recently (McGrath *et al.*, 1963) to spread the chromosomes for detailed microscopic and autoradiographic study. The tissue is immersed 4–6 minutes in sodium citrate to swell the cells and separate the chromosomes and sister chromatids, fixed 5–30 minutes in 50% acetic acid, and then squashed with considerable pressure between a slide coated with potassium chrome alum subbing (Boyd, 1955) and a No. 1 cover glass. The slide is immersed immediately in liquid nitrogen until the bubbling stops, the cover glass pried off, and the slide immersed at once in 95% ethanol. After 1–3 minutes the slide is removed and allowed to dry in air. Cytoplasmic stainability may be prevented by hydrolysis in 1 *N* HCl at 60°C for 5 minutes, followed by a 1 minute rinse in distilled water, and air-drying.

A useful staining procedure for these squashes is to immerse them 5–30 seconds in 0.1% toluidine blue in citrate buffer at pH 5.0. (Staining time is determined by the stain intensity desired; overstained preparations may be destained with glycerin.) They are rinsed in tertiary butyl alcohol for 0.5–2.0 minutes and air-dried. If they are thoroughly dried they may be mounted directly in Euparol or Permount. If some water remains in them, they may be mounted in the following mixture, which has an aqueous base: 3.0 gm gelatin; 0.2 gm potassium chrome alum; 80 ml distilled water; 20 ml glycerin; 0.1 gm toluidine blue dye. Preparations are blotted to remove excess mounting medium.

B. Sections

Preparation of the grasshopper embryo for sectioning with the rotary microtome can be accomplished for most purposes with the routine procedures used for many animal cells. Except where noted, we have found that hard paraffin (melting point of 58–60°C) gives excellent results in serial sectioning. A weak polonium source placed directly over the block during sectioning reduces static electricity and facilitates obtaining a complete ribbon. Given below are some of the fixatives, stains, and enzyme digestion techniques we have used with success on sectioned embryos, as well as some procedures we have found useful in particular studies on the neuroblast.

1. Fixatives

Carnoy's (3 parts absolute alcohol and 1 part glacial acetic acid), 50% acetic acid, and Bouin's or Allen's B15 fixatives give good results with the grasshopper embryo. Since the embryo is small, fixation times can be brief; for example, we routinely fix in Carnoy's for sectioning for only 5 minutes. For fixation in Bouin's or Allen's B15 fixative, we usually allow the embryos to stand for 30–60 minutes. In the case of embryos fixed in Carnoy's solution, enough eosin is added to the 95% alcohol in the alcohol series so that the embryos take on a slight pinkish color, which facilitates seeing them during solution changes and embedding.

2. Staining

The neuroblasts in sectioned material up to at least 10μ in diameter stain well in Feulgen (Gaulden, 1959; McGrath, 1963), methyl green-pyronine (Gaulden and Carlson, 1951), mercuric bromphenol blue (Kawamura, 1960), azure B-bromide (Stevens, 1962), and crystal violet. Staining the neuroblast in sections with Feulgen obviates the difficulties of handling whole embryos after hydrolysis and staining. (Section IX, A, 1, b).

3. Enzyme Treatment

Digestion of deoxyribonucleic acid and ribonucleic acid in neuroblasts can be performed on sections up to 10μ thick or on squash preparations. The enzymes used should be free of proteolytic action and all water should be Pyrex-distilled. The slides should be shaken frequently during the digestion period to free air bubbles that will sometimes collect on the slides over the sections.

a. *Buffer Solutions.* It is important that the enzyme solutions be buffered. For DNase an exact pH of 6.5 is recommended for the best results. This pH is in the optimal region for buffer action and is near optimum (pH 6.8) for DNase activity. Solutions of 0.01 *M* Na_2HPO_4 and 0.01 *M* KH_2PO_4 can be used as follows to make the two buffer solutions needed: (1) 1 part of the Na_2HPO_4 solution and 2 parts of the KH_2PO_4 solution give a 0.01 *M* phosphate solution at pH 6.4–6.5; (2) 1 part of Na_2HPO_4 solution and 1 part of KH_2PO_4 solution give a 0.01 *M* phosphate solution at pH 6.8.

b. *Digestion with DNase.* Slides with sections on them are placed for 2 hours at 37°C in the following solution: 10 ml buffer solution (1), 90 ml water, 0.123 gm $MgSO_4$, 0.10 gm bovine albumin, and 0.01 gm DNase (crystallized at least once).

After digestion the slides are transferred to cold 5% trichloroacetic acid for 3 minutes, rinsed with distilled water, and then treated as desired.

The bovine albumin in the DNase solution stabilizes the enzyme, but for best results it is recommended that the DNase solution be made fresh before using.

c. *Digestion with RNase.* Sections on slides are placed in a 0.05% RNA solution in buffer solution (2) at 37°C for 2 hours. In contrast to DNase, RNase is very stable and can be stored in solution for repeated use. It can be stored in the refrigerator but should not be frozen. Ribonuclease needs no metal ions for action, and it will act well from pH 6.0 to pH 7.5.

4. Special Techniques

a. *Reidentification in Serial Sections of Cells Studied in Living Condition.* To follow the incorporation of specific labeled precursors into cell structures at given mitotic stages, it is necessary to be able to relocate in an autoradiograph particular cells that were studied when living. For example, if one wishes to know whether thymidine is incorporated during a given mitotic stage, a cell in a culture preparation is identified by number (Section VII, E, 3) and observed until it reaches the beginning of that stage. The medium surrounding the embryo is then replaced with medium containing labeled thymidine. Observations on the cell are continued until it reaches the end of this stage, when it is fixed. A useful fixation procedure is to place the cover glass with its hanging-drop culture over a depression containing a drop of a 1% solution of osmic acid. After 60 seconds the embryo is transferred with a pipette to Carnoy's fixative. This procedure of fixation, together with gentle handling, insures that the ventral surface of the embryo remains flat. The embryo is embedded in a drop of paraffin on a glycerin-coated glass slide so that the position of the ventral surface is known. In an alternative procedure (McGrath, 1963), the embryo is allowed to remain attached to the cover glass from fixation through the alcohol series into paraffin. The paraffin block is trimmed while still remaining attached to the cover glass and then placed on a cold surface (4–5°C). The temperature change loosens the block from the cover glass. The previously studied neuroblasts are now situated within 30–40μ of the surface; if deeper, they could not have been observed accurately in the living tissue. If the sectioning is done at 6–8μ, therefore, all portions of the neuroblasts to be re-examined will be included in the first seven sections at most. It may be desirable to cut a few additional sections, on the chance that some of the deeper neuroblasts will be needed to determine the exact position of the previously studied cells.

b. *Thin Serial Sections.* For some types of studies it is necessary to have thin serial sections of the embryo, as for example, in autoradiographic studies of the nucleolus, which is 1μ in diameter when fixed.

The following technique (Stevens, 1962), though somewhat laborious, gives fairly uniform 1 or 2μ sections in ribbon form. Embryos are fixed in Carnoy's for 5 minutes, dehydrated, cleared in benzene, and placed in a mixture of equal parts of benzene and hard paraffin (60–62°C) overnight at room temperature or for shorter periods at 65°C. The embryos are then transferred to the following mixture at 63–66°C for 6–12 hours: 5 gm beeswax, 5 gm gum damar, and 90 gm hard paraffin (60–62°C). To prepare this mixture, the waxes are melted and mixed, then the powdered damar is added and mixed thoroughly. The mixture is filtered through several layers of mirror cloth prior to use. Embryos are embedded so that the position of the ventral surface is known (Section IX, B, 4, a). Sections are cut on a rotary microtome with a Schick razor blade sharpened according to the method of Sjöstrand (1956). As the ribbon comes off the blade, it floats onto a 0.2% sodium chrom glucosate solution contained in a Lucite trough that is fastened onto the razor blade holder (Gettner and Ornstein, 1956). Use of the paraffin mixture and dry ice to cool the trough solution prevents crumbling of the thin sections. Sodium chrom glucosate prevents rusting of the razor blade.

C. Autoradiographs

Autoradiographs can be made of squashed or sectioned neuroblasts containing radioactive labeled compounds (Gaulden, 1959; McGrath, 1963; McGrath *et al.*, 1963).

Slides are cleaned in bichromate-sulfuric acid mixture or 95% ethanol and subbed by dipping them in chrome alum-gelatin solution at 21–26°C (Boyd, 1955). The slides are drained and dried in a vertical position. If sections are used, paraffin is removed with two rinses of xylene, and slides are hydrated with an ethanol-water series. If thin squash preparations (Section IX, A, 2) are used, the slides are air-dried before application of emulsion.

Emulsion in the form of stripping film or liquid may be used. The AR10 film of Kodak Limited, London, has an emulsion of a uniform thickness of 5μ. Liquid emulsion (Kodak NTB, NTB-2, or NTB-3), is easier to handle than stripping film and, because of its fluidity, surrounds the cells more thoroughly than does the film.

Stripping film is applied to slides according to the technique described by Doniach and Pelc (1950). For application of liquid emulsion, the slides are dipped in the emulsion at 40–50°C. After application of either type of emulsion the slides are dried in a vertical position and stored for the desired exposure time at 4–17°C in light- and air-tight boxes containing Drierite or silica gel. The preparations are processed at 17–18°C. They are placed in Kodak D-19 developer for 4–5 minutes, rinsed in distilled water for 15 seconds, immersed in full strength Kodak acid fixer for 5 minutes, and rinsed 20 minutes in running tap water and then in distilled water. The use of fixer without hardener permits better penetration of some stains.

Neuroblasts can be stained with Feulgen reagent before the emulsion is applied. Other stains, such as methyl green-pyronine, azure B bromide, or toluidine blue, are leached out by the developer and fixer and must, therefore, be used after processing of the emulsion.

Autoradiographs of neuroblasts can be made into permanent preparations by dehydrating and covering them with a thin solution of standard mounting medium and a cover glass. For mounting with an aqueous base medium the technique described in Section IX, A, 2 is recommended.

D. Electron Microscope Techniques

It has generally proved difficult to obtain good preservation of the cells of embryonic tissues of most organisms and of invertebrate tissues at any stage of development. For analysis of these difficulties and details of methods for achieving excellent preservation of the grasshopper neuroblast fine structure, the reader is referred to the work of Stevens (1962).

X. Radiation Techniques

Certain features of neuroblasts make them particularly advantageous for radiation studies. The closeness of these cells to the surface makes them accessible to poorly penetrating radiations such as alpha, beta, and ultraviolet radiations. Their constant number over many cell generations simplifies the use of counts of different stages to determine effects on mitosis. Their constant position in relation to one another makes it possible to select certain cells before irradiation and to reidentify these cells repeatedly over long periods of time in culture and ultimately in fixed preparations.

A. Irradiation Methods

The details of techniques for exposing neuroblasts to different types of radiation and to agents modifying their response to radiation are described in published reports; therefore, only salient points will be mentioned here.

1. X and Gamma Rays

Grasshopper embryos may be exposed to the highly penetrating X- and γ-rays *in vivo*, i.e., within the intact chorion of the egg, or *in vitro* in hanging-drop cultures or suspended in culture medium (Carlson, 1938a, b, 1940, 1941a, b, 1942, 1954; Carlson *et al.*, 1949, 1953; Carlson and Harrington, 1955; Gaulden *et al.*, 1953; Gaulden and Kokomoor, 1955;

Harrington and Koza, 1951; St. Amand, 1956; Shaw, 1956b; Tipton and St. Amand, 1954).

It should be noted that the osmotic pressure of neuroblasts changes immediately after exposure to 100r or more of X-rays (Harrington and Koza, 1951). Culture medium isotonic to untreated cells is hypotonic to them after irradiation, and a measurable increase in their diameter occurs.

2. Beta Particles

A technique has been devised by Gaulden *et al.* (1952) for exposing neuroblasts to a known amount of beta radiation. Phosphorus-32 bakelite plaques are used as a source of pure beta radiation of uniform high intensity.

Embryos dissected for hanging-drop cultures (Section VII, D, 3) are placed ventral surface down in the center of an exposure dish. The dish consists of two metal rings assembled in such a way that the inner one carries with it a 0.001 inch rubber hydrochloride membrane that forms the bottom of the dish. The inside dimensions of the inner ring, 33 mm diameter and 12 mm depth, exceed the maximum range of P^{32} β-rays in water. The ventral surface of the embryo is held against the bottom of the dish by affixing the freshly cut edges of the embryo to the membrane with gentle pressure. The embryos are covered with dissecting medium to a depth of 1 cm to insure that the amount of radiation scattered back from the culture medium to the cells is exactly the same as that contributed by the radiation scattered by the polystyrene electrodes used for calibrating the plaques. This aqueous layer also has essentially the same absorption and scattering properties as the cells.

The exposure dish is placed in a chamber that is designed to bring the bakelite plaque beneath the dish and in contact with the membranous bottom of the dish, and at the same time to protect the worker from exposure. Since the neuroblasts are separated from the source only by the membrane, the uncertainties of extended depth dose calculations are eliminated, and an accurate determination of the amount of beta radiation reaching the cells can be made.

Following exposure the embryos can be easily detached from the membrane for hanging-drop preparations or for fixing.

3. Alpha Particles

A method of treating neuroblasts with alpha particles has been developed and described by Rogers (1955). Because of the high linear energy transfer and short paths of alpha particles, it is necessary to prepare the hanging drop on a layer of high quality mica that can be split into sheets as thin as 2.5–5μ. The mica is fastened with paraffin to one surface of a small polystyrene ring, which is then inverted and sealed to a plain glass slide. Such preparations are optically suitable for study with the oil immersion objective of the microscope.

The radiation source may be prepared by electrochemical deposition (Haïssinsky, 1937; Kanne, 1937) or, if a strong source is needed, by the distillation technique (Rona and Schmidt, 1928). Rogers (1955) used the former. By varying the time of deposition on silver or palladium rods, 1, 2, and 4 mm in diameter, sources varying in strength from 10^3 to 10^6 particles per second per square millimeter were obtained. All rods had shanks 4 mm in diameter that could be fitted into a common source holder (Fig. 12). This consists of a brass-enclosed polystyrene cylinder threaded at the

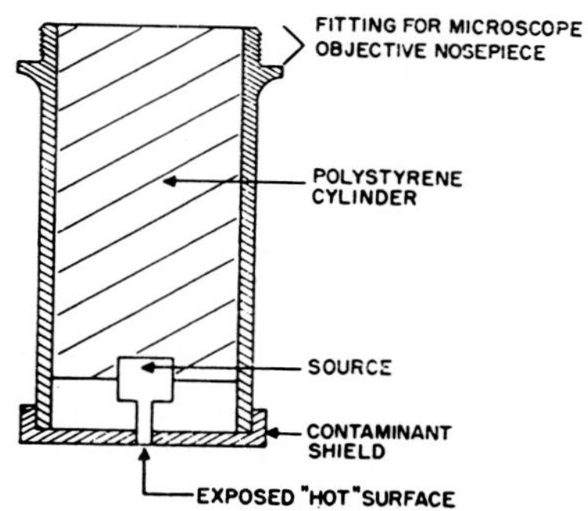

FIG. 12. Alpha particle source and microscope-adapted mount (from Rogers, 1955).

upper end to fit the threads of a microscope nosepiece. Fitted over the lower end of the source holder is a brass cap with a central hole exactly the size of the source, through which the source extends. The lower surfaces of the cap and source are flush.

The area to be treated is centered under the microscope. With the use of a special calibration of the focus adjustment knob of the microscope the source can be quickly adjusted for any preselected distance, swung into place over the hanging drop, and the cells irradiated for the desired time.

For a discussion of dosimetry of alpha particles in investigations of this type the reader is referred to the paper by Rogers (1955).

4. Ultraviolet Radiation

Neuroblasts can be used for the experimental study of the effects of whole surface radiation (Carlson and Hollaender, 1944, 1945, 1948; Carlson and McMaster, 1951; Carlson, 1954; Roberts, 1955) and microbeam radiation (Gaulden and Perry, 1958; Gaulden, 1960; Carlson *et al.*, 1960). Either polychromatic or monochromatic ultraviolet radiation can be used to treat the neuroblast, the latter being easily obtained by interposing a monochromater between the radiation source and the cells.

a. *Whole Cell Irradiation.* Hanging-drop preparations of embryos are made on quartz cover glasses. Half of the embryo is shielded from radiation by attaching a small piece of black paper to the surface of the cover glass with rubber cement in such a way that the edge of the paper coincides with the midventral line of the embryo. Thus the cells on one side of the embryo can serve as controls for those irradiated on the other side. Following irradiation, the black paper can be easily removed. Only those irradiated cells are used for observation which lie against the cover glass and are not shielded by the dermatoblast nuclei that sometimes lie over the neuroblast and shield it from ultraviolet radiation. Neuroblasts situated close to the midventral line are not used because of the possibility that those on the control side received some scattered radiation and those on the treated side were partially shielded.

b. *Microbeam Irradiation.* Parts of the neuroblast can be irradiated with a microbeam of ultraviolet radiation by using the apparatus originally described by Uretz and Perry (1957). The reflecting objective recommended by them, however, limits considerably the optical properties of the microscope, so a Zeiss Ultrafluor objective, the lenses of which are corrected for visible and ultraviolet wavelengths, is preferred. The image of the aperture on which the ultraviolet radiation falls is focused on a fluorescent plate and adjusted to coincide with cross hairs in the eyepiece of the microscope. After the ultraviolet beam has been cut off with an opaque shield or shutter, the image of the part of the cell to be irradiated is made to coincide with the cross hairs, and the desired exposure given. Subsequent study can be carried out under another microscope, if desired.

5. Modification of Radiation Effects

a. *Heat.* To determine the effects of pretreatment and posttreatment with heat on X-ray-induced chromosome breakage, eggs are immersed in water at the temperature and for the time desired (Gaulden, 1949).

b. *Oxygen.* The effects of oxygen on the mitotic response of neuroblasts to X-rays has been determined by exposing whole eggs to different concentrations of gaseous oxygen as well as to nitrogen or carbon dioxide, or by evacuation of the exposure chambers (Gaulden *et al.*, 1953). Moistened eggs are placed in small polystyrene containers, the lids of which are sealed with vacuum grease. The exposure dishes are alternately evacuated to a few millimeters of mercury and flushed with a given gaseous mixture three times prior to irradiation to insure that the atmosphere around the eggs is the intended one. Each container is connected with a manometer to allow checks on pressure. With the exception of those eggs irradiated *in vacuo*, irradiation is done at a few millimeters positive pressure to permit detection of leaks in the system.

c. *Sodium Hydrosulfite.* Shaw (1956b) has reduced oxygen tension by exposing neuroblasts *in vitro* to sodium hydrosulfite, which quickly combines with molecular oxygen in solution. Dissected embryos are placed in sealed chambers containing freshly prepared sodium hydrosulfite in Shaw's medium 3–5 minutes before irradiation. Within 2 minutes after irradiation the embryos are returned to dishes of dissecting medium to remove the sodium hydrosulfite and its decomposition products. The embryos are then made into hanging-drop cultures for examination.

d. *Yolk.* The influence of embryonic yolk on the ability of neuroblasts to recover from the mitotic effects of X-rays has been investigated by Gaulden and Kokomoor (1955). Having determined that one-fourth of the yolk in an embryo gives the best mitotic activity in unirradiated embryos in Carlson's medium, they studied irradiated cells in cultures containing one-fourth yolk and in cultures containing no yolk.

e. *Hypertonic Medium.* The influence of hypertonic medium on the response of cells to X-radiation has been tested with the neuroblast (Gaulden, unpublished data). Hanging-drop cultures of embryos are irradiated in Carlson's medium isotonic to them. Immediately after irradiation (within 30–60 seconds), the isotonic medium is replaced with medium hypertonic to the cells, that is, it contains 1.2 times the salt concentrations of the isotonic medium, and observations on the cells are begun.

f. *Light.* The only agent affecting the response of neuroblasts to ultraviolet radiation is photoreactivating light, that is, light of wavelengths 3000–5000 Å. Carlson and McMaster (1951) used as the criterion of effect the spheration induced by ultraviolet in the nucleolus of the neuroblast. Exposure to the ultraviolet is performed as outlined above in Section X, A, 4. To determine the response of the neuroblast nucleolus in the absence of photoreactivating light, cultures are prepared under room lights filtered by yellow cellophane, exposed to monochromatic ultraviolet radiation, and observed with light passed through a Corning filter No. 3482 to absorb all wavelengths of light below 5350 Å. To detect photoreactivation, other hanging-drop preparations are irradiated in white light and observed with unfiltered light (except for copper sulfate solution) of a ribbon filament research lamp.

B. Methods for Making Observations

Observations on irradiated neuroblasts can be made on living cells in hanging-drop cultures or on fixed and stained cells. Time-lapse photography has been used in only one study (Roberts, 1955).

1. Culture Studies

Mitotic effects can be determined by either of two methods. Individual cells in desired stages of mitosis can be selected (Section VII, E, 3), irradiated immediately, and followed for hours or days with records made of the time and stage of mitosis at as frequent intervals after irradiation as desired for the particular problem under study. Alternatively, counts of neuroblasts in a given mitotic stage per embryo can be made at regular intervals to determine the number of cells passing through that stage over a period of time after irradiation. This method requires selection of a stage or stages whose duration is known to be unaffected by the radiation. The combined stages prometaphase, metaphase, and anaphase, with a duration of 22± 1 minute at 38°C, are useful because they are quite resistant to ionizing radiations and can be quickly identified in the rapid survey made at each counting interval. If 22 minutes is selected as the counting interval, the counts will include all the cells that pass through these stages.

Morphological effects are determined by careful observation of individual cells. Chromosome aberrations can be observed with a certain degree of accuracy in living cells (St. Amand, 1956) but can best be analyzed in fixed-stained cells.

2. Fixed Cell Studies

Cells that have been treated within the intact chorion of the egg with X- or γ-rays or in hanging-drop preparations with any type of radiation may be squashed or sectioned for study. The techniques used are the same as those given in Section IX, A, B. In the irradiated cell the mitotic and morphological picture can be quite different at different times after irradiation. It is necessary, therefore, to fix embryos at varying time intervals after irradiation so that the consecutive series of events can be reconstructed from a study of the different preparations. In studies of the mitotic effects of irradiation it is often useful to make counts of certain mitotic stages in embryos fixed at regular time intervals after treatment. For this purpose acetocarmine squash preparations are used and all the neuroblasts per preparation are examined.

Fixing and staining of a given cell in a hanging-drop culture can be easily accomplished by adding a small drop of acetocarmine to the hanging drop. Dilution of the carmine by the culture medium prevents intense staining of the cells underlying the neuroblasts, and the chromosomes of the latter cells can be readily observed. For fixation alone the ideal procedure is to place a drop of 1% osmic acid in the depression of the hanging-drop preparation. To prevent blackening of the cells by the osmic acid vapor, the cover glass carrying the dissected embryo is transferred after 1 minute to a clean depression slide for observation.

XI. Chemical Techniques

The effects of a chemical on the neuroblast can be easily determined by adding it to the culture medium. Embryos can be treated in large numbers in a dish of dissecting medium or individually in hanging-drop preparations. Only those chemicals can be used that do not, at desired concentrations, alter the osmotic pressure of the medium. Small changes in osmotic pressure can be corrected by adjusting the concentration of medium components. Details of the use of several compounds on the neuroblast are reported elsewhere: colchicine (Gaulden and Carlson, 1951), versene (Sarkar, 1957), agmatine (St. Amand *et al.*, 1960), and sodium hydrosulfite (Shaw, 1956b). The uptake of labeled amino acids, deoxyribosides, and ribosides has been studied by adding them to the culture medium of hanging-drop preparations (Gaulden and Perry, 1958; Gaulden, 1959; McGrath, 1963).

XII. Gas Techniques

The influence of a gas on the neuroblast *in vitro* can be determined by passing it through a small exposure chamber on top of which is suspended a hanging-drop preparation (Gaulden *et al.*, 1949). The sides of the exposure chamber consist of two semicircular pieces of glass made by cutting in half a 5 mm length of glass tubing of 15 mm inside diameter. The tubing is affixed with vacuum grease to the surface of a glass slide with the two halves separated to admit on opposite sides the ends of two pipettes (2 mm outside diameter). Vacuum grease is used to close the space between the two halves of tubing and to seal on top of the chamber a cover glass carrying a hanging-drop preparation of an embryo. A large drop of culture medium placed in the bottom of the chamber helps maintain correct osmotic pressure in the hanging-drop. The desired gas is passed continuously through water and into and out of the exposure chamber by way of the pipettes. If the gas is admitted to the chamber under low pressure, the vacuum grease will hold its seal.

XIII. Microdissection

Embryos are dissected and oriented in a hanging drop in the usual way. The cover glass, instead of being sealed over a depression slide, however, is sealed with mineral oil over an opening in the top of a special moist chamber made of plastic (Fig. 13). The three plastic sides of the chamber

FIG. 13. Microdissection moist chamber.

are fused with the surface of a plastic base that can be clamped in the mechanical stage of the microscope. The top of the moist chamber is sealed to the sides with petrolatum. The open side of the chamber is closed with a wall of petrolatum, built up after the microdissection needles are positioned. The interior dimensions of the chamber we have used are 30 mm square × 10 mm high.

The microneedle is made by first drawing out a glass rod to a diameter of about 1 mm in a coarse flame and then pulling it apart in the tiniest flame that can be kept lighted. A small hypodermic needle can be used as a burner. The microneedle is bent at a right angle a few millimeters back from the tip, so that when the shaft is attached horizontally in the holder of the microdissection apparatus, the tip will be in a vertical position. The shaft must be as near horizontal as possible and the tip as near vertical as possible, for the needle has to pass through many underlying layers of cells to reach the neuroblasts. Unless it moves parallel to the axis of the tip, the tissues are pulled sideways as the needle penetrates them. The Chamber's microdissection instrument has proved to be the most satisfactory instrument tried, because the motion can be controlled to a fraction of a micron, and when the force applied to the needle is removed there is no back motion of the needle. A disadvantage of this instrument is the difficulty in making coarse adjustments of the needle.

The succession of procedures by which the apparatus and material is prepared for microdissection follows. The base plate of the moist chamber with attached sides is inserted in the mechanical stage and the approximate center of the moist chamber is brought under the center of the microscope objective. Small strips of absorbent paper folded to form several layers are placed against the three sides of the chamber and soaked with water to provide an abundance of water vapor for the moist chamber. The shaft of a microneedle is fastened with sealing wax to a piece of glass rod. This rod should be large enough in diameter to be held in the clamp of the microdissection instrument and long enough to permit the tip of the needle to be centered under the objective of the microscope. With the aid of the low power objective the needle is brought to the center of the field, where it is locked by tightening the screws of the clamp. The cover of the moist chamber is sealed in place with petrolatum with its centrally located hole centered under the objective. The tip of the needle is brought just below the upper surface of this cover by the coarse vertical adjustment. Because the needle tip is too small to be seen with the naked eye, this is a difficult procedure. It can best be done by (1) lowering the needle well below the top of the chamber cover, (2) placing a cover glass over the hole of the moist chamber cover, (3) focusing the objective on the lower surface of the cover glass, (4) removing the cover glass, (5) bringing the tip of the microneedle up to the focal plane of the objective, and (6) lowering it about a half turn of the vertical fine adjustment. With a spear-shaped dissecting needle, a wall of petrolatum is built up at the open side of the moist chamber through which the microneedle shaft passes. The hanging drop is now prepared, and the cover glass containing this is sealed with mineral oil over the hole in the top of the moist chamber. The embryo is centered under the objective by manual movement of the cover glass or by the mechanical stage.

The cell to be investigated is now centered in the field of the oil immersion objective and the microneedle raised with the vertical fine adjustment until it touches the tissue. The movement of the cells as the needle touches them tells the observer whether the needle is directly under or to one side of the selected cell. If necessary, it is lowered again and moved with the horizontal motion adjustment. When it is thought to be in the right position, it is brought upward again till it contacts the cell in the desired place.

Horizontal movements of 10–15μ can be made with the needle in the tissue; for greater movement the needle should be removed from the tissue, adjusted horizontally, and raised again. There is evidence to indicate that the microneedle does not actually penetrate the cell membrane, but that it merely pushes the membrane ahead of itself into the cell, as one might push one's finger into the side of a toy balloon without puncturing it (Carlson, 1952). The membrane is apparently sufficiently elastic that the microneedle can be moved about from one side of the cell to the other without rupturing the membrane.

If one wishes to microinject rather than microdissect the cell, a micropipette, drawn from glass tubing, is substituted for the microneedle. The micropipette must, of course, be connected by tubes with a syringe, so that fluids can be drawn into and forced out of it. We seal the shaft end of the micropipette inside the cone end of a tapered ground glass joint. This joint is coated with petrolatum and inserted in the sleeve member of the joint which is held in the clamp of the microdissection instrument. One micropipette can be easily exchanged for another at this joint. The free end of the sleeve member of the joint is joined through the base of a hypodermic needle to a Luer adapter. From this, a 1 mm diameter polystyrene tube is connected with another Luer adapter, which in turn is attached to a syringe. The apparatus is shown in Fig. 14. In use, the whole

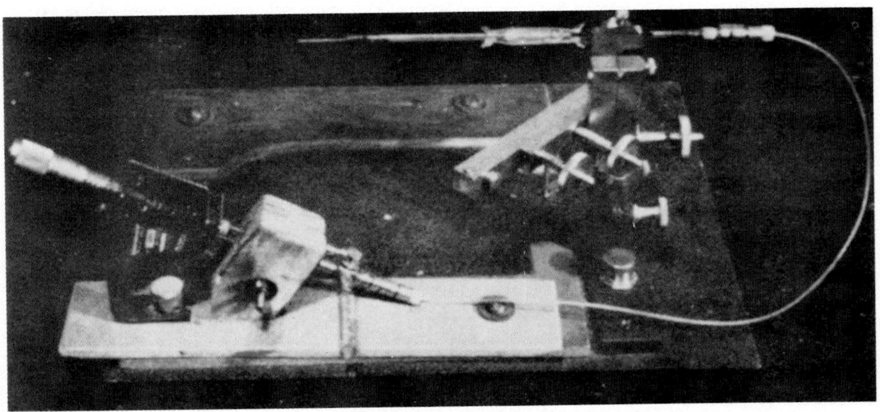

FIG. 14. Microinjection apparatus.

system must be filled with a fluid, such as water. This can be done most easily if a three-way connector with stopcock is inserted between the syringe and the Luer adapter, as shown in the illustration.

Acknowledgments

The authors acknowledge indebtedness to many former students, assistants, and associates, who in their research developed new techniques or improved old ones. In particular they express their appreciation to present co-workers and students Richard A. McGrath, William M. Leach, and Stefan O. Schiff, not only for contributions to technique, but also for timely help in preparing and criticizing this manuscript. They wish to thank Elliot Volkin for helpful advice on methods of DNA and RNA digestion.

References

Bodine, J. H. (1929). *Physiol. Zool.* **2,** 459.

Boyd, G. A. (1955). *In* "Autoradiography in Biology and Medicine," p. 209. Academic Press, New York.

Carlson, J. G. (1938a). *Genetics* **23,** 596.

Carlson, J. G. (1938b). *Proc. Natl. Acad. Sci. U. S.* **24,** 500.

Carlson, J. G. (1940). *J. Morphol.* **66,** 11.

Carlson, J. G. (1941a). *Proc. Natl. Acad. Sci. U. S.* **27,** 42.

Carlson, J. G. (1941b). *Cold Spring Harbor Symp. Quant. Biol.* **9,** 104.

Carlson, J. G. (1942). *J. Morphol.* **71,** 449.

Carlson, J. G. (1946). *Biol. Bull.* **90,** 109.

Carlson, J. G. (1952). *Chromosoma* **5,** 199.

Carlson, J. G. (1954). *In* "Radiation Biology" (A. Hollaender, ed.), Vol. I, pp. 763–824. McGraw-Hill, New York.

Carlson, J. G. (1961). *Ann. N. Y. Acad. Sci.* **95,** 932.

Carlson, J. G., and Harrington, N. G. (1955). *Radiation Res.* **2,** 84.

Carlson, J. G., and Hollaender, A. (1944). *J. Cellular Comp. Physiol.* **23,** 157.

Carlson, J. G., and Hollaender, A. (1945). *J. Cellular Comp. Physiol.* **26,** 165.

Carlson, J. G., and Hollaender, A. (1948). *J. Cellular Comp. Physiol.* **31,** 149.

Carlson, J. G., and McMaster, R. D. (1951). *Exptl. Cell Res.* **2,** 434.

Carlson, J. G., Hollaender, A., and Gaulden, M. E. (1947). *Science* **105,** 187.

Carlson, J. G., Synder, M. L., and Hollaender, A. (1949). *J. Cellular Comp. Physiol.* **33,** 365.

Carlson, J. G., Harrington, N. G., and Gaulden, M. E. (1953). *Biol. Bull.* **104,** 313.

Carlson, J. G., Gaulden, M. E., and Jagger, J. (1960). *In* "Progress in Photobiology," Proceedings of the 3rd International Congress on Photobiology (B. Chr. Christensen and B. Buchmann, eds.), pp. 251–253. Elsevier, Amsterdam.

Carothers, E. E. (1923). *Trans. Am. Entomol. Soc.* **49,** 7.

Doniach, I., and Pelc, S. R. (1950). *Brit. J. Radiol.* **23,** 184.

Gaulden, M. E. (1949). *Hereditas* (*Suppl.*), p. 579.

Gaulden, M. E. (1959). *In* "Mitogenesis" (N. S. Ducoff and C. F. Ehret, eds.), pp. 38–39. Univ. of Chicago Press, Chicago, Illinois.

Gaulden, M. E. (1960). *In* "The Cell Nucleus" (J. S. Mitchell, ed.), pp. 15–17. Butterworths, London.

Gaulden, M. E., and Carlson, J. G. (1951). *Exptl. Cell Res.* **2,** 416.

Gaulden, M. E., and Kokomoor, K. L. (1955). *Proc. Soc. Exptl. Biol. Med.* **90,** 309.

Gaulden, M. E., and Perry, R. P. (1958). *Proc. Natl. Acad. Sci. U .S.* **44,** 553.

Gaulden, M. E., Carlson, J. G., and Tipton, S. R. (1949). *Anat. Rec.* **105,** 16.

Gaulden, M. E., Sheppard, C. W., and Cember, H. (1952). *Nature* **169,** 228.

Gaulden, M. E., Nix, M., and Moshman, J. (1953). *J. Cellular Comp. Physiol.* **41,** 451.

Gettner, M. E., and Ornstein, L. (1956). *In* "Physical Techniques in Biological Research" (G. Oster and A. W. Pollister, eds.), Vol. 3, pp. 627–686. Academic Press, New York.
Haïssinsky, M. (1937). *In* "Les Radiocolloides." Hermann, Paris.
Harrington, N. G., and Koza, R. W. (1951). *Biol. Bull.* **101**, 138.
Kanne, W. R. (1937). *Phys. Rev.* **52**, 380.
Kawamura, K. (1960). *Exptl. Cell Res.* **21**, 1.
Kawamura, K., and Carlson, J. G. (1962). *Exptl. Cell Res.* **26**, 411.
McGrath, R. A. (1963). *Radiation Res.* **19**, 526.
McGrath, R. A., Leach, W. M., and Carlson, J. G. (1963). *J. Roy. Microscop. Soc.* **82**, 55.
Nelsen, O. E. (1931). *J. Morphol.* **51**, 467.
Parker, J. R. (1930). *Univ. Montana Agr. Exptl. Sta. Bull. No.* **223**, 1.
Roberts, H. S. (1955). *J. Exptl. Zool.* **130**, 83.
Rogers, R. W. (1955). *Radiation Res.* **3**, 18.
Rona, E., and Schmidt, E. A. W. (1928). *Sitzber. Akad. Wiss. Wien Math. Naturu. Kl. Abt. IIa* **137**, 103.
St. Amand, W. (1956). *Radiation Res.* **5**, 65.
St. Amand, G. S., and Tipton, S. R. (1954). *Science* **119**, 93.
St. Amand, G. S., Anderson, N. G., and Gaulden, M. E. (1960). *Exptl. Cell Res.* **20**, 71.
Sarkar, I. (1957). *Cytologia* **22**, 370.
Shaw, E. I. (1955). *Exptl. Cell Res.* **9**, 489.
Shaw, E. I. (1956a). *Exptl. Cell Res.* **11**, 580.
Shaw, E. I. (1956b). *Proc. Soc. Exptl. Biol. Med.* **92**, 232.
Sjöstrand, F. (1956). *In* "Physical Techniques in Biological Research" (G. Oster and A. W. Pollister, eds.), Vol. 3, pp. 241–298. Academic Press, New York.
Slifer, E. H. (1932). *J. Morphol.* **53**, 1.
Stevens, B. J. (1962). The fine structure of the grasshopper neuroblast cell during mitosis Ph.D. Thesis, Radcliffe College, Cambridge, Massachusetts.
Tipton, S. R., and St. Amand, G. S. (1954). *Physiol. Zool.* **27**, 311.
Uretz, R. B., and Perry, R. P. (1957). *Rev. Sci. Instr.* **28**, 861.
Wheeler, W. M. (1893). *J. Morphol.* **8**, 1.
Whiting, P. W. (1915). *Entomol. News* **26**, 239.
Zirkle, C. (1937). *Science* **85**, 528.

Chapter 14

Measurement of Material Uptake by Cells: Pinocytosis

CICILY CHAPMAN-ANDRESEN

The Physiological Department of the Carlsberg Laboratory, Copenhagen, Denmark

---

I. Introduction

In this paper "uptake of material by cells" is designed to express the different types of uptake which accompany interiorization of part of the external cell membrane, together with the material ingested. Uptake by penetration through the cell membrane, by means of diffusion, facilitated diffusion or active transport, will not be taken into consideration, except where there is ambiguity concerning the exact method of intake. The uptake of particles, visible in the light microscope, by means of the classically defined process of phagocytosis (Metchnikoff, 1883) will not be dealt with in detail, except in so far as it is comparable with pinocytosis.

The term "pinocytosis," coined by Lewis in 1931 to describe the uptake of fluid droplets from the surrounding medium by omental macrophages, was considered by Lewis to represent an uptake of fluid, and the same term and meaning were applied by Mast and Doyle (1934) to a similar process in amebae; again, fluid uptake was considered to be the important part of the process. More recent reports, especially on amebae (Brandt, 1958; Schumaker, 1958; Chapman-Andresen and Holter, 1961) but also on mammalian cells (Gosselin, 1956; Policard and Bessis, 1958) have indicated that the uptake of solute may be the more significant feature of the process, since considerable amounts of solute may be adsorbed to the outer surface of the cell, as the first phase of pinocytosis.

This type of uptake of material "in bulk," accompanied by ingestion of cell membrane, has been reported in many different cell types, and a special terminology has been developed to denote variants of the process. Terms such as rhopheocytosis (Policard and Bessis, 1958), athrocytosis (Gérard and Cordier, 1934), ultraphagocytosis (Gosselin, 1956), phagotrophy (Seaman, 1961; Rudzinska and Trager, 1959), *colloidopexie* (Volkonsky, 1933) and *chromopexie* (Bratianu and Llombart, 1929) are considered here to describe essentially the same process as pinocytosis. Also the terms potocytosis (Meltzer, 1904) and cytopempsis (Moore and Ruska, 1957), designed to convey the concept of vesicular transport through cells, are considered to define similar processes. For the purpose of convenience in this paper an arbitrary limit will be set between pinocytosis and phagocytosis—although the author considers that this is physiologically incorrect—by defining the size of the particles ingested in each case: Pinocytosis describes the uptake of solutes and particles not visible under the highest magnification obtainable with the light microscope, while phagocytosis is defined as the uptake of particles which are visible by bright field light microscopy. The size of the vacuoles in which material is enclosed during pinocytosis varies from several microns to a few millimicrons, ranging from those visible with light microscope (Chapman-Andresen and Prescott, 1956) down to those visible only with the electron microscope (Farquhar and Palade, 1962).

Various aspects of pinocytosis have been reviewed by Holter (1959, 1960, 1961, 1962), Marshall *et al.* (1959), and Rustad (1961). The stream of recent reports on pinocytosis in many different cell types, from slime mold (Guttes and Guttes, 1960) to embryonic axons (Godina, 1955; Hughes, 1953) emphasizes the interest in pinocytosis as a means of uptake of material. The theories which have been put forward (Bennett, 1956;

Palade, 1956; Novikoff, 1960) concerning vesicular uptake stress the need for more detailed and quantitative experimental data in this field.

II. Demonstration of Pinocytosis

A. Protozoa

1. Amebae

For demonstration of pinocytosis in living amebae, one of the best media is a simple solution of an inorganic salt, e.g., a 0.125 *M* solution of sodium chloride in 0.01 *M* phosphate buffer at a pH between 6.5 and 7.0. When *Amoeba proteus* is immersed in this solution at room temperature, pinocytosis begins after 2 or 3 minutes and continues for 20 to 30 minutes, which is the normal period for a cycle of pinocytosis in this species. To avoid compression, the amebae are placed in a simple chamber consisting of two cover slips fixed onto a glass slide with paraffin such that a wide groove is formed between them; a cover slip forms the lid over the groove.

Although the excellent observations of Mast and Doyle (1934) were made without the aid of phase contrast microscopy, the use of a phase contrast microscope at a magnification of 200 to 400 times facilitates the visualization of single channels in this species. The membrane movements are especially easy to follow with the Reichert Anoptral phase contrast system (Wilska, 1954).

The use of basic dyes (Rustad, 1959; Rustad and Rustad, 1961; Chapman-Andresen, 1962) or of fluorescent-labeled compounds (Holter and Marshall, 1954; Brandt, 1958; Chapman-Andresen and Holtzer, 1960) facilitates demonstration of pinocytosis in amebae when these compounds are used at suitable pH values and concentrations (see Section III, A). Pinocytosis in other species of free-living amebae, e.g., *Chaos chaos* (*Pelomyxa carolinensis*) and *A. dubia*, can be demonstrated by the same methods.

Figure 1 illustrates the appearance of specimens of *A. proteus* during intense pinocytosis in three different inducing solutions; these three phase contrast photographs of living amebae show the types of pseudopodia and channels characteristic for pinocytosis in acid protein solutions, inorganic salt solutions, and basic dyes.

Some species of small amebae can be observed to take up droplets of fluid from complex culture media, e.g., *Acanthamoeba* sp. Neff (Adam, 1959), *Hyalodiscus simplex* (Wohlfarth-Bottermann, 1960).

Pinocytosis has been studied in fixed material by identification of

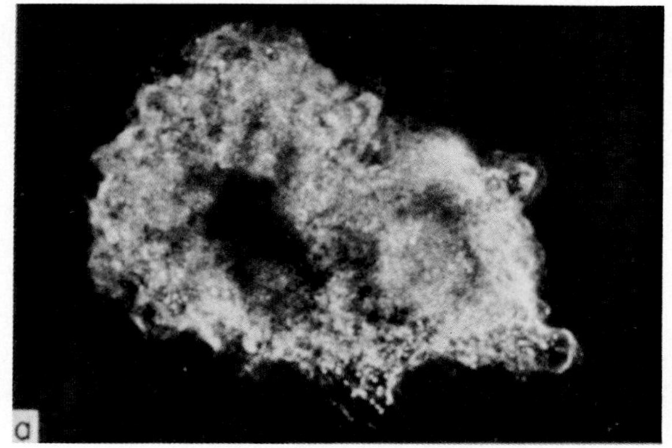
a

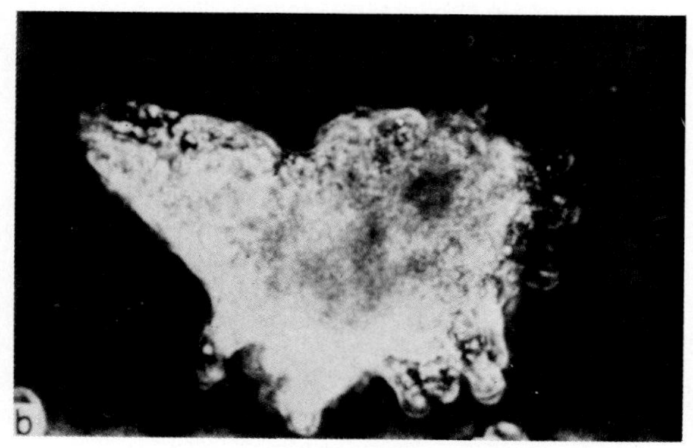
b

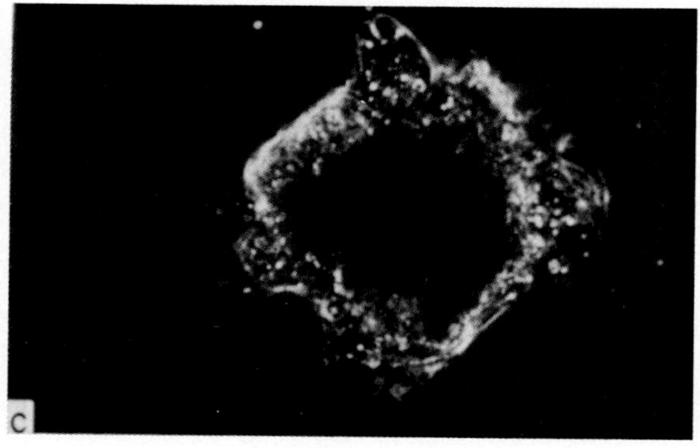
c

material of extracellular origin in membrane-bound vacuoles and by light microscope studies with fluorescent-labeled material (Holter and Marshall, 1954; Brandt, 1958; Chapman-Andresen and Holtzer, 1960), and also by electron microscopic studies using suitable labels (Nachmias and Marshall, 1962; Marshall and Nachmias, 1960; Brandt and Pappas, 1960). Electron microscopic studies on the fine structure of pinocytosis channels and vesicles have been reported by Chapman-Andresen and Nilsson (1960), by Roth (1960), and by Brandt and Pappas (1962).

2. Ciliates

Tetrahymena has been observed to form vacuoles at the base of the gullet when immersed in 2% solutions of proteose-peptone, the normal medium used for the culture of this ciliate (Chapman-Andresen, cited by Seaman, 1961). Cultures in the log phase of growth show this effect best, and preparations are made by placing the ciliates in a drop of medium on a glass slide, covering carefully with a cover slip, so that the organisms are not compressed, and then gently removing excess fluid with lens paper wicks placed at the edges of the cover slips until the cells are trapped between slide and cover slip, but still living and slightly compressed; it is then possible to count the vacuoles. Seaman (1961) used the dye trypan blue to facilitate observation of "phagotrophic" uptake in this species; within an hour all the vacuoles contained within the *Tetrahymena* were blue. This author notes that care must be used in placing the cover slip on the drop of fluid containing the organisms, since they are easily ruptured.

The Reichert Anoptral phase contrast system, and also the American Optical Co. dark L phase contrast objective, give good visualization of the vacuoles in *Tetrahymena*.

Gold colloid particles added to the proteose-peptone medium are reported by Cohen (1959) to be ingested.

3. Parasitic Forms

Bird (1961) reported that pinocytosis occurs at the tail region of entamebae, and Chapman-Andresen (unpublished observations) noted that pinocytosis vacuoles were constantly formed at a region just anterior to the uroid in *Entamoeba invadens*.

FIG. 1. Characteristic shape and channel form in *Amoeba proteus* after induction of pinocytosis by three different inducing solutions. (A) Five minutes after immersion in 1% bovine plasma albumin at pH 4.4. Fine channels on small pointed pseudopodia. (B) Ten minutes after immersion in 0.125 *M* NaCl at pH 6.5. Wider channels than in (a) and on longer and less pointed pseudopodia. (C) Ten minutes after immersion in 0.1% acridine orange at pH 8.0. Both channels and pseudopodia are coarser than in (b), and the total number of channels less (from Chapman-Andresen, 1962).

The uptake of cytoplasm from host blood cells by malarial parasites has been reported from electron microscopic studies by Rudzinska and Trager (1959); recently, the same authors (1962) found that a similar process takes place in erythrocytes parasitized by *Babesia rodhaini* and noted that this process is similar to pinocytosis and could be described as "intracellular pinocytosis."

Electron microscopic studies by Steinert and Novikoff (1960) on *Trypanosoma mega* showed that this parasite ingests ferritin by means of vacuoles formed at the gullet.

B. Mammalian Cells

For the demonstration of pinocytosis in living mammalian cells, the most convenient material is perhaps omental cells of rat (Lewis, 1931; Holtzer and Holtzer, 1960) or peripheral or peritoneal exudate leucocytes (Bessis, 1954, 1959; Chapman-Andresen, 1957; Wittekind, 1961; Holter and Holtzer, 1959). These cells are readily obtained and can survive and pinocytose at room temperature. Whole heparinized blood is centrifuged to separate the leucocytes. A suspension of these leucocytes or of peritoneal leucocytes is diluted with physiological saline solution, the suspension placed in special glass or plastic vessels with inclined sides ("Freixa vessels," Bessis *et al.*, 1953), the cells allowed to sediment onto cover slips which are placed against the inclined walls at 37°C for an hour. The cover slips are then removed, the backs of the slips gently cleaned, and then inverted over a drop of saline solution on a glass slide to form a simple chamber, two opposite sides of which are sealed with molten paraffin, leaving two opposite sides unsealed for perfusion of solutions through the chamber. Various protein solutions can be passed through the chamber by the simple expedient of placing a drop of solution at one of the unsealed sides and pulling the fluid through the chamber by placing a wick of lens paper at the other unsealed side. Observation of the cells with phase contrast oil immersion objectives shows the cells in saline solution extended (étalement, Bessis and Bricka, 1952) on the slip; perfusion with 2–10% plasma protein solutions causes the cells to round up and form pinocytosis vacuoles at various areas at the periphery of the cell. The use of phase contrast microscopy and cinemicrography (Robineaux and Pinet, 1960) facilitates the observations, as does the use of fluorescent compounds (Wittekind, 1961).

Ascites tumor cells from mice have been observed to show engulfment of droplets of fluid *in vitro* (Easty *et al.*, 1956; Chapman-Andresen, unpublished observations), and large cells from chicken Rous ascites tumor, at an early stage in development, are good objects for such studies.

By means of electron microscopic studies, electron-dense material of extracellular origin, present in membrane-bound vacuoles and vesicles, has been observed in many types of cells (Odor, 1956; Ryser *et al.*, 1962; Hayward, 1962). The recent report of Easton *et al.* (1962), using ferritin-conjugated antibody, gives an excellent demonstration of pinocytosis in ascites tumor cells.

The epithelial cells from the jejunum of infant mice were found by Clark (1959) in electron microscopic studies to show invaginations and vesicle formation, while uptake of fluorescein-labeled protein in droplets was demonstrated in the same cells by Holtzer and Holtzer (1960). The latter authors tested the response of a wide range of mature mammalian cells for their response to fluorescein-labeled protein solutions. Table I shows the types of cell tested and summarizes the results of these experiments. The recent demonstration by Farquhar and Palade (1962) of channel systems and membrane-bound vesicles in certain cells of the renal glomerulus is most convincing and supports the theory that uptake of material in membrane-bound vesicles is a process of normal and physiological occurrence.

C. Other Cells

Indications that pinocytosis might occur in plant cells have been put forward by Buvat (1958) and Buvat and Lance (1957) from electron microscopic observations on apical meristems of various plants, in which invaginations from the cell membrane were observed. Weiling (1961) presented evidence for the formation of pinocytosis vacuoles from the plasmalemma of pollen mother cells by means of invaginations from the plasmalemma. Studies on the uptake of radioactive proteins by root tips, by means of autoradiography (Jensen and MacLaren, 1960), indicated that proteins entered the cells and were found mainly in the region just inside the plasmalemma. In light and electron microscopic studies with the copper phthalocyanine dye, Alcian blue (Haddock, 1948), Ashton, Chapman-Andresen, and Jensen (unpublished observations) found that the epidermal cells took up the stain in small discrete vacuoles, but the fate of these vacuoles could not be followed owing to the toxicity of the dye to the roots.

III. Inducers of Pinocytosis

The extent to which pinocytosis can be considered as a normal means for the entry in bulk into cells of substances which cannot, or cannot in

TABLE I

REACTION OF TISSUE CELLS TO LABELED PLASMA PROTEINS[a]

Type of preparation[b]	Normal globulin	Antimyosin	Bovine albumin
Reticulo-endothelial cells	+[c]	+	+
Ileum (newborn)	+	+	+
Kidney	+	+	+
Liver	0	0	0
Cardiac muscle	0	0	0
Skeletal muscle	0	0	0
Smooth muscle	0	0	0
Stomach	0	0	0
Colon	0	0	0
Bladder	0	0	0
Lung	0	0	0
Thyroid	0	0	0
Adrenal	0	0	0
Pancreas	0	0	0
Fat	0	0	0
Red blood cells	0	0	0
Skin	0	0	0
Cornea	0	0	0
Fibroblasts	0	0	0
Cartilage	0	0	0
Tissue culture and cell suspensions			
HeLa	+	+	+
Peritoneal exudate	+	+	+
Ascites tumor	+	+	+
Kidney	0	0	0
L cells	0	0	0
Cynamologus (heart cells)	0	0	0
Fibroblasts	0	0	0
Human amnion	0	0	0

[a] From Holtzer and Holtzer (1960).

[b] Cells exposed to fluorescein-labeled proteins for 2–6 hours; living cells examined in ultraviolet microscope immediately after washing free of label.

[c] + denotes incorporation in cytoplasmic vacuoles of labeled plasma proteins. Following deliberate injury all cells take up the proteins by direct permeation, with consequent diffused staining of cytoplasm and nucleus or nucleus alone.

sufficient quantity, enter the cell through the membrane has not so far been determined, but recent reports such as those of Farquhar and Palade (1962) and Easton *et al.* (1962) certainly lend considerable support to this supposition. Pinocytosis can be "induced" in certain types of experimental material by immersing the cells in various solutions, which in the case of amebae are now fairly well defined. The situation for mammalian cells is not so clear, since less data have been presented, probably owing partly to the lower tolerance of such cells to variations in the composition of the medium. A review by Holter (1960) on induction of pinocytosis gives a survey of the position at that time.

A. Amebae

Although some authors report that amebae do not pinocytose in clean culture solution (Chapman-Andresen and Prescott, 1956; Chapman-Andresen, 1962), Rustad (1961) considers that slight and occasional pinocytosis takes place under normal cultural conditions. Intense pinocytosis is induced by transferring the amebae to various solutions. They then respond to the presence of certain solutes in the environment by the formation of pinocytosis channels. An inorganic salt solution (dilute sea water) and a protein solution (egg albumin) were the first media shown to cause pinocytosis in amebae (Mast and Doyle, 1934); it was later shown that both the monovalent and divalent cations from sea water were inducers (Chapman-Andresen and Prescott, 1956), and also, a solution containing a single inorganic salt would induce pinocytosis in amebae (Chapman-Andresen, 1958).

Proteins were found to differ in their inducing properties; the γ-globulin used by Holter and Marshall (1954) was found to be a more consistent inducer in *C. chaos* than the bovine plasma albumin used by Chapman-Andresen and Holter (1955). Further studies on the inducing properties of proteins of different molecular weights and isoelectric points (Chapman-Andresen, 1962) showed that for the species of ameba tested, *A. proteus*, the isoelectric point of the protein was decisive for its inducing properties, while the size of the molecule was unimportant. These results are illustrated in Fig. 2, in which the pH of the protein solution is plotted against the intensity of the pinocytic response to the protein solution, as determined according to the method described in Section IV,A,1. It can be clearly seen that although all the proteins tested (with the exception of pepsin, which has a very acid isoelectric point) induce pinocytosis in amebae at pH values of between 4.0 and 4.8, only the proteins with alkaline isoelectric points induce channel formation when tested in neutral or alkaline solutions. It appears that proteins induce pinocytosis when they are present mainly in the cationic state, i.e., on the acid side of the isoelectric point.

The inducing properties of a series of amino acids, tested in solutions of different pH, are shown in Fig. 3. Acidic and basic amino acids as well as neutral amino acids were tested. The figure shows that acidic and basic

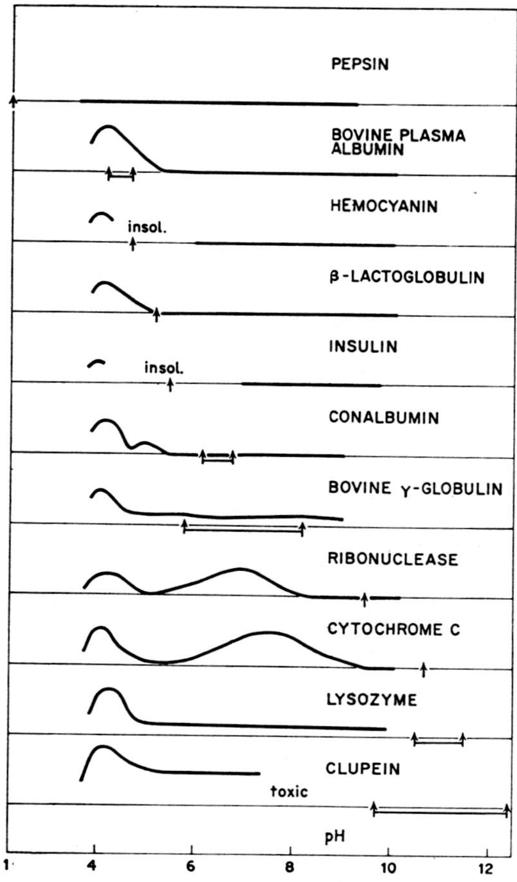

FIG. 2. Effect of pH of inducing solution on response of *Amoeba proteus* to solutions of proteins of different molecular weights and isoelectric points. Abscissa: pH of protein solution. Ordinate: response of amebae, estimated according to Section IV,A,1. The isoelectric regions of the proteins are indicated by arrows. Concentrations of protein solutions about 1×10^{-4} *M*, with the exception of hemocyanin, which was 1×10^{-6} *M* (from Chapman-Andresen, 1962).

amino acids induce pinocytosis with a maximal effect at pH 8, but the neutral amino acids do not act as inducers within the pH range tested. The different pH values of the solutions tested were obtained by the addition of acid (HCl) or base (NaOH). With acidic amino acids, NaOH equal to one equivalent must be added to obtain a solution with pH 8; hence the solution tested corresponds to a solution of the sodium salt of the amino acid. Similarly, with the basic amino acids an equivalent of

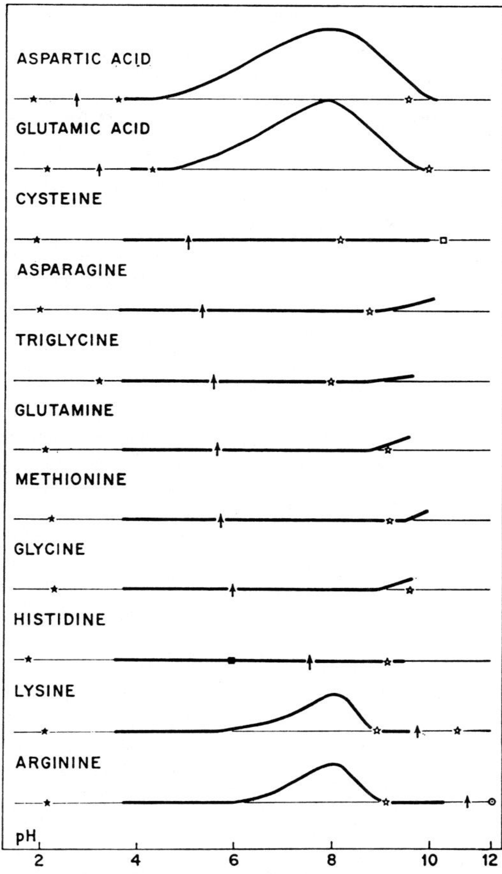

FIG. 3. Effect of pH of inducing solutions on response of *Amoeba proteus* to solutions of different amino acids. Abscissa: pH of amino acid solution. Ordinate: response of amebae, estimated according to Section IV,A,1. The symbols indicate: ★ p*K* (COOH); ☆ p*K* (NH_3); ⊙ p*K* (Guan.); ■ p*K* (Im.); □ p*K* (SH); the p*I* values are indicated by arrows. The concentration of amino acids equals 0.063 *M* (from Chapman-Andresen, 1962).

acid must be added to adjust the solution to pH 8, hence the basic amino acids are present in a solution which corresponds to that of the chlorides. It may be concluded that the amino acids act as inducers when they are present in solution as salts. This hypothesis was confirmed by testing the inducing properties of the hydrochlorides of histidine and cysteine; these salts, when neutralized with NaOH to pH 8, induced pinocytosis, but solutions of the free amino acids did not.

TABLE II

LIST OF COMPOUNDS REPORTED TO INDUCE PINOCYTOSIS IN AMEBAE

Substance	Concentration	Reference
Sea water	25%	Mast and Doyle (1934); Chapman-Andresen and Prescott (1956)
Neutral solutions of inorganic salts	0.01–0.2 *M*	Chapman-Andresen and Prescott (1956); Chapman-Andresen (1958); Brandt (1958)
Buffer solutions	0.01–0.1 M	Chapman-Andresen (1962)
Calcium gluconate	"Hypertonic"	Mast and Doyle (1934)
Sodium oleate	0.006 *M*	Chapman-Andresen (1962)
Slightly alkaline solutions of acidic and basic amino acids	0.01–0.2 *M*	Chapman-Andresen (1962)
Basic dyes	0.01%	Rustad (1959); Chapman-Andresen (1962); Rustad and Rustad (1961)
Protein solutions	0.5–5%	Mast and Doyle (1934); Holter and Marshall (1954); Chapman-Andresen and Holter (1955, 1961); Brandt (1958)
Acid solutions of proteins with IP[a] above 4	0.1–5%	Chapman-Andresen (1960b); Nachmias and Marshall (1962)
Neutral solutions of protein with IP above 6	0.1–5%	Chapman-Andresen (1960b); Rustad (1959)
Enzymes with alkaline IP	0.002–1%	Schumaker (1958); Rustad (1959); Chapman-Andresen (1962); Brandt and Pappas (1960)
THO_2	0.05–0.5%	Brandt and Pappas (1960)
Versene	0.001 *M*	Brandt (1958)

[a] IP = isoelectric point.

Table II summarizes the compounds which have been found to induce pinocytosis in amebae. These substances or mixtures all contain some charged groups, and while in the case of amino acids and salts, both negatively and positively charged molecules are present, proteins act as inducers under conditions where the predominant charge is positive, i.e., on the acid side of the isoelectric point.

Compounds which have been tested and found not to give pinocytosis in amebae, include carbohydrates (Mast and Doyle, 1934; Chapman-Andresen, 1961) whatever the concentration or pH of the solutions tested, nucleic acids (Chapman-Andresen and Prescott, 1956) and solutions of neutral amino acids. Ethyl alcohol and urea, over a wide pH range and concentration, have also been found to be negative. While gold colloid was reported by Brandt and Pappas (1960) not to induce a surface reaction in *C. chaos*, Chapman-Andresen and Danes (cited in Holter, 1959) found that amebae took up the colloid. The inducing properties of gold colloid may depend to a large extent on the concentration and type of gelatin added as stabilizer to the commercial gold colloid solution.

Induction of pinocytosis in *A. proteus* by exposure to ultraviolet irradiation has been reported by Rinaldi (1959).

B. Mammalian Cells

Little evidence is available on the induction of pinocytosis in mammalian cells by solutions of single pure substances, as these cells require a more complex medium to retain their morphological integrity. There are, however, some indications that globulins are more efficient inducers than are albumins (Chapman-Andresen, 1957; Sorkin, 1960; Wittekind, 1961). This is interesting in view of the detailed data of Northover (1961) on the effect of different proteins in the medium on the phagocytic response of leucocytes to bacteria. Albumin inhibits phagocytosis, while globulin promotes the process; acetylation of the proteins, which increases the negative charge on the proteins, promotes the inhibiting effect of albumin and decreases the enhancing effect of globulins.

Insulin has been reported by Barrnett and Ball (1960) to have a specific promoting effect on pinocytic uptake in rat adipose tissue, and Paul (cited by Barrnett and Ball, 1960) found that cells in tissue culture responded to small concentrations of insulin in the medium by increased pinocytosis. Low pH values in the medium, and also the addition of cortisone, were found to increase uptake of protein by ascites tumor cells (Ryser *et al.*, 1960).

Although Holtzer and Holtzer (1960) reported that various tissue cells tested with fluorescein-labeled proteins showed no difference in the uptake of albumin and globulin, Ryser *et al.* (1962) reported that ascites tumor cells ingested large amounts of ferritin but took up little colloidal gold. They consider that these results indicate a discrimination by the cells between particles of similar size, but different properties. The question of uptake of colloidal gold will be further discussed in Section V.

C. Other Cells

1. Ciliates

The uptake of droplets of proteose-peptone, the usual culture medium for *Tetrahymena*, by formation of vacuoles from the base of the gullet was noted by Chapman-Andresen (cited by Seaman, 1961). Seaman and Mancilla (1961) isolated from proteose-peptone a long chain polypeptide, containing a high proportion of arginine, which is active as an inducer of "phagotrophy" in *Tetrahymena.*

2. Plant Cells

The presence of ribonuclease (Jensen and MacLaren, 1960) or Alcian blue (Ashton, Chapman-Andresen, and Jensen, unpublished observations) within root tip cells, and observations of concentration of these compounds at or near the cell membrane, cannot be taken as definite evidence that these substances are acting as inducers of pinocytosis in plant cells. Vacuoles and invaginations have been observed in normal cells (Buvat, 1958; Weiling, 1961), and if these are due to pinocytosis, then this is induced by some normal extracellular component present in the tissue.

IV. Quantitative Estimation of Pinocytic Uptake

A. Amebae

1. Quantitation of Intensity of Pinocytosis

One method of estimating the intensity of pinocytosis is to count the number of channels formed during one cycle of pinocytosis, after induction under standard conditions by a given inducer. This approach has been used by Chapman-Andresen (1962) for the small fresh water amebae, and is suitable for *A. proteus*, *A. dubia*, and small specimens of *C. chaos*. The amebae are starved for 2 days before the experiments, since starved amebae have been found to react more intensely to inducers than fully fed amebae (Chapman-Andresen, 1962), and are transferred to fresh culture medium before the experiment. Using a braking pipette with a fine tip (Holter, 1943), a group of fifty amebae is transferred to a salt cellar in minimal (ca. 5 μl) culture solution containing the inducing solution, the concentration and pH of which are known. The salt cellar is rocked gently to mix the contents, and at least twenty amebae are transferred with another braking pipette, which has previously been rinsed three times with the inducing solution, to a simple chamber of the type described in Section II,A,1. A stop watch is started at the time of immersion of the amebae in the inducing solution. The position of the first ameba is found and recorded by means of the vernier system of the microscope stage, and the number of channels counted and recorded, the time being noted by the stop watch. The second ameba is then found, its position recorded and channels counted, and so on until ten amebae have been found and their channels counted. The time at which the count was made on the first and last ameba is recorded, and then the amebae are relocated from the recorded positions, the channels recounted, and the procedure continued until each ameba has been observed five times in the course of about 20 minutes. The total number of channels is then calculated, and the figure divided by the number of amebae gives the mean channel number found per ameba during the counting period. It has been found that the variation within groups of amebae from the same culture tested on the same day, and tested with the same inducing solution, is of the order of 20%. The variation between groups counted on different days may be up to 100%, probably owing to slight variations in the physiological state. In this way the effect of pH or concentration of an inducing solution or the effect of temperature on the response of the amebae can be tested (Fig. 4a, b, c).

Variations in response have been observed between different races of *A. proteus*, and within the same race fed on different diets and starved for different periods (Chapman-Andresen, 1960a, 1962).

For the "Bristol" strain of *A. proteus*, as cultured at the Carlsberg Laboratory, it was found that feeding on *Tetrahymena*, according to Prescott and James (1955), and starvation for 2–6 days resulted in a maximal response to the standard NaCl inducing solution.

2. Measurement of Uptake

a. Radioactive tracers. Glucose-C^{14} which like other carbohydrates tested is not an inducer of pinocytosis in amebae, and to which the plasmalemma is only slightly permeable, was used by Chapman-Andresen and Holter (1955) in experiments to measure the amount of fluid taken up by *C. chaos* during pinocytosis of bovine plasma albumin. The amebae were immersed for varying periods in the glucose albumin solutions, removed and rinsed well in culture medium before measurements of radioactivity were made

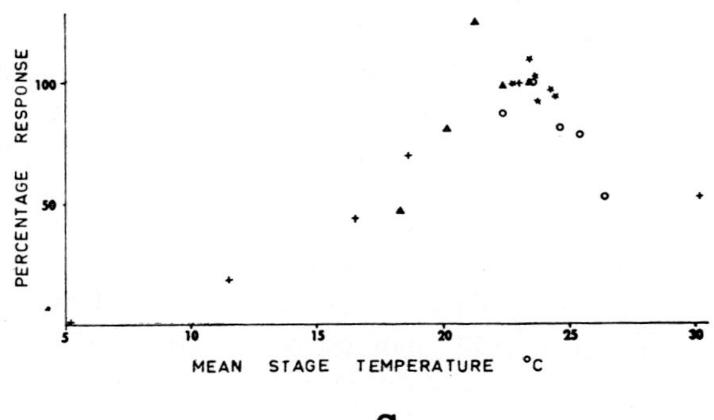
PERCENTAGE RESPONSE
100
50
5
10
15
20
25
30
MEAN STAGE TEMPERATURE °C

a

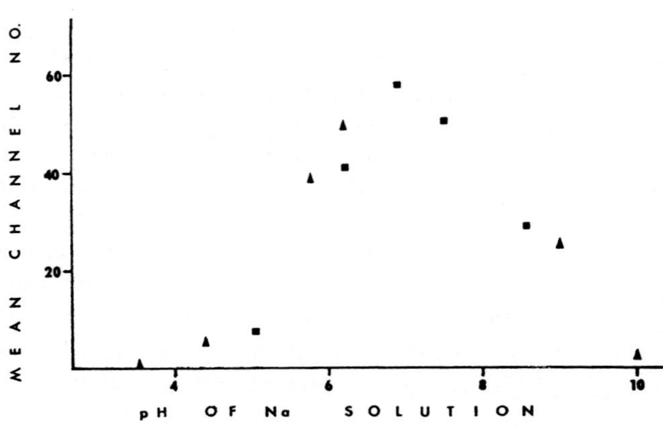
MEAN CHANNEL NO.
60
40
20
4
6
8
10
pH OF Na SOLUTION

b

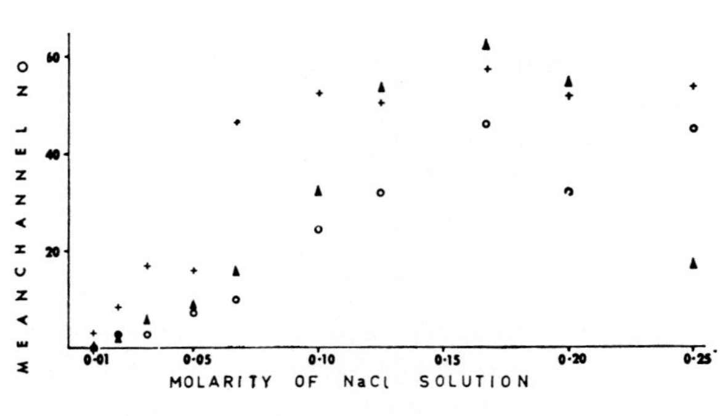
MEAN CHANNEL NO
60
40
20
0·01
0·05
0·10
0·15
0·20
0·25
MOLARITY OF NaCl SOLUTION

c

on groups of amebae disintegrated on a planchet with NaOH, and dried. The results were rather variable; the volume ingested, expressed as a percentage of the average volume of an ameba, ranged from 1 to 10%. The variability of these results is doubtless due in part to the fact that the pH of the inducing solutions varied somewhat and also to differences in the amount of protein adsorbed to the surface. The results of Chapman-Andresen and Prescott (1956), using a similar technique with S^{35}-labeled methionine, which again, is not an inducer of pinocytosis, but to which the plasmalemma is permeable, showed that more methionine enters the cell when protein is added and that more labeled methionine is incorporated into the proteins of the cell.

The use of radioactive salts, $Na^{22}Cl$ and $NaBr^{82}$, which in suitable concentrations are inducers of pinocytosis, and to which the membrane of amebae is permeable, by Chapman-Andresen and Dick (1961, 1962) showed that the amount of salt solutions pinocytically ingested corresponded to approximately 1–10% of the volume of an ameba. These values were obtained as a difference between the total amount taken in by the amebae, and the amount which entered by diffusion through the plasmalemma, calculated by influx measurements.

When radioactive proteins are used as inducing solutions (Schumaker, 1958) and measurements of the amount of material ingested made in a similar way, the volume of solution ingested would have corresponded in percentage of the mean ameba volume to several hundred times the normal volume of an ameba. Schumaker pointed out that this must be due to a considerable adsorption of protein to the surface, followed by interiorization of the solute-loaded membrane. About half of the protein was lost on washing for periods of several hours. Another approach to this problem was made by Chapman-Andresen and Holter (unpublished), who used two labeled compounds, glucose-C^{14} to measure the volume of fluid ingested, and I^{131}-labeled serum albumin to measure the ingestion of inducing solute. By the use of metal filters placed between the sample and the device for measuring radioactivity, the relative amount of the two

---

FIG. 4. Effect of temperature, pH of inducing solution, and concentration of solute on pinocytosis of NaCl in *Amoeba proteus*. (a) Response to 0.125 *M* NaCl at different temperatures; Abscissa: mean stage temperature in °C. Ordinate: response of amoebae, estimated according to Section IV,A,1. (b) Response to 0.125 *M* NaCl at temperature of 21.5°C, to solutions at different pH values. (c) Response to NaCl solutions of different molarity, and in different diluents, at pH 6.5 and temperature of 21.5°C; Abscissa: molarity of NaCl solution. Ordinate: response of amebae estimated according to Section IV,A,1. NaCl solution diluted with ○ distilled water; + phosphate buffer; ▲ maleate buffer (from Chapman-Andresen, 1962).

tracers in the inducing solution and in the amebae after immersion for various periods can be determined. The use of different pH values for the washing solutions, and different temperatures for the period of induction enables one to differentiate between the amounts of material ingested and the amount adsorbed to the surface. In the case of protein inducers which are effective only at acid pH, washing in culture solution at the same pH as that of the inducing solution will retain the surface adsorbed material, while washing at neutral pH will remove this surface-bound layer and give a measure of the ingested material (Chapman-Andresen and Holtzer, 1960). Periods of immersion in the cold, at about 4–5°C, a temperature at which *A. proteus* does not form channels (de Terra and Rustad, 1959; Chapman-Andresen, 1962), but at which surface adsorption takes place, will give the surface adsorbed material alone, if washing is carried out at acid pH, while washing with neutral solutions will remove this layer.

For measurements of the radioactivity of single living specimens of *C. chaos*, the chamber devised by Chapman-Andresen and Robinson (1953) is convenient, since repeated measurements can be made of the radioactive content of the same specimens at intervals after uptake of the tracer. Volume measurements can also be made at the same time on the same specimen.

b. Fluorescent compounds. The first uptake measurements to be made on pinocytosis in amebae were those of Holter and Marshall (1954), who used fluorescein-labeled γ-globulin to determine the uptake of protein during pinocytosis in *C. chaos*. These authors employed squashes and freeze-dried sections of normal or centrifuged amebae to determine the distribution of the ingested labeled protein in the fluorescence microscope, and the total amount of label in homogenates of single amebae by means of a microfluorometric technique. They found that the amebae would ingest on the average 80 mμg of protein in 3 hours of feeding and that the labeled material had disappeared completely in 5–6 days.

Fluorescein-labeled protein was also used by Brandt (1958) for measurements on pinocytic uptake in *C. chaos*, in addition to a fluorescent antibody technique which affords a precise localization of the protein.

Using *A. proteus* and fluorescein-labeled bovine plasma albumin, Chapman-Andresen and Holtzer (1960) found that it was possible to follow uptake of the labeled protein by examination of living amebae for short periods under the ultraviolet microscope, and to determine by this means the factors affecting the surface binding. These authors found that with fixation in formol-calcium, the fluorescent label was leached out or displaced in specimens which were fixed more than a few hours after removal from the protein solution. It was considered that the lability of the label might be due either to a change in the permeability of the walls of the pinocytic vacuoles, or to an enzymatic breakdown of the labeled protein into smaller molecules which cannot be fixed by formalin.

c. Colored compounds. As first reported by Rustad (1959), basic dyes are inducers of pinocytosis in amebae. These dyes can be used to give a demonstration of pinocytosis, but the fate of the ingested material is not easy to follow with such dyes, e.g., acridine orange, to which the plasmalemma is permeable. Chapman-Andresen (1962) showed that when amebae, which have pinocytosed in acridine orange solution, are fed with ciliates on the following day, the dye present in the ameba penetrates through the walls of the newly formed food vacuoles and stains the captured ciliates.

The copper phthalocyanine dye, Alcian blue, which was first developed for textile dyeing by Haddock (1948) and later shown to be an excellent stain for mucin (Steedman, 1950), is also an excellent inducer of pinocytosis in amebae. It has the advantage that the dye, once bound to the outer surface of the mucous coat of the amebae, cannot be washed off and remains in an insoluble state until finally eliminated from the amebae by defecation. This dye, again unlike many basic dyes, can be retained *in situ* in amebae fixed by conventional methods, such as ethyl alcohol or formol-calcium

Alcian blue was used by Chapman-Andresen (1962) to quantitate and follow the fate of the pinocytic vacuoles formed after induction of pinocytosis by this dye in *A. proteus*. The amebae were immersed for 1 minute in 1:10,000 aqueous solution of the dye at pH approximately 6, and the dye diluted with culture medium several times before removing the amebae from the vessel, since they are sticky and difficult to pipette directly from the dye solution. Amebae were then fixed in ethyl alcohol (96%) for 10 minutes, taken through three changes of absolute alcohol to cedar wood oil, and examined in this medium at about $\times 400$ magnification. The number and size of the blue vacuoles were assessed in groups of ten amebae fixed at intervals of from 60 minutes to 195 hours after immersion for 1 minute in the dye. Channel counting on a batch of the same amebae enabled a correlation to be made between the number of channels and the number of vacuoles formed in the same solution. It proved impossible, however, to count individual vacuoles in amebae fixed within 1 hour after removal from the Alcian blue solution, since the vacuoles were clumped together in a mass. This corresponds to the period after pinocytosis when the amebae are "digesting" and not indulging in locomotory streaming (Chapman-Andresen, 1960b). After this period, when locomotory streaming has recommenced, the vacuoles become distributed, together with the other inclusion bodies, within the cytoplasm. Coalescence of vacuoles could be followed during the period between 6 and 24 hours after ingestion, and defecation of the blue vacuolar contents was observed.

Table III summarizes some results obtained on uptake of various

TABLE III

COMPARATIVE DATA ON QUANTITATIVE ESTIMATION OF UPTAKE BY PINOCYTOSIS IN AMEBAE[a]

Ameba species	Inducer	Label	Mean uptake expressed as: volume percentage of mean ameba volume[b]		Mean uptake expressed as: weight of compound as percentage of mean ameba dry weight[c]		Reference
Chaos chaos	Rabbit γ-globulin	Fluorescein (coupled to globulin)	30–40		5.0		Holter and Marshall (1954)
	Bovine plasma albumin	Glucose-C^{14} (added to albumin solution)	1–10		0.8		Chapman-Andresen and Holter (1955)
	NaCl	Na^{22}	1–9		0.5		Chapman-Andresen and Dick (1961, 1962)
	NaBr	Br^{82}	1–9		1.0		
	Gold colloid stabilized with gelatin	Au^{198}	ca. 25		0.2		Chapman-Andresen and Danes (cited by Holter, 1959)
Amoeba proteus	Ribonuclease Cytochrome c	I^{131}-labeled protein	5000 (2500)[d]		17 (8.5)[d]		Schumaker (1958)
	Bovine plasma albumin		Acid wash	Neutral wash	Acid wash	Neutral wash	
		I^{131}-labeled albumin	53–200	23	66	7.5	Chapman-Andresen and Holter (1961)
		Glucose-C^{14} added	3–5	2	0.0001	0.00005	
	Alcian blue	Blue color of dye	0.5				Chapman-Andresen (1962)

[a] From Chapman-Andresen (1962).
[b] Mean volume of *C. chaos*, 0.04 μl; mean volume of *A. proteus*, 0.002 μl.
[c] Mean dry weight of *C. chaos*, 2.4 μg; mean dry weight of *A. proteus*, 0.12 μg.
[d] Measurements made 2 hours after removal from inducing solution; all other determinations made shortly after removal from inducing solution.

substances by pinocytosis in amebae; data on the two species *A. proteus* and *C. chaos* are included. The difference in uptake found by the use of different inducing solutions is very large and depends to a large extent on the degree of binding of the inducing solute to the outer surface of the amebae, and also on the interval between immersion in the inducer and recording the measurement. The significance of these differences has been pointed out in the preceding sections (IV,A,2, a, b, c), which describe the methods used for these different inducers.

B. Mammalian Cells

1. Quantitation of Intensity of Pinocytosis

From measurements of the size and number of pinocytic vacuoles entering macrophages in studies with time lapse cinefilms, Lewis (1931) reported that these cells may take up a volume of fluid corresponding to about one third of their own volume. Later, Lewis (1935, 1937), using the same method, observed that cells in tissue culture may ingest volumes of fluid corresponding to several times their own volume within a few hours.

Analysis of cinemicrographic records of leucocytes (Frédéric and Robineaux, 1951) and tissue culture cells (Pomerat *et al.*, 1954; Gey *et al.*, 1954, 1955; Rose, 1957) may also give quantitative determination of pinocytic activity.

2. Measurement of Uptake

a. Radioactive tracers. The technique of obtaining rabbit peritoneal macrophages by injection of 10% sterile gum acacia in 0.1 *M* NaCl [2 intraperitoneal injections of 150 ml at an interval of 4 days (Gosselin, 1956)] gave a good yield of almost exclusively large mononuclear cells. Chilling the exudate and mixing with sodium hexametaphosphate to a final concentration of 0.375% in the exudate suspension prevented fibrin formation and aggregation of the cells. This material was used to study the uptake of radioactive colloidal gold in a suspension fluid consisting of 10% phosphate buffer, 20% rabbit serum, and 70% isotonic saline at pH 7.4; the cells were incubated in Vaseline-sealed watch glasses without agitation, and the supernatant fluid, obtained by gentle centrifugation of the cell suspensions, was used to assay the amount of gold removed by the cells by a spectrophotometric method. The gold present in the cells after incubation was determined by spectrophotometric measurement of cells lysed by shaking in distilled water and using as blank the same quantity of cells incubated for the same period in the absence of gold. Gosselin (1956) found that populations of exudate leucocytes exposed to gold under the same conditions also took up the colloid, but at a much slower rate than the macrophages, indicating a significant difference in the uptake between these two cell types.

From measurements of the radioactivity of washed cells measured at intervals after incubation with Au^{98}-colloid, Chapman-Andresen and

Danes (cited in Holter, 1959) found that L strain mouse fibroblasts in tissue culture took up the colloid. Suspension cultures, continuously agitated, took up appreciably more of the colloid than did sheet cultures, even when the latter were agitated during incubation with the gold.

Using a similar method, Thomason and Schofield (1961), in studies on the uptake of I^{131}-labeled albumin by Ehrlich ascites tumor cells, considered that only damaged tumor cells took up the protein and that some of the uptake measured might be due to that of the leucocytes, which are always present in ascites cell populations. Chapman-Andresen (unpublished observations) also found that ascites tumor cells took up some I^{131}-labeled albumin, but that I^{131}-labeled globulins were ingested to a considerably greater extent by both ascites tumor cells and by peritoneal cells from guinea pigs and rabbits.

b. Fluorescent compounds. Holtzer and Holtzer (1960) used three different fluorescein-labeled proteins in their studies on the uptake of proteins by mature mammalian cells. These authors point out the importance of dialysis of the labeled material to remove any free label, and of filtering and sterilization, e.g., through a Millipore filter type AA (Millipore Co., Bedford, Massachusetts) to remove all particulate matter.

Three types of preparations were used for examination of living cells:

(1) Tissue slices, pieces about 0.5 mm^3, were placed in 0.2 ml of labeled protein, the watch glass placed in a moist chamber, and the tissue incubated at 37°C for 2–6 hours, stirring the solutions every 30 minutes. After incubation the tissue was well washed in a 1:1 mixture of Tyrode's solution and normal tissue culture medium and examined as a squash preparation.

(2) Tissue culture cells were grown on cover slips to give a monolayer, and the labeled protein was placed over the cells, which were then incubated in a moist chamber. The washing procedure was the same as in the previous method.

(3) Cell suspensions (0.2 ml) were placed in centrifuge tubes and 0.2 ml of labeled protein added; the tubes were shaken every 30 minutes. After incubation the cells were washed, concentrated by repeated centrifugations and resuspensions, and slide–cover slip preparations of the cells were made. The living cells were examined by phase contrast or ultraviolet microscopy, and the numbers and sizes of the fluorescent vacuoles present in individual cells were measured.

In cells from the reticuloendothelial system, exposed to the labeled protein solution for 2–6 hours, over 60 vacuoles were counted in a single cell, and in some cells the vacuoles occupied over 50% of the cell volume. Holtzer and Holtzer (1960) note that damaged cells present a characteristic pattern of distribution of fluorescent material, which can be readily distinguished from the pattern given by true uptake by living cells. The latter contain sharply delimited vacuoles, while injured cells show diffuse fluorescence with staining of the nucleus.

c. Cytochemical techniques. Straus (1958), in studies on the uptake of protein *in vivo*, used the technique of injection of horse radish peroxidase into rats, followed by localization of the injected enzyme in extracts of various tissues by means of colorimetric analysis with *N,N*-dimethyl-*p*-phenylenediamine. Later this author (1961), using a cytochemical technique, followed the distribution of this enzyme within the cells of the rat kidney and found that the size and shape of the peroxidase-containing bodies was related to the amount of protein injected.

A similar technique was employed by Maeir (1961), using the benzidine reaction on peritoneal exudate cells in culture on cover slips. Both of these techniques could be used to give quantitative determinations of uptake of the peroxidase by counting and sizing the colored reaction products within the cells. The distribution of iron dextran in L strain fibroblasts was followed by Danes and Struthers (1961) using the Prussian blue reaction to localize the iron complex within fixed cells.

C. Other Cells

The method given in Section II,A,2 for the counting of vacuoles ingested by living specimens of *Tetrahymena* gives an estimate of the amount of fluid taken up by the cells. The trypan blue method of Seaman (1961) determines the total amount of dye ingested. Seaman notes that the vacuoles, when first formed, are bright blue, while the dye solution in which the organisms are placed is practically colorless. This indicates a considerable concentration of the dye adsorptively accumulated in the vacuoles. Hence bound dye, in addition to dye in solution in the droplets, is measured. In this method an equal volume of cells in suspension and stock dye solution[1] are mixed. At intervals organisms were freed of extracellular dye by gentle centrifugation. Attempts to release the dye from the cells by means of organic solvents, acids or alkalis proved unsuccessful, hence a procedure was adopted which consisted of sonicating the organisms. This procedure did not release the dye but enabled measurements to be made and compared with a standard curve, obtained by measuring the optical density of normal sonicated organisms to which known amounts of trypan blue had been added. A total dye uptake corresponding to a volume of 0.036 ml per hour per 10^6 cells was found. Later, Seaman (1962) found that if cells were washed briefly with 0.02 *M* potassium phosphate

[1] The concentration of the stock trypan blue solution was adjusted so that a 1:15 dilution gave an optical density of 0.42 at 650 mμ in a Beckman DU spectrophotometer, using a cuvette with a light path of 1.0 cm.

buffer, until the supernatant was free of dye, and then resuspended in a measured volume of the buffer for an hour, the dye is released into the buffer solution and may be measured directly in the spectrophotometer. Fixation with Baker's formol-calcium solution preserves the integrity of the vacuole membranes for 3–4 hours, long enough to permit examination of the specimens and to count vacuole numbers.

Seaman (1961) reports that *Tetrahymena,* when cultured in synthetic medium, contains few vacuoles, and that specimens washed with synthetic medium or phosphate buffer immediately prior to immersion in trypan blue do not take up the dye.

V. Significance of the Values Obtained and Errors Likely to be Encountered in the Different Methods

It is clear from the data presented in Table III, which summarizes uptake experiments with amebae, that the results obtained are very divergent, and that this divergency is due partly to the differing inducing solutes used and partly to the differing time intervals between immersion in the inducer and the measurement. In addition, the conditions of removal of the excess extracellular solution before the measurement and the temperature at which the experiments are carried out will influence the uptake measured. For example, when *A. proteus* is immersed in acid solutions of bovine plasma albumin (pH 4.0–4.5), and the uptake measured immediately after washing in acid culture medium, the result will indicate a high uptake, while immersion of amebae in the same concentration of albumin at pH 7.0 followed by washing in neutral culture solution will give a negligible uptake. If sodium chloride is added to the acid albumin solutions, pinocytosis will be inhibited. The degree of inhibition is inversely proportional to the concentration of sodium chloride added (Chapman-Andresen, 1962). Care should be exercised when testing the pinocytic effect of mixed solutions, since the use of phosphate and maleate buffers in the range between pH 6 and 7 may result in spurious pinocytosis due to the pinocytic effect of the buffer and not of the inducing solute under test. The conditions under which mammalian cells respond to different inducing solutions are so far less clearly defined, but salts and proteins normally are present in test solutions and the proportions of these constituents may be expected to affect the response. It is to be expected that different cell types require different inducers, and that these may vary with the age of the cell and be influenced by hormonal conditions. It should be noted that in some uptake experiments the label followed and the inducer are not the same compound, as for example in the glucose-C^{14} experiments of Chapman-Andresen and Holter (1955). The differences found between the uptake of colloidal gold by biological materials used by various authors may mean that the colloid is not an inducer, and that its presence or absence within cells is due to the inducing or noninducing properties of other constituents of the media. While Brandt and Pappas (1960) reported that the colloid did not attach to the outer surface of *C. chaos*, Chapman-Andresen and Danes (cited by Holter, 1959) found that a considerable amount was ingested by this species. In the case of ascites tumor cells, Ryser *et al.* (1962) reported that very little colloid was taken up, while the results of Harford *et al.* (1957) with HeLa cells, and those of Gosselin (1956) with macrophages and of Parks and Chiquoine (1956) with hepatic phagocytes showed that these cells took up large amounts of the colloid. This difference may be due to genuine differences in the capacity of the cells for uptake of this substance, but it might also be due to differences in the composition of the colloids used and especially to the concentration of gelatin used as stabilizer for the colloid. Gelatin is an inducer of pinocytosis in amebae, and excess gelatin in colloid solutions enhances uptake. However, the addition of extra gelatin to gelatin-stabilized gold colloid solutions injected into rats was found by Murray and Katz (1955) to retard the rate of disappearance of the colloid from circulating blood, presumably owing to the formation of a gelatin-gold-plasma complex.

Many types of tracers, suitable for study of individual cells and of mass cultures are now available, and more detailed and especially quantitative data on uptake by cells should soon be forthcoming.

REFERENCES

Adam, K. M. G. (1959). *J. Gen. Microbiol.* **21,** 519.

Ashton, M. E., Chapman-Andresen, C., and Jensen, W. A. In preparation.

Barrnett, R. G., and Ball, E. G. (1960). *J. Biophys. Biochem. Cytol.* **8,** 83.

Bennett, H. S. (1956). *J. Biophys. Biochem. Cytol. Suppl.* **2,** 99.

Bessis, M. (1954). "Traité de Cytologie sanguine." Masson, Paris.

Bessis, M. (1959). "Kinetics of Cellular Proliferation." Grune & Stratton, New York.

Bessis, M., and Bricka, M. (1952). *Rev. Hematol.* **7,** 407.

Bessis, M., Freixa, P., and Bricka, M. (1953). *Rev. Hematol.* **8,** 71.

Bird, R. G. (1961). Ph.D. Thesis. Univ. London.

Brandt, P. W. (1958). *Exptl. Cell Res.* **15,** 300.

Brandt, P. W., and Pappas, G. D. (1960). *J. Biophys. Biochem. Cytol.* **8,** 675.

Brandt, P. W., and Pappas, G. D. (1962). *J. Cell Biol.* **15,** 55.

Bratianu, S., and Llombart, A. (1929). *Compt. Rend. Soc. Biol.* **101,** 299.

Buvat, R. (1958). *Ann Sci. Nat. Botan. Biol. Vegetale* [11] **19,** 121.

Buvat, R., and Lance, A. (1957). *Compt. Rend. Acad. Sci. Paris* **245,** 2083.

Chapman-Andresen, C. (1957). *Exptl. Cell Res.* **12,** 397.

Chapman-Andresen, C. (1958). *Compt. Rend. Trav. Lab. Carlsberg Ser. Chim.* **31,** 77.

Chapman-Andresen, C. (1960a). *Lunds Univ. Årsskr.* **2, 56,** 15.
Chapman-Andresen, C. (1960b). *Intern. Congr. Soc. Cell Biol. 10th, Paris, 1960.*
Chapman-Andresen, C. (1962). *Compt. Rend. Trav. Lab. Carlsberg* **33,** 73.
Chapman-Andresen, C., and Dick, D. A. T. (1961). *Compt. Rend. Trav. Lab. Carlsberg* **32,** 265.
Chapman-Andresen, C., and Dick, D. A. T. (1962). *Compt. Rend. Trav. Lab. Carlsberg* **32,** 445.
Chapman-Andresen, C., and Holter, H. (1955). *Exptl. Cell Res. Suppl.* **3,** 52.
Chapman-Andresen, C., and Holter, H. (1961). *Compt. Rend. Trav. Lab. Carlsberg.* In preparation.
Chapman-Andresen, C., and Holtzer, H. (1960). *J. Biophys. Biochem. Cytol.* **8,** 288.
Chapman-Andresen, C., and Nilsson, J. R. (1960). *Exptl. Cell Res.* **19,** 631.
Chapman-Andresen, C., and Prescott, D. M. (1956). *Compt. Rend. Trav. Lab. Carlsberg Ser. Chim.* **30,** 57.
Chapman-Andresen, C., and Robinson, C. V. (1953). *Compt. Rend. Trav. Lab. Carlsberg Ser. Chim.* **28,** 343.
Clark, S. L., Jr. (1959). *J. Biophys. Biochem. Cytol.* **5,** 41.
Cohen, A. I. (1959). *Ann. N. Y. Acad. Sci.* **78,** 609.
Danes, B. S., and Struthers, M. (1961). *J. Biophys. Biochem. Cytol.* **10,** 289.
De Terra, N., and Rustad, R. C. (1959). *Exptl. Cell Res.* **17,** 191.
Easton, J. M., Goldberg, B., and Green, H. (1962). *J. Cell Biol.* **12,** 437.
Easty, D. M., Ledoux, L., and Ambrose, E. J. (1956). *Biochim. Biophys. Acta* **20,** 528.
Farquhar, M. G., and Palade, G. E. (1962). *J. Cell Biol.* **13,** 55.
Frédéric, J., and Robineaux, R. (1951). *J. Physiol. Paris* **43,** 732.
Gérard, P., and Cordier, R. (1934). *Biol. Rev. Biol. Proc. Cambridge Phil. Soc.* **9,** 110.
Gey, G. O., Shapras, P., and Borysko, E. (1954). *Ann. N. Y. Acad. Sci.* **58,** 1089.
Gey, G. O., Shapras, P., Bang, F. B., and Gey, M. K. (1955). "Fine Structure of Cells." Noordhoff, Groningen.
Godina, G. (1955). *Z. Zellforsch. Mikroskop. Anat.* **42,** 77.
Gosselin, R. E. (1956). *J. Gen. Physiol.* **39,** 625.
Guttes, E., and Guttes, S. (1960). *Exptl. Cell Res.* **20,** 239.
Haddock, N. H. (1948). *Research (London)* **1,** 685.
Harford, C. G., Hamlin, A., and Parkes, E. (1957). *J. Biophys. Biochem. Cytol.* **3,** 749.
Hayward, A. F. (1962). *Z. Zellforsch. Mikroskop. Anat.* **56,** 197.
Holter, H. (1943). *Compt. Rend. Trav. Lab. Carlsberg Ser. Chim.* **24,** 399.
Holter, H. (1959). *Ann. N. Y. Acad. Sci.* **78,** 524.
Holter, H. (1960). *In* "Biological Approaches to Cancer Chemotherapy" (R. J. C. Harris, ed.). pp. 77–88. Academic Press, New York.
Holter, H. (1961). *In* "Biological Structure and Function" (T. W. Goodwin and O. Lindberg, eds.), Vol. I, pp. 157–168. Academic Press, New York.
Holter, H. (1962). *In* "Enzymes and Drug Action," Ciba Foundation Symposium, p. 30. Little, Brown, Boston, Massachusetts.
Holter, H., and Holtzer, H. (1959). *Exptl. Cell Res.* **18,** 421.
Holter, H., and Marshall, J. M., Jr. (1954). *Compt. Rend. Trav. Lab. Carlsberg Ser. Chim.* **29,** 7.
Holtzer, H., and Holtzer, S. (1960). *Compt. Rend. Trav. Lab. Carlsberg* **31,** 373.
Hughes, A. F. (1953). *J. Anat.* **87,** 150.
Jensen, W. A., and MacLaren, A. D. (1960). *Exptl. Cell Res.* **19,** 414.
Lewis, W. H. (1931). *Johns Hopkins Hosp. Bull.* **49,** 17.

Lewis, W. H. (1935). *Harvey Lectures* **31**, 214.

Lewis, W. H. (1937). *Am. J. Cancer* **29**, 666.

Maeir, D. M. (1961). *Exptl. Cell Res.* **23**, 200.

Marshall, J. M., Jr., and Nachmias, V. T. (1960). *Science* **132**, 1496.

Marshall, J. M., Jr., Schumaker, V. N., and Brandt, P. W. (1959). *Ann. N. Y. Acad. Sci.* **78**, 515.

Mast, S. O., and Doyle, W. L. (1934). *Protoplasma* **20**, 555.

Meltzer, S. J. (1904). *Am. Med.* **8**, 191.

Metchnikoff, E. (1883). *Biol. Zentr.* **3**, 560.

Moore, D. H., and Ruska, H. (1957). *J. Biophys. Biochem. Cytol.* **3**, 457.

Murray, I. M., and Katz, M. (1955). *J. Lab. Clin. Med.* **46**, 263.

Nachmias, V. T., and Marshall, J. M., Jr. (1962). *In* "Biological Structure and Function" (T. W. Goodwin and O. Lindberg, eds.), Vol. II, pp. 605–619. Academic Press, New York.

Northover, B. J. (1961). *Nature* **189**, 574.

Novikoff, A. B. (1960). *Biol. Bull.* **119**, 287.

Odor, D. L. (1956). *J. Biophys. Biochem. Cytol.* **2**, *Suppl.*, 105.

Palade, G. E. (1956). *J. Biophys. Biochem. Cytol.* **2**, *Suppl.*, 85.

Parks, H. F., and Chiquoine, A. D. (1956). *Proc. Congr. Electron Microscopy, Stockholm*, p. 154, *1955*.

Policard, A., and Bessis, M. (1958). *Compt. Rend. Acad. Sci.* **246**, 3194.

Pomerat, C. M., Lefeber, C. G., and Smith, McD. (1954). *Ann. N. Y. Acad. Sci.* **58**, 1311.

Prescott, D. M., and James, T. W. (1955). *Exptl. Cell Res.* **8**, 256.

Rinaldi, R. (1959). *Exptl. Cell Res.* **18**, 70.

Robineaux, R., and Pinet, J. (1960). "Cellular Aspects of Immunity," Ciba Foundation Symposium, p. 5. Churchill, London.

Rose, G. G. (1957). *J. Biophys. Biochem. Cytol.* **3**, 697.

Roth, L. E. (1960). *J. Protozool.* **7**, 176.

Rudzinska, M. A., and Trager, W. (1959). *J. Biophys. Biochem. Cytol.* **6**, 103.

Rudzinska, M. A., and Trager, W. (1962). *J. Protozool.* **9**, 279.

Rustad, R. C. (1959). *Nature* **183**, 1058.

Rustad, R. C. (1961). *Sci. Am.* **204**, 121.

Rustad, R. C., and Rustad, L. C. (1961). *Intern. Biophys. Congr., 1st, Stockholm*

Ryser, H., Caulfield, J. B., and Aub, J. C. (1960). *Intern. Congr. Soc. Cell Biol. 10th, Paris, 1960.*

Ryser, H., Caulfield, J. B. and Aub, J. C. (1962). *J. Cell Biol.* **14**, 255.

Schumaker, V. N. (1958). *Exptl. Cell Res.* **15**, 314.

Seaman, G. R. (1961). *J. Protozool.* **8**, 204.

Seaman, G. R. (1962). *J. Protozool.* **9**, 335.

Seaman, G. R., and Mancilla, R. (1961). *Proc. Intern. Conf. Protozool., 1st, Prague, 1961.*

Sorkin, E. (1960). *In* "Mechanisms of Antibody Formation" (M. Holub and L. Jarošková, eds.), pp. 61–69. Publishing House of the Czechoslovak Academy of Sciences, Prague (distributed by Academic Press, New York).

Steedman, H. F. (1950). *Quart. J. Microscop. Sci.* **91**, 477.

Steinert, M., and Novikoff, A. B. (1960). *J. Biophys. Biochem. Cytol.* **8**, 563.

Straus, W. (1958). *J. Biophys. Biochem. Cytol.* **4**, 541.

Straus, W. (1961). *Exptl. Cell Res.* **22**, 282.

Thomason, D., and Schofield, R. (1961). *Exptl. Cell Res.* **24**, 457.

Weiling, F. (1961). *Naturwissenschaften* **48**, 411.

Wilska, A. (1954). *Mikroskopie* **9,** 1.
Wittekind, D. (1961). *Z. Zellforsch. Mikroskop. Anat.* **54,** 631.
Wohlfarth-Bottermann, K. E. (1960). *Protoplasma* **52,** 58.
Volkonsky, M. (1933). *Bull. Biol. France Belg.* **67,** 135.

Chapter 15

Quantitative Autoradiography

ROBERT P. PERRY

The Institute for Cancer Research,
Philadelphia, Pennsylvania

I. Introduction

One of the most useful methods for studying *in situ* biochemical reactions on the level of the individual cell is autoradiography. In this technique a specimen containing radioactive material is covered with a layer of photographic film of a type designed particularly for this purpose. A great variety of specimen material may be used: for example, individual whole cells and microorganisms, tissue sections, squashes, and even sagittal sections of entire animals. The specimen and film are in contact for a certain exposure period during which the radioactive atoms decay. The emitted radiation (usually β-rays) strikes the photographic emulsion and activates silver halide grains, forming a latent image which, upon development of the emulsion, will depict the distribution of radioactive material within the specimen. The developed image contains two distinct elements of information: first, its location relative to certain observable structures in the specimen, and second, its intensity, which bears a definite relationship to the amount of radioactivity present. In this chapter we will concern ourselves with the latter element.

A. Relative and Absolute Measurements

Autoradiography is designated as quantitative if a law of correspondence can be established between the relative amounts of radioactive material in particular regions of a specimen and the relative grain (or track) densities associated with these regions. In addition, it is sometimes possible to calculate, from the grain density data, the exact amount of isotope incorporated; this is referred to as an absolute measurement.

In general, relative measurements are considerably easier to make than are absolute measurements. The latter usually involve some sort of calibration against a standard source, and it is often difficult, if not impossible, to make the calibration under conditions which are identical to those of the measurement. Fortunately, in most cases relative measurements, i.e., quantitative comparisons, are entirely sufficient for elucidation of the phenomena under investigation.

B. Factors Influencing Quantitative Measurements

The factors which are involved in making a quantitative autoradiographic measurement are: (1) the specimen geometry and its relation to the photographic emulsion, (2) the density of the specimen, (3) the energy spectrum of the β-rays which are emitted from the particular radioactive atom, and (4) the thickness and sensitivity characteristics of the emulsion. In addition, the grain number should be adjusted to an optimum which is high enough relative to background for statistical accuracy and yet low enough so that "coincidence" events are at a negligible level.

The interplay of factors (1–4) is illustrated in Fig. 1. In the ideal case, Fig. 1a, there is a one-to-one mapping of radioactive atoms at points P into silver grains at points Q, such that differences in the grain density profile faithfully represent differences in the amount and distribution of the radioactive material. The grain distributions are, in this case, unaffected by varying the specimen or emulsion thickness. In reality, however, the grain distribution is distorted owing either to the spread of the image

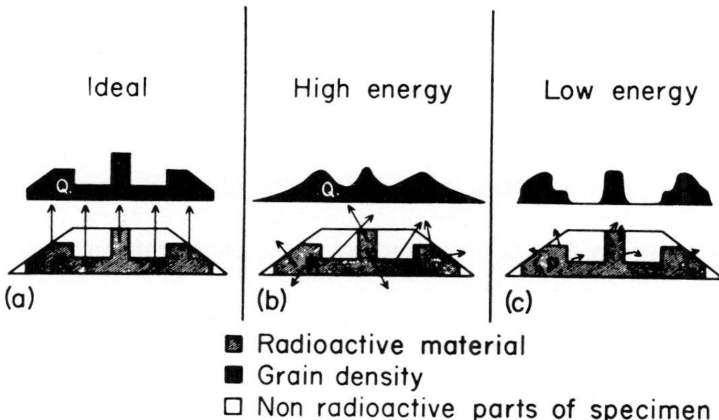

FIG. 1. Schematic illustration of the relationship between the amount of radioactive material incorporated in a specimen (outlined below) and the autoradiographic grain density (in black above). The emulsion is in contact with the upper surface of the specimen. In the ideal case, (a), there is a perfect image of the distribution of radioactivity so that grains at Q bear an identical relation to the whole as do their source points, P. In the high energy case, (b), electrons emitted at P may give rise to grains, Q, which are at other points in the image. This leads to image broadening and loss of contrast. Note the diminution in the narrow central peak compared to the broader peaks at each end. In the low energy case, (c), many electrons, especially those emitted from the part of the specimen distant from the emulsion, would be absorbed in the specimen and hence not reach the emulsion. This will greatly improve the resolution, but it will result in a distribution which is distorted in a way which depends on the proximity of different regions to the emulsion.

when relatively high energy emitters are used, or to self-absorption by the specimen when very low energy emitters are used.

Electrons from emitters such as P^{32} (maximum energy, 1.7 Mev; average range in water, 1250μ), S^{35} (0.167 Mev; 50μ), and C^{14} (0.155 Mev; 40μ) are ejected in all directions and suffer little or no attenuation in passing through comparatively thin specimens. Consequently, electrons emitted from a certain region of the specimen are likely to give rise to grains at points which do *not* lie directly over the region (Fig. 1b). This gives rise to image spread—hence poor resolution—and to loss of contrast due to "crossfire." These effects vary greatly with the specimen thickness, emulsion thickness, thickness of the separating layer (gap), and the effective radii of the regions to be resolved. Evaluations of their magnitude have been made by several authors (Doniach and Pelc, 1950; Gross *et al.*, 1951; Lamerton and Harriss, 1954) (cf. Section II,A).

The situation with an emitter such as H^3 (0.018 Mev; 1μ) is somewhat different. The electrons emitted by tritium have an average range in fixed biological material of a few microns at most. Since this is of the same order as the average specimen thickness, the most important factor to be considered is the absorption of these electrons by the specimen material itself. It is highly probable that an electron emitted from a point, *P*, in a region of the specimen a few microns distant from the emulsion will not give rise to a grain at all (Fig. 1c). The grain density will thus have an extremely marked dependence on specimen thickness and density, and on the proximity of the radioactive regions to the emulsion. The analysis of this effect, which proceeds along different lines than that for electrons of high energy, will be treated in detail in Section II,B.

II. Theoretical Considerations

A. Image Spread and Crossfire

For isotopes emitting electrons of relatively high energies the determination of the amount of image broadening is essentially a geometrical calculation in which it is assumed that grain density is proportional to the radiation intensity, which varies inversely as the square of the distance from the source. Very extensive calculations of this type were presented by Lamerton and Harriss (1954). They made use of theorems concerning the distribution of radiation around sources of different shapes to calculate the image spread from finite sources of various linear dimensions. Values were obtained for various thicknesses of specimen, emulsion, and gap.

Of perhaps greater interest here are their calculations regarding contrast or "crossfire." A uniformly active specimen in the form of an infinite disc of given thickness was considered in contact with an emulsion of a given thickness, and the mean grain density was determined. A cylindrical volume of given radius in the emulsion was then chosen and the relative contribution to the mean grain density found (a) from the part of the specimen immediately underlying this volume of emulsion, and (b) from the more distant parts of the specimen. Two different formulas for the β-ray absorption within the specimen were used and gave essentially similar results. Table I (from Lamerton and Harriss, 1954) summarizes these calculations. There is a relatively high crossfire correction in the case of small structures because many of the electrons originating from these structures dissipate a large part of their energy in more distant parts of the emulsion.

For example, it can be seen that with the relatively "soft electrons emitted by S^{35}, a thin specimen, and an emulsion 2μ thick, an object 5μ in diameter which exhibits a grain density twice that of its surroundings

TABLE I

CALCULATED CROSSFIRE FOR VARIOUS GEOMETRIES[a]

Conditions	Radius of cylinder (μ)	Ratio of grain density contributions from the activity within the given structure to that from more distant parts of the specimen	
		For P^{32} electrons	For S^{35} electrons
5μ specimen	5	0.09	0.23
5μ emulsion	10	0.19	0.60
2μ specimen	1	0.03	0.06
2μ emulsion	5	0.20	0.50
	10	0.35	1.08
2μ specimen	1	0.02	0.04
5μ emulsion	5	0.13	0.33
(or vice versa)	10	0.25	0.79

[a] Data from Lamerton and Harriss (1954).

may in reality have a concentration of radioactive material which is 4 times that of its surroundings. Similarly, an object 1μ in diameter would have to contain over 33 times as much radioactivity per unit volume in order to give an autoradiographic image which was twice as dense as its surroundings. Approximately the same is true for C^{14} electrons which are only slightly less energetic than those from S^{35}.

A further source of error should be considered if liquid emulsions are used. When a liquid emulsion is applied to a small isolated specimen in a layer which is not much thicker than the specimen itself, it is important to realize that the thickness of the emulsion immediately over the specimen may be less than that on either side of it. This is especially important when high energy emitters such as P^{32} are used. A consideration of this phenomenon was made by Bleecken (1961), who found that an error in grain density of approximately 25% is encountered when 5μ thick emulsion layers are applied to P^{32}-labeled Basidiomycete hyphae 2μ in diameter. This error is not significant with stripping film which follows the contours of the specimen.

A very general "matrix theory" has been developed by Odeblad (1959) for considering geometrical effects. One writes:

$$D_i = XS_{ij}P_jV_j \qquad (i = 1,2 \ldots N, j = 1,2 \ldots n) \tag{1}$$

where D_i is the grain density at point i in the emulsion (indexed over the number of measured areas, N), P_j and V_j are, respectively, the concentration and volume of radioactive material at point j in the specimen (indexed over the number of different areas in the specimen, n), X is a proportionality factor, and S_{ij} express the geometrical and self-absorption relations between specimen and emulsion. The advantage of this method is that the problem is stated completely in a single, rather simple matrix equation. However, the calculation of the factors S_{ij} involves the same type of calculations and integrations and the same assumptions concerning absorption functions as those used by Lamerton and Harriss (1954).

B. Calculations for Tritium

1. Interaction of H^3 Electrons with Matter

In the case of H^3 β-rays the inverse square geometrical effects lose importance relative to the reduction in grain production due to specimen self-absorption. Before discussing specific calculations of the self-absorption, it is worthwhile to consider briefly the basic aspects of the interaction of H^3 β-rays with matter.

As the electrons emitted by tritium pass through matter they lose energy due to a large number of inelastic collisions with atomic electrons. Their mean energy loss per unit path length, derived from the theory of Bohr, may be written as:

$$\left\langle\frac{dE}{dx}\right\rangle = \frac{NZ\pi e^4\overline{B}}{E} \tag{2}$$

where E is the energy of the incident electron, e the electronic charge, N the number of atoms per unit volume, Z the number of electrons per atom, and $\overline{B}$ the "stopping power" of the material. The total range, R_i, of an electron of initial energy E_i is then:

$$R_i = \int_0^{E_i} \frac{-dE}{\langle -dE/dx\rangle} = \frac{A}{N_{Av}\rho Z\pi e^4} \int_0^{E_i} \frac{E}{\overline{B}}\, dE \tag{3}$$

where we have used the relation $N = \rho N_{Av}/A$; ρ is the density in gm/cm^3, A is the atomic weight, and N_{Av} is Avogadro's number.

The stopping power, $\overline{B}$, is itself a function of E but varies only very slowly (as the logarithm of E). In water, for example, it ranges from about 6 at 1 kev to 12 at 20 kev (Fano, 1954). Therefore to a first approximation it can be taken outside the integral sign. A/Z is about 2.5 for most biological macromolecules and thus evaluating constants one may write:

$$R_i \simeq \frac{0.31E_i^2}{\overline{B}\rho} \tag{4}$$

where the R_i are in microns and the E_i are in kev.

From Eq. (4) we see that the distance which a given electron will travel in matter is proportional to the square of its energy and inversely proportional to the density of the matter. Table II lists the ranges in matter with

TABLE II

THEORETICAL RANGE AND EMISSION FREQUENCIES FOR THE TRITIUM β-RAYS[a]

Energy E_i (kev)	Range R_i (μ)	Emission frequency ν_i ($\times$ 100)	Fraction of electrons with energy $> E_i$
1	0.04	10.8	—
2	0.14	11.1	0.89
3	0.28	10.7	0.78
4	0.45	10.5	0.67
5	0.66	9.5	0.57
6	0.91	8.4	0.47
7	1.19	7.6	0.39
8	1.49	6.5	0.31
9	1.82	6.1	0.25
10	2.16	5.2	0.186
11	2.60	4.5	0.135
12	3.06	3.1	0.089
13	3.57	2.6	0.058
14	4.10	1.7	0.032
15	4.68	0.90	0.015
16	5.26	0.48	0.0061
17	5.90	0.13	0.0013
18	6.55	0.005	0.00005

[a] Range calculated for a material of density 1.3.

density 1.3 (e.g., dried protein films) for electrons with energies corresponding to those emitted by tritium. Using the tritium emission spectrum (Curran *et al.*, 1948) we have tabulated the frequencies, ν_i, of electrons in each energy range. In addition Table II shows the fraction of electrons which have energies greater than E_i—and hence ranges greater than R_i. It should be remarked that ranges calculated in this way give the entire length of the electron path, which is indeed very tortuous since it results from numerous collisions. The straightline distance from the beginning to the end of the path will always be considerably shorter than these calculated ranges.

2. Self-absorption Corrections

The foregoing has illustrated the way in which two properties—density and thickness—determine the amount of self-absorption in a biological specimen. Thus, significant variations within the specimen or among comparable specimens of either of these parameters must be measured before quantitative measurements can be made. In the case of carefully sectioned material of uniform thickness one need consider only the density contributions, whereas with uneven material such as tissue culture cells growing on glass the influence of both thickness and density should be assessed.

In an elegant study Maurer and Primbsch (in press) have evaluated the amount of self-absorption which occurs in biological material of various densities. They sought specifically to determine the relative self-absorption associated with nucleoli, nucleoplasm, and cytoplasm in tissue sections. However, their results are of sufficient generality so that they may be applied to any material in which an estimate of the density or dry mass is obtainable. Their method was essentially as follows. Sections of varying thickness (0.25–6μ) were cut from methacrylate-embedded mouse liver cells which had been labeled with tyrosine-H^3 or cytidine-H^3. The methacrylate was dissolved and autoradiographs were made using AR-10 stripping film. The grains per square micron over each cell compartment were then counted and plotted against section thickness. Saturation, i.e., no further increase in grain density for increasing section thickness, was observed at roughly 0.25μ for the nucleolus and at about 1μ for nucleo- and cytoplasm.

Then using the data from dry mass measurements (cf. Section III,A), they converted the values for section thickness of each compartment to values of dry mass, expressed in mg/cm². This enabled them to express the data for all three compartments on a single graph (Fig. 2a), and in so doing to obtain a curve applicable to desiccated biological material in general. The ideal number of grains per unit area, i.e., that number which would be produced if there were no self-absorption, is obtained from the slope of the curve extrapolated to infinite thinness. Furthermore, differentiation of the curve yields an "absorption curve" (Fig. 2b) which gives the fraction tritium electrons which will pass through a given mass of dried tissue and produce silver grains. This is useful for determining the "overlay effect," i.e., the effect of a layer of nonradioactive material interposed between the specimen and the film. Finally, by taking the ratio of the measured to the ideal number of grains in Fig. 2a, one can obtain a curve for the self-absorption coefficient (Fig. 2c). This curve illustrates the way in which the number of grains produced by a given amount of radioactivity depends on the total dry mass of the material which contains the radioactivity. It is seen for example that the measured activity will be only 40% of the ideal activity if the radioactivity originates from a layer of material whose dry mass is 0.05 mg/cm². This would

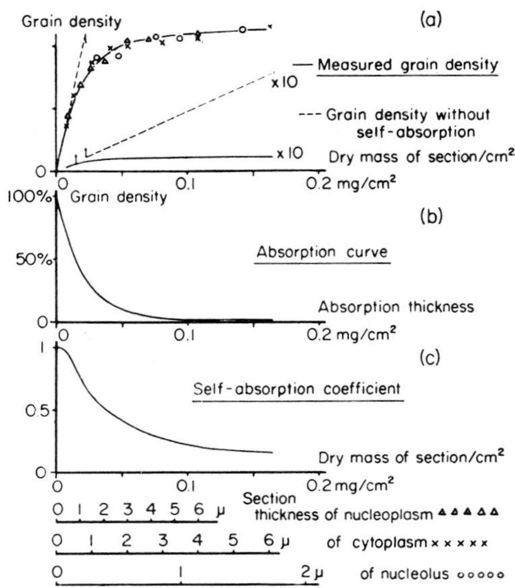

FIG. 2. (a) Grains per unit area (ordinate) vs. dry mass of sections in mg/cm² (abscissa). Experimental points: O, nucleolus; Δ, nucleoplasm; X, cytoplasm. All points fall on the single curve (solid line) which is valid for desiccated biological material. Dotted curve is extrapolation to an infinitely thin section and gives the grains per unit area which would obtain if there were no self-absorption. (b) Absorption curve, obtained from the solid curve of (a) by differentiation. (c) Self-absorption coefficient, obtained by plotting the ratio of the solid to the dotted curves of (a). Scales at bottom illustrate the thickness in microns of each cell compartment which corresponds to the abscissa values of dry mass in (a), (b), and (c). From Maurer and Primbsch (in press).

correspond to less than 3μ of nucleoplasm, 2μ of cytoplasm, and 0.6μ of nucleolus.

In the case of a specimen of uneven thickness such as the tissue culture cell depicted in Fig. 3, a knowledge of the average cell profile is required. A method for determining the average profile is discussed later (cf. Section III,A). One may consider each of the three compartments (nucleolus, nucleus, and cytoplasm) as a disc of a characteristic thickness which is roughly equal to the average for the compartment. The minimum distance between the compartment and emulsion, Z_1, the maximum distance, Z_2, and the density of the compartment can then be used to ascertain the magnitude of the self-absorption correction.

In a previous publication (Perry *et al.*, 1961) we used the principles discussed in Section II,A together with measurements of cell profiles to derive a set of relative correction factors, E, relating the measured grain count over a cell compartment, g^*, to the ideal grain count in the absence

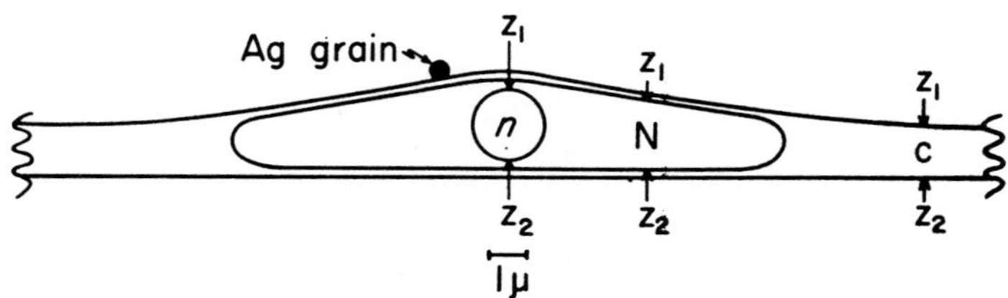

FIG. 3. Profile of average HeLa cell in an autoradiograph preparation, drawn to scale. *n* is nucleolus, N is nucleus, C is cytoplasm, and Z_1 and Z_2 are the respective average minimum and average maximum distances from the emulsion. A silver grain of a size representative of Ilford G.5 emulsion is shown for comparison.

of self-absorption, $g:E = g/g^*$ (Table III). In the derivation we assumed that all compartments have a density equal to that of dried protein film (i.e., $\rho = 1.3$). We did not take into account the fact that the different cell compartments, having different dry mass concentrations *in vivo*, might be expected to contain different amounts of air space when desiccated. Unfortunately, one cannot assume that densities in desiccated cells are proportional to the respective dry mass per unit volume *in vivo* because different parts of the specimen will undergo different amounts of compression upon dehydration (cf. Stenram, 1961). Therefore one cannot use density determinations made under one set of conditions with profile measurements made under other conditions. Both measurements must naturally be made on material fixed and treated in the same way. Since this has not yet been done for tissue culture cells, we cannot predict to what extent the density corrections would modify the $\bar{E}$ value given in Table III. However, since nucleolar densities are always found to be at

TABLE III

PARAMETERS OF RADIOAUTOGRAPH EFFICIENCY FOR HELA CELLS[a]

Compartment	Z_1 Minimum distance from emulsion μ	Z_2 Maximum distance from emulsion μ	$\bar{E}$ Normalized efficiency factors
Cytoplasm	0	1.4	1.0
Nucleus	~0.2	2.0	1.6
Nucleolus	~0.4	2.3	2.3

[a] Perry *et al.* (1961).

least 3 times that of the other cell parts (Stenram, 1961), one can predict that the true factor for the nucleolus is probably somewhat greater than 2.3.

C. Optimal Number of Grains

1. Grain Density

For quantitative evaluation of autoradiographs the number of grains per unit area over any particular specimen must be controlled, by adjusting either the exposure time or the concentration of isotope administered, so that the probability of coincidence is relatively small. By "coincidence" we mean that two or more disintegrations result in a single observable silver grain. When one is considering large areas and large numbers of grains, the saturation effect may be seen as the deviation from linearity at the high exposure end of the conventional *H-D* curve. As with ordinary photographic procedures one adjusts conditions so as to be on the linear portion of the curve.

In the case of a small discrete quantity of grains one may treat the problem as follows: The maximum number of resolvable grains per unit area is designated as n_{max}. The value of n_{max} depends on (a) the grain size, which in turn depends on the type of emulsion used and on the conditions of development, and on (b) the number of layers of grains which can be activated by a particular β-ray. Thus if we consider a monolayer of grains, 0.5μ in diameter, $n_{max} = 4\mu^{-2}$; for two layers $n_{max} = 8\mu^{-2}$. For a monolayer of grains, 0.25μ in diameter, $n_{max} = 16\mu^{-2}$.

It may be shown[1] that the observed number of grains, n_{obs}, is related to the true number of grains in the absence of coincidence, n_{true}, by

$$n_{obs} = n_{max}\left[1 - \left(\frac{n_{max}-1}{n_{max}}\right)^{n_{true}}\right] \tag{5}$$

[1] Equations (5) and (6) are derived as follows: The true number of grains, i.e., those resulting from all "effective" disintegrations in the absence of coincidence is

$$n_{true} = n_{max} \sum_{k=1}^{n_{true}} kP_k$$

where the P_k are calculated from the binomial or Poisson distribution,

$$P_k = C_k^{n_{true}}\left(\frac{1}{n_{max}}\right)^k \left(\frac{n_{max}-1}{n_{max}}\right)^{n_{true}-k} \xrightarrow[n_{max}\to\infty]{} e^{-n_{true}/n_{max}} \left(\frac{n_{true}}{n_{max}}\right)^k \Big/ k!.$$

The number of grains actually observed is

$$n_{obs} = n_{max} \sum_{k=1}^{n_{true}} P_k = n_{max}(1 - P_o) =$$

$$n_{max}\left[1 - \left(\frac{n_{max}-1}{n_{max}}\right)^{n_{true}}\right] \xrightarrow[n_{max}\to\infty]{} n_{max}\,(1 - e^{n_{true}/n_{max}}).$$

or when n_{max} is large

$$n_{obs} \to n_{max}\,(1 - e^{-n_{true}/n_{max}}). \tag{6}$$

In Figure 4, Eq. (5) has been used to plot n_{obs} vs. n_{true} for 3 values of n_{max}. Also shown are the values of the ratio, n_{obs}/n_{true}, for all possible values of n_{obs}/n_{max}. This latter curve has been plotted using the approxima-

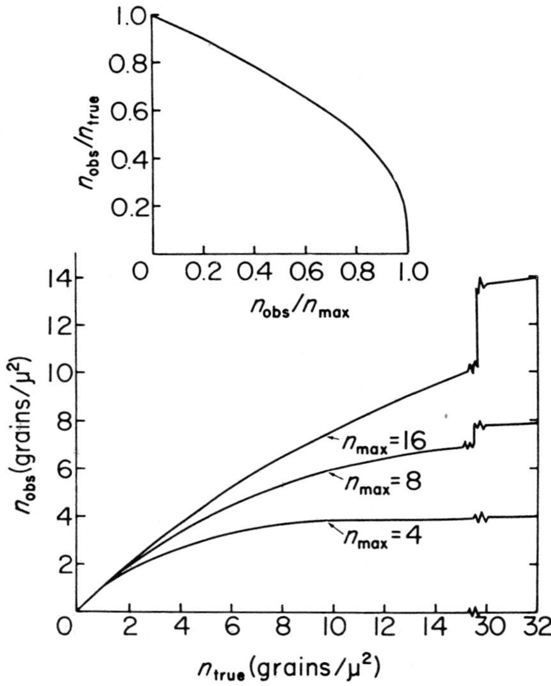

FIG. 4. Coincidence corrections. Lower curves: n_{obs} vs. n_{true} for three values of n_{max}, calculated from Eq. (5). Upper curve: n_{obs}/n_{true} (the fraction of the true count which is actually observed) vs. n_{obs}/n_{max} (the number of grains observed per unit area expressed as a fraction of the number of resolvable grains which would completely cover the area).

tion of Eq. (6). It can be seen from these curves that if the observed number of grains is to be greater or equal to 80% of the true number then the grain density cannot exceed 0.37 of the maximum possible density. For an n_{max} of $8\mu^{-2}$ this corresponds to an observed grain density of slightly less than 3 grains/μ^2.[2]

[2] Recently developed techniques in which reduced grain size is achieved by rapid treatment in selected developers and in which autographs are observed in the electron microscope (Caro, 1962) obtain resolutions with tritium of 0.1μ. Consequently, for these conditions the allowable value of n_{obs} is increased to 37 grains/μ^2.

2. Total Grains

If all the samples of a particular specimen contain the same amount of radioactive material then the variation in grain count among samples is due solely to the randomness of radioactive decay.[3] In this case the total number of grains which must be counted for a given accuracy to be attained may be calculated from well-known statistical formulas.

For instance, the per cent standard error (% S.E.) is

$$\% \text{ S.E.} = \frac{100}{\sqrt{G}} \tag{7}$$

where G is the total number of grains counted.[4] The standard error is that deviation from the true average count which a given count has a 31.7% probability of exceeding. For example, if one sample of a given specimen is found to have 4 grains associated with it then the % S.E. $= 100/\sqrt{4} =$ 50%, and the true average count has a 31.7% probability of being greater than 6 or less than 2. If 100 samples of this same specimen are counted and yield a total count $G = 400$, then % S.E. = 5% and the average count has a 31.7% probability of being greater than 4.2 or less than 3.8.

When the background count, B, forms an appreciable fraction of G then Eq. (7) must be modified so that the % S.E. in G-B, the net count, is:

$$\% \text{ S.E.} = 100\sqrt{G}\left[\frac{G + B}{(G - B)^2}\right]. \tag{8}$$

D. Grain Count Distributions

The spread of grain counts for a population of cells is usually significantly greater than that for a Poisson distribution about a single mean (which one might expect from the statistical nature of the radioactive decay). It is customary to attribute this increased spread as being due to some form of biological variation, although in some cases inanimate radioactive specimens have also produced apparent departure from the Poisson distribution (Levi and Nielsen, 1959). An analysis of grain count distributions which allows important conclusions to be drawn concerning the nature of the synthetic processes at the cellular level has been made by Lajtha *et al.* (1960).

Figure 5 illustrates four different types of grain count distribution which

[3] Uniformity among samples is not usually realized in practice, however, because of uncontrollable biological variation (cf. Section II,D).

[4] This applies to grain counting where *not more* than one grain is attributed to a disintegration. In the case of track counting, G refers to disintegrations, not grains (Levi, 1957).

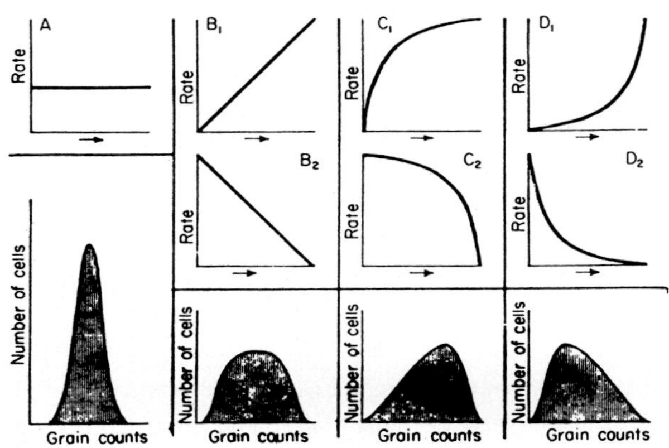

FIG. 5. Cell-to-cell grain count distributions to be expected from various forms of rate-time curves. A: constant rate, B: linearly changing rate, C: rate high over most of cell cycle, D: rate low over most of cell cycle. From Lajtha *et al.* (1960).

might be encountered depending on the characteristic curve for the rate of incorporation of tracer as a function of time in the cell's life cycle. For a nongrowing population of cells a steady rate of uptake such as that shown in Fig. 5A may indicate a steady rate of synthesis or turnover of a compound. However, a standard deviation greater than that predicted by an ideal Poisson distribution can be expected since this average rate is itself a distribution of rates between young and senescent members of the population. For example, Lajtha *et al.* (1960) find that data for the incorporation of methionine-S^{35}, into the small lymphocytes of human leukemic blood fit a normal distribution with standard deviation of 30% [15% for a mean grain count of 45 grains per cell and 25% for biological variation, $S_{\text{total}} = \sqrt{(S_1)^2 + (S_2)^2}$]. For an asynchronous growing population of cells all four types of distribution are possible as well as combinations thereof. Discontinuous processes such as deoxyribonucleic acid synthesis are also analyzable by this method since grain counting is confined to those members of the population which are truly labeled.

III. Practical Considerations and Techniques

A. Determination of Parameters for Self-absorption Corrections

1. CELL PROFILES

The method which one uses to determine specimen geometry will of course be dictated by the particular material involved. It is especially important to make these measurements if one wishes to make quantitative autoradiographs of material of uneven thickness, for example, tissue culture cells growing on glass or squashes of different types of material.

It is possible to make preparations of tissue culture cells which not only allow one to draw a scale diagram of the average cell such as that shown in Fig. 3, but also allow a direct visualization of the effect of variable cell thickness on grain production (Perry *et al.*, 1961). The technique is essentially as follows: HeLa cells are grown on Millipore filters (in Petri dishes), incubated with a tritium-labeled compound (cytidine-H^3,) fixed in acetic acid: ethanol for 30 seconds, washed in 70% ethanol, dried, and layered with liquid emulsion. After development, fixing, and washing, the "sandwich" of filter, cells, and emulsion is dehydrated in an alcohol series and embedded in paraffin. Sections 3μ thick are cut at right angles to the filter plane and affixed to slides. The cells are stained with methyl green-pyronine (Unna) and the dye effectively removed from the emulsion by a 5 minute treatment with *n*-butyl alcohol.

Examples of the profiles so obtained are shown in Fig. 6. Under the conditions of this experiment the nucleoli contain the highest *concentration*

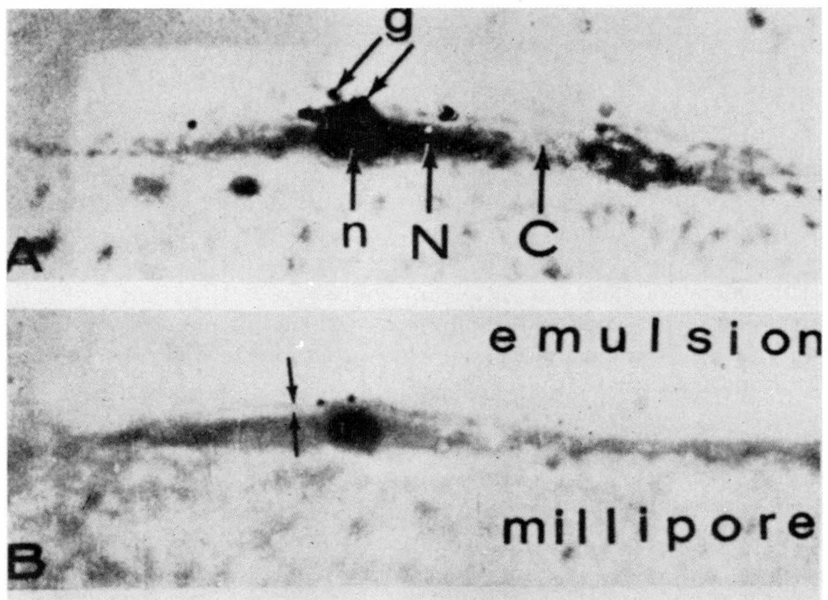

FIG. 6. Profiles of autoradiographs. Adjacent cells on the same preparation. A: cell with nucleolus (*n*) practically touching emulsion. Note large grain density, (*g*). *N* is nucleus, *C* is cytoplasm. B: cell with nucleolus buried beneath 0.8μ layer (arrows) of nucleo- and cytoplasm. Note scarcity of grains.

of label. The grain count is much lower in Fig. 6B than in 6A because in the former there is a 0.8μ layer of nucleoplasm and cytoplasm intervening between nucleolus and emulsion. Also obvious from these profiles is the fact that the *average* thickness of cytoplasm is less than that of the nucleus or nucleolus. Measurements from 50 cells gave rise to the average profile depicted in Fig. 3.

2. Measurement of Cell Densities

The most practical method for determining the densities of the different cell compartments is microinterferometry. A very thorough account of this technique has been given by Barer (1956). For reasons discussed earlier (Section II,B) it is necessary to make the determinations on material treated in the same way as that used for profile measurements. The particular problems associated with measurements on fixed material are discussed at length by Stenram (1961), and the reader should refer to this paper for further details.

B. Adjustment of Grain Number

In Section II,C we discussed why it was necessary to work with grain densities which fall within a certain optimal range. One is sometimes confronted with a situation where a series of specimens to be studied can be expected to incorporate widely varying amounts of the label. This might be the case in a kinetics experiment carried out over a large time range, or in an experiment in which an inhibitor greatly reduces the number of grains observable in a control. One would like to adjust conditions in a precise way—analogous to diluting samples for an assay—so that measurements are made over a certain limited range of counts.

The two practical possibilities for this are the adjustment of the specific activity or concentration of isotope which is administered to the organism and the adjustment of the exposure time of the autoradiographs. The first of these methods can be used if one employs a range of concentrations in which a linear relation exists between grains produced and isotope concentration. In kinetic experiments we have succeeded in achieving linearity over a 50-fold range of concentrations (Perry *et al.*, 1961).

The second method can be used if one is careful to maintain constant conditions of development and to avoid exposures which are so long that loss of activated grains due to latent image fading occurs. We have found that autoradiographs stored at 24°C in desiccated boxes for as long as 10 days show no detectable latent image fading. Baserga and Nemeroff (1962) have reported similar data on this effect. If longer exposures are necessary, then special techniques such as those mentioned by Ray and Stevens (1953) or Herz (1959) are suggested.

C. Methods of Assay

There exist three different methods for the quantitative assessment of an autoradiograph: (1) measurement with a microdensitometer or similar instrument of the degree of blackening in a given area, (2) visual counting of individual grains, and (3) track counting.

1. Densitometry

This method is most useful where large specimens of areas $10^4\mu^2$ or larger are concerned. Several instruments have been designed specifically for use with autoradiographs (Dudley and Pelc, 1953; Mazia *et al.*, 1955; Gullberg, 1957; Tolles, 1959; Rogers, 1961). The more promising of these use incident dark field illumination to measure the light reflected from the silver grains (Gullberg, 1957; Rogers, 1961). However, no instrument has yet demonstrated sufficient accuracy or practicality in the measurement of small objects so that it could supplant visual counting as the standard technique for studies involving single cells.

2. Visual Grain Counting

The most accurate method for most purposes, especially in studies involving objects of cellular size, continues to be visual grain counting. In practice it is not difficult for trained investigators to count autoradiographs with a precision of better than 10%. Certain special methods, designed to reduce the fatigue, remove some of the subjective elements, and to increase the precision of grain counting, have been suggested (Micou and Goldstein, 1959; Ostrowski and Sawicki, 1961). With these methods counts are made either on the projected image of the specimen or on a focal series of photographs.

3. Track Counting

A very valuable technique for the counting of specimens labeled with isotopes other than tritium is that of track counting. This method, developed principally by Levi and co-workers (Levi and Hogben, 1955; Levi, 1957; Levi and Nielsen, 1959), can be used with moderately labeled samples (<50 tracks/$100\mu^2$) to achieve a precision of about 4% (Levi and Hogben, 1955). One must use an emulsion of appropriate sensitivity and thickness (easily obtainable with liquid emulsions) and must set a practical lower limit on the number of contiguous grains which is to be counted as a track. Levi uses 4 for this latter figure (Levi, 1957). The track technique is particularly useful when one is dealing with specimens of very low activity since only a few tracks emanating from a restricted area are readily recognizable.

D. Nonrandom Arrays of Grains

One sometimes observes that the distribution of grains over a tritium-labeled specimen is not homogeneous but rather that the grains occur in clumps or rows. The questions arise: Is this an artifact of the preparation, or is there a localization of radioactive molecules on some submicroscopic structure? Should a distinction be made between these grains and ones which are homogeneously distributed? Consideration of this problem in model systems has shown that the possibility of preparation artifact does indeed exist (cf. Levi and Nielsen, 1959, and discussion following). However, a direct test on the material in question is clearly more definitive.

The following method has been devised for testing inhomogeneous grain distributions (Perry, in press). The specimen is affixed to a membrane of Formvar [approximately 75 mμ thick as measured by the interference color test (Peachy, 1958)] which is held in some substantial frame.[5] The frame is dipped into liquid emulsion so that a layer of film coats both sides of the Formvar. All further treatment is identical to that for conventional autoradiographs. Figure 7 shows an example of this type of preparation made with HeLa cells labeled for 30 minutes with cytidine-H^3. The fact that the label is confined to submicroscopic threadlike structures, most likely the interphase chromosomes, is clearly seen by comparing upper and lower layers of grains. The probability that a random or artifactual cluster of grains would give a comparable pattern on both sides of the cell is extremely low. It might also be mentioned here that if a 750 mμ thick Formvar membrane is used instead of one 75 mμ thick, then the number of grains produced on the film layer touching the cell is 7 times greater than on the layer separated by the Formvar. This attenuation could be predicted by the principles discussed in Section II,B,1.

E. Absolute Calibration

As stated in the introduction, absolute measurements present the autoradiographer with a considerably more formidable task than do relative

[5] The choice of method for affixing the specimen to the Formvar will depend on the type of material being studied. For tissue culture cells, thin rectangular pieces of mica, the size of Leighton Tube cover slips, were punched with 1- and 2-mm holes and used as supports for the Formvar. The cells were grown and labeled directly on these supports. Those cells which grew on the Formvar covering the holes were selected for observation in the final preparation.

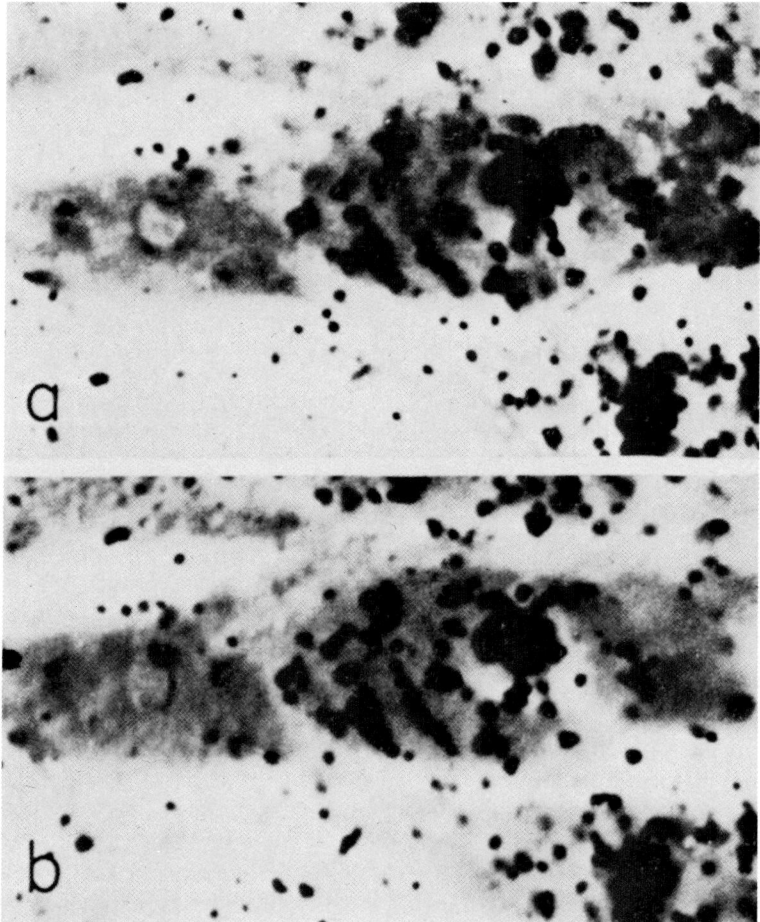

FIG. 7. Grain patterns on a two-sided autoradiograph. (a) Grains on film layer above cell; (b) grains on film layer beneath the thin Formvar supporting membrane. Note that certain long "strings" of grain show continuity partly above and partly below. This would be expected if radioactive molecules were on strands which had a wavy configuration. Labeling: 30 minutes with cytidine-H^3 (>90% of the incorporation is into ribonucleic acid).

measurements. The general method is to consult tables of grain yield which give the conversion from plate density or grain number[6] to number of electrons impinging on the emulsion, and then to calculate the original

[6] Density, D, and grain number, N, can be interconverted by means of Nutting's equation: $N = D/0.4343\bar{a}$, where $\bar{a}$ is the mean projected area of the grains.

number of emitted electrons using the considerations discussed in Section II. From this number, the decay constant of the isotope, and the exposure time, the absolute amount of activity in the sample can be calculated. Grain yields taken from the compilation of Herz (1959) and the data of Beischer (1953) are shown in Table IV. Since these values are based on monolayer

TABLE IV[a]

GRAIN YIELD[b]

Isotope	Emulsion	Grain yield	Author(s)
H^3	Ilford G.5	0.7	Beischer
H^3	Kodak NTB-3	0.6	Beischer
C^{14}	Kodak AR-10	2	Levi
S^{35}	Kodak AR-10	1.8	Lamerton
Fe^{59}	Kodak AR-10	1.6	Cormack
I^{131}	Kodak AR-10	1.8–1.9	Cormack, Herz
P^{32}	Kodak AR-10	0.8	Cormack, Herz

[a] From Herz (1959) and Beischer (1953).
[b] Number of grains rendered developable per incident electron.

and source-impregnated emulsions, they may differ slightly from the values actually applicable to cellular sources.

Alternatively, for any given system one may assay the total amount of radioactivity in a known quantity of substance by some independent means such as gas-phase counting, and then compare this with autoradiographic data on the same material. However, an efficiency factor obtained in this way is valid only for material whose geometrical characteristics and internal distribution of radioactivity resemble very closely those of the material used for calibration. Kisieleski *et al.* (1961), using stripping film autoradiographs of 3μ sections of lung labeled with thymidine-H^3, arrive at a factor of 100–200 disintegrations per developable silver grain. This value is roughly 0.1 of a similar factor calculated by the above-mentioned methods. The discrepancy has not been satisfactorily explained.

IV. The Problem of "Intermediates"

It is perhaps appropriate to conclude with what is usually the final aspect of any autoradiographic study, the interpretation of data.

Conventional autoradiographic techniques do not measure tracer which is in the form of water-soluble compounds because these are washed out in the fixation and subsequent treatment of the specimen. This means that the original precursor which is freely diffusible, and all soluble intermediates,[7] are not detected in the autoradiographic experiment. In this way autoradiography differs fundamentally from biochemical experiments in which measurements of metabolic pools can often be made. New "dry"-mount techniques designed to localize these precursors and intermediates are being developed (Fitzgerald, 1961), but as yet they are not in widespread use.

If the cells or organisms are in a steady state metabolically they will contain at the beginning of the experiment intracellular pools of unlabeled precursors and intermediates. The time necessary for the labeled precursor to be converted to the product depends on the size of these pools and on the rate constants and enzyme affinities of the reactions involved. Thus two different locations within a cell or homologous locations in two different organisms may exhibit different amounts of incorporation within a given period of time simply because they contain different amounts or kinds of pre-existing intermediate pools which must be consumed before the label can be incorporated into the product. It is essential to recognize the possibility of this phenomenon when interpreting autoradiographic data and, if possible, to design ancillary experiments which will determine its relative importance.

References

Barer, R. (1956). *In* "Physical Techniques in Biological Research" (G. Oster and A. W. Pollister, eds.), Vol. III, p. 30. Academic Press, New York.

Baserga, R., and Nemeroff, K. (1962). *Stain Technol.* **37**, 21.

Beischer, D. E. (1953). *Nucleonics* **11**, (12), 24.

Bleecken, S. (1961). *Atompraxis* **7**, 321.

Caro, L. (1962). *In* "Proceedings of the Fifth International Congress for Electron Microscopy" (S. S. Breese, ed.), Vol. II, p. L-10. Academic Press, New York.

Curran, S. C., Angus, J., and Cockcroft, A. L. (1948). *Nature* **162**, 302.

Doniach, I., and Pelc, S. R. (1950). *Brit. J. Radiol.* **23**, 184.

Dudley, R. A., and Pelc, S. R. (1953). *Nature* **172**, 992.

Fano, U. (1954). *In* "Radiation Biology" (A. Hollaender, ed.), Vol. I, p. 1. McGraw-Hill, New York.

Fitzgerald, P. J. (1961). *Lab. Invest.* **10**, 846.

Gross, J., Bogoroch, R., Nadler, N. J., and Leblond, C. P. (1951). *Am. J. Roentgenol.* **65**, 420.

Gullberg, J. E. (1957). *Exptl. Cell Res. Suppl.* **4**, 222.

Herz, R. H. (1959). *Lab. Invest.* **8**, 71.

Kisieleski, W. E., Baserga, R., and Vaupotic, J. (1961). *Radiation Res.* **15**, 341

Lajtha, L. G., Oliver, R., Berry, R. J., and Hell, E. (1960). *Nature* **187**, 919.

Lamerton, L. F., and Harriss, E. B. (1954). *J. Phot. Sci.* **2**, 135.

Levi, H. (1957). *Exptl. Cell Res. Suppl.* **4**, 207.

[7] Soluble in the fixed tissue but not diffusible from the living organism.

Levi, H., and Hogben, A. S. (1955). *Kgl. Danske Videnskab. Selskab Mat. Fys. Medd.* **30,** No. 9.
Levi, H., and Nielsen, A. (1959). *Lab. Invest.* **8,** 82.
Maurer, W., and Primbsch, E. *Exptl. Cell Res.*, In press.
Mazia, D., Plaut, W. S., and Ellis, G. W. (1955). *Exptl. Cell Res.* **9,** 305.
Micou, J., and Goldstein, L. (1959). *Stain Technol.* **34,** 347.
Odeblad, E. (1959). *Lab. Invest.* **8,** 113.
Ostrowski, K., and Sawicki, W. (1961). *Exptl. Cell Res.* **24,** 625.
Peachey, L. D. (1958). *J. Biophys. Biochem. Cytol.* **4,** 233.
Perry, R. P. *Proc. European Conf. Autoradiography, Rome, 1961,* In press.
Perry, R. P., Errera, M., Hell, A., and Dürwald, H. (1961). *J. Biophys. Biochem. Cytol.* **11,** 1.
Ray, R. C., and Stevens, G. W. W. (1953). *Brit. J. Radiol.* **26,** 362.
Rogers, A. W. (1961). *Exptl. Cell Res.* **24,** 228.
Stenram, U. (1961). *Exptl. Cell Res.* **22,** 545.
Tolles, W. E. (1959). *Lab. Invest.* **8,** 99.

Chapter 16

High-Resolution Autoradiography

LUCIEN G. CARO[1]

The Rockefeller Institute, New York, New York

I. Introduction

Descriptive cytology, using the electron microscope as its major tool, has made rapid progress during the last decade and has revealed within

[1] Present address: Laboratoire de Biophysique, Université de Genève, Switzerland. This work was supported by a grant from the National Science Foundation. The experimental evidence and much of the discussion presented in this chapter have been described previously by Caro and van Tubergen (1962) and Caro (1962). The illustrations are reprinted with the kind authorization of the publishers of the *Journal of Cell Biology.*

the cell a complex network of fibers, particles, and membranes. The structure of the organelles which form this network is often known almost down to the macromolecular level. Little has been found, however, about the precise function of many of these structures and about their interplay in the various cellular functions. This lack of knowledge is due, for the most part, to the paucity of suitable analytical tools. Autoradiography could provide a simple, easily interpreted method of analysis of cellular function but has in the past been limited, in its applications to cellular biology, by its lack of resolution. We shall describe in this chapter methods for autoradiography, using light or electron microscopy, which give sufficient resolution for studies at the intracellular level.

The first approach toward improving resolution in autoradiography might be to select an isotope emitting particles of low energy, and therefore short range. Tritium has considerable and well-recognized advantages in this respect (Fitzgerald *et al.*, 1951). A decrease in the size of the silver bromide crystals of the emulsion is another obvious approach. Highly sensitive emulsions with grains as small as 0.1μ are available commercially. Their advantage has not always been fully recognized, mostly because in such emulsions the size of the final autoradiographic grains is small and counting grains becomes a difficult task even with the best light microscopes. The necessity for a close contact between emulsion and specimen was recognized early. The damaging effect on resolution of even small separations was calculated by Doniach and Pelc (1950) and demonstrated experimentally by Stevens (1950).

The effect of the thicknesses of the specimen and of the emulsion on resolution is considerable. As we shall try to demonstrate in Section IV, extremely thin specimens covered by fine grained emulsions of comparable thinness result in preparations with much higher autoradiographic resolution than the conventional techniques. Such preparations cannot be observed conveniently in the light microscope: the size of the photographic grains can be decreased well beyond the resolving power of light optics, the specimen becomes too thin to provide sufficient contrast, and the resolution of the microscope becomes inferior to that of the autoradiographic process. For such preparations electron microscopic observation becomes essential. The use of the electron microscope in autoradiography is therefore dictated by the conditions which lead to high autoradiographic resolution.

In one of the earliest attempts to visualize tracks from radioactive decays at the electron microscope level, Comer and Skipper (1954) noticed that the probability for a long track from a single radioactive particle was low, but these authors were not concerned with problems of resolution and did not therefore examine the question further. The first application of electron microscopic autoradiography to biological specimens by Liquier-Milward (1956) did not demonstrate a striking increase in autoradiographic resolution. In another pioneering attempt O'Brien and George (1959) mentioned that this technique led to improved resolution and showed some evidence for this. Using bacteria labeled with tritiated thymidine and a fine grain emulsion (Kodak V-1055), van Tubergen (1961) was the first to demonstrate clearly a resolution superior to that obtained by conventional techniques. By using thin sections of tissue labeled with tritium and thin layers of fine grain emulsions (Ilford K.5 and L.4) we have obtained autoradiographic resolutions at the subcellular level with little loss in image quality (Caro, 1961a; Caro and Palade, 1961, 1963). Comparable results have been obtained by several authors using a number of variations of the techniques of Liquier-Milward and O'Brien and George (Przybylski, 1961; Pelc *et al.*, 1961; Revel and Hay, 1961; Harford and Hamlin, 1961; Hampton and Quastler, 1961; Granboulan *et al.*, 1962; Silk *et al.*, 1961).

In this article we shall describe techniques for autoradiography which have given good resolution in light microscope preparations and resolutions of the order of 0.1μ in electron microscope preparations (Section II). We shall present some experimental justification and general comments on the various steps used in these techniques and show the final results obtained (Section III). We shall then derive a theoretical expression for the expected distribution of grains around a point source and verify this relation experimentally (Section IV). The methods to be described here were designed for high resolution rather than quantitation. Although they give reproducible relative results they might not always be the best for absolute quantitation. We have tried to stress simplicity and avoid complicated techniques. These methods have been used by a number of workers in this laboratory and applied to a number of biological problems. They have in general given consistent and reproducible results.

II. Methods

A. Light Microscope Techniques

1. Preparation of Slides

Pre-cleaned slides, with frosted end, are dipped in a subbing solution, dried vertically in a dust-free area, and stored in plastic slide boxes. [The subbing solution is made by dissolving gelatin, 1 gm per liter (Kodak purified calfskin gelatin), in hot distilled water, cooling, and adding 0.1 gm per liter chromium potassium sulfate. It is stored in a refrigerator].

2. Preparation of Specimen

The labeled specimens are fixed and embedded in methacrylate using standard techniques (Pease, 1960). Sections are cut at 0.4μ and spread with xylene (Satir and Peachey, 1958). They are picked up on the wet tip of a sharpened wooden stick (toothpick or applicator) and floated on a drop of clean distilled water placed in the center of a subbed slide. After drying the slide completely at 45°C, the methacrylate is removed by dipping for 10 seconds in amyl acetate. The position of the sections is indicated by a light scratch with a diamond pencil. In all these operations cleanliness is essential. Care should be taken not to touch the slide except on its frosted end.

3. Preparation and Application of Emulsion

The Ilford Nuclear Research emulsions K.5 and L.4 are used. They come in gel form (and have the shape and consistency of short pieces of cooked spaghetti). They can be handled under yellow-green light (A 10-minute exposure of a slide coated with K.5 to a 25-watt safelight with filter AO at a distance of 2 meters did not significantly increase the background). It is best, however, to keep the exposure to light at a minimum. Before use, the emulsions are normally stored in the refrigerator. They have a limited shelf life and after a while, background builds up to a very high level. The useful life of an emulsion is quite variable, but in general we have used K.5 up to 2 months and L.4 up to 4 months after the date of manufacture indicated on the bottle. To avoid possible complications (postmaturation, high background, clumping, etc.), emulsions which have been melted and diluted are used only once and discarded. To prepare the emulsion, 20 gm of K.5 or L.4 are put in 20 ml of distilled water in a Coplin jar and melted at 45°C for 15 minutes. After stirring gently but thoroughly with a glass or plastic rod, the emulsion is cooled at room temperature for 30 minutes. The slides are dipped and withdrawn with a slow and uniform motion. The excess emulsion is drained and the slides set to dry in a vertical position. A gentle stream of warm, filtered air helps to accelerate the process. When the emulsion begins to dry, it appears quite uniform and without streaks, provided the slide was not dirty (finger grease, etc.).

4. Background Eradication

Background is almost never produced during exposure if proper precautions are taken. It is sometimes present in the emulsion, especially with K.5, and builds up with time. It is recommended that a test slide be developed, for any preparation, immediately after the emulsion is dry. If the background is objectionable it can be removed in the following manner, derived from a method proposed by Yagoda (1949): The bottom of a 3 × 4 inch staining dish is covered with 5 thicknesses of filter paper wet with 10 ml of freshly made 3% hydrogen peroxide. The slides to be eradicated are placed on a glass holder in the dish, taking care that they do not touch the wet paper; the dish is covered tightly and placed in a light-proof box. The slides are exposed to H_2O_2 vapors for 4–6 hours, then dried thoroughly to eliminate all traces of H_2O_2.

5. Storage during Exposure

The dry slides are stored in a black plastic slide box (25 slide size). Two such boxes fit in a light-proof Kodak cardboard container for $6\frac{1}{2} \times 9$ cm photographic plates. A small package of Drierite is also placed in the container, which is then wrapped in light-proof cloth and stored in a 4°C refrigerator or at room temperature.

6. Photographic Processing

The slides, if cold, are allowed to come to room temperature before processing. The various solutions are placed in 3 × 4 inch staining dishes and the slides processed 10 at a time in a standard glass holder. All solutions are kept at 20°C ± 1°. The following schedule is recommended:

Developer: Kodak D-19. 2 minutes for K.5, 4 minutes for L.4. Or Kodak D-19 + 0.012% Benzotriazole (Kodak Anti-Fog No. 1). Six minutes for K.5.
Stop Bath: 1% acetic acid. 10 seconds.
Fixer: Kodak Rapid Fixer. 5 minutes.
Wash: Running water, 5 minutes; distilled water, 1 minute.

Following this the slides are dried completely and stored in a plastic slide box.

7. Examination and Storage

For examination a large No. 1 cover slip is mounted with a drop of water or a solution of glycerin (the contrast of the image can be decreased by increasing the concentration of glycerin) and the slide examined in phase contrast with an oil immersion objective. After examination the cover slip is removed, the slide washed in distilled water, dried, and stored. With reasonable care this process can be repeated many times without damage to the slide. Slides have been stored in this manner for 2 years without deterioration. Mounting of the cover slip with one of the usual permanent mounting media results in an almost complete loss of contrast because of the high index of refraction of these media.

The gelatin of the emulsion does not usually interfere very much with the phase contrast image. If needed, it can be cleared to a considerable extent, without effect on the grains, by a treatment of a few minutes in 0.05 *N* NaOH.

B. Electron Microscope Techniques

1. Preparation of Specimens

Methacrylate-embedded material is generally used, although specimens embedded in Epon have also given satisfactory results. Thin sections (pale gold) are picked up on a screen coated with a collodion film backed by a thin carbon layer. The section must be perfectly flat and smooth. This also holds for the collodion film and the grid supporting it. Electroplated grids, such as the Athene models, have been found particularly good in this respect. After drying, the screens are attached by a small portion of their edge to a small piece of double coated masking tape (Scotch No. 400) fixed to a microscope slide. Three to four grids, close to each other, can be put on each slide. Here again cleanliness is essential.

2. Preparation and Application of Emulsion

a. *First method.* Ten grams of Ilford L.4 are melted in 20 ml of distilled water in a 300 ml beaker at 45°C for 15 minutes. After thorough stirring, the beaker is placed in an ice bath for 2–3 minutes, then at room temperature for 30 minutes. The emulsion should now be very viscous. A loop of thin wire (platinum, silver, or copper) 4 cm in diameter is dipped in the emulsion and withdrawn slowly, forming a thin film in the loop. This film should then gel almost immediately. The loop is touched to the surface of the slide and the gelled film falls on the grids and adheres to them very firmly. If the gelling of the film does not take place rapidly, or if electron microscopic examination reveals gross unevenness in the distribution of silver halide crystals, the time of cooling in the ice bath should be increased slightly. If the viscosity of the emulsion is so high that a film cannot be formed, the emulsion can be melted at 45°C and the process repeated with a shorter cooling time in the ice bath. After a few cycles of melting and gelling the emulsion becomes lumpy and should be discarded. In the electron microscope the preparation should appear as a tightly packed monolayer of silver halide crystals.

b. *Second method.* A 2% solution of purified agar in distilled water is poured to a thickness of 0.5 cm in Petri dishes. After hardening it is stored in a refrigerator. Before use the agar plate is removed from the dish and rectangles 2 × 3 cm are cut and placed on microscope slides. These slides are warmed to 37°C for a few minutes to remove surface moisture. The agar blocks are then flooded with 0.2% parlodion in amyl acetate and the slides dried in a vertical position. Subsequent manipulations are done in the darkroom. An emulsion is prepared as in the previous method, but using 10 gm of L.4 to 40 ml of water, and simply cooled to room temperature. The loop is used to form a film which is applied to the collodion-agar surface without waiting for gelling. Because of the smoothness of the surface and of the diffusion of the water from the emulsion to the agar (through the collodion membrane), drying artifacts are prevented and very uniform distributions of silver halide crystals are obtained. When dry, the collodion-emulsion membrane is floated on a water surface (emulsion side up). Thin sections of the material to be examined had been previously picked up on grids without a supporting membrane. They are placed on a piece of fine meshed metal screening in the water, brought under the collodion-emulsion membrane, and lifted out of the water. After drying they are attached to a glass slide as described above.

3. Storage during Exposure and Photographic Processing

The preparations are handled and stored in exactly the same manner as the light microscope slides. Background can be eradicated similarly, but this is rarely necessary because of the extreme thinness of the emulsion and the generally low background of L.4. Photographic processing is the same except for development. For routine work Kodak Microdol-X is used for 5 minutes at 20°C. If the highest possible resolution is needed, the following "physical" developer is employed: a 1 *M* solution of sodium sulfite is dissolved in distilled water at 50°C; *p*-phenylenediamine is added to a concentration of 0.1 *M*; the solution is cooled and filtered. Development is for 1 minute at 20°C. This developer should be made just before use, since it is unstable.

4. Staining and Examination

Electron microscope preparations can be stained after the photographic processing. Since the presence of a gelatin layer over the specimen reduces the contrast of the image, a strong staining is necessary. A solution of 1% uranyl acetate mixed before use with absolute alcohol to give a final concentration of 30% ethanol (Gibbons and Grimstone, 1960) and applied for 10–45 minutes gives good results. Lead stains can also be used but it should be remembered that many formulas are strongly alkaline and will tend to remove the gelatin (Revel and Hay, 1961). The Karnovsky (1961) stain has been found generally satisfactory (see Section III).

When the gelatin remains in place, the specimen is relatively thick; we have used high electron microscope voltages (80 or 100 kv) to minimize damage and reduce chromatic aberration which is particularly noticeable because of the thickness of the preparation.

III. Discussion of the Methods

A. Choice of Emulsion

The photographic emulsions commonly used in autoradiography are nuclear research emulsions composed, in approximately equal volumes, of crystals of silver halide and of gelatin. Two considerations guide the choice: (a) the emulsion must be capable of registering electron tracks, since most isotopes used in autoradiography are β-emitters, and (b) the size of the silver halide crystals must be small. Among the commonly used emulsions the Kodak NTB and NTB-3 and the Ilford G.5 have a fairly large grain size (0.23–0.33μ) which precludes their use in high-resolution work. The Kodak Ltd. stripping film emulsion AR-10, its equivalent in bulk form, the experimental emulsion V-1055, and the Ilford Nuclear Research emulsion in gel form K.5 have a grain size of the order of 0.2μ. The finest grained, electron-sensitive emulsions which we have used were the Ilford L.4, and an emulsion made in the laboratory by Dr. Pierre Demers (1958) at the Université de Montréal. Both have grains slightly larger than 0.1μ. (We are grateful to Dr. Pierre Demers for the gift of some of his emulsions.)

Little information exists regarding the response of various emulsions to β-particles from tritium. The sensitivity of nuclear emulsions is usually measured by the number of developable grains per unit distance in the track of particles at minimum ionization. Any such measurement depends, of course, not only on the sensitivity of individual grains but also on their density along the track. (The smaller the grain size, the higher the concentration of grains, and therefore the higher the possible number of grains in a track.) Studies concerned with autoradiographic responses have usually been made with isotopes such as P^{32}, I^{131}, C^{14}, or S^{35} which produce long range ionizing particles. We have tried to obtain a direct and practical indication of the response to H^3 decays by determining the autoradiographic sensitivity of a number of emulsions. The method of preparation was identical to that described in the next paragraphs. The sources of tritium were cells of *Escherichia coli* fully labeled with leucine-H^3, that is to say, grown in the presence of leucine-H^3 for more than 7 generations. The sensitivity was determined by counting the average number of grains per cell. A total number of at least 300 cells on 3 different slides were counted for each emulsion, the average grain count per cell varying between

2 and 4 grains. Development was in D-19 for 2 minutes at 20°C, except for L.4, for which it was 4 minutes. A number of such experiments were performed and in each case the response of K.5 was used as a base line and arbitrarily set at 100. Table I summarizes the results.

TABLE I

GRAIN SIZE AND RELATIVE SENSITIVITY OF VARIOUS NUCLEAR EMULSIONS[a]

Emulsion	Grain diameter (μ)	Relative sensitivity
Ilford L.4	0.12	132
Demers	0.12	61[b]
Ilford K.5	0.18	100
Kodak V-1055	0.17	51
Kodak AR-10	—	57
Kodak NTB-3	0.23	48
Kodak NTB	0.27	—
Ilford G.5	0.32	—

[a] The grain diameter was measured in the electron microscope and is accurate to ±10%. The relative sensitivity was measured by taking the average grain count per cell in autoradiographs of bacteria uniformly labeled with tritiated leucine. Development was for 2 minutes, in D-19 at 20°C, except for L.4 (4 minutes). The differences in autoradiographic response reflect, in part, differences in grain size, since an emulsion with large silver halide crystals has few of them per unit volume.

[b] This value was obtained without sensitization. When the emulsion was sensitized with triethanolamine, as specified by Demers (1958), the sensitivity became equivalent to that of L.4.

On the basis of these results, L.4 was chosen as the most suitable emulsion for electron microscopic autoradiography. For light microscopic autoradiography, it has the disadvantage of showing frequent tracking (several grains caused by one decay) when used in thick layers with tritium. This complicates grain counts in quantitative work. (This tracking largely disappears, for reasons which will appear later, when the emulsion is applied as a monolayer of crystals, such as is obtained in electron microscopic preparations.) For this reason we have usually selected K.5 for light microscopic preparations on the basis of its high sensitivity, low tracking, and similarity in composition with L.4.

B. Specimen Preparation

The preparation of the labeled specimen is identical to that of ordinary material for electron microscopy: fixation in buffered osmium, dehydration in graded alcohols, embedding in methacrylate or epoxy resin, and sectioning on an ultramicrotome (Pease, 1960). The blocks are cut somewhat larger than usual to give a better sampling of the specimen. It is always advisable to verify that the incorporated label is preserved during the preparation. This is done by sampling each processing solution and counting the amount of released tritium in a scintillation counter. In some published experiments (Caro, 1961b; Caro and Forro, 1961) we have found, for example, that with bacteria labeled either fully or with a pulse of tritiated leucine, uridine, cytidine, or thymidine, the loss was extremely low. But any new situation should be investigated in this respect.

For autoradiography at the phase contrast microscope level, methacrylate is the preferred embedding material. Methacrylate sections as thin as 0.2–0.3μ can be seen clearly in phase contrast when the embedding medium is removed. This removal cannot be done conveniently with epoxy resins and much thicker sections are needed to provide sufficient contrast. In general, methacrylate-embedded materials have also given better results at the electron microscopic level. Since a fairly large number of sections are needed to provide enough specimens for testing exposure, staining, etc., and to give a meaningful sample of the material, the greater ease of sectioning given by methacrylate is a distinct advantage. Of some importance too is the better contrast it provides, over the various epoxy compounds, in the electron microscopic image. For these reasons we have used methacrylate-embedded material for both light and electron microscopic preparations in all cases when it was not made impossible by the nature of the specimen.

C. Application of Emulsion

This is probably the most critical step of the procedure, especially in the electron microscopic method. A number of methods have been proposed: Comer and Skipper (1954) spread a liquid emulsion on the surface of a Formvar coated slide and recovered the film, after processing, by floating on ethylene chloride. Liquier-Milward (1956) simply touched the grid to the surface of a liquid emulsion, a method used also by Harford and Hamlin (1961). O'Brien and George (1959) used a thin wire loop to produce a film which was then applied to the sections. This method was also used by Revel and Hay (1961). Caro (1961a) used a bubble of emulsion. Przybylski (1961) applied a drop with a brush or a pipette. Pelc *et al.* (1961) poured the emulsion on a formvar-coated slide.

All of these methods involve the application of a liquid film of emulsion to the specimen.

For electron microscopic preparations the applied emulsion should consist of a monolayer of silver halide crystals, closely and uniformly packed. The appearance of the final preparation is illustrated in diagrammatic form in Fig. 1. Microscopic examination, after drying, of emulsions ap-

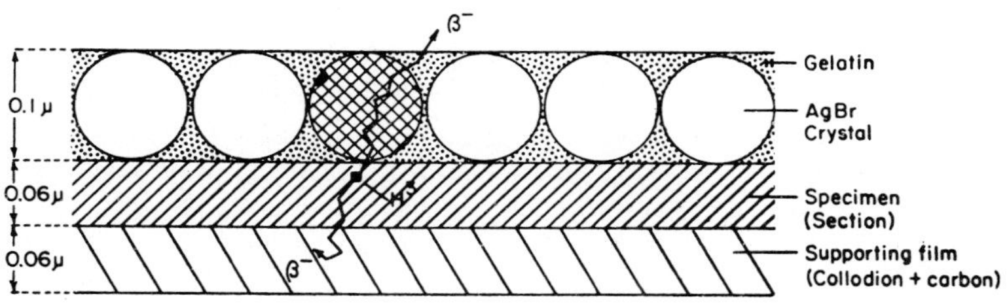

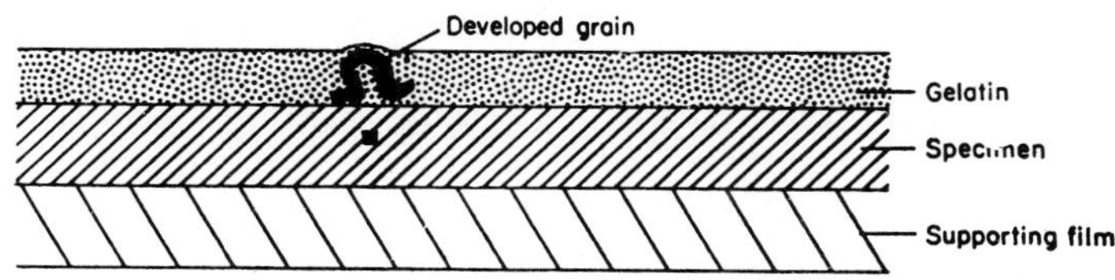

FIG. 1. Diagrammatic representation of an electron microscope autoradiograph preparation. *Top:* during exposure. The silver halide crystals, embedded in a gelatin matrix, cover the section. A β-particle, from a tritium point source in the specimen, has hit a crystal (cross-hatched) causing the appearance of a latent image on the surface (black speck on upper left region of crystal). *Bottom:* during examination and after processing. The exposed crystal has been developed into a filament of silver; the nonexposed crystals have been dissolved. The total thickness has decreased because the silver halide occupied approximately half the volume of the emulsion.

plied in the sol state reveals that the grains are distributed in a nonrandom manner over the specimen and outline the surface irregularities (Caro and van Tubergen, 1962). Another common defect of this method of application is that the thickness of the emulsion is very uneven due to drying stresses. To avoid these defects, the emulsion must be applied after it has gelled, as suggested by van Tubergen (1961). A method using gelled films was also used by Caro and Palade (1961). The first method described here consists in the application to the specimen of a pre-formed, gelled film of emulsion, thereby avoiding a displacement of the grains with respect to the surface features of the specimen. With a little practice it gives a uniform distribution of the grains and good reproducibility; because of its simplicity, it is used in all routine work. The second method is based on the observation that, with a clean wire loop and a well-mixed emulsion, extremely uniform films can be produced and maintained for a few seconds before convection currents begin to destroy this uniformity. The method of diffusion into an agar block through a collodion membrane has been used in the past to insure uniform distributions of bacteria (Houwink and van Iterson, 1950) or viruses (Kellenberger and Arber, 1957) in suspension. If the film of emulsion is applied to the collodion surface as soon as it has been formed, a very uniform distribution is obtained. The number of layers of silver halide crystals can be modified by chainging the dilution of the emulsion. When used as described this method will result in a good approximation of a monolayer. It has the disadvantages of more complicated manipulations in the darkroom and of interposing between the specimen and the emulsion a thin layer of collodion, thereby decreasing the resolution. It is possible to apply small, particulate specimens, such as viruses, directly on the emulsion, thereby avoiding this disadvantage. This cannot be done in the case of sections, since then the emulsion would be sandwiched between collodion and methacrylate and the photographic processing would be incomplete and irregular. Because it gives very uniform films, this method is preferred when attempts at quantitative work are made.

Although both methods described here were designed for high resolution rather than quantitation, their reproducibility is satisfactory. As an example, Table II gives the relative grain counts over various cellular structures for 4 different preparations of pancreatic exocrine tissue 20 minutes after intravenous injection of tritiated leucine. Another test for the linearity of the autoradiographic response is the distribution of grain counts over uniform specimens. We have shown that cross sections of bacteria uniformly labeled with uridine-H^3 provide such a specimen, and that a Poisson distribution of grain counts over them is obtained with stripping film emulsions (Caro, 1961b). The situation remains true at the electron microscope level, as shown in Table III.

The method of Silk *et al.* (1961), consisting of the bromination of an evaporated film of silver, seems to offer some advantage with respect to uniformity. However, the results obtained by these authors suggest the possibility of an artifact, since they find grains grouped in large clumps and exclusively over the cytoplasm of tissue culture cells labeled with thymidine-H^3. It is possible that, because of the intimate contact between the specimen and the unprotected silver bromide crystals, chemical reactions can take place readily between them and result in reduced grains. Some evidence for such an effect was obtained by Dr. Gershon M. Goldberg (1962, personal communication). In spite of this, it is likely that a modification of this technique might produce good results.

TABLE II

REPRODUCIBILITY OF GRAIN COUNTS IN ELECTRON MICROSCOPIC AUTORADIOGRAPHY[a]

Cell region	Section number				Average (%)
	1	2	3	4	
Golgi	74	71	78	72	73
Zymogen	15	10.5	3	11	10
Rough e.r.	7.5	9	16	12	11
Total grains counted:	67	208	100	144	Total grains 519

[a] Reproducibility of grain counts made over various regions of pancreatic exocrine cells, for 4 different preparations from the same block. In this specimen DL-leucine-H^3 was injected intravenously and the pancreas was fixed 20 minutes later. For more details on this work see Caro and Palade (1961).

Although a certain amount of biological variation is probably superimposed on the methodological error, the reproducibility of such relative grain counts is good and well within the range of expected statistical variation. (For the first line $\chi^2 = 0.479$, $P = 0.80$.)

D. Background Eradication

The major cause of background grains is the presence on some of the silver halide crystals of a latent image, due to accidental exposure to radiations, to light, to heat, or resulting from chemical or mechanical

TABLE III

DEMONSTRATION OF A POISSON DISTRIBUTION OF GRAIN COUNTS[a]

Number of grains	Number of sections	Expected from Poisson
0	219	223
1	184	176
2	72	69.5
3	18	18.3
4	1	4
$\chi^2 = 0.936$	$P > 0.5$	

[a] Autoradiographic grain counts over thin cross sections of *B. subtilis* labeled with uridine-H^3 in an electron microscope preparation. The fact that a Poisson distribution is obtained shows that the autoradiographic response is fairly uniform over the various areas surveyed (50 fields in 3 thin sections). This compares favorably with results obtained in light microscope preparations with stripping film emulsion.

effects. This latent image is not normally distinguishable from that caused by the passage of a β-particle and consists of a speck of reduced silver. The treatment with H_2O_2 oxidizes and therefore eradicates all latent images, that of autoradiographic grains as well as that of background grains. It can therefore be applied only at the beginning of exposure. Figure 2 shows

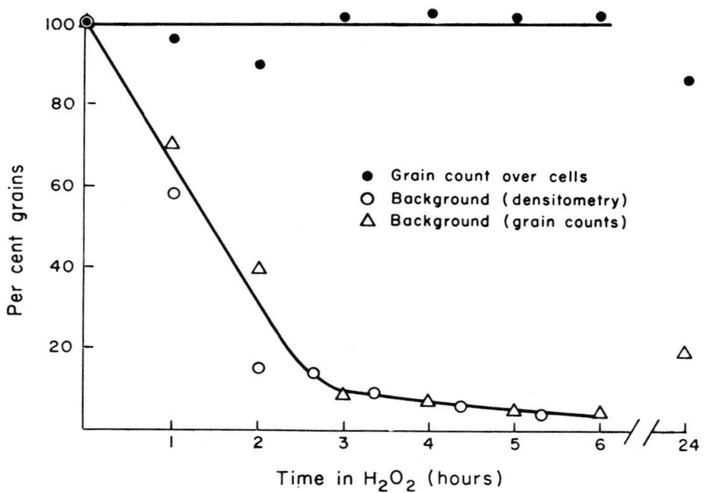

FIG. 2. Background eradication in H_2O_2 atmosphere. Grain counts on preparations of *E. coli* labeled with leucine-H^3 and treated for various lengths of time in H_2O_2 vapors. Background was measured as number of grains per $100\mu^2$ or by densitometry. In both cases the values were measured relatively to the value at time 0. The sensitivity, measured as the average grain count per cell, did not change during the first 6 hours of treatment, while the background decreased by 95%. All slides were given the same exposure after eradication.

the effect of a H_2O_2 treatment, such as that described in Section II, on the sensitivity and the background of autoradiographs of uniformly labeled bacteria, using K.5 emulsion. The sensitivity is measured by the average grain count per cell. A treatment of 5–6 hours decreases the background by 95% and leaves the sensitivity unaffected. A 24 hour treatment results in a slight reversal of this effect.

It is extremely important to establish that the incorporated label is not affected by H_2O_2. Thus we found that in osmium-fixed bacteria or in pancreatic tissue, exposure to H_2O_2 did not affect incorporated leucine-H^3, uridine-H^3, and thymidine-H^3. This was shown by the fact that treatment in H_2O_2 did not affect the grain count over the cells, nor did it cause release of radioactive material into the emulsion. The possibility of creating an artifact should not, however, be ignored. It is known, for example, that osmium-fixed lipids are solubilized by H_2O_2 (Baker, 1960), and it was found that incorporated choline-H^3 was released from osmium-fixed membranes due to exposure to H_2O_2 and diffused into the emulsion (Dr. David Luck, 1962, private communication), causing a decrease in grain counts and an increase in apparent background.

E. Storage and Exposure

The storage conditions during exposure will affect (a) the sensitivity of individual crystals, (b) the regression of the latent image, and (c) the background. The second of these effects has received the most attention and it is generally accepted that regression (that is to say the disappearance of the latent image from a previously exposed crystal) is due to an oxidation of the silver speck constituting the latent image and can be minimized by storage in CO_2 or nitrogen (Herz, 1959; Ray and Stevens, 1953) and storage at low temperature (LaPalme and Demers, 1947). We have measured the over-all autoradiographic response of K.5 and L.4 under various storage conditions (by counting grains over uniformly labeled bacteria). The results, shown in Table IV, seem to differ from what might be expected from the regression effect alone (Herz, 1959). Storage in CO_2 does not seem to affect markedly the sensitivity, while temperature has a definite effect.

It is possible that in these preparations, with a thin, well-dried emulsion exposed to slow and therefore highly ionizing electrons, the regression of the latent image is not an important factor, and the major effect of storage conditions is on the sensitivity of individual crystals. On rare occasions background has been found to increase for the storage conditions which resulted in higher over-all sensitivity, but in general it is not affected by any of the storage conditions used here for periods as long as 3–4 months.

The exposure time depends on the amount of label incorporated, its distribution in the specimen, and many other factors. It can therefore be predicted only on rare occasions and is usually determined by developing test slides at regular intervals. Because of the thinness of the layers, the electron microscope method has extremely low sensitivity. A simple rule can be used to estimate the necessary exposure in the type of preparations described above: if a light microscope preparation from a 0.4μ section gives a suitable autographic response in 1 week, a useful preparation for the electron microscope will need a 2–4 months exposure. The sensitivities of the two methods differ therefore by a factor of 10, approximately.

TABLE IV

EFFECT OF VARIOUS STORAGE CONDITIONS ON THE OVER-ALL AUTORADIOGRAPHIC RESPONSE OF K.5, L.4, AND V-1055 EMULSIONS[a]

Storage conditions					
Temperature	−20°C	4°C	4°C	4°C	20°C
Atmosphere	Air	CO_2	Air	Air	Air
Drying agent	Drierite	Drierite	Drierite	$ZnCl_2$[b]	Drierite
Emulsion (and exposure time)					
K.5 (2 days)	36	60	100	112	136
K.5 (5 days)	83	80	100	100	116
K.5 (7 days)	100	106	100	—	121
L.4 (7 days)	85	114	100	—	140
V-1055 (19 days)	78	82	100	102	114

[a] The grain count per cell has been normalized with respect to the value found for storage in air at 4°C over Drierite (set arbitrarily at 100). The cells used in the various experiments had different amounts of label and the average grain counts varied from 1.5 to 3 grains per cell. In each series all slides were developed together in D-19 at 20°C for 2 minutes, except for the L.4 emulsion which was developed 4 minutes. Each point represents the average of 300 cells on 3 different slides.

The fact that, in the K.5 experiments, the differences between various storage conditions are less pronounced on longer exposure times might indicate that the length of the exposure is also an important factor in determining the best storage conditions.

[b] Excess $ZnCl_2$ in contact with saturated solution, giving approximately 10% relative humidity.

F. Photographic Processing

A photographic developer reduces rapidly to metallic silver grains the exposed silver bromide crystals which carry a latent image. The nonexposed grains are also affected but the reaction takes place with some delay. If it is interrupted early enough by placing the slides in a solution of sodium thiosulfate (hypo) the nonexposed crystals are dissolved, leaving only the reduced grains in the emulsion. Typically, the number of developed image grains (from exposed crystals) increases rapidly at the beginning of the reaction, then reaches a plateau (Demers, 1958), the only subsequent change being an increase in size (James, 1954). The behavior of background grains is opposite: they remain at a fairly constant level at the beginning and then increase in number very rapidly as the reaction progresses (Demers, 1958). For practical purposes we tried to determine the conditions of development which give a maximum number of grains without an undue increase in background. This was done for L.4 and K.5, using uniformly labeled bacteria to measure the autoradiographic response, and developing the preparations in D-19 at 20°C (Figs. 3 and 4). Similar curves for the stripping emulsion AR-10 have been shown by van Tubergen (1959).

In the case of K.5 we find that a plateau in the grain count is not reached

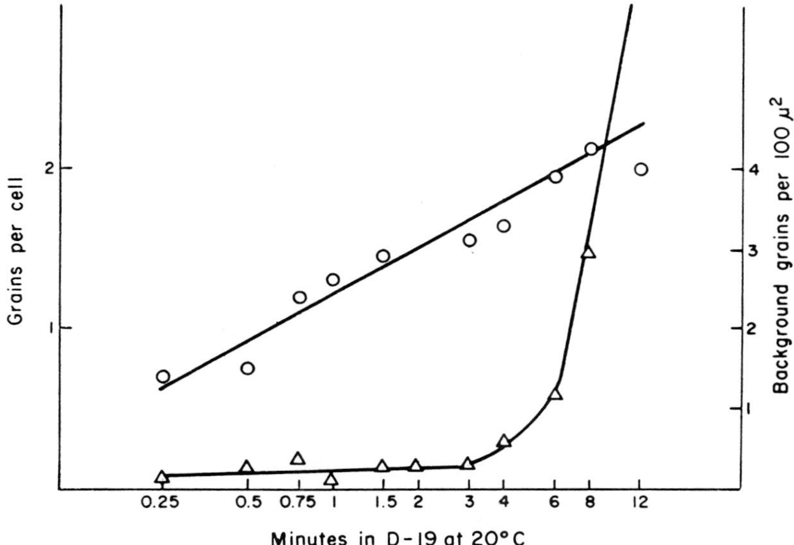

FIG. 3. Development curve for K.5. The grain counts were made on preparations of *E. coli* labeled with leucine-H^3. The average grain count per cell increases with developing time. The background remains low for the first 3 minutes of development and then rises suddenly. A 2-minute development time gives low background and good sensitivity. Since the slope of the grain count per cell curve has a low value (notice that the time scale is logarithmic), reproducible results can be obtained.

before the background becomes objectionable. The time of development was therefore arbitrarily chosen at 2 minutes, and a careful control of temperature and time of development was exercised when the reproducibility of the results was important. Recent results have shown that a plateau could be reached, while keeping the background at a low level, by adding Kodak Anti-Fog No. 1 to the D-19. For L.4 a plateau is reached after approximately 2 minutes, and a 4 minute development time was found to give good results.

We can also apply the information gained from the type of development curves described above directly to the electron microscope level. There, however, we encountered other problems more directly related to high resolution, the first one being the relation between the original event, the

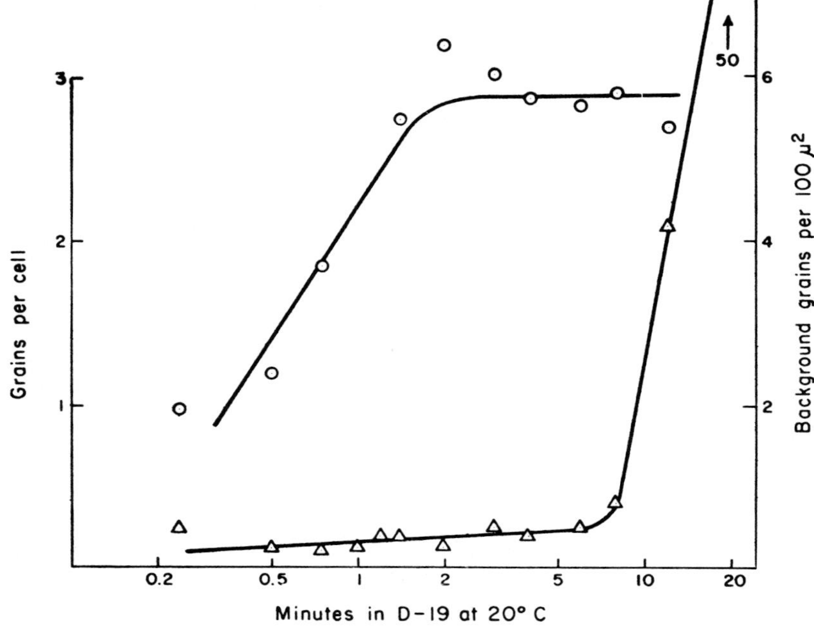

FIG. 4. Development curve for L.4. The grain count per cell reaches a plateau after 2 minutes in D-19 at 20°C, while the background does not rise significantly until 6–8 minutes. The development time chosen was 4 minutes.

passage of a charged particle through a crystal of silver halide, and the final event, the grain of silver which we observe in the microscope.

Following the passage of a charged particle through a crystal of silver halide, a latent image, probably formed by a few molecules of reduced silver (Demers, 1958), appears on the surface of the crystal. There does not seem to be a direct relationship between the position of this latent image and the path of the particle. For example, we have found that a single hit from a β-particle from tritium could produce as many as three separate developable latent images in one single crystal (see p. 346). There is a certain amount of uncertainty, therefore, in the localization of a β-decay inherent to this phase of the process and which does not seem capable of being improved except by reduction of the size of the crystals.

The next step is the growth, in the developer, of a silver grain by reduction of silver ions, in a reaction which is believed to be catalyzed by the silver speck of the latent image (James, 1954). There are two basic types of developer: the so-called "chemical" and "physical" developers. A chemical developer, such as D-19, reduces the silver halide crystal itself.

The final result is a long filament of silver which grows out of the surface of the crystal and coils randomly in a process that is not well understood. This coil can have, in the case of L.4 developed in D-19, a diameter of 0.3–0.4μ. A fine grain developer such as Microdol-X (Eastman Kodak) produces in general a single strand of silver, rather than a coil (Figs. 5 and 6). There does not seem to be any good way to decide which end of this filament originated on the silver halide crystal. We therefore used the middle point of a line drawn between the two extremities of the filament as the estimated position of the original latent image. This will impose, on the average, an error on the position of a single grain which, in our estimation, will be less than 1000 Å. In cases when the highest possible resolution is not required, this is quite acceptable. We have therefore used Microdol-X as a routine developer for electron microscopic autoradiography.

Other fine grain developers have been tried, in particular Ansco 110, Ansco Finex-L, Unibath, a chlorohydroquinone developer proposed by Demers (1958), and a hydroquinone developer proposed by Loveland (quoted in James, 1954). In all cases the grains were longer and more complex than with Microdol-X. In some cases they were thinner but this does not result in higher resolution. When a dilute developer is used, as proposed by Przybylski (1961), or when the temperature of the developer is lowered, the over-all sensitivity decreases and the filaments are not shortened but they become much thinner. This has a major disadvantage: either spontaneously or under the electron beam, such long, thin filaments tend to disintegrate into a number of small silver particles giving only the appearance of finer grains without really improving resolution since they originate from the familiar filamentous form.

To arrive at a better definition of the position of the latent image we relied on the other type, or "physical" development described by Lumière *et al.* (1911). We have used the pre-fixation type (James, 1954) in which the developer dissolves the silver bromide crystals, leaving only the latent image upon which silver ions present in the solution are then attached. The best formula among the variations which we have tried was a solution of 1.0 M sodium sulfite and 0.1 M *p*-phenylenediamine as the reducing agent. The variations tried, and discarded, were changes in the ratio of the two components and addition of various amounts of silver nitrate. With a development of 1 minute at 20°C, the resulting grains are extremely small, either spherical or comma-shaped (Figs. 7 to 11). It can be demonstrated that the pointed end of the comma corresponds to the origin of the grain (see below). Therefore, either because the grain is small or because we know its orientation with respect to the original speck of silver, we can define the position of the latent image that produced it with an error which we estimate at approximately 200 Å.

Although this developer gives good resolution and sensitivity, it is unstable and less reproducible than Microdol-X. In particular the size of the grains, while generally small, is difficult to control. It is of interest, therefore, only when the highest possible resolution is required.

We have conducted a few simple experiments in order to obtain a better understanding of the relation between β-decay and photographic grain. In one such experiment leucine-H^3 was mixed with the emulsion, which was then applied as a uniform monolayer of crystals. The exposure was calculated to give less than one grain per 25 μ^2, so that the probability of having two distinct registered decays separated by less than 0.5μ was close to zero. After development in Microdol-X the preparation was scanned for the presence of tracts (2 or more grains separated by less than 0.5μ). It was found that only 1.8% of the grains were double, and no tracks of more than two grains were found. Since approximately 30% of the decays from tritium would give enough energy to expose more than one grain, it seems that in a monolayer of silver bromide crystals, a hit by a tritium beta on a crystal reduces the probability of another hit by the same particle on a second crystal to an almost negligible value. This is probably an important contribution to resolution. The situation would be quite different if there were several layers of grains. Indeed with the thicker emulsions used at the light microscope level, tracks from tritium decays as long as 4–6 grains are commonly found in L.4.

When the physical developer already described was used to develop a similar preparation (emulsion to which leucine-H^3 has been added) it was found that (a) the number of developed grains was comparable to that obtained with Microdol; (b) approximately 6% of the grains carried two latent images and gave rise to two developed grains very close to each other, while approximately 1% had three latent images and produced three grains; (c) when several grains grew from separate latent images on the same crystal their origin (assumed to be the point at which the separate grains are closest to each other) was always the point of the comma.

We have no direct information concerning the sensitivity of individual crystals. It seems likely, though, that the probability that a crystal hit by a tritium beta will produce a developed grain is fairly close to one. The response of K.5 to β-decays from tritium was found to be approximately 1 grain per decay (1962, unpublished observations). Since tracks are rare, this implies that one hit on a crystal gives a grain. In the case of L.4, tracks are more frequent but the number of grains per decay is higher than one so that the situation with respect to individual crystals is approximately the same.

G. Final Steps

Removal of the gelatin has been practiced by several authors as a means to enhance contrast of the final image. The procedures used include proteolytic digestion (Comer and Skipper, 1954; Przybylski, 1961), alkaline digestion (Revel and Hay, 1961), and warm water after fixation in a nonhardening hypo (Silk *et al.*, 1961). In our experience all these procedures have the disadvantage of causing, on occasion, a displacement of the grains and almost always some loss of grains. The most useful procedure seems to be that of Revel and Hay (1961), which combines lead staining and clearing of the gelatin and which we have found to cause a displacement of the grains only rarely.

H. Results

Thin sections of labeled bacteria and small viruses provide convenient discrete sources of tritium of known geometry and have been found useful as test specimens. Some examples of the results obtained are shown in Figs. 5–11. The cells used were from a thymine-less strain of *Bacillus*

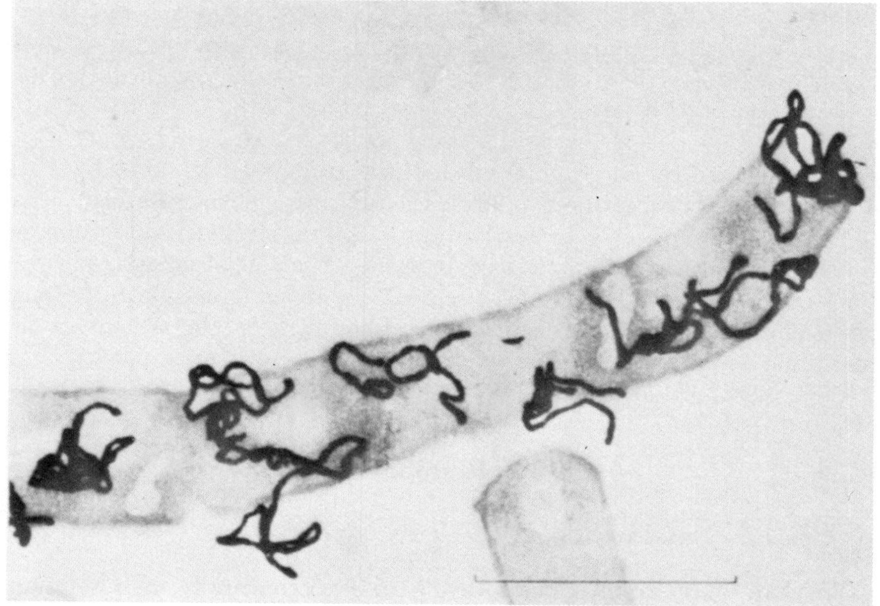

FIG. 5. Autoradiograph of thin sections of *B. subtilis* labeled fully with uridine-H^3. The section was stained in uranyl acetate. Development in Microdol-X. There is no obvious localization of the label. ×23,100.

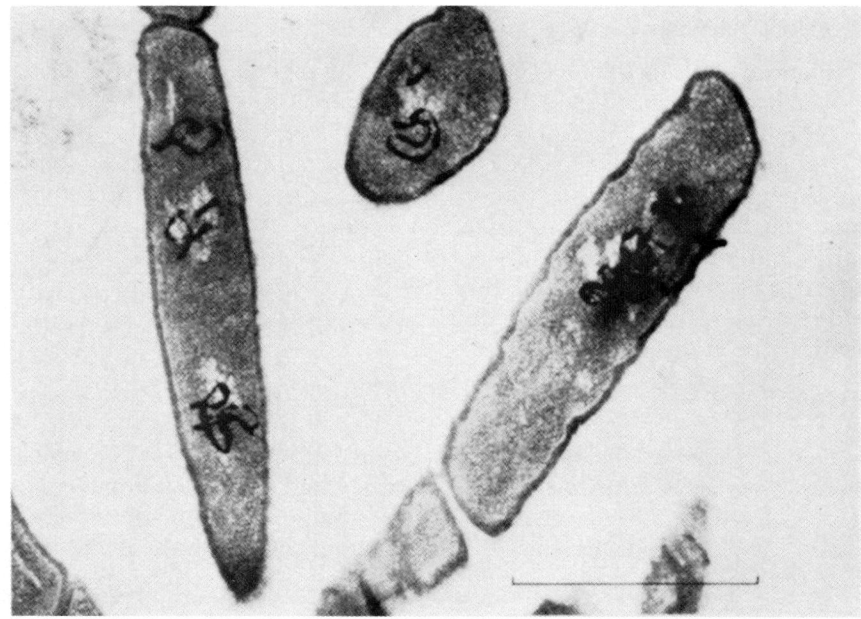

FIG. 6. Thin sections of *B. subtilis* labeled fully with thymidine-H^3. Stained in uranyl acetate. Development in Microdol-X. The grains seem closely associated with the nuclear region. $\times$21,780.

subtilis (isolated by Dr. Romig) labeled with uridine-H^3 or thymidine-H^3. The difference between the two labels is clear, and even in these small cells ($0.6 \times 2\mu$) it is possible to resolve autoradiographically cellular details (in this case nuclear region versus cytoplasm). The bacteriophage preparations are described in Section IV. Figures 7–11 give an example of the fine grain physical type of development described earlier. The advantage in resolution as well as in the clarity of the image is clear.

IV. Resolution

A. General Considerations

We shall try to examine theoretically and experimentally the resolution of which the methods of electron microscopic autoradiography are capable. Several theoretical analyses of resolution in autoradiography have been published (Doniach and Pelc, 1950; Nadler, 1951; Gomberg and Schlesinger, 1955). The results of these various calculations cannot, however, be applied directly to the present situation since they make assumptions which, while legitimate for conventional methods and fast β-particles, become invalid with low energy β-particles and layers of emulsions whose thickness is comparable to the size of the grains. In particular, the range limitations of the β-particles cannot be ignored, and the emulsion cannot be treated as a continuous medium.

We shall derive, in this section, a theoretical expression for the expected distribution of exposed grains around a point source of tritium, calculate from this the distribution for a small extended source, and verify this experimentally. Only an outline of the calculations will be given here. A more extended treatment can be found in a published article (Caro, 1962).

Three elements of uncertainty combine to limit resolution. The first is the relation between the source of β-particles and the crystals hit by these particles. The second is the relation between the passage of an electron through a crystal and the position of the latent image formed. The third

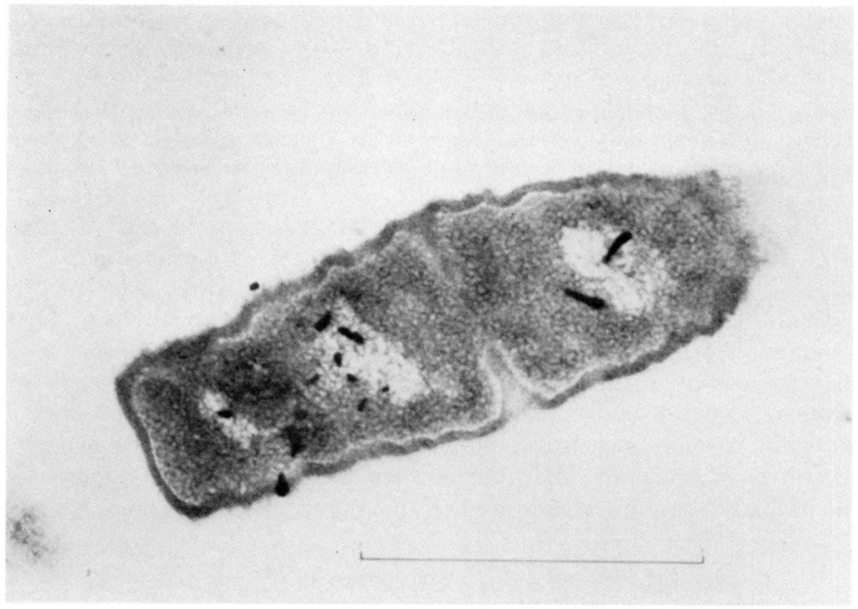

FIG. 7. Thin sections of *B. subtilis* labeled fully with thymidine-H^3. Stained in uranyl acetate. Development in fine grain "physical" developer. Notice small size and good localization of the grains with respect to the nuclear regions. ×31,350.

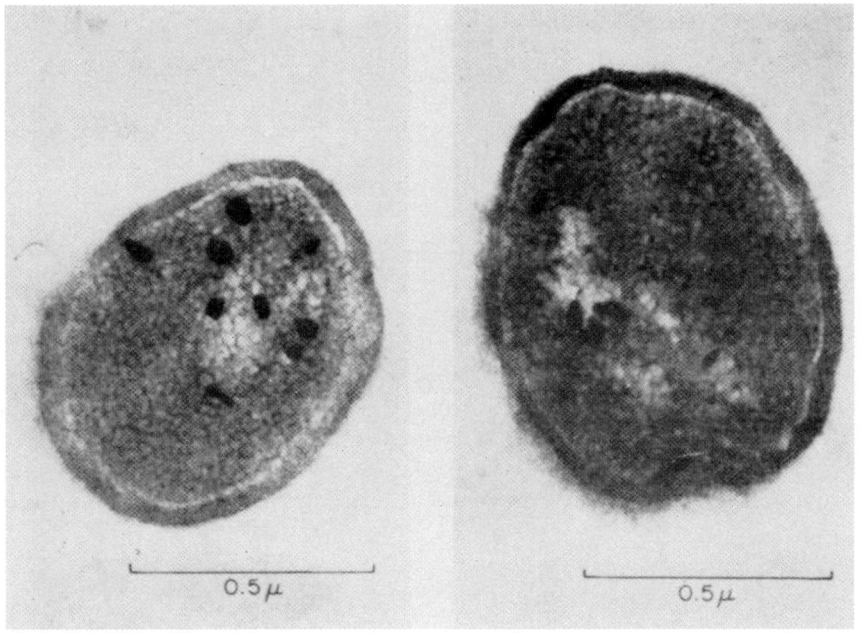

FIGS. 8 and 9. Autoradiographs of thin cross sections of *B. subtilis* labeled with thymidine-H^3. Fine-grain "physical" development. Although grains are found outside the nuclear region almost all of them occur very close to it. ×44,220.

is the relation between the final image observed: a deposit of silver of variable size and shape, and the latent image that produced it. We have seen in Section III that by using a special fine grain developer the position of a given developed latent image could be located with great accuracy. We have also seen that it was not possible to determine from this the position of the center of the corresponding crystal of silver halide with an accuracy better than 500 Å. This last degree of uncertainty is probably beyond our control and can only be decreased by reducing the size of the crystals. We shall therefore study the first part of the process: the probable position, with respect to the source, of the centers of exposed crystals.

B. Distribution of Exposed Crystals around a Point Source

We shall first consider the simple case, illustrated in Fig. 12, of a point source 500 Å away from an emulsion consisting of a monolayer of silver bromide crystals 0.1μ in diameter. In order to calculate the expected density of exposed grains around that source we shall evaluate the probability that a grain at a given distance will be hit by an electron emitted by the source. This will depend on the range of the electron and on the geometry of the preparation.

1. Range Distribution of β-Particles from Tritium

The distribution of particles having at least a given range is shown in Fig. 13. This is based on the energy spectrum of tritium decays (Robertson and Hughes, 1959), the calculated range of electrons (Lea, 1955), extrapolated to material of the density of methacrylate (1.1), and corrected for the curved path of electrons (Williams, 1930). The distribution of ranges would be very similar for tissue or for paraffin since the densities of these media are not very different from 1.1. One fact emerges clearly from such elementary considerations: if a source of tritium betas is placed 1μ away from the emulsion, only 20% of the emitted betas will reach the

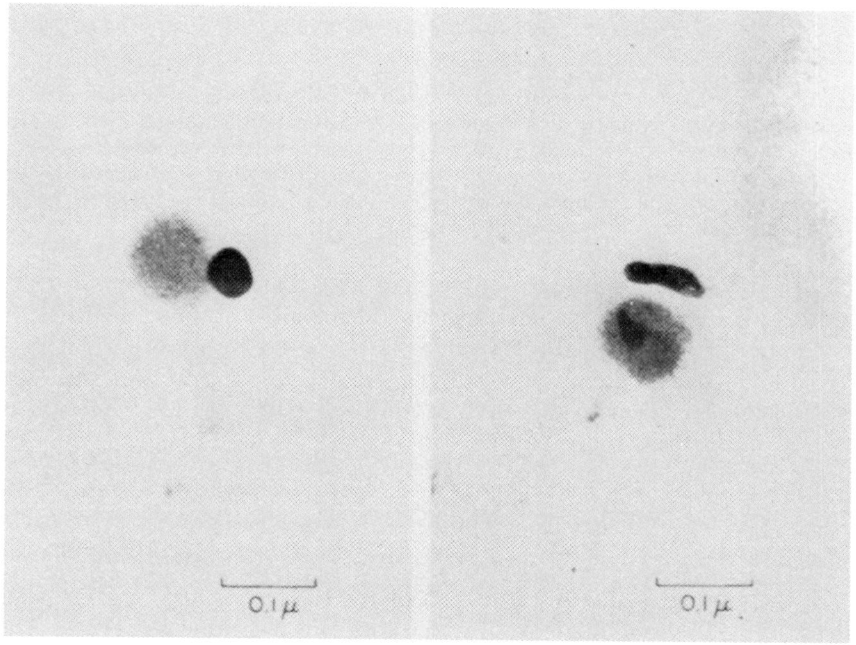

Figs. 10 and 11. Autoradiographs of T-2 bacteriophages labeled with thymidine-H^3. The fine grain "physical" developer described in the text was used. The phages were stained with uranyl acetate (only the head of the phage, containing the nucleic acid, is normally stained, but occasionally the tail can be made visible, as in the upper left). ×82,500.

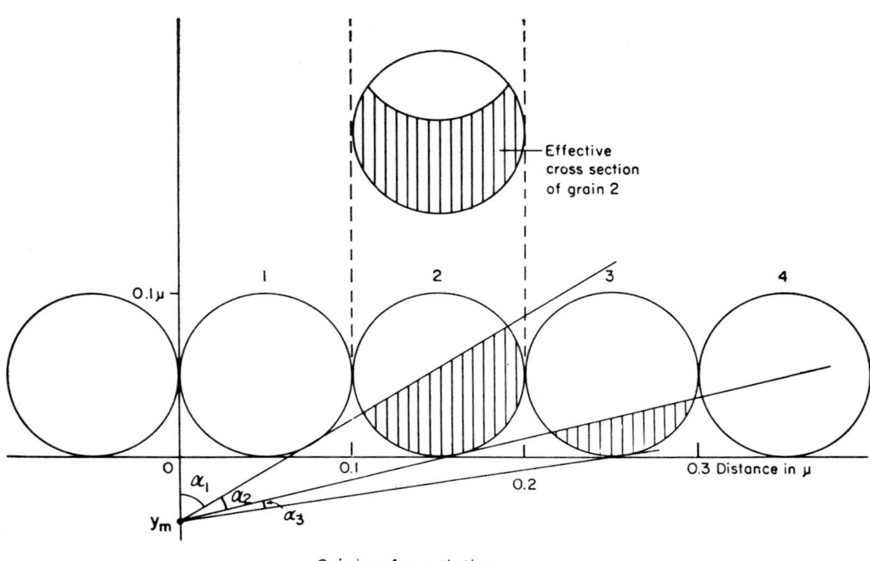

FIG. 12. Diagrammatic representation of the situation investigated in the resolution calculations given in the text. A point source of tritium is placed at y_m, 500 Å away from a monolayer of silver halide crystals 0.1μ in diameter. The effective cross section of a crystal is decreased by the presence, in the path of the electrons emitted, of other crystals. For example, if grain 2 is immediately behind grain 1, its cross section will be decreased by the projected shadow of grain 1 (see text).

emulsion; at 2μ the proportion becomes 2%. This means that in a conventional autoradiograph of a normal histological section, 5μ thick for example, the autoradiographic image is produced by a very thin upper layer and therefore represents only a minute fraction of the structures seen in the microscope. This obvious source of artifacts and misinterpretation is considerably reduced when thin sections are used in light microscope preparation and almost completely eliminated at the electron microscope level with sections thinner than 1000 Å.

2. GEOMETRY

If the photographic crystals were isolated the probability of a hit would decrease as the solid angle from which they are seen from the source, that is to say, as the square of the distance from the source. Since they are closely packed we might expect that because of the relatively high density of silver bromide, crystals which are close to the source will partially shield those which are farther away. It can be assumed, therefore, that if an electron hits a crystal, the probability that it hits a second crystal in the monolayer is close to zero. This can also be demonstrated experimentally (see Section III). This effect contributes to the resolution by decreasing the available target area of remote grains. Its contribution was evaluated graphically (Caro, 1962).

The probability that a grain situated at a given distance will be hit is then a product of these three factors: (a) probability that the electrons emitted will have a sufficient range in methacrylate to reach the grain (gelatin is assumed to have a density close to that of methacrylate), (b) the solid angle, and (c) the effective target size of the grain. The expected density of exposed grains around the source is plotted in Fig. 14. It can be described, as a first approximation, by a relation of the form $D = D_o e^{-1.6x}$, where D is the density of exposed grains, D_o this density at the origin, and x the distance in units of $1/10\mu$. If we use for resolution a definition similar to the Rayleigh criterion of classical optics, the value will be approximately twice the distance at which the density decreases to 50% of its maximum value. The resolution predicted on this basis is 860 Å, or approximately 0.1μ.

Similar calculations were made for various situations and the results plotted in Fig. 15. It is clear from these curves that resolution could be

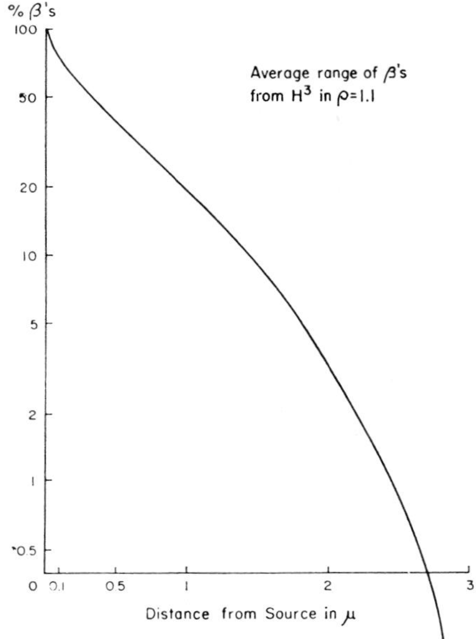

FIG. 13. Expected distribution of ranges of β-particles from tritium in a medium of density 1.1 (methacrylate). This distribution is based on the energy spectrum of tritium decays and on the calculated range of electrons, corrected for the curvature of the path.

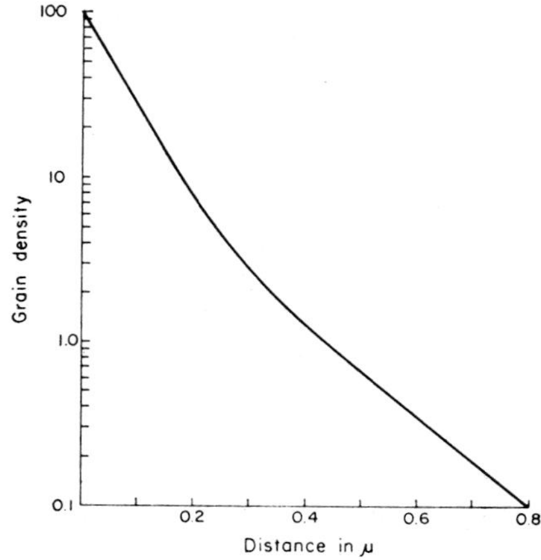

FIG. 14. Expected density of grains, as a function of distance from the origin, for a point source 500 Å away from the emulsion (grain diameter 1000 Å). The probability that a crystal will be hit falls to less than 30% of its value at the origin within 0.1μ and to less than 10% within 0.2μ. The density distribution curve appears as the sum of two exponential functions but can be approximated by the simple relation $D = D_o e^{-1.6x}$ where x is the distance from the origin in units of 0.1μ.

improved considerably by a combined decrease in emulsion thickness (and therefore in crystal size) and specimen thickness.

In order to evaluate the distribution of grains with respect to a given structure, the density distribution is integrated over the area of the structure. Such an integration can be done by graphic or numerical methods with an accuracy sufficient for most purposes. This was done, for example, over the volume of a sphere equivalent to the size of a bacteriophage head. The results are shown in Fig. 16 (continuous curve). It should be noted that for convenience we have plotted here the radial distribution of grains, i.e., the total number of grains expected at a certain distance. This corresponds to the density multiplied by the number of grains expected to be found at that distance (a factor which increases proportionally to the distance).

C. Experimental Demonstration of Resolution

T-2 bacteriophages labeled with thymidine-H^3 were used as test specimens. (We are grateful to Dr. Phyllis Kahn for providing the labeled bacteriophages.)

The preparations were made by the agar collodion filtration technique described by Kellenberger and Arber (1957): A drop of the phage suspension was spread over a thin collodion membrane coating a 2% agar surface, the particles were fixed by a brief exposure to OsO_4 vapors, and the preparation was placed in a Petri dish until diffusion of the liquid into the agar was complete. The collodion film was then floated on a water surface, specimen grids placed on top of it (on the phage side of the film), and the film picked up with a square of copper mesh lowered on its upper

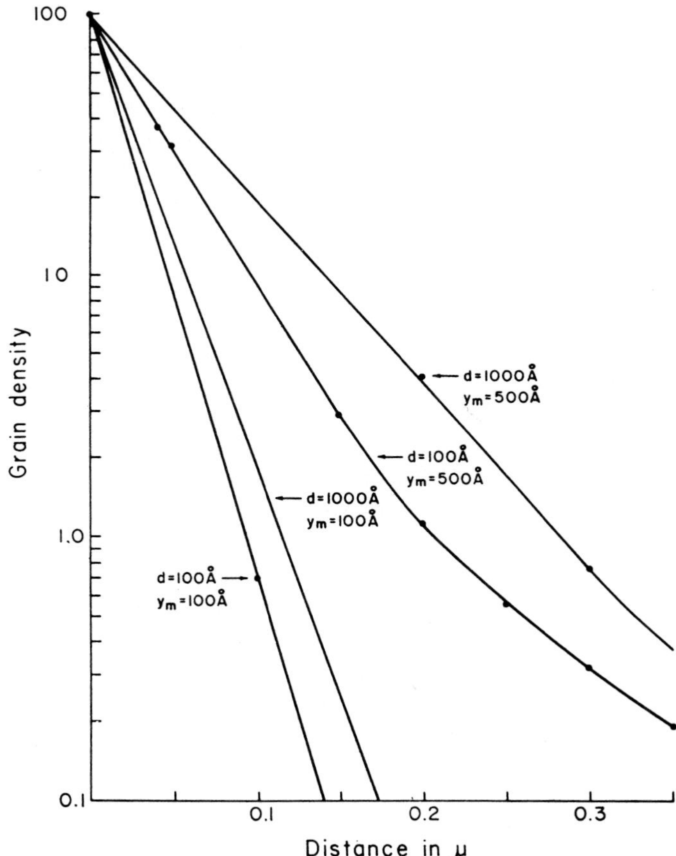

FIG. 15. Expected grain density distributions, calculated as explained in the text, for a variety of situations: (a) crystal diameter 1000 Å, source 500 Å from emulsion; (b) crystal diameter 100 Å, source 500 Å from emulsion; (c) crystal diameter 1000 Å, source 100 Å from emulsion; (d) crystal diameter 100 Å, source 100 Å from emulsion. It is seen that resolution will increase if either the diameter of the silver halide crystals or the thickness of the specimen is decreased. For reasons mentioned in the text, a decrease in crystal diameter would have a more important effect on the resolution than would appear from this graph.

surface. An emulsion was placed on each screen by the loop method already described (Section II). The final preparation consisted therefore of a monolayer of silver halide crystals separated from the phage particles by a thin collodion membrane. This membrane had approximately the same electron scattering properties, judged from its apparent density in the electron microscope, as a very thin Epon or Araldite section and was probably of comparable thickness, i.e., approximately 500 Å. The exposure was calculated to give an average grain count per phage slightly lower than one. After exposure the preparations were developed in the fine grain physical developer described in Section II. The bacteriophages were then stained for 20 minutes in 2% uranyl acetate. Photographs of all phage particles (Figs. 10 and 11) having at least one associated grain were taken and the distance from the grain to the center of the phage measured. As we have mentioned already, the grains are either small and spherical or larger and comma-shaped. In the first case the center of the grain and in the second case the pointed end of the comma were used to indicate the position of the corresponding latent image. The resulting distribution is shown on the histogram of Fig. 16. It is found to coincide fairly well with the expected distribution.

We find therefore than an experimental distribution of grains around phage particles follows closely the expected distribution of exposed crystals. This expected distribution was, in turn, calculated from a theoretical point source distribution. This gives therefore an experimental verification of the theoretical distribution and a justification of the resolution estimated from it.

It might be of some practical interest to determine the distribution of grains over more extended areas. To this end we have used thin sections of *Bacillus subtilis* labeled with thymidine-H^3 and measured the distribution of grains on either side of the edge of the nuclear region on cross sections of the cells (Figs. 8 and 9). The resulting distribution is shown in Fig. 17. It is clear that if we had two regions of similar size separated by a distance of 0.1μ they would be resolved autoradiographically.

D. The Influence of Crystal Size on Resolution

We might consider first the effect of grain size on resolution. We have seen that if an electron hits a crystal the latent image can appear anywhere on the surface of this crystal and can therefore be as far as 500 Å away from the center. This introduces an additional uncertainty in our distribution, which was based on the expected position of the center of exposed crystals. In an experiment such as the one with the bacteriophages described above, where the exposure was calculated to produce a very small

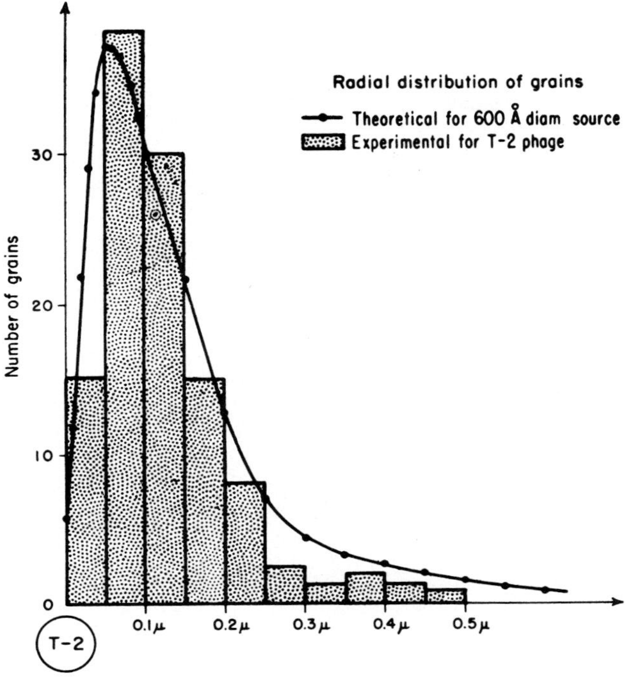

FIG. 16. Radial distribution of grains around a tritium-labeled bacteriophage. The theoretical curve was calculated by graphic integration of the point source distribution shown in Fig. 14 over a sphere 600 Å in diameter. The experimental distribution was measured on 100 photographs such as those shown in Figs. 10 and 11. This plot represents the total number of grains (not the density) found at a given distance from the origin.

number of grains for each source, we do not expect that the distribution over a large number of sources will be affected greatly. If we consider, for example, an exposed crystal whose center is 1000 Å away from the source, it is clear that the probability that the latent image will appear closer than 1000 Å to the source is almost equal to that of appearance further away. It is only when we come very close to the source that this situation changes significantly. Therefore, without going into a detailed analysis, we might expect a change in the shape of the density distribution curve only near the origin, very little change after 1000 Å, and only a slight over-all effect on resolution. This conclusion is supported by the experimental distribution which fits clearly the predicted distribution for the centers of crystals. It is also confirmed at the light microscope level and on a different scale by the results of Bleeken (1961).

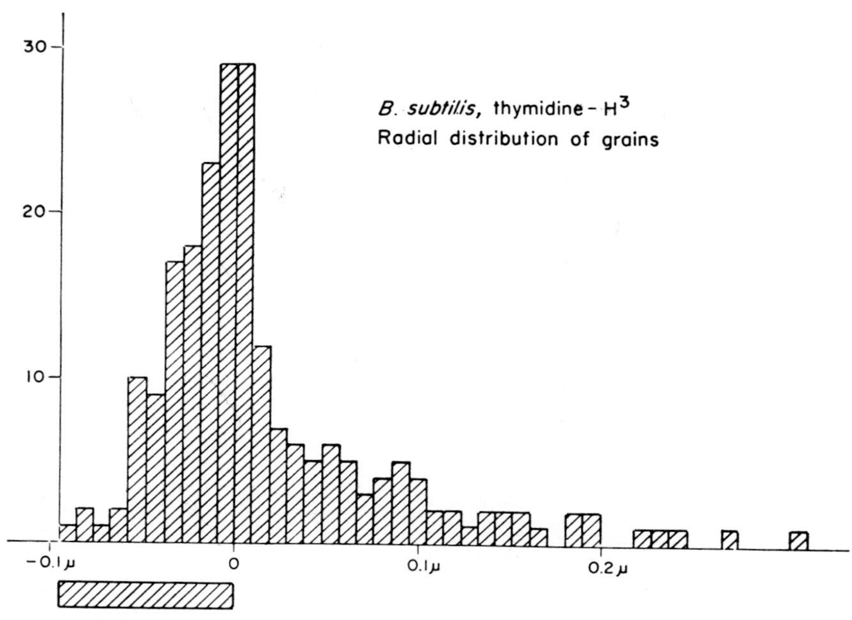

FIG. 17. Distribution of grains over the nuclear regions in thin cross sections of *B. subtilis* such as those shown in Figs. 8 and 9. Distances were measured with respect to the edge of the nuclear region, the counts on the left of the origin representing counts over the nuclear region. As might be expected, because of increasing areas, the highest probability of a grain occurs at the edge of the nuclear region. Approximately 89% of 220 grains counted were found within 0.1μ of the nuclear region or over it.

The crystal size, however, will clearly affect resolution in cases when the number of grains per source must be high. If we want to separate autoradiographically two point sources separated by 1000 Å, there must be enough grains developed to give a statistical meaning to the concept of grain density. If the diameter of a crystal is 1000 Å we can, at most, have two grains between the two sources. This will not be sufficient to define them. If the diameter of the crystals were reduced to 100 Å (without changing the shape of the density distribution) it would be possible to have enough grains to define the two sources and the resolution of approximately 1000 Å would again become a meaningful concept. Another factor, related to the density of grain counts needed, is that as the exposure increases, a crystal immediately above a point source might be hit a number of times but still produce only one grain, while grains further away have an increasing probability of having been hit at least once, thereby decreasing the resolution (Doniach and Pelc, 1950). In conclusion, therefore, if we assume a certain predicted resolution, an emulsion with a crystal size of the same order as the resolution expected will be good enough to separate extended sources (such as the nuclear regions of bacteria considered above) but for smaller sources a finer grained emulsion will be needed.

On the basis of energy loss relationships Pelc *et al.* (1961) have proposed that 100–500 Å would be a limiting crystal size for registering tritium β-particles. This estimate seems reasonable since Perfilov *et al.* (1961), for example, have described a nuclear emulsion having a grain size of 500 Å and a high sensitivity to electrons at minimum ionization. (The rate of energy loss with respect to distance for a charged particle decreases with higher energies until a minimum is reached. For electrons this minimum occurs at 1 Mev. An emulsion capable of registering 1 Mev electrons will be sensitive to electrons of any energy.) β-Particles with the average energy for tritium (5.7 Kev) will have a rate of energy loss approximately 17 times higher than 1 Mev electrons (Nelms, 1956; Herz, 1951) and therefore a much higher probability of being registered in a given emulsion (Demers, 1958). A decrease in the size of the crystals therefore seems to provide a promising approach toward improving resolution to some extent, although this will be limited by the size of a silver halide crystal still capable of registering one decay (Pelc *et al.*, 1961).

We have therefore reached the following conclusions: On the basis of the geometry of the preparation and the range distribution of tritium β-particles we can predict a resolution of the order of 0.1μ when the methods of autoradiography outlined in Section II are used. The calculated distribution of exposed grains leading to this prediction has been verified experimentally using bacteriophages as a test specimen. When using emulsions having grains with a diameter of 0.1μ, the number of grains per unit area proves to be a practical limit to the resolution if small sources are to be separated. With extended sources of simple geometry, the resolution achieved comes close to the predicted limit. It therefore seems that using the present methods on tissue sections, we can expect a limit in resolution of the order of 0.1μ. A significant improvement of this limit will require a considerable decrease in both the specimen thickness and the size of silver halide crystals.

From a practical point of view we reach the following conclusions: If the problem investigated required the identification of sources of various sizes separated by relatively great distances, very satisfactory results can be expected, the grains being found over or very close to the sources. Such a situation was found, for example, in the case of labeled zymogen granules in pancreatic exocrine cells (Caro and Palade, 1961). A good discrimination of the grain counts will also be obtained with extended sources separated by at least 1000 Å. If, however, closely spaced small sources are to be separated, finer grained emulsions will be needed. In any case it is clear that the present techniques are sufficient for their application to a large number of problems at the subcellular level.

V. Discussion

A. General Conclusions on the Methods of High-Resolution Autoradiography

1. Light Microscope Methods

As we have seen in Section IV, resolution in autoradiography can be increased by reducing the thickness of the emulsion and of the specimen. The use of a low energy β-emitter such as tritium is a contributing factor but not absolutely essential. We have obtained, with either S^{35} or C^{14} (1962, unpublished observations), resolutions which were sufficient to study processes at the subcellular level.

At the light microscope level the techniques described here given an improvement in autoradiographic resolution over the classical methods, but the main advantages lie in the quality of the specimen. The use of methacrylate-embedded material allows for much thinner sections than paraffin embedding. The quality of the image, in phase contrast, is excellent and many small cellular details such as mitochondria, zymogen granules, and fat droplets are easily seen in the autoradiographs. The thinness of the section eliminates to a great extent the problem of superimposition of structures always present in paraffin sections several microns thick. The reproducibility of grain counts in such preparations is good and comparable to that obtained with stripping emulsions (Caro and van Tubergen, 1962).

2. Electron Microscope Methods

On the basis of our experience with the method of electron microscopic autoradiography and of the experiments described in Sections III and IV, we have reached the following general conclusions:

(a) Because of its small grain size and high sensitivity to electrons, Ilford L.4 Nuclear Research emulsion seems to be the most suitable commercial emulsion of those tested.

(b) Specimen preparation does not present any special problem but the thin sections should be prepared with more than routine care.

(c) The emulsion should be applied in such a way that a monolayer of silver halide crystals is formed and that the distribution of these crystals is uniform and not affected by the specimen.

(d) Background is usually low at the electron microscope level but when present it can be eliminated by a simple method described in the text.

(e) Preparations should be stored with a drying agent either at room or refrigerator temperature.

(f) Photographic processing is a critical step. For routine applications Microdol-X was found to be a good developer. For the highest possible resolution a special developer, of the "physical" type, is preferred. Its formula and mode of application are given in the text.

(g) The sections should be stained in order to obtain sufficient contrast. This is done, through the gelatin, after photographic processing. Uranyl acetate is employed most frequently. Alkaline lead stains have been used occasionally to improve image quality, but they should be used cautiously since they partially remove the gelatin and might disturb the position of grains.

B. Applications of High-Resolution Autoradiography

The application of the electron microscope to autoradiography, a major step in the development of high-resolution techniques, is very recent and the techniques are still in a fairly crude stage. In spite of this, the present techniques are reliable enough to warrant their application to a large number of problems at the subcellular level. They offer, in addition to autoradiographic resolution, some important advantages: the optical resolution of the microscope allows us to see and recognize clearly the labeled structure, even if it is beyond the resolving power of the light microscope (as in the case of bacteriophages for example); to see photographic grains much below this resolving power; and to measure with great accuracy the distance between the grain and the structure. In addition, the great depth of focus of the electron microscope permits one to obtain a complete photographic record of both grains and structures. For these reasons accurate grain counts can be performed and, as we have seen, relative quantitation is obtained with good reproducibility. With some improvement in methodology, absolute quantitation is not beyond the scope of this technique. Its main drawbacks are that it is time consuming and has very low sensitivity, thus requiring high levels of labeling.

Most of the articles published so far on this subject were simple demonstrations of the technique and only a few attempts were made to obtain results of biological significance. Revel and Hay (1961) demonstrated the incorporation of thymidine-H^3 in a homogeneous fibrous component of the interphase nuclei of *Amblystoma* larvae. Caro (1961) and Caro and Palade (1961, 1963) used this method in a detailed study of the synthesis, transport, and secretion of proteins in the exocrine cell of the guinea pig pancreas. Such limited applications suffice, however, to demonstrate the potentialities of the technique and its usefulness as a new analytical tool in cell physiology.

References

Baker, J. R. (1960). "Cytological Technique," 4th ed. Methuen, London.

Bleecken, S. (1961), *Atompraxis* **7**, 321.

Caro, L. G. (1961a). *J. Biophys. Biochem. Cytol.* **10**, 37.

Caro, L. G. (1961b). *J. Biophys. Biochem. Cytol.* **9**, 539.

Caro, L. G. (1962). *J. Cell Biol.* **15**, 189.

Caro, L. G., and Forro, F., Jr. (1961). *J. Biophys. Biochem. Cytol.* **9**, 555.

Caro, L. G., and Palade, G. E. (1961). *Compt. Rend. Soc. Biol.* **155**, 1750.

Caro, L. G., and Palade, G. E. (1963). *J. Cell Biol.* In press.

Caro, L. G., and van Tubergen, R. P. (1962). *J. Cell Biol.* **15**, 173.

Comer, J. J., and Skipper, S. J. (1954). *Science* **119**, 441.

Demers, P. (1958). "Ionographie. Les Émulsions Nucléaires. Principes et Applications." Les Presses Universitaires de Montréal, Montréal.

Doniach, I., and Pelc, S. R. (1950). *Brit. J. Radiol.* **23**, 184.

Fitzgerald, P. J., Eidinoff, M. L., Knoll, J. E., and Simmel, E. B. (1951). *Science* **114**, 494.

Gibbons, I. R., and Grimstone, A. V. (1960). *J. Biophys. Biochem. Cytol.* **7**, 697.

Gomberg, H. J., and Schlesinger, M. J., Jr. (1955). *Proc. Intern. Conf. Peaceful Uses Atomic Energy, Geneva, 1955* **14**, 266.

Granboulan, P., Granboulan, N., and Bernhard, W. (1962). *J. Microscop.* **1**, 75.

Hampton, J. H., and Quastler, H. (1961). *J. Biophys. Biochem. Cytol.* **10**, 140.

Harford, C. G., and Hamlin, A. (1961). *Lab. Invest.* **10**, 627.

Herz, R. H. (1951). *Nucleonics* **9**, No. 3, 24.

Herz, R. H. (1959). *Lab. Invest.* **8**, 71.

Houwink, A. L., and van Iterson, W. (1950). *Biochim. Biophys. Acta* **5**, 10.

James, T. H. (1954). *In* "The Theory of the Photographic Process" (C. E. K. Mees, ed.). Macmillan, New York.

Karnovsky, M. J. (1961). *J. Biophys. Biochem. Cytol.* **11**, 729.

Kellenberger, E., and Arber, W. (1957). *Virology* **3**, 245.

LaPalme, J., and Demers, P. (1947). *Physiol. Rev.* **72**, 536.

Lea, D. E. (1955). "Actions of Radiations on Living Cells," 2nd ed. Cambridge Univ Press, London and New York.

Liquier-Milward, J. (1956). *Nature* **177**, 619.

Lumière, A., Lumière, L., and Seyewetz, A. (1911). *Compt. Rend.* **153**, 102.

Nadler, N. J. (1951). *Can. J. Med. Sci.* **29**, 182.

Nelms, A. T. (1956). *Natl. Bur. Standards (U. S.) Cir.* **577**.

O'Brien, R. T., and George, L. A. II. (1959). *Nature* **183**, 1461.

Pease, D. C. (1960). "Histological Techniques for Electron Microscopy." Academic Press, New York.

Pelc, S. R., Coombes, J. D., and Budd, G. C. (1961). *Exptl. Cell Res.* **24**, 192.

Perfilov, N. A., Novikova, N. R., Zakharov, V. I., and Vikhrev, Yu. I. (1961). *Atomnaya Energ.* **11,** 543.

Przybylski, R. J. (1961). *Exptl. Cell Res.* **24,** 181.

Ray, R. C., and Stevens, G. W. W. (1953). *Brit. J. Radiol.* **26,** 362.

Revel, J. P., and Hay, E. D. (1961). *Exptl. Cell Res.* **25,** 474.

Robertson, J. S., and Hughes, W. L. (1959). *In* "Proceedings of the First National Biophysics Conference" (H. Quastler and H. J. Morowitz, eds.), pp. 278–283. Yale Univ. Press, New Haven, Connecticut.

Satir, P. G., and Peachey, L. D. (1958). *J. Biophys. Biochem. Cytol.* **4,** 345.

Silk, M. H., Hawtrey, A. O., Spence, I. M., and Gear, J. H. S. (1961). *J. Biophys. Biochem. Cytol.* **10,** 577.

Stevens, G. W. W. (1950). *Brit. J. Radiol.* **23,** 723.

van Tubergen, R. P. (1959). Ph.D. Thesis, Yale University.

van Tubergen, R. P. (1961). *J. Biophys. Biochem. Cytol.* **9,** 219.

Williams, E. J. (1930). *Proc. Roy. Soc. London A* **130,** 310.

Yagoda, H. (1949). "Radioactive Measurements with Nuclear Emulsions." Wiley, New York.

Chapter 17

Autoradiography with Liquid Emulsion

D. M. PRESCOTT

Biology Division, Oak Ridge National Laboratory,[1]
Oak Ridge, Tennessee

I. Introduction

The autoradiographic method is becoming more useful partly because of the growing list of compounds labeled with radioisotopes (especially tritium and carbon-14) that are now commercially available and partly because of various technical advances, for example, the introduction of autoradiography into electron microscopy. In addition, a number of improvements in techniques at the level of light microscopy and the availability of reliable liquid emulsions have helped to simplify the procedures. The stripping film technique is still used in a number of laboratories, but for almost all purposes this somewhat tedious and time-consuming method can be replaced by the easier method of liquid emulsion coating.

Most descriptions of procedures of autoradiography contain many detailed steps and lists of special requirements, and in some instances this has resulted in rejection of the method as too intricate or requiring too much special equipment. Quantitative autoradiography does require special precautions (see Perry, this volume, Chapter 15) but semiquantitative or purely qualitative autoradiography is relatively simple and in this laboratory is looked upon as a detail at the end of a tracer experiment.

[1] Operated by the Union Carbide Corporation for the United States Atomic Energy Commission.

II. Emulsions

We use the liquid emulsions NTB, NTB-2, and NTB-3 manufactured by Kodak (Rochester, New York) almost exclusively. The size of the silver grains decreases and sensitivity and resolution increase in the order, NTB, NTB-2, NTB-3. The interrelations between sensitivity, grain size, and resolving power have been discussed in detail by Caro (this volume, Chapter 16). Caro has also made some comparative measurements of the sensitivity and grain size of several emulsions, including NTB and NTB-3. NTB-3 has about the same sensitivity as the Kodak (London) stripping film, AR1O. The choice of emulsion depends upon the requirements of the particular experiment. NTB is suitable for highly radioactive samples and also has such a low intrinsic background that corrections are not necessary if grain counting is undertaken. NTB-3 is more efficient with samples containing low activity but tends to have more background. For information on other commercially available emulsions, see Caro (this volume, Chapter 16).

The emulsion stocks are kept at room temperature, and no increase in background has been noticed under these conditions even during periods as long as 4 months. Frequently, diluted emulsion is used (one part distilled water to one part of emulsion) if the biological material is very flat, e.g., sectioned material, isolated chromosomes. The diluted emulsion gives a thinner coat and makes staining through the emulsion easier. For preparations that have an uneven surface, the full-strength emulsion covers better. In some instances multiple coating may be required.

III. Procedure

The emulsion is a gel at room temperature and is melted in a water bath at 42°–45°C. The circular Technicon constant temperature water bath (diameter, 27 cm) is convenient for this step because it is small, portable, and has a convenient depth (6 cm). The indicator light on the bath should be covered with a piece of black tape to avoid accidental exposure of emulsions. Each new bottle of emulsion (118 ml) is tested by melting the full bottle in the water bath and dipping a clean slide directly into the bottle. It is important to allow the emulsion to come to the temperature of the water bath to avoid lumpy or uneven coating of the slide. The test slide is allowed to dry (2 or 3 hours in a light-tight box), then developed, and checked for background. If the background is suitably low (see Fig. 1 for example), the emulsion can be used for several months without concern about intrinsic background. One bottle of emulsion is enough to coat 1–3000 slides. At the time the new bottle is melted for testing, generally

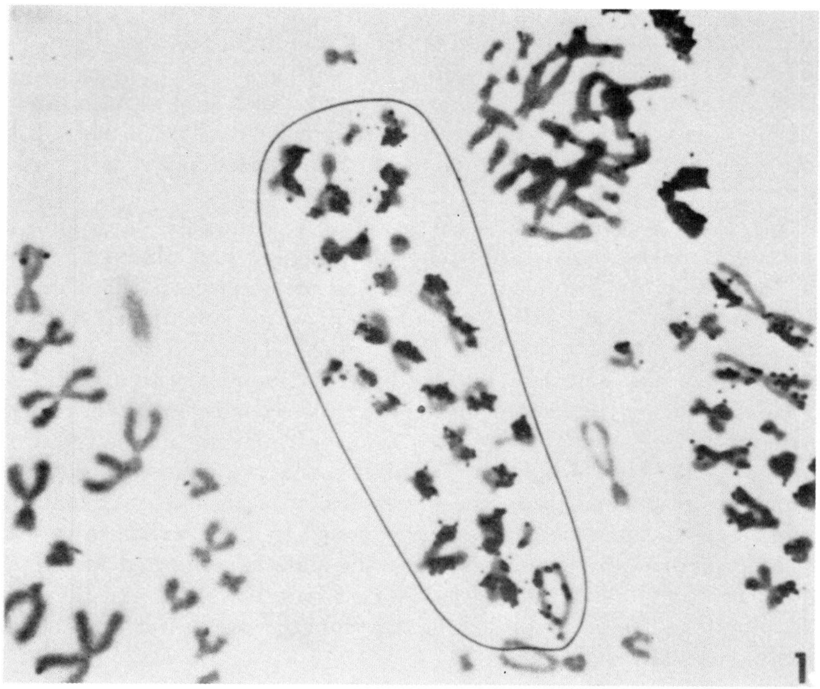

FIG. 1. An autoradiograph of isolated chromosomes from a Chinese hamster tissue culture cell labeled with tritiated thymidine. The chromosomes are from the second metaphase after labeling and demonstrate semiconservative segregation of deoxyribonucleic acid. A few sister chromatid exchanges are present. Note the low background of this emulsion (NTB-2). For reports of the experiments, see Prescott and Bender (1963) and Marin and Prescott (1963).

about half of the emulsion is poured into a separate, clean bottle to simplify subsequent handling, e.g., melting. The stock bottle of emulsion is melted each time slides are to be coated and the amount of emulsion to be used is poured into a special emulsion vessel (see below). For all darkroom operations, a Wratten series Number 1 safe light filter (red) with a 15 watt bulb is used and work carried out at a minimum of 3 feet from the light.

The Kodak emulsions adhere well to clean slides and it is no longer necessary to use slides subbed with gelatin (see Caro, this volume, Chapter 16). However, biological materials are sometimes more easily affixed to subbed slides, and occasionally such slides are used for this purpose. For dipping slides, emulsion is poured into a vessel shaped to take two microscope slides arranged upright and back-to-back with the biological material facing out (see Fig. 2). This type of vessel is described by Boyd (1955). The main advantage of the vessel is that a minimum amount of emulsion is needed to provide the proper depth for coating.

Dipping two slides at a time speeds up the task and also causes the emulsion to rise higher in the vessel. The emulsion vessel is held in the water bath by an ordinary clamp with rubber-faced jaws, as shown in Fig. 2. If the biological material is placed on the lower half of the slide (see Fig. 2), less emulsion is needed. Before entering the darkroom, the slides are arranged in back-to-back pairs (Fig. 2) and placed in Coplin jars. It is easier to obtain an even coating of emulsion if the slides are dry when dipped, but slides can be kept in water and dipped wet. The jars are placed in the water bath to warm the slides and thereby reduce the cooling of the emulsion during dipping. Each pair of dry slides is dipped once, being left in the emulsion for 4–5 seconds. As a pair of slides is withdrawn from the emulsion, it is held for a moment at the top of the vessel to drain. After dipping and draining, the two slides are separated and placed upright in a neoprene-coated test tube rack to drain and dry. The openings in the rack are just large enough to allow a slide to be fitted diagonally across the openings so that the slide is supported at one end and at the edges. With these procedures, about 100 slides can be coated in 15 minutes. The emulsion left in the dipping vessel after all slides are coated is normally discarded.

The test tube racks are placed in a light-tight box, and after the slides are thoroughly dry (usually slides are left overnight, but this is much longer than necessary), they are transferred from the racks to black bakelite slide boxes (capacity of 25) for prolonged storage. Normally, no drying agent is enclosed in these boxes. The slide boxes should be sealed with opaque tape to eliminate any light leaks between the box and its lid. These boxes are kept at room temperature (22°–24°C) without further precautions.

Ordinarily, development of a test slide after a few days will give enough information to permit a good estimation of how long the slides should be allowed to expose. The latent image formed by β-particles may eventually fade, and extremely long exposure times may be ineffective in producing an autoradiographic image of the predicted intensity. However, we have used exposure times of 8 months with no detectable fading.

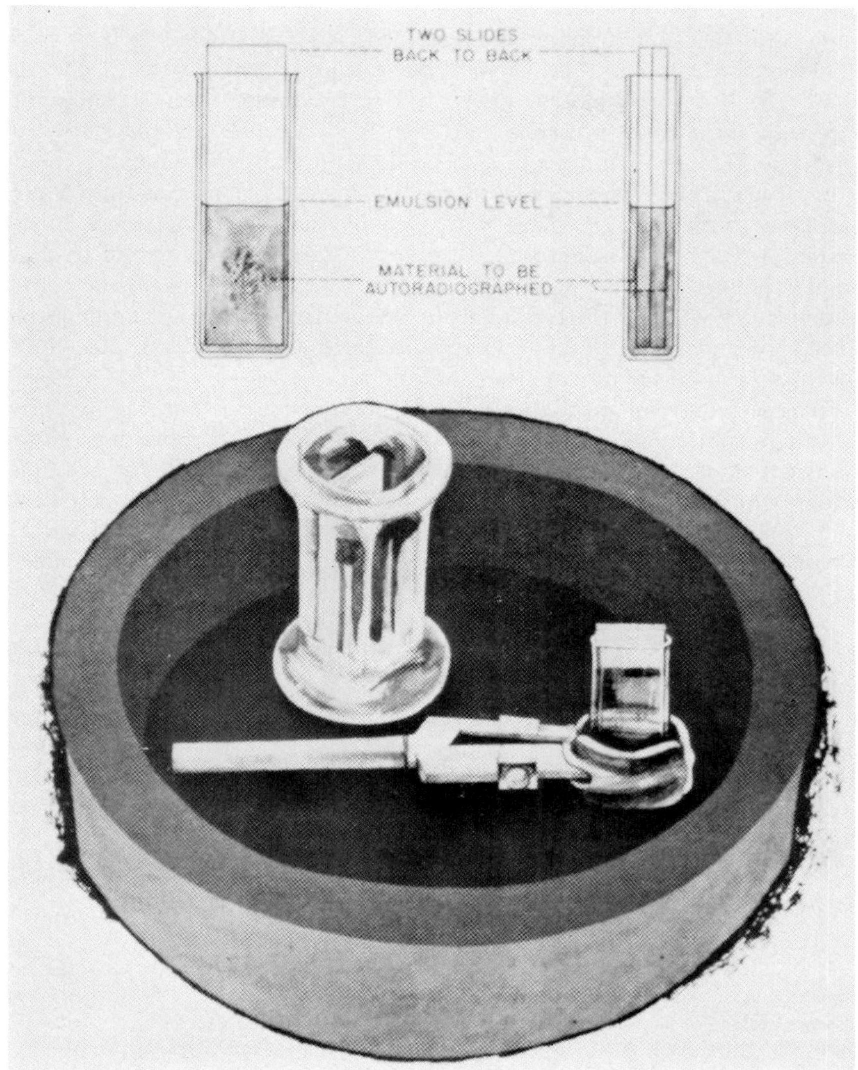

FIG. 2. Basic equipment for liquid emulsion autoradiography. See text for explanations.

The slides are developed for 2 minutes in either D-11, D-19, or Dektol (Kodak) at room temperature (22°–24°C), rinsed once in water, and fixed for 2–5 minutes in Kodak acid-fixer. After fixing, the slides are rinsed in running water for 20 minutes, given a final rinse in distilled water, and dried. The dried slides can be stored at this point or can be stained and made into permanent mounts. Most materials are stained well through the emulsion with an aqueous solution of toluidine blue (0.25% w/v) at about pH 6 or with methyl green and/or pyronine. After staining, the excess toluidine blue is washed off with 95% alcohol and the slides are air-dried. Giemsa staining can also be done through the emulsion (Gude *et al.*, 1955). The slides can be stored in this condition or mounted permanently with a cover glass with one of the usual mounting media (Euparol, Canada balsam, etc.). In many instances, staining can be done before the emulsion is applied, but any new procedures should be tested to determine whether the treatment causes artifacts in the autoradiograph. Aceto-orcein, lacto-orcein, and Feulgen staining are examples of procedures that can be used before emulsion coating.

In processing biological specimens in preparation for autoradiography, materials that might inactivate or otherwise distort the reaction of the emulsion must be avoided. If formaldehyde or picric acid, for example, are present in the fixative or the fixed material is extracted with perchloric acid, thorough washing is necessary to remove all traces of these chemicals because they will inactivate the emulsion. Perchloric acid is particularly difficult to leach out of cells, and, in general, trichloroacetic acid extraction is preferable.

Most of our tracer experiments utilize radioactive amino acids or nucleosides, and usually fixation is done with 70% alcohol or 95% alcohol: acetic acid (3:1). After fixation, the material (monolayers of cells or tissue sections) is extracted with 5% trichloroacetic acid at 0°C for 5 minutes, followed by washing in several changes of 70% alcohol over a period of several hours. This is followed by alcohol dehydration, air-drying, and autoradiography.

A valuable review and discussion of liquid emulsion autoradiography has recently been presented by Kopriwa and Leblond (1962).

REFERENCES

Boyd, G. A. (1955). "Autoradiography in Biology and Medicine." Academic Press, New York.

Gude, W. D., Upton, A. C., and Odell, T. T., Jr. (1955). *Stain Technol.* **30,** 161.

Kopriwa, B. M., and Leblond, C. P. (1962). *J. Histochem. Cytochem.* **10,** 269.

Marin, G., and Prescott, D. M. (1963). *J. Cell Biol.* In press.

Prescott, D. M., and Bender, M. A. (1963). *Exptl. Cell Res.* **29,** 430.

Chapter 18

Autoradiography of Water-Soluble Materials

O. L. MILLER, JR., G. E. STONE,[1] AND
D. M. PRESCOTT

Biology Division, Oak Ridge National Laboratory,[2]
Oak Ridge, Tennessee

I. Introduction

A method has been developed for autoradiographic detection of radioactive cellular materials which are ordinarily removed with water or other solvents during standard autoradiographic procedures. The method includes a technique which permits extraction of acid- or water-soluble materials followed by their deposition around a cell on a microscope slide so that the amount of both the soluble and insoluble radioactive materials can be estimated for the same isolated cell. In addition, a dry autoradiographic procedure for intracellular localization of soluble materials has been elaborated.

The use of dry autoradiography as a method for detecting water-soluble compounds within cells or tissues has been largely limited to frozen or

[1] NIH Postdoctoral Fellow.

[2] Operated by Union Carbide Corporation for the United States Atomic Energy Commission.

frozen-dried sections (see references marked with an asterisk). Certain methods are not suitable for tritiated precursors because of the short range of tritium radiation (see, for example, Chapman-Andresen, 1953; Eisen and Harris, 1957; Guidotti and Passalacqua, 1956). Some of the proposed methods are complex (Canny, 1955; Fitzgerald *et al.*, 1961) or are limited to special situations (Feinendegen and Bond, 1962). None of the published methods allow quantitative detection of both acid-soluble and acid-insoluble radioactivity in a single cell. In addition to permitting the latter measurements, the method described here is simple to use and should be applicable to a wide variety of cell types, experimental situations, and preparative schedules. We have used it successfully with several types of protozoa and with mammalian tissue culture cells.

II. Procedures

In its complete form the method involves three independent, parallel procedures: (a) analysis of cells extracted with acid, water, or other solvent to demonstrate only insoluble or incorporated activity according to the usual, standard method of autoradiography; (b) analysis by dry autoradiography of cells from which the soluble radioactive material has not been removed, thereby demonstrating intracellular localization of the soluble material; and (c) analysis by autoradiography of cells from which the soluble material has been extracted and deposited by drying in a delimited area surrounding the cell. In the latter, both the soluble radioactive material around the cell and the insoluble radioactive material within the cell are detected. NTB-3 liquid emulsion (Kodak, Rochester) has been used throughout the development of this method, but other liquid emulsions should work equally well.

A. Completely Extracted Cells

This procedure is carried out in the usual way by extracting preparations with relatively large volumes of solvent (acid, acid-alcohol, water, etc.), drying, and coating with liquid emulsion for autoradiographic exposure.

B. Unextracted Cells

For successful application of this method the cells must be prepared for autoradiography so that the soluble materials are not lost. For most types of microorganisms this can be accomplished by air-drying of cells directly from a physiological medium or by freeze-drying of wet smears on microscope slides. Tissues and tissue cultures can be prepared by the standard freeze-drying procedures.

The dry preparations are autoradiographed as follows: Forty to 50 ml of emulsion are melted in a 45°C water bath, poured into a 100-ml beaker or 50-ml Coplin staining jar, and cooled to near 30°C. A thin film of emulsion is obtained by dipping a wire loop, some 3.5–4 cm in diameter, into the emulsion (we are indebted to Caro, this volume, Chapter 16, for the loop technique which he devised for electron microscopy-autoradiography). The loops may be made simply by twisting size 22 nickel-chrome alloy wire around the base of a bottle of the proper diameter and affixing a microscope slide to the wire handle of the loop with tape, as shown in Fig. 1. The attachment of the slide allows the loop to be set on a flat surface for air-drying. The loop films air dry in 15–30 minutes (the films are sufficiently dry if there is no adherence when the film is touched to the surface of a glass slide).

A slide (the experimental material should be near one end) is held so that the area of the slide containing the radioactive material may be placed inside the wire loop with the end of the slide touching the film and the rest of the film overlaying the specimen area of the slide (Fig. 1). Holding the slide and film in contact, warm moist air (breath) is blown at the por-

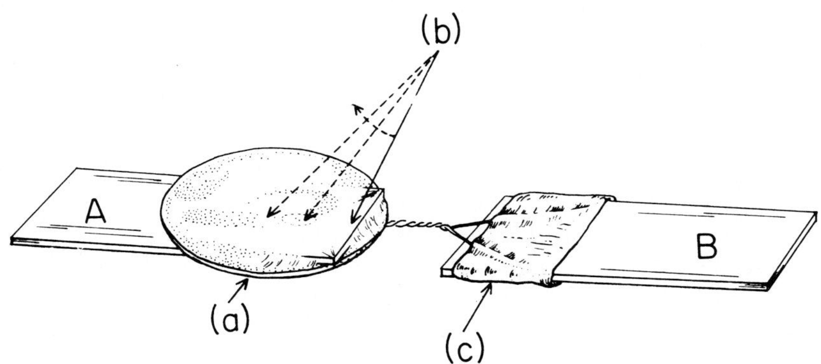

FIG. 1. Illustration of method of applying dry emulsion film to a slide. The specimen end of slide A is brought under and inserted into the wire loop (a) holding the film until the two corners stretch the film and project slightly over the top of the loop. The rest of the loop and film is held firmly in contact with the specimen area of the slide. Breath (b) is blown lightly and evenly on the film, beginning at point of contact and moving toward the specimen until the major portion of the film sticks to the slide. Slide B is pushed further onto slide A until the adhering film detaches from the loop, then slide A is withdrawn and stored for exposure. The wire loops are attached to slides with tape (c) previous to dipping in emulsion and placing on a flat surface for drying.

tion of film touching the end of the slide. This softens the emulsion and causes it to become sticky. When the film begins to adhere to the end of the slide, the direction of blowing is moved up the slide until the film adheres for most of its extent along the surface of the slide. The loop is pushed around the slide until the nonadhering portion of the emulsion has torn away. The slide is then withdrawn from the loop and stored as usual for exposure. Tests with H^3-nucleosides dried in spots on slides show that the slight amount of moisture entering the film from the breath is not sufficient to cause detectable displacement of water-soluble compounds. With the exception of bubbles formed when the film begins adhering simultaneously in more than one area or infrequent bubbles over specimens, the film adheres smoothly to the slide and experimental materials and does not wrinkle or shift during subsequent processing. Bubble formation can be minimized by applying the loop films to slides as soon as possible after the emulsion has dried.

C. Detection of Soluble and Insoluble Radioactivity

The detection and quantitation of soluble radioactive materials in cells can be done in two ways:

1. Diffusion in Wet Film

A wet but gelled film of emulsion is applied to the slide in a manner which allows water soluble materials to diffuse out of the cell and be spread in a limited area around the cell (probably within the wet emulsion). A film of emulsion (diluted 1:1 with water) is obtained by dipping a wire loop as described in the previous section. The film, which gels quickly at room temperature, is cooled over an ice bath in air (air temperature, 15°–20°C). The gelled film is applied to slides kept at about the same temperature and stored for exposure at 10°C in light-tight boxes containing a drying agent such as Drierite. This portion of the method is of limited usefulness because the efficiency of extraction and the diffusion spread of extracted material cannot be controlled very well.

2. Limited Area Extraction

In this method a circle is drawn around the specimen with a fine-pointed glass marking pencil (wax pencil). In the case of single cells the circle should be 1 mm or less in diameter. The thin layer of wax forms a barrier which will retain the extraction fluid in the defined area. A small amount of extraction solvent (for example, acetic acid-alcohol) is dropped onto the cell with a fine bore pipette. The solvent will fill the area within the circle, the materials extracted from the cell will be spread relatively evenly in this area when the solvent has dried. The extraction can be repeated several times if there is reason to doubt that complete extraction was achieved with one application of solvent. Dry autoradiography is then carried out as described in Section II, B. Determinations of relative amounts of extracted and unextracted materials for the same cell can be made with grain counts.

III. Experimental Example

Thymidine-H^3 Labeling

The uptake of thymidine-H^3 into the nucleotide pool of *Tetrahymena pyriformis* during different stages of the cell life cycle has been studied with the methods described in this paper. Small groups of dividing cells were obtained by selecting individual dividing cells from a log phase culture as described by Stone and Cameron (this volume, Chapter 8). Cell samples were given a brief incubation in thymidine-H^3 (10μc/ml, sp. act. 6.6 c/mmole) at different points of the cell cycle. Following this treatment, the cells were quickly and thoroughly washed with nonradioactive medium to remove exogenous thymidine-H^3. Cells were dried on slides immediately or at various intervals after washing.

Cells engaged in micro- or macronuclear deoxyribonucleic acid (DNA) synthesis at the time of thymidine-H^3 incubation and dried onto slides immediately after washing free of radioactive medium showed only nuclear labeling after complete extraction as shown in Figs. 2 and 3 (Section II, A). When similar cells in macronuclear S were subjected to the wet film autoradiography (Section II, C, 1), radioactivity was distributed in a halo over the cytoplasm and around the cell in addition to macronuclear labeling (Figs. 4 and 5). If such cells were extracted with acetic acid alcohol according to the wax ring method (Section II, C, 2) and autoradiographed by the dry film method, the extracted materials were evident as a halo of radioactivity around the cell (Fig. 6). The macronucleus showed the usual autoradiograph (radioactivity incorporated into DNA). Finally, cells not extracted at any point and then covered with emulsion by the dry film method showed radioactivity only in the nucleus (Fig. 7). Since our other studies have shown that such cells contain a soluble pool of thymidine-H^3 derivatives, we must assume that this soluble nucleotide pool is normally localized in the nucleus. This conclusion agrees with other evidence (Feinendegen and Bond, 1962; Branton and Jacobson, 1962) that the pool of thymidine derivatives is localized in the nucleus.

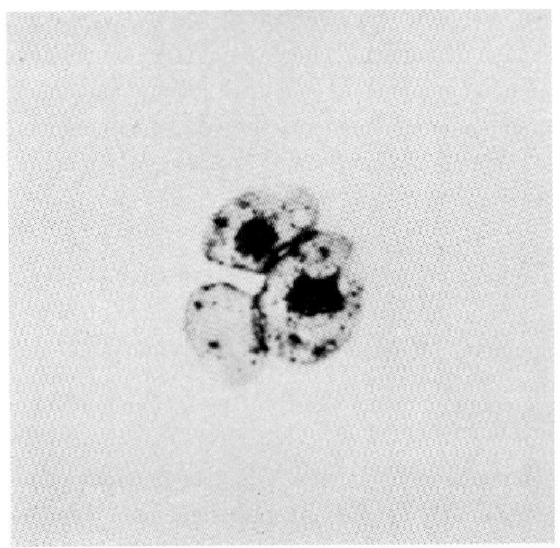

FIG. 2. Cells completely extracted by acetic acid-alcohol (Section II, A) after thymidine-H^3 incubation and washing. Two cells were in macronuclear S during labeling and show grains over the macronucleus, while the remaining cell was in G1 and shows no incorporation of label into DNA.

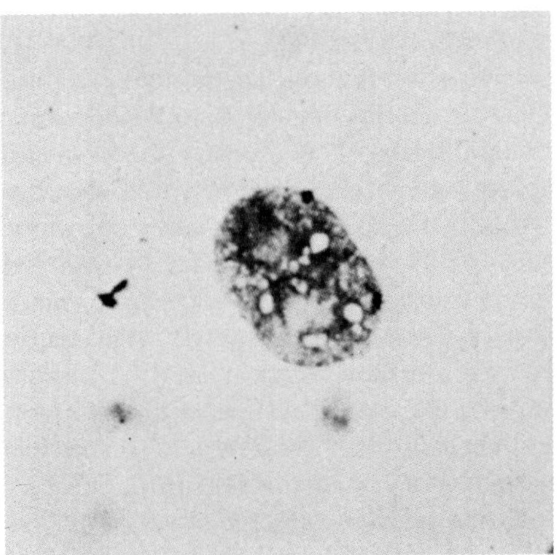

FIG. 3. A cell treated similar to those shown in Fig. 2 except that thymidine-H^3 was supplied during micronuclear S. The two daughter micronuclei separate previous to cell division; both show label in acid insoluble DNA.

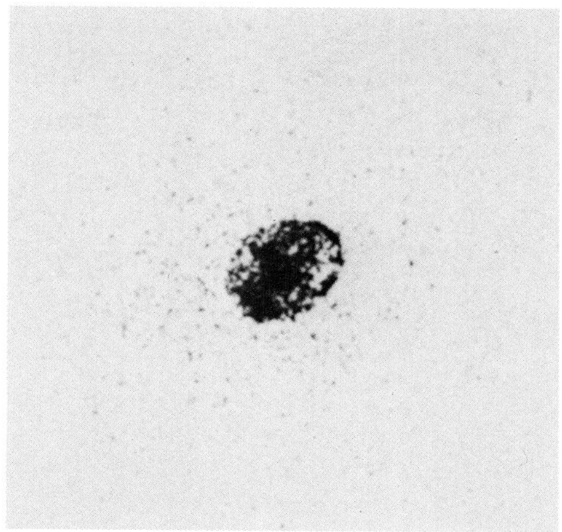

FIG. 4. Autoradiograph of cell coated with wet, gelled emulsion (Section II, C, 1) following thymidine-H^3 incubation, washing, and drying without extraction. Much of the water-soluble thymidine derivative pool has been extracted from the cell by the wet film but has remained within a relatively small area around the cell.

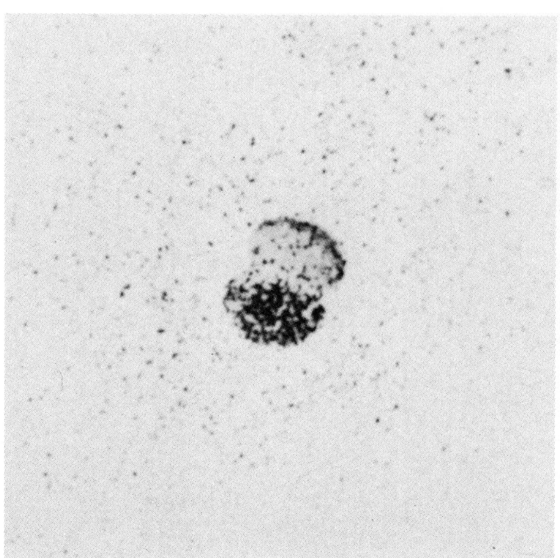

FIG. 5. Cells treated similar to that shown in Fig. 4. The upper cell was in G1 and exhibits no pool or macronuclear label, while the lower cell which was in early macronuclear S shows an extracted pool. Label over the macronucleus is light relative to pool label, suggesting that the exogenous precursor may enter the intracellular thymidine nucleotide pool an appreciable time prior to its incorporation into DNA.

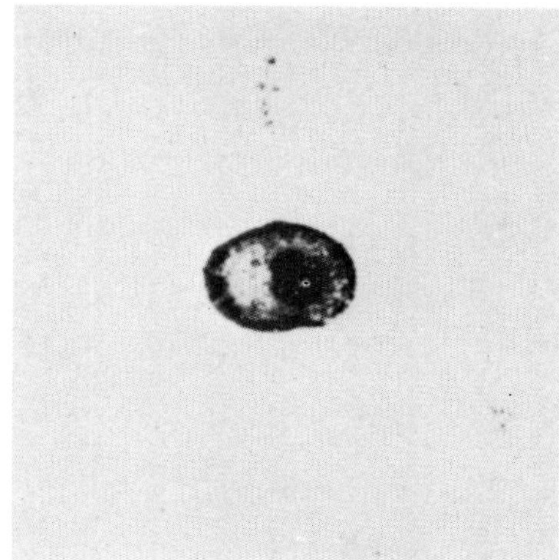

FIG. 6. A cell extracted by acetic acid-alcohol within a delimiting circle marked with a wax pencil (Section II, C, 2). The cell exhibits dispersed acid-soluble materials plus heavy incorporation of label in the acid-insoluble DNA of the macronucleus.

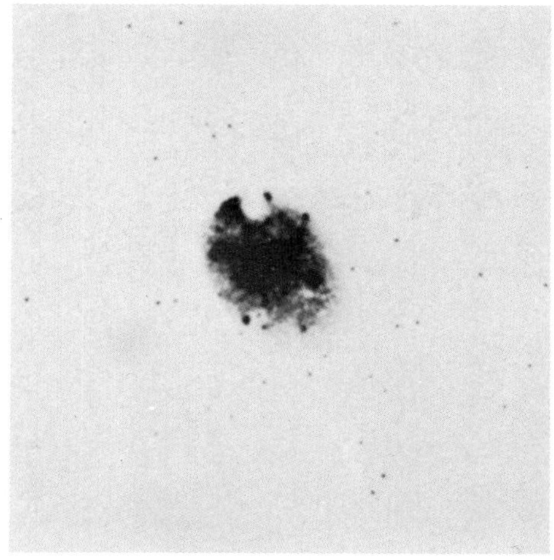

FIG. 7. Cell incubated in thymidine-H^3, washed, and dried previous to coating with dry emulsion (Section II, B). Labeling is localized in the macronucleus. Since water-soluble (Section II, C, 1) or acid-soluble (Section II, C, 2) material can be demonstrated in similar cells, it is concluded that most, if not all, of the soluble thymidine derivative pool is located in the nucleus of the living cell.

References

References marked with asterisk indicate publications in which frozen or frozen-dried sections were used in attempting dry autoradiography. These are cited as a group in the Introduction of this chapter.

*Blank, H., McCarthy, P. L., and DeLamater, E. D. (1951). *Stain Technol.* **26,** 193.
*Branton, D. and Jacobson, L. (1962). *Stain Technol.* **37,** 239.
Canny, M. J. (1955). *Nature* **175,** 857.
Chapman-Andresen, C. (1953). *Compt. Rend. Trav. Lab. Carlsberg, Ser. Chim.* **28,** 529.
*Edwards, L. C. (1956). *Intern. J. Appl. Radiation Isotopes* **1,** 184.
*Edwards, L. C., and Udupa, K. N. (1957). *J. Biophys. Biochem. Cytol.* **3,** 757.
Eisen, V. D., and Harris, F. T. C. (1957). *Nature* **180,** 440.
Feinendegen, L. E., and Bond, V. P. (1962). *Exptl. Cell Res.* **27,** 474.
*Fitzgerland, P. J. (1961). *Lab. Invest.* **10,** 846.
Fitzgerald, P. G., Ord, M. G., and Stocken, L. A. (1961). *Nature* **189,** 55.
*Gage, R. S., and Aronoff, S. (1960). *Plant Physiol.* **35,** 65.
*Gallimore J. C., Bauer, E. C., and Boyd, G. A. (1954). *Stain Technol.* **29,** 95.
Guidotti, G., and Passalacqua, F. (1956). *Experientia* **12,** 117.
*Harris, J. E., Sloane, J. F., and King, D. T. (1950). *Nature* **166,** 25.
*Hassbroek, J. J., Noggle, J. C., and Fleming, A. L. (1962). *Nature* **195,** 615.
*Holt, M. W., and Warren, S. (1950). *Proc. Soc. Exptl. Biol. Med.* **73,** 545.
*Holt, M. W., and Warren, S. (1951). *Proc. Soc. Exptl. Biol. Med.* **76,** 4.
*Holt, M. W., Cowing, R. F., and Warren, S. (1949). *Science* **110,** 328.
*Huang, T. (1960). *Intern. J. Appl. Radiation Isotopes* **8,** 234.
*Mellgren, J. (1952). *Exptl. Cell Res.* **3,** 689.
*Oster, H., Kundt, H. W., and Taugner, R. (1955). *Arch. Exptl. Pathol. Pharmakol.* **224,** 476.
*Russell, R. S., Sanders, F. K., and Bishop, O. N. (1949). *Nature* **163,** 639.
*Smitherman, T. C., Debons, A. F., Pittman, J. A., and Stephens, V. (1963). *Nature* **198,** 499.
*Sterling, C., and Chichester, C. O. (1956). *Stain Technol.* **31,** 227.
*Taugner, R., and Wagenmann, U. (1958). *Arch. Exptl. Pathol. Pharmakol.* **234,** 336.
*Winteringham, F. P. W., Harrison, A., and Hammond, J. H. (1950). *Nature* **165,** 149.
*Witten, V. H., and Holmstrom, V. (1953). *Lab. Invest.* **2,** 368.

Chapter 19

Preparation of Mammalian Metaphase Chromosomes for Autoradiography

D. M. PRESCOTT AND M. A. BENDER

Biology Division, Oak Ridge National Laboratory,[1]
Oak Ridge, Tennessee

I. Introduction

In autoradiographic studies on labeling of deoxyribonucleic acid (DNA), ribonucleic acid (RNA), and proteins of mammalian chromosomes with tritiated precursors, we devised a procedure for preparing cytoplasm-free metaphase chromosomes. The method has the following advantages: (1) several hundred to several thousand sets of chromosomes can be affixed to a single slide, (2) the chromatids are well separated and autoradiographic resolution of label between sister chromatids is excellent, (3) no cytoplasmic layer is present between the chromosomes and the autoradiographic emulsion, thereby increasing the sensitivity and resolution of the autoradiographic detection of incorporated label, and (4) autoradiographic determination of labeled RNA and protein in chromosomes is possible because of the absence of "background" radioactivity from non-chromosomal RNA and protein. The method has been described in principle in a previous paper (Prescott and Bender, 1961); several improve-

[1] Operated by Union Carbide Corporation for the United States Atomic Energy Commission.

ments have been added in the account below, and a few illustrations of autoradiographic results with chromosomes are shown in three accompanying figures. The method has been used mainly with the Chinese hamster "fibroblast"-line CHEF 125 (Prescott and Bender, 1962a), but it works equally well with several other mammalian cell types.

II. Procedure

The cells are cultured in 55 mm Petri dishes, and colchicine is added to the culture (to 10^{-6} M) several hours before isolation of chromosomes. Just before the isolation, the medium is decanted and the cells washed once with balanced salt solution. The solution is then replaced by hypotonic saline (10 to 15% of full-strength, phosphate-buffered Hank's balanced salt solution) at room temperature. An important part of these steps is the complete removal of serum proteins from the culture. After 3 or 4 minutes in the hypotonic medium, cells arrested in metaphase become dislodged from the glass (Axelrad and McCulloch, 1958). They are then concentrated in the center by very gently swirling the medium. The cells remain in good condition in the hypotonic medium at room temperature for about 1 hour. While the Petri dish is being observed under a dissecting microscope, several hundred to several thousand metaphase cells in about 0.5 μl of medium are drawn into the tip of a braking pipette (see Stone and Cameron, this volume, Chapter 8, for description of braking pipettes) controlled by mouth through a rubber tube. The tip of the pipette is dipped into a reservoir of glacial acetic acid, and an equal volume of the acid is drawn up. After 5 to 10 seconds the entire contents are expelled onto a clean microscope slide over which a drop of 3:1 (100% alcohol:acetic acid) fixative has been allowed to spread a few seconds earlier. [We have not found it necessary to use "subbed" slides for autoradiography when using either NTB, NTB-2, or NTB-3 (Kodak) liquid emulsion.] After a few seconds the drop of acetic acid and medium spreads, leaving behind individual, isolated chromosomes and well-spread, partial, and complete complements of chromosomes uncontaminated by cytoplasm. Just as the chromosomes are about to dry, they are rinsed with another drop of the 3:1 fixative. The fixative accumulates along the edges of the slide and should be wiped off with gauze to prevent reflowing of the fixative over the chromosomes. The slides are air-dried and, at this point, are ready for emulsion-coating.

III. Examples and Variation of Technique

A set of chromosomes from a third metaphase after labeling with thymidine-H^3 is shown in Fig. 1. The radioactivity is restricted to one

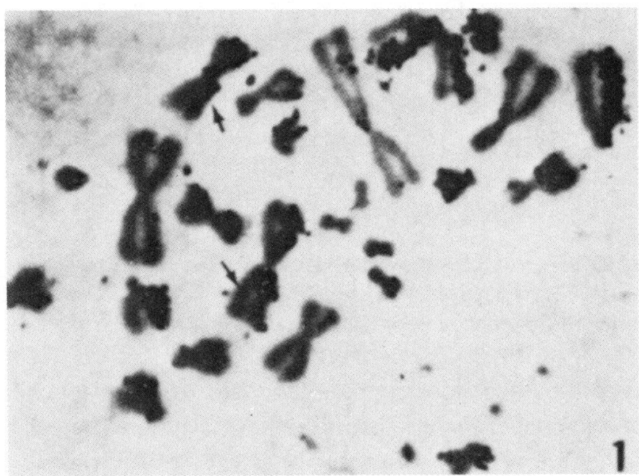

FIG. 1. A complement of chromosomes from a Chinese hamster cell isolated at the third metaphase after incubation in thymidine-H^3. Autoradiographic resolution between chromatids is good. Evidence of sister chromatid exchanges during previous cell cycles are indicated by arrows. For a full discussion of the experiments, see Prescott and Bender (1963) and Marin and Prescott (1963).

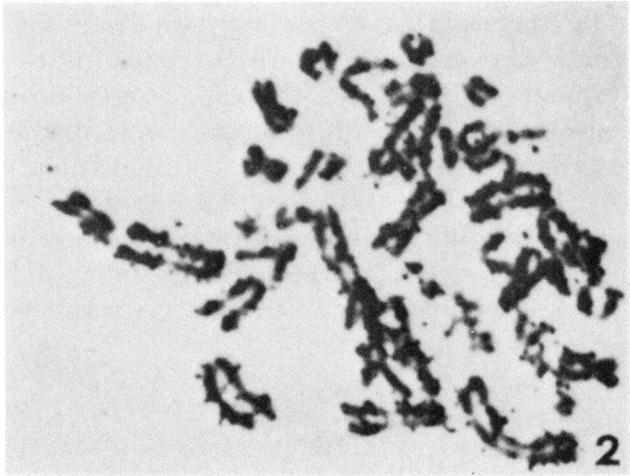

FIG. 2. A complement of chromosomes from a Chinese hamster cell isolated at the first metaphase after incubation in H^3-labeled amino acids.

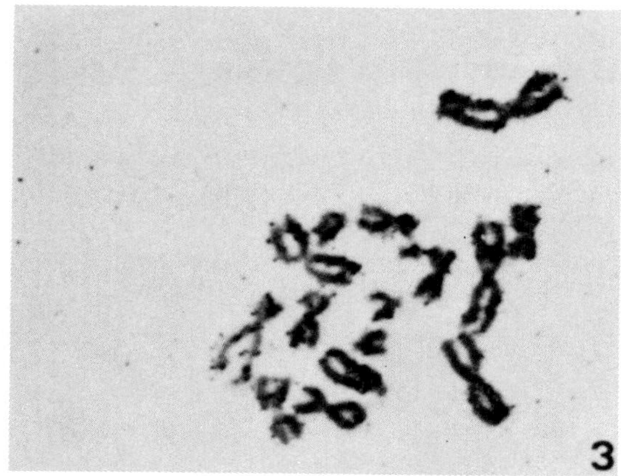

FIG. 3. A complement of chromosomes from a Chinese hamster cell isolated at the first metaphase after incubation in uridine-H^3. The uridine-H^3 was present during the G_2 period, and the radioactivity represents incorporation into RNA only.

chromatid in those chromosomes still containing radioactivity. Since the segregation of labeled DNA is semiconservative, some chromosomes are no longer labeled at the third metaphase but a few sister chromatid exchanges have occurred (see Prescott and Bender, 1963).

Treatment with the acetic acid takes out much of the protein and RNA from the chromosomes. This loss of material was greatly decreased by substituting a short fixation with neutral formalin for the glacial acetic acid treatment and disrupting the cells with 3:1 fixative. The sequence of steps was modified as follows: Living cells are drawn up into the tip of a braking pipette in the usual 0.5 μliter of medium. An equal volume of 10% neutral formalin is drawn up and allowed to remain in the pipette for 60 seconds. Next about 1 μliter of 100% alcohol:acetic acid fixative (3:1) is drawn into the pipette and the whole mixture immediately expelled onto a clean slide covered a few seconds previously with a drop of the alcohol:acetic acid fixative. Subsequent steps are as described for the acetic acid method. Complements of chromosomes in the first metaphase after labeling with H^3-amino acids or uridine-H^3 are shown in Figs. 2 and 3, respectively. For a brief description of these experiments see Prescott and Bender (1962b).

REFERENCES

Axelrad, A. A., and McCulloch, E. A. (1958). *Stain Technol.* **33**, 67.
Marin, G., and Prescott, D. M. (1963). *J. Cell Biol.*, in press.
Prescott, D. M., and Bender, M. A. (1961). *Exptl. Cell Res.* **25**, 222.

Prescott, D. M., and Bender, M. A. (1962a). *Exptl. Cell Res.* **26,** 260.

Prescott, D. M., and Bender, M. A. (1962b). *Abstr. 2nd Ann. Meeting Am. Soc. Cell Biol., San Francisco* p. 146.

Prescott, D. M., and Bender, M. A. (1963). *Exptl. Cell Res.* **29,** 430.

Chapter 20

Methods for Measuring the Length of the Mitotic Cycle and the Timing of DNA Synthesis for Mammalian Cells in Culture

JESSE E. SISKEN

Department of Experimental Pathology,
City of Hope Medical Center,
Duarte, California

I. Introduction

In order to proceed from one division to the next, the proliferating cell must carry out a multitude of activities, a few of which have been observed to occur in some sort of pattern. Thus, for many types of cells, deoxyribonucleic acid (DNA) is synthesized during only a part of interphase which is called the S period. Between the end of telophase and the beginning of S there is a period called G1, and between the end of S and the beginning of prophase a period called G2 (Howard and Pelc, 1953).

In many kinds of studies, for example, those designed to determine the effects of various agents on the growing cell, it is important to be able to measure not only rates of proliferation but also the length of the different parts of the mitotic cycle. In this chapter, we present some methods for measuring intermitotic times of individual cells, average intermitotic times of cultures, and the length of each of the parts of the mitotic cycle. Not all of the known methods are described, and those which are included are covered in varying degrees of detail. While the emphasis is on mammalian cells *in vitro*, many of the techniques outlined in this chapter can be applied equally well to material *in vivo*. Indeed, some of the techniques have been more commonly used and most thoroughly investigated in relation to their employment with cells other than those in culture.

II. Measurements of Intermitotic Times by Time-Lapse Cinemicrography

This technique has been used by many investigators (for example, Olivo and de Lorenzi, 1928; Fell and Hughes, 1949; Jacoby, 1958; Hsu, 1960; Sisken and Kinosita, 1961b; McQuilkin and Earle, 1962), and in each case the cell type, method of culture, and instrumentation was different. The procedure described below is the one used in our laboratory.

A. Setting Up the Cultures

For this type of measurement, the basic requirements of the culture are that enough cells be present to constitute a good sample and that they do not wander out of the microscopic field. This method works best, therefore, with epithelial-like cells which are seeded in clusters. To keep them this way, they are scraped from the inner surface of stock culture bottles with a rubber policeman and drawn into a syringe through a 15-gauge hypodermic needle. Depending on the concentration of cells, 0.01–0.05 ml of this suspension is injected into a pre-assembled Rose chamber (Rose, 1954) which is then filled with medium. The chamber, which contains approximately 5000–10,000 cells per milliliter, is placed in an incubator with the glass cover slip which will be closest to the microscope objective facing down to allow cells to settle and attach to it. Photography can begin 12–24 hours later.

B. Photography and Instrumentation

We use the 16-mm Ciné Kodak Special II camera together with a commercial timer, drive unit, and stand.[1] A standard microscope is used with phase contrast optics, but because of the thickness of the Rose chamber, a long-focus top element has been substituted for the standard one on the substage condensor. We use a Gevaert black and white reversal film[2] which has a fine grain and good contrast and which was designed for time-lapse cinemicrography of cells in culture. Photography is carried out at low magnification at the rate of one frame per minute.

Culture temperature is maintained during photography by means of a thermistor controller[3] which feeds a continuously variable voltage to an infrared heating lamp. Cultures are shielded from the direct rays of the heating lamp by a strip of aluminum foil, and air circulation around the microscope stage is restricted. The bead of the thermistor probe is oiled directly to the outer surface of the cover slip of the Rose chamber approximately 1 cm from the cells to be photographed. Advantages of this kind of temperature control are that the system reaches a very stable ($\pm 0.1°C$) equilibrium quickly, and temperatures other than 37°C can be selected with great precision. Of course, for many experimental situations, other types of temperature regulators serve just as well.

Analyses of the developed film can be carried out on any one of several commercially available 16-mm editing units which measure the length of film between events as observed on a viewer. When the number of frames exposed per unit time during photography is known, film length can be converted to absolute time.

C. Determination of Intermitotic Time

For measurements of intermitotic time, the event which usually marks the beginning or end of a mitotic cycle is the separation of chromosomes at the beginning of anaphase. By recording the intermitotic time for many cells, this method can be used to determine the average intermitotic time of a culture. Necessary conditions for this are: (1) most, if not all, of the cells must be part of the proliferating population; (2) the degree of variability in intermitotic times must be relatively low; and (3) photography must be carried out long enough and with a large enough population so

[1] Electro-Mechanical Development Co., Houston, Texas.

[2] Texas Photo Supply Co., Houston, Texas.

[3] Oxford Laboratories, Redwood City, California.

that a significant number of intermitotic times can be recorded. Care must also be taken to avoid a bias due to cells with longer mitotic cycles not having a chance to divide. One way to do this is to omit data from the last section of the film where cells are followed to the end without dividing. This part of the film is easily delimited if all cells are part of the proliferating population. In addition, the probability of such a bias declines and the size of the sample increases as photography of the colony is prolonged. But then the possibility arises of a change in average intermitotic time due to the action of the cells on the medium. When a vigorous cell line is employed, this problem might be avoided by seeding small numbers of cells in the culture chamber. In our experiments, we use approximately 5000–10,000 cells per milliliter, and judging by changes in pH, at least, the medium remains within a usable range for up to 6 days. While the quality of the medium can also be judged by changes in average intermitotic time, the occurrence of such a change does not necessarily indicate that culture conditions are becoming worse. For example, we observed one line of cells in a pedigree which maintained constant generation times for five cell generations while another line developing from the same parent cell in the same microscopic field had a more variable and increasing generation time (Sisken, 1963b).

III. Measurements of Growth Rates of Cultures

The word "growth" can refer to several phenomena, but for the purposes of this chapter we define growth as increase in cell number and, therefore, an expression of intermitotic time. The methods which have been developed to measure growth rates of cultures depend upon the various possible criteria of growth, and while each is valid and useful for what it measures, as will be pointed out, they are not all equally good indicators of increase. In general, these methods involve analyses of changes in cell numbers, in a chemical constituent of the cells, or in some physical dimension of the culture. Since such methods have often been described in detail, they will be mentioned here only briefly with references to more complete descriptions.

A. Changes in Cell Number

1. Direct Counts

The number of cells per unit volume in an appropriate suspension can be counted either directly in a hemacytometer (Merchant *et al.*, 1960;

Parker, 1961) or with an electronic cell counter (Kuchler and Merchant, 1958; Harris, 1959), which has the advantage of being much faster and of lowering sampling error. While the counts are generally higher than those obtained in a hemacytometer, correction factors can be applied if desired.

2. Plate Counting

Growth rates can also be determined by measuring the time required for the average number of cells per colony to double (Puck and Marcus, 1955). This is done by preparing replicate plates seeded with suspensions of single cells, and, at specific intervals, counting the number of cells per colony in representative plates. This method combines some of the advantages of cinemicrography with those of mass culture techniques so that variability within a population of cells as well as over-all rates of growth can be studied.

3. Nuclear Counting

This method, designed by Sanford *et al.* (1951) for counting L-cells growing on surface substrates, involves digestion of the cytoplasm with citric acid and enumeration of the nuclei thus released with a hemacytometer. Modifications of the original method are cited by Parker (1961). While the presence of multinucleated cells may lead to slightly higher counts, this is not always a disadvantage since certain kinds of cellular activities, such as nuclear syntheses, are perhaps more realistically measured on a per nucleus rather than a per cell basis.

B. Increase in Physical Dimensions

Growth rates of cells have been determined by measuring such culture characteristics as colony area (Ebeling, 1921), packed cell volume (Waymouth, 1956), and total wet and dry weights (see White, 1954). The major difficulty with these methods is the wide variability in each of these characteristics between individual cells, particularly in a proliferating population. While these methods may provide valid indications of growth rates in logarithmic phase cultures (for example, see Kuchler and Merchant, 1958), changes can occur in each of them under certain conditions without any change in cell number.

C. Changes in Chemical Constitution

Many studies have employed increases in certain cell constituents as indications of growth rates. The amount of DNA present is probably the most useful of these criteria (Davidson *et al.*, 1949), but there remain the problems of increases in DNA during interphase, heteroploidy, and polynucleation. Measurements of ribonucleic acid (RNA) and protein have also been made (for example, Salzman, 1959) but their relationships to cell multiplication are even less specific. Again, as in the case of physical dimension, changes in the amounts of each of these substances can occur under certain conditions without any change in cell number so that the usefulness of these methods is largely confined to measuring cell multiplication in logarithmic phase cultures.

IV. Measurement of Parts of Interphase

The usual methods for measuring the various parts of interphase take advantage of the fact that tritiated thymidine, a specific precursor of DNA (Reichard and Estborn, 1951), is stably incorporated only into actively replicating chromosomes (Taylor *et al.*, 1957). As shown below, this phenomenon can be utilized in several different ways.

A. Curve of Labeled Mitoses Following a Pulse Label

1. Basic Procedure

In our laboratory, we usually seed 50,000–100,000 human amnion cells (Fernandes, 1958) on cover slips in Leighton tubes with 2 ml of medium. Twenty-four hours later, after the cells have become attached, approximately 7 ml of medium is added to each tube and the tubes stood upright. This permits the experiment to be carried out in a water bath, where temperature can be more easily controlled. When the cultures are 48–72 hours old, the cover slips bearing the cells are placed in medium containing tritiated thymidine for 10 minutes. When measuring only the G2 period, we use a concentration of 1 μc/ml (specific activity, 1.9 c/mmole). This gives a sufficient number of grains after a 2 week exposure so that there is seldom any question as to whether a metaphase is labeled or not. While this concentration produces no signs of radiation damage in short-term experiments, such damage would occur in studies extended over a longer period. Therefore, if this method is to be used to measure S and G1, the much lower concentration (0.05 μc/ml) recommended by Painter and Drew (1959) should be employed. After exposure to isotope, the cells are rinsed in fresh medium containing unlabeled thymidine (approximately 100 times more concentrated than the isotope solution) and then incubated in their original medium to which a similar concentration of unlabeled thymidine has been added. At specific intervals after this exposure, cells are fixed with ethanol-acetic acid (3:1). (If a fixative such as Bouin's is used, which precipitates protein around the cells, the cover slips should be rinsed in a balanced salt solution prior to fixation.) Approximately 1 hour later the cells are rinsed three times in 100% ethanol and air-dried. Each cover slip is attached to a glass slide cell-side up with Permount or HSR (Painter and Drew, 1959), and when the mounting medium is thoroughly dry, the slides are stained with Feulgen, and stripping film (AR10, Kodak Ltd.) or liquid emulsion applied.

2. Variations on This Procedure

This procedure can be varied at almost every step. For example, to incubate cells under controlled atmospheric conditions, cells can be seeded on cover slips on the floor of Petri dishes. Advantages of this method are that less medium is required and culture conditions tend to be more uniform. There are, however, some disadvantages. Fluctuations in incubation conditions due to the opening and closing of both the incubator and the Petri dishes can occur, as well as physical destruction of cells due to cover slips sliding across each other when the dish is moved.

Suspension cultures, which have the advantage of uniform conditions, can also be used. A sample would be withdrawn, smeared on a slide, and air-dried. Fixation would be done before smearing or just prior to staining or preparing the autoradiograph. The disadvantage of this method is that the media-changing procedures are somewhat more complicated.

3. Analyses of the Slides

Labeled cells should be scored in as well-defined and as short a stage as possible. Because early prophases and late telophases are difficult to identify in cultured cells, metaphases plus anaphases, or, for better precision, only metaphases, are generally counted. Figure 1 is a curve of labeled metaphases as a function of time after exposure to the isotope. The time at which the first labeled cell arrives at metaphase is the minimum time required for a cell to go from the end of the period during which DNA is synthesized through G2 + prophase (P) to metaphase. Since all cells do not pass through this or any other part of the mitotic cycle at identical rates, there is a finite time between the entry of the first labeled cell into metaphase and the time when the maximum percentage of metaphases is labeled: the time at which the 50% level is reached is usually considered the mean time of G2 + P.

The curve reaches a plateau at a maximal value when the cells which had been in S at the time of labeling are passing through mitosis and then descends at the entry into mitosis of G1 cells, i.e., those which had not

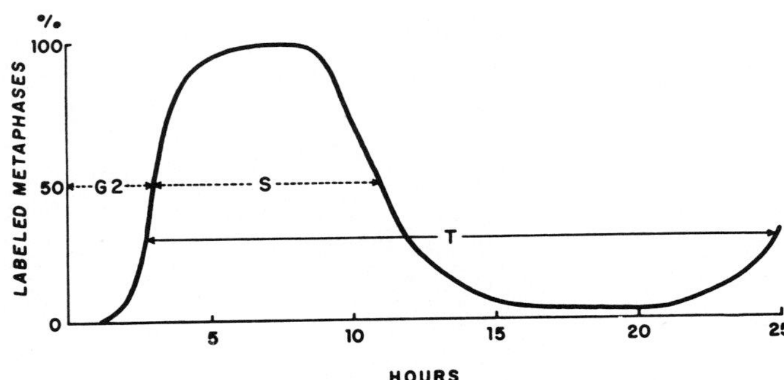

FIG. 1. A hypothetical curve of labeled metaphases vs. time since exposure to tritiated thymidine based on those results published by Painter and Drew (1959). See text for detailed explanation.

yet reached their period of DNA synthesis while tritiated thymidine was available. The width of the plateau is considered a measure of the S period and is usually determined by measuring the distance between the 50% levels on the ascending and descending lines on either side of the plateau (Painter and Drew, 1959; Cattaneo *et al.*, 1961; Lesher *et al.*, 1961; Young, 1962). Johnson (1961), however, measured the S period by determining the time between the first rise of the curve prior to the plateau, and the beginning of the decline after the plateau. While the height of the plateau tends to approach 100% labeled metaphases, it may not actually reach this point due to lagging mitotic or G2 cells and to unlabeled G1 cells which are quick to reach division.

Because some of the cells which had been in S at the time of labeling are arriving in mitosis for a second time, the descending line may approach but not reach a trough at zero before the curve ascends again. The time between comparable points on the two ascending lines is considered a measure of total intermitotic time (Painter and Drew, 1959; Cattaneo *et al.*, 1961; Lesher *et al.*, 1961; Young, 1962). By subtracting S and G2 + P from this total, a measure of G1 is obtained.

4. DISCUSSION OF THE METHOD

In the light of the variability which is always observed between cells, the precision of measurements thus obtained should be accepted with some caution. Considering specifically the measurement of G2 + P, it is apparent that a curve is obtained instead of a straight vertical line because of at least two factors: variations in the length of the G2 + P phase, and variations in the lengths of the times during which cells are in the mitotic stage which is being scored. Since metaphase is generally short, the shape of the curve can be considered the result of the distribution of the lengths of G2 + P. If this distribution is symmetrical, the 50% level of labeled metaphases may well represent the population. However, Stanners and Till (1960) have shown that this is not always the case. A frequency distribution of G2 times derived from one of their experiments was skewed and indicated a modal G2 value of approximately 4 hours while the 50% labeled level was about $5\frac{3}{4}$ hours, a difference, therefore, of approximately 40%. After the plateau, the line is generally found to descend at a shallower rate than the rising line prior to the plateau, as shown in Fig. 1. This is due to the variations in S being added to the variations in G2 and mitotic stages (Quastler, 1960). Studies (Sisken, unpublished) of curves presented by other investigators indicate that the distribution of S values may also have some degree of asymmetry. Since the accuracy of determinations of an average S measured by this method depends upon the symmetry of the distributions of G2 and S times for individual cells, and since the degree of symmetry may vary, the precision of such measurements may also vary.

For similar reasons, this kind of measurement of total intermitotic time and therefore of G1 must also be accepted with some reservation. By measuring the time between comparable points on the two ascending curves, one is measuring the time between the arrival in mitosis of the fastest cells to progress from the end of S through G2 + P to metaphase and the shortest time required for labeled cells to enter metaphase for a second time. Since the second rise is usually much shallower than the first, the intermitotic times thus derived will vary according to what levels on the curve are chosen. If again there is a problem with skewness (see Kubitschek, 1962), measurements thus obtained may not be representative. The accuracy of this method could be checked, however, by performing this experiment in parallel with an experiment to measure growth rates under exactly the same conditions.

B. Estimation of S Based on the Percentage of Cells which Can Be Labeled during an Instantaneous Exposure to Tritiated Thymidine ($T\text{-}H^3$)

The fraction of cells in any given part of the mitotic cycle has often been considered equal to the fraction of the whole mitotic cycle taken up by that period. According to this hypothesis, if 30% of the cells are in S at any given moment, then 30% of the total cycle is taken up by the S period. This would be correct if cells were equally distributed throughout the mitotic cycle. As many investigators have shown, however (Scherbaum and Rasch, 1957; Painter and Robertson, 1959; Stanners and Till, 1960;

Edwards *et al.*, 1960; James, 1960; Johnson, 1961), this is not true in an exponentially growing population and is probably not true in most other growth situations (see Fig. 2). This will, however, hold true for systems

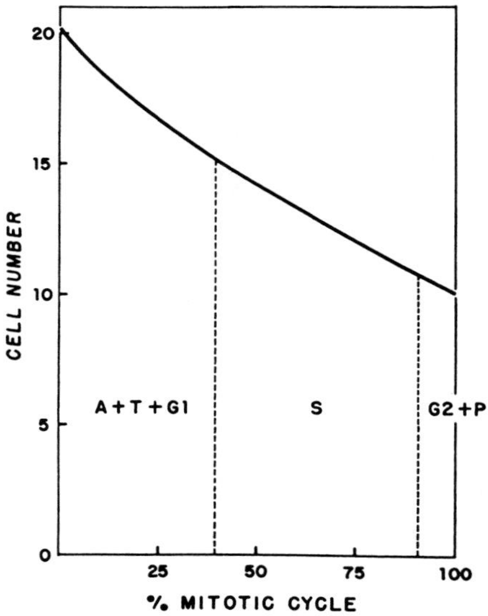

FIG. 2. Frequency distribution of cells in various parts of the mitotic cycle. Abscissa: total intermitotic time in per cent. Ordinate: relative number of cells. The percentage of cells in any part of the cycle is equal to the percentage of the total area under the curve which lies over that part of the cycle. Redrawn from Sisken and Kinosita (1961a) and based upon the curve in Scherbaum and Rasch (1957).

where the increase in cell number is linear and where cells which will not repeat the cycle are distinguishable from those that will immediately after mitosis (Quastler, 1960). As far as this author is aware, only the intestinal epithelium (Quastler and Sherman, 1959) has been shown to have both of these characteristics.

The length of S can be determined from the number of cells synthesizing DNA when the distribution of cells in the different parts of the mitotic cycle, the total intermitotic time, and the period from the end of DNA synthesis to mitosis are known. Johnson (1961) and Stanners and Till (1960) have published equations relating the mean intermitotic time, and the length of S and its place in the cycle, to the fraction of cells which are in S. An example of a graphical determination from a frequency distribution is shown in Fig. 2. Stanners and Till (1960) point out that this method of measuring S is very sensitive to synchronization, a phenomenon which probably occurs often in cultured cells (Sisken, 1963a), and present a method for correcting their calculations for the degree of synchrony.

C. Estimation of S by Determining the Time Required for Cells to Attain Maximum Label

This procedure is based on the supposition that maximal labeling by T-H^3 will occur only in those cells which spend their entire S period in the presence of isotope. Stanners and Till (1960) incubated tissue-cultured cells continuously in the presence of T-H^3 and determined the elapsed time from exposure to isotope to the arrival at metaphase of cells with the maximum amount of label. This gives the length of S + G2 + P. Because different parts of the cycle vary in length and individual cells vary in the rate of incorporation of label, and because of autoradiographic variations, the following procedure was adopted: samples were taken at various times after exposure to isotope, and frequency distributions of the number of grains over metaphases plotted for each sample. Those samples taken 4 hours or more after addition of isotope were found to have normal distributions of grain counts. They then replotted each distribution on probability paper where the peak grain count is given by the 50% intercept of the line; the peak values for each distribution were then plotted as a function of time since exposure to T-H^3. The time at which the curve reaches a maximum is a measure of S + G2 + P. By subtracting the length of G2 + P as determined according to Section IV, A, a value for S can be obtained.

D. Measurements of G1 and S by Combination of Cinemicrography and Autoradiography

The principle of this method (Sisken, 1959; Sisken and Kinosita, 1961a) is to relate the incorporation of tritiated thymidine as determined in an autoradiograph to the place of the cell in the mitotic cycle as determined in a time-lapse cinemicrographic recording. This method is a modification of one by Walker and Yates (1952), who combined cinemicrography with quantitative microphotometry. More recently, Seed (1962) made interferometric determinations of dry mass, photometric measurements of Feulgen staining, and autoradiographic determinations of incorporated tritiated thymidine all in the same cells whose mitotic histories had been recorded by cinemicrography.

1. Procedure

In this method, cultures are prepared as in Section II, A. Photography of a single colony of cells is carried out for about one and a half to two generation times, after which the medium is replaced with a prewarmed medium containing tritiated thymidine (1 μc/ml, 1.9 c/mmole). Photography is resumed for 10 minutes, and the cells fixed by substituting fixative (alcohol-acetic acid, 3:1) for the isotope-containing medium. The chamber is replaced on the microscope stand and a photograph made of the same field. A diamond pencil may be used to scratch a circle around the colony. After an hour of fixation, the cells are washed three times with 100% ethanol, the chamber disassembled, and the cover slip attached with Permount cell-side up on a 2 × 3 glass slide. When the Permount is thororoughly dried, the cells can be put through the Feulgen staining procedure and stripping film or liquid emulsion applied. Autoradiographs are usually developed after a 2 week exposure. Enlarged prints are made of the last frame on the film prior to fixation and of the frame taken after fixation, to help identify the cells in the colony. After locating the scratch with phase contrast, the colony is identified by comparison to the enlarged prints. Each cell in the colony is judged to be labeled or not and, after identification in the last frame of the motion picture film, is traced back to determine when it last divided. Average generation time for the colony is determined from the same film as in Section II.

2. Analysis of the Data and Evaluation of the Method

Individual labeled and nonlabeled cells are plotted against the time since the previous division of these same cells (Fig. 3). Since labeled cells will have been in S for varying amounts of time, their points will fall within a time range. The earliest point is assumed to be from a cell just beginning to synthesize DNA when label was applied, and therefore to indicate the time from division to the beginning of DNA synthesis. Since anaphase and telophase are short, the measure for most purposes may be considered G1. The possibility that by chance none of the labeled cells had *just* entered S might tend to bias G1 slightly toward the long side. However, this is counterbalanced by the fact that since G1 varies widely among individual cells and since our measure of G1 depends on the earliest cell to acquire label, we are probably observing cells from the short side of the distribution of G1 values; therefore, our measure of G1 tends to be somewhat less than the average for the colony. When sample sizes are large, this may even be overbalancing, and occasionally a cell with an extremely short G1 is observed (Sisken and Kinosita, 1961a). Such cells generally stand so far apart from the others in the distribution that they are disregarded.

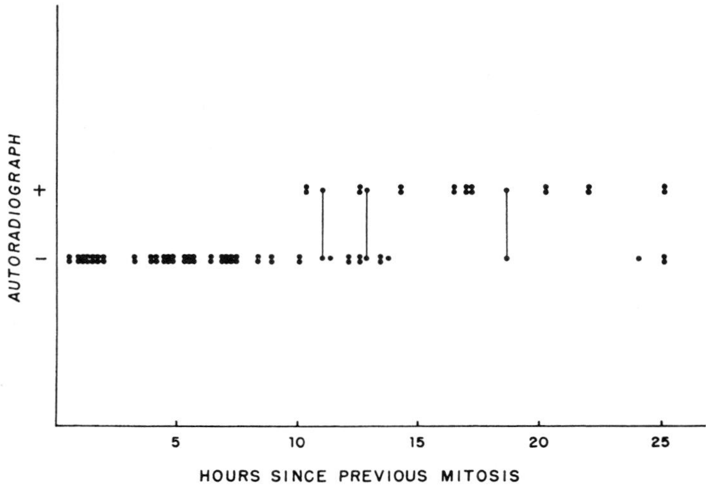

FIG. 3. A plot of whether or not cells are labeled vs. time since their previous division. Vertically paired points are sister cells. Redrawn from Sisken and Kinosita (1961a).

By subtracting G1 from average intermitotic time which is obtained for this same colony of cells by analysis of the motion picture, one obtains a value for S + G2 + P which tends to be slightly longer than the average S + G2 + P. If average G2 + P is measured in a separate experiment according to the method in Section IV, A, and subtracted from S + G2 + P, a value of S can be obtained which also will be on the high side. In an attempt to get a more accurate value for S, we subtracted our value of G1 and the minimum G2 + P (Sisken and Kinosita, 1961a) from a "minimum" intermitotic time (average intermitotic time minus one standard deviation). We were able to predict the number of cells which should be in S (by the method outlined in Section IV, B) for each set of calculations. Since, in these experiments, cells are exposed to isotope for very short periods, the percentage of cells in S could be determined directly in each experiment. For two separate experiments, the observed values were 3.3 and 3.8% lower than those predicted on the basis of the first type of calculation, and 0.5 and 0.9% higher than those predicted on the basis of minimums. Therefore, both methods appear to give acceptable results with the true value of S being somewhere between those thus derived.

Advantages of this method are that the measurement of G1 is direct and not dependent upon experimentally derived values for S and G2, and that it is relatively insensitive to synchrony. Since the history of each of the cells in the culture is recorded on film, other information concerning the cells can also be obtained. For example, analyses of the film will determine whether cells are synchronized (Sisken, 1963), and if the cells are treated with some physical or chemical agent, effects on the morphology of interphases and mitotic cells can be observed as well.

V. Summary

Methods of measuring the intermitotic time of individual cells and the average intermitotic time of cultures by means of time-lapse cinemicrography were described. Some techniques for determining growth rates of cultures were mentioned and their usefulness as indicators of intermitotic time considered briefly. Several methods for measuring G1, S, and G2 were described, all of which are based on the labeling of cells in S with tritiated thymidine.

Acknowledgment

The author's work was supported in part by Grant C-4526 from the National Cancer Institute, U. S. Public Health Service, and Grant G-9850 from the National Science Foundation.

References

Cattaneo, S. M., Quastler, H., and Sherman, F. G. (1961). *Nature* **190,** 923.

Davidson, J. N., Leslie, I., and Waymouth, C. (1949). *Biochem. J.* **44,** 5.

Ebeling, A. H. (1921). *J. Exptl. Med.* **34,** 231.

Edwards, J. L., Koch, A. L., Youcis, Pauline, Freese, H. L., Laite, M. B., and Donalson, J. T. (1960). *J. Biophys. Biochem. Cytol.* **7,** 273.

Fell, H. B., and Hughes, A. F. (1949). *Quart. J. Microscop. Sci.* **90,** 355.

Fernandes, M. V. (1958). *Texas Repts. Biol. Med.* **16,** 48.

Harris, M. (1959). *Cancer Res.* **19,** 1020.

Howard, A., and Pelc, S. R. (1953). *Heredity* **6,** Suppl., 261.

Hsu, T. C. (1960). *Texas Repts. Biol. Med.* **18,** 31.

Jacoby, F. (1958). *In* "Dynamics of Proliferating Tissues" (D. Price, ed.), pp. 16–17. Univ. Chicago Press, Chicago, Illinois.

James, T. W. (1960). *Ann. N. Y. Acad. Sci.* **90,** 550.

Johnson, H. A. (1961). *Cytologia* **26,** 32.

Kubitschek, H. E. (1962). *Exptl. Cell Res.* **26,** 439.

Kuchler, R. J., and Merchant, D. J. (1958). *Univ. Mich. Med. Bull.* **24,** 200.

Lesher, S., Fry, R. J. M., and Sacher, G. A. (1961). *Exptl. Cell Res.* **25,** 398.

McQuilkin, W. T., and Earle, W. R. (1962). *J. Natl. Cancer Inst.* **28,** 763.

Merchant, D. J., Kahn, R. H., and Murphy, W. H., Jr. (1960). "Handbook of Cell and Organ Culture." Burgess, Minneapolis, Minnesota.

Olivo, O. M., and de Lorenzi, E. (1928). *Rend. Reale Accad. Naz. Lincei* **7,** 936.

Painter, R. B., and Drew, R. M. (1959). *Lab. Invest.* **8,** 278.

Painter, R. B., and Robertson, J. S. (1959). *Radiation Res.* **11,** 206.

Parker, R. C. (1961). "Methods of Tissue Culture," 3rd ed. Harper (Hoeber), New York.
Puck, T. T., and Marcus, P. I. (1955). *Proc. Natl. Acad. Sci. U. S.* **41,** 432.
Quastler, H. (1960). *Ann. N. Y. Acad. Sci.* **90,** 580.
Quastler, H., and Sherman, F. G. (1959). *Exptl. Cell Res.* **17,** 420.
Reichard, P., and Estborn, B. (1951). *J. Biol. Chem.* **188,** 839.
Rose, G. G. (1954). *Texas Repts. Biol. Med.* **12,** 1074.
Salzman, N. P. (1959). *Biochim. Biophys. Acta* **31,** 158.
Sanford, K. K., Earle, W. R., Evans, V. J., Waltz, H. K., and Shannon, J. E. (1951). *J. Natl. Cancer Inst.* **11,** 773.
Scherbaum, O., and Rasch, G. (1957). *Acta Pathol. Microbiol. Scand.* **41,** 161.
Seed, J. (1962). *Proc. Royal Soc. London B* **156,** 41.
Sisken, J. E. (1959). *Genetics* **44,** 536.
Sisken, J. E. (1963a) *Nature* **197,** 104.
Sisken, J. E. (1963b). *In* "Cinemicrography in Cell Biology" (G. Rose, ed.). Academic Press, New York.
Sisken, J. E., and Kinosita, R. (1961a). *J. Biophys. Biochem. Cytol.* **9,** 509.
Sisken, J. E., and Kinosita, R. (1961b). *Exptl. Cell Res.* **22,** 521.
Stanners, C. P., and Till, J. E. (1960). *Biochim. Biophys. Acta* **37,** 406.
Taylor, J. H., Woods, P. S., and Hughes, W. L. (1957). *Proc. Natl. Acad. Sci. U. S.* **43,** 122.
Walker, P. M. B., and Yates, H. B. (1952). *Proc. Royal Soc. London B.* **140,** 274.
Waymouth, C. (1956). *J. Natl. Cancer Inst.* **17,** 305.
White, P. R. (1954). "The Cultivation of Animal and Plant Cells." Ronald Press, New York.
Young, R. W. (1962). *Exptl. Cell Res.* **26,** 562.

Chapter 21

Micrurgy of Tissue Culture Cells

LESTER GOLDSTEIN and JULIE MICOU EASTWOOD

Department of Biology, University of Pennsylvania, Philadelphia, Pennsylvania
and
Department of Zoology, University of California, Berkeley, California

I. Introduction

The attractive features of tissue culture (t. c.) cells for the study of a variety of cell biology problems are well recognized (Pomerat and Sevringhaus, 1954). It is not always clear, however, that the value of t. c. cells for studies of certain subcellular structure characteristics is fully appreciated. We should like to call attention to the fact that very few cell types, indeed, can surpass t. c. cells as material upon which micrurgy can be performed *and* that are excellent for the study of much fine cytological detail (see Fig. 1).

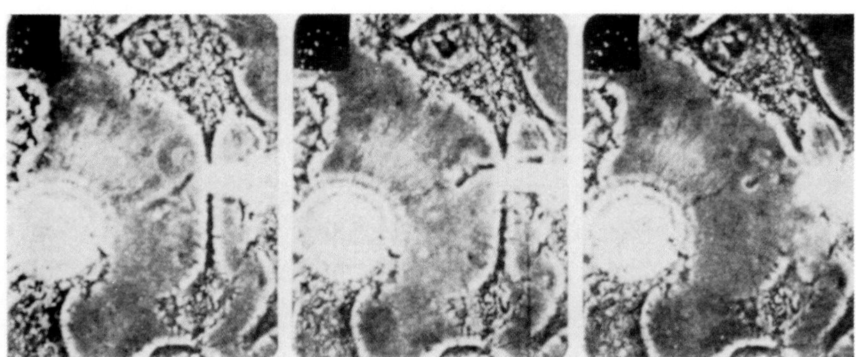

FIG. 1. Three phase-contrast photomicrographs, at 15-second intervals, showing effect of micrurgy on mitochondrial appearance. Human amnion cell is being severed into two parts, a nucleate fragment (upper) and an enucleate fragment (lower). Note particularly the change in contrast of the mitochondria in enucleate fragment. Approximately × 900. (From Goldstein *et al.*, 1960a.)

Very little micrurgy has been performed on t. c. cells; consequently, we shall concentrate here largely on our own experiences in this area. We believe a description of our methods should provide a useful background for those setting out to perform similar or related operations. Successful t. c. cell micrurgy is more dependent, as are many other techniques, on proper equipment than on unusual manual skills; therefore, we shall emphasize the instrumentation needed for satisfactory operations.

II. Equipment

Although it may be possible to perform micrurgy on t. c. cells with equipment that is standard in most cell biology laboratories, the operations are greatly facilitated by the use of specialized apparatus that can be quite complicated (Crocker and Goldstein, 1958). The equipment to be described here, however, is probably the simplest that is consistent with reasonable performance.

A. Microscope

There can be little doubt that for micrurgy of t. c. cells an inverted rather than a standard microscope is preferred. There are several reasons for this choice (see Kopac, 1959). For our purposes, the great value derives from the ability to employ an operating chamber in which the cells are covered with a "lying drop" of medium rather than with a "hanging drop," as would be necessary with a standard microscope.

The use of an inverted microscope permits simplified construction of the operating chamber, simplified access to the chamber interior, and easy maintenance of a seal between the cell medium and the atmosphere. These points will be enlarged upon in Section II,C; let us here cite merely the optical advantages of the inverted microscope in dealing with living cells.

With an inverted microscope one may use a deeper chamber for operations on cells that cannot be made to adhere ("upside down") to an upper surface of a chamber. Similar concerns apply to cells—such as t. c. cells—that can continue to adhere to a surface when inverted but that may become dislodged during operations and fall out of the objective focal range of a standard microscope. This obviously would not happen on an inverted microscope with cells lying on the bottom of the chamber. With the availability of relatively long working distance condensers for phase-contrast microscopy, rather thick chambers may be employed and or abundant space can be provided between the condenser and the operating chamber to permit ready entrance of microtools into the chamber. Another advantage of the inverted microscope is that the lying drop is usually flat at the surface and thus does not induce any serious optical distortion, whereas with a standard microscope and a hanging drop—unless the chamber is very thin (and the drop of medium is squeezed between the upper and lower surfaces of the chamber)—there is likely to be curvature at the drop surface that causes particularly serious distortion in a phase-contrast optical system. A further advantage is that a "lying drop" can be enlarged to cover an unlimited area of the cover glass, thus providing access to many cells in one chamber.

Several problems are encountered even with an inverted microscope, although most of these have been solved to some extent (Crocker and Goldstein, 1958). There are two that deserve particular attention. The first concerns the manner in which the microscope is focused. Once the microtools are in operating position it is urgent that the microscope stage be moved vertically at best only a few microns; thus, one should like to employ a microscope that focuses by movement of the objective rather than the stage. This is particularly necessary for the coarse focus but is not always found with inverted microscopes. When focusing is accomplished by movement of the stage, it is necessary to focus the microscope before introducing the microtools into the chamber, a process that then requires great care.

The second problem derives from the fact that on an inverted microscope only the optics are inverted, while the stage is constructed much the same as on a standard microscope. As a result it is frequently not possible to rotate the objective nosepiece below the microscope stage, thus making it difficult to change magnification after the microtools are in position in the operating chamber. One solution to this problem is to substitute a clutch mechanism (used normally to permit precise centering of objectives) for the rotating nosepiece and to use "shock mounted" objectives that are modified so that the objectives may be shortened by pressure on a lever (Crocker and Goldstein 1958) during exchange of lenses.

B. Micromanipulator

Since it is likely that most t. c. cell micrurgy will be performed on cells that grow firmly attached to glass, the tool requirements will be such that probably any good micromanipulator will serve for the operations. This is true because in a situation where a cell is attached to the substratum no tools are needed to hold the cell in position, a circumstance that greatly simplifies the operating requirements. Thus, for cell-cutting procedures (see Section III,C) only one microtool is necessary and the motion used is relatively simple, permitting one to employ successfully even a manipulator that imparts a motion to the tool by direct mechanical connections. Most of the latter type provide a motion in the same direction as that in which the operator's hand moves, with the result that the image in a compound microscope moves in a direction opposite to that of the operator's hand; this makes the learning of complex motions, but not of the simple cutting motion mentioned above, difficult.

Unquestionably, a micromanipulator that does not have direct mechanical connections between control levers and microtools—such as the de Fonbrune (1949) and the Ellis (1962)—provides greater flexibility in many respects and may also be more comfortably mounted for the operator (see Crocker and Goldstein, 1958). These instruments, because of their indirect controls, also do not transmit vibrations from the hand of the operator. Unfortunately, however, the de Fonbrune instrument (at least as furnished in the United States) is poorly constructed and the Ellis micromanipulator is not commercially available.

Our experience has been largely with the de Fonbrune manipulator, upon which we have made several modifications. To make the manipulator head more stable, a heavy steel base was clamped to the bottom of the original base. To provide greater sensitivity of the pneumatic fine controls, the volume of the pneumatic systems was increased by the incorporation of flasks into the tubes leading from the control pistons to the aneuroid diaphragms of the manipulator head. To overcome, to some extent, imprecision in the movement of the microtools, adjustments were made in the wire connections of the yoke uniting the 3 aneuroid diaphragms, the manipulator head was leveled carefully, and efforts were made to select front-end aneuroid diaphragms that provided strictly horizontal movements. (For further details of these modifications see Crocker and Goldstein, 1958.) The quality of the horizontal coarse controls can be improved by substituting one of a variety of microscope mechanical stages for the mechanism furnished with the de Fonbrune instrument.

If complicated operating motions are not required instruments such as the Zeiss and Leitz micromanipulators (whose quality of manufacture is high) may be desirous, particularly for the initial positioning of the microtools with the "coarse" controls. It may also be possible to construct relatively simple remote controls for these instruments to move the control sticks and thus overcome most of their drawbacks.

It seems probable to us that any micromanipulator that provides a reasonable reduction of motion from the operator's hand and that can provide smooth and relatively vibrationless movement can be adapted for operations that require only simple motions. More complicated operations, such as those involved in nuclear transplantations, might require several sophisticated instruments at one time; but, in any event, such complicated operations do not appear to be practical for critical experiments on t. c. cells at this time, although Kopac (1959) reports some progress in this direction.

C. Operating Chamber

Probably any one of a great number of differently designed culture chambers can be successfully used in t. c. cell micrurgy, but only one, which we consider highly satisfactory, will be described. The chamber that we have used has proven to be practical and versatile enough (in its unmodified version) for a variety of uses other than micrurgy; it is the so-called Rose chamber (Rose, 1954). The modified version that we have employed is shown disassembled in Fig. 2. The chamber is assembled as follows: The cover glass is placed on top of the bottom plate, the sponge rubber gasket (upper right) is placed on top of the cover glass, the top plate (right) is placed on top of the gasket, and finally the complete unit fastened together with the 4 screws. An assembled chamber is pictured in Figs. 3 and 4. When in use we find on the interior the following: a layer of cells growing on the cover glass, approximately 2 mm of growth medium above the cells, and covering the growth medium approximately 1 mm of sterile mineral oil, which serves to reduce evaporation and the passage of gases and air-borne

FIG. 2. Photograph of disassembled operating chamber. Upper left: bottom cover glass; upper right: rubber gasket; lower left: bottom plate; lower right: top plate; and bottom row: 4 screws for holding assembled unit together. (Courtesy Dr. T. T. Crocker.)

FIG. 3. Photograph of an assembled operating chamber without any contents. Cutting microtool is shown in approximately normal position. (Courtesy Dr. T. T. Crocker.)

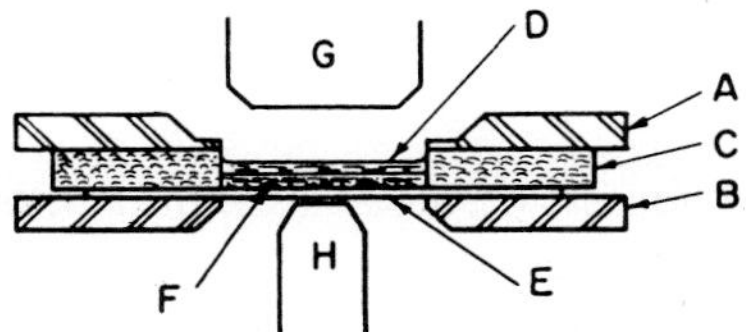

FIG. 4. Diagram of the cross section of an assembled operating chamber with contents. (A) Top plate; (B) bottom plate; (C) rubber gasket; (D) layer of mineral oil; (E) bottom cover glass (shown too thick); (F) cell growth medium; (G) microscope condenser; and (H) microscope objective.

materials between the culture and the atmosphere. (It is possible, of course, to operate in a well-equilibrated, germ-free, gassed, and humified box or room but this would be a rather expensive arrangement.[1])

Note that the chamber has been modified for operation purposes from the original Rose design in the following respects: (1) the top cover glass has been removed and replaced by a layer of mineral oil (which is penetrable by microtools), and (2) part of the gasket and part of the top plate have been cut away on one side to allow easy entrance of the microtool into the operating area (see Figs. 2 and 3). In practice the cells are prepared for the operations by growth in the standard Rose chamber with the only modification being the presence of the altered gasket. When the cells are ready, the chamber is partially disassembled, the top cover glass removed, the standard top plate replaced by the modified version, and a layer of sterile mineral oil placed on top of the growth medium (which may also have been exchanged for a fresh or modified medium).

Aside from facilitating the operation procedures, the chamber construction also permits the handling of the cell-carrying cover glass in subsequent manipulations, such as those used in cytochemical processing. The position of the experimental cells can be marked by scratching the underside of the cover glass with a diamond point "objective" immediately following an operation while the chamber is still in position on the microscope stage. This mark then allows for simplified location of specific cells after the chamber has been disassembled.

[1] In subsequent work it was found that complete removal of the mineral oil prior to fixation and other cytochemical processing of the cell was difficult to accomplish; consequently, modifications were developed to eliminate the need for an oil seal. These included affixing a cover glass with petrolatum to the *top* surface of the top chamber plate until immediately before the microtool was to be introduced into the chamber and replacing this cover glass immediately after micrurgy was completed (usually within 1 hour of the removal of the top cover glass). Further incubations were carried out in a gassed and humified incubator. Under such conditions, with the operations performed at room temperature, evaporation and contamination are insignificant even in the complete absence of antibiotics (Crocker and Eastwood, 1963).

D. Microtools

A variety of microtools can be made, and many have been described by de Fonbrune (1949). These, however, need not be considered in detail here because most are intended primarily for other kinds of operations. What concerns us are the specific requirements for the apparatus and operations discussed in this chapter. For these purposes, and assuming that only one microtool will be used during any operation, the needs are quite simple.

A glass rod, about 1–2 mm in diameter, is bent twice as shown in Figs. 3 and 5. The bends can be performed with a microburner (gas) and are

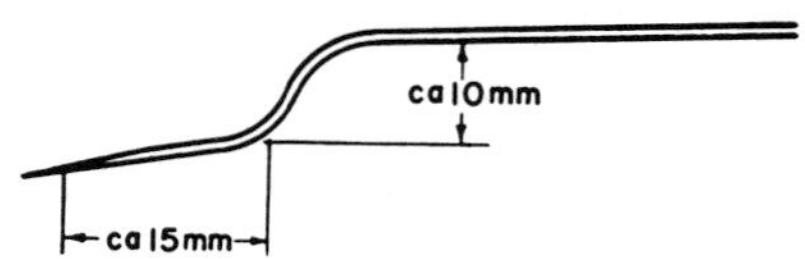

FIG. 5. Diagram of side view of microtool for cell micrurgy.

necessary to assure that the microtool does not come in contact with the microscope condenser and that the tip of the operating tool does not enter the cell chamber at too steep an angle. Should more than one tool be required it may be necessary to make an additional bend or two in a different plane so that the tools do not collide with one another during the operations. After the bends are made further work on the operating tip is performed on a microforge (preferably the de Fonbrune type).

For our work we have been concerned only with cutting cells in two, and for this purpose the operating tip should be pulled out to a diameter of about 2–5μ and a length of about 10–20μ on the microforge. The tool should be constructed to enter the chamber in such a fashion that the tip forms an angle with the cover glass of about 5–10°.

E. Incubation Equipment

If an operation can be completed within a few minutes, it is probably unnecessary to be concerned about temperature control since the sojourn at room temperature would be quite brief. Should the operation require relatively lengthy intervals it may be desirous (although not always) to maintain a controlled temperature throughout the experiment.

Maintenance of a suitable incubation temperature can be achieved in a number of ways; 3 general methods will be cited. One may carry out the entire incubation and operation in a constant temperature room. This is by far the simplest if such a room is available, but the incubation temperature for mammalian tissue culture cells is likely to cause discomfort to the experimenter. Maintenance of the complete operating apparatus—*sans* the operator—in a constant-temperature box also can be effective but such an arrangement is frequently rather awkward and introduces several obstacles to the manipulations. Not so restricting but slightly difficult to construct and providing somewhat less than ideal temperature regulation is an arrangement for heating the microscope stage, which in turn heats the operating chamber (Crocker and Goldstein, 1958). With a small thermistor (wired into the electrical system of the temperature control apparatus) inside the operating chamber to regulate the heat output, the system can be made to work satisfactorily without discomforting the operator or making access to the cells and tools awkward.

We believe that, if suitable experimental controls are maintained, in most cases no temperature regulation is necessary for operations of even 2 to 3 hours outside the incubator. Perhaps a reduced environmental temperature even may be beneficial in that a lowered metabolism may minimize surgical "trauma."

III. Handling of Cells

Having discussed the apparatus needed for micrurgy of t. c. cells, let us now turn to matters concerned with the handling, preparation, and processing of the cells themselves.

A. Preparation of Cells Suitable for Micrurgy

As far as we are aware the only extensive micrurgy that has been performed on t. c. cells has been that of cutting a cell in two, one part with a nucleus and the other without (Goldstein *et al.*, 1960a). Many other operations can be imagined, but it is likely that few will be widely employed until improved preparative methods are available or until special cell strains are found or developed. In the light of these circumstances, it appears judicious to consider only those preparative methods for cells that can be reasonably severed into two fragments.

It was found early that to recover viable enucleate and nucleate fragments from an operation, a cell could only be cut through a segment less than 5μ wide. [This is true for mammalian cells but may not be for others, such as amphibian cells (Wachtel and Ornstein, personal communication, 1957).] Thus, the ideal dissectable cell is one that is dumb-bell shaped (see Fig. 1). To achieve a dumb-bell shape, even of a small proportion of the cells in a culture, it is necessary to do the following.

Cells must be cultured at a sufficiently low concentration to prevent growth of a confluent sheet, since crowding tends to compress the cells and inhibit movement. It is this movement that appears to cause the cells to form dumb-bell shapes, probably by differential adhesion to the glass. For a similar reason the cells should be thoroughly dispersed when inoculated into a growth chamber so as to prevent the formation of compact clumps of cells.

Normal cultures of HeLa and human amnion cells when treated as above produce a low proportion of "cuttable" cells, and conceivably other cell strains may produce higher proportions without additional manipulations. We were able to increase considerably the number of "cuttable" cells in a chamber by reducing the serum content of the medium the day before the planned micrurgical operations. Trypsin dispersed cells were planted at a concentration of 4000–6000 cells per milliliter in a medium containing 20% human serum in medium 199 and Hank's balanced salt solution; after 2 days the old medium was exchanged for fresh medium and after an additional 1–3 days, depending on when the micrurgy was to be performed, the medium was exchanged for one containing only 10% human serum. This method enabled us to locate 20–30 "cuttable" cells in suitable orientation for micrurgy within one chamber in a relatively brief time period.

B. Operating Medium

Since the chamber, when ready for micrurgical operations, is no longer tightly closed against the atmosphere, some modifications of the chamber contents must be made. (We have already noted that a layer of mineral oil can be used to "replace" the removed top cover glass, but this may be insufficient for the needs of the system.) Even with a layer of mineral oil over the chamber medium, a fair degree of gas exchange may occur between the medium and the atmosphere, and one cannot, therefore, rely completely on such commonly used buffers as bicarbonate for pH control. We have found (Goldstein *et al.*, 1960a) that glycyl-glycine at 10^{-3} M serves reasonably well for a few hours in the maintenance of the pH at about 7.4.

Because of the more exposed condition of the operating chamber contents, it also has been found worthwhile to increase the concentration of penicillin and streptomycin in the medium when possible (Goldstein *et al.*, 1960a). Microbial contamination was rarely a problem when these higher concentrations of the antibiotics were used.

C. Cutting of Cells

The operation for cutting a cell in two is remarkably simple. After the tip of the microtool is positioned (with coarse and fine micromanipulator controls) in the microscope field a few microns above the cell layer, the microscope stage is moved until a cell suitable for cutting is located. The tool is then lowered with the fine micromanipulator control until it comes in contact with the cytoplasmic strand of the dumb-bell shaped cell, and the strand is severed either by pressing it between microtool and cover glass or by drawing the microtool across the cytoplasmic strand (see Fig. 6). The cell is then in two parts.

D. Marking Location of Cells

Under ordinary conditions the cell fragments of interest will be fairly closely surrounded by numerous uncut cells, a circumstance that makes it rather difficult to relocate the experimental fragments when only periodic observations are made, since the fragments and the untreated cells are in constant movement and change orientation with respect to one another. Furthermore, this difficulty is compounded when numerous experimental cell fragments are to be observed in one operating chamber. To facilitate relocation of cut cell fragments two steps are taken:

(1) All the untreated cells within approximately 50–100μ of the cell fragments are swept away from the field with a microtool, leaving the experimental fragments very conspicuous in the midst of a clear area of the chamber.

(2) The above area is marked by a circle scratched (with a microscope "objective" that has a piece of diamond in place of the lens) on the underside of the cover glass. This mark also serves well to help locate the cell fragments for observation on another microscope after the cover glass has been removed and processed for cytochemical purposes.

E. Fixation and Cytochemical Processing

Should examination of fixed cells be desired, the operating chamber may be easily disassembled and the cover glass immersed in a fixation medium. Any further processing for cytochemical purposes may be carried out in the usual fashion with only the caution that the cover glass be handled with care because of its fragility.

F. Some Applications of Tissue Culture Cell Micrurgy

A few examples of experiments in t. c. cell micrurgy will be cited here to give a view of progress in this field. It will be a brief section since advances

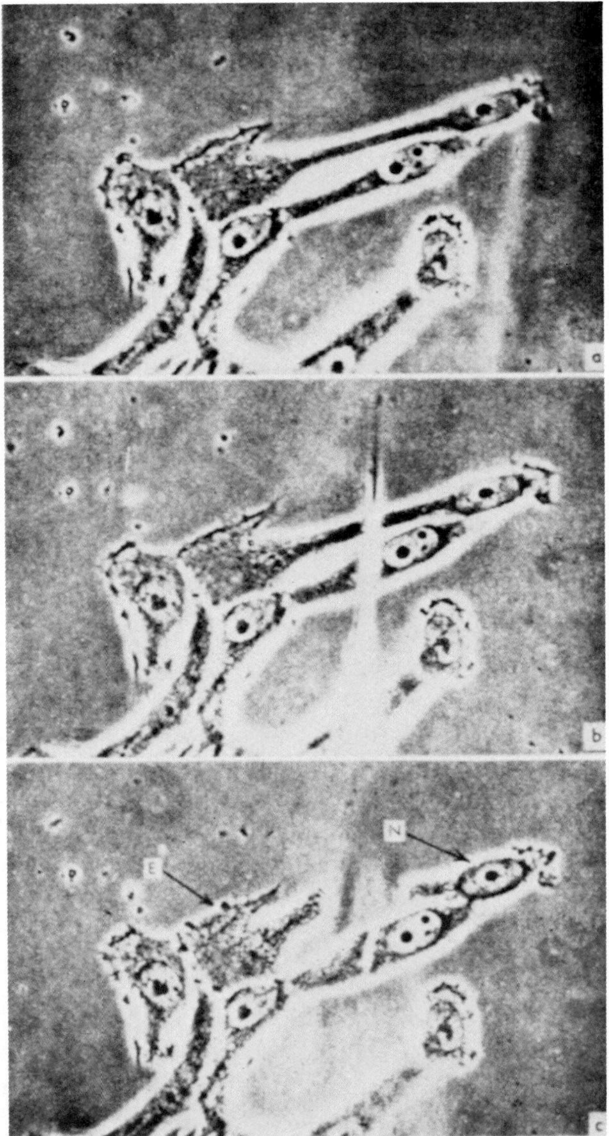

FIG. 6. Three phase-contrast photomicrographs, at 15 second intervals, demonstrating cell micrurgy operation as the microtool is pulled across cytoplasmic strand. (N) Nucleate fragment; (E) enucleate fragment. Approximately × 1000. (From Goldstein *et al.*, 1960a.)

have been scanty, largely because technical development has been relatively meager.

Early attempts at microdissection of t. c. material were performed by Chambers and Fell (1931) working on several cell types. They punctured, prodded, tore, and cut various parts of cells and studied the responses of the cells and cell parts to these insults. From this pioneering work only purely descriptive observations were made and few meaningful generalizations could be developed.

Duryee and Doherty (1954) reported some preliminary experiments with amphibian t. c. cells in an effort to learn something of their physical properties. Apparently little knowledge of general usefulness has been obtained subsequently, since further evidence has not been published.

Kopac (1959) also described some preliminary micrurgical experiments with t. c. material but again there apparently has not been sufficient progress to warrant detailed publication. Kopac's experiments are potentially very exciting, for they represent the first promising attempts to transplant *sub*nuclear components from one cell to another or from one part of a cell to another.

Goldstein *et al.* (1960a) carried out an extensive study of the microscopic behavior of micrurgically produced enucleate cell fragments and found that they behaved much like normal cells in many respects. The enucleate fragments showed normal motility, motion of cell surfaces, and pinocytosis but survived for only about 20 hours. There were some intracellular changes, the most marked being the appearance of a new structure characterized as a "granular ring."

In further studies from the same laboratory (Goldstein *et al.*, 1960b) an investigation was made of some metabolic activities in enucleate cell fragments. These were able to incorporate radioactive amino acids (presumably into protein) at a rate comparable to that of normal whole cells but were unable to incorporate any of a number of radioactive ribonucleic acid precursors that were available in the culture medium.

Crocker and Eastwood (1963) have examined the infection with ornithosis virus of micrurgically produced enucleate cell fragments and discovered that viral attachment, penetration, growth, and some maturation is possible in the absence of a cell nucleus. The synthesis of viral deoxyribonucleic acid was also observed, thus demonstrating that viral replication is not directly dependent on the host's genetic apparatus.

IV. Conclusion

Given the proper equipment, various kinds of t. c. cell micrurgy can be relatively straightforward operations; some operations, such as nuclear transplantation, seem impossible by present methods. The most difficult part of all the methodology appears to be microtool manufacture, but even this is relatively simple compared to the microtool requirements for other purposes. The important simplifying feature of t. c. cells for micrurgy is their ability to adhere well to a glass substratum so that no accessory tools are necessary to hold the cells in position during microdissection (although this advantage may be lost in mitotic cells, which do not adhere well to glass during division). The biggest handicap to successful t. c. cell microdissection probably is the difficulty involved in getting cells in a condition suitable for the operations. It does not seem possible to perform operations on t. c. cells as readily as on other cells, e.g., amebae and *Acetabularia*, but this deficiency is compensated for by the greater suitability of tissue culture material for a variety of cytological observations.

References

Chambers, R., and Fell, H. B. (1931). *Proc. Roy. Soc. (London) Ser. B* **109,** 380.
Crocker, T. T., and Eastwood, J. M. (1963). *Virology* **19,** 23.
Crocker, T. T., and Goldstein, L. (1958). *Mikroskopie* **12,** 315.
de Fonbrune, P. (1949). "Technique de Micromanipulation." Masson, Paris.
Duryee, W. R., and Doherty, J. K. (1954). *Ann. N. Y. Acad. Sci.* **58,** 1210.
Ellis, G. W. (1962). *Science* **138,** 84.
Goldstein, L., Cailleau, R., and Crocker, T. T. (1960a). *Exptl. Cell Res.* **19,** 332.
Goldstein, L., Micou, J., and Crocker, T. T. (1960b). *Biochim. Biophys. Acta* **45,** 82.
Kopac, M. J. (1959). *In* "The Cell" (J. Brachet and A. E. Mirsky, eds.), Vol. I, pp. 161–191. Academic Press, New York.
Pomerat, C. M., and Sevringhaus, E. L., eds. (1943). *Ann. N. Y. Acad. Sci.* **58,** 971–1326.
Rose, G. G. (1954). *Texas Rept. Biol. Med.* **12,** 1074.

Chapter 22

Microextraction and Microelectrophoresis for Determination and Analysis of Nucleic Acids in Isolated Cellular Units

J.-E. EDSTRÖM

Department of Histology, University of Gothenburg, Gothenburg, Sweden

I. Introduction

The determination of nucleic acid content and base composition by the biochemical methods described in this paper is performed on specific cellular structures isolated by microdissection. The nucleic acids are extracted from these structures and analyzed under defined physico-chemical conditions—the essential principles of biochemical work. For the determination of nucleic acid content (Edström, 1958; Pigon and Edström, 1959; Edström and Kawiak, 1961), this approach has necessitated some sacrifice in sensitivity as compared with that attainable with direct photometric measurements on histological sections, but has the distinct advantage in that absolute amounts can be quantitatively determined. The methods are nevertheless suitable for work on the single cell scale (with particularly favorable material even the single gene scale).

Fresh or frozen-dried tissue, advantageous in some cases to minimize postmortem artifacts, may be used by the present methods. Usually, fixed tissue is preferred as it is possible with suitable procedures to preserve the nucleic acids quantitatively and it is advantageous to be able to resort to simple preparative procedures as well as to store the material in paraffin blocks.

For the determination of nucleic acid base composition, microelectrophoresis is employed (Edström, 1956, 1960a). The technical basis of the electrophoretic separation of nucleic acid components in small amounts is the reduction in length, width, and thickness of the supporting medium, with the traditional basis for the evaluation of the individual compounds, ultraviolet light absorption, being retained. This means that the increased sensitivity is obtained by measuring the absorption in smaller areas. However, scaling down the electrophoretic procedure by reducing the dimensions must be accompanied by certain modifications in technique because of the resulting steepening of the concentration gradients of the migrating compounds. Compared to traditional systems the concentration changes per unit length are increased due to the action of two factors: (1) the reduction in linear dimensions causes an inversely proportional increase in the slope of the concentration gradients; and (2) the concentration (weight of the migrating compound per unit volume of the supporting medium) is increased in proportion to the reduction in thickness of the supporting medium. Combined, these two factors give rise to gradients which are of the order of 25,000 times steeper than in traditional zone electrophoresis. This is the main methodological consequence resulting from the reduction in linear dimensions in electrophoresis, and the micro-electrophoretic technique consists, in principle, of the practical measures for handling and preserving such gradients. The term *microphoresis* was introduced for electrophoresis in a scale involving bases and nucleotides in amounts of about 10^{-10} gm (Edström, 1956).

The methods whereby ribonucleic acid (RNA) and deoxyribonucleic acid (DNA) content are determined in microscopic tissue units may perhaps be considered as side products of the elaboration of the microphoretic technique. In these cases the optical density of the extracts in ultraviolet light is determined directly after they have been evaporated to dryness and redissolved to form lens-shaped droplets.

II. Methods

A. Preparation of the Biological Material

The cellular units used for microchemical investigation may be isolated either from fresh or fixed tissue, if not initially free like blood cells and protozoa. For fresh tissue, freehand manipulation is usually employed, whereas dissection of fixed tissue is best carried out with the aid of a micromanipulator. For freehand isolation the technique will vary depending upon the type of material. Fresh spinal ganglion cells with or without capsules were isolated by Pigon (Hydén *et al.*, 1958; Edström and Pigon, 1958) in 0.25 *M* sucrose with the aid of iridectomy scissors and a scalpel. Hydén uses stainless steel microspatules to lift nerve cells and glial tissue from fresh brain sections with the aid of a binocular dissecting microscope (Hydén and Pigon, 1960). Zajicek and Zeuthen (1956) found that the tendency of fresh tissue units (in their case megakaryocytes) to stick to glass surfaces and get lost could be prevented by coating the glass with agar.

By treating isolated neurons with phenol and ethanol, Hydén and Egyhazi (1962) obtained cytoplasm-free nuclei which subsequently were individually collected and pooled for RNA base analysis. Freehand procedures are used to isolate dipteran giant chromosomes (Edström and Beermann, 1962) as well as various nuclear components, including lampbrush chromosomes from urodele oocyte nuclei (Edström and Gall, 1963) for RNA analysis.

The use of fixed tissue has several advantages. So far only Carnoy and formalin fixation have been employed (see Appendix 1.1 and 1.2); the former is particularly useful. In several tests it has been shown that Carnoy fixation preserves RNA if carried out under controlled conditions and short fixation times (Edström, 1953; Hartleib *et al.*, 1956; Lagerstedt, 1957; Edström *et al.*, 1961). These types of fixation allow the subsequent enzymic removal of all RNA. For DNA, only Carnoy-fixed material has been used.

Embedded material can be stored for months without any measurable fall in RNA content. For the isolation of cellular units, sections of a suitable thickness are cut (thick enough to include whole structures, i.e., up to

100–120μ). The sections are mounted on glycerol-egg albumen (1:1)-coated cover glasses (12 × 30 × 0.17 mm) and flattened by heat. The use of water is avoided. The cover glasses can be stored in labeled test tubes or fastened with two strips of tape onto a conventional glass slide, on which identification data can be applied.

Prior to dissection with the micromanipulator, a section is deparaffinized with chloroform for 5 minutes and transferred to successive baths of 100% ethanol and 0.01 *N* acetic acid, 5 minutes in each. One must blot the hydrated section to remove excess acetic acid. This leaves the section fully hydrated and covered with a thin liquid layer. In the case of units previously isolated freehand and placed on cover glasses, and which one wants to arrange further with the micromanipulator, it is necessary to use a micropipette to wet the units individually.

B. Micromanipulation

A cover glass with a section or other biological material is placed, with the material facing downwards, over a groove in a thick slide. A space is formed which is surrounded on four sides by the groove and the cover glass and is accessible from two opposite sides. This space is filled with liquid paraffin (Paraffin liquid for injections, E. Merck A. G., Darmstadt, Germany, No. 7162) which is held in place by capillary force. This arrangement has been adopted from de Fonbrune (1949) and is called an oil chamber (see Fig. 1). Arranging a cover glass over the groove without any

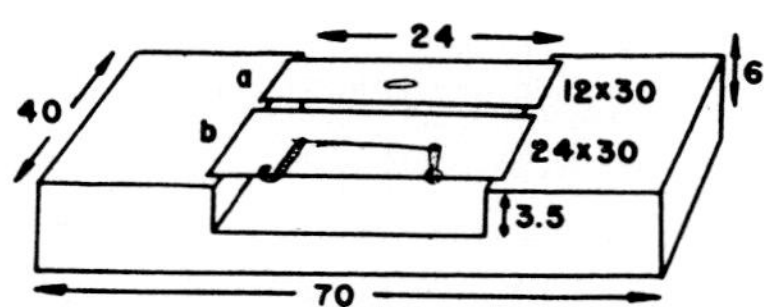

FIG. 1. A combined chamber for microdissections consisting of a paraffin-filled part (a) and a dry part with a fiber and buffer bridges (b). Dimensions in millimeters. From Edström (1956).

liquid paraffin forms a dry chamber, which is often useful. Finally, one may combine in the same grooved slide a chamber filled with liquid paraffin and a dry chamber (combined chamber). In such a case it is necessary to keep the two cover glasses apart, leaving about a millimeter between the edges to prevent the paraffin from spreading from one to the other.

For isolating tissue units from a hydrated section in an oil chamber, two dissecting needles (see Appendix 2.1) directed by the de Fonbrune micromanipulator (Etablissements Beaudouin, 1 et 3 rue Rataud, Paris

5e) are used. The microscope used in combination with the micromanipulator is a Zeiss Standard microscope equipped with phase contrast optics, phase contrast usually being preferred to other kinds of optical systems during the micromanipulation.

The oil chamber can be conveniently extended with a second clean cover glass marked on the upper side with India ink, on which to place and keep isolated samples. Small hydrated tissue pieces become more transparent after a time in the oil chamber, due to the loss of water. It is therefore essential to have their locations well marked. In other respects the drying is advantageous since it permits the storing of the isolated samples.

For work with two needles attached to the same micromanipulator receiver, the left hand is used for the gross vertical adjustment screw on the stand of the receiver to change the vertical position of both needles, and the right hand to move the manipulator lever for three-dimensional control of the movable needle. The second needle, connected to the encasement of the receiver and which cannot be manipulated independently, is mainly used for holding.

C. Extraction

Micropipettes can be used in the oil chamber and can be operated by a connection via a rubber tube to a 2-ml air-filled syringe with a two-way stopcock. The second outlet of the stopcock permits the intake or ejection of air (see Appendix 3.1). Two kinds of pipettes are used, one for extractions and hydrolysis and another for obtaining measured volumes. The former kind, with a tapering distal end, is used when only the order of the volumes handled need be known, in which case a rough volume calibration can be done. A column of oil is expelled into a drop of water or glycerol and the diameter of the resulting spherical oil drop is measured, as well as the length of the oil column in the pipette. For standardization and testing of various procedures it is often necessary to transfer accurately determined volumes for which a pipette with a distal nontapering part of several hundred microns and a diameter of 10–12μ is used (see Appendix 2.2).

Prior to the enzymic extraction of RNA, the free nucleotides must be removed. Units that are isolated from fresh tissue or collected freehand onto glass cover slips are treated with cold 1 *N* perchloric acid (0°–4°C), usually for 5 minutes. The perchloric acid is removed with 0.01 *N* acetic acid in three changes during 5 minutes under agitation. The cover slip is then transferred to a test tube containing 96% ethanol, in which it is stored. Prior to use the material is treated with chloroform, absolute ethanol, and 0.01 *N* acetic acid as described for tissue sections. It is not necessary to include a special treatment for removing free nucleotides when using fixed tissue since it has been found that these are eliminated during the hydration of the tissue for the micromanipulation (Edström, 1953).

Much attention has been devoted to the question of the suitability of Carnoy-fixed tissue for histochemical tests since the control solutions (solutions without enzyme; more properly containing inactivated enzyme) may also result in the removal of some RNA (Stowell and Zorzoli, 1947). In the present microchemical work this is unimportant. The way in which RNA is removed when it is collected for analysis is not crucial in itself, but it is imperative that a quantitative removal take place, both for the determination of absolute amounts and for the base analysis. In the latter case, it must be recognized that ribonuclease hydrolyzes the different nucleotides from RNA at different rates. The fact that pancreatic ribonuclease leaves a nondialyzable core rich in purines, has not been found in several tests to prevent complete extraction (Edström, 1953; Lagerstedt, 1956; Sandritter *et al.*, 1957; Edström *et al.*, 1961). It is desirable to make the extraction as specific as possible, i.e., to reduce the extraction of non-RNA constituents. In a quantitative investigation it was found that extraction as recommended by Brachet (1940), i.e., ribonuclease in distilled water at pH 6.0, is ideal in this respect and much superior to an electrolyte-containing solution at pH 7.6 which removes some protein from fixed tissue (Edström *et al.*, 1961). Unfortunately, the former solution is not always efficient for complete RNA removal when used in small volumes like those employed for microextractions. On this account and because some contamination with the relatively lower ultraviolet-absorbing protein can be tolerated both in determinations of nucleic acid content and for electrophoresis, a buffered solution is usually employed. In some kinds of material where the concentration of RNA is low, ribonuclease in distilled water at pH 6.0 may have particular value (Edström *et al.*, 1962). For microphoresis it is necessary to obtain RNA extracts free from buffer electrolytes. This is achieved by using volatile electrolytes in the ribonuclease solution used for extractions (see Appendix 1.3).

Isolated tissue samples placed in an oil chamber are incubated in droplets of enzyme solution about ten times their volume. A large supply drop of enzyme solution is placed in the oil chamber by means of a capillary pipette bent at the tip and operated by mouth. Droplets of the desired size for incubation are removed from the supply drop by the micropipette and placed near each sample. After the micropipette has been emptied, it is used to transfer these individual droplets, each to its sample. The oil chamber is now placed in a Petri dish, the bottom of which is covered with a filter paper moistened with a few drops of the volatile buffer, and is then kept in an incubator at 37°C for 30 minutes. After this time a new supply drop of enzyme solution is introduced into the chamber. New volumes for the second extraction are taken with the micropipette from this drop and placed near each incubated object. A dry cover glass is also added, giving a combined chamber. Each original extract is then individually transferred to the dry cover glass where it is evaporated to dryness. After the delivery of an extract the pipette is used to transfer the prepared second incubation volume to the extracted cell. In this way the pipette is washed and the washings included in the following extract. A second digestion at 37°C for 30 minutes is then carried out, after which extracts are evaporated to dryness and new volumes of enzyme for the third extraction applied as after the first incubation period. Three extractions are usually performed. Extracts from the same sample are evaporated close together. During the incubations in a humid dish the dry cover glass is removed from the chamber. The times are doubled for formalin fixed tissue.

For determination of nucleic acid content the pooled and dried extracts should be kept within as small an area as possible. Extracted tissue units may be stained afterward for control of the digestion, identification, etc., by removing the paraffin with chloroform and drying the glass. If the glass is placed in a test tube with a hole in the bottom, it is conveniently handled in a staining procedure.

D. Hydrolysis

Prior to an electrophoretic separation, the extracted nucleic acid is hydrolyzed with hot 4 *N* HCl to liberate the purine bases and pyrimidine nucleotides from ribopolynucleotides. The problem of maintaining small volumes of aqueous solutions at high temperature is solved by performing the hydrolysis in a micropipette of the type that is used for extractions. In such a pipette, 4 *N* HCl is first introduced as a column several millimeters long followed by a volume of liquid paraffin large enough to give a safe separation between the long column of hydrochloric acid and the hydrolyzate which is to follow next. The extract is dissolved in a volume of 4 *N* HCl, in which the concentration of RNA in the hydrolyzate does not exceed about 1%. After the hydrolyzate a series of small alternating volumes of liquid paraffin and 4 *N* HCl is introduced into the tip to prevent evaporation of the hydrolyzate and enable transportation of the pipette for hydrolysis (see Fig. 2). The hydrolysis is done at 100°C in a bath of liquid paraffin saturated with 4 *N* HCl. A cylindrical vial (weighing tube) of 80 mm height and 35 mm diameter is filled two-thirds with liquid paraffin and the bottom covered with a layer of 4 *N* HCl, 0.5–1 cm high.

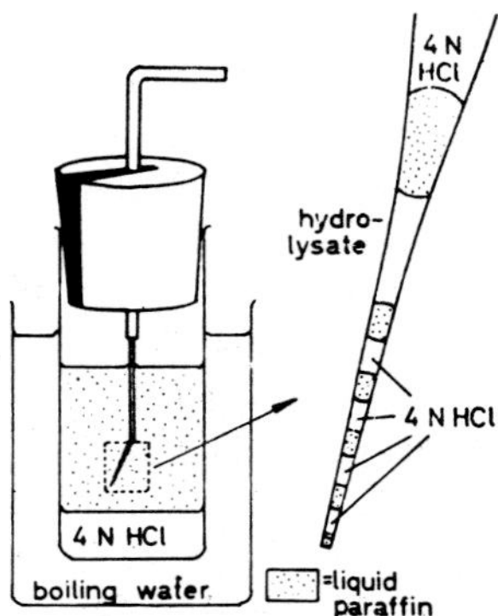

FIG. 2. Arrangement for microscale hydrolysis of RNA. From Edström (1960a).

The vial is shaken and placed overnight in an oven at 100°C. It is taken directly from the oven to a boiling water bath. The pipette is mounted in a slit of a rubber stopper and inserted into the vial so that the tip reaches the lower half of the liquid paraffin (see Fig. 2). After 30 minutes the hydrolyzate is extruded in an oil chamber (the plugging volumes of HCl may be included in the hydrolyzate) and afterward evaporated to dryness using a combined chamber. When used for electrophoretic analysis the dry hydrolyzate is dissolved in a minimal volume of 4 *N* HCl in an oil chamber. As a guide to finding a suitable volume, it is recommended to take about twice the volume necessary to dissolve the substance. Dried hydrolyzates must not be stored under liquid paraffin, since this may cause a loss of purines.

In preference to 1 *N* HCl, traditionally used for hydrolysis (Smith and Markham, 1950), 4 *N* HCl was chosen. In contrast to the former, it dissolves RNA extracts quickly at room temperature. For hydrolysis of RNA 1 *N* HCl is generally used for 60 minutes at 100°C. The use of 4 *N* HCl for only 30 minutes compensates for the increased acidity but may be a somewhat stronger treatment. However, in quantitative tests it has not been possible to measure any difference in results of the two hydrolytic procedures (Edström, 1960a).

E. Electrophoresis

Electrophoresis on a microscopic cellulose fiber is employed to separate the RNA constituents in amounts of 10^{-10} gm (i.e., 500–1000 $\mu\mu$g RNA) from each other. The medium in which the electrophoretic migration occurs consists of two phases, one of which is the supporting framework of cellulose molecules, and the other a solution, the electrophoretic buffer, in which the applied compounds dissolve. This system gives the compounds a specified ionization and allows the migration of ions in an electric field. In the microphoretic work the electrophoretic buffer is characterized by certain properties prerequisite for obtaining sharp separations on a microscopic scale. These properties are a high viscosity (4000–5000 cp); a relatively high conductivity, approximately $0.7 \cdot 10^{-3}$ mho/cm, and for the special case where purines are involved, a high acidity (around pH 0) to increase the solubility of these compounds. The basis for detection and determination of the microphoretically separated nucleic acid constituents is their absorption of ultraviolet light at 257 mμ. It is essential that the electrophoretic buffer has no more than a moderate absorption at this wavelength. An electrophoretic buffer meeting the specifications enumerated above is prepared from sulfuric acid, glycerol, and glucose as described in Appendix 1.8.

The supporting cellulose framework is obtained from artificial silk produced according to the cuprammonium method, designation: "Cupresa HW Naturglanz, ungedreht im Strang," 0.8 den. per filament (Farbenfabriken Bayer A.G., Dormagen, Germany). The individual fibers of the silk thread are used after they have been induced to swell by treatment with alkali (see Appendix 1.7). In an untreated state they have a diameter of 9μ and in the final state, during electrophoresis, 25–30μ. After treatment, the fibers are kept in the electrophoretic buffer.

To isolate individual fibers from the bundle of entangled fibers obtained after the alkali treatment, one first obtains a free fiber end by pulling the bundles apart with a needle. Such an end may be taken by rotating it onto the tip of the needle. It is slowly pulled free of the other fibers and placed onto a clean glass slide, with one free end protruding over the edge of the glass. Excess electrophoretic buffer is removed by transferring the isolated fiber successively to new parts of the slide, whereby a wet track of decreasing thickness is left each time. After six or seven such transfers, the fiber is usually ready for use as evidenced by thin and uniform tracks resulting from the later transfers.

For microphoresis the fiber is placed, slightly stretched to keep it straight, on a quartz glass, 25 × 30 × 0.5 mm (obtained from W. C. Heraeus GmbH., Hanau, Germany), parallel to the longest side. A fiber length of 12–20 mm and a diameter of 25–30μ is suitable. Buffer bridges are applied from the ends of the fiber toward the long edge of the quartz glass, the bridges ending about 5 mm from the corners with a hook over the edge. The buffer bridge is used in the form of a paste made by mixing the electrophoretic buffer with finely powdered SiO_2 to a consistency such that it can be smeared out but will not flow out along the fiber. The fiber is then ready to be used for the application of hydrolyzates. The quartz glass, with the fiber underneath, is placed behind a cover glass with hydrolyzates in an oil chamber to give a combined chamber. The microscope is equipped with a small heater used during the application of hydrolyzates (see Appendix 3.2). While initially heating the fiber for a few minutes, suitable application points for hydrolyzates are marked by applying droplets of liquid paraffin with the micropipette to the quartz glass close to the desired application points. Although the fiber is not even along its whole length, several uniform segments (one separation requiring about 500μ) are usually available on a given fiber. The markings are made at places where the fiber shows an even diameter for at least 500μ in the direction of the cathode. Hydrolyzates are applied by touching the lower side of the fiber lightly with the tip of the micropipette, applying to the syringe a slight positive pressure which is increased as the column of hydrolyzate is shortened. The pipette is emptied as completely as possible of the hydrolyzate. Often some liquid paraffin flows out and spreads along the fiber, but paraffin in such small quantities is not apt to cause any inconvenience. The hydrolyzate should stay as a slightly bulging concentrated spot at the point of application. It takes 5–10 seconds to apply an extract to the fiber, which is used for several hydrolyzates as a rule. It is usually possible to find six or seven suitable locations for separations on a fiber of 15 mm length.

After the application of hydrolyzates, the fiber is in a relatively dry state and the viscosity of the electrophoretic buffer is far above the required one. The correct viscosity in the fiber is obtained by exposing it to an atmosphere of 42% relative humidity for 5 minutes in a constant humidity chamber specially constructed for this purpose (see Appendix 3.4). The quartz glass is introduced into this chamber without disturbing the relative humidity and brought into contact with the electrodes. After 5 minutes in the chamber, equilibrium has been reached and the electrophoretic buffer has absorbed the amount of water required to give the right viscosity for successful separations. The fiber is covered with liquid paraffin while in the chamber and 2 kv applied for a time that is proportional to the fiber length (about 0.7 $\times$ fiber length in mm, expressed in minutes, i.e., 8–14 minutes for a fiber 12–20 mm long). A current of the order of 10 μa is obtained at 2 kv measured with a "Scalamp" galvanometer, model 7904/S (W. G. Pye & Co. Ltd., New Market Road, Cambridge, England). An extra high power supply is used delivering 2 or 4 kv (see Appendix 3.3).

F. Photography and Photometry

After complete electrophoretic separations have been obtained, the quartz glass is taken to the ultraviolet microscope (see Appendix 3.5 and 3.6) for inspection and photography at 257 mμ.

Photography is carried out with a low power lens (16-mm quartz monochromate, corrected for 275 mμ, N.A. 0.20) and a 10× quartz ocular. A fluorescent eyepiece is used for focusing. A bellows length of 25 cm providing a total magnification of 93× is used. It is not necessary to include regularly a reference system since the absorbing bands are evaluated by comparison with each other. A picture of a separation in ultraviolet light is shown in Fig. 3, together with its densitometer tracing.

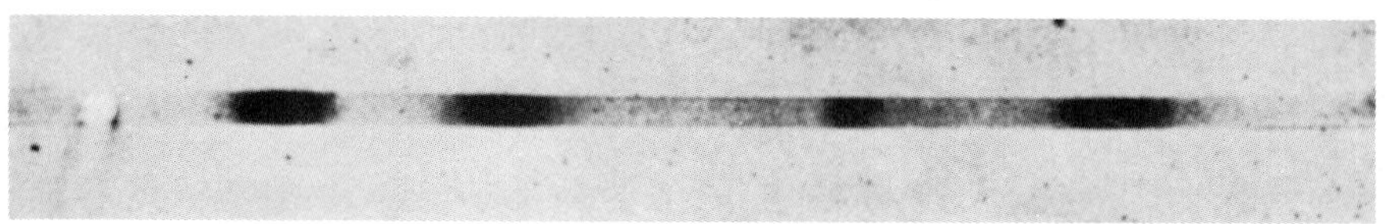

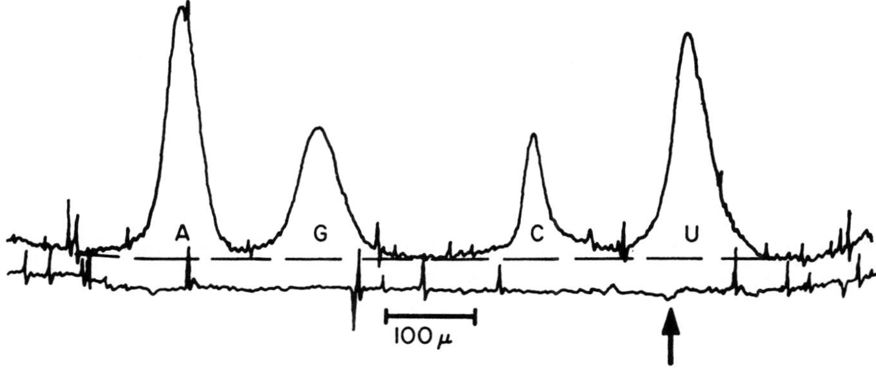

FIG. 3. A microphoretic separation of an RNA hydrolyzate from isolated lampbrush chromosomes viewed at 257 mμ (Edström and Gall, 1963). A, G, C, and U stand for adenine, guanine, cytidylic acid, and uridylic acid, respectively. The application point is indicated by the arrow.

Certain precautions must be taken during photography. Excessive illumination of the fiber exerts a selective destructive action on uridylic acid and a consequent reduction in its optical density (OD) at 257 mμ. Consequently, a standard time of 10 seconds illumination has been introduced for all focusing before photography, and the exposure time for the plates has been standardized to 30 seconds. The time for film exposure will of course vary depending upon the type of illumination; a time has to be selected by trial which will allow the absorbtion by the four separated bands to fall within the linear part of the photographic blackening curve. The characteristics of the latter may be determined with the aid of a reference system (see Appendix 3.7). Kodak O 250 plates are used, developed for 2 minutes in a Kodak D72 developer, afterward rinsed with water, and fixed with a Kodak F52 solution.

The exposed plates are scanned in the recording microdensitometer described by Walker (1955) (Joyce, Loebl & Co. Ltd., A8, Princesway, Team Valley, Gateshead on Tyne 11, England). The picture of the fiber is scanned with a 16-mm objective along its length at an arm ratio of 1:2 and with a gray wedge extending from 0.5 to 2.5 OD units. A slit covering about half the diameter of the fiber is used for the scanning beam of light. The background along the separation is recorded as close to the fiber as possible.

G. Calculations

Before integrating the areas under the peaks of the curve, a base line is drawn parallel to the background tracing through parts of the curve representing nonabsorbing segments of the fiber. The areas under the peaks are evaluated from the weight of copies prepared on transparent paper. Since in microphoresis only the quotients between the integrated areas are of interest, it is sufficient to determine their relative size. (For calculations of quotients see Appendix 4.1.) The reference OD values have been taken from the absorbtion curves published by Beaven *et al.* (1955). For the purines the values are based on the curves for solutions in 6 N HCl. In quantitative tests it has been found that the use of these constants gives a recovery close to 100% (Edström, 1960a). Hot acid hydrolysis gives approximately 5% dephosphorylation of the pyrimidine nucleotides (Markham and Smith, 1951). For uridylic acid this is unimportant since uridine stays at the same place as the nucleotide and has the same absorption properties. Cytidine migrates faster than cytidylic acid but occupies a place that lies closer to cytidylic acid than to guanine. Unless very extended separations are used, the similarly absorbing cytidine will, therefore, be included with cytidylic acid.

H. Determination of Nucleic Acid Content

A relatively simple method is available for the determination in microscopic tissue units of the RNA content in amounts down to 25 $\mu\mu$g. The ribonuclease extracts are collected on a quartz glass in a combined chamber. The quartz glass, of the same kind as used for microphoresis, is pretreated to remove all water from its surface. (Storing of the cleaned and dried glass in a dry organic liquid like chloroform or decane for a couple of days.) It is necessary to remove the quartz glass from the oil chamber during the digestions of RNA in a humid dish as described in Section II, C.

The quartz glass with the collected RNA extracts is used to make an oil chamber. The extracts, when dissolved in a glycerol-containing buffer (see Appendix 1.5), form round lens-shaped drops of a regular outline (see Fig. 4). To decrease the contact area between the pipette tip and the drops,

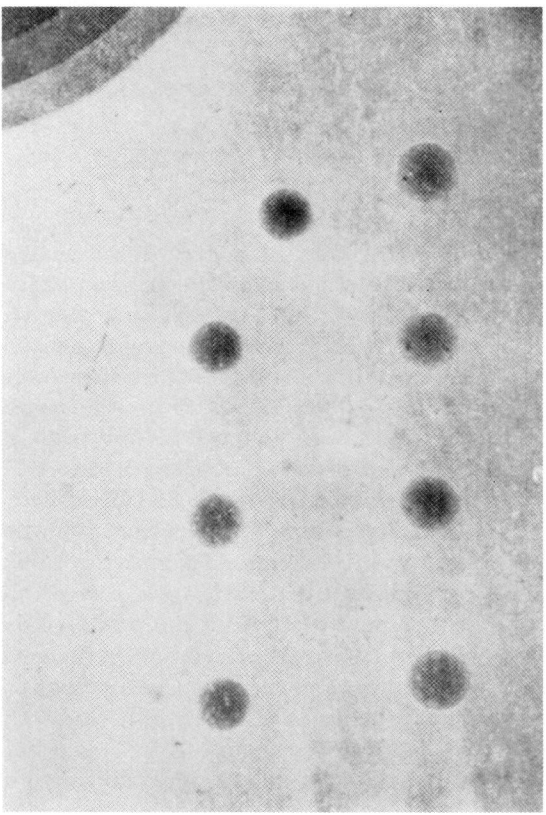

FIG. 4. RNA extracts from individual Purkinje nerve cell bodies of the rat photographed at 257 $m\mu$ and containing RNA amounts between 94 and 123 $\mu\mu g$. The reference system gives steps differing by 0.1505 optical density units. ×175.

a pipette with an angle of 45°–50° toward the horizontal plane and a tip diameter of only 6–7μ is used for the applications of the glycerol-containing buffer. The nucleic acid spots on the quartz glass are photographed in ultraviolet light at 257 $m\mu$ with a reference system giving steps with differences in optical density of 0.1505 (at a magnification of 130×). A fluorescent eyepiece is used for focusing. The pictures of the spots are investigated by photometry at a further magnification of 2, 5, or 10×, depending on the size of the spots. Two tracks are run through the center at 90° to each other and superimposed. A mean curve is drawn on transparent paper, and it is then possible with the aid of a device for integration of the absorption (see Appendix 4.3) to determine the amount of RNA in the spots (see Appendix 4.2). This method also works for DNA extracted with deoxyribonuclease (Edström and Kawiak, 1961) (see Appendix 1.4). In this case four extractions, 1 hour each, are performed at 37°C.

III. Accuracy

The microphoretic method has been scrutinized in several tests for recovery and accuracy. The method should be checked with RNA of known composition, such as yeast RNA, from time to time. As an aid to others in locating artifacts, some potential sources of error will be pointed out. Incomplete extraction tends to increase the ratio of pyrimidines to purines. Incomplete hydrolysis (which may result from the use of unsaturated paraffin in the bath or too small volumes of hydrochloric acid for the hydrolyzate) increases the absorption at the position of cytidylic acid, since unhydrolyzed purine compounds will be localized here and measured as cytidylic acid. Incomplete delivery of an extract from the micropipette may give rise to a transfer of varying efficiency for different hydrolysis products. Extracts contaminated with large amounts of proteins give increased absorption at the application point, i.e., at the position of uridylic acid. This error can be lowered by storing the isolated material in 96% ethanol for several days. Low uridylic acid values are obtained by excessive illumination in ultraviolet light. A small spectral bandwidth of the light during photography is important for quantitative work, but this source of error is easy to avoid in ultraviolet microscopes utilizing illumination with a discontinuous spectrum, such as the Köhler ultraviolet microscope. On account of the differences in the OD of the separated bands, care must be taken that the linear part of the photographic blackening curve is utilized and that due regard is paid to stray light. Finally, unsharp and extended zones may arise from several sources, the most important of which are (1) overloading of the fiber with hydrolysis products, (2) insufficiently swollen fibers, (3) defective heating during the application of extracts, and (4) lag of time between the completion of a separation and photography.

There is a random error between individual analyses within a hydrolyzate as well as between different hydrolyzates from the same material, of which the latter variation is of greater interest. For biological material an average coefficient of variation (V) between hydrolyzates of 5% was found by Egyhazi and Hydén (1961) and 7% was determined by Edström (1956) on yeast RNA.

An analysis of the different steps in the procedure for determination of RNA content shows that the errors involved are quite low (Edström, 1953, 1958). The photographic-photometric part of the procedure has been tested with measured amounts of RNA. The values obtained in this way show a quantitative recovery and a V-value of about 5%. An idea of the total random error in the method may be obtained by using homogeneous biological material. Determination of the RNA content in single nerve cells from the cochlear ganglion cells of the guinea pig (data in Table I, from

TABLE I

THE RNA CONTENT IN ISOLATED COCHLEAR GANGLION CELLS FROM THE GUINEA PIG DETERMINED FOR SINGLE CELLS OR FOR CELLS IN GROUPS OF TEN[a]

Single cells				Cells in groups of ten			
Animal number	n^b	Mean ($\mu\mu$g)	V	Animal number	n^b	Mean ($\mu\mu$g)	V
I	8	26	18.6	XIII	5	323	5.1
II	8	29	10.5	XIV	5	335	6.1
III	8	31	10.3	XV	5	334	9.6
IV	7	31	24.1	XVI	5	371	5.2
V	7	36	6.2	XVII	5	352	5.4
VI	8	35	6.5	XVIII	5	375	4.6
				XIX	5	395	3.2
Average			12.7				5.6

[a] Data from unpublished work by O. Hallén and J.-E. Edström.
[b] n = number.

unpublished work by O. Hallén and J.-E. Edström) gives values with an average V-value of 12.7%. By analyzing groups of ten cells the biological variation is reduced by a factor of $1/\sqrt{10}$. From the average V-value for group data the random error of the method can be calculated. The results show that 4.1% of the variation is due to the method, 12.0% being the V for the biological variation between single cells.

The method for the determination of total amounts of DNA is easier to check because more favorable material is available, such as nondividing cell nuclei. It seems likely that spermatocytes and spermatids show an insignificant biological variation. With these cells as well as groups of calf thymocytes and rat spermatids, V-values of 6–10% were obtained (Edström and Kawiak, 1961). Mean values for calf thymocytes of 7.7–8.1 $\mu\mu$g were measured. Since biochemical analyses (for reference, see Davidson, 1950) have given values of 6.4–7.5 $\mu\mu$g per nucleus, the possibility exists that this method contains a positive systematic error of 10–15%, although an analysis of the method failed to show any cause for such an error.

IV. Applications

The nucleic acid methods have found a special application in two fields: the study of the RNA of different cellular organelles and chemical studies on the central nervous system.

A consistent finding has been the similarity in base composition between nucleolar and cytoplasmic RNA (Edström, 1960b; Edström *et al.*, 1961; Edström and Beermann, 1962), a finding that agrees with radioautographic and other evidence for a nucleolar origin of at least a part of the cytoplasmic RNA (see Perry *et al.*, 1961). In the nucleus, in addition to the nucleoli, nuclear sap and chromosomes may be separately analyzed in suitable material (Edström and Gall, 1963). In the giant chromosomes of the chironomids it is possible to analyze pooled Balbiani rings, which are products of the activity of single genes (Beermann, 1961), to obtain information on the base composition of their RNA (Edström and Beermann, 1962). A compilation of analytical results in this field is given in Table II.

The nervous system is a tissue in which the need for microchemical procedures is particularly evident because of its complex morphology and associated complex function. Evidence that the central nervous system possesses biochemical differentiation of a similar order of complexity has been accumulating for several years. As part of broader metabolic studies of the nervous system, Hydén and co-workers have been using the microchemical methods for the determination and analysis of RNA. In functional and pharmacological studies it has been found that neurons and glia demonstrate quite specific changes in RNA content and composition after various kinds of treatments (Egyhazi and Hydén, 1961; Hydén and Egyhazi, 1962). The fact that the neuronal RNA is comparatively resistant to postmorten changes (Jarlstedt, 1962) and that fixed and embedded material can be used is of value for investigation of clinical material. Gomirato and Hydén (1963) found that RNA in glia of basal ganglia is grossly abnormal in patients with Parkinson's disease.

TABLE II

BASE COMPOSITION OF RNA FROM COMPONENTS OF VARIOUS CELLS[a]

	Oocyte, *Tegenaria domestica* (Edström, 1960b)			Oocyte, *Asterias rubens* (Edström *et al.*, 1961)			Salivary gland cell, *Chironomus tentans* (Edström and Beermann, 1962)		
	Nucleolus	Nucleoplasm	Cytoplasm	Nucleolus	Nucleoplasm	Cytoplasm	Nucleolus	IV chromosome segment with Balbiani ring	Cytoplasm
Adenine	25.2 ± 0.2	28.4 ± 0.6	25.1 ± 0.5	23.7 ± 1.3	35.7 ± 1.3	23.5 ± 0.2	30.6 ± 0.8	38.0 ± 0.6	29.4 ± 0.4
Guanine	29.8 ± 0.9	28.5 ± 1.3	30.2 ± 0.5	33.4 ± 0.3	24.8 ± 0.9	31.9 ± 0.3	20.1 ± 0.5	20.5 ± 0.6	22.9 ± 0.3
Cytosine	22.9 ± 1.0	20.3 ± 0.8	21.9 ± 0.6	24.3 ± 0.4	16.5 ± 0.5	24.8 ± 0.3	22.1 ± 0.6	24.5 ± 0.6	22.1 ± 0.4
Uracil	22.2 ± 0.7	22.7 ± 0.5	22.9 ± 0.7	18.5 ± 0.5	23.0 ± 0.8	19.7 ± 0.3	27.1 ± 0.6	17.1 ± 0.6	25.7 ± 0.3

[a] Mean values of molar proportions in per cent of the sum ±SEM.

V. Concluding Remarks

Although microphoresis has to the present been used mainly for the base analysis of RNA, it is evident that several other applications remain. Thus it can be used with advantage for the determination of the adenine: guanine quotient in DNA (Edström and Beermann, 1962). A combination of microphoresis and radioautography may prove particularly useful. An enzymological application by Sierakowska and Edström (unpublished) on the ribonuclease and phosphatase activities in subcellular parts of starfish oocytes has commenced. Subcellular parts isolated in a nonpolar medium are placed in the oil chamber into small incubation droplets containing suitable substrates (cyclic cytidylic acid for ribonuclease and noncyclic nucleotide for phosphatase). After incubation the contents of the droplets are analyzed by microphoresis, and enzyme activity is revealed by the presence of decomposition products.

One may want to know whether still greater sensitivity of the microphoretic technique is to be expected. Theoretically the lower limit is set by the solubility of the migrating compounds in the impregnated silk fiber. With the use of ultraviolet absorption for detection and measurement and on the assumption of a minimal efficient OD of 0.3 for the separated bands, a maximal solubility of 10 mM and an optical molecular density per centimeter (ϵ) of 10,000, it can be calculated that a cuvette depth of 33μ is necessary. The most sensitive procedure and the only one currently feasible is to use the supporting medium as a cuvette during the absorption measurements. Using a medium of cylindrical shape (fiber) and assuming an efficient zone length of twice the diameter, it can be calculated that an amount of about 1 $\mu\mu$mole can be separated and determined. This figure gives only the order of the sensitivity, in practice it has been possible to obtain reasonably good separations involving nucleic acid components in amounts corresponding to about half of this value. It is evidently not possible to obtain a fundamental improvement in sensitivity by applying the present principles for the separations. For this purpose it is necessary to modify the procedure in an essential aspect, e.g., by sharpening the bands (to give discs), or using more sensitive methods of quantitation (e.g., measurement of induced fluorescence or radioactivity).

With regard to the determination of nucleic acid content, it seems reasonably possible to obtain a higher sensitivity by adapting the shrinking droplet technique of Ornstein and Lehrer (1960).

VI. Appendices

Appendix 1: Solutions and Chemical Treatments

1.1. Carnoy Fixation

The following procedure is recommended for tissue pieces 2–3 mm thick: Immersion in freshly prepared fixative according to Carnoy (absolute ethanol-chloroform-glacial acetic acid, 6:3:1, by volume) for 90 minutes at room temperature, followed by absolute ethanol and benzene, 90 minutes each and infiltration with paraffin for 4–18 hours.

1.2. Formalin Fixation

Tissue pieces, 2–3 mm thick, are fixed for 3 hours in Lillie's buffered formalin (100 ml commercial formalin, i.e., 37–40% formaldehyde; 900 ml distilled water; 4.53 gm $NaH_2PO_4 \cdot 2H_2O$ and 7.23 gm $Na_2HPO_4 \cdot 2H_2O$) at room temperature, followed by running tap water overnight, dehydration in 96% and absolute ethanol, 90 minutes in each, benzene and paraffin as above.

1.3. Ribonuclease Solution with Volatile Electrolytes

Dissolve 0.4 mg of pancreatic ribonuclease (Worthington Biochemical Corporation, Freehold, New Jersey) in 1 ml 0.2 *M* ammoniumbicarbonate-acetate buffer, pH 7.6. The latter solution is prepared by dissolving 1.58 gm ammoniumbicarbonate in 100 ml distilled water and adjusting with 0.2 *M* acetic acid to pH 7.6. It is stored in the refrigerator after addition of a few drops of chloroform. The pH is checked before use and adjusted with acetic acid if necessary. Freshly dissolved enzyme is used.

1.4. Deoxyribonuclease Solution

Pancreatic deoxyribonuclease (Worthington) is used in a concentration of 0.4 mg per milliliter 0.02 *M* phosphate buffer pH 7.0, containing 0.003 *M* $MgCl_2$, 0.0025 *M* hydroxylamine as hydrochloride (not 0.005 *M* as stated in the original paper, Edström and Kawiak, 1961), and 0.1% gelatin. The buffer solution is kept in the refrigerator and should be renewed monthly. Only freshly dissolved enzyme is used.

1.5. Glycerol-Containing Buffer for RNA

A solution is made of 2 parts by volume of 0.2 *M* Na, K phosphate buffer, pH 7.6, and 5 parts of water-free glycerol, specific gravity 1.26. The OD at 257 mμ (or the wavelength used for photography in the ultraviolet microscope) is measured in a spectrophotometer in 1-cm cuvettes and compared with the OD of the liquid paraffin used. The OD of the liquids, if not agreeing within 0.3 OD units, should be made equal, e.g., by dissolving adenine in the usually less absorbing buffer.

1.6. Glycerol-Water Mixture for DNA

Since the DNA extracts contain buffer salts, it is sufficient to use a glycerol-water mixture (6:1, by volume) for these. The OD at the wavelength used for ultraviolet photography should be checked and adjusted as for the glycerol-containing buffer for RNA.

1.7. Alkali Treatment of Cellulose Fibers

Cupresa silk thread is cut in about 30 pieces, 2 cm long, which are placed in a beaker with distilled water. They are transferred to 1.5 *N* NaOH when wet and 2 minutes later to 2.25 *N* NaOH. The treatment with the latter solution is carried out at 10°C for 5 minutes under gentle stirring with a glass rod. Since the fibers become too soft during the immersion in the 2.25 *N* NaOH to be lifted without tearing, it is necessary to empty the beaker into a larger volume of distilled water, from which it is possible to lift the fibers with a glass rod to three subsequent changes of distilled water, 2 minutes each. The fibers, after excess moisture has been removed with filter paper, are finally placed in the electrophoretic buffer and shaken for an hour on a mechanical shaker and then placed in a refrigerator. A preparation can be used from the day of its preparation for a couple of months (it was earlier incorrectly believed that the fibers could be used only during the first 3 days, Edström, 1960a).

1.8. Electrophoretic Buffer

The electrophoretic buffer has been modified since it was first described (Edström, 1956). The sulfuric acid concentration has been increased and the heating time shortened. It is prepared as follows: 20 ml 8 *N* sulfuric acid, 8 ml distilled water, 33 gm glycerol (specific gravity 1.26) and 72 gm water-free D-glucose are mixed in a flask and heated in a water bath at 100°C under stirring until the sugar dissolves. After 20 minutes the flask is removed, cooled rapidly, and stored at −20°C, where it will keep for months.

Appendix 2: Microinstruments

2.1. Glass Needles

Glass needles are prepared from 3-mm soda glass which is pulled to give a 5 cm length of 1 mm diameter adjoining 3 cm of the thicker piece. The end of the thin part, softened in the de Fonbrune microforge (Etablissements Beaudouin, 1 et 3, rue Rataud, Paris 5e) by contact with the heated platinum wire, is pulled at 50°–60° from the axis to a cone with a blunt tip. The working field is then cooled by applying a stream of air and the electrical heating of the wire increased correspondingly. The needle is brought in contact with the wire a second time but now barely touching the tip. By removing the needle from the wire a sharp tip can be obtained.

2.2. Micropipettes

The starting material is 8- to 9-mm pyrex glass tubing, maximal wall thickness 1 mm. Care must be exercised during the different stages of pulling that the relative wall thickness is not increased by heating. Capillaries about 1 mm in diameter are first pulled in a hydrogen burner and cut in approximately 10 cm lengths. At 2 cm from one end the capillary is heated with an alcohol flame and pulled to give a short local thinning of about 0.5 mm diameter. A hook is made by heating the capillary near its end, distal to the thinning. The capillary is then introduced into the long arm of a glass holder made of 3-mm tubing with right angle arms of 2 and 4 cm length. The short arm is to be connected to the syringe used for maneuvering the pipette. The holder with the capillary sealed in by picein is inserted in the microforge holder and placed in a vertical position with the hook and the short glass holder arm extending toward the right. A 2.5–3 gm weight is hung on the hook and the glass instrument inclined 25° from the vertical position. The capillary is then heated with the platinum wire (which should not be allowed to touch the glass) about 1 mm above the point where the capillary shows the maximal thinning. After the capillary has bent, the angle is increased a further 10° (to a total of 35°) and heated at its thinnest point, where it is kept at about half the distance of a capillary diameter. Heat is applied in such a manner that the capillary will become extended slowly to a pipette tube of microscopic dimensions and break after 10–20 seconds of heating. A useful shape can be found by experience. If the micropipette is too long (too much heat) it has inconveniently high resistance during its operation due to capillary forces; if it is too short, it is readily broken. An orifice of 8–10μ in diameter is suitable for most types of work. A smaller opening, for the application of glycerol-buffer droplets to RNA and DNA extracts, is obtained by using lighter weights.

Satisfactory pipettes for delivering measured volumes (after calibration) are obtained by stopping the heating of the pipette before it breaks, moving it upwards 2–3 mm, and approaching it again with the heated wire until it breaks, this time using the air stream to obtain localized heating. This kind of pipette is given a total inclination of about 10°. To calibrate it, a column of liquid paraffin is trapped between the tip and a column of water behind the paraffin, a very small volume of water also being used to seal the tip. The paraffin column length is measured with an eyepiece micrometer, after which the column is expelled into a droplet of glycerol stained with methylene blue. From the diameter of the sphere formed by the paraffin the volume corresponding to the measured length of the pipette can be calculated.

With the use of an air-filled system an explosive delivery may occur due to the resistance towards expulsion of a volume of water solution suddenly being overcome as the positive pressure increases in the syringe. The use of thin-walled pyrex tubing decreases this tendency; contaminations on the inner pipette surface enhance it. Clean thin-walled pipettes of the shapes and sizes described above seldom cause difficulties of this kind. For the preservation of good functional pipettes they should be made slightly hydrophobic with liquid paraffin, which is kept in their distal parts for a day before they are used for water solutions. This paraffin is of further use as a column behind the pipetted volumes of aqueous solutions, preventing evaporation and liquid losses toward the rear. It is also essential for proper functioning of the pipette that the meniscus between the paraffin and the water solution is not moved so fast that droplets of any phase are left behind. The pipette is rinsed with 4 *N* HCl from a droplet in the oil chamber after being used, all aqueous solutions expelled, and the pipette stored with liquid paraffin in its distal end.

Appendix 3: Apparatus and Equipment

3.1. Syringe for Pipetting

The micropipette is connected by means of a rubber tube to a 2-ml "Inaltera" syringe with a three-way stopcock (Georg A. Henke, Tuttlingen, Germany). The stopcock plug is fastened onto a cone-shaped brass stand fixed to a wood platform on which both the microscope and the micromanipulator are placed. The stopcock body with the syringe can be moved around this axis. Use is made only of two outlets, one outlet is for the rubber tube, the other one is left free for the intake or expulsion of air.

3.2. Heater for Drying Fibers and Hydrolyzates

A platinum wire, 6 cm long, 0.6 mm in diameter, and spirally wound, is housed in a metal cylinder, 2 × 6 cm, with an open slit a fourth of its circumference wide except for shorter pieces at the ends, which are left intact. The wire, connected to electrical cables leading to a variable transformer by means of metal adaptors located in the ends of the cylinder, is insulated from the latter by ring-formed porcelain insulators. The insulators are glued to the cylinders and the adaptors by means of litharge cement. The cylinder, with the opening facing toward the object field, is attached to the microscope stand near the objective nosepiece. The platinum wire is fed from a variable transformer unit consisting of a transformer 220 v/3 v, maximum effect 45 w. It has a fixed resistance of 300 ohm and a variable one of 1000 ohm on the primary side. The radiator is shown in Fig. 5.

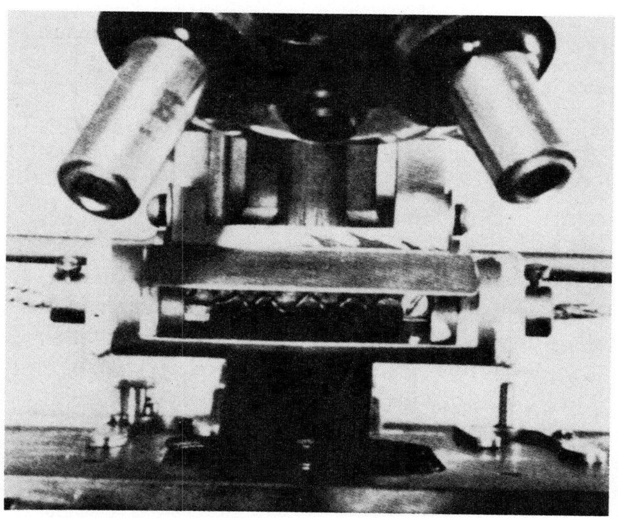

FIG. 5. The heater used for drying fibers and hydrolyzates for microphoresis. From Edström (1956).

3.3. HIGH VOLTAGE SUPPLY

A unit delivering 2 or 4 kv, constructed for this purpose, is shown in Fig. 6. As the output of the instrument is only 100 μa when short-circuited, it is safe in spite of the high voltage.

3.4. CONSTANT HUMIDITY CHAMBER

A chamber (Edström and Pilhage, 1960) providing constant humidity conditions for the microphoretic separations and constructed for this purpose is shown in Fig. 7. Chambers, as well as other microphoresis equipment, may be obtained from Rudolph Grave AB, Box 43, Mölndal 1, Sweden.

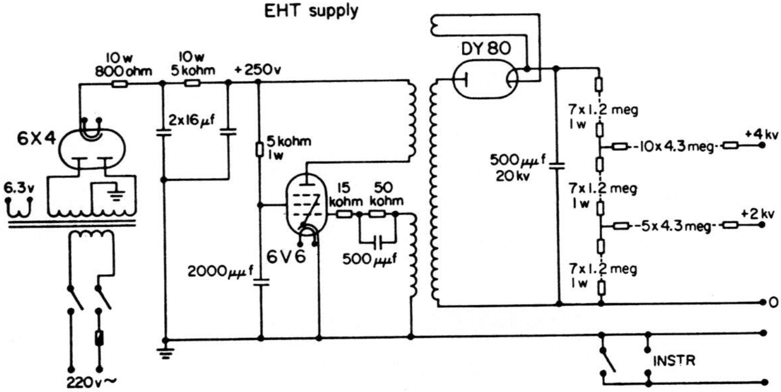

FIG. 6. High voltage unit circuit.

3.5. Optical Equipment for Ultraviolet Microscopy

Apart from the usual demands on a microscope arrangement for photography in monochromatic light, the microphoretic procedure and the subsequent quantitative determination of the ratios of the separated compounds impose certain restrictions on the choice of equipment. A practical advantage is to be able to include the whole separation in one plate which requires low power lenses. The area that is reproduced by a 16-mm objective and 10× ocular is large enough to include a whole separation and enough background. Such a quartz monochromate, corrected for 275 mμ, as used in my work, is made by VEB Carl Zeiss, Jena, Germany. Monochromates corrected for 254 or 275 mμ may also be obtained from Cooke, Troughton & Simms, York, England. The latter firm also provides a quartz substage condensor with removable front lens for work with the 16-mm quartz monochromate. A suitable eyepiece is a 10× quartz ocular; a fluorescent eyepiece must be used for direct viewing of the field in ultraviolet light. Both kinds are supplied by the British firm. Before the equipment is set up, it must also be ascertained that the light intensity is such that the exposure times will be moderate. As it is desirable to run simultaneously several separations and as there is free diffusion in the fiber, each exposure has to be so short that all photographic work can be finished within 20–30 minutes after the completion of the separations. (This factor may be of importance if direct photometry in the ultraviolet is tried.)

I have been using as a light source the spark generated between rotating cadmium electrodes used by Köhler (1904). The spectral lines are dispersed by means of two 60° water-filled quartz prisms. The line at 257 mμ, purified by means of a filter according to McFarland *et al.* (1958)

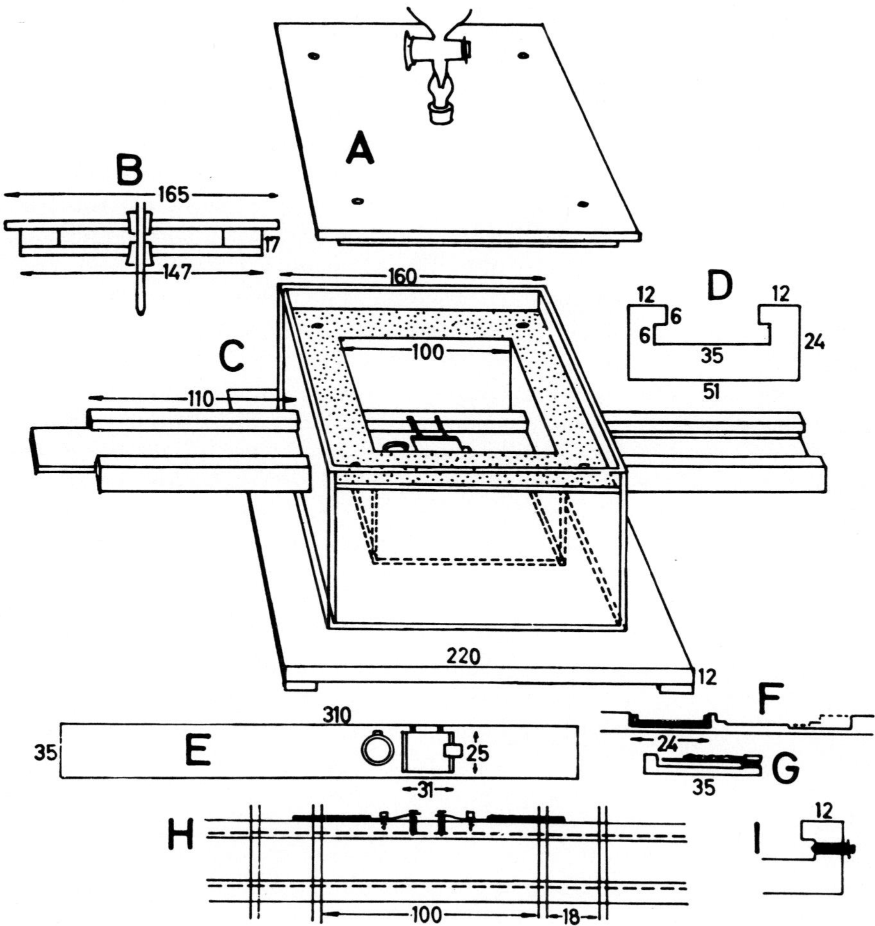

FIG. 7. Constant humidity chamber for microphoresis. (A) The lid in perspective; (B) Cross section through the lid at the center; (C) The chamber in perspective with guide and slide in position for microphoresis; (D) Cross section of the guide; (E) The slide with trough and cup for collection of liquid paraffin; (F) Longitudinal section through the slide along the axis. The profile of the trough at an out-of-axis section indicated by a broken line; (G) Cross section of the slide through the trough and one of the brass nails. A quartz glass in position with a buffer bridge is also shown; (H) View from above of the central part of the guide and the electrical connections; (I) Cross section of the guide through one of the brass nails. (D), (F), (G), and (I) have been drawn twice the size of (B), (E), and (H). (A) and (C) are shown in approximately the same scale as the latter three. From Edström and Pilhage (1960).

(see Appendix 3.6), is used for the quantitative work. This light source involves motors to rotate the electrodes; a transformer 200 v/5 kv, maximal effect 4 kw; and a converter from 50 to 500 cycle per second. As the cadmium spark generates poisonous fumes it has to be well housed and evacuated. The equipment seems unnecessarily complicated today and complete ultraviolet microscopes with low power optics are now supplied by Cooke, Troughton & Simms, as well as by Carl Zeiss, Oberkochen, Germany. If it is possible to choose wavelengths, 265 mμ is recommended since it is located relatively near the absorption maxima of all four ultraviolet-absorbing compounds. It should be pointed out that particularly in the case of microphoretic separations, it is essential that the spectral bandwidth of the light used be low since the error in the quantitative evaluation grows at different rates for the different compounds with increasing bandwidth. A lamp generating high intensity ultraviolet light is valuable in combination with a monochromator since it permits a low bandwidth to be used. The illumination should be kept as low as possible also to reduce photodecomposition of uridylic acid. Scott (1955) and Walker (1956, 1958) give detailed information on microscopy and measurements in ultraviolet light.

3.6. Filter for Isolating Ultraviolet Light

A suitable filter for combination with the cadmium light source or a mercury low pressure lamp to purify the lines at 257 and 254 mμ, respectively, has been described by McFarland *et al.* (1958). Polyvinylalcohol, 98% hydrolyzed [Matheson, Coleman and Bell, Norwood (Cincinnati), Ohio, USA], is mixed with water at a concentration of 10% (w/v) and heated in a water bath until the polymer dissolves. The liquid is poured onto a glass plate as a film 0.25 mm thick after drying. According to the recommendations of McFarland *et al.* the film is stained after it has been peeled from the plate, but I have found it easier to stain the film while on the plate. The stain solution consists of 1 gm iodine and 2 gm potassium iodide in 100 ml distilled water. A treatment time of 5 seconds is recommended but this, as well as the concentration of the dissolved compounds, may be varied to give filters of different densities. The relative amounts of iodine and potassium iodide must be kept constant.

3.7. Reference System

A reference system for calibrating blackening may be obtained by using a rotating disc with zones having apertures differing by a constant logarithmic ratio. Since most low power quartz monochromates give rise to a slight amount of stray light, it is desirable to compensate for this error by means of a rotating disc in the following way: the OD of heavy concentrates of nucleic acid in spots of the size used for microchemical determination is evaluated by comparing their density with a part of the photographic plate exposed for a fraction of the total exposure time. (In the absence of stray light the OD of such spots is infinite.) As an example one may find that such spots have the same blackening as emulsion exposed for one fortieth of the total exposure time. This means that the stray light is 2.6% of the refracted light. The resulting error, small at low OD values, increases with increasing densities. Objects with an OD of 0.5 will be measured with a 5% negative error in this case if no compensation is made. The rotating disc used for calibrating blackening can be constructed to compensate for such stray light. A suitable OD difference between each adjoining zone is 0.1505, i.e., log $\sqrt{2}$. In an uncompensated system the ratio between each outer aperture to that of its inner neighbor will, consequently, amount to $\sqrt{2}$. Correction for stray light gives ratios equal to

$$(100 + s):(100/\sqrt{2} + s),$$

where s is the amount of stray light in per cent of the incident light, the measured apparent OD in the uncorrected system of the opaque spot being log $(100 + s):s$. A sector compensating for 4.1% stray light and giving differences in OD of 0.1505 is shown in Fig. 8. It is rotated at 1500 rev per minute.

FIG. 8. Disc with zones having apertures which give optical density differences of 0.1505, when the disc is rotated in a light path. It is corrected for 4.1% stray light. From Edström (1958).

It is known that a rotating sector may give rise to errors such as an intermittency effect and interference with the intensity variations of the light source (Thorell, 1947). There is no need for a special check on this point since the whole photographic-photometric procedure can be tested directly with measured amounts of nucleic acid.

Appendix 4: Calculations

4.1. Calculations of Base Ratios

The relative areas circumscribed by the peaks of the photometer curve (Fig. 3) and the base line are determined as previously described (Section II, G) for the separated compounds. The values are divided by the corresponding ϵ-value at the wavelength in question. At 257 mμ the ϵ-values $\times 10^{-3}$ are 11.2, 9.6, 5.15, and 9.5 for adenine, guanine, cytidylic acid, and uridylic acid,[1] respectively (values from the curves published by Beaven *et al.*, 1955). The resulting quotients are added and the percentage of the sum that each quotient constitutes is calculated.

4.2. Calculation of Total Amounts of Nucleic Acid

The formula for the calculation of the amount of nucleic acid in an extract is:

$$x = \frac{\Sigma h \cdot f^2 \cdot s \cdot 0.1505}{a \cdot d}$$

where x is the amount of nucleic acid in $\mu\mu$g; Σh is the sum of the mean zone heights in millimeters as determined with the aid of the absorption integrating device (half of the sum of values from both sides), see Appendix 4.3; f is the number of microns corresponding to 1 cm of the horizontal dimension of the photometer curve, i.e., 10,000 $\times$ the inverted value for the magnification in the photometer curve; s is the value in square centimeters of the central circular area, i.e., the area common to all zones in an absorption integrating device; a is the height in millimeters of each step of the reference system; 0.1505 is the difference in OD units between each step of the reference system; d is the OD at 257 mμ of 1 $\mu\mu$g nuclease-digested

[1] I have calculated a maximal destruction of 3.2% of the total amount of uridylic acid during our exposure conditions. This might explain the fact that the values obtained for uridylic acid by microphoresis are slightly lower than those obtained in the macroscale (as seen in Table II of Edström, 1960a, and confirmed in unpublished work). In view of the large amount of data calculated already with the value of 9500 for uridylic acid, I have preferred to retain this constant in my work although one of 9200 may be more correct.

To decrease the random error between individual analyses, a correction factor for variations in fiber width may be used with advantage, particularly when the number of analyses from a hydrolysate is small and the fiber shows variations in width exceeding $\pm 5\%$ of the average width. In this case each quotient is multiplied by the value for the fiber width at the point of maximal absorption.

nucleic acid per square micron. This value is 2.93 for RNA (Edström, 1953) and 2.57 for DNA (Edström and Kawiak, 1961).

4.3. Absorption Integrating Device

The picture of the lens-shaped nucleic acid extracts are considered as consisting of a number of concentric zones and a central circular area, with all zones having the same area as the latter. The average OD of each zone is determined and the values can be added together since they are representations of absorption from areas of equal size. It is possible to calculate the OD from the steps of the reference system. From the value for the magnification and the specific OD constant for the nucleic acid in question, the amount contained in a spot is determined. This procedure is carried out with the aid of an absorption integrating device (Fig. 9) constructed as follows: A horizontal line, representing background blackening, is drawn on millimeter paper. A vertical line to represent the center of the extract is drawn upwards from the middle of this line. Vertical lines are then placed on both sides of the central line at such distances that they will each divide a zone into areas of the same size. If the central circular area is given a radius of r, the distances of the zone-dividing lines from the center will be $r \cdot \sqrt{0.5}$, $r \cdot \sqrt{1.5}$, $r \cdot \sqrt{2.5}$, etc. The intersection points of the mean curve of the two superimposed photometer curves, drawn on transparent paper,

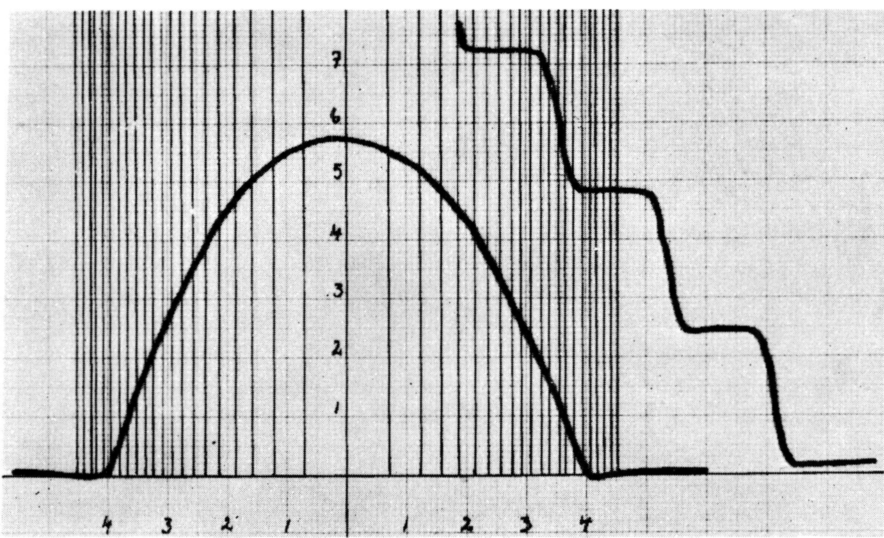

Fig. 9. Absorption integrating device with superimposed photometer curve and reference system tracing for determination of the RNA content in an extract. From Edström (1958).

and the zone-dividing lines (the central line should not be included) are registered in millimeters from the base line. The values on both sides are added, and the sum will constitute an integral of the blackening of the extract. Since it is suitable to divide an extract into about ten zones and since the value for each zone represents four points, the integration is based on about forty measuring points. It is practical to have three absorption integrating devices having radii for the central circular area of 0.5, 1, and 1.5 cm, respectively. As the arm magnification of the densitometer can be varied (2, 5, or 10×), it is always possible to find combinations which give a suitable number of measuring points. An absorption integrating system with superimposed photometer curve is shown in Fig. 9.

Acknowledgments

Figures 1 and 5 are reproduced here by permission of the Editors of *Biochimica et Biophysica Acta,* Figs. 2 and 7 by permission of the Editors of the *Journal of Biophysical and Biochemical Cytology,* and Figs. 8 and 9 by permission of the Editors of the *Journal of Neurochemistry.*

I wish to thank Dr. Ray Iverson, Department of Zoology, University of Miami, and Professor Folke Skoog, Department of Botany, University of Wisconsin, for revising the English text of the manuscript.

Financial support for the original work has been given by the Swedish Medical Research Council and the Swedish Cancer Society.

References

Beaven, G. H., Holiday, E. R., and Johnson, E. A. (1955). *In* "The Nucleic Acids" (E. Chargaff and J. N. Davidson, eds.), Vol. I, pp. 493–553. Academic Press, New York.

Beermann, W. (1961). *Chromosoma* **12,** 1.

Brachet, J. (1940). *Compt. Rend. Soc. Biol.* **133,** 88.

Davidson, J. N. (1950). "The Biochemistry of the Nucleic Acids," 1st ed. Methuen, London.

de Fonbrune, P. (1949). "Technique de micromanipulation." Monographies de l'Institut Pasteur. Masson, Paris.

Edström, J.-E. (1953). *Biochim. Biophys. Acta* **12,** 361.

Edström, J.-E. (1956). *Biochim. Biophys. Acta* **22,** 378.

Edström, J.-E. (1958). *J. Neurochem.* **3,** 100.

Edström, J.-E. (1960a). *J. Biophys. Biochem. Cytol.* **8,** 39.

Edström, J.-E. (1960b). *J. Biophys. Biochem. Cytol.* **8,** 47.

Edström, J.-E., and Beermann, W. (1962). *J. Cell Biol.* **14,** 371.

Edström, J.-E., and Gall, J. G. (1963). *J. Cell Biol.* In press.

Edström, J.-E., and Kawiak, J. (1961). *J. Biophys. Biochem. Cytol.* **9,** 619.

Edström, J.-E., and Pigon, A. (1958). *J. Neurochem.* **3,** 95.

Edström, J.-E., and Pilhage, L. (1960). *J. Biophys. Biochem. Cytol.* **8,** 44.

Edström, J.-E., Grampp, W., and Schor, N. (1961). *J. Biophys. Biochem. Cytol.* **11,** 549.

Edström, J.-E., Eichner, D., and Edström, A. (1962). *Biochim. Biophys. Acta* **61,** 178.

Egyhazi, E., and Hydén, H. (1961). *J. Biophys. Biochem. Cytol.* **10,** 403.

Gomirato, G., and Hydén, H. (1963). *The Brain.* In press.

Hartleib, J., Diefenbach, H., and Sandritter, W. (1956). *Acta Histochem.* **2,** 196.
Hydén, H., and Egyhazi, E. (1962). *J. Cell Biol.* **15,** 37.
Hydén, H., and Pigon, A. (1960). *J. Neurochem.* **6,** 57.
Hydén, H., Lövtrup, S., and Pigon, A. (1958). *J. Neurochem.* **2,** 304.
Jarlstedt, J. (1962). *Exptl. Cell Res.* **28,** 501.
Köhler, A. (1904). *Z. Wiss. Mikroskop.* **21,** 129.
Lagerstedt, S. (1956). *Experientia* **12,** 425.
Lagerstedt, S. (1957). *Z. Zellforsch. Mikroskop. Anat.* **45,** 472.
Markham, R., and Smith, J. D. (1951). *Biochem. J.* **49,** 401.
McFarland, R. H., Anderson, R. A., Nasim, M., and McDonald, D. G. (1958). *Rev. Sci. Instr.* **29,** 738.
Ornstein, L., and Lehrer, G. M. (1960). *J. Histochem. Cytochem.* **8,** 311.
Perry, R. P., Errera, M., Hell, A., and Dürwald, H. (1961). *J. Biophys. Biochem. Cytol.* **11,** 1.
Pigon, A., and Edström, J.-E. (1959). *Exptl. Cell Res.* **16,** 648.
Sandritter, W., Pillat, G., and Theiss, E. (1957). *Exptl. Cell Res. Suppl.* **4,** 64.
Scott, J. F. (1955). *In* "Physical Techniques in Biological Research" (G. Oster and A. W. Pollister, eds.), Vol. I, pp. 131–203. Academic Press, New York.
Smith, J. D., and Markham, R. (1950). *Biochem. J.* **46,** 509.
Stowell, R. E., and Zorzoli, A. (1947). *Stain Technol.* **22,** 51.
Thorell, B. (1947). "Studies on the Formation of Cellular Substances during Blood Cell Formation." Kimpton, London.
Walker, P. M. B. (1955). *Exptl. Cell Res.* **8,** 567.
Walker, P. M. B. (1956). *In* "Physical Techniques in Biological Research" (G. Oster and A. W. Pollister, eds.), Vol. III, pp. 402–487. Academic Press, New York.
Walker, P. M. B. (1958). *In* "General Cytochemical Methods" (J. F. Danielli, ed.), Vol. I, pp. 164–217. Academic Press, New York.
Zajicek, J., and Zeuthen, E. (1956). *Exptl. Cell Res.* **11,** 568.

Author Index

Numbers in italics indicate the page on which the reference is listed.

Subject Index

8 D 9 E 0 F 1 G 2 H 3 I 4 J 5